P9-AFN-233

TRANSPERSONAL PSYCHOLOGIES

Perspectives on the Mind from
Seven Great Spiritual Traditions

Charles T. Tart, Editor

HarperSanFrancisco
A Division of HarperCollinsPublishers

To the many who have seriously asked questions
and sought answers about man and the spiritual

Acknowledgment is made to the following for permission to reprint copyright material:

JONATHAN CAPE, LTD. for passages from *The Dermis Probe, The Magic Monastery, Tales of the Dervishes*, and *Thinkers of the East*, by Idries Shah, reprinted by permission of Jonathan Cape, Ltd.

E.P. DUTTON & CO., INC. for passages from *Tales of the Dervishes* by Idries Shah, copyright © 1969 by Idries Shah, reprinted by permission of the publishers, E.P. Dutton & Co., Inc.

TRANSPERSONAL PSYCHOLOGIES: *Perspectives on the Mind from Seven Great Spiritual Traditions.* Copyright © 1975 by Harper & Row Publishers, Inc. Copyright © 1992 by Psychological Processes, Inc. All rights reserved. Printed in the United States of America. No part of this book may be used or reproduced in any manner whatsoever without written permission except in the case of brief quotations embodied in critical articles and reviews. For information address HarperCollins Publishers, 10 East 53rd Street, New York, NY 10022.

THIRD EDITION

Transpersonal pychologies : perspectives on the mind from seven great
    spiritual traditions / Charles T. Tart, editor.— 3rd ed.
        p. cm.
    Includes bibliographical references and index.
    ISBN 0–06–250856–3 (alk. paper)
    1. Transpersonal psychology. I. Tart, Charles T.
BF204.7.T73 1991
    150.19—dc20   89–46448
                                                                   CIP

92 93 94 95 96 MAL 10 9 8 7 6 5 4 3 2 1

This edition is printed on acid-free paper that meets the American National Standards Institute Z39.48 Standard.

Harper San Francisco and the author, in association with the Rainforest Action Network, will facilitate the planting of two trees for every one tree used in the manufacture of this book.

CONTENTS

INTRODUCTION TO THE 1992 EDITION

So many of us are rich—and it doesn't satisfy.

In our materialistic culture, each of us has been repeatedly exposed to the message that material wealth will buy happiness. Yes, we still have far too many people who suffer from material want in this world. Yet vast numbers of us in the West, even many who consider ourselves "poor", live far more materially comfortably and secure lives than almost every human being who ever lived in the past. Indeed, many millions of us live much better materially than the kings and queens of old.

And it still doesn't satisfy.

Part of the reason our material riches do not satisfy is that we have come to realize that we are a part of the ecosystem of the planet, not independent, unchecked exploiters, and we will have to pay stiff prices to restore a viable balance. Materiality also imposes inherent limits, such as vulnerability, sickness, and death. But the more important reason material riches alone don't satisfy is that something inherent and vital in our beings has been left out of the "everything = matter" doctrine.

What can you do when you're unhappy?

You can blame other people or situations—"It's all their fault!"—or you can look inward to see what you are contributing to your dissatisfaction. Psychotherapy is one way to look inside. Most people who have sought help from counseling and psychotherapy have done so because they want to be "normal." They want to feel comfortable with others, hold a job, be part of a family, have friends, be respected, feel materially safe and secure, and the like.

In the 1950's and 1960's, however, therapists began seeing a new type of "patient." An interview would show that the person was materially and socially well off. "I am vice president of the Gross and Jumbo Corporation, I have job security and authority, I love my spouse and family and they love me, my kids are doing OK, my sex life is satisfying, I am respected in the community and in my profession, I have friends, I own a big house, three TV sets, two cars, and I have money in the bank." Their actions in life were intelligent and adaptive, and they were successful by the standards of our culture. Then why were they coming to a therapist? These people have gotten the rewards that society had said would make them happy. Nevertheless, they reported things such as "My life is empty." Or, "There must be more than this," Or, "It doesn't mean anything much." Or, "I feel hollow inside."

The new syndrome was dubbed "existential neurosis," unhappiness centered around unanswered questions of *meaning*. This dis-ease is even more widespread today, as so many additional people have gotten the material rewards and then found them wanting. Many more people are striving desperately to get their share of material rewards, not knowing that they will probably also find them wanting.

It is strange to call this dis-ease an existential *neurosis*. To consider it a form of illness is to implicitly accept the cultural norm that material and social success should naturally lead to happiness in "normal" people. But to be locked into the assumptions of our culture, to fail to transcend it, is to be personally vulnerable to the suffering inherent in our culture's contradictions. Indeed, from a transpersonal point of view, this kind of existential discontent can be the beginning of real growth, and it would be a tragedy to "cure" it.

To return to our new breed of patients, the two long-dominant branches of orthodox Western psychology, behaviorism and the psychoanalytic/psychiactric approach, have little to offer them. Both systems have very limited world views about what is possible for humans beyond material gratification. A new field, humanistic psychology, has evolved as one response to these new patients, who now often become "client" or "student." In humanistic psychology, creativity, emotional vitality, authenticity, and finding meaning beyond material gratification are central concerns.

To put it more personally, since that is really where all this matters, back in the 1960's, some of us discovered that in addition to having clever heads, we have *hearts* and *bodies*. We found it lonely to live only in our intellects. It is also stupid. Real intelligence, we discovered, is not just a matter of cognitive, intellectual processes: there is an "intelligence" and a life of the heart and of the body as well. These other kinds of intelligences and experiences have to be searched for, discovered, accepted, nourished, and developed, and eventually integrated into a higher level of holistic functioning.

Humanistic psychology was the social manifestation of our attempts to grow wise hearts and bodies, as well as wise minds. Becoming a better-balanced human of this sort is not easy, but we are learning more about both the science and the art of how to develop our selves and about how to apply this development in creating a more peaceful and fulfilling society.

We got very excited by these discoveries, rightfully so. Many of our lives were greatly enriched by humanistic growth work. But, by and large, humanistic psychology did not generally go beyond the limited "all is material" view of our culture. There still tended to be an implicit, underlying worldview that thought, emotions, and the body are all ultimately reducible to and equivalent to physical matter reactions, and thus limited by them. Thus humanistic psychology tended to neglect another part of human development, our fourth aspect, the *spirit*. Not "spirit" in the limited sense of vitality or authenticity, but as something *real* behind the material manifestations of life, something we get fleeting glimpses of in "mystical experiences," the vital energy underlying religions before they all too often ossify into mechanisms for social control. *Transpersonal psychology*, the study of the parts of our nature that are beyond (*trans*) our ordinary, limited, personal self, is the social manifestation of trying to understand and develop this fourth aspect.

Like humanistically developing the intelligence of the heart and body, the personal and social development of a transpersonal psychology is not easy. Mixed in with the most profound transpersonal experiences and realities is a lot of fantasy, dreaming, immaturity, and psychopathology. The New Age movement is our current illustration of this, where genuinely useful transpersonal knowledge and techniques that we badly need are mixed in with nonsense and immature fantasy.

Although still in its infancy, transpersonal psychology aims eventually to grow so it can separate sense from nonsense and address questions like the following:

- Does the experience of so-called higher consciousness actually deal with a reality, or it is just a kind of delusion?
- Is love nothing but a matter of intelligent, biological self-interest, the plotting of a "selfish gene," or is it, as the mystics have said, a genuinely transpersonal energy?
- Is the mystical experience of *oneness* a genuine transcendence of the limits of body and matter, or is it just an intoxicating dream of an all-too-finite creature actually consisting of nothing but a physical, inherently separate body that will ultimately die, taking with it into nothingness that which we call mind, heart, and personality?
- How can we make the mystic experience the common property of humans, instead of the almost accidental experience of a few?
- How can we guide the aftereffects of transcendental experience so they result in greater psychological maturity, rather than religious fanaticism?

The answers to these kinds of questions are vital to everyone, not only those who characterize themselves as interested in spiritual matters. They will play a major role in determining whether humanity survives on this planet. If we are indeed nothing more than chemical accidents limited to nothing but the physical dimension of reality as "scientism," the influential materialism-made-dogmatic-religion of our times says, then personal gratification in the material realm is our individual primary concern. Go for maximum material gratification and the devil take the hindmost! (See my *Open Mind, Discriminating Mind: Reflections on Human Possibilities* for a detailed discussion of this.)

If, on the other hand, there is a real spiritual dimension linking us, so that we are all brothers and sisters in some profound and loving way, then we have a vital basis for creating peace in the world and genuinely caring for each other's welfare. Insofar as we discover the reality of the transpersonal, we will be rich in a much more important way than in the material dimension and these riches will transform our world for the better.

The original publication of this book in 1975 helped to stimulate the growth of transpersonal psychology as a social movement.* It was also helpful to many individuals in introducing them to alternative ways to view themselves and their world, and thus increased their potential to grow. The fundamental human questions the various chapters deal with are just as vital today as they were then, and I hope this new edition will be of value to you personally and to all of us transpersonally.

For technical reasons, one chapter from the original edition, on the Arica training has been dropped.

Charles T. Tart
March, 1991
University of California
Davis, California
and
Institute of Noetic Sciences
Sausalito, California

---

*Those interested in keeping up with and/or joining in these developments should contact the Association for Transpersonal Psychology, PO Box 3049, Stanford, California 94305. The ATP is an organization of both psychological professionals and interested lay people that publishes a general newsletter and the professional Journal of Transpersonal Psychology, as well as holding an annual meeting in California where experiential as well as intellectual knowledge of developments can be gained.

INTRODUCTION TO THE ORIGINAL EDITION

CHARLES T. TART

TRANSPERSONAL PSYCHOLOGY is the title given to an emerging force in the psychology field by a group of psychologists and professional men and women from other fields who are interested in those *ultimate* human capacities and potentialities that have no systematic place in positivistic or behavioristic theory ("first force"), classical psychoanalytic theory ("second force"), or humanistic psychology ("third force"). The emerging Transpersonal Psychology ("fourth force") is concerned specifically with the *empirical*, scientific study of, and responsible implementation of the findings relevant to, becoming, individual and species-wide meta-needs, ultimate values, unitive consciousness, peak experiences, B-values, ecstasy, mystical experience, awe, being, self-actualization, essence, bliss, wonder, ultimate meaning, transcendence of the self, spirit, oneness, cosmic awareness, individual and species-wide synergy, maximal interpersonal encounter, sacralization of everyday life, transcendental phenomena, cosmic self-humor and playfulness, maximal sensory awareness, responsiveness and expression, and related concepts, experiences, and activities. As a definition, this formulation is to be understood as subject to *optional* individual or group interpretations, either wholly or in part, with regard to the acceptance of its content as essentially naturalistic, theistic, supernaturalistic, or any other designated classification.

—Anthony Sutich, in the first issue of
the *Journal of Transpersonal Psychology*,
Spring 1969.

Robert Ornstein, in the introduction to his recent book *The Nature of Human Consciousness: A Book of Readings* (1973), said:

Psychology is, primarily, the science of consciousness. Its researchers deal with consciousness directly when possible, and indirectly, through the study of physiology and behavior, when necessary. Psychologists are now returning to the essential questions of our discipline: How does the mind work? What are the major dimensions of human consciousness? Is consciousness individual or cosmic? What means are there to extend human consciousness? These questions have not yet had a full treatment within academic science, having been ruled out of inquiry by the dominant paradigm of the past 60 or so years.

Yet there is a cultural and scientific evolution, if not revolution, in process. Academic people, being members of their culture, reflect the general interest in "Altered States" of consciousness, meditation, drug states, and new and old religions. The intent of this book is to assist in a small way in regaining a lost perspective in psychology. Often teachers and their students become sidetracked in their study, and wind up investigating One Minor Aspect of One Possible Means of Approaching Psychological Problems. The central aim, the context, the original impetus to study consciousness may become forgotten. There is, therefore, a continuing need to reestablish the basis of psychology and to link current research with that of other students of consciousness, such as William James and Carl Jung, and with the "esoteric" psychologies of other cultures, such as Sufism, Yoga, and Buddhism. [p. xi]

The call to link our psychology with other psychologies, to understand our minds, is not simply of academic interest: our culture is in the midst of a crisis that may be resolved by nuclear annihilation, mass starvation, and the partial or total collapse of civilization. We look at economics, politics, ecology, crime, and so on to find the villains, but *we* are the villains. Ordinary man, man who does not know himself, neurotic man, psychotic man—all project their psychological inadequacies and conflicts out on the world, finding the villains out there and retaliating against them. Economics, politics, ecology, crime—these are all manifestations of how *we* behave, how *we* (mis)perceive, how *we* distort. Psychology is not merely an interesting academic study: it is the ultimate key to understanding ourselves and, hopefully, saving ourselves.

Western psychology, as a science, is not very old. Almost all of it has been done in the last few decades. The problems involved in studying human nature, the human mind, have been found to be enormous. Progress? Yes, there has been excellent progress in psychology. But, compared to what we need to know about man, scientific psychology is in its infancy.

We do not know enough psychology to find good solutions to world problems today. Yet if we do not build an adequate psychology, we will never build a good world.

One of the reasons for the slow growth and inadequacies of our psychology is that it is culture bound; it is linked to and frequently limited by the multitudes of (implicit) assumptions that create the consensus reality of the Western world in the twentieth century. It particularly fails to deal adequately with human experience in the realm we call the spiritual,* that vast realm of human potential dealing with ultimate purposes, with higher entities, with God, with love, with compassion, with purpose. The "enlightened rationalism" and physicalism that have been so successful in developing the physical sciences have not worked very well in psychology, for reasons discussed in Chapter 1.

In spite of the fact that our present science has not dealt adequately with these vital aspects of human experience, I have a deep conviction that science, as a method of sharpening and refining knowledge, can be applied to the human experiences we call transpersonal or spiritual, and that both science and our spiritual traditions will be enriched as a result. In particular, we will create a scientific transpersonal psychology, or psychologies, a truly Western understanding of the spiritual.

The creation of this transpersonal psychology is a long-term undertaking. Fortunately, however, we do not start from a total lack of observations and conceptualizations, but from a very rich heritage of spiritual traditions and disciplines. Although they are unknown to most Westerners, these traditional transpersonal psychologies, which I shall call spiritual psychologies in this volume,

---

*I use the term "spiritual" in preference to "religious" because I feel the former term implies more directly the *experiences* that people have about the meaning of life, God, ways to live, etc., while "religious" implies too strongly the enormous social structures that embrace so many more things than direct spiritual experience, and which have often become hostile to and inhibiting of direct experience. When I hear "religious," I get all sorts of associations of priests, dogmas, doctrines, churches, institutions, political meddling, and social organizations. Thus I shall always use the term "spiritual" in preference to "religious," as we generally are not dealing with the socialization and institutionalization of spiritual experience in this book. On those rare occasions when I use "religious," I do mean the more institutionalized version of spirituality.

have grappled with vital human problems for many centuries. If we use them as sources of inspiration, neither embracing them uncritically nor rejecting them unthinkingly, we shall have a good head start on developing our own indigenous transpersonal psychologies.

This book is an attempt to start bridging the gap between "orthodox, Western psychology" and a number of transpersonal psychologies, psychologies that are integral parts of various spiritual disciplines.

What is a psychology? It is an interrelated set of (inherently unprovable) assumptions about the world and human nature, bodies of observations about human nature, theories about the meaning of those observations, and techniques for learning more. We are familiar with "scientific" psychology, our orthodox, Western brand. We think it is based on "scientific facts." But, as discussed in Chapter 1, there are no simple "facts" just lying around waiting to be discovered: our implicit assumptions affect the way we look and control what we will find to be the "meaningful" facts. So our orthodox, scientific psychology has its assumptions, assumptions often so implicit, so removed from conscious awareness, that we don't know we have them.

As Westerners we have little appreciation for the fact that there are many other psychologies. Zen Buddhism has a psychology; so do Yoga, Christianity, and Sufism. These psychologies are working bodies of knowledge which, to some extent, can be looked at independently of the religious belief system ordinarily associated with them, just as orthodox, Western psychology can, to some extent, be looked at outside the context of twentieth-century Western culture.

Orthodox, Western psychology has dealt very poorly with the spiritual side of man's nature, choosing either to ignore its existence or to label it pathological. Yet much of the agony of our time stems from a spiritual vacuum. Our culture, our psychology, has ruled out man's spiritual nature, but the cost of this attempted suppression is enormous. If we want to find ourselves, our spiritual side, it is imperative for us to look at the psychologies that have dealt with it. Not that there will be some simple solution of finding that Spiritual Psychology #3 is right and our psychology is wrong, of simply converting to a different belief system. We *are* twentieth-century Westerners, with science in general and scientific psychology in particular as important parts of our backgrounds. Some of us may be able to drop that background and accept a particular transpersonal psychology as our primary frame of reference. But for many of us, what we learn about the spiritual side of ourselves must at least coexist with, and preferably *integrate with,* our heritage of Western science and culture. So I think our job will be to bridge the spiritual and our Western, scientific side.

In the first chapter of this book I attempt to start this kind of bridging by looking at the nature of science, arguing that we have unnecessarily confused the powerful *tool* of scientific method with a *philosophy* of physicalism that keeps our science from adequately dealing with spiritual experiences and altered states of consciousness. If we return to practicing the *essentials* of scientific method, we may, in the best sort of scientific way, develop state-specific sciences. The kinds of human experiences dealt with in the spiritual psychologies are not incompatible with the essence of science. Indeed the spiritual psychologies presented later may be state-specific sciences themselves. Even if they are not what we Westerners would call sciences, they have an immense amount to teach us.

In the second chapter I try to make *explicit* many of the *implicit* assumptions that underlie orthodox, Western psychology. This constitutes a kind of review of our psychology to put the spiritual psychologies in perspective. Many of these assumptions block progress in understanding the transpersonal. I hope my chapter may do more than academically list assumptions: as long as assumptions are implicit, we don't question them and we have no opportunity to escape from their controlling influence over us. By making many of them explicit, we may be able to see their consequences and question them; we may be able to look at the spiritual psychologies with a more open mind.

It is easy to think that, however interesting the spiritual psychologies may be in dealing with odd aspects of *subjective* experience, *our* orthodox, Western psychology is based on hard science and deals with what's *real.* In the third chapter I briefly look at the data of modern parapsychology in order to show that the physicalistic view of the universe held by most psychologists (and Westerners generally) is quite narrow: certain phenomena, such as telepathy, have been shown to exist by the *best* sort of scientific work, and such paranormal phenomena suggest that the spiritual psychologies are talking about things that can be every bit as real as the ordinary physical world, not "just" subjective experience.

The most important part of the book is the remaining eight chapters, in which eight experts in various spiritual disciplines present their spiritual disciplines as psychologies.

The traditional spiritual psychologies stress the importance of direct experiential knowledge of their subject matter. In asking people to contribute chapters on particular spiritual psychologies, I kept this requirement in mind, and searched for contributors who not only had an excellent "scholastic" knowledge of their spiritual discipline, but who also practiced the particular spiritual path as a personal discipline. The search bore excellent fruit, as Chapters 4 through 11 will attest. Each contributor took on an unusual task: to present his spiritual discipline as a *psychology,* rather than in the traditional way. This proved arduous, requiring a masterful "translation" from the traditional concepts into "psychologese," into a language familiar to and comprehensible to the average, educated Westerner. Language is limited, of course, and can serve only as a pointer *toward* experience for many of the most valuable things, but the contributors have done an excellent job. Indeed, many contributors wrote afterward that carrying out the task of translation, difficult as it was, was quite rewarding, for it enriched their own understanding of their disciplines.

I gave each contributor* an outline to follow in preparing his or her chapter, an outline asking that areas of traditional interest to Westerners be talked about, as well as what was central to the particular spiritual tradition. The outline was intended as an aid, though, not a straitjacket, so it has been modified to various degrees by various contributors. By and large, however, each chapter will deal with most of the topics traditionally considered important in Western psychology. These topics are: a brief history of each spiritual path and a look at its current activity; basic philosophy and assumptions about the nature of the universe, the nature of man, man's place and function in the universe, his relationship to higher and lower entities, and the basic nature of human consciousness; the path's teaching on personality, emotion, motivation, memory, learning, mind-body relationship, psychopathology, perception, social relationships, cognitive processes, potential new faculties, altered states of consciousness, and death; and an overview of each particular spiritual path, its methods, the way of contacting the living tradition, and the dangers of each path.

In trying to decide what the most logical sequence for these chapters would be, I eventually gave up believing there was some "logical" sequence, and decided to arrange them to follow roughly the course of the sun as it leaves California, circles the globe, and returns. So after my California-written chapters we move across the Pacific to Japan to learn of Zen Buddhism, then farther west for a deeper look at the Buddha's teachings on higher states of consciousness and meditation, then to India for Yoga, then through the Middle East for Gurdjieff's system, the Arica Training (both of which owe much to Eastern and Middle Eastern sources), and Sufism. From the Middle East we go to Europe and America for the Christian Mystical Tradition and the Western Magical Tradition, so completing our circuit of the globe.

This sampling of eight spiritual psychologies is far from complete, as space has precluded dealing with such important ones as Taoism, Alchemy, the Cabalistic Tradition, Tibetan Buddhism, and so on. I hope to organize a second volume to rectify these omissions.

I trust the impact of the traditional spiritual psychologies will stimulate us to ask some questions about our psychology, widen our conception of what a psychology is, and develop our own scientific, transpersonal psychologies.

---

*The one exception to each contributor preparing his chapter especially in terms of the outline for this book was Daniel Goleman's chapter on the Buddha's teachings on higher states of consciousness (Chapter 5), which appeared in the *Journal of Transpersonal Psychology* while this book was in preparation. It was so relevant to the theme of the book that I have been very pleased to be able to include it here; it could well have been written expressly for the book.

1 SCIENCE, STATES OF CONSCIOUSNESS, AND SPIRITUAL EXPERIENCES: THE NEED FOR STATE-SPECIFIC SCIENCES

CHARLES T. TART

The last several hundred years in the West have seen a continuous struggle between science and orthodox religion, with conventional religionists decrying the godlessness of science and feeling threatened as its discoveries contradicted traditional religious dogma, and, on the other side, many scientists feeling that religion was the main source and maintainer of superstitious thought that held back man's progress. There have been many important individual exceptions to this, religious men who have seen the value of science, and scientists who have had a strong religious faith, but, by and large, there has been marked polarization between these two ways of approaching the universe.

Until a generation ago, it would have seemed that science and its technological marvels were clearly emerging as the dominant force among the educated segment of the population. Judaism and Christianity were often given lip service, but increasingly people pinned their faith for a better life on science and its products, and many educated people had no formal religious faith at all. In retrospect, we can see that science was (and still is) used by many as a religion, a source of hope and faith in human progress.

Today we see a quite different picture. T. Blackburn (1971), writing in *Science*, noted that a large proportion of our most talented young people are "turned off" by science and technology. I see the same rejection of science and scientific culture by many of the brightest students in the universities, and the whole counterculture is an outcome of this. When a tool as useful as science is rejected by a large proportion of the most intelligent young people, we have a major cultural crisis.

The causes of the rejection of science are quite complex and varied, as with any major social movement, but a very basic cause of the alienation I want to discuss here is the widespread experience of altered states of consciousness (ASCs) by young people, and the spiritual experiences often occurring in ASCs, combined with the fact that orthodox science almost totally rejects the experiences and knowledge gained from ASCs. Blackburn himself, while asking us to recognize the validity of a more sensuous-intuitive approach to nature, still exemplifies this rejection of experiences from ASCs when he says: "Perhaps science has much to learn along this line from the disciplines, *as distinct from the content,* of Oriental religions" (my italics).

As an illustration, a Gallup poll several years ago (Newsweek, Jan. 25, 1971, p. 52) found that approximately half of American college students had tried marijuana, and a large number of them were using it fairly regularly, thus experiencing a particular kind of ASC. They do this at the risk of having their careers ruined and going to jail for several years if they are caught. Why? Conventional research on the nature of marijuana intoxication, the "facts" of orthodox science, tell us that the major effects of marijuana are a slight increase in heart rate, reddening of the eyes, some difficulty with memory at high levels of intoxication, and rather small decrements in performance on complex psychomotor tests.

Would you risk going to jail to experience these?

An intelligent marijuana smoker, hearing a physician or scientist talk about these effects as the important, "scientific" data about marijuana intoxication will simply sneer and have his antiscientific attitude reinforced, for it is clear to him that scientists have no real understanding of what marijuana intoxication is all about. I carried out an extensive study of the experiential nature of marijuana intoxication (Tart, 1971b) which details what people experience in this ASC, but these sorts of experiences are generally dismissed as "subjective" or "pathological" by orthodox science and not worthy of extended investigation. When most psychologists label something as "subjective" today, they mean it is unreliable, nonscientific, and unimportant. Yet these *experiences* are the reason people use marijuana, not for the physiological effects and increased errors on complex performance tasks. So the important human experiences are overlooked or considered not worth serious investigation by orthodox science.

To put this more formally, a large proportion of intelligent people are experimenting with ASCs in themselves, and finding that the experiences they have are of extreme importance in creating a philosophy and a style of life. The conflict between the experiences and philosophies resulting from these ASCs and the attitudes and intellectual-emotional systems that have evolved in our ordinary state of consciousness (SoC) are a major factor behind the increased alienation of many people from conventional science. To stay with our example of marijuana intoxication, for example, it is relatively common for experienced users to feel themselves to be more childlike and open and filled with wonder at the universe, to find sexual love a union of souls as well as bodies, to feel nonphysical kinds of energy flowing in the body, to feel at one with the world, and to feel that time comes to a stop. Not quite as common, but still frequent, are experiences of mind-to-mind contact with others (telepathy) and feeling in touch with a higher power or God (Tart, 1971b). These types of experiences are not limited to ASCs induced by drugs, of course, but can occur in meditative states and other kinds of ASCs. Yet these kinds of experiences of ecstasy, other "dimensions," mystical union, rapture, beauty, space-and-time transcendence, and transpersonal knowledge are simply not dealt with adequately in conventional scientific approaches. They either are not dealt with at all or are swept into the wastebasket category of "subjective" and "pathological" experiences. These kinds of experiences will not disappear if we crack down more on psychedelic drugs (an obviously impossible task—obvious to everyone but the government), for immense numbers of people are now practicing various nondrug techniques, such as meditation and yoga, for producing ASCs.

Thus people's experiences in ASCs are creating intense spiritual experiences that must be dealt with in their lives. Conversely, desire for religious experiences, increased by the breakdown of the traditional value system of our culture, is responsible for people seeking out ASCs by various means.

Now, we must look at the question: Will the traditional conflict between science and religion remain, with people polarizing into a "straight" technological scientism on the one side and an irrational kind of faith and superstition on the other side? Or can the traditional conflicts between science and religion be reduced, so that the two areas of human endeavor can interpenetrate and enrich each other? I believe the latter can take place, and have proposed that we create state-specific sciences to do so (Tart, 1972). In this chapter I shall say something about the nature of ASCs, discuss the essence of scientific method, show that, in principle, we can develop sciences of ASCs, and then discuss how the spiritual psychologies described in this book may be such sciences, or the beginnings of such sciences.

Note that while our focus here will be on ASCs and the experiences occurring in them, many of the experiences of ASCs are not necessarily spiritual, and spiritual experiences are not limited to occurring in ASCs. Nevertheless, because so many of the living, religious experiences do take place in or are facilitated by ASCs, our focus on ASCs is highly appropriate in laying the groundwork for a scientific approach toward spiritual experience.

STATES OF CONSCIOUSNESS

The terms "state of consciousness" (SoC) and "altered state of consciousness" (ASC) are coming into fairly widespread use in our culture now. The common-sense idea behind the terms is recognition of the existence of a *state* of consciousness, a pattern, an organizational style of one's overall mental functioning at any given time. It is analogous to the idea of crossing from one physical state to another (say, New Jersey to California), where there are some common features from one state to another, but the overall organization is different in quite important ways. There are different laws which are supposed to govern one's behavior, there are different styles of life, and so on. When the experiential "feel" of one SoC differs radically from another, we then talk about an altered SoC, an ASC.

Unfortunately, as often happens when terms get into common use, they tend to be used so generally and imprecisely that they lose their descriptive value, and this is rapidly happening with SoC and ASC. Many people, for example, now use SoC to simply mean what's on their mind at any particular moment, and ASC to mean that what's on their mind at this moment is different from what it was a moment ago. If I were to use the terms this way, I would now say that at this instant of writing I am in "bookcase consciousness" because I am looking at a bookcase, and now I move my eyes and I am in "clock consciousness" because I am looking at my clock, and now I am in "window consciousness" because I am looking at the window. So I shall introduce more specific terminology, in line with my own theory of the nature of states of consciousness (Tart, 1970; 1973b; 1974a; 1975), to use through the remainder of my chapters.

A *discrete state of consciousness* (d-SoC) will be defined as a specific *pattern* of functioning of the mind, recognizing that this pattern may show a range of variation in its specifics while still remaining the same overall pattern. Thus we recognize a variety of objects as automobiles even though they vary in shape, size, color, and other specific features. A *discrete altered state of consciousness* (d-ASC) is a *radical* alteration of the overall patterning of consciousness (compared to some reference d-SoC, usually our ordinary waking d-SoC) such that the experiencer of the d-ASC (or perhaps an observer) can tell that different laws are functioning, that a new, overall pattern is superimposed on his experience. That is, *within* a d-SoC, particular parts of the pattern, particular psychological functions, may function faster or slower, more or less efficiently, or show a change in the particular content they are working with, but the *overall* pattern remains the same. To go back to our earlier example, as I looked around the room the content of my particular perceptions changed from a bookcase to a clock to a window, but I was in my ordinary state of consciousness all the time. I felt basically the same while looking at all three different things, my mind continued to function by a certain set of rules for reasoning and processing information, and so forth.

A d-ASC, on the other hand, would be illustrated by a state like dreaming, intoxication with a drug, or a possible result of meditative techniques. I might, for example, have had a dream of looking at the bookcase, then at the clock, then at the window. The specific content and sequence might have been the same as in my ordinary d-SoC, yet (on awakening) I would clearly recognize that the overall patterning of my mental functioning had been quite different from what it ordinarily is. Thus d-ASCs are d-SoCs that feel distinctly different to the experiencer from his ordinary, waking d-SoC; they are *radical* alterations, not just minor shifts in content or quantitative changes of functioning. Remember that a d-SoC is an overall pattern of functioning: "radical" changes in the parts that constitute the pattern may include major quantitative shifts in the range of functioning of psychological/physiological functions such as memory, reasoning, sense of identity, and motor skills, and the temporary disappearance of some functions and emergence of new functions not available in the ordinary d-SoC.

Almost all ordinary people experience two d-ASCs in addition to their ordinary, waking state: the dreaming state and the transitional states between waking and sleeping (hypnagogic and hypnopompic states). Many other people experience another d-ASC, alcohol intoxication, and, the newest to our culture, d-ASCs produced by marijuana intoxication and more powerful psychedelic drugs. Other people also experience d-ASCs produced by meditative techniques, so-called spirit possession states, and hypnotic or autohypnotic states.

A simple analogy with computer functioning can make the nature of d-SoCs and d-ASCs clearer. Imagine a very simple kind of computer which can be programed to do one sort of function on numbers fed into it. One program might be to serially add all numbers fed into it. This would be a d-SoC. It might also be that this computer could be adjusted to take more or less time to do the addition, that is, to run faster or slower, or to work with various degrees of accuracy. This would correspond to the kind of quantitative variations we have in any d-SoC, such as feeling cheerier or sadder, sleepier or more awake, in our ordinary d-SoC. But basically all the computer program does is add; it maintains an overall pattern in spite of quantitative variations in it.

Now suppose we reprogram the computer so that it will multiply each number that is fed into it by the result of all previous multiplications of numbers fed into it. We have a new pattern, a new d-SoC, a d-ASC with reference to the previous program. Again, we might adjust it to do this faster or slower, more or less accurately, but now the way it processes information, the kind of operations it performs on stimuli coming into it, is very different. This is the nature of d-SoCs: they are like different programs in a computer. The human mind and brain are, of course, infinitely more complex than this simple example given here. Two or more d-SoCs may show some features in common: for instance, one might be able to add a column of numbers while dreaming, while in your ordinary, waking state of consciousness, and while intoxicated with marijuana. Yet the *overall patterns* of mental functionings of these d-SoCs are very different.

If we look at the techniques of the spiritual psychologies from this perspective, we see that two of the many things they do are to alter particular aspects and contents of our mental or physical functioning *within* our ordinary, waking d-SoC, and to temporarily alter our ordinary d-SoC so we experience one or more d-ASCs. The first process is to "purify" our ordinary d-SoC: for example, by eliminating certain neurotic patterns or disabusing us of wrong ideas. The latter process would be to have us reach, say, a certain meditative state in which quite different kinds of experiences could occur.

It is important to recognize that a d-SoC is an *active* way of coping with reality, with incoming information both about the external world and about one's body and own experiences. Our commonsense idea of consciousness is that we somehow perceive things as they are and do the obviously sensible things to them in terms of reasoning, feeling, evaluating, acting, and such. Modern psychological research has shown this to be a completely false notion. Any d-SoC is an *arbitrary* way of working with information,* of selectively taking in certain kinds of information and rejecting other kinds, selectively giving importance to it in terms of various kinds of value systems, and doing things or experiencing things in certain ways as a result. So there is no "normal," biologically given state of consciousness that is somehow the natural, optimal state of mind that a person could be in, although there are probably biological restrictions of possibilities. Rather, our ordinary d-SoC is a *construction* built up in accordance with biological and cultural imperatives for the purpose of dealing with our physical, intrapersonal, and interpersonal environments. A d-ASC is a radically different way of handling information from the physical, intrapersonal, and interpersonal environments, yet the d-ASC may be as arbitrary as our ordinary d-SoC.

I say this semi-arbitrariness to highlight the common (implicit) assumption that our ordinary state of consciousness, the so-called normal d-SoC, is somehow the optimal one, and all d-ASCs are inferior versions of it. Some d-ASCs are certainly not as adaptive or useful for dealing with *certain kinds* of situations as our ordinary d-SoC, but some may be far more useful in other kinds of ways. Indeed, one might say that one of the primary claims of the spiritual psychologies is that certain d-ASCs are far more useful and "true" for understanding certain kinds of problems, such as man's relationship to the rest of life, than our ordinary d-SoC. We shall consider this question of evaluating qualities of d-SoCs later on.

STATES OF CONSCIOUSNESS AND PARADIGMS

Thomas Kuhn (1962), a historian of science, introduced the idea that science functions under the control of *paradigms.* Since his concept of paradigms is similar in many ways to my concept of d-SoCs, and since each spiritual psychology is a paradigm for dealing with reality, it will be worthwhile to look at this idea.

A paradigm is a major intellectual achievement that underlies normal science

---

*In the long run a d-SoC cannot be *completely* arbitrary in the way it processes information, as we do have to deal with an environment that may kill us for nonadaptive actions.

and attracts and guides the work of an enduring number of adherents in their scientific activity. It is a kind of "supertheory," a theory or formulation about the nature of reality of such a wide scope that it seems to account for most or all of the major known phenomena in its field. Copernican or heliocentric astronomy, for example, the idea that the planets revolve around the sun, is an example of a paradigm that still guides astronomy. When it was introduced, it seemed to organize all the data of astronomy in a much more useful way than the former theory of the planets in the heavens revolving around the earth (Ptolemaic or geocentric astronomy). While seeming to explain most or all of the important phenomena in its field in an overall sense, however, a paradigm is open-ended: there are important subproblems to be solved within that framework, gaps and details in the overall picture to be filled in, so there is plenty of work for scientists to do.

In principle, an ordinary scientific theory is always subject to further tests. A paradigm, however, is so successful after its introduction that it undergoes a *psychological* change that scientific theories are not supposed to undergo. A paradigm becomes an *implicit* framework for most scientists working within it; it becomes the "natural" way of looking at things and doing things; it is the obviously "sensible" way to think about problems in its field. Once it becomes "obviously sensible," it no longer seriously occurs to adherents of the paradigm to subject it to further tests, and, having become implicit, it then acquires tremendous controlling power over its adherents. You do not think about rebelling against something that seems like the natural order of the universe; you do not realize you are controlled by your concepts.

For example, when you were taught physics in high school did anyone explain the *theory* of gravity to you? No, of course not. You were taught the *law* of gravity. It really is the *theory* of gravity, but it has worked so immensely well for so long that it has become accepted as totally true and called a law instead of a theory. Now, what happens when someone claims he has invented an antigravity machine? He is automatically dismissed as a crackpot, because everyone knows that the *law* of gravity rules out things like that.

It may be useful to automatically dismiss inventors of antigravity machines as crackpots. Certainly the idea of "defying" the "law" of gravity is nonsensical to people working within the generally accepted physical paradigm, and it may save scientists a lot of time that would be wasted on blind alleys. Paradigms do serve to concentrate attention on areas that are likely to pay off in research results. Nevertheless, a paradigm is also a set of blinders. Since it automatically, implicitly defines certain kinds of problems and endeavors as trivial or impossible or meaningless, one never looks there, and so never comes up with data that is inconsistent with the paradigm. The great scientific revolutions, which Kuhn discusses so admirably, the major breakthroughs to entirely new pictures of the universe, come when someone continues to concentrate on the "trivial" or anomalous kinds of data, and shows that there are indeed discrepancies in the paradigm when it is pushed beyond certain limits, and that there is an alternative way of looking at the universe, a new paradigm. The great innovators in science have often been considered crackpots for a while, and during periods of what Kuhn calls paradigm clash, when a new paradigm is being advanced against an old paradigm, there is much antagonism and very poor communication between the factions. Indeed, Kuhn says that often the only way a new paradigm in science gets really general acceptance in the scientific academic world is when the staunch adherents of the old paradigm die off and are replaced in their positions by younger people!

This does not sound like the "cold rationality" that science is supposed to operate with, and it is not. Rationality is a goal of science, but science is practiced by human beings who have other qualities in addition to (some) rationality.

A paradigm and a d-SoC are quite similar. Each constitutes a complex, inter-related set of rules and theories that enable a person to interact with and interpret experiences within an environment. In both cases, the rules become largely im-plicit: the scientist forgets that his paradigm is a theory and subject to further testing; the person experiencing a d-SoC forgets that it is an arbitrary way of organizing consciousness and comes to think it is simply a natural way of perceiv-ing things. By not recognizing the tentativeness or arbitrariness of either a para-digm or a d-SoC, one becomes almost completely controlled by them.

Kuhn's concept of a paradigm has far wider applications than to formal scien-tific theories guiding the investigatory activities of scientists. We all have para-digms, world views, about different areas of reality. We have personal and cultural paradigms about economics, politics, religion, sexuality, aggression, and so on. And, almost all of these are *implicit* belief systems, sets of rules for interpreting things, thinking about things, acting on things, so we no longer know what the rules are that govern our reactions. A d-SoC is an overall organization of our mind that is like a paradigm, although it may have specific subparadigms for dealing with specific content areas within it. Changing the program in a com-puter, changing one's state of consciousness from one d-SoC to a d-ASC, and looking at the world from two different paradigms are very comparable actions. They give us quite different understandings of things.

PARADIGM CLASH BETWEEN "STRAIGHT" AND "HIP"

People become emotionally attached to the things which give them pleasure, and a scientist making important progress within a particular paradigm becomes emotionally attached to it. People getting satisfaction from life within a particular cultural framework, another kind of paradigm, become attached to it. People doing well within a particular d-SoC become attached to it. When data which make no sense in terms of the (implicit) paradigm, whether it be scientific, cultural, or d-SoC, are brought to a person's attention, the usual result is *not* a reevaluation of the paradigm, but a rejection or misperception of the data. This rejection seems "rational" to others sharing that paradigm, so one has lots of social support for his position. It seems "irrational" to others committed to a different paradigm. Think of some of your friends who share a different political view from you, and how they seem to be "reasonable" in so many areas but just totally unreasonable in that one, and then realize that they feel the same way about you.

The conflict now existing between those who have experienced certain d-ASCs (whose ranks include many young scientists as well as young people generally) and those who have not is very much a paradigmatic conflict. A person has a mystical experience in a d-ASC, for example, and later tells others that the fundamental principle of the universe is love, that we are all immersed in it as if we were drops of water in the sea. An orthodox psychiatrist, committed to a different paradigm linked to his ordinary waking d-SoC, hears this statement and "obviously perceives" that the person experienced a temporary episode of infantile regression with subsequent deterioration of reality testing. Or a subject in an experiment takes LSD and tells his investigator, "You and I, we are all one; there are no separate selves." The investigator reports that his subject showed a "confused sense of identity and distorted thinking processes." The mystic or experimental subject is reporting what is obviously true to him; the investigator is reporting what is obvious to him. The psychiatrist's or investigator's (implicit) paradigm, based on his scientific training, his cultural background, and his ordinary d-SoC, indicates that a literal interpretation of the mystic's or experimental subject's statement cannot be true, and therefore must be interpreted as mental abnormality on the part of the subject. The mystic or experimental subject, his paradigms radically changed for the moment by being in a d-ASC, reports what is obviously true to him, and perceives the investigator as being mentally subnormal, since he seems incapable of perceiving the obvious.

Historically, Kuhn has shown that paradigm clashes have been characterized by bitter emotional antagonisms and total rejection of the opponent. In addition to cool, rational, scientific debate of the "facts," an immense amount of emotional antagonism develops. We are currently seeing the same sort of process between the orthodox social and medical sciences and those seeking and having spiritual experiences: the orthodox psychologist or psychiatrist, who would not take any of those "psychotomimetic" drugs himself or sit down and do that regressive meditation process, carries out research to show that drug takers and mystics are escapists. The drug taker or meditator views the same investigator as narrow-minded, prejudiced, and repressive. If he is a student, he may drop out of the university, or otherwise not engage in any meaningful dialogue. Communication between the two factions tends to be subtle or not so subtle name calling, rather than useful discourse.

Must the people who experience d-ASCs continue to see scientists as concentrating on the irrelevant, and scientists see the experiencers of d-ASCs as confused* or mentally ill? Or can science deal adequately with the experiences people have in d-ASCs? Let us now look at the nature of knowledge and the essence of scientific method to show that we can.

THE NATURE OF KNOWLEDGE

Science (from the Latin *scire,* to know) deals with knowledge. Philosophers have quarreled over what knowledge is from time immemorial, but for our immediate purposes I shall define knowledge as an immediately given, experiential feeling of congruence between two different kinds of experiences, a feeling of matching. One set of experiences may be regarded as perceptions of something, the external world, others, or oneself. The second set may be a theory, a scheme, a system of understanding, a memory, or a belief. The feeling of congruence is something immediately given in experience, although many more formal criteria of matching have been proposed.

For example, as I write I catch a movement out of the corner of my eye, turn and look, and see that it is a small, hairy animal with four legs, tail, and pointed ears. Some part of my mind says "cat," and I feel that I know what I have perceived. The immediate sensory experience is felt to be matched with internal criteria, so then I "know" something.

All knowledge is experiential knowledge. We tend to think that knowledge about the physical world is somehow different, but it is not so. *My* knowledge of the law of gravity is something I experience, and I have no certainty whether it exists independently of me, even though I choose to make that assumption. All my knowledge of the physical world can be reduced to this: given certain sets of experiences which I (by assumption) attribute to an external world activating my sensory apparatus, it may be possible for me to compare them with purely internal experience (memories, previous knowledge) and predict with a high degree of reliability other classes of experiences, which I again attribute to the external world. Because my ability to predict what will happen in the class of experiences I attribute to the external world is so remarkably high (I know that every time

---

*Certainly some d-ASCs show certain kinds of deterioration of psychological functions on the part of the experiencers, but such specific decrements are quite different from the blanket rejection of d-ASC experiences caused by paradigm bias.

I walk into the experience I call a closed door, I will have the experience I call a bumped nose), I have come, like everyone else, to believe that the physical world exists independently of my experience of it, but that belief says something about my psychology, not necessarily anything about the ultimate nature of reality.

Science as an organized social effort has been incredibly successful in dealing with the set of experiences we attribute to physical reality, and it has historically become associated with the philosophy of physicalism, the belief that physical reality exists independently of our perception of it, and is the ultimate reality. Thus the philosophy of physicalism says that a good explanation is an explanation which describes things in terms of physical matter and its properties and interaction. So, for example, if I can say that your anger in a situation is due to the chemical action of adrenalin flowing in your bloodstream, this is considered a good explanation in terms of physicalism, much more fundamental than my talking about your psychological reactions to something else.

Unfortunately (for those accepting physicalistic philosophy), the vast majority of important phenomena of d-ASCs and spiritual phenomena have no known physical manifestations: they are purely internal experiences. Thus, to a physicalistic philosophy they are epiphenomena, not very worthy of study unless they can be reduced to a physical basis. Science has not had any important degree of success in reducing any of these phenomena to a physical basis, so the result has been that they are ignored by not being studied. But, insofar as science deals with *knowledge,* it can distinguish itself from the philosophy of physicalism and deal with experiential knowledge.

ESSENCE OF SCIENTIFIC METHOD

People have long recognized that in spite of their strong conviction that they know something or other, they may be wrong. In fact, we are often wrong. What at first seems like matching between our ideas and our experiences later turns out to not match, or to be a coincidental matching when looked at from a larger perspective. We have learned that our reasoning is often faulty, our observations are often incomplete or mistaken, and that emotional and unconscious factors can seriously distort our reasoning and observation. Reliance on other people as authorities and reliance on "rationality" or intellectual "elegance" are not certain criteria for achieving knowledge that is true, knowledge that always produces concepts which match with experience. The development of scientific method may be seen as a determined effort to systematize the process of acquiring knowledge and refining knowledge in such a way as to minimize the various pitfalls of observation and reasoning, and produce a steady, if erratic, movement toward truth in the long run.

Scientific method can be reduced to four basic principles: (1) good observation; (2) the public nature of observation; (3) the necessity to theorize logically; and (4) the testing of theory against predicted, observable consequences. In a sense, this is "common sense." The scientist is someone who is more aware of and committed to these rules than the ordinary man. The repeated application of this method and the particular sets of "facts" thus built up constitute the scientific enterprise. Let us look at these rules in detail, and see how dropping unnecessary accretions from physicalistic philosophy will allow them to be applied to spiritual and d-SoC phenomena so that we may develop state-specific sciences.

OBSERVATION

A scientist is committed to observe as well as possible the phenomena of interest in his field, to constantly try to find better ways of making these observations, to observe more systematically and precisely and accurately. If one asks, "What kind of body of observation does Western science have about spiritual and d-SoC phenomena?" the answer is a very sketchy, inaccurate one. Why?

The major problem is that the physicalistic philosophy attached to science has constituted a paradigm which has discouraged science from observing these kinds of phenomena, which have been labeled ephemeral, subjective, unreliable, unscientific. When scientists use the word "mystical," they are generally using it as a pejorative. The first step in bridging the gap between science and the spiritual, then, is that we must recognize that since all knowledge is fundamentally experiential, the observation of experience and the refinement of this kind of observation is legitimate and is the foundation of any psychological sciences we will build in this area. We cannot ignore data that is not physical.

Although the orthodox scientist makes an error in dismissing a priori the data of spiritual experience and d-ASCs because of his paradigmatic commitments, many people who would consider themselves on the spiritual side of the controversy make an equal error. They say, "He who tastes, knows." This is undoubtedly true: the only way to really know an experience is to have the experience, but there are degrees of *knowing* it. He who tastes without paying very much attention to what he is doing knows only a little bit about it, and he who tastes with strong (implicit) preconceptions about what the taste will be like may distort his perceptions and fulfill his expectations. So there is great need to refine observations here.

In general, the physical sciences have been immensely more successful than the psychological sciences because the data are far easier to observe. If you want to investigate the law of gravity, you can drop objects from various heights almost any time you wish to, make the measurements at your leisure, and repeat them as often as you like. Psychological phenomena, on the other hand, disappear if you are in the wrong mood, take on a different coloration if you've just had an argument with a friend, and so forth.

A traditional idea in the old physical sciences, which was adopted wholesale by psychology in its attempt to imitate success, was that of the "detached observer," whose act of observing had no effect on the phenomena observed. Thus he could study the "pure" phenomena. Modern physics has come to believe that this idea is completely wrong at subatomic levels (Heisenberg's uncertainty principle), and possibly wrong at all levels. But psychology has been slow in recognizing this. The topic is now getting some general attention under the rubrics of experimenter bias (Rosenthal, 1966) and demand characteristics (Orne, 1962), in which experiments have shown that the expectations of the psychologist-experimenter definitely affect the performance of subjects, usually in a way to falsely "prove" the experimenter's hypothesis. The object falling under the influence of gravity falls at the same rate regardless of the mood of the experimenter (at least this is still an unquestioned belief for most physicists), but the subject in a psychological experiment is indeed affected by the mood of the experimenter. This is also true if the experimenter is trying to observe himself: our observations of ourselves may alter our selves to various degrees. So, we must recognize that every act of observation may affect the observed and try to take this into account except in specific cases in which we can definitely show otherwise.

We must also recognize that every observer has his own characteristics that become superimposed on his observations. As we said about a state of consciousness earlier, it is an *active* way of grasping the environment, not just a passive observation of what is. If you and I observe the same phenomena, we may come up with quite different descriptions of it because you have unknowingly attended to only certain parts of it and not to others, and have confused your own characteristics with those of the observed, and I have done the same thing. If we cling steadfastly to a myth of our objectivity, or at least if I believe that *I* am objective and you believe *you* are objective, we have problems. If you don't agree with me, but I have an emotional investment in believing I am objective (as most of us do), then I must think you are wrong, or vice versa. We must recognize that the characteristics of the observer may not only alter the phenomenon itself but certainly affect the observer's perception of it. We can then try to understand the characteristics of the observer, take them into account in understanding his observations, and thus obtain a more comprehensive and accurate picture.

In terms of our current scientific data on spiritual phenomena and d-SoCs, virtually none of the above conditions have been met. Generally the reports come from people who are not trained observers in the first place, who often do not have a conscious commitment to good observation but only to a particular theory or belief system of their own they want to prove, and we usually know nothing about those observers' particular characteristics. While in principle good observation will lay the data foundation for scientific understanding of spiritual and d-SoC phenomena, in fact our present data base is quite poor, a mixture of what are probably a few good observations and many, many poor ones.

FREE COMMUNICATION: THE PUBLIC NATURE OF OBSERVATION

In science, observations must be *public* in the sense that they are repeatable by any properly trained observer. This means that the original observer communicates his observations freely and fully to others interested in the phenomena so they may attempt to repeat them. The original observer must try to describe the (experienced) conditions surrounding his observations with sufficient clarity and detail that another may attempt to set up or find similar (experienced) conditions, and make an observation which is essentially identical with what was originally reported. If the other observer sets up what seem to be similar conditions, but then does not have the experience of what was originally reported, the original observation, this means that the original investigator gave an incorrect description of the conditions necessary to make his observations and/or that he was not aware of certain essential aspects of these conditions and so described them incorrectly or incompletely.

For example, someone reports that there is a phenomenon he calls the "Northern Lights," a play of colors in the sky which he has observed. He must also point out that it must be night time to observe this phenomenon, one must be looking north, and he must be at a high latitude in order to see it. Someone else is then able to set up the same conditions: he arranges his physical environment so his experience is of being in a northern latitude and looking at the northern night sky, and he may then also have the experience of seeing the Northern Lights. If our second observer does not see them when these conditions are set up, it may mean that the original observer forgot to specify, for instance, that they are more likely to be seen at certain seasons of the year than others. Our second observer is in the right place at the wrong time; he had an incomplete description of the conditions necessary to observe the phenomenon.

When a second observer has the same sort of experiences as the first observer under specified conditions, we speak of this as *consensual validation.* By obtaining consensual validation we have a much higher confidence that reported observations have indeed been described accurately, rather than possibly being a product of one observer's distorted way of perception.

The physicalistic addition to the methodological rule of consensual validation is that since physical data are the only data that are ultimately "real," internal or experiential phenomena, being inherently unreliable and unreal, must be reduced to physiological or behavioral data to become reliable. If they cannot be so reduced, they are generally ignored. This came about historically because experiential data are much harder to get consensual validation on: I may go to a concert and say that a particular piece of music produced great joy in me; you may go and hear the same piece played and experience no joy at all. Physical data, historically speaking, have simply been much easier to work with. You can adequately describe all the conditions necessary, and replication can be obtained by a trained observer much more easily. To return to our example of feeling joy at hearing a particular piece of music, I was probably wrong to ascribe the feeling of joy to merely the condition of hearing a particular piece of music played. It would also be necessary to describe, under the heading of necessary conditions, something about the particular mood I was in when I went to the concert, and something about my personal history that has created the possibility of certain kinds of experiences. Insofar as I am not able to discern these as necessary conditions, or fail to include them in my report of an observation, it is unlikely that another will be able to consensually validate my experience. The fact that experiential phenomena take place under much more complex conditions than physical phenomena and so are inherently more difficult to describe adequately, however, does not mean that they should be ignored in favor of concentration only on the easier, physical phenomena.

There are various examples, scattered throughout the psychological literature, which suggest that consensual validation of purely experiential phenomena can be quite good, but these are generally too scattered to make much of an impact on science. To take one example, Erma Kvetensky and I (Tart and Kvetensky, 1973) carried out a questionnaire study of experienced marijuana users, asking them to take eight experiential phenomena commonly associated with the d-ASC of marijuana intoxication and rate, from their own experience, the minimum level of intoxication necessary to experience these phenomena. Level of intoxication was also a purely experiential measure which is not the same thing as drug dosage. We then compared these results with those obtained from an earlier group of experienced users (Tart, 1971b) to see how reliable these internal observations were. Figure 1 presents the two charts which summarize these results, and shows that there was an extremely high degree of agreement on two sets of experiential ratings. The overall correlation between them was .95, an exceptionally high correlation for psychological research.* This finding is particularly striking because we were not dealing with the observations of highly trained observers, but ordinary, college-educated people for the most part.

---

*Correlation means the degree of relationship between two things: a correlation of zero would mean no discernible relationship, while a correlation of one would mean a perfect relationship; i.e., if you know the value of one variable you know exactly the value of the other.

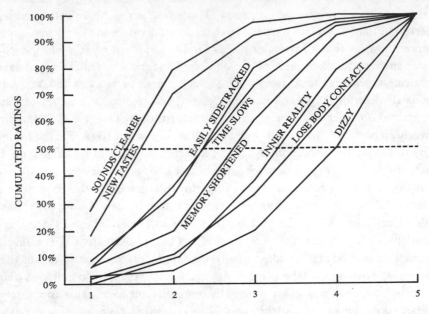

MINIMAL EXPERIENTIAL LEVEL OF INTOXICATION,
as reported by the subjects (Tart, 1971b)

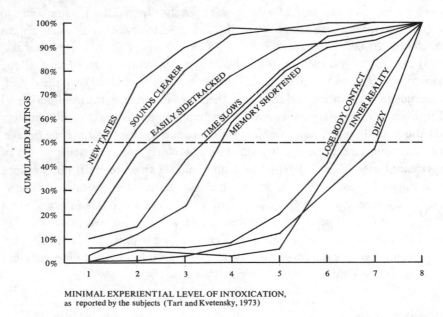

MINIMAL EXPERIENTIAL LEVEL OF INTOXICATION,
as reported by the subjects (Tart and Kvetensky, 1973)

Fig. 1: Reliability of scaling various experiential phenomena of marijuana intoxication.

A science, as a human enterprise shared by a number of people, builds its foundation on a body of consensually validated observations, the data base or "factual" base of the science. As long as one cannot get any reasonable degree of agreement among different observers, one cannot build a science. In terms of our scientific knowledge about d-ASCs, we start from a poor data base. Very few investigators have looked to see how consistent reports by individual observers were, so most of what we have as a data base at this time is simply an overall impression that certain types of phenomena are common in various d-ASCs. We know almost nothing about the exact nature of these phenomena and the particular experiential conditions necessary to produce them.

The emphasis on the public nature of observation in science has had a misleading quality, which the example above unfortunately reinforces: that *any* intelligent man can replicate a scientist's observations. This might have been true in the early days of various sciences, but certainly has not been true for a long time. I cannot go into a modern physicist's or biologist's laboratory and confirm his observations: I don't know what many of his terms mean, I don't understand how to use his apparatus, and I would probably just make a mess of things.

Given the great complexity of spiritual phenomena and d-ASC phenomena, and their significance, the need for replication by trained observers to form a data base for future sciences is of exceptional importance. This will not be easy to accomplish. It generally takes four to ten years of intensive training to produce a scientist in any of our conventional sciences, so we should not be surprised if it takes as long or longer for future sciences of d-ASCs.

We cannot specify now what adequate training would be for the state-specific sciences I propose. There will be many years of trial and error and controversy before various kinds of useful training patterns begin to emerge clearly, before some of these patterns are seen to produce observers who can agree well with each other and build sciences, and others which do not. There will undoubtedly be many people undertaking such training who will not be able to complete it also: we must recognize that possibly only a few people have the necessary qualities to complete such training successfully. Some people do not have the necessary characteristics to become physicists or mathematicians, and some undoubtedly do not have the characteristics to become, say, scientific investigators of meditative states.

Public observation, then, always refers to a limited, specially trained public of scientists working in a particular area. It is by basic agreement about observations among these specially trained people that a data base is developed that becomes the foundation for a science. That laymen cannot replicate the observations of this science (unless they wish to undergo the requisite training to become the necessary kind of scientists rather than laymen) is of no relevance in judging the validity of the science. This is important to point out, as I have seen many scientists who have read descriptions of spiritual phenomena or d-ASC phenomena, sat down and tried one of them for ten minutes, had no result, and then proclaimed loudly that there was nothing to this whole area. This is a layman's opinion of a very complex field, and has no relevance. Psychology generally has had many problems from the assumption almost every human being makes that he is an expert psychologist.

Another major problem in obtaining the needed consensual validation to form the data base for sciences of spiritual phenomena and d-ASCs is that of *state-specific communication*. This is a concept predicted by my theory of d-ASCs (Tart, 1975), but not yet investigated empirically. Given that a d-ASC is an overall qualitative and quantitative shift in the complex functioning and *pattern* of consciousness, such that there are new "logics," new ways of perceiving, a paradigm shift, it is quite likely that communication between two observers in the same d-ASC may take a different pattern from what it would ordinarily take between the same two people in their ordinary d-SoC. Such a shift might make for improved or worsened communication, depending on the particular subject matter they were attempting to communicate about within the common d-ASC.

Even if two observers had become relatively fluent in communicating in a particular d-ASC, an "outside" observer, an observer in a different d-SoC, might not be able to follow the communication between our first two observers. Indeed, he might feel that their communication had "deteriorated." There is an implicit assumption here, made by almost all of us, that if I cannot understand what other people are talking about, they are probably talking nonsense!

Practically all investigations of communication by experimental subjects in d-ASCs have yielded a "deterioration" of communication, as evaluated by ortho-dox investigators. These investigators have not taken the possibility of state-specific communication into account in designing their studies. If I am listening to two people in any d-SoC, speaking in English, and they suddenly begin to intersperse words and phrases in French, I, as an outside (that is, a non-French-speaking) observer will probably conclude that there has been a gross deteriora-tion in communication, "infantile regression to nonsense sounds." To the two observers, or to an observer who also speaks French, they may be communicating *more* fluently because of the ability of French to express certain concepts that English cannot. Adequacy of communication between people in the same d-ASC, and the accuracy of communication across different d-SoCs, must be empirically determined. Some criteria for this are discussed elsewhere, along with a complete presentation of my theory on the nature of states of consciousness (Tart, 1975).

Thus the consensual validation which forms the data base of a science may be restricted by the fact that only observers/scientists who can enter that particular d-ASC and learn to communicate fully in it can participate in consensual valida-tion. It may be impossible for someone not able to enter that d-ASC to ever be able to understand the nature of the phenomena.*

The idea of state-specific communication and the incomprehensibility of it to an outside observer is well illustrated in a Sufi teaching story about a Sufi mystic and the Mulla Nasrudin, a figure who is simultaneously rascal, idiot, and sage. Both of them are able to function in various d-ASCs and have their ordinary d-SoC quite changed as a result.

A Sufi mystic stopped Nasrudin in the street. In order to test whether the Mulla was sensitive to inner knowledge, he made a sign, pointing at the sky.

The Sufi meant, "There is only one truth, which covers all."

Nasrudin's companion, an ordinary man, thought: "The Sufi is mad. I wonder what precautions Nasrudin will take?"

Nasrudin looked in a knapsack and took out a coil of rope. This he handed to his companion.

"Excellent," thought the companion, "we will bind him up if he becomes violent."

The Sufi saw that Nasrudin meant: "Ordinary humanity tries to find truth by methods as unsuitable as attempting to climb into the sky with a rope." [Shah, I., 1966]

THEORIZING

Like people in general, scientists are not content simply to observe what happens, simply to look at the data. They want to know what the observations *mean,* what concepts account for what has been observed, what the origins, goals, mechanisms, and consequences of things are. If we see two people quarreling, for instance, we are seldom content simply to note that they are quarreling and let it go at that: we want to know *why* they are quarreling, what the meaning of this particular observation is. So we theorize, to put it in a formal way, we search among the concepts that are stored in our mind to find a set of concepts which "explains" the observations we have just made, and/or we modify our old concepts and create a new set to explain the observations.

The third methodological rule of science is that theorizing about observations must be *logical:* the conceptual links between observations and the set of concepts put forward to explain them be of such a nature that anyone who knows the logics generally accepted in the culture or science, whether they are linguistic, math-

---

*A state-specific scientist, one able to enter a particular d-ASC and carry out scientific work there, might find his own work somewhat incomprehensible when he is back in his ordinary d-SoC or some other d-ASC because of the phenomena, for which experimental evidence is now accumulating, of *state-specific memory.* That is, not enough of his work would transfer to his ordinary d-SoC to make it comprehensible to him in that d-SoC, even though it would make perfect sense when he was again in the d-ASC in which he did his scientific work. To put it humorously, when the scientist returned home his wife might ask, "What did you do in the laboratory today?" and he would honestly reply that he had no clear idea at all, but when he was there he knew that his work was progressing nicely!

ematical, or whatever, can see that the thinking steps have been performed correctly. It is like requiring, for example, that before we accept a prediction about economic possibilities we want to know that the arithmetical calculations used in developing the prediction have been carried out correctly.

In the ideal case, then, the scientist observes a certain group of phenomena that interests him and then comes up with a new concept which links all of these observations together, explains them in a simplified way. Some data may, for logical reasons, be considered to not fall under the heading of this theory. The theory may not be intended to be totally comprehensive, but for the data that it clearly is relevant to, it should explain all the observations that have been made so far. When this theory is communicated to another scientist, the other scientist should be able to agree that the rules of the particular logic have indeed been followed in developing this theory, that the theory is *logically valid,* even though he may not wish to accept the theory as "true" for other reasons, such as believing that there is some other theory that handles the same data in a more elegant fashion.

The requirement to theorize logically and consistently with the observed data is not as simple as it looks, however. A common, generally implicit assumption in our culture is that there is one true "logic," and that all intelligent people know what this is. Any logic (and there are many of them) is a set of *assumptions* and a set of rules for manipulating information based on these assumptions. The assumptions are, to a large or total extent, arbitrary. Change the assumptions and the rules for working with these assumptions, and you have a different logic.

The example familiar to most readers of different logics would be the three different geometries mentioned in many high school geometry courses. The geometry we use most, Euclidean geometry, makes an assumption that parallel lines always maintain exactly the same distance from one another, no matter how far they are extended, even to infinity. Two other geometries make different assumptions. One assumes that as parallel lines are extended to infinity they tend to converge and eventually meet. The other assumes that as parallel lines are extended to infinity they gradually diverge and eventually are an infinite distance apart from one another. Now each of these three assumptions is perfectly valid, they are purely mental constructs, and there is no way of declaring one inherently more valid than another. On an earthly level, dealing with small-scale material objects that cannot come anywhere near extending to infinity, Euclidean geometry provides the best working fit to the other sensory data about these objects that we have, although not fitting purely visual data which sees railroad tracks come together in the distance. But this merely says something about the usefulness of a particular application, not about the inherent validity of an assumption. An assumption is *assumed.* You may talk about the consequences of assumptions being more or less useful in relation to some other standards, but there is no way of "proving" or "disproving" an assumption.

A theory that works well tends to become implicit and, being implicit, has a tremendous control over us. I find, for example, that I *really* think the two other geometries are nonsense, that everyone knows that parallel lines are parallel by definition! If I take care to think about it logically, I'm not caught by this assumption, but emotionally I really believe in Euclidean geometry and I tend to automatically dismiss the other two (and my visual experience with railroad tracks) as not serious.

A paradigm and d-SoC are also both logics, sets of interlocking assumptions and rules for working with information, that tend to become implicit. Indeed, the better a paradigm works in explaining things, or the better a d-SoC works in making us feel comfortable in the reality we have to deal with, the more it becomes implicit and simply feels as if it were the truth or the "natural" order of things.

For example, suppose you have immense numbers of observations on the

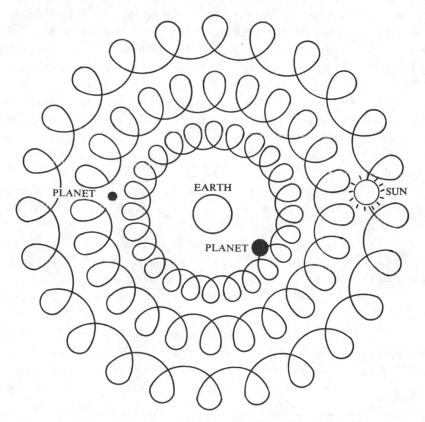

Fig. 2: The universe as conceived in Ptolemaic or geocentric astronomy, with various planets revolving in epicycles around the earth.

positions, over the course of time, of the planets and the stars, and you wish to know how these planets and stars move. If you use the "obvious" paradigm that was accepted in our culture for the longest period of time, the Ptolemaic, geocentric astronomical paradigm, which says that the earth is obviously still and in the middle of things, and all the heavenly bodies go around it, then you make "sense" out of the data by making drawings like Figure 2, showing the heavenly bodies going around the earth in a very complex fashion. They go around not simply in circles, for there are discrepancies between observations and what you would predict from drawing circles, but in what are called epicycles, circles on top of circles. This is the "obviously sensible" explanation of the data.

Today this kind of drawing of planetary paths looks silly: we "know" that the sun is the center of the solar system, and our earth, along with the other planets of the solar system, rotates about it. After all, we were taught it in school! So the kind of drawing of elliptical paths around the sun, shown in Figure 3, is the "obviously sensible" way to reduce the data to us.

As an intellectual exercise, one can see the arbitrariness of the geocentric and heliocentric paradigms for astronomy, can see that the data could be cast in either one. In the history of science, the geocentric astronomical paradigm was eventually rejected because it became incredibly cumbersome to make observation and theory fit: astronomers were having to superimpose epicycles on the epicycles on the epicycles. The heliocentric paradigm, when it was generally accepted, provided a much simpler and more elegant way of matching observations and concepts. *But,* the heliocentric paradigm has sunk in much deeper than that: we can look at the geocentric drawing in Figure 2 and *know* that it is not true! We have developed an automatic, deep commitment to the heliocentric paradigm that borders on an emotional, rather than just an intellectual, acceptance of it.*

The difference between the geocentric and heliocentric paradigms is a shift in the particular intellectual content within a single d-SoC, our ordinary state of consciousness. Suppose we think of the same phenomena viewed from two different d-SoCs: we will find similar things to viewing data from two different paradigms, but with even greater complexity, for the nature of logic may change in a d-ASC. It is as if parallel lines *obviously* stay the same distance apart in one d-SoC and *obviously* converge in a second d-SoC. Certain assumptions are automatically made in one d-SoC by virtue of its inherent nature, but different assumptions are made in the other d-SoC. In the d-ASCs we know of, of course, there is a fair amount of overlapping content. Two plus two equals four in a hypnotic state as well as in an ordinary state, for example (although it can be

---

*Let me stress that scientifically we do *not know* that the earth rotates about the sun; this view merely fits the data far better and more "elegantly" than the alternative.

altered quite readily to make it equal something else in the hypnotic state).

Let us now consider the case in which a scientist enters d-SoC #2, makes certain observations while in that state, and, while remaining in d-SoC #2, theorizes as to what they mean. In order to avoid the possibility of errors in his theorizing, failure to follow the logic inherent in d-SoC #2, he wishes to have another scientist check on him. So he finds a second scientist who can enter d-SoC #2 and communicate fluently in it. The first scientist communicates his observations and his theorizing to the second scientist, who can then comment on whether the first scientist has followed the logic for d-SoC #2 correctly— whether he has played according to the rules of the game for d-SoC #2. Thus we have a validation of the correctness of the theorizing which is specific to d-SoC #2.

Suppose the scientist who has created this theory now reorganizes his consciousness so that he is back in d-SoC #1 (which might be our ordinary state of consciousness, but could be any d-SoC), and then attempts to communicate his observations and theories to another scientist who is also in d-SoC #1. He may find that he cannot adequately recall or understand or communicate his own observations and theories because of the phenomena of state-specific memory and state-specific communication. Thus his attempts to communicate to this new scientist who is in d-SoC #1 are a failure. Or, suppose that the first scientist remains in d-SoC #2 and attempts to describe his theory to a third scientist who is in d-SoC #1. Although the scientist now understands what he is saying, the third scientist in d-SoC #1 may not be able to comprehend what the first scientist is saying because of the communication problems. Thus the third scientist who is not in the same d-SoC cannot comment on the inherent *validity* of the first scientist's theorizing. He may comment on its *communicability*, he may say that

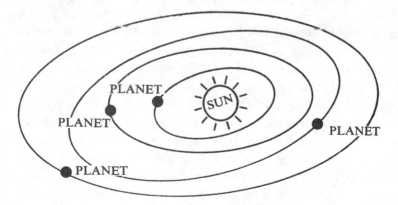

Fig. 3: The solar system as conceived in the Copernican or heliocentric paradigm. The sun is considered the center of the solar system, and the planets are seen as revolving in elliptical paths about it.

what the first scientist is saying makes no sense at all or does seem to make some sense in d-SoC #1, but in order for him to comment on the inherent validity of the theory, the third scientist must also be able to enter d-SoC #2 and communicate fluently in it. So, scientists who can enter the same d-SoC and learn to communicate may comment on the inherent "logical" validity of one another's theories, but the "outsider," the person who cannot enter and work in that d-SoC, cannot comment on its inherent validity.

Let us apply this reasoning to spiritual phenomena. If I read, for example, a bit of Buddhist writing on the nature of consciousness, it may not be comprehensible to me. But, given that this was probably developed from a d-ASC (as Goleman argues in Chapter 5), I would be foolish to say it is inherently wrong. I can only accurately say that I do not understand this. Only if I can learn to achieve the d-ASC that the original writer was in can I have a hope of saying anything about its inherent validity, its state-specific validity.

I must emphasize again that this idea of state-specific theorizing and state-specific logics flies very much in the face of our "commonsense" or, more precisely, ordinary d-SoC assumption that there is only one kind of *real* logic, and that I (including you) am a master of it. If you find yourself at all agitated over this section, it would be well to reread it and try to see what sorts of assumptions lie behind the agitation.

TESTABILITY

Because of a recognition of the fact that the feeling that "I know" or "this is obviously true" may have little relation to reality, even though it pleases the person experiencing it, the fourth methodological rule of science is that a theory must not only consistently account for the observed data and have a logical structure, it must also make predictions about further data to be observed under new conditions. That is, a scientific theory must have *testable* consequences that go beyond what has already been seen, and these consequences must eventually be tested. If the predicted observations do not occur, then the theory must be rejected or modified, no matter how elegant, "rational," or satisfying it is.

To put this in a more formal way, one of the prime characteristics of the human mind seems to be an ability to create patterns out of arrays of stimuli coming into it. This has great survival value in many ways: a few bits of shading and color in the background of many bushes were turned into the patterns of a tiger by perceptual processes, and our ancestors froze or crept away. The tiger wasn't always there, but it might have been, and escaping was a very adaptive kind of behavior.

The problem is that this patternmaking mechanism works so well that it often creates patterns in our perception where none exist in the external (or internal) world. For example, one can devise a random process to generate numbers and come up with a number like 80119797907168851212564954889O. There is a mathematical theorem that shows one can then devise a formula, a mathematical function, which will generate this particular string of numbers, thus implying that the numbers were not randomly generated at all but are only a complex pattern. The catch is that this mathematical function will not predict (beyond chance expectation) what the *next* number in the series will be. Thus it is with our minds: we can generate wonderful patterns, theories, concepts, but that does not guarantee that these theories will predict the next event coming along. So one of the major strengths of science is its insistence that theory must have testable consequences, and the commitment to go ahead and test these consequences.

The association of science with physicalism has led us to think that testing a theory means looking at physical consequences, things we can measure with instruments. We predict on theoretical grounds, for example, that two chemicals will react strongly and produce heat, then we actually mix the two chemicals and insert a thermometer to see if heat is generated. But, in accordance with our earlier theoretical position that all knowledge is basically an experience in our minds, there is no need to feel that a physical consequence is somehow a "better" validation of a theory than a purely experiential consequence. Physical things are generally much easier to verify, but this does not eliminate the need to achieve testability of our theories about spiritual phenomena and d-ASC phenomena.

Let us construct a hypothetical example to show how this is done. Suppose that in a certain d-ASC numerous observers report being able to experience certain kinds of tingling, pulsing, or warm sensations that can move readily about in the body, to which they give a generally agreed-upon name, "psychic energy." Suppose they further report that when they have been physically ill while in that d-ASC, with some kind of illness that affects one part of the body more than another, they find they can feel less of this psychic energy in the afflicted part of the body than in the rest of their body. Now, an observer/investigator might theorize that this hypothesized psychic energy is important in the general, healthy functioning of the body, and is an underlying basis of physical health. This is a simple theory consistent with the observed observations, namely that a deficiency of the psychic energy is associated with physical afflictions and spells out a possible underlying mechanism.

Now, it is a straightforward step to reason that if one could deliberately control this energy (experience moving it about at will) in the d-ASC, and one then deliberately created a deficiency of this energy in a certain part of the body (a specification of conditions for observation), that part of the body would be liable to come down with a physical affliction. Or, conversely, if a given part of the physical body was ill, and one deliberately "took" psychic energy from the rest of the body (that is, had the experience of doing this) and moved it into the ill part, the ill part should heal. Both of these are testable predictions. If the conditions were met and observations showed that the predicted effects were indeed produced, this would be a good theory.

This is, of course, a very simple example, and there might be alternative theories to explain the same phenomena, but it is basically the type of thing that constitutes the scientific enterprise. The requirement of testability is also a basis for choosing among alternative theories that all explain initial data equally well: which one is best validated as its scope is extended and the resulting predictions tested?

Figure 4 summarizes in diagrammatic fashion the essence of scientific method. Given a certain segment of reality that is our field of interest (it could be called biology, physics, meditative state #10, dreams, whatever), we make observations of that field, with a commitment to continually refine and expand our observations. We also theorize about what our observations mean, with a similar commitment to theorize logically and refine our theorizing. We then make further predictions based on our theory, committing ourselves to make these as accurately as possible, and, applying these predictions back to the segment of reality of our interest, observe whether they are correct.

The process sketched so far, shown by the outer circle of arrows in Figure 4, can all go on in one person's mind. The open and comprehensive communication with other scientists, represented by the middle circle, brings a power into the process that allows avoidance of many errors and, in the long run, produces accomplishments well beyond what a single mind can do. Thus our observations are communicated with others who either validate or do not validate them, who extend them, giving us a further stimulus to refine our observations. Our theories are communicated with others, who agree or don't agree that we have followed certain logic processes without error, and further stimulate us to refine our theorizing. Our predictions from our theory are shared with others, who again indicate whether we have correctly followed the appropriate logic in making these predictions and further stimulate us about other predictions, perhaps making other predictions themselves, thus further refining the predictive process. This overall pattern of interaction with scientific peers and with the segment of reality of interest constitutes the scientific method. Metaphorically, it constitutes a kind of communication with reality. It is not a static process, but one repeated over and over again, eventually leading to more and more congruence between our concepts and our observations of (experiences of) reality, or what in older terms we would call a closer and closer approximation to truth. The particular d-SoC in which all this process is carried out is what constitutes the state-specificity of the process.

EMOTIONAL INVOLVEMENT AND SCIENCE

One of the popular stereotypes of the scientist, popular among scientists as well as among lay people, is that the scientist is a very cool character, he is not emotionally involved with what he studies, and this makes him "objective." How can we reconcile this apparent need for emotional uninvolvement with the intensely emotional experiences that take place in various d-ASCs?

The first step of reconciliation is to realize that this stereotype is false in many ways. The scientist, being human, gets excited by what he's doing, is pleased and satisfied when results seem to prove his own theories, is angry or depressed when results go against his favorite theories. Indeed, it sometimes is the emotional attachment to proving his own theory that provides the driving force that makes him into a hard-working researcher. So a very large amount of emotion occurs in ordinary state of consciousness science.

In spite of his emotional involvement with his subject material, the scientist is

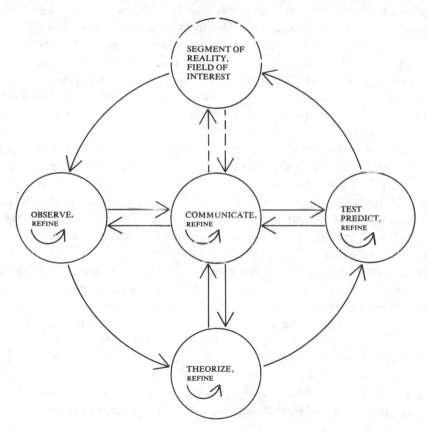

Fig. 4: The essence of scientific method.

still committed to observation, open communication, logical theorizing, and testing the consequences of his theory. If he wants to be recognized as a scientist by his colleagues, he must communicate his results and conduct his experiments in such a way that they meet the essence of scientific method, discussed earlier. Although he may have been very excited and pleased with a certain result, he writes a scientific report that leaves out his own excitement and simply communicates the way to make certain kinds of observations, the observations, the theorizing about them, and ways in which he may have tested the theory.

This kind of communication is perfectly adequate in most of the physical sciences: the apparatus you are using to measure something does not respond to your emotional mood. When we get into psychological processes, however, especially d-ASC processes and observations and manipulation of one's own internal state, we often find that it can't be done unemotionally. That is, a certain kind and intensity of emotion is necessary as the energy source and/or catalyst to make a particular experience come about. So the tactic here is not to pretend that emotion is unnecessary, but to specify clearly and exactly why and in what manner emotions are necessary in order to make certain observations.

One might legitimately argue that emotions are very dangerous things once they get aroused in connection with a person's work, as it is not very easy to turn them on and off at will. They can become part of one's long-term personality structure and can seriously distort work. How can we develop state-specific sciences in which emotion is involved, when the emotions might bias our investigators so much?

While recognizing the real dangers of implicit and uncontrolled emotionality, I think the answer lies in realizing that while we have not trained ourselves to understand and control our emotions in our culture, this does not mean that we must always be the slaves of emotions. We do not have to adopt the physical sciences' model of pretending that emotions are not part of science, nor try to suppress all emotions, as that would kill off many phenomena we are trying to study. We need to really recognize the importance of emotions and continue to develop various kinds of psychotherapeutic and personal growth techniques that will both allow a person full access to his emotions and give him a more stable personal basis on which to deal with emotions without becoming overly attached to them. Indeed, I am inclined to believe Gurdjieff's idea (Ouspensky, 1949) that our emotional system constitutes a whole "brain," potentially as intelligent and important as our "thinking" brain, but that the failure of our culture to adequately develop, educate, and integrate all three of our "brains" (Gurdjieff also treats the body as a "brain," a way of evaluating data) leaves us controlled by poorly understood and feared emotions, rather than master of them.

STATE-SPECIFIC SCIENCES

When we think of a branch of science, we usually have an image something like this: centered on interest in some particular subject matter, a number of highly selected, talented, and rigorously educated people spend considerable time making detailed observations on the subject matter of interest. They may or may not have special places (laboratories), instruments, or methods to assist them in making finer and more extended observations. They speak to one another in a technical vocabulary that often amounts to a special language, which they feel conveys precisely the important data and concepts of their field. Using this language, they confirm and extend mutual knowledge of data basic to the field. They theorize about such basic data and construct theoretical systems to explain these data. They validate, reject, or refine the theories by recourse to further observation. These trained people all have a long-term commitment to constant extension and refinement of their observations, and extension and refinement of their theories. Their activity is often incomprehensible to laymen or scientists in other branches of science.

This overall description of a science is equally applicable to a wide variety of sciences, or areas that could become sciences, whether we call such areas biology, physics, psychology, genetics, chemistry, experimental mysticism, or drug-induced state of consciousness. The particulars of research activity might look very different, but the basic scientific method, summarized in Figure 4, would be seen running through all of them.

What I proposed in originally writing about this area (Tart, 1972) was that we begin to create various *state-specific sciences,* sciences particular to various d-ASCs. If such sciences could be created, we would have groups of highly skilled, trained, and dedicated practitioners able to achieve certain d-ASCs, and able to agree with one another that they had attained the common state. While in a particular d-ASC, the group of scientists might want to investigate other areas of interest, such as internal phenomena of the particular d-ASC that had not yet been explored, the interaction of that d-ASC with ordinary physical reality, the interaction of people in that d-ASC, the interaction of that d-ASC with other d-SoCs, and so on. By analogy, it's as if a group of investigators could find some way of getting to a state called California (to use a very "mystical" example!), could agree to mutual satisfaction that they were all in California, and then begin individual explorations of California, sharing their observations and theories about what these observations meant, with the eventual hope of "explaining" California.

Some people who feel that science is hostile to their particular interest area would say that science can never comprehend or add anything to our knowledge of spiritual phenomena, just as some would say that California is a phenomenon too complex to be understood by human minds. The important thing is that we must try this and find out how successful we will be, not abandon the attempt a priori.

The fact that the scientist should be able to function skillfully in a particular d-SoC in which he is attempting to develop a state-specific science does not mean that he would always be the observer or the subject in experimental work. While he might often be observer, subject, and experimenter simultaneously, he could also collect data in experimental work with other subjects in that particular d-SoC, and/or be in that d-SoC himself at the time of data collection, and/or be in that d-SoC himself for data analysis and theorizing.

When this proposal for creating state-specific sciences was first presented, some readers asked for examples of state-specific sciences. Aside from the fact that examples are not possible because we have not yet developed any state-specific sciences (we will deal later with the question of whether the spiritual psychologies presented in this book are state-specific sciences), any example that would make good sense to the readers of this chapter (who are, presumably, all in an ordinary d-SoC) would fail to illustrate the uniqueness of a state-specific science. If it did make sense, it would be an example of a problem area that could be approached adequately from both our ordinary d-SoC and the d-ASC, and thus it would be too easy to see the entire problem in terms of accepted ordinary-consciousness scientific procedures and miss the point about the necessity for developing state-specific sciences.*

Ordinary science is, of course, a state-specific science, specific to our ordinary d-SoC.

STATE-SPECIFIC TECHNOLOGIES

It is important to distinguish the proposed state-specific *sciences* from what we might call state-specific *technologies*. A technology is a body of knowledge about *how* to accomplish certain things, often coupled with a certain amount of innovation for accomplishing accepted purposes more efficiently. There are times when the exact border between a science and a related technology is unclear, especially since the progress of a science often depends on the progress of its associated

---

*It is possible that readers who have themselves not experienced any d-ASC other than ones in which their mind seemed to be functioning in a "deteriorated" fashion (drunkenness or dreaming, e.g.) may fail to appreciate the need for developing state-specific sciences. This was succinctly illustrated when this proposal was first presented (Tart, 1972). Among the many letters to the editor commenting on my proposal was a pair of letters (not selected by the editors of *Science* for publication) from a psychiatrist. His first letter was severely critical of the proposal, arguing that it could not improve on the ordinary state-of-consciousness science we already have. His second letter, written a few days after the first, stated that he had been in a d-ASC the night before, had thought about this proposal, and, *from the perspective of that d-ASC,* saw that it made perfect sense! It was embarrassing for him to write the second letter, and he tried to reason away this experience, but his scientific honesty compelled him to write it.

technology, but generally we can emphasize that the important thing in a science is to *understand,* and to continually search for further understanding, while the primary purpose of a technology is to *accomplish* already accepted goals, with new understanding being a secondary consideration or, sometimes, of no importance at all. So we may have an expert group of technicians who learn to manufacture needed medicines or needed bullets more efficiently, or who learn to use psychological techniques to increase the reading ability of disadvantaged children, or sell more (useless) products through improved advertising. In all these cases technicians accept that what they are doing is good and useful, and concern themselves with doing it well. They are not particularly concerned with understanding the overall effects of bullets or medicines or improved advertising or improved reading skills in society as a whole or in their relation to the overall nature of man, or in understanding *why* these things work as they do.

The distinction between a science and a technology is further confused in our society because many scientists are essentially technicians, plying a trade they have learned rather than really being interested in finding new knowledge, while some technicians have the curiosity and commitment to searching for truth that characterizes science.

From the Western scientific point of view, we do not have any state-specific sciences (unless some of the spiritual psychologies are state-specific sciences), but there clearly are many state-specific technologies scattered through the world, even though our scientific knowledge of them is meager. That is, there are bodies of knowledge about inducing particular d-ASCs and then controlling experience within those d-ASCs to produce results considered useful in terms of certain accepted goals. As a Western example, consider the practice of hypnotherapy. Elaborate techniques exist for inducing hypnosis in many people defined as ill, and for then manipulating the d-ASC of hypnosis to maximize various kinds of medical and psychiatric therapeutic processes. Hypnotherapy is an example of a state-specific technology coupled with a science, because there has been a reasonable start on an ordinary d-SoC science of hypnosis, and considerable research is going on in this area to expand this knowledge. We do not have a state-specific science of hypnosis, however.

Let us consider two examples of state-specific technologies which do not seem to be coupled with any science. One such state-specific technology can be seen at many revivalistic meetings. Given the goal of the revivalist that converting people to Christianity is a good thing, a good revivalist skillfully induces extreme emotions about guilt and sin in many people at the revival. Inducing extreme emotions is an excellent way of destabilizing one's ordinary d-SoC so that it may become unstable and be replaced by a d-ASC.* The expectational context of the

---

*The process of inducing d-ASCs has been discussed in detail elsewhere (Tart, 1973b; 1975).

Christian tradition, combined with the specific suggestions inherent in the preaching at the revival, then guides the content of whatever d-ASC is produced into a specifically Christian form, producing very powerful emotional experiences in some sort or sorts of d-ASCs. These emotional d-ASC experiences often have a carryover effect of producing conversion and keeping it active for some period of time, perhaps a lifetime: the d-ASC experience may seem miraculous by ordinary consciousness standards.

In using this as an example, my aim is not to antagonize Christians, who, also having accepted the idea that conversion to Christianity is a good thing, may not see what is "wrong" with such techniques. I do not wish to judge whether this is right or wrong, but merely to point out that technological knowledge for inducing and controlling a d-ASC is used in the service of an already accepted goal: the goal is not questioned, nor is the d-ASC or the spiritual experiences therein explored to increase knowledge, but only used to maximize the effectiveness of attaining the goal.

A second example, supposedly historical but possibly mythical, stems from the explanation frequently given of the origin of the word "assassin." The word supposedly derives either from hashish, the potent resin of the marijuana plant, or from a Middle Eastern sheik named Hussain, who reportedly used the following state-specific technology. Acting in the role of an Islamic religious leader, he recruited followers to use as assassins against his enemies by promising them that loyalty to him would guarantee them entry into the kingdom of heaven when they died. Hussain then "proved" this claim, in order to make absolutely loyal followers, by inviting the potential follower to a banquet at which the potential follower's food was drugged, presumably with hashish and certainly with some other drugs that put him to sleep before the effects of the hashish became noticeable. On awakening, the potential follower found himself in a beautiful garden which was hidden in the sheik's castle. He was now extremely intoxicated, in a d-ASC from the effects of the hashish. Being in a beautiful garden, surrounded by beautiful women, having all his perceptions psychedelically enhanced, and being told he was in heaven produced a conviction in him that he was. After a period of time he was again drugged into sleep and taken back into his ordinary surroundings. Upon awakening he had a memory of having visited heaven, just as his leader had promised he would, and became a loyal follower even at the risk of his life, since he *knew* that he was guaranteed entry into heaven.*

Whether this story is historically true or not, it makes perfect sense in terms of illustrating the uses to which a state-specific technology can be put, as well as

---

*Presumably the potential follower had no previous familiarity with the effects of hashish, or he would recognize he was drugged and be suspicious.

showing that the "obvious" perception of truth in a d-ASC can be false.

Manipulating people through the use of d-ASCs depends on their being ignorant of their actual condition. I hope that increasing familiarity with d-ASCs and the development of state-specific sciences will make people less susceptible to such manipulation.

RELATIONSHIPS BETWEEN STATE-SPECIFIC SCIENCES

I mentioned earlier that, in older terminology, the repeated application of scientific method ultimately leads us toward truth, but I felt rather uncomfortable using this phrase. While it is a noble idea, it reinforces a common misperception of science, a misperception shared by many scientists themselves. It is the idea that in our ordinary d-SoC we are capable of comprehending everything in the universe, and that the progress of science is a steady, albeit sometimes erratic, march toward the ultimate reduction of everything to simple, elegant, comprehensible theories, whose applications explain literally everything. This has often been put in the metaphor of the ultimate mathematical formula to which everything reduces, and the expansion of which yields all phenomena. An implicit corollary of this, given the way people's minds work, is that phenomena which do not seem to fit in with this wonderful linear march toward truth are dismissed as unimportant or attacked as superstition and nonsense.

While it is possible that there may be some d-SoC in which *everything* can be observed and understood, this does not fit with what we have observed so far. Certain kinds of phenomena, especially those we call spiritual phenomena, seem quite incomprehensible in our ordinary d-SoC, although they seem much more comprehensible in certain d-ASCs. If there is some one d-SoC in which everything can be understood, perhaps this is some sort of ultimate enlightenment, but it certainly is not our ordinary d-SoC. Let us look at the relationship between the various state-specific sciences that may be developed for various d-ASCs, and see what this can tell us about the possibilities of ultimately understanding everything.

Any state-specific science consists of two parts, a body of observations and a body of theories about the observations. The observations are what can be experienced relatively directly; the theories are the inferences and explanations about nonobservable factors that account for the observations. The fact that my car runs, for example, is an observation for me. The chemical theory to explain the combustion of gasoline and air underlying the running of the car is not directly observable by me—it is a theory.

In considering two separate d-SoCs, what may be theory in one d-SoC may be observation in the other, or vice versa. For example, the phenomenon of *synes-*

thesia (for example, seeing vivid colors as a consequence of hearing sound, without any physical visual stimuli) is a theoretical idea for me in my ordinary d-SoC: I cannot experience it, and can only think of theories about what it might mean, based on other people's reports. If I were under the influence of a psychedelic drug such as LSD or marijuana (Tart, 1971b), I might directly experience synesthesia, and so what is theory to me in one d-SoC would become direct observation in a second d-SoC.*

Figure 5 shows some possible relationships between three state-specific sciences, two of which show considerable overlap in their content, the third of which shows no overlap at all with the other two. The area labeled O_1O_2 is one which permits direct observation, direct experience in both state-specific sciences. The area labeled T_1T_2 is one of theoretical inferences about subject matter common to the two state-specific sciences. In area O_1T_2, by contrast, theoretical propositions of state-specific science #2 are matters of direct observation for the scientist in d-SoC #1, and vice versa for the area labeled T_1O_2. State-specific science #3 is a body of observation and theory exclusive to that d-SoC, and has no overlap with the other two sciences.

We cannot say that when there is an overlapping area of subject matter, work in one state-specific science either *validates* or *invalidates* the work of a second state-specific science, even though our (implicit) assumption that everything ought to be understandable in terms of our ordinary d-SoC inclines us to think so. In the physical sciences the concept of *complementarity* had to be introduced when it was found that light could be explained equally well as either a wave or a particle, that the two ways of explaining it both gave valid, useful results, and that there was no way of ever choosing between the two explanations, of ever proving that one was true and the other was false. Each is a kind of paradigm with unique properties of its own. With state-specific sciences, given what we now know about the uniqueness of d-ASCs, the sciences developed will have uniquenesses and may be complementary when subject matters overlap, but probably will not be reducible to one another.

Let us consider as an example the longstanding controversy between explaining present-day life on earth by evolution based on random selection versus explaining it as a divinely guided process. In many ways, ultimately "proving" one or the other position is impossible. Rather, it may be the case that the idea of divine guidance of the evolutionary process is a certain kind of observation or theory that makes "obvious" sense in a certain d-ASC, while the chance selection idea makes "obvious" sense in our ordinary d-SoC. Insofar as this may be true, there

---

*I hesitate to use examples from drug-induced d-ASCs so frequently, as they reinforce an incorrect assumption that drugs are the main cause of d-ASCs, but this is the area in which most of the scanty scientific knowledge of d-ASCs occurs, and so provides ready examples.

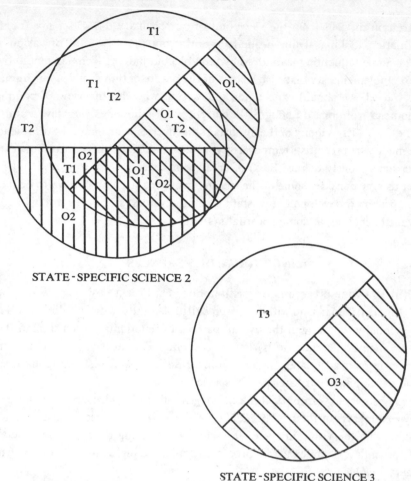

STATE - SPECIFIC SCIENCE 1

STATE - SPECIFIC SCIENCE 2

STATE - SPECIFIC SCIENCE 3

Fig. 5: Possible relationships between three state-specific sciences.

will never then be a resolution in which one or the other is completely proven and the other disproven. As Kuhn points out, in the case of a clash between two competing paradigms, it is not so much that the one which is superseded is totally *disproven* as that it is obviously less useful than the paradigm which replaces it, but the new paradigm may not account for every thing that the old one accounted for.

Thus the development of state-specific sciences may give us complementary views of man and nature that greatly enrich our overall scope, but attempts to reduce any of them to another one may be wasted energy.

Complementarity is a concept which must be shown to be useful *empirically* in the long run, not proclaimed a priori. I am not attempting to discourage research on d-ASCs from the viewpoint of our ordinary d-SoC science (or, for that matter, looking at our ordinary d-SoC from the viewpoint of various d-ASCs). Some reduction may indeed by possible, but judging from current knowledge, complementarity may also be part of the nature of things, given our humanness. Indeed, we should expect rich interaction whereby the view of common phenomena from one d-SoC greatly enriches and stimulates the view from the other d-SoC, just as many of the important discoveries of ordinary d-SoC sciences were made when scientists temporarily entered a d-ASC, such as dreaming or (the rather ambiguously defined SoC) of creative reverie.

Let us now consider some of the specific problems which will have to be faced in the proposed development of state-specific sciences, since they are also quite relevant to looking at some spiritual systems.

INDIVIDUAL DIFFERENCES

There is a widespread, implicit assumption that because two people are "normal" (not certified insane within a given cultural context), their ordinary d-SoCs are essentially the same in the overall pattern of functioning, even though there may be many differences in particular contents. This questionable assumption prevents us from adequately understanding d-SoCs, as well as standing in the way of the development of state-specific sciences.

Some people, for example, think in images, others in words. Some can voluntarily make parts of their body numb; most cannot. Some recall past events by remembering the visual image of the scene and looking at the relevant details, while others use complex verbal processes, remembering words, with little visual imagery involved.

This means that person A may be able to have certain kinds of experiences in his ordinary d-SoC that person B cannot experience in his ordinary d-SoC, no matter how hard B tries. This may result in B's thinking that A is insane, too imaginative, or a liar, or B may feel inferior to A. Conversely, if A takes B as a standard of normality, he may himself feel odd or abnormal.

Sometimes B may be able to enter a d-ASC and there experience some of the sorts of things that A has reported experiencing in his ordinary d-SoC. Thus a realm of knowledge and experience that is "ordinary" for A is then state-specific for a d-ASC for B. Conversely, some of B's experiences in a d-ASC may not be available to A in his ordinary d-SoC.

Synesthesia may again serve as an example. A few, rare individuals can experience synesthesia in their ordinary d-SoC, but most do not. Yet in surveying the experiences of veteran marijuana users (Tart, 1971b), I found that 56 percent of them experience synesthesia at least occasionally while in the d-ASC induced by marijuana. Similarly, certain kinds of spiritual experiences may be readily available for one individual in his ordinary d-SoC, yet they are totally unavailable for another individual unless he goes into a d-ASC. This may cause great misunderstanding, for the first individual may teach the second the techniques that always work for him in inducing certain spiritual experiences, and not understand why they do not work for the latter. We would say that the technique depends on a certain aspect of mind which is state-specific for the second individual, and so he will not experience it unless he knows that first he must alter his d-SoC.

This lack of recognition of individual differences appears in the scientific literature in the form of controversies over whether the concept of a "state" of consciousness is necessary to explain various phenomena. In at least one case, a proponent of the idea that the concept of a state of hypnosis is unnecessary himself experiences many phenomena in his ordinary d-SoC that most people have to enter the d-ASC of hypnosis to experience (Barber, 1972).

Another important source of individual differences which is little understood at present is the degree to which an individual may first have a particular experience/observation or concept in one d-SoC and then be able to reexperience it in or transfer it to a second d-SoC. That is, sometimes an item of information may be state-specific on initial learning or for many experiences, but, for reasons we know almost nothing about now, eventually be transferable to a different d-SoC. So some people may have a spiritual experience occurring only in a particular d-ASC for a while, but then find it becomes part of their ordinary d-SoC. We know almost nothing scientifically about the degree to which such transfer can take place, the conditions favoring or hindering it, or the fullness of the transfer. Most studies so far have been interested only in the persistence of ordinary d-SoC skills (such as writing, speaking, arithmetic ability) into d-ASCs. A comprehensive knowledge of d-SoCs will eventually involve comparing every d-SoC with every other, rather than choosing only our ordinary d-SoC as a base line of comparison. Again, there will probably be major differences between individuals in their ability to transfer, related to the enormous differences hidden under the assumption that our ordinary d-SoCs are essentially alike.

PROBLEMS AND PITFALLS ASSOCIATED WITH d-ASCs

If we use the historical experience of Western man with d-ASCs as a guide, the understanding of d-ASCs and the development of state-specific sciences will be difficult. Some of the difficulties are not different in kind from those associated with our ordinary d-SoC but are exaggerated by the qualities of d-ASCs. Others may be unique to particular d-ASCs. There are two general classes of difficulties: general methodological problems stemming from the inherent nature of some d-ASCs, and those concerned with personal perils to the investigator. I shall discuss state-related problems first and deal with personal perils in the next section.

The first important problem in the proposed development of state-specific sciences is the "obvious" perception of the truth. Many times in d-ASCs, one's experience is that one is obviously and lucidly *directly* experiencing The Truth, with total certainty and no questions at all. This sort of phenomena is usually expressed as: "I *know* X!"

This feeling of absolute certainty is very gratifying: as was mentioned earlier, though, one of the historical reasons for developing science was a recognition that the conviction of certainty does not guarantee that one is correct. Suppose that being able to live with uncertainty is a necessary step in approaching truth. The individual who follows a spiritual path or tries to reach truth in a d-ASC may settle for the feeling of certainty rather than pressing on with his investigations. The experience of certainty may inhibit or extinguish the desire for further questioning of experience.

Further, the experiencing of certainty, while it may not necessarily prevent the individual investigator from extending his experience, may inhibit his desire for consensual validation: he feels no need for validation, and he doesn't want to risk invalidation: Since one of the greatest strengths of science is its insistence on consensual validation of basic observations and the logic of theorizing, the feeling of certainty can be a serious drawback in the development of state-specific sciences or in one's personal growth. Although too much distrust can become as much of a neurotic game as too much credulousness, investigators attempting to develop state-specific sciences will have to learn to distrust the obvious or, more precisely, to accept the feeling of certainty as a real *experience,* as data, but not let it blind them to the need for further investigation.

A second major problem in developing state-specific sciences is that in some d-ASCs one's abilities to visualize, or imagine are enormously enhanced compared to an ordinary d-SoC, so that whatever one imagines is so vivid that it seems like a *perception,* not like imagination. Thus one can imagine that something is being observed and classify it as "data," but this classification is a mistake.

If one can essentially conjure up anything one wishes, without being aware of the willfulness involved in it, how can we ever get at the truth? How can we be protected from simply building fantasy worlds while believing we are studying reality?

Let us suppose, for example, that for implicit, compelling, personal reasons I believe that sound and light are manifestations of the same energy, but that in our ordinary d-SoC we are too insensitive to realize this. Suppose I now enter, for example, some meditative d-ASC whose properties are such that the phenomenon of synesthesia is possible. Without realizing that my desire is causing it, I can now create a sound, such as turning on the radio, and see distinct flashes of light coming out of the loudspeaker. Or I might turn on a light bulb and hear sound associated with it. Believing that my theory has now been confirmed by direct observation, I feel very happy and may communicate this to other people interested in similar things. If they do not experience the same thing, I might conclude that there is something wrong with them that makes them an inferior observer compared to me. How do we get around such subjectivity?

One way of looking at this problem is to realize that the ability to unknowingly imagine things so vividly that they are thought of as perceptions *is* data. That is, it is useful to know that desires can influence perceptions so strongly in a particular d-ASC, and it may be further useful to find out what the limits of this influence are, and how it might differ from one d-ASC to another. We should not a priori hypothesize that anything could be imagined with equal facility in any d-ASC; thus, investigating these relationships may tell us some important things about the nature of various d-ASCs and the human mind. The "error" here is not in seeing lights associated with sound and vice versa, but in taking this as a complete observation; for I have failed to observe that compelling belief in this phenomenon is a necessary precondition of observation, a part of the phenomenon.

More fundamentally, the way to approach this problem of subjectivity is to realize that it is not unique to d-ASCs, even though it may affect persons in d-ASCs somewhat more strongly. One can have various illusions, misperceptions, and false beliefs, based on personal qualities, in one's ordinary d-SoC. Before the rise of modern physical sciences, all sorts of things were imagined about the nature of the physical world that could not be directly refuted: the world really does look flat, for example. The same techniques that eliminated these false beliefs in the physical sciences will also eliminate them in state-specific sciences dealing with experiential, nonphysical data. All observations will have to be subjected to consensual validation; their theoretical consequences will have to be examined; and alternative theories and explanations will have to be tested to see which is best. Insofar as some experiences are completely arbitrary imaginings, reflecting only one individual's unique psychology, they will not show consistent patterns across people and so will not be replicated by other observers. This will distinguish them from phenomena which do show the general lawfulness and tell us something about the d-ASC generally. Too, the more self-knowledge an investigator develops the more he may be able to observe all the (personal) factors affecting his observations.

A special problem arises: being a member of a particular culture has taught one to shape experiences in terms of its cultural norms. This can lead to a consensual validation by the state-specific scientists of a given culture that again is an instance of the way experience *can* be patterned, and as such is useful data, but is not properly explained by attributing it to the d-ASC per se. Cross-cultural investigation by scientists from varied cultures is the way this will have to be looked at. For example, a Westerner may experience seeing a creature we can call an angel while in a certain d-ASC, but his vision does not necessarily imply that angels exist in reality and that one can see them in a certain d-ASC, or that angels are an archetypal product of the human mind, because almost all Westerners have had a number of specific beliefs about the nature of angels communicated to them in childhood, even though they may later have consciously rejected them.

Let us return to our example of believing that light and sound are the same energy and always accompany each other if one is sensitive enough to see it. That I or someone else could see light produce sound and sound produce light is certainly data. We might prefer to explain it with an alternative theory that expectation is the cause of the observation, not an inherent quality of the physical world or man's mind. You could choose which of the two theories is more satisfactory by setting up an experiment in which expectation was deliberately varied. If you can find people who could enter the requisite d-ASC and who did not have any prior expectations about the association of light and sound, you could have them make observations to see if light and sound went together. Or you could systematically give some observers expectations that they do go together, and other observers expectations that they never go together. By examining the outcomes of this, you could decide between the two theories. The first theory, that light and sound always go together, would predict that the observers with no preconceptions would see light and sound going together, as well as those who were given the preconception that light and sound work together. The second theory would predict that those with no preconceptions would not see light and sound going together, and the other two groups would behave exactly according to their experimentally induced preconceptions.

This illustrates another major way of dealing with the question of subjectivity caused by the enhanced ability to imagine in some d-ASCs, namely that one continues to build up theories from whatever one's data base is, even if it is contaminated by subjectivity, and goes on and tests the consequences of the theories. Theories that are largely based on subjectivity should have less predictive ability in the long run than those which are not so subjective, and eventual refinement can take place toward less and less subjectivity, as it does in any branch of science.

A third major problem in developing state-specific sciences may be that they cannot be developed for all d-ASCs. Some d-ASCs may depend on or result from genuine deterioration of observational and reasoning abilities, or a deterioration of the will, such that one could not very well carry out any kind of investigative program. Those d-ASCs for which state-specific sciences can probably be developed will be discussed later, but what should be emphasized now is that the development of each science must really depend on attempting to do it, not on an a priori decision based on reasoning in our ordinary d-SoC.

A fourth major problem is that many spiritual and d-ASC experiences are described as "ineffable," beyond our ability to conceptualize. We should make some further distinctions here. Some experiences may be ineffable in the sense that a person may experience them and be unable to conceptualize them even to himself: these would be completely ineffable experiences. A second class of experiences may be ineffable in the sense that a person may not be able to communicate them adequately to anyone else, but it may be very clear to himself what the experience is all about. A third class of experiences may be ineffable in the sense that they cannot be communicated from one d-SoC to another d-SoC but are communicable within the d-SoC by state-specific communication. Phenomena of the first sort may be completely inaccessible to scientific investigation, while phenomena of the second type may be accessible to scientific investigation only in the limited sense that a single individual may try to follow the rules of science in his own mind. But, insofar as he has lost all the advantages of consensual validation, he may not be able to develop a very powerful, individual science. Phenomena of the third sort are exactly the kind that make state-specific sciences necessary.

Some phenomena which we now believe to be ineffable may not be so in reality: it may simply be that not enough attempts have been made to communicate them and develop an adequate vocabulary to communicate them. English, for example, is an excellent language for dealing with physical reality, but it is poor for communicating the subtler aspects of ordinary d-SoC phenomena and has almost no vocabulary at all for communicating d-ASC phenomena. Some languages, such as Sanskrit and Tibetan, are supposed to be much more adequate for communicating about experiential and d-ASC data. We shall have to develop more adequate languages to communicate about spiritual and d-ASC phenomena, and we must make this attempt before finally deciding that certain phenomena are ineffable.

Finally, we should recognize the possibility that some of the phenomena of d-ASCs are too complex for us to understand. The capacity of our minds may simply be too limited. This should not discourage us from trying, but should balance an implicit arrogance we often have in assuming that we can understand everything and that what we cannot understand is not worth understanding.

PERSONAL PERILS

Personal perils are those that stem more from an investigator's particular personality than from the nature of d-ASCs per se, although the two interact. We will consider personal perils under two general categories here, those stemming from a negative experience in a d-ASC, what we would colloquially call a bad trip, and those stemming from too good a reaction, a good trip.

Bad trips in a d-ASC and/or long-term negative aftereffects from a d-ASC often stem from the fact that our cultural upbringing has not prepared us to deal with radical alterations in our ordinary d-SoC. We become dependent on and attached to stability, we fear the unknown, and we develop personal rigidities and various kinds of social and personal taboos. Insofar as this rigid structure of our personality fits in with the prevailing cultural norm, we are rewarded for this in a variety of ways by our peers and are called "normal." Too, our culture generally considers d-ASCs to be some sort of insanity, so we do not have a very good cultural heritage for beginning to work with d-ASCs, either personally or as state-specific scientists.

In addition to exposing an individual to types of experiences he may be unable to handle because of the above sort of rigidities, some d-ASCs can also cause a bad trip because the structure or functioning of the psychological defenses is altered or lowered, and unacceptable personal material from a person's past is presented to consciousness with resulting emotional upset. This potentiates with the likelihood that the person may not know how to cope with anxiety in the d-ASC, so it may rise to more frightening levels than if the same thing happened in his ordinary d-SoC. Thus the individual who wishes to explore d-ASCs personally or become a state-specific scientist should be a relatively mature and stable* person to begin with. Even if one starts from a good base, considerable psychological growth work is probably necessary to minimize the risk of serious adverse consequences, as well as to help make a potential investigator aware of his own needs and implicit biases that may distort his experiences and observations in d-ASCs.

Good trips may also "endanger" a potential state-specific scientist in that they may produce experiences that are so ecstatic and rewarding that they again interfere with the scientific activity of the investigator. We have already mentioned the perception of "obvious truth," and its effect of eliminating the need for further investigation or consensual validation. Similarly, if a certain kind of experience is exceptionally rewarding, the investigator may be content with it and reluctant to investigate it further, since this might endanger his source of ecstasy. That is, people may settle for getting "high," rather than trying to see the truth that may lie behind feeling high.

The ability to imagine things with incredible vividness in some d-ASCs further contributes to this particular danger: a person's most longed-after desires may come true in the form of fantasies which seem like reality. Because of the satisfy-

---

*I use "mature and stable" in a much wider sense here than simply fitting in with local cultural norms, being "normal."

ing nature of such visions, the potential investigator does not want to see what lies behind them.

The psychological complexities of any given individual are much more subtle than we are able to discuss here, of course.

These personal perils further emphasize the necessity of developing training programs for potential state-specific scientists. Although it is difficult to envision from our present knowledge what such a training program would be like, it would not be very much like conventional scientific training. The undergraduate and graduate university training that almost all scientists receive today devalues personal knowledge, enhances personal rigidity, discourages emotional feelings, and pays more lip service than actual service to openmindedness. The training faculties are taken as models of mature scientists, and the students are rewarded for imitating them. Any great deviance from these training models in "unconventional" directions can often eliminate the chance that a person will acquire the credentials necessary to work as a scientist in a given field. Much of the necessary training programs for d-ASC work would have to be devoted to the potential scientist's understanding of himself through psychotherapeutic and psychological growth techniques.

Many of us have known people, ordinary people and scientists included, who have become personally involved with d-ASCs, and some of them have become very ineffective people or experienced deep psychological crises afterward. This is not unlikely, given the poor preparation for d-ASCs in our culture. But it would be premature to conclude that such unfortunate consequences cannot be avoided with the proper selection, training, and discipline. In the early history of all the currently established sciences, many practitioners were very nonobjective and partisan about their investigations—by contemporary standards, they were fanatics. Nevertheless, as a social institution, particular branches of science did progress. Not all experiencers of various d-ASCs develop pathology as a result: indeed, many of them become considerably more mature, especially when these experiences are integrated with a program of personal growth. Only by actually attempting to develop state-specific sciences will we be able to determine which d-ASCs are suitable for such development, and which kinds of people are best suited for this kind of work. There will undoubtedly be psychological casualties along the way, but d-ASCs and the spiritual phenomena connected with them are too important to be ignored because there is some risk.*

---

*The question of the risk of experiencing d-ASCs is very confused because of a general, implicit assumption that *not* experiencing them is a low-risk state. Look at the ordinary d-SoC culture around you to see the fallacy of this.

PROSPECTS FOR STATE-SPECIFIC SCIENCES

Throughout history human beings have been influenced by spiritual and mystical factors, many of which were originally experienced in d-ASCs, although they came to most people in diluted form through organized religions. Because of the experiences occurring in d-ASCs, and subsequent social transformations of them, untold numbers of both the noblest and the most horrible acts of which mankind is capable have been committed. We are at present in a time of cultural crisis: the old spiritual foundation of our culture has become too weak to uphold it, and more and more people are desperately searching for some kind of a spiritual foundation. This situation in which we find ourselves is the primary argument for our need to develop state-specific sciences.

The educated people of our culture held a hope for many generations that religions were simply a form of superstition that would be left behind in our "rational" age. This hope has failed, and our understanding of the mind now indicates that such a hope can never be fulfilled. Reason is a *tool,* and a tool that is used in the service of assumptions, belief systems, and needs which are *not* subject to reason. The irrational or, to express it better, the *a*-rational, is not going to disappear from the human situation. The more we try to deny its existence, the more we fall under its implicit power.

Our great success in the development of the physical sciences has not been particularly successful in formulating better philosophies of life or increasing our real knowledge of ourselves: indeed, the physical sciences have created many problems as well as solving many. The sciences we have developed to date are not very human sciences. They tell us *how* to do things, but give us no scientific insights on questions of what to do and not to do, ultimate goals, *why* to do things.

The youth of today, as well as increasing numbers of mature people and scientists, are turning to meditation, Oriental religions, and personal use of psychedelic drugs. Indeed, much of the so-called drug problem in this country is basically a spiritual quest, even though the form of its expression is often quite clumsy and immature. The phenomena encountered in the d-ASCs that are becoming more prevalent in our culture provide more satisfaction and are more relevant to the formulation of a philosophy of life and finding a feeling of one's place in the universe than "pure reason" (Needleman, 1970). Yet of the many scientists who are now personally exploring d-ASCs, few of them connect this with their role as scientists. They have not really begun to develop state-specific sciences, in spite of the need.

I find it difficult to predict what our chances are of developing state-specific sciences: they depend too much on cultural fads and prejudices that are hard to assess, rather than simply on need. Also, our knowledge of d-ASCs is too diffuse, and much of it is simply ordinary d-SoC views of d-ASCs. But I believe that with effort we can develop state-specific sciences for such d-ASCs as autohypnosis, meditative states, lucid dreaming (Tart, 1969), self-remembering (Ouspensky, 1949), reverie, marijuana intoxication (Tart, 1971b), low levels of alcohol intoxication, some psychedelic drug states, and biofeedback-induced states. In all of these d-ASCs volition seems to be retained so the investigator can carry out experiments on himself and direct his observations. There are other d-ASCs in which the ability to explore the state volitionally may disappear during the d-ASC, but which could be explored by preparing oneself beforehand, such as by suggestion. These would be states like ordinary dreaming, hypnagogic and hypnopompic states, and high dreams (Tart, 1969).

Let us now consider the relationship of the spiritual psychologies to the state-specific sciences I proposed.

THE SPIRITUAL PSYCHOLOGIES: STATE-SPECIFIC SCIENCES?

Are the spiritual psychologies presented in this book state-specific sciences or the beginnings of state-specific sciences?

First, let me emphasize that the spiritual psychologies that we talk about are the bodies of technique, spiritual discipline, and philosophical framework presented in later chapters, and not the watered-down versions of these that have turned into the mass religions. These spiritual psychologies emphasize the necessity of experiencing various spiritual things for oneself, rather than just believing them, and provide various kinds of techniques for altering one's state of consciousness in order to experience directly the bases of the spiritual path.

At a *minimum*, the spiritual psychologics presented in this book are state-specific technologies. They have sophisticated techniques for altering content and state of consciousness and for guiding experience within d-ASCs. The apparent complexity of the various spiritual psychologies as state-specific technologies varies greatly, from the relatively straightforward practices of Zen and Christianity at one extreme to the complex technologies of Sufism or the Western magical tradition at the other extreme.

It also seems clear that, regardless of whether any of these spiritual psychologies are state-specific sciences or not, they can certainly be used by some of their adherents and practitioners simply as state-specific technologies. That is, some practitioners of a particular spiritual technology may give lip service to the need to personally acquire basic knowledge and to question assumptions, but in practice they may have very fixed and rigid a priori goals and beliefs, and only selectively use parts of a spiritual psychology to reinforce their own belief systems. Entering a d-ASC is no guarantee that anything fundamental will change in a person: indeed, many or perhaps all of one's neurotic patterns and games can be transferred into the spiritual life. The Sufi tradition, as expressed by Idrics Shah, seems particularly aware of many possible psychopathologies of the spiritual path, and the reader is referred to Shah's writings for many teaching stories illustrating these pitfalls (see Bibliography).

Note carefully that the problem of using a system of understanding to support one's beliefs in a neurotic way is hardly unique to the spiritual psychologies. Abraham Maslow, in his brilliant book *The Psychology of Science* (1966), has shown how science can be either one of the best neurotic defense mechanisms devised by man or an open-ended personal growth system, depending on how the individual scientist uses it. I cannot recommend Maslow's book too highly.

It is clear that the spiritual psychologies, as state-specific technologies, form an immense reservoir of information, techniques, and heuristic theories that we shall draw on in developing our own state-specific sciences. An immense amount of exploration of d-ASCs has been done in the spiritual psychologies, whether it fits the Western concept of science or not.

But are the spiritual psychologies state-specific *sciences?* Have they been, and are they, dedicated to a constant refinement of observation, a constant questioning of the obvious, to consensual validation of observation and theorizing? Again, many practitioners of the spiritual psychologies, even if they intend to operate in the mode we would call state-specific sciences, may have succumbed to the various pitfalls talked about earlier, such as becoming fixated at some state of knowledge that produces emotionally satisfying experiences, rather than continuing to question. But, as a whole, are the spiritual psychologies state-specific sciences?

As a specific example, I recall many years ago reading Swami Vivekananda's book (1956) presenting yoga to the West for one of the first times. Vivekananda claimed that yoga was a science, and constantly pointed out that he was not asking for any faith on the part of the reader that what he said was true. Rather, he presented techniques for producing various d-ASCs and spiritual experiences, and urged the reader not to *believe* that he would get results but to try them and experience the results, the data, for himself.

At first glance, this was a commendably scientific attitude. When one looks at it more closely, however, Vivekananda did present many yogic ideas about the nature of the mind along with the techniques, and we now realize through psychological research that one cannot simply set aside all one's expectations and preconceptions by a simple act of will. It is a very difficult feat to discover what one's preconceptions are and then hold them in abeyance. The teaching presented by Vivekananda may have acted as suggestions which could structure d-ASC experience and so produce a kind of artificial verification. Perhaps yoga, then, was a "crude" or young science, "unsophisticated" in not taking this biasing possibility into account? Perhaps not.

I do not really know whether some, or any, or all, of the spiritual psychologies presented in this book are actually state-specific sciences. I do not know because I look on them as an outsider, not as one who has been intimately involved in the training and disciplining and experiencing of the d-ASCs involved and the spiritual experiences involved. In terms of the spiritual psychologies, I and practically all other Westerners must consider ourselves as laymen. Just as I, as a layman, cannot take a tour through a physicist's or a biologist's laboratory and decide whether I am seeing a science in action, or perhaps only a technology, or perhaps a set of superstitions with fancy apparatus that will impress me, so as a layman I cannot decide whether the spiritual psychologies are state-specific sciences or not. They are certainly state-specific technologies, and I suspect that many or most of them are indeed at least partially state-specific sciences: this is why they have been included in this book.

Do you feel frustrated not to have a final answer on whether these spiritual psychologies are state-specific sciences or not? Fine! I hope this frustration will induce many readers to learn more about the spiritual psychologies, to explore d-ASCs, and to help found the state-specific sciences that we so badly need.

THIS IS ALL VERY INTERESTING, BUT . . .

I would like to address myself to the category of questions that say the idea of developing state-specific sciences is interesting, but, for various reasons, there is no need for it or it can't be done. The main arguments, coming from beliefs currently active in our culture, are that: (1) everything worth knowing has already been discovered or revealed in some spiritual discipline or other, and it's a matter of being faithful to that spiritual discipline if you want to know; or (2) that we are incapable of knowing or forbidden to know these things, with the corollary that therefore we don't need to develop such sciences.

The general answer to these objections lies in remembering that no man is an isolated island, but part of a culture, no matter how much he may overtly try to reject certain aspects of his culture. As Westerners, we are part of a culture that has science as a very powerful force within it, a force that cannot be ignored. Cultures consist of many parts, and the parts interrelate to one another in subtle, complex, and powerful fashions. We may overtly reject a particular part of our culture, but because of these interrelationships we generally pay a price for such rejection.

Rejection of science is very powerful in our culture today, especially among the young. And many others, feeling that science has become too antihuman, take a stand in a particular spiritual/religious tradition and try to deal with all their life from that point of view. So we have objections that the scriptures of a certain religion already contain all truth, or the teachers of that religion or the practices of that religion will give a person all that is necessary. One can then try to reject the scientific culture totally or, more commonly, try to selectively integrate only those parts that do not conflict with one's religious beliefs. But this means closing one's mind off to a good deal of valuable human knowledge about reality.

A philosophy of life that depends on active rejection of parts of human knowledge leaves a good deal to be desired.

This selective rejection of parts of human knowledge can be seen as a defensive maneuver, and so basically neurotic. Particularly, the implications of scientific findings which tend to discredit religious experiences (as discussed in Chapter 3 on the paranormal basis of the spiritual traditions) come to be seen as a threat, and so must be selectively misperceived or rejected.

But we *are* Westerners, and science is a part of our personal heritage and our cultural heritage. It is likely that some spiritual traditions, particularly those not indigenous to our culture, will take root in our culture and thrive, while rejecting science, but there will be a price for this. I have no doubt that many sacred scriptures contain a great deal of valuable information and wisdom, and I am certain that many spiritual teachers have a great deal to teach us that is of *immense* value, but even the greatest sorts of of spiritual teachings must be adapted to the culture of the people they are presented to if they are to really connect with their whole psyches.*

Thus this proposal to develop state-specific sciences is an attempt to begin the integration of the best of our scientific tradition with the vast, uncharted (to science) sea of human potentials we can call man's spiritual potentialities. This whole book is an attempt at starting to bridge the gap between the spiritual and the scientific.

The realm of the spiritual, and the connected realm of altered states of consciousness, is one of the most powerful forces that shape man's life and destiny. I think attempting to keep these realms and the realm of science separate is dangerous, and I hope we will go on to develop state-specific sciences and similar endeavors that will start building bridges between them. To those who think it can't be done, I can only reply that we have to find that out by trying, not by limiting ourselves in advance by preconceptions.

---

*I also believe that the application of scientific method and its progressive refinement within the traditional spiritual disciplines may result in important advances within those disciplines themselves. All the dangers besetting the development of state-specific sciences probably apply to progress in traditional spiritual disciplines, so that in spite of the important information in them, they have errors of many sorts. I shall not develop this idea further here, however, because I am an "outsider" with respect to many important aspects of the spiritual disciplines.

2 SOME ASSUMPTIONS OF ORTHODOX, WESTERN PSYCHOLOGY

CHARLES T. TART

Every action we undertake and every thought we have rests on an assumption —and usually many assumptions. As I sit down at my typewriter to work on this book, I assume that the typewriter will turn on when I throw the switch, that its mechanism will function properly, and that I will have my usual command of the English language, to mention just a few of the assumptions underlying this instant. If someone asks me for advice about a problem, I assume that I am capable of understanding the problem, and I further assume that I am wise enough to give him good advice. In both of these examples, I speak of assumptions because I do not *consciously* sit down and *hypothesize* that the typewriter will work and that I am smart enough to give advice; I just assume that I can. These kinds of assumptions are *implicit,* acts of faith that we practically never give any conscious thought to.

In the example of sitting down at the typewriter, the assumptions seem, to a commonsense view, quite warranted, and it would be rather foolish to bring them into consciousness each time and question them. In the second case of giving advice, it is not quite so obvious that the assumptions are always warranted, even though we make them just as frequently as we make the former assumptions. Technically speaking, the assumptions about the typewriter and my command of the language are based on personal experience, personal data, and if we consider them as scientific hypotheses or theories they seem like very good theories indeed: they have had many, many confirmations. As for the example of giving advice, I would consider the assumptions not to be terribly good as scientific theories, and they may not be confirmed by experience so much as being assumptions that I have an emotional attachment to, so I have never seriously looked at outcomes which might contradict them. That is, I may be rather poor at giving advice, but it may be important to me to believe that I am good at it, so I don't notice the poor outcome of my advice giving.

What matters in either case, however, is that the assumptions are *implicit,* not subject to conscious scrutiny, and therefore exert an immense amount of power over me. If I don't know that I assume something, I will have no idea that I have been affected by implicit assumptions unless I get into a situation in which the assumptions have very clear-cut, contradictory consequences. If I assume I can walk through the wall, and therefore I get up and walk rapidly into the wall, I shall have an experience of crashing into it, which will cast considerable doubt on my assumption. If I assume I am a good advice giver, I may get very little feedback on the validity of this implicit assumption, because human problem situations are generally so complex and have so many different kinds of outcomes springing from the same actions that it is generally easy to rationalize that my advice was good, and so I am not forced to question my assumption about being a good advice giver.

Considering these two factors, namely (1) that in human life, situations are often not clear-cut and (2) that we have much emotional attachment to the systems of assumptions that underlie our ordinary state of consciousness, we can see how we can go through our entire life having our experience slanted in certain directions because of interlocking sets of implicit assumptions, and it may never occur to us to question any of these assumptions. By not making them clearly conscious and questioning them, we have little opportunity to determine their validity or free ourselves from their power over us.

This is not simply a philosophical argument. My own experience, through self-observation and psychological growth techniques, has been of finding many areas in which my actions and thoughts were controlled by lifelong assumptions which had been completely unconscious. There is an immense amount of evidence from psychological experimentation in general to support this position. Innumerable examples through all areas of psychology can be found by looking at any elementary psychology textbook. One of the earliest studies, for example, showed that poor children tend to perceive coins as being larger than rich children do, a case in which perception was altered by value judgments that constitute sets of assumptions. Psychoanalysis provides numerous examples from individual therapy in which people's reactions to others are based on distorted perceptions stemming from transference reactions to parents. Innumerable examples from social psychology show that people's perceptions of and reactions toward others are often based on stereotypes and prejudices, inculcated in childhood, which have sunk below the level of consciousness.

The thing that constantly amazes me, however, is that while psychologists are quite familiar with innumerable pieces of evidence supporting this picture of human beings as constantly controlled by implicit assumptions, they practically never apply it to their personal lives or to their scientific work, or they apply it in one small area of their life or work and implicitly assume that they personally are not controlled by large numbers of implicit assumptions in all the rest of their areas of life and work. Yet if one begins to apply this idea to psychological research, it is clear that much of what we consider our "data" may be only relatively true; it is data only in the sense that it applies within the context of certain generally shared cultural assumptions, certain generally shared assumptions in the psychological domain, and the particular personal involvement and motivation of the subjects and the experimenters involved.

Because psychologists have been fighting an uphill battle for prestige in the scientific hierarchy for some time, this is an idea which is seldom seriously considered. To give an example, several years ago Robert Rosenthal (1966) published a series of experiments showing that the expectations of the psychological experimenter, even though never overtly or knowingly communicated to the subjects by the experimenter, nevertheless influenced subjects' behavior in ways that tended to confirm the hypothesis or expectations of the experimenter.

In many experiments, Rosenthal trained assistant experimenters to administer subjects a picture rating test. This was a series of photographs, originally selected to be quite neutral in terms of how "successful-looking" the photographed persons were. Subjects were asked to rate how successful each subject looked on a plus ten (very successful) to minus ten (very unsuccessful) scale. The training of all assistant experimenters was identical except that for one group of them, Rosenthal offhandedly remarked that subjects, on the average, scored about plus five. For another group he offhandedly remarked that subjects generally averaged a score around minus five. The assistant experimenters never said anything explicitly like this to the subjects: they administered identical, written instructions that they read to all subjects. But this slight biasing operation to the assistant experimenters consistently pulled subjects' responses in one or the other direction, so most assistant experimenters had their expectation confirmed, and felt that they were collecting "good" data. While not aware of it, the assistant experimenters behaved in subtle ways that influenced their subjects' behavior.

Most psychologists do not accept Rosenthal's work, for a very wide variety of reasons. Some of these reasons seem to be valid critiques of details of experimental design, but I am convinced that the basic rejection of Rosenthal's data is due to its implications. If, as I am certain, the implicit assumptions and biases and expectations of the experimenter are an important factor in *every* psychological experiment, then a large amount of our psychological experiments, perhaps 90 percent or more, will turn out to have very limited validity. They will have shown mainly that an experimenter with an investment in a hypothesis, a set of assumptions, can subtly influence subjects and obtain support for his hypothesis whether it is "true" in some larger sense or not. As psychologists we certainly do not want to have much of our data base cut away from underneath us. Further, we have a great investment in the "objectivity" and "scientificness" of our field, so emotionally we cannot tolerate the implications of experimenter bias. And since we are clever, we can find good reasons for rejecting studies that we don't want to accept anyway. So only a minority of psychologists have accepted the problem in experimental design created by experimenter bias, and begun to set up their experiments in ways which will take this into account.

I came into psychology with an odd background, a long-term interest in altered states of consciousness and extrasensory perception. I had to suppress the expression of much of this interest during my undergraduate and graduate training because it was clearly at variance with what many of my professors "knew" to be true; that is, it conflicted with a variety of widely accepted assumptions in the psychological community. This made me aware of how many things which were "self-evidently true" to my colleagues were not "self-evidently true" to many other people outside of orthodox, Western psychology, and so sensitized me to question some of the assumptions that we make. Editing this book on spiritual psychologies has brought many more of the assumptions of orthodox, Western psychology into consciousness for me, through seeing how quite different assumptions underlie many of the spiritual psychologies.

I stress again that as long as an assumption is *implicit,* as long as it is operating outside of conscious awareness, you are unlikely to ever question it, and so you are totally in the power of that assumption. Given that human behavior is incredibly complex, and that within a given cultural context shared implicit assumptions will make for commonalities of behavior and so seem to "validate" these assumptions, I believe that our orthodox, Western psychology, the psychology taught in universities, is full of a very large number of *relative* truths, *relative* facts. I have sufficient faith in the scientific method to believe that in the long run the consequences of the assumptions producing this relativity will start coming out in experimental data and force us to confront these assumptions and modify them. Unfortunately, the "long run" may take thousands of years, given our attachment to our assumptions and our ability to falsely validate them among people who share the same assumptions.

What I wish to do in this chapter is to state *explicitly* a large number of the implicit assumptions that are part of orthodox, Western psychology (and of Western, educated people in general). This will serve a purpose of making clearer the background many of us have and from which we look at the spiritual psychologies, but my real hope for trying to bring these assumptions into consciousness is to make it possible for us to ask questions about them.

I am going to present these assumptions in the form of articles of faith, blunt statements that such and such is true, and then make some comments on differing ways of looking at these "obvious truths" from the viewpoint of the spiritual psychologies.* I believe one of the commonest assumptions of many

---

*It is arrogant for me to state what the spiritual psychologies generally assume about certain things, given my limited knowledge of them, but I hope the potential usefulness of this chapter in getting readers to question their assumptions will outweigh my errors in speaking for the spiritual psychologies.

readers will be on the order of: "That's not an assumption, that's a *fact!*" I then invite the interested reader to take a further step, however, and ask himself some questions. How do I *personally* know that this statement is true? Have I validated it for myself, or did I simply passively accept it because it was taught to me by someone I regarded as an authority and/or because it was generally accepted by my peers? How strongly do I react emotionally to the idea of questioning this statement? Do I have an emotional investment in this statement's being true? Am I really willing to look to see if I have an emotional investment in this statement's being true? Am I just intellectually saying, "Okay, this is an assumption," as a quick means of dismissing it from my mind so I do not have to actually think about whether this might be only an assumption, and not true? If I am a psychologist, is much of my work which establishes my reputation based on this assumption? If so, am I willing to question it when it is so important to me? Am I classifying this discussion as "philosophy," which to a psychologist means that one doesn't have to pay much attention to it because one deals with the "facts"?

I suggest that a *real* questioning of the assumptions of orthodox, Western psychology is an extremely difficult thing to do, but one which could have an extremely high payoff in freeing us to see more of reality.

I should further note that the assumptions we will consider in this chapter have almost never been taught as assumptions. At no point in our training as psychologists (or even as members of Western civilization) have we been asked to sit down and swear allegiance to these assumptions as articles of faith—on the contrary, most of them were never taught explicitly at all. For example, I do not believe any of my teachers in psychology explicitly stated that mystical experiences were inherently pathological, one of the common assumptions of orthodox, Western psychology. There was no need to state it explicitly: the subject was practically never mentioned at all, and on those rare occasions when it was, it was usually mentioned in the context of a discussion on psychopathology, or, if it came up in informal discussions, the slight, superior sneers of my "scientific" colleagues and peers were sufficient to convey the message.

Further, many of these assumptions were presented as *facts.* But we were never invited to prove these facts for ourselves; it was assumed that they had been proven a long time ago. Indeed, there is good evidence for many of the things I shall present as assumptions, and if they were being treated as scientific *hypotheses,* with a certain amount of evidence supporting them and a certain amount of evidence not supporting them, all would be well and good. But whether they were introduced as hypotheses and evidence collected for and against them to begin with, they are not being treated as hypotheses in the minds of psychologists, but have sunk to the level of implicit assumptions.

We are almost completely controlled by every assumption that has become implicit and so beyond the power of questioning. Let us now begin to look at many assumptions which have become implicit in the minds of orthodox, Western psychologists, in the hope that by making them explicit we may be able to question them.

Note that I say implicit in the minds of many or even the majority of orthodox, Western psychologists. Psychology is far from a completely unified discipline, and one can find particular schools of psychology and particular psychologists who will take exception to practically every assumption that we will deal with. But in spite of the importance of these exceptions and their growing importance in such developments as humanistic and transpersonal psychology, most of the assumptions we will discuss are implicitly held by the majority of orthodox, Western psychologists today.

I have grouped the assumptions in the same sort of categories that guided the contributors in writing about the spiritual psychologies. This listing of common assumptions is probably far from complete.

THE NATURE OF THE UNIVERSE

Assumption: The universe was created accidentally or created itself or has always been around, and there is no purpose or reason for the universe existing.

Members of Western scientific culture in general, as well as psychologists specifically, basically assume that the universe in which they live has no reason for its existence. Because this is a somewhat depressing idea, we seldom give any thought to it. This assumption and other assumptions about the nature of the universe as a whole are incredibly audacious assumptions when one realizes they are made by a creature which lives on one little planet in a rather remote portion of one galaxy and has possessed the rudiments of science for only a couple of centuries.

The spiritual psychologies generally assume a purpose for the universe, covering such alternatives as its having been created by some kind of a god, to the universe itself being some kind of living entity or being which is expressing itself, or the universe as a whole having a purpose and that it is evolving toward a higher level of consciousness and action. These are not mutually exclusive ideas.

Assumption: The universe is dead; life is only an infinitesimal, insignificant part of the universe.

In terms of sheer bulk, life *as we know it* does indeed take up only a small portion of our world, and it is assumed that this is true all through the universe. Further, life is seen as an accidental development of lifeless physical forces and as having no real function in the universe. Given the universe as basically purposeless, what function could life have? This assumption fits well with the stance of so much of our Western culture of man standing alone, surrounded by vast, merciless, inanimate forces.

Many of the spiritual psychologies assume the universe is either mostly alive or completely alive. For example, the Gurdjieff system assumes that the planets are alive and evolving, but their life takes place on such a vast time scale compared to ours that it is impossible for us to notice this in an ordinary way. Most of the spiritual psychologies not only assume purpose for the universe but, seeing it as alive and evolving, give the universe the same properties as life in general. A consequence of this is that man's relationship to a living, interconnected, and evolving universe is quite different than if he assumes the universe is dead and purposeless.

Assumption: Physics is the ultimate science, because physics is the study of the real world.

Psychology, of course, then becomes a very derivative science, studying secondary or tertiary or quarternary or even more derivative phenomena. Since the universe is nothing but physical matters and energies operating in a space-time framework, human experience is then in some sense ephemeral and not real. The man who speaks of an experience about love is dealing with dreams or unimportant, derivative phenomena, while the man who builds an atomic bomb is dealing with what is *real.* Human experience thus becomes "subjective," a term which, for psychologists, is very pejorative, meaning unreal and unscientific. "Good" explanations/theories are those which reduce to statements about matter, energy, space, and time. To be a "real" science, then, psychology must ultimately reduce all its psychological and behavioral ideas to physiological data and then to the physical data underlying physiology.

The spiritual psychologies may or may not accept the "reality" of the physical world, but they postulate a psychological or psychical reality as just as real or even more real than physical reality. Physical reality may be seen as simply a particular manifestation of a psychological reality which is even more real. Thus there is no need for physical justification of spiritual realities: indeed, this may be seen as an attachment to the senses which can hinder spiritual progress. The ultimate test of reality is not whether you can build a weapon with which to strike your opponents over the head. I deliberately use this crude example because it seems to obtain so frequently in the world in which we live, despite talk about truth and experimental validation.

For the spiritual psychologies, then, consciousness and experience and life become basic factors, rather than relatively unimportant derivatives, in understanding the universe.

Assumption: What is real is what can be perceived by the senses or by a physical instrument, and what can be perceived by the senses can be detected by a physical instrument.

This is an alternative way of looking at some of the assumptions above, but one which seems to operate almost independently of the others and so deserves to be expressed separately. It comes out in this attitude: If you make a claim, show me your proof with my physical senses or my instruments. If, for example, someone claims to see rays of light radiating from a saint, we say show it to me with my eyes, and if I can't see it with my eyes then put a physical instrument there, and if that doesn't detect it, it is not real.

The spiritual psychologies assume the reality of things which are not real in the physical sense. For our example of seeing rays of light streaming from around a saint, a phenomenon often called the aura, the answer from the spiritual psychologies' point of view might be that indeed this was an illusion at some times on the part of the perceiver, but at other times it is a perfectly real perception through faculties that are different from the ordinary senses, which do not rely on the energies of the physical universe as we know it. So nonphysical things can be just as real as physical things. Such nonphysical realities may or may not show interaction with the physical world, but their realities are not to be judged by whether or not they have a physical manifestation.

The orthodox assumption is somewhat depressing if you think about its consequences, for many of the things which are most important in our life, such as love, charity, intelligence, and pleasure, are mental concepts that we infer from behavior or things we experience directly, but nothing we can *directly* detect with physical instruments.

Assumption: Only the present moment exists.

This linear view of time permeates all our Western thinking. The past is gone and dead, the future does not yet exist, and all we have is this infinitesimally narrow portion of the temporal continuum we call the present, which is continually fading to become the past and the future.

It is an assumption that I completely believe in, even though I can intellectually question it. I have no real conception of any other kind of time, yet many of the spiritual psychologies see the past and the future as just as real, just as existent, as the present. Indeed, the excellent evidence for precognition that we have collected in Western science (see Chapter 3) indicates that the future can affect the present and/or that our division of time into past, present, and future is only an arbitrary construct of our mind, only part of a larger reality. Our use of this commonsense view of time to produce spectacular results in the physical sciences has strongly reinforced our view that it is really the way time is, not merely a cultural construct, but our great success may be more a matter of limiting the application of the concept to the physical sciences rather than its universal validity.

> *Assumption: We can understand the physical universe without understanding ourselves.*

Physicists are not required to take courses in psychology or self-awareness* as part of their training to become physicists. They are studying the "outside" physical world, using their instruments and their intellects, and their own personalities and spiritual natures are not taken into consideration. To put it extremely, a first-class physicist making excellent progress in the physical sciences may torture children for a hobby. It is unlikely to affect his progress as a physicist unless he lets his emotions "interfere" with his work. The individual investigator's personality, as long as it is not so neurotic as to interfere with the application of his intellect to his work, is not considered particularly relevant in doing scientific work.

Many of the spiritual psychologies assume, to the contrary, that one's nature, one's personality, or one's level of spiritual being will have a profound effect on his understanding of the universe. Many of them suggest that one's level of being, if low, will not only affect his cognitive processes and so systematically distort the way he sees the universe and restrict his intellectual formulations, but may further react on the universe itself, thus giving a kind of false validation to his view. This is easy to see in, say, the social sciences. If you believe that men are inherently selfish because you are inherently selfish, it is easy to observe selfish behavior among the vast panorama of human activity and confirm your view. This confirmation may be a useful contribution to scientific knowledge insofar as you collect good observations and come up with hypotheses to explain various forms of that selfish behavior. That is as far as one would take that view as long as one assumes that the universe is basically dead. But if the universe is in some way alive and responsive, then your own level of being may affect not only your perceptions, evaluations, and ways of interacting with your fellow men, it may also have direct effects on the physical universe about you.

---

*For that matter, orthodox, Western psychologists are almost never required to take any courses in self-awareness as part of their training.

ASSUMPTIONS ABOUT THE NATURE OF MAN

Assumption: Man is his body and nothing more.

Put more fully, we assume that a man is his skeleton, muscles, tendons, blood supply, internal organs, sense receptors, and nervous system: that the concept of man is essentially totally defined by the physical parts which constitute him. If we had a different array of physical equipment—say, a different nervous system and different senses—we would not be man as we know him. So, to ultimately understand man, one must understand the physical, physiological systems that comprise him. Given our culture's hyperintellectuality, this particularly means that we must understand the functioning of the brain and nervous system.

The spiritual psychologies do not accept this assumption but always consider that man is something else in addition to a physical body, or at least potentially something else. Thus we have the concept of a soul—some nonphysical portion, very much the essence of man, which may be able to exist independently of physically embodied man. Or we have the idea that man is essentially a mental being, and while he may or may not possess an individual soul, he is capable of contacting and merging with nonphysical things outside his physical body. Or the idea that man may come, through proper psychological work, to develop something other than the purely physical in himself, which then becomes very much a part of his reality. The various spiritual psychologies may see the body as relatively unimportant or as a very important shaper of experience, but as only one *component* of the total nature of man.

Assumption: Man exists in relative isolation from his surrounding environment. He is an essentially independent creature.

Here we see man as living on the earth, but not really part of it. We know he has to eat and breathe air and that severe natural disturbances like earthquakes will definitely affect him, but psychologically we act as if man were essentially independent. We have an abundance of scientific evidence that this is not true: quite aside from the ecology movement as a protest against the view of man as not part of his environment, we are slowly collecting scientific evidence to show that man responds to many natural forces outside of himself that we have not previously suspected (Ornstein, 1972; 1973), such as lunar cycles or atmospheric ionization. But the vast majority of us seldom take into account the possibility that we are part of the world around us: if I want to build a house *here,* I bulldoze the earth and build it *here* because I want it *here;* there is no real question of how this fits in with the functioning of the rest of the world.

The spiritual psychologies usually emphasize that man is very much a part of his world, that as a creature of life he has some kind of psychic or spiritual connection to all other forms of life, is both influenced by them and influences them, and consequently has responsibilities. Insofar as the ecology movement gains momentum, we will gradually come to think of ourselves as more a part of the environment, but the spiritual psychologies take this much further than the obvious physical dependence on our environment. The spiritual psychologies see man as a cosmic creature, related to the universe in a far vaster and nonphysical way than even our most ardent ecologists see him.

Assumption: Man starts life "fresh," except for limitations set on him by his genetic inheritance, his cultural environment, and accidental happenings, all modified by his reactions to them.

This says that a human being's life starts essentially at birth, is determined almost totally by physical factors (the influence of culture and other people as mediated by physical factors), and ends in death. It is a very clear span, with the hope of understanding all the factors that influence it in between.

Spiritual psychologies often take the view that man does not start fresh this way: they may believe in previous lives, that a man starts life with an inheritance, both favorable and unfavorable, from his experiences in previous lives. They may see human life as extending on in some form after death. Thus an individual may come into life with a mission or purpose. Trying to understand a man's life in terms of just the actual physical span of it can be seen as very incomplete, even though not insignificant.

Assumption: Man is completely determined by his genetic inheritance and environment.

In discussing the previous assumption, I was rather vague about man's responses to the factors impinging on him and affecting the course of his life. Orthodox, Western psychology assumes that man is completely determined ultimately by the physical processes that constitute his own nature and the nature of the environment around him. This goes to the extreme that if one had a complete understanding of a man's genetic makeup at birth and all of the physical-psychological forces impinging on him, every event in his life would be understandable and predictable. In practice this is considered a goal unlikely of attainment, since the sheer number of factors impinging on a man is enormously large and too much for even supercomputers to handle. But, in practice, it is certainly felt that the general outlines of a given individual's life should be predictable to a very high degree of accuracy. Man is not free. Free will is an illusion that we have, but everything is determined by the play of matter and energy within the space-time framework. Similarly, the concept of responsibility makes no ultimate sense, since everything is determined and happens the only way it could happen.

Many of the spiritual psychologies recognize that this deterministic view is partly true but not complete. They give man a definite amount of responsibility and free will, and argue that spiritual development may increase a man's responsibility and free will. A man may allow himself to be almost totally determined in his life, but he has an option of doing something about it, even though doing something about it may be very difficult.

Assumption: Even though we believe man is completely determined, in practice we must act as if he has free will.

When someone does something I don't like, I immediately think it's his *fault*, and all abstractions about men having no choice and doing only what could be done fade into irrelevance. That selfish, inconsiderate bastard should be punished! The theory of total determinism seems to actually flourish only for brief moments in psychological laboratories, and psychologists *act* as if other people have a great deal of free will. Indeed, I suspect most psychologists never apply the idea of determinism to themselves except when they want to shirk responsibility, and they assume they have free will in the vast majority of their actions. Not to assume we have free will would be depressing, so we rationalize that we must believe and act as if we did to keep up a positive approach to life.

The spiritual psychologies do not take this attitude, but instead emphasize that by heedlessness and attachment to various physical and emotional things we are indeed almost totally determined in much that we do. If we do not have some kind of psychological and spiritual awakening, which must first start with recognizing our limitations, we will be trapped in recurring psychological patterns throughout our lives, and perhaps through an afterlife or other lives to come.

Assumption: We have a rather good understanding of the history of man.

Our libraries are filled with history books, and archaeological evidence fills in the general picture for periods of man's history before the widespread deployment of written records. So if you want to get a general picture of history, you can go to the library and read about it. Many theories about the psychology of man, such as his innate degree of aggressiveness, are based on this generally accepted history.

Many of the spiritual psychologies have quite different views of the history of man, sometimes referring to civilizations of which we have no scientific record. They often depend more on oral traditions than written records. It is interesting to note our tremendous preference on physical records in writing history: if a single manuscript says that A is true and many oral traditions (among the "peasants") say that B is true, we will often accept A. It is amusing to think that a few liars in previous times who knew how to write could have far more influence on us than people who accurately remembered and passed down what had happened.

We believe, based on our idea of history, that we have been making progress: some of the spiritual psychologies believe we have been going downhill from far more psychologically and spiritually advanced civilizations of the past, although these civilizations may not have produced much in the way of physical artifacts. The assumption that we are making progress is a very important one to us, so we label as crackpots those people who take the idea that earlier civilizations were ahead of us.

Assumption: We understand the origin and evolution of man.

The orthodox assumption is that man evolved by a series of accidents from life on this planet, which in turn had evolved from a series of physical accidents or inevitable consequences of the physical environment. Our origin, basically, is that it just happened that way because that's the way it had to happen, given the prevailing conditions. Our evolution has been in the pattern we have deduced, from ape to man.

Some of the spiritual psychologies have a theory of evolution for man which is not a blind evolution but an evolution guided by nonphysical forces, or by a divine creator or creators, or by the inherent aliveness and purposefulness of the universe. Others postulate either a special creation of man or that man is a representation of higher levels of being acting on this earth, rather than a product of the earth itself, even though by being physically embodied he is very much of the earth.

Assumption: We can't expect too much from a creature like man, or there are no limits on man's attainments.

Both of these assumptions are held by individual psychologists, and sometimes alternate rapidly from time to time in the same psychologist. The pessimistic one, showing man as merely an animal that accidentally evolved in a purposeless universe and full of the frailties shown by history, is probably generally held when things are not going well. When we are successful, on the other hand, we tend to think of man as absolutely godlike and, primarily through his technology, capable of conquering the entire universe and achieving anything. American culture on the whole tends to take the optimistic, technological-progress-to-infinity point of view.

Many spiritual psychologies emphasize how much either of these assumptions may blind us to the reality of what we are. Many would emphasize, for example, that an incredible degree of evolutionary progress is possible to man, albeit not in the technological sphere, *if* he will make the effort to evolve. But this evolution must begin by a recognition of what a person actually is, including his spiritual potentials. The spiritual psychologies do not take the pessimistic view that you can't expect much from a creature like man, but rather emphasize the importance of real humility: not an artificial breast-beating and bewailing our fate, but an actual *experiential* understanding of our limits and our insignificance in relation to the whole cosmos. Many of the spiritual psychologies emphasize that real humility is needed before man can play a more important part in the functioning of the cosmos.

Assumption: Each man is isolated from all others, locked within his nervous system.

Given the view that consciousness is the function of the physical operation of the nervous system, and that the physical is what is real, any knowledge of anatomy will show that one nervous system is completely isolated from *direct* contact with another nervous system. The only way we can contact one another is through the intermediary of making changes in our bodies which affect other physical energies which affect receptors in the other person and are turned into nervous impulses that will affect his or her consciousness, a very tenuous and indirect link, subject to many errors. So each man is an island, and a totally isolated island. The best we can do to find happiness and meaning is to modify our own nervous system functioning (thinking, feeling, imagining) or try to have desirable kinds of sensory stimulation from the world and others reach us, and not have undesirable kinds reach us.

The spiritual psychologies, in not accepting man as strictly physical, also open the possibility of *direct* contact between one human being and another, contact between the spiritual essence of each that is not limited by the physical properties of the nervous system. The contact of love, for example, may be a chemical-neural infatuation between two people in many instances, but sometimes it may be far more. Love may be an energy or reality that actually bridges the gap between people, not just an arbitrary way of reprograming the human biocomputer.

Assumption: Psychological energy is completely derived from physical energy, as expressed in physiological processes in the body.

All our energy, all our feelings of aliveness or deadness, tiredness or ability to do, come from the metabolism of our food and stored food products within the body. We may tinker with the efficiency of energy metabolism within the body by drugs and the like, but ultimately we are completely dependent on food intake into our bodies for energy. This means there are definite upper limits to what a human being can do, these upper limits being not too far above the ordinary.

Many spiritual psychologies assume, on the contrary, that the physical energy we take in through food is only one source of energy for the human being, and there are important, nonphysical sources of energy that can be tapped. Indeed, many postulate that if these nonphysical sources of energy were turned off we would die: it is their functioning which makes us alive and human, for we are not simply machines for the conversion of food into muscular activity and fantasy. Within the Western scientific tradition good evidence now exists for nonphysical kinds of energy that can affect human beings (see Chapter 3), but this evidence is little known and does not affect the thinking of most psychologists.

ASSUMPTIONS ABOUT MAN'S FUNCTION IN THE UNIVERSE

Assumption: Man has no function in a purposeless universe.

With all reality being nothing but matter and energy operating in the space-time framework, purpose is an idea that exists only in human brains, this idea itself being only a function of the workings of various physical processes. Man has no purpose at all in terms of the universe. He may invent his own purposes, as will be discussed in some of the assumptions following, but there is no purpose in terms of the real universe.

The spiritual psychologies give man a function in the universe. The nature of the function may vary. It may be to attain salvation for the glory of God; it may be to become more conscious as an integral expression of the evolutionary urge of the universe; it may be to act as a channel for higher evolutionary forces to reach our levels, and so on.

Assumption: The only real purpose of life is to maximize pleasure and to minimize pain.

Since the orthodox, Western psychological assumption is that man has no function in terms of the real universe, he then invents a function for himself. Man has a psychological need to believe in meaning. Since we like pleasure and dislike pain, all goals and purposes in life can be seen as some variant on seeking pleasure and avoiding pain. Because we are complex organisms, the particular expression of this may vary enormously, so what is pleasurable to one person for his own psychological reasons may seem painful to another person. Even "finding meaning" in life, or scientifically trying to understand the universe, can be seen as a kind of pleasure seeking. Since this life is all we have, why not get as much pleasure as possible out of it?

Some of the spiritual psychologies, such as yoga, see this seeking of pleasure and avoidance of pain as the root cause of the human predicament. Since life invariably brings misfortunes in one way or another, becoming attached to seeking pleasure and avoiding pain psychologically heightens the impact of both pleasure and pain on one. As some pain is inevitable, the psychological need to avoid it allows us no rest, and keeps us constantly tied up in illusion. The spiritual psychologies stress that we must learn to transcend our attachment to pain and pleasure, and/or that pain must be faced with full conscious awareness because it contains the seeds of important learning and growth.

Assumption: The universe is a harsh, uncaring, unresponsive place.

This may be partly a modern version of the widespread Christian religious belief that matter is essentially evil and a temptation keeping us from God. If the universe is purposeless, how can we have any connection with it except to try to avoid the misfortunes that would otherwise occur? And we certainly can't expect the universe to care about us: the best human beings can do is provide for their own preservation and pleasure individually and in groups.

The spiritual psychologies may assume that the universe is harsh, but it is not uncaring. Harshness can be seen as justice and lawfulness. Insofar as we are important parts of an interrelated, evolving universe, we are receiving lessons from being in this universe, if we will pay heed to it. Indeed, the universe may be quite responsive, with our level of spiritual being attracting various events which are appropriate. This is particularly expressed in Gurdjieff's psychology in a way which, if you think about it, can be seen as very wonderful or very frightening. The idea is that your level of spiritual being attracts your life, that the universe is very responsive to "prayer," in the sense that what you want sets up nonphysical forces that tend to bring things about physically. The problem is, in Gurdjieff's view, that we are so psychologically messed up, and have so many contradictory and self-destructive wishes, that getting what we "want" may be very unpleasant.

Assumption: We are here to conquer the universe.

This seems to follow from the previous assumptions about the nature of the universe and man's place and function in it. If we want to ensure our survival, maximize our pleasure, and minimize our pain, we must take a harsh, uncaring universe and shape it to our needs as we see them. This assumption is so widespread that I think it will be very hard to see how much it affects our behavior. After all, didn't our country become great by *conquering* the harsh, primeval wilderness and the savages who dwelt in it? Isn't the next great human adventure the *conquest* of space?

The spiritual psychologies would generally feel that we are here to understand our place in the universe and to harmoniously fulfill our function in it once we understand it, not to try to shape the universe to fit with our limited view of what is good for us.

Assumption: We are by far the supreme life form on earth, and are probably the only intelligent life form in the whole universe.

This is an incredibly arrogant assumption, but we make it all the time. It certainly seems true with respect to this planet, since, after all, we possess the power to kill any other life form. I recall how impressed I was with John Lilly's book, *The Mind of the Dolphin* (1967), and his argument that dolphins may be just as, or more, intelligent than we are in the sense of having a brain capable of handling an enormous amount of data, but that their intelligence is in a form very alien to us, being adapted to a life in the sea. I spoke about this idea with many colleagues and found practically none who could take it at all seriously. After all, dolphins were *animals,* and had no tools, and anyway, if they were so smart, why didn't they try to communicate with *us?*

The spiritual psychologies all assume that there are beings (usually nonphysical, but including possible extraterrestrial beings) that are far more intelligent than we are, and far more evolved in a large variety of ways, such as being truly loving and compassionate, or very powerful. We may sometimes be able to learn through psychical contact with such creatures. But, primarily, the spiritual psychologies tend to stress how much we tend to live in a state of illusion, not beginning to use the intelligence we do have to anywhere near its full extent.

Note also that the assumption that we are the smartest creatures around has a corollary that there is no help: we depend entirely on our own efforts. The spiritual psychologies stress that we must make enormous efforts, but help is available.

Assumption: Lower organisms exist for man's benefit.

Since we are the smartest creatures around in a purposeless universe, the only limits on exploiting other organisms for our benefit are economic and ecological reasons—that is, we don't want to overexploit and disrupt the ecosystem and consequently suffer for it later. But there is no inherent reason for not exploiting other creatures. Practically, our cultural conditioning makes many of us squeamish about *personally* killing or inflicting pain on animals, but there is no inherent reason for not exploiting all other life forms in the most effective way possible.

The spiritual psychologies see man as having obligations toward lower life forms, as well as obligations toward higher life forms. Man, as part of an overall, evolving, *interrelated* universe needs to discover and fulfill his function in it, not define it in any arbitrary way he wants, such as maximizing his own benefit.

ASSUMPTIONS ABOUT THE NATURE OF HUMAN CONSCIOUSNESS

Assumption: Only human beings are conscious.

Most psychologists see all other organisms, even the higher animals, as essentially automatons, reacting mechanically to stimuli in terms of innate or learned patterns. In principle, one could make a computer program to simulate the behavior of any animal. Man alone is held to be conscious in the sense of being aware of *himself* in addition to being aware of stimuli that impinge on him. One consequence of this is that it justifies the exploitation of other life forms mentioned above, for insofar as they have no consciousness, they cannot really suffer no matter what we do to them. The orthodox assumption that only humans are conscious relates closely to the assumption that we are by far the smartest creatures on the planet.

The spiritual psychologies generally accept the idea that higher, nonphysical creatures also possess full consciousness, and such psychologies often attribute various degrees of consciousness, albeit in forms quite different from human consciousness, to lower organisms. These may include collective consciousness in species in which no one individual has well-developed consciousness. If one takes the perspective that consciousness can appear in a variety of life forms, then consciousness is worth studying as a general principle in itself, whereas if one assumes it is unique to human beings, then it is seen as a specialized problem and possibly not as important as a more general understanding of the world.

Assumption: Man is conscious.

All normal human individuals are presumed to be conscious, that is that they sense things, they are aware of their discrete identity as they sense things, and they may think about perceptions and exercise volition. A variant of this implicit assumption is that *I* am conscious, but other people may be treated as if they were unconscious automatons, although this attitude is covered up because of the adverse social consequences of showing it. The holder of that attitude may not be consciously aware of it.

Some of the spiritual psychologies seriously question this assumption, holding that the state we call ordinary consciousness does not possess the properties we ascribe to consciousness at all, namely being aware of oneself as well as the stimuli coming in, and exercising volitional choice over one's reaction to the stimuli. Gurdjieff's psychology (Chapter 7), for example, states flatly that ordinary men are not at all conscious: they are complete automatons, completely programed by their environment to automatic reactions, and they do not maintain awareness of themselves as discrete entities and react with free volition, even though the *potentiality* for this is available. Other spiritual psychologies commonly describe man's ordinary state of consciousness as one dominated by illusion and day-dream, but again stress that real consciousness is *possible*.

The assumption that you are conscious is a particularly difficult one to seriously question: Gurdjieff noted that as soon as you accuse people of not being conscious, they actually become conscious for a moment while indignantly saying no, but then almost instantly slip back into their ongoing dreams and lose awareness of themselves. Only prolonged attempts at observation of your consciousness will show you that you almost always forget to try to observe yourself, and you immediately lose track of yourself after starting to observe as you fall back into your ordinary state of little or no self-awareness.

Assumption: Consciousness is produced by the activity of the brain, and there-fore the activity of consciousness is identical with the activity of the brain.

This is more formally called the psychoneural identity thesis. Since reality is ultimately physical in nature, consciousness itself must be a product of that physical activity. All the intricacies and subtleties of consciousness therefore represent intricate patterns of neural firing within the brain and, to some extent, within the nervous system generally. This supports the orthodox, Western psychological assumption that each of us is completely alone: since consciousness is a function of nervous system activity and nervous systems are not connected, we are doomed to be forever alone (until some supersurgeon of the future starts connecting nervous systems together).

The spiritual psychologies generally treat the brain and nervous system as an *instrument* of consciousness, but classify consciousness as a factor every bit as real in its own right as physical things. William James argued a good many years ago that there was no logical way of distinguishing by observation whether conscious-ness was *generated* by the brain or was a *transmitter* of it. The important conse-quence of not identifying consciousness with brain activity, no matter how much consciousness may be affected by working through the brain, is that consciousness may then exist independently of the brain. There is actually excellent scientific evidence for this hypothesis, inferentially through the phenomena of extrasensory perception, and directly in out-of-the-body experiences, as discussed in Chap-ter 3.

ASSUMPTIONS ABOUT ALTERED STATES OF CONSCIOUSNESS

Assumption: Altered states of consciousness are simply a temporary reorganization of brain functioning.

In the same way that ordinary consciousness is assumed to be identical with brain functioning, any radically different functioning, a discrete altered state of consciousness (d-ASC) is considered to be a different way of nervous system functioning. Although the experiences of the d-ASC may include the kind of things we call mystical or paranormal, such as contact with higher beings or telepathic interaction with others or predicting the future, all such functioning is considered illusory, since the events described are physically impossible. Thus while a person might experience something we could call a "spiritual truth" in a d-ASC, the orthodox psychological view is that this in no way demonstrates its reality—it simply shows how unusually the brain can function in d-ASCs.

The spiritual psychologies view the brain as primarily a *transmitter* of consciousness, and so a d-ASC may have a profoundly different meaning than merely the rearrangement of brain functioning. It may represent new psychic faculties (nonphysical in nature) beginning to operate, it may represent the intervention or gift of higher powers, or it may represent a loosening or altering of the ordinary relationship between mind and body, as when the mind becomes partially or wholly free of the body. Thus the experiential data of a d-ASC are to be looked at seriously rather than dismissed as mere aberrations caused by disordered brain functioning.

> *Assumption: Our ordinary state of consciousness is generally the most adaptive and rational way the mind can be organized, and virtually all altered states of consciousness are inferior or pathological.*

It is amazing how widespread the assumption is that our ordinary state of consciousness is somehow the "best." I have seen it lying behind all sorts of arguments at scientific meetings, although it is almost never voiced explicitly. I am trying to promote a more conservative psychological view that the "goodness" of any particular d-SoC depends on whom it occurs in and what particular task one wishes a person to perform: thus state A might be very good for some things and very bad for other things for a given person. To use just one concrete example, it would seem that our ordinary d-SoC is certainly superior to the state of marijuana intoxication if one is adding up long strings of numbers, as, say, in balancing one's checkbook. If, however, the task is to visit an art museum and appreciate the paintings, reports indicate that the state of marijuana intoxication is definitely superior to the state of ordinary consciousness (Tart, 1971b) for many experienced marijuana users. What we need is a large-scale mapping of which d-SoCs show which properties with respect to various tasks instead of making such global statements as that ordinary consciousness is superior; but we do not have it yet, and almost everyone assumes that his ordinary state of consciousness is superior. Psychologists give some lip service to the idea that there might be "creative states" that seem to be good for geniuses to use in their work, but there is considerable ambivalence about the degree to which these "creative states" border on the pathological.

While the spiritual psychologies recognize that there are states of consciousness inferior to ordinary consciousness (drunkenness, for example), they nevertheless believe that many d-ASCs are clearly superior to our ordinary state, particularly the higher mystical states. Various d-ASCs are often seen as necessary to understand certain aspects of the spiritual path which cannot be comprehended in our ordinary state of consciousness. This has been discussed at greater length in Chapter 1 on states of consciousness and state-specific sciences. As with holding that a d-ASC may be more than simply a change in brain functioning, this wider view of the spiritual psychologies encourages one to take a more serious look at the things experienced and learned in d-ASCs.

Assumption: A person who spontaneously goes into altered states of consciousness is probably mentally ill.

Such people are generally labeled "schizoid," meaning that they are not quite odd enough to be completely labeled schizophrenic (a terribly vague but widely used diagnostic category), but they are certainly a little too abnormal to be trusted. For an orthodox, Western psychologist, once a person has been labeled schizoid, one no longer has to take anything he says seriously. If he makes a telling argument that goes against what one believes, that simply demonstrates the cleverness of the paranoid mentality!

This orthodox, Western psychological assumption is very much culture bound: in many other cultures a person who spontaneously goes into d-ASCs is considered to be gifted and selected for special training to help him develop his talent.

If a psychologist himself occasionally goes into d-ASCs, he is very careful to keep quiet about it if he doesn't want his professional reputation destroyed.

The spiritual psychologies are more open toward spontaneously occurring altered states of consciousness. It *may* mean that a person is poorly adjusted, but it may also mean a natural talent (or one inherited from a past life) which can be cultivated and can lead to important spiritual understanding. Each case must be judged on its individual merits.

Assumption: Deliberately cultivating altered states of consciousness is also a sign of psychopathology.

Given the orthodox assumption that our ordinary d-SoC is already optimal for practically all human functions, why should any sane person deliberately try to induce an inferior state of consciousness in himself? Again, a psychologist who deliberately cultivates d-ASCs in himself, such as by meditating, still has to keep it quiet. Such cultivation is easily seen as flirting with psychosis, and indicates the person is not well adjusted to reality and must be seeking some kind of escape.

Deliberate cultivation of d-ASCs is, of course, an essential technique of many of the spiritual paths, not simply cultivating any state, but cultivating certain states for specific ends.

ASSUMPTIONS ABOUT THE RELATIONSHIP BETWEEN MIND AND BODY

Assumption: The body is a relatively passive servo-mechanism for carrying out the orders of the nervous system.

The orthodox, Western psychological assumption is that consciousness and volition reside in the central nervous system, and the body is primarily a device for carrying out those orders. I (my brain) think and decide, my body is my slave. I need to take adequate care of it, as I would any good slave, so it can carry out my orders effectively, and I should know its capacities and limitations, but it is certainly not to be consulted on making decisions.

Some of the spiritual psychologies share something of this attitude, but others take a quite different position, viewing the body as a kind of brain or mind in and of itself, capable of providing important information and making decisions. Further, in some spiritual disciplines like yoga, it is believed that the functioning of the body has a profound effect on the mind. *Mudras,* for example, the symbolic gestures that yogis often practice, are held to create a certain state of mind as a result of putting the body in a certain posture. This idea apparently also was important in early Christianity. C. S. Lewis puts it rather amusingly in his *Screwtape Letters* (1960), in which he has an older devil advising a younger devil on how to tempt humans. The old devil advises that it is important to tempt humans to think that they can pray in any old comfortable position, because this will keep them out of positions which actually make a prayer more effective.

I am glad to say that significant breaks in the orthodox façade are appearing with the renewed interest in the body and its effect on psychological functions in humanistic and transpersonal psychology.

Assumption: The physical body is the only body we have.

This seems absolutely self-evident, yet quite different positions are taken in the spiritual psychologies. Most of the spiritual psychologies assume we have at least one other, nonphysical body, which is like our physical body but possesses somewhat different abilities, including the ability to survive bodily death. Other spiritual psychologies assume we have many bodies, existing on different, nonphysical levels of existence, and affecting each other in certain kinds of ways. Others believe that we may have only our physical body ordinarily, but through spiritual efforts we can create other bodies capable of surviving death. Just as many spiritual psychologies would not consider the physical body as simply a passive servo-mechanism, but an active partner in the development of our consciousness, so these nonphysical bodies should not be considered as simply passive.

ASSUMPTIONS ABOUT DEATH

Assumption: Death is the inevitable end of human life.

This is not something we like to think of: death is a taboo topic in psychology, often not even to be found in the indexes of books on psychology, much less given any real treatment. But we all believe that the physical body will eventually malfunction sufficiently so that we will die. Medical science may prolong life, but death is inevitable, despite science fictionish dreams of medically produced immortality.

Some spiritual psychologies, however, believe that while physical death is certainly the common lot, some spiritually developed individuals may be able to alter the life processes in their body to achieve life spans of hundreds of years or even relative immortality. Particularly in some of the alchemical traditions, such as the Chinese alchemical tradition, this has been stated as a goal which has been attained by some of the older adepts. The general principle is that greatly enlarged physical life span or immortality is not attained by medical means, but by understanding, controlling, and balancing the nonphysical energies that constitute the essence of life, but which are ordinarily misused. Note, however, that prolonging physical life is not considered useful unless corresponding spiritual growth takes place, and even then it may not be desirable.

Assumption: Physical death is the final termination of human consciousness.

Since consciousness is a by-product of the electrochemical functioning of the brain and nervous system, and physical death means the complete, irreversible breakdown of the nervous system, obviously consciousness ceases once the breakdown has gone beyond a certain point, and can never exist again. Thus the end point of all human consciousness, all striving, all joy and sorrow, all search for meaning, is death. It is not a very heartening view, and we do not think of it. Indeed, so repressed is the thought of one's own personal death that many psychologists have remarked that each human being acts as if he or she were immortal.

The spiritual psychologies have a wide range of beliefs about death. Classical Buddhism, for example, considers speculation about whether consciousness survives death or not to be a waste of time: the issue is to obtain enlightenment *now*, since the now is the only time that is real to one. Most of the spiritual psychologies assume that something about a human being survives the physical death of the body. This something may retain consciousness and personal identity in some systems, or be something more basic but less personal in other systems. Other spiritual psychologies, such as Gurdjieff's, assume that survival of the individual consciousness is generally not the case, but can be brought about through sufficient spiritual work. Many assume that the something that survives is not the individual personality. This is common in the idea of reincarnation, that in a given lifetime some deep aspect of the human individual learns something, or fails to learn important lessons, and this deeper aspect reincarnates and forms a new personality in another lifetime, with the consequences of learning or failure to learn in previous lifetimes manifesting as one goes along. The idea of learnings from previous lifetimes manifesting in present ones is the idea of karma, the law of cause and effect.

By now the reader may have got back into a frame of mind that regards these as rather interesting ideas, but certainly it's *obvious* that we have only one lifetime, and that the various assumptions of Western, orthodox psychology are simple statements of *fact*. They are not simply statements of "fact"; they are *theories* about the meaning of life. For some there has been good empirical evidence to support them as useful scientific theories, but let me ask you again: How much have you simply passively accepted these opinions because they were taught to you and they were socially acceptable, and how much have you actually evaluated them for yourselves? With regard to reincarnation, for example, have you actually read any of the scientific investigations of cases of alleged memories of previous incarnations, such as Stevenson's (1966) excellent collection? Have you actually looked at the parapsychological studies of mediums claiming to bring back specific messages from deceased individuals to prove their continuing identity, which are extensively chronicled in the annals of parapsychology?

Neither survival of physical death nor reincarnation has been well "proven" by the few scientific researches that have been done into it, but enough rather convincing evidence has been collected that, for one wishing to be truly scientific, it should remain an open question rather than one settled a priori by automatic assumptions. So, I remind you, whether there is evidence for any or many or all of the various assumptions of orthodox, Western psychology, all of them are questioned by one sort of evidence or another, and the fact that they have sunk below the level of a consciously held hypothesis and become implicit assumptions gives them enormous power over you.

ASSUMPTIONS ABOUT PERSONALITY

Assumption: An individual's personality is what makes him unique, skilled, worthwhile, and gives him his sense of identity.

The concept of personality is central in Western psychology in talking about any individual's uniqueness, your own feeling of being who *you* are, rather than just a faceless stranger in the crowd. Personality is generally thought of as long-term skills, attitudes, memories, behaviors, beliefs, and emotions that give consistency to your own experience and a consistency of who you are to others so that they say they *know* you. A great emphasis in the orthodox, Western notion of personality is on the way it makes one individual unique, different from others. Indeed, we often pejoratively describe a person as having no personality when we mean that he seems to have no (valued) characteristics that distinguish him.

Consequent with this assumption, we seek to develop our personalities, to maintain, strengthen, and extend those qualities in us which we think are unique to us. Statements such as: "He's a real personality" are often considered very complimentary in our society.

The spiritual psychologies may see this kind of attachment to and development of personality as either a minor consideration or a positive hindrance to spiritual development. The level of personality is generally seen as a lower level of human development, and putting more and more energy into it is a diversion from man's spiritual goals. Most spiritual psychologies speak of a deeper self or an essence or a soul that lies behind the relative surface reality of personality and that is responsible for man's craving for spiritual growth and is also the thing that actually grows. Some spiritual disciplines, such as the monastic ones, deliberately minimize personality characteristics, while others emphasize that one should not be attached to them. These attitudes result in a very different deployment of psychological energy from the orthodox, Western practice.

> *Assumption: A sense of personality, personal identity is vital, and its loss is pathological.*

The term "depersonalization" is used to describe psychiatric difficulties, and, in general, any marked fading of the sense of personal identity is considered pathological. A major exception is when a person becomes relatively identified with a "good cause," a cause we approve of, and then we consider it a healthy sign that the person can be so devoted. If a friend says, "I'm not sure who I am —I have questions about my identity," we are liable to refer him to a psychiatrist.

While given cases of changes in personal identity may be pathological, the spiritual psychologies would also see this as a possible sign of real questioning necessary to spiritual growth. As long as one accepts the surface identity, the personality brought about by one's particular upbringing and particular culture, he is not really turning attention to his deeper self. There are meditation techniques which involve repeatedly asking the question: "Who am I?" and questioning each answer more and more deeply. At the higher levels of spiritual experience, personal identity temporarily disappears altogether as the person becomes aware of and identified with higher spiritual forces or entities. Failure to lose one's sense of personal identity is frequently regarded as failure to achieve success in the spiritual discipline. After profound mystical experiences, involving union with the highest levels of the universe, the personality may reappear in the person's subsequent life, but it is now only a collection of characteristics of no great importance, a *style* or *tool* of expression rather than the basic nature of the person, who is now in touch with and identified with something much deeper.

Assumption: The basic development of personality is finished and complete in adulthood, except in the cases of neurotics or other mentally ill persons.

While we can see that people may learn specific bits of knowledge and specific skills all through their lives, their basic structure, their basic personality, is considered to be relatively complete by the time of young adulthood. Assuming an average life span of sixty-some years, the first third of life then is devoted to acquiring basic psychological skills and attitudes, and the rest of life to living within that framework. We may work on changing and developing the external environment in our maturity, but our own psychological growth is done with, our basic personality is fairly rigid and won't change, except in the case of neurotics who have to make up for improper and missed development from the first third of their life. Another way of saying this is that if we are an adult we then assume we are mature.

The spiritual psychologies all take the view that development is not over on reaching adulthood, that development to be an adequately functioning member of society is only a preliminary groundwork to beginning real spiritual development. Personality should not remain at this relatively shallow and culturally bound level, but the individual should begin to contact deeper and deeper levels of himself in the course of his spiritual growth. Lifelong growth is the goal. The idea that because we are an adult we are mature is laughable. Too, development and growth do not necessarily stop with one lifetime. The potentials of men are so vastly greater than those represented by the ordinary adult's adjustment to his culture that the feat of adjusting to one's culture is of no great consequence.

Assumption: A healthy personality is one which allows the individual to be well-adjusted in terms of his culture.

This is a widely held assumption with respect to one's own culture, although we question it when an individual is adjusting to a culture we don't like. So the orthodox American psychologist feels that someone who is well adjusted to American culture is indeed healthy, but the Nazi who was well adjusted to his society was not so healthy. Scientists try not to make value judgments about different cultures, since this supposedly interferes with their objectivity, but we make them anyway. This assumption is congruent with the idea that we have only one life, which ends with the death of the physical body, so being well adjusted to one's culture clearly allows one to get the maximum of pleasure and the minimum of pain from it.

The spiritual psychologies, taking a longer and wider perspective, would see adjustment to one's society as a relatively minor achievement, and, if the culture perpetuates patterns judged as delusory or evil, then someone who actually wishes to grow spiritually should definitely *not* be well adjusted to his culture, although he may have to dissimulate adjustment in order to avoid friction and harassment that would divert energies from his spiritual goals. An old Sufi saying describes a common attitude of the spiritual psychologies quite well: "In the world, but not of it."

> *Assumption: A normal adult has a fairly good degree of understanding of his own personality.*

There is some inherent contradiction here among orthodox, Western psychologists, for in theory many of them hold that we do not understand ourselves very well, but in practice they and we expect other people to have some understanding of themselves and take responsibility for themselves, and we act consequent with this assumption. If the normal adult is a person who has had some psychotherapy, especially if he is a psychologist or a psychiatrist, we expect him to have quite a bit of understanding of his personality.

The spiritual psychologies would generally regard an ordinary person's understanding of his personality, or even a psychologist's for that matter, as a relatively trivial and often very distorted understanding of a not too important level of human functioning. Many of the spiritual psychologies emphasize over and over that the ordinary human being and his society live in and mutually reinforce a world of illusion, and their "understanding" of themselves and others within this world of illusion is itself mainly illusory. Since various reinforcement systems are set up for appropriate behavior within this world of illusion, and since most of us are attached to seeking pleasure and avoiding pain, there is a strong force not to question the illusionary world and our understanding of it, so few do question it. But questioning the obvious, questioning the socially agreed-upon consensus reality, is vital for spiritual (and scientific) progress.

> *Assumption: Personality is a relatively unified structure in normal adults.*

We assume that a given person is relatively consistent with himself, that he constitutes *one* person with various characteristics, traits, and so on. Thus you call yourself by one name, with the implication that you are indeed one person even though you have a range of moods and feelings. People who show severe contradictions between parts of their personality are labeled neurotic. In rare cases of multiple personality, quite different sets of characteristics hang together in discrete clusters (rather like d—SoCs) and call themselves by several names:

they are regarded as very abnormal indeed.

Some of the spiritual psychologies question this view strongly. Gurdjieff's system, for example, says that we actually have many quite discrete subpersonalities, each one of which calls itself "I" when it happens to be activated by appropriate environmental stimuli, but that we have no unity of personality at all except in the sense that all the various subpersonalities are associated with the same physical body and name. A major developmental stage in many spiritual psychologies is to become aware of the contradictions within us (such as finding that one part of us is very interested in seeking enlightenment, one is terribly afraid of it, and another simply wants to be comfortable) and to develop a unified whole for a personality.

ASSUMPTIONS ABOUT COGNITIVE PROCESSES

Assumption: Reasoning is the highest skill possessed by man.

The ability to think and to think *logically* (ignoring, for the sake of this discussion, the fact that there are many logics) is considered the unique ability of man, that which separates him from the animals and gives him dominion over the earth. For our orthodox, Western psychologists, it is the skill which brings the most reward in the profession in general, and this is generally true for scientists and academics as a whole.

The spiritual psychologies would certainly agree that reasoning is a valuable skill, but many would disagree that it is the highest skill. Some would call intuition the greatest skill possessed by man; others would call the ability to love the highest skill. The importance of these differences in assumptions will become clearer as we go on.

Assumption: Developing the logical mind, one's reasoning abilities, is the highest accomplishment a person can aim for.

Put in another way, the more one becomes like a professor, the better. The more one's mind becomes like a vast computer, capable of flawless reasoning and with immense data banks to draw on, the more one is developed. With the notable exception that some reinforcement is given to developing "clinical skills" in the training of clinical psychologists and psychiatrists, all one's training in psychology rewards intellectual skills and the use of words that that entails. A graduate student trying to get a Ph.D. in experimental psychology who starts talking about his increased ability to empathize, for example, is going to be in for difficulties at most graduate schools.

A closely related assumption of orthodox, Western psychology is that information or knowledge exists in isolation from the person who has it. Thus the formula

$E = MC^2$ is equally valid when held in the mind of an American nuclear physicist or a Russian nuclear physicist; their personalities have nothing to do with it.

We have already mentioned that in many of the spiritual psychologies, developing such faculties as intuition or the ability to love or will power are considered just as important as or more important than developing intellectual skills. Further, there is a belief that in the spiritual realm, the most important realm of human knowledge, knowledge does not exist in isolation from the personality or level of spiritual being of the knower. The example of the physical formula used above is an example of a certain kind of knowledge that is independent of personality, but many of the most important kinds of human knowledge cannot be known unless there is a corresponding level of spiritual development of the knower.

For example, in many spiritual psychologies it is pointed out that the emphasis on morality connected with religion is not simply an isolated injunction to make people good; it is a *technical practice* designed to alter the level of being of the spiritual seeker, which is essential to opening certain domains of knowledge. Certain kinds of knowledge can be apprehended only when a certain kind of emotional balance is reached or, as another example, when the body has been educated to function as a "brain." Certain kinds of vital spiritual knowledge then are closed to, say, the man who may be a brilliant professor in the intellectual realm but has let his body deteriorate and goes home and (psychologically) beats his wife each night.

Assumption: Extension of our basically sound knowledge and cognitive processes is the way to greater knowledge and wisdom.

We generally assume that what we *already* know and the cognitive skills we *already* possess are basically sound. If we are dissatisfied and we need to know more or achieve more meaning in life, we must *add* to what we already have. Particularly, we generally assume that our ability to reason and use other cognitive skills is quite adequate, that what we need is more *information* on how to properly handle situations in which we are not now satisfied with our performance.

Many of the spiritual psychologies emphasize that if we want to grow we must question, modify, and *get rid of* a lot of what we feel we already know. We must stop exercising some of the "skills" that we already have, since they are the cause of our trouble. Others may additionally emphasize that we must develop quite new cognitive faculties that are qualitatively different from those we currently possess, such as developing our intuition rather than learning to reason better or faster. M. Nicoll, one of the teachers in the Gurdjieff tradition, gives an apt example of a man with a garden full of weeds asking what he should do to grow fine food, what he should plant in his garden. The answer is that at this stage he cannot think about planting anything: he must stop lovingly watering the weeds. It's not what he must *do,* but what he must stop doing (Nicoll, 1952–56).

> *Assumption: Knowledge is a hypothesis, a concept in the mind, and there is no direct, certain knowledge of anything.*

Given the orthodox assumptions that consciousness is identical with neural activity in the brain and nervous system, and that the final nature of reality is physical events, the belief that knowledge is always indirect is quite congruent, for our consciousness is totally locked up and isolated within the brain, from which it *interprets* certain neural events as belonging to the outside world. Thus I can look up from where I am writing and say that I "know" the front door is closed because I "see" that it is closed, but what I am really saying is that I'm experiencing a certain pattern of neural events, *presumably* mediated through my eyes, to which I give the label "seeing that the door is closed." I can have no absolute certainty that the door even exists, for the whole thing could be a malfunctioning of my brain. Thus knowledge is seen as only a kind of hypothesis, supported by sensory evidence. But, since we never have *direct* contact with anything but our own neural processes, we can never be certain about *anything,* no matter how reliable it has been in our experience or how many other people (with whom, of course, we have no direct contact either) we can get to agree with us about this state of affairs.

The spiritual psychologies generally believe that while experience of the physical world is ordinarily derivative in this same way, there are modes of *direct* knowledge and experience of both the physical world and the spiritual world. Meditation, in many traditions, is seen as a way of becoming one with the object meditated on, whether that object is an external, physical object or a spiritual object or concept, and thus one has a direct knowledge of it. If the meditation object with which one merges is a higher-level spiritual being or God, one may, know certain basic truths with absolute certainty, not inferentially.

> *Assumption: Philosophers are the ultimate authorities about the nature of knowledge.*

Psychologists generally have a certain awe about philosophers, believing them to be the authorities on what knowledge is all about and believing that basic questions about how we acquire valid knowledge have been worked through by philosophers long ago. In actual fact, most psychologists have almost no formal knowledge of philosophy at all and practically never draw on philosophy in their day-to-day work. Further, many psychologists feel that philosophers finished their work in helping to lay the foundations for scientific method: the basic problems of what is knowledge and how to acquire it were thus solved long ago, and living philosophers are sort of quaint relics from an older age whose problems have now been solved. They seldom say this directly to philosophers, as philosophers are known to often have sharp tongues and bad tempers.

The spiritual psychologies would see this assumption as a very relative truth, for, as we have already discussed, rational thinking is only one of many types of human knowledge, and a type of knowledge which can be extremely misleading when highly developed but not used in harmony with other developed human skills like intuition, love, and will. In the spiritual disciplines, the person who has developed direct, *experiential* knowledge of spiritual realities is the real authority, not the one who has not had the experience but has done a lot of reasoning about it. And the function of the real authorities is not to *tell* others what the ultimate nature of reality is, but to teach people how to experience it for themselves so that their knowledge will be direct.

> *Assumption: Almost all important knowledge can be transmitted by the written word, and the written word is the least ambiguous, most accurate way of transmitting it.*

Most of the business of the academic world proceeds on this assumption, and innumerable mountains of paper are generated and shuffled from place to place every day in its practical application. Lecturing in the course of teaching is given much lip service, but the real way to rise in the academic world, outside of administrative routes, is to write, to write many words which gain acceptance in prestigious academic publications. If a student has a "hunch" or a vaguely formed idea about a researchable topic, his professors ask him how can he translate this into a written grant proposal or into an experiment whose results and procedures can be clearly described in written form in an academic journal.

I was very taken in by this assumption in extreme form for the first twenty years or so of my life, when I in effect believed that everything written in a book was true. After all, a book was practically sacred—it was inconceivable that people would put an untruth or a lie into a book! I still am taken in by this assumption most of the time, even though I can intellectually question it.

Within orthodox, Western psychology some recognition is given to the ability of pictures and art forms to transmit certain kinds of information, but this is generally felt as an unnecessary evil or an inferior form of information transmission that can certainly be improved upon when we learn how to adequately conceptualize these areas in language. With so much veneration given to the written word, then, it is not surprising that psychologists often talk about ways of improving language so that it communicates even more precisely than it does now.

There is little doubt that science has progressed enormously, primarily the physical sciences, using the written word and the logic inherent in it as a primary tool of communication, especially that very precise form of the written word, mathematics. But the physical sciences have also stressed that observable results are even more important than the beauty and convincingness of language.

The spiritual psychologies would emphasize that language is only one way of communication, a way suited to certain kinds of information but not to others. Particularly, the spiritual psychologies believe that language is highly inadequate for conceptualizing or communicating most of the really important dimensions of spiritual experience. Language may be useful, but its usefulness is limited, and people are constantly warned against believing that because they can express something in language they actually understand it. Many alternative forms of communication are used, such as symbolic drawings and actions, touch, and, in some systems, a direct mind-to-mind communication of spiritual experience by some form of what we would call telepathy. This may include, in some systems, a direct transmission of something that alters a person's state of consciousness and makes him directly experience certain truths.

Our orthodox, Western assumption is that if someone makes a great discovery he builds a device and/or writes a book about it. In a spiritual psychology someone who makes the highest kind of discoveries may write, but he is just as likely to carve a statue, teach a dance, bake good bread, or paint a picture to express his knowledge and communicate it.

> *Assumption: Logical inconsistencies in the expression of something indicate its invalidity.*

One of the first things a lawyer does to discredit the opposition, or a psychologist who doesn't like someone else's theory does to disprove it, is to look for logical inconsistencies in its expression. Even if the apparent inconsistency turns out to be incomplete or poor phrasing rather than a real, logical inconsistency, the person who shows logical inconsistencies is greatly discredited. Logical inconsistencies are greatly frowned upon in science especially, although they may sometimes be tolerated between two theories when complementarity (see the discussion in Chapter 1) is necessary.

Often in the spiritual psychologies material is presented which contains logical inconsistencies, but since logic is looked upon as only one form of knowledge, such logical inconsistencies may not be important. The rational, verbal expression of a spiritual truth is seen as only a poor approximation to the actual truth itself, and if it comes out as logically inconsistent, that is no great problem. It says something about the shortcomings of logic, not the validity of the spiritual truth being expressed.

Indeed, some spiritual disciplines often deliberately introduce logical inconsistencies into their teachings as a training and selection device. As a selection device, it will antagonize those who insist that all new knowledge be coherent with their own already formed opinions, so they will go away and not waste the time of the spiritual teacher. As a training device, if the student takes the material seriously but nevertheless sees the logical inconsistencies in it, it will force him to begin actually looking at his own system of logic instead of passively accepting it at an implicit level.

> *Assumption: When people agree with me they are being rational; when they disagree they are probably irrational.*

Psychologists have no monopoly on this one: we all do it all the time, and everyone deplores it, but it's a good thing to be reminded of it.

> *Assumption: Fantasy is a part-time cognitive activity, usually done in our leisure hours.*

The orthodox picture of man is that he spends most of his time working, reasoning, perceiving, and problem solving, and that only in neurotics and other abnormal people is much time outside of leisure time spent in fantasy. This is a fitting picture of a "rational creature," such as we believe we are.

The spiritual psychologies generally stress that we spend almost all of our time in fantasy activity, that almost all our interactions with the world and other people around us are tinged more or less with fantasy. Within a culture many fantasies are shared and thought of as realities, so ordinary social interaction seldom gives us feedback on how much fantasy we are engaged in. Prolonged self-observation will show that many times we are living almost in a dream world. We skillfully and automatically blend inputs from reality into it in accordance with our needs and defenses. This is a tremendous waste of energy, and must be reduced and eventually eliminated to grow spiritually.

> *Assumption: Faith means believing in things that are not real or that you have no solid evidence for.*

Faith is a negatively loaded word for most Western psychologists, indicating that people believe the most irrational, nonsensical things possible and, perversely, are proud that they believe in such things. Things like the existence of God, for example. When faith is of something you are sure is true and will eventually be provable, even though you do not have enough evidence yet, the attitude is not quite so negative, but faith is not considered to have any really appropriate part in the scientific process. Tentative belief in postulated hypotheses, yes, but faith, with its smackings of religiosity, no.

Within the spiritual psychologies, faith is often seen as standing for irrational belief also, including such irrational beliefs as faith in the unlimited power of rationality. But faith is also used to indicate guiding one's actions through evidence about things that are not physical. That is, faith can represent a conviction based on very substantial evidence about spiritual realities which can never be translated into readily observable, physical manifestations. Thus faith in religious teaching brought about by witnessing miracles, for example, can be seen as a rather inferior form of faith because it still uses physical reality as its ultimate testing point, while the faith that has an experiential basis in spiritual realities alone can be a very important tool in spiritual growth.

Assumption: Intuition is a word we use for lucky guesses, coincidences, or rational processes that are outside of conscious awareness but are nevertheless rational.

Orthodox, Western psychologists have always had a difficult time with the idea of intuition. It's not so bad when intuition comes up with the same conclusion as reason, but when intuition goes against reason then intuition is liable to be dismissed. Rational processes which go on outside of consciousness are considered to be probably sloppy and inferior, as is generally assumed about all d-ASCs, even though they may occasionally be very creative. Intuition is a good "random factor" to have in creative geniuses, but we certainly don't encourage it among psychologists. I can recall little encouragement to anyone to develop his or her intuition in graduate school when I was a student.

Many spiritual psychologies conceive of intuition as one or more powerful cognitive faculties that work on principles other than logical rationality, and that work "outside" of conscious awareness, outside in the sense that only the answer to a problem is present, not the awareness of the functioning of the intuition process itself. Further, intuition is seen as something that can be cultivated, and as something that can give a more profound understanding of many things than reason.

Assumption: Symbols are nothing but physical objects with emotional meaning, or electrophysiological patterns within the brain.

A symbol is something you look at that has some kind of meaning for you, such as a figure of a Buddha or a crucifix. Psychologically, a symbol has reality only in one's mind, which, since the mind is seen to be identical with brain processes, means that symbols are reduced to patterns of electrical activity in the brain. As such, they may affect the brain in which they exist, or they may affect other brains if properly communicated through the senses, but they have no reality beyond that.

Some of the spiritual psychologies, on the other hand, believe that certain symbols have an existence and power of their own over and above the mind that experiences them. Rather than being exclusively generated within the mind of man, symbols may appear in the mind as a manifestation of a spiritual reality outside the mind. Thus they form a connection between the individual experiencing them and an outside reality, and may thus be transformers or converters of energy to other levels of existence. The veneration for symbols and the many sophisticated techniques developed for their usage is seen as more than "just" a psychological technique in many spiritual psychologies.

Assumption: Our beliefs and psychological experiences affect only ourselves, not the "real" world, except when expressed by motor activities.

This is similar to the idea that the mind is essentially totally isolated within the confines of the nervous system, but it also has an element of security to it: no matter how dumb or crazy or afraid I get in my own mind, good old solid physical reality will not be affected by it unless I use my body to affect it, so I can always depend on good old solid physical reality. If the walls begin to melt around me, I know that it's just a trick of my mind, since walls don't really melt. If a demon attacks me, I know it's just a projection of my psychological conflicts, since nonphysical creatures like demons can exist only within my mind.

Spiritual psychologies do not always make this assumption of the physical world being real and all mental things being unreal, and indicate that sometimes a mental process may have a direct, parapsychological type of effect on physical reality, as well as on other people's mental reality. Thus many experiences occurring in mystical and other d-ASCs are not considered as existing only within the mind, but as affecting this reality or other levels of reality. One can push this to the extreme of thinking about the possibility that "reality"—or, more accurately "consensus reality"—is as much a function of a widely shared belief system directly influencing it as of its own intrinsic nature. Whether this concept seems exciting or frightening will say something about our humanness.

ASSUMPTIONS ABOUT EMOTION

Assumption: Emotions are electrical and chemical shifts within the nervous system.

This assumption is similar to the ones that thoughts or symbols are "nothing but" electrochemical patterns in the nervous system. Emotions are reduced to "nothing but" neurohumoral chemicals in the bloodstream interacting with various brain processes in specific areas of the brain, like the hypothalamus and limbic system. This kind of assumption leads directly into the "chemical psychiatry" approach to achieving happiness. If emotions are nothing but chemical and electrical patterns, then injecting the right chemical substance in the bloodstream can clearly enhance desired emotions and suppress undesired emotions.

The spiritual psychologies do not make this reduction of emotional events strictly to physical events. Emotion is viewed as a type of consciousness energy and/or as the activation of particular parts of the mind and nervous system, and as potentially having far greater consequences than merely electrochemical shifts within the brain and body. Emotion, for example, can be seen as a kind of "fuel" which, if used properly, can allow the attainment of higher states of consciousness and consequent spiritual growth. As with thought, many of the spiritual psychologies assume that emotion can have a direct effect on others and external reality, that it is not totally confined within the nervous system unless expressed by overt motor acts.

Assumption: Emotions interfere with logical reason and make man irrational; therefore they should generally be suppressed or eliminated except for recreational purposes.

This is the idea of a completely rational man, using some kind of logic that is the optimal way of approaching all situations. It contains a further assumption that if one really understands the facts, and reasons about them logically, the most true and useful solution will almost inevitably result. Abundant psychological evidence exists to show that reasoning can be subtly (and sometimes not so subtly) influenced by whatever emotions happen to be dominant at the time.

The spiritual psychologies in general certainly see emotion as being able to interfere with rationality, and as being a cause of great difficulties, but the spiritual psychologies do not see emotion per se as necessarily bad, only undesirable and poorly controlled emotions. Rather than having the ideal of suppressing emotion, the ideal is to suppress or alter emotions which interfere with spiritual growth, but to develop and purify other kinds of emotions which may constitute fuel for higher states of consciousness, and help keep motivation high for working difficult spiritual practices. Further, some of the spiritual psychologies see emotion as a way of evaluating information that is quite different from intellectual evaluation, but every bit as valid and necessary. That is, certain truths can be apprehended only through proper use of certain kinds of emotions, and they can never be understood intellectually. The completely intellectual man, with his emotions suppressed, would be seen as highly pathological in the spiritual psychologies. I should underscore the importance of this orthodox, Western assumption: although in formal psychological theories the balanced emotional life is allowed for, in practice if a psychologist's peers feel he is "highly emotional" or "passionate," he will have difficulty in succeeding in the academic world, as he will not be trusted or readily promoted.

Assumption: Emotions have no place in scientific work, or while they may motivate individuals, they must be filtered out of the final product.

While scientists admit that the average man certainly tends to get rather emotional and irrational, they pride themselves on being rational and relatively unemotional themselves. This is the basis of their "objectivity." While it is admitted that an "irrational" desire may motivate the scientist to work hard and he may then usefully accomplish something, that emotional tone must not appear in his scientific report on his work. After all, scientists work with the "facts" and the logical consequences of theories, not with whether they like or dislike something.

Some psychologists have now recognized that there is a lot more emotional motivation in science than we give lip service to, and that the suppression of it in final scientific reports gives a misleading impression of a totally intellectual activity. Emotionality is seen as a consequence of our human frailty and so must be recognized in spite of its undesirability.

As we discussed above, the spiritual psychologies see emotions as a key tool for understanding certain kinds of truths, and so eliminating them makes certain kinds of knowledge impossible. Further, most of the spiritual psychologies would see even the scientific enterprise as being extremely emotional, with the degree of emotionality being suppressed from the consciousness of the individual scientist, rather than being absent. I am greatly impressed by this degree of probable suppression when I attend various sorts of academic meetings. Even in psychology departments, no application of psychological knowledge is made in faculty meetings: rather the whole thing proceeds on the assumption that everyone there is a rational being, holding a strictly logical discussion to find the optimal solution to problems, rather than seeing that the interaction among various partially suppressed emotions may be the dominant determinant of what goes on, with the "reasoning" serving mainly as rationalization for expressing feelings.

Assumption: Negative emotions are the inevitable lot of man.

Emotions such as anxiety, fear, sorrow, depression, anger, jealousy, and the like are seen as built into our human nature, built into our physiology, and although we try to avoid them, even a relatively well-adjusted person is expected to experience these emotions occasionally. This partially contradicts the assumption above about rational man having few emotions, but we have many contradictory assumptions that alternate or sometimes work simultaneously. If someone claims not to have these emotions, we suspect that he is lying or simply unaware of himself. Freud's psychology has had a major hand in strengthening this assumption, and although few psychologists would call themselves Freudians, almost all have been influenced by Freud to a greater or lesser extent. The Freudian view of man is that under a thin veneer of civilization and control lurk primitive drives for sexual expression and self-aggrandizement that must be at least partially satisfied within the compromise structures that civilization allows. One has to expect a fair amount of negative emotions in such a creature.

The spiritual psychologies certainly recognize these negative emotions, but often point out that we set up conditions to help bring about their fulfillment. We may learn from these negative emotions if we have a goal of spiritual growth and/or we may learn to completely eliminate these negative emotions. The ordinary range of negative human emotions is not considered inevitable in many of the spiritual psychologies.

Assumption: There are no higher emotions; all emotions are basically self-serving and animal.

This ties in with the previous assumption that we know the range of real human emotions, they are mostly negative, and the best we can do is try to minimize the negative emotions and enjoy and increase the positive emotions such as joy, pleasure, and excitement. Reports of "mystical ecstasy" or "higher emotions" are looked upon either as myths or as possible indicators of serious psychopathology.

Some of the spiritual psychologies stress, on the contrary, that the range of emotions that most human beings go through is the lowest range of emotions for human beings, and that there are higher emotions such as love, compassion, and ecstasy that are far more real to those who experience them than the ordinary human emotions. The orthodox, Western assumption about love is that one should be suspicious of it: it is a combination of sexual desire and other desires for pleasure attached to another person and rationalized as being selfless, when actually it is quite self-serving. The spiritual psychologies generally recognize this about ordinary love, but do insist that there is a higher form of love which is indeed selfless and far more powerful than ordinary love.

Assumption: Play is for children.

Have you ever seen a psychologist* playing? Or almost any adult, for that matter? You may fairly often see adults indulging in "entertainment" or "recreation," but the element of spontaneous, childlike play is almost totally missing from adult life. The little of this element that is left takes stylized, narrow forms. It is "inappropriate" to simply play with anything and everything in this serious, grownup world we live in. While theoretical value is accorded to the spontaneity, spontaneity and playing are, for all practical purposes, almost never manifested in the professional activities of orthodox, Western psychologists.

Many of the spiritual psychologies have a far more open attitude toward play, stemming from a feeling that children quite often have a higher degree of purity and spirituality, since their being has not yet been overlaid by the deadening attachment to the world that gradually saps our life. Indeed, some spiritual systems see the whole world as a kind of divine play, even though we, in our

---

*My apologies to some child psychologists.

limited perspective, may see it as deadly serious or evil. Yoga psychology (see Chapter 6), for example, sees how a person who has reached enlightenment may not renounce the world but may take part in it as an expression of the divine play of the living universe. A number of observers have also reported that highly spiritual people often seem to have a delightful capacity to simply play, to take a childlike, joyous delight in the here and now.

Assumption: Pain is bad and should be avoided.

While orthodox, Western psychology recognizes that pain can be a useful danger signal, warning us to attend to physical illness or to escape from a threatening situation, pain is otherwise looked upon as something to be avoided at all costs. If you have a pain, you not only go to your doctor to be cured of any underlying physical illness but to have the pain eliminated. If you experience mental anguish, it is widely accepted to go to your doctor or psychiatrist for a tranquilizer or other psychoactive drug that will still your mental pain. On the nonmedical side, alcohol is consumed in incredible quantities in our culture to escape from psychic pain of various sorts. The older, puritanically oriented ethic seemed to see pain as something to be borne, and that it was good not to give in too easily to pain, but the obviously neurotic and masochistic elements in the puritan attitude toward pain do not recommend it.

Indeed, a guiding implicit philosophy of life of many people in our culture today is to maximize pleasure and minimize pain. We call it hedonism when it is an explicit philosophy. While few people will take that position explicitly, vast numbers of us do implicitly.

The spiritual psychologies generally have a quite different attitude: they stress that the problem of human suffering *is brought about* by this desire to escape pain and maximize pleasure. Since a certain amount of pain and misfortune is the inevitable lot of every human being in an imperfect world, this attitude of escaping pain and pursuing pleasure makes us more the slave of pleasure when we manage to get it or when we are seeking it, and more the victims of pain when we cannot avoid it. Many spiritual systems stress the cultivation of nonattachment, transcending attachment to pleasure and pain. This does not mean that practical steps to avoid noxious situations are not taken, or that one does not enjoy life, but it does mean that one's internal attitude toward pleasure and pain changes vastly.

Both pain and pleasure can be seen as capable of teaching important lessons in a spiritually growing person if some degree of nonattachment to them is possible, but basically they are seen as inherent parts of a continuum: *pursuit* of or attachment to pleasure automatically makes one more vulnerable to pain. The greater the pursuit and attachment, the greater the vulnerability.

ASSUMPTIONS ABOUT LEARNING

Assumption: Learning is a matter of permanent and semipermanent electro-chemical changes in the brain and nervous system.

This assumption is so widely accepted as accounting for all learning that vast sums are spent on research in brain function to try to find what portions of the brain are responsible for what kinds of learning. Although we have very little *specific* evidence that a given bit of learning takes place at a particular location of the human brain, this lack of data is assumed to be a result of the immense complexity of the human brain and one that will certainly yield to research in the future.

Insofar as the spiritual psychologies do not assume that the human mind is limited only to the functioning of the brain and nervous system, learning would not be so narrowly defined as "nothing but" electrochemical changes in the nervous system. The whole idea of reincarnation and the theory of karma, for example, clearly require that what is learned in a given lifetime must (at least partially) transfer to some nonphysical entity which acts as a carrier vehicle to transmit this learning to another lifetime. This also has a corollary that what you learn is very important, for it will not be "erased" completely with the disintegration of the brain and nervous system, but will have far longer-term consequences.

Assumption: Learning is a matter of accumulating knowledge.

Orthodox, Western psychologists recognize, in formal discussions of learning, and in many laboratory experiments, that learning is more complicated than this, for it is also a matter of unlearning incorrect responses and incorrect concepts. But, in terms of how each of us, including psychologists, conducts our daily lives, we almost always operate on the implicit assumption that we need to learn *more*. If we have some kind of problem and can't solve it, we very seldom question whether the concepts we have to begin with about the problem are correct, rather we think: What *more* do I need to learn? We have a vast educational industry that we support, designed to give us more and more and more information about innumerable topics. The neurotic and the person with school difficulties are the people who may have bad habits that have to be unlearned, but we almost always act as if we simply need more information to add to our wisdom—we assume that what we know now is basically all right and needs only to be supplemented in areas in which we are not succeeding.

Many of the spiritual psychologies put the emphasis on *un*learning, and point out that most of our problems arise not from lack of information but from an abundance of incorrect information, either factually incorrect or incorrect in its interpretation. We have strong emotional attachments to these faulty learnings which make it difficult for us to consider that they might be in error or to reevaluate them. Stripping away is more important than accumulating in many spiritual disciplines, to let our more basic spiritual nature underneath come through.

> *Assumption: Intellectual learning is the highest form of learning, and a person with a very high IQ has the potential to learn practically everything of importance.*

Orthodox, Western psychologists also have such categories as motor learning for learning coordinated kinds of motions such as might be involved in sports, and may theoretically recognize the possibility of some emotional learning, but I don't believe there is any graduate school program in orthodox, Western psychology that spends any time at all on teaching a student to educate his emotions or his body. The university is a hyperintellectual system, and one gets ahead in it by making words. Someone very much involved in athletics and the like is liable to be referred to as a "jock," and not command much respect among scholars. So even though other categories of learning are recognized, intellectual learning is acclaimed as the ultimate form of learning in almost every action taken by orthodox, Western psychologists.

The spiritual psychologies generally consider intellectual learning as only one form of learning, and hardly the most important. The difference in attitudes might be understood by looking at the distinction Gurdjieff made in classifying spiritual systems or ways, as he called them. One way was the way of the body, the way of the fakir, in which through prolonged and extraordinary discipline of the body the will was developed. The second way was the devotional way, the way of the monk, in which the emotions were developed. The third way, the way of the yogi, was the intellectual way, in which the mind was developed, although not just intellectually in the Western scholastic sense of the term, but involving the attainment of various d-ASCs. Gurdjieff felt that each of these ways was a very important way and could lead to valuable results, although each developmental way in isolation also contained the possibility of grossly imbalanced development which would not be useful in the long run; he referred to his own teachings as stemming from a fourth way that involved a balanced development of body, mind, and emotions. I have found Gurdjieff's conception here very useful: if you look at orthodox, Western psychology, or Western culture in general, you see that we have greatly overstressed intellectual development and given little real thought to the education and development of our emotional and bodily nature.

Assumption: Learning is a matter of taking in sensory impressions and applying cognitive processes to them.

This assumption is perfectly congruent with the physicalistic view of man. The only way new information can get into a human being is via the senses, and he may then use what cognitive skills he has to learn things from this information. Therefore if we want to teach someone else or ourselves to be better learners, we can focus either on learning to be a better observer or on learning to use our basic cognitive processes more effectively.

The spiritual psychologies generally would broaden this conception by emphasizing that some very important learning comes not from information that comes in through the senses, but from material that comes in in some kind of extrasensory way and/or from uncovering information already existent in the depths of our nature, but ordinarily buried. The most important learning in most spiritual growth processes would come from this totally interior working and discovery of aspects of our deeper self, which are also related to the living universe in general.

Note that all the various psychological functions we will be discussing in other sections contain assumptions that they are ultimately reducible to electrical and chemical processes in the brain and nervous system, and this has important consequences on how one tries to study these things. I will not emphasize the point further for each class of assumptions separately.

ASSUMPTIONS ABOUT MEMORY

Assumption: Memory is not very reliable: it is far better to depend on an objective record.

At first glance this seems like a fairly good assumption: we have a great deal of psychological research demonstrating that memory can fail to retrieve all sorts of information and that memory has many distortions involved in the retrieval of other information that makes it quite inaccurate. The tricky part of this assumption, however, is the attribution of truth or virtual infallibility to "objective" records, to written accounts or photographs or movies or video tapes or audio tape recordings. When an "objective" record apparently verifies what we want to be true, we forget how much the making and interpreting of "objective" records are affected by human desires.

I believe the spiritual psychologies would generally emphasize that we make a fetish of "objectivity" because this happens to meet various current desires, but we are not at all that objective. Indeed, it could be argued that "objective" records are not very important, since they cannot store some of the most vital aspects of information with respect to human life in general and the spiritual in particular. Thus human memories must be the standard for certain kinds of experiences, and it is believed that in various higher states of consciousness memory may function with far greater accuracy than in ordinary life.

Assumption: The only memory we have is of impressions in this life up to the present moment.

The assumption that man is born as a tabula rasa, a blank tablet, as far as memory is concerned is generally implicitly held. Impressions start coming in from the moment of birth, although they are not really organized in the infant and so not available later as memories. But as cognitive processes begin to create order out of the infant's world, he starts storing up memories of what has happened to him, what he has been told, what he has read. That is all there is in memory.

Many of the spiritual psychologies would not limit memory to this life. Some believe that memories of infancy can be recalled under proper circumstances, and that memories of intrauterine life can also be recalled. Further, some assume that racial memories, actual memory information passed on to us as part of our heritage of being human beings, can be recalled, and others believe that information about previous lives can be recalled. All of the spiritual psychologies then grant man a much wider span of memories to be drawn upon in the course of spiritual development. The Buddha, for example, is reported to have remembered all of his past incarnations while he was working through his enlightenment experience, and to have then made further personality changes in himself as a result of this recall, solidifying and expanding his enlightenment.

Assumption: The only memories we have direct access to are our own.

That is, the only thing that can exist in *our* personal memories is what has come in through *our* personal senses. We have only indirect access to others' memories through what they have told us or written or indicated by their behavior about themselves. This is perfectly congruent with the assumption that the only information that comes in is through the senses.

Many of the spiritual psychologies do not assume this ultimate isolation within our own nervous system, and believe that under appropriate circumstances we may have direct access to memories other than our own. This may include extrasensory communication with other people, providing a kind of direct access to their memories, and may include extrasensory, spiritual communication with nonhuman entities, both higher and lower in terms of spiritual development. In the Western magical tradition, for example, it is believed that one can have access to memories stored in objects such as trees and stones, as well as the knowledge of nonphysical entities of various sorts.

ASSUMPTIONS ABOUT MOTIVATION

Assumption: Desiring things is the basic motivation that keeps a person's life functioning, and lack of desire for things is pathological.

The orthodox, Western psychological view of motivation is that it stems from lack of something essential for life. The most basic lacks are those physical ones necessary to sustain the functioning of the body, such as air, food, and water. Similarly, avoiding situations which threaten damage to the body, such as painful stimuli and physical attack by animals or others, constitutes basic motivations. These are all maintenance needs and safety needs. When these basic levels of need are actually filled, psychologists say other motivations may become important, such as sexual desires and social motivations like needing to belong to and be accepted in some group, and more individual motivations such as a need to have a philosophy about the universe that gives one's life meaning. These latter sorts of needs are usually seen as subservient to the more basic maintenance and survival needs; that is, if most people have to make a choice between protecting their life and filling some social goal that will gain peer group acceptance, the former goal is chosen. People who put ideals ahead of their own comfort and survival are looked upon with mixed feelings: we are glad that *they* did it, but we are not so sure that we would do it.

In practice this psychological conceptualization of motivation becomes more general and we implicitly assume that people want things all the time, material things, psychological things. Indeed, our economy is based on this assumption and on the advertising game designed to keep these assumed needs running at a high level. If a person says he is not interested in earning more money or having a nicer home or achieving more recognition and the like, we speak of this as an "amotivational syndrome," and suspect that something is very wrong with the individual.

The spiritual psychologies see the extent to which we are always wanting something or other as a primary way of trapping us at our current level of development and preventing further spiritual development. This constant desire for things may be called greed or attachment, and it functions to keep an individual locked within a certain understanding of the universe which is consistent with fulfilling his motivations for more things. On many spiritual paths renunciation is practiced as a technical procedure: in deliberately disciplining oneself to not want things, one can then have them or not have them, but not be trapped by being intensely motivated to get them and keep them.*

The spiritual psychologies then would see giving up many of our "basic motivations" for various kinds of things as essential. Almost all the things we think we need are not really essential. Decreasing desire for various worldly goods and achievements is not seen as pathological, but as an important step forward in spiritual growth.

> *Assumption: The primary motivations affecting people are desires for power and desires for sexual pleasure, along with an avoidance of pain.*

Although few psychologists would call themselves Freudians or Adlerians, the psychoanalytic concepts developed by Freud and extended by Adler that sexual gratification and power over others are primary motivations are accepted by a large number of psychologists. These are conceived of as unconscious needs or motivations, things which the individual would seldom admit to consciously; he is not aware of how important they are. The Freudian picture of man tends to be that of a person driven by sexual and power needs, but needing to compromise in obtaining gratification of these in order to fit in with his social group. One need only look through the advertisements in any magazine to see how much sexual desires and desires to feel socially approved of, powerful, and belonging are used to sell goods to people.

The spiritual psychologies would generally recognize the importance of security needs, sexual needs, and social needs, but would add that a basic *spiritual* need, the need to know one's true nature and one's place in the universe, is just as important if not far more important than these other needs. Indeed, the need for spiritual growth is considered far more important: all other needs may be subordinated to it, although these other needs must not be pathologically denied.

The orthodox, Western psychological position about needs for understanding oneself and life, these spiritual needs, is that they are something of a luxury, all right to be used once basic survival and social needs are met, but far from primary. The spiritual psychologies, on the other hand, would see spiritual needs as so primary that insofar as they are not given enough attention, man must exist in a neurotic, pathological state. The spiritual psychologies would say that most people today, by virtue of lacking a spiritual goal and working discipline, are in a very pathological state, and this accounts for the sad state of the world. The orthodox, Western psychological approach of denying that such spiritual needs exist does not fulfill them, and cannot provide any ultimate guides to a full life and a better world.

---

*We should note that the practice of renunciation has often become pathological in the practices of spiritual paths, becoming an end in itself rather than a tool.

ASSUMPTIONS ABOUT PERCEPTION

Assumption: The only things there are to perceive are the physical world and the sensations from the internal operations of our body and nervous system.

For the orthodox, Western psychologist, the external world and the internal world of our body and nervous system are a total listing of all there is to perceive. The physical world here would include both those aspects of it that we can directly perceive with our senses as given and those aspects we can perceive indirectly by having an instrument translate physical energies that we cannot perceive directly with our sense organs into energies which we can.

The spiritual psychologies do not limit reality, either external or internal, to what can be reduced to physics. Thus there are large, highly important aspects of reality existing external to us which can be perceived by various kinds of extrasensory perception, and, since the mind is not assumed to be limited to the nervous system, there are psychological realities beyond those produced by brain and body processes which are also possible to perceive. Thus the spiritual psychologies postulate a much wider world for perception to handle.

Assumption: The nature of our sense organs determines the nature of our perceptions.

Vision then is a function of the way the eyeball and its connecting nerves are constructed, hearing is a function of the way the ear is constructed, and so forth.

Some spiritual psychologies take a different view, namely that the categories of perception we know of are functions of the mind, and while they ordinarily operate through sense organs constructed in certain ways and with certain characteristics, they may operate independently of such sense organs. Thus in certain states of consciousness one is supposed to be able to see things at a distance, although certainly no physical eye and associated nervous connections are there to transmit the information. The course taken by parapsychologists, the small minority of Western scientists who take this area seriously, of calling such phenomena *extra* sensory perception does not explain it, only labels it. When one implicitly assumes that the nature of perception is always shaped by the appropriate sense organ, one will not bother to look for other kinds and modalities of perception if there is no obvious sense organ functioning.

Assumption: Perception is somewhat selective and biased, but generally gives us a very good picture of the world around us.

This is a particularly interesting assumption, for it is implicitly made all the time by orthodox, Western psychologists in spite of a wealth of evidence they themselves have collected to show that perception is extremely selective and biased, depending on one's upbringing, needs, and all sorts of nonconscious processes. All that evidence, though, applies to subjects in experiments: when I, as a psychologist, look at something, I pretty much see it the way it is. This assumption is hardly limited to psychologists.

The spiritual psychologies generally take a position much more toward the view that most perception is quite biased and distorted by our desires and wishes. Thus, instead of beginning with an idea that we have a relatively good picture of ourselves and the world, spiritual psychologies start with the conception that we have a very poor picture of ourselves and the world, and the manifold selective processes and distortions in our perception must slowly be stripped away in the course of spiritual development.

ASSUMPTIONS ABOUT SOCIAL RELATIONSHIPS

Assumption: The selfish, neurotic, unreasonable actions of others are the major cause of our personal suffering.

It is very easy to see how unreasonable others are in what they want, in their reasoning, in their actions. If other people weren't so neurotic, our own lives would go much more happily and smoothly. This assumption is hardly unique to psychologists. Indeed, psychologists, through knowledge of the voluminous psychological evidence on the psychopathology of everyday life, may hold it slightly less than the man in the street, but still psychologists are very much affected by it.

Many of the spiritual psychologies, while recognizing the reality of suffering created by the selfish and evil actions of others, nevertheless stress that by far the primary cause of our personal suffering is our own psychological attitudes and actions. There are relatively rare times in our lives when someone else actually does something harmful to us, but these are quite rare in terms of the innumerable times we take offense or feel hurt because someone has done something that upset our *ego.* Someone does not give us proper respect, or makes a slighting remark or the like: these actions can only be "hurtful" if you have a certain psychological investment in the image of yourself that is incongruent with these actions. The Gurdjieff system, for example, stresses that we are responsible for *all* of our suffering, and the blame cannot be put on anyone else.

Assumption: No normal person likes to suffer.

This seems obvious: pain is bad, suffering is bad, and we do all we can to avoid them. We see that certain neurotic people seem to have some causal effect in creating their suffering, but since we are normal that does not apply to us.

Many spiritual psychologies stress that we are actually attached to our suffering, not only in the sense that the attachment to pleasure per se automatically brings about the conditions for displeasure, but that we actually satisfy certain ego needs by suffering in particular ways. Again drawing an example from Gurdjieff's system, Gurdjieff stresses that only one thing needs to be sacrificed to really begin on the spiritual path, and that is one's own suffering, but that this is the hardest possible thing for a person to give up. A person will give up anything but his own suffering. It takes prolonged self-observation to actually see how attached we are to our own suffering.

Assumption: Progress comes from improving society.

We are always putting our energies into educating the masses or selected groups, trying to make the social system run better, correcting injustices, believing if we could do this we would make true progress.

The spiritual psychologies generally emphasize that the only real progress that can be made is that which comes from individual spiritual development. Insofar as a number of individuals show great spiritual development, their social relationships and their effect on those about them will also show marked improvement. Some of the spiritual psychologies particularly emphasize that any attempts at social improvement that do not stem from an inner growth on the part of the person will be perverted and result in no real progress at all. Indeed, putting lots of one's energy into social reform and the like can be seen as a substitute for one's personal spiritual development, and a substitute that simply perpetuates the game it purports to cure. Social systems are seen to be one of the primary creators and maintainers of the illusory view of the world that blocks real spiritual progress. Again, the old Sufi admonition to be "in the world but not of it" characterizes one of the main orientations of the spiritual psychologies. This does not mean that the spiritual psychologies are uninterested in how people relate to one another: they emphasize that improved social relations must ultimately come from improved relations with one's own spiritual potentialities. It is too easy to concentrate on the faults of others and the system in order to avoid seeing one's own responsibility.

SOME MISCELLANEOUS ASSUMPTIONS

Assumption: Scientific progress is cumulative.

This follows from a view that science "discovers" facts which are lying around out there waiting to be found, and its changes are mainly in the theories used to account for these facts. So we build up more and more facts, and our old facts are still good, even though we may want to interpret them in new ways. This is similar to the assumption discussed earlier that the way to become more knowing and wise is to add new facts to those you already know, assuming that what you already know is correct.

This view of science has been strongly challenged from within science, particularly in Thomas Kuhn's (1962) idea that science has paradigms, overall views with corresponding assumptions about reality that determine what we see as *relevant* facts and how we interpret them. This has been discussed more fully in Chapter 1. Facts, then, are not lying around out there waiting to be discovered, but are in a sense created by the way we look for things. In spite of excellent evidence to support this view that science does not simply cumulatively progress but undergoes major revolutions in which old "facts" now become irrelevant data, most orthodox, Western psychologists are still stuck in the implicit assumption that scientific progress is simply cumulative.

A consequence of questioning this assumption might be that we would have to unlearn much of what we now think of as the *basis* of our psychological knowledge, and the unattractiveness of this prospect helps make the idea that we might have to raise such questions seem silly.

I'm not sure what the view of most spiritual psychologies would be on this matter, except that it would probably be along the general line of feeling that our orthodox, Western psychology is still so vastly incomplete in the vital areas of man's spiritual development that it is premature to talk about whether any cumulative progress has been made. The spiritual psychologies also stress the importance of *un*learning old conceptual systems.

Assumption. Our civilization (and its psychology) is the greatest civilization that ever existed on this planet.

After all, we have conquered by various means all "primitive" countries, and other countries which are becoming powerful are those that are becoming industrialized and following our general pattern of Western civilization. This means that ideas about psychology from other cultures and past cultures are interesting and quaint, and may even contain a few grains of truth at times, but they certainly cannot compare with modern scientific psychology.

Many of the spiritual psychologies feel that the sources of their teachings come from people who lived at a time when civilization was more advanced than it is now, not more advanced in terms of gadgetry and material wealth, but more advanced in the level of psychological and spiritual development of some of its members. No one denies that technology has been developed to a very high level today, but when one looks at the way people live, it is not clear that technological development goes along with being "civilized." Thus many of the spiritual psychologies see their systems as being far more sophisticated and advanced than the knowledge and methods of orthodox, Western psychology.

We should be aware of how much the assumption that material riches is a sign of progress is with us: I believe many psychologists look at pictures of, say, a yogi wearing a loincloth, sitting on the ground, and think (at some level of themselves): How could anyone who can't even own a good house, much less the conveniences of modern life, have anything worthwhile to teach us? I suppose our hypothetical yogi might look at an orthodox, Western psychologist sitting among his apparatus, his TV set, his car, and wonder how anyone who was so attached to such an incredible quantity of material goods could hope to make any real progress in understanding his spiritual self.

Assumption: Our civilization (and our psychology) are steadily progressing.

The belief in steady progress is a deeply rooted assumption for Americans, and psychologists share it. Our civilization has already advanced greatly, and it is continuing to advance every day: it is only a matter of time until problems like poverty and war and ignorance will be eliminated.

Spiritual psychologies do not necessarily share this view, and some see our civilization as static or retrogressing rather than progressing. Gurdjieff points out that every age has thought of itself as more advanced than the previous one and well on the way to solving social problems, but if you look at history you will see that human life has remained essentially the same. So many wars, for example, are fought with the motivation that this would be the war to bring about final peace, yet history is primarily a matter of unceasing wars.

Assumption: An active, conquest-oriented approach is the way to make progress in understanding and controlling the universe.

We are a very active culture; we identify with the masculine principle; we speak of *conquering* disease, *conquering* ignorance, and the like. Orthodox, Western psychology is primarily a matter of manipulating events and seeing what results occur, actively pushing things in various directions (the independent variable), seeing what comes out (the dependent variable). We often measure "progress" by the ability acquired to manipulate things at will. Our sciences as a whole are very masculine, active sciences.

The spiritual psychologies generally have stressed that there is another attitude toward understanding reality, a passive, receptive, feminine attitude. This is not to say that the masculine attitude is wrong in any sense, but it is one of two attitudes, and the optimal approach to understanding oneself and reality is to use both of these approaches, selecting which one is appropriate for the occasion. This is very difficult for us to do as Westerners: we are so used to the active attitude that most of us find it quite difficult to be receptive and passive and, as it were, let nature or our deeper selves teach us a lesson. Yet the spiritual psychologies stress that many of the most important spiritual realities cannot be taken by force;

we must develop a receptivity and humility if we ever wish to learn certain kinds of things.

Assumption: Being a scientist and being a mystic are incompatible.

If a person is a good, competent scientist, the orthodox, Western assumption is that he cannot be a mystic, doing "weird" things inside his head at the same time. A great gulf is considered to exist between the types of mentalities necessary for these two roles. Since being a mystic is considered pathological by most orthodox psychologists, this gulf is a good thing. One of the most deprecating remarks you could make about a scientist's work is to say that it shows signs of being "mystical."

In spite of this assumption, there are many historical examples of scientists who have also been mystics. Pascal, for example, had mystical experiences of considerable intensity. I do not believe the spiritual psychologies would see anything necessarily incompatible with being both a scientist and a mystic; it is a matter of balance, just as the active, conquering and the passive, receptive attitude must be balanced in the individual.

One of the most interesting demonstrations of this compatibility is a study by LeShan (1969) on the similarities in world view between physicists and mystics. In a fascinating article, LeShan took statements about the ultimate nature of reality made by some of the greatest mystics and some of the greatest physicists, and mixed them together without indicating whether a statement came from a scientist or from a mystic. Most people, including myself, are unable to accurately discriminate the source of the statement. Does the following statement, for example, come from a scientist or a mystic? ". . . the reason why our sentient, percipient and thinking ego is met nowhere in our world picture can easily be indicated in seven words: because it is ITSELF that world picture. It is identical with the whole and therefore cannot be contained in it as part of it" (LeShan, 1969, p. 6).

This concludes our all too brief and incomplete look at some of the implicit assumptions of orthodox, Western psychology. Note that I am *not* saying the implicit assumptions of orthodox, Western psychology are *wrong* and those of the spiritual psychologies are *right:* I do not know where the balance of rightness and wrongness lies. But it is clear that as long as assumptions are implicit, we have no opportunity to question them and possibly escape from their controlling power over us. If this chapter succeeds in raising some serious questions about implicit assumptions for some readers, it has served its purpose.

3 THE PHYSICAL UNIVERSE, THE SPIRITUAL UNIVERSE, AND THE PARANORMAL

CHARLES T. TART

A great achievement of our Western civilization has been in the physical sciences. We have built up an elegant, consistent, and exceptionally powerful world view based on the notion of *physicalism,* a notion that all events are ultimately reducible to lawful interactions of matter and energies within the space-time continuum. There can be no doubt of the power of this view: a look at skyscrapers, antibiotics, atomic weapons, and the like is sufficient to remind us that this world view has resulted in unprecedented taming and conquest of the physical world.

I want to evaluate the spiritual psychologies from this orthodox, physical science world view. I do this because the challenge faced by the spiritual psychologies in taking root in our civilization is very much a challenge of accommodating themselves to this physicalistic world view.

From this physicalistic position, most of what will be presented in this book is nonsense. We know that all human experience is ultimately reducible to patterns of electrical and chemical activity within the nervous system and body. Some day our science will probably be advanced enough to further reduce these electrical and chemical events in the nervous system to even more fundamental atomic and subatomic events. Thus if someone enters a discrete altered state of consciousness (d-ASC) and has an experience, say, of energy flowing through his body and feeling it exuding from his fingertips (as often happens in paranormal healing), we must say that this is a "hallucinatory" experience. There is no such nonphysical energy, and this experience is simply an unusual pattern of firing within the individual's nervous system. A person may have had a profoundly moving mystical experience, he may have felt in direct communion with God, the experience may have totally changed the pattern of his life and made a new man of him. Nevertheless, we must say that since the idea of God makes no sense at all in physical terms, that "contact with God," whether it affects one profoundly or not, is another example of how flexible the biocomputer that constitutes our brain is. It can be programed to give convincing simulations of things that are totally nonsensical. God is nothing but an electrochemical pattern in the brain.

The orthodox scientific attitude has been that it would be much better for human beings to stop having these irrational, hallucinatory, "mystical" experiences and settle down to be completely rational. "Completely rational" meant having experiences and acting in a way according to the physicalistic, scientific world view. I think there has been some loosening of this attitude to the extent that some psychologists and psychiatrists (who basically accept this physicalistic world view) would nevertheless say that as man is constructed now, he seems to have a need for a certain amount of irrational experience. So hallucinations, *if kept within socially appropriate bounds,* may be good for mental health. Therefore if the masses need to go to church and believe in nonphysical entities who will do favors for them, that's fine—it keeps society running on an even keel. But this is a grudging acceptance, because even tolerating this much of a departure from "reality," much less the more radical departure of directly experiencing the things religions talk about, is basically irrational and conducive to social disorder and insanity.

If, from the orthodox position, we grudgingly accept that at least some people need to have these kinds of unusual experiences, it is rational to conclude that they should have them in the least socially disruptive manner, in ways which have the fewest unhealthy side effects. If you have this irrational need to "talk with God," perhaps psychedelic and hypnotic drugs, given in the proper context of suggestion and expectation, will keep you happy: they wear off quickly so you can become "normal" again. If you want to feel happy, progress has now been very rapid in direct electrical stimulation of the brain: within a decade you will be able (probably illegally, but later legally) to have some electrodes permanently implanted in your brain and a little stimulator in your pocket. Every time you push the button you can feel pleasure. If visions are your thing, the proper electrodes connected to your stimulator can give you wonderful visionary kinds of experiences.

I am quite serious in saying this: the rapid progress, technologically speaking, in direct electrical stimulation of the brain will make this sort of thing not only theoretically but economically practical in the not too distant future. Since some drug and electrical stimulation will undoubtedly produce experiences apparently similar to those reported as resulting from the more arduous practices of the spiritual path, why should one go to all the trouble of meditating through a lifetime and undertaking all sorts of strenuous, demanding disciplines when technological progress will put the experience within most people's reach much more easily and quickly?

The traditional answer from the "orthodox" religious side of such a controversy is that science is only a limited set of knowledge and certain spiritual truths are already known, and if you don't pay attention to them you will be in trouble.

In its strongest form this takes forms like: "Believe in God and do what He says, or you'll go to hell or have a bad reincarnation," or whatever. For those for whom a religious belief structure is much stronger than the influence of the physicalistic world view, this may be a sufficient answer. But it essentially means you have to choose to selectively ignore much of the scientific world view and its power. There are many of us with scientific training who cannot simply ignore the scientific world view: it's too obviously successful in too many areas, and when it says the spiritual view cannot be true, we must listen seriously.

As we discussed earlier in connection with developing state-specific sciences, we should be suspicious of ways of "adapting" oneself to the world that involve ignoring major areas of human knowledge. I believe the orthodox scientific attitude of ignoring the spiritual is just as unadaptive and pathological as the orthodox religious attitude of ignoring all areas of science that conflict with one's belief system.

This conflict need not exist. A closer look at certain aspects of science will sketch the outlines of a settlement of this apparent conflict between the scientific world view and the spiritual world view, and it is the basis of this potential settlement that this chapter is devoted to outlining.

Before considering the major grounds for reducing the conflict between the spiritual and the scientific, we should remind ourselves that science is still in its infancy. Almost all the major progress in science has been made in the physical sciences. We have not developed a good psychology, we have not developed state-specific sciences, nor have we made really thorough attempts to study the compatibility of the spiritual and physicalistic views of the universe. Because of the astounding success of physical science, and human attachment to that which is successful, we have had a psychological overinvestment in the physical world view, such that for many people it has become a religion. Like most religions, it defames its rivals. A certain amount of humility as to how much we really know about the universe is appropriate.

THE PHYSICALISTIC WORLD VIEW AND PARANORMAL PHENOMENA

The basic approach for reconciling the physicalistic and spiritual views of the world comes from that very small and almost unknown branch of science called parapsychology, literally meaning the investigation of things which are beyond *(para)* ordinary psychology. The term is more specific than that, for its primary focus is on investigating those aspects of human experience which make no apparent sense at all in terms of the physical world view, phenomena such as telepathy, clairvoyance, precognition, and psychokinesis. That is, parapsychology deals with the investigation of direct mind-to-mind communication (telepathy), the direct contact of mind with physical objects without intervening sense data (clairvoyance), the prediction of the future when it cannot be inferred from known physical events (precognition), and the direct influence of the mind on matter without the intervention of the body or known physical energies (psychokinesis). Telepathy, clairvoyance, and precognition are collectively referred to as extrasensory perception (ESP), and ESP and other paranormal kinds of perception and action are collectively called psi phenomena.

Parapsychology is a relatively new science. Its history as an *experimental* science hardly goes back beyond the beginning of our own century. Its inception primarily resulted from the conflict between a spiritual view of the world and the rapid rise of modern physical science which debunked such a view.

The founding of the Society for Psychical Research in London in 1882 can be considered the major event marking the birth of parapsychology. It was called psychical research then. The founders of this Society for Psychical Research were scientific, scholarly, and literary figures in England, many of whom were spiritualists. I use "spiritualists" in the restricted sense of the term to mean people who believed that surviving spirits of deceased persons could communicate through special people, mediums, during a d-ASC, mediumistic trance. Some of the founders were devout Christians. Most were people who were well versed in the scientific world view and appreciated its power. Some believed, for various reasons, in a whole realm of spiritual phenomena, but realized these views would have to be reconciled. All recognized the importance of the spiritual. The things on which they founded their religious beliefs, their philosophies of life, were being declared as impossible and nonsensical by the science of their day (and our day).

We will not deal with the history of parapsychology since there are many excellent books in print which do treat this subject as well as providing excellent overviews of the field (Broad, 1962; Gudas, 1961; Heywood, 1959; Murphy and Dale, 1961; Pratt, 1966; Pratt et al., 1966; Rao, 1966; Rhine, 1964; Schmeidler, 1969; Smythies, 1967; Soal and Bateman, 1954). The history is a long, involved one of a few men struggling against enormous prejudice in the scientific community, where the general opinion was that they shouldn't be allowed to even investigate these phenomena at all. The data of parapsychological research, although still rejected by a majority of the scientific community, have shown beyond any reasonable doubt that our current physicalistic view of the universe is vastly incomplete, and certain phenomena do indeed exist which may constitute a basis of spiritual experiences.

The importance of parapsychology, then, is that from *within* the scientific enterprise, using the most refined scientific methods, a foundation has been created for scientists and educated Westerners in general to seriously consider the claims of the spiritual psychologies. I believe it is this scientific basis which will be increasingly important in deciding whether the spiritual psychologies do indeed become an integral part of our civilization, or remain philosophies and belief systems which are split off from our technological civilization.

PARAPSYCHOLOGY AND THE SCIENTIFIC COMMUNITY

It is well to note that parapsychology and its findings are not accepted by the great majority of scientists today, even though there is now considerably greater acceptance than there was a decade ago. To put it bluntly, this is not a matter of rational rejection of poor experimentation and insufficient data on the part of an educated scientific community, but a simple case of prejudice. Almost all scientists are simply totally ignorant as to what the data of parapsychology are, and prejudiced against looking at it.

The attitude of many scientists was summed up in 1955 in an article in *Science,* one of the nation's most prestigious scientific journals. Under the title "Science and the Supernatural," a chemist, George Price, wrote a review article the essence of which was: no intelligent man can read the evidence for the existence of extrasensory perception and doubt that it exists, *but,* since we *know* it is impossible, we must conclude that all this evidence is due to error and fraud.

At the time the article came out, I and many parapsychologists were highly incensed at the overall unfairness and selectivity of the review. I have since come, however, to at least appreciate the straightforwardness of Price's attitude. He states quite clearly that he is certain as to how the universe works and when confronted by evidence contradictory to his accepted view, he will simply deny the evidence. At least he is very much up front about his position!

My statement that scientific rejection of parapsychology is based on ignorance and prejudice will make many of my colleagues angry. But if you are one of these colleagues and you think the idea of extrasensory or psychic phenomena is nonsense, ask yourself some questions and give yourself honest answers. First, how much have you actually *thought* about the possibility of such phenomena versus how much have you simply and automatically accepted the prevailing attitude? Second, how much have you actually read of the *scientific* literature on parapsychology? Not the popularizations, which leave a great deal to be desired, but the original scientific reports which now number in the thousands?

I'm afraid the almost universal answer will be that you simply accept the belief common in the scientific community without ever having given much thought to it, and that you have never looked at the scientific evidence which might contradict this belief. Indeed, the pattern I find among most colleagues is that they know a priori that there are no such phenomena, therefore they never bother to read any evidence which might indicate there was, and then say they have never seen any evidence to contradict their belief.

On the more positive side, scientific acceptance of the legitimacy of doing parapsychological research has increased greatly, so many scientists do think it's all right to look, and some have even looked themselves and accepted the findings. There are still only a few dozen parapsychologists, many of them part-time, working in the whole world, but they have for many years filled three scientific journals* with excellent evidence about extrasensory perception, so there is a very large backlog of data. The general situation is that there are now several basic psi phenomena whose existence has been established beyond any reasonable doubt. In this chapter I will discuss these four basic, well-proven phenomena, mention some others for which there is good but not yet indubitable evidence, and talk about their implications for some of the phenomena reported in the spiritual psychologies.

METHODOLOGY OF PARAPSYCHOLOGY

Parapsychology originally focused on the study of what are called spontaneous cases, things happening to ordinary people in the course of their lives which seem to be inexplicable in terms of the physicalistic world view. A mother in England, for example, might have a dream about her son, stationed in India, being killed by a rampaging elephant. If the mother had no reason to expect that anything like this would happen, if it was the only frightening, intense dream she had had about her son in ten years, and the dream actually occurred within a few hours of the actual death of her son caused by a rampaging elephant, it would appear to be some kind of communication that makes no sense at all in terms of the physicalistic world view. The parties are separated by too much distance.

Of course there are "coincidences"; two things "just happen" to coincide, but there is no meaningful relationship between them. While spontaneous cases provide some reason to believe in the existence of paranormal phenomena, coincidence is a problem, so many of the original studies were concerned with collecting spontaneous cases in which coincidence could not reasonably seem to play a part. If every day I have vague feelings that something is wrong somewhere, they are bound to coincide with actual events of relevance to me occasionally, and that does not mean much. Or perhaps I actually overheard a conversation about some event and then forgot it: having some ideas about the event later is not evidence for psi. Many of the original studies of spontaneous cases were evaluated by

---

*For the reader who would like to keep up with current parapsychological research, these are the *Journal of the American Society for Psychical Research* (5 W. 73d St., New York, NY 10023), the *Journal of the Society for Psychical Research* (1 Adam & Eve Mews, London W86UQ), and the *Journal of Parapsychology* (Box 6847, College Station, Durham, NC 27708). The *International Journal of Parapsychology* is no longer published, but back issues can be found in major libraries.

weighting procedures in which conflicting explanations were sifted, and the event was considered paranormal only when all ordinary explanations and coincidence seemed to be very improbable. No researchers based the existence of paranormal phenomena on any one case, no matter how impressive, but on large collections of such events. Thus early in our century many members of the Society for Psychical Research felt that spontaneous cases seemed to indicate the definite existence of various psi phenomena.

Nevertheless in spontaneous cases happening in the real world we are basically doing *retrospective* investigations of *reports,* and so we do not have the kind of control over things that is so important in science. We are two steps removed from the actual phenomena. It is difficult to rule out totally alternative explanations and coincidence. So, although one can build a good case for the existence of psi phenomena from spontaneous case data, it would be much more satisfactory to have data collected in the laboratory where all alternative explanations can be distinctly ruled out. Being able to study psi phenomena at first hand is even more important when one wants to investigate *how* they work. The early workers in the field were aware of this, and the science we call modern parapsychology is primarily a laboratory science, even though there is still much study of spontaneous cases: they can give suggestions about the effects of psychological variables that are difficult to deal with in the laboratory. For example, many dramatic psi cases are connected with the death of someone, but one can scarcely set out killing people in the laboratory to see if the "experiment" results in a telepathic transmission.

The basic laboratory procedures in parapsychological experiments, regardless of the particular paranormal phenomenon studied, are designed to exclude all known physical energies that might account for the phenomena, so that if anything then happens it must be attributed to some other, "nonphysical" form of action. Thus if you are trying to investigate paranormal communication between two people it is essential that they be physically isolated from each other in such a fashion that no known physical energies could transmit the required information between them. Two subjects in a telepathy experiment are almost never put in the same room, for example, as this might allow them to perceive unconscious (or conscious) gestures or sounds or actions from each other that would account for information transmission.

Another major aspect of laboratory studies in parapsychology is that great precautions are taken to prevent conscious cheating on the part of the experimental subjects. This came about for two reasons. First, spiritualism was making many spectacular claims at the time psychical research got started, but there were many quite scandalous cases of individual mediums resorting to plain old-fashioned fraud to produce their effects. Thus they might tell a sitter at a séance many accurate things about his background, supposedly as a result of the spirit control talking through them, but it would turn out that they had hired a private detective to investigate the background of a sitter from whom they might hope to get monetary contributions if he were convinced of the reality of spiritual phenomena. Or many "physical" mediums, those producing physical phenomena that were apparently inexplicable (such as objects floating in the air), used conjuring tricks of one sort or another to fraudulently produce these phenomena. Such deliberate cheating seems rare, but since parapsychologists do not like to be fooled or waste their time, it is important to make cheating virtually impossible, and this is standard operating procedure in parapsychological experimentation.

A third feature characteristic of parapsychological laboratory work is the use of statistical evaluations of almost all experiments. This came about because of the question of whether coincidence might account for results in various experiments. If you ask me to guess which cards of an ordinary deck, spread out face down on the table, are black and which are red, and after I make my guesses we find that I got twenty-nine right, is this what we would expect from coincidence or chance variation, or is this such an unusual score as to mean that I'm using ESP?

Evaluating what chance coincidence is in spontaneous cases is extremely difficult. How unlikely is it to dream of a friend receiving a minor injury? Being happy? Dying? Winning money?

To deal with the problem of coincidence, parapsychological experiments generally use repeated guessing techniques such as card guessing, in which the score one would get by chance and the variation of that score by chance alone are *precisely* known according to the best sort of mathematics underlying much of modern science. If one gets any particular score, one can then precisely say what the odds against the chance of getting a score like that are, and if the score is very improbable, then one can conclude that something paranormal happened. So you may guess at a deck of cards and get a score that would happen one in ten times by chance alone. This is not considered very striking, but if you get a score that would happen only one in a hundred times by chance alone, it is more reasonable to think that something actually happened, rather than the result being due to chance. The more improbable the scores get, say, if the odds are a million to one against chance, the more likely you are to believe that some paranormal effects have occurred. We will flesh out these examples as we now consider particular paranormal phenomena.

TELEPATHY

Telepathy literally means mind-to-mind communication, a thought of my mind being perceived by your mind when there is neither any sensory communication to convey the thought nor any likely way in which you could infer from previous knowledge of what was happening to me what I would be likely to be thinking about at this moment. Many people have had experiences when they think about a particular subject and a companion starts talking about exactly the thing they were thinking about. In many instances this is probably not telepathy, but common trains of thought which by coincidence happen to have arrived at the same thing. If two ardent football fans happen to drive past a football stadium and one suddenly asks how the other thinks a big game that weekend is going to come out, it is not really very unusual if the other person was just beginning to think about how that game was going to come out. There are other instances in people's experience when they cannot see such an obvious reason for thinking the same thing, but in all these spontaneous cases it is difficult to rule out what is a likely or unlikely thought.

Many laboratory studies of telepathy have been conducted which rule out all alternative explanations. The typical kind of study is for an experimenter to randomly shuffle a deck of cards without looking at them, so the order is unknown to anyone. Ordinary playing cards or special cards may be used. Then one subject, called the sender or agent, looks at the cards one by one, usually every five seconds or on some such fixed time schedule. The experimenter keeps a written record of the order of the cards. A second subject, generally seated in another room and often at a considerable distance, so that no sensory cues can reach him, knows the time schedule of the experiment and writes down or reports whatever impression comes into his mind about a card each time the sender is looking at one. A written record is made of the receiver's calls, they are then compared, the number correct scored, and the answers statistically evaluated. There are now many dozens of experiments, conducted in the most rigorous manner, in which the scores have been far beyond what would be expected by chance, often with odds of hundreds of millions to one or more against a chance explanation. From this kind of experiment, the reality of telepathy has been established beyond any reasonable doubt.

The reader will note that when I say "beyond any reasonable doubt" I imply that people who disagree with me are unreasonable. Within the rules of scientific procedure, this has been the case in all of my experience. The people who disagree with me about the existence of telepathy have simply never bothered to read even a small fraction of the evidence for it, and I do not believe a person who knows nothing about an area directly but nevertheless has strong opinions about it is being reasonable in any scientific sense.

The fact that telepathy has thus been established in this way does *not* mean that every time you think something that someone else is thinking it is telepathy, or that every experiment of the sort described above is successful. A survey that Burke Smith and I did several years ago (Tart, 1973a) found that approximately one out of every three parapsychological experiments was successful in yielding scores that were significantly different from chance. Statistically speaking, there should be far more than one hundred unsuccessful experiments for every successful one if we were merely dealing with experiments that happened to come out by chance alone.

The successful telepathy experiments usually involve groups of subjects. If you look through results of individual subjects, many of them never show anything beyond chance scoring, and even those who do often show a very low level of scoring. Most of the time subjects in telepathy and other kinds of ESP experiments are guessing, but every once in a while ESP adds something and alters the overall average score. But even the best subjects are not uniformly successful, and often lose their ability after a time.

Other ways of testing and studying telepathy have included the sender's making drawings, with techniques used to ensure that the object to be drawn is selected at random rather than depending on common associations of sender and receiver,* and attempts to telepathically influence the dreams of sleeping subjects. Both types of experiments have been highly successful. In order to avoid the subjectivity of deciding whether the sender's and receiver's drawings really match beyond coincidence, they are usually evaluated by a blind judging technique. A judge or judges are given a series of drawings that were targets to be sent and a series of drawings that were responses, without any indication of which targets were supposed to go with which responses. The judges are asked to match the targets and responses on degree of similarity, and the results can be objectively evaluated statistically.

As with the other basic psi phenomena to be described below, telepathy has been generally found to be unaffected by physical variables. It does not seem to make any difference how close or how far away the sender and receiver are, whether there is any kind of shielding between them, or the like. Occasional physical effects have been reported, but seldom found to be reliable or replicable. On the other hand, psychological variables do make a major difference in the functioning of telepathy. Things like the subject's desire to cooperate or not cooperate, his mood, the emotional relationships between sender and receiver, and the like can greatly affect the level of operation of telepathy. We will consider the general findings about psychological variables in more detail later.

---

*One of the commonest ways to make sure the drawing to be made is randomly selected is to use a table of random numbers to decide which page a dictionary will be opened to, and then draw the first drawable object on the page opened to.

CLAIRVOYANCE

The word "clairvoyance" comes from the French and literally means clear seeing. It refers to a kind of ESP in which the subject or receiver does not try to pick up the thoughts of another person, but rather the state of physical affairs of some object. In the standard kind of card guessing test for clairvoyance, the cards are thoroughly shuffled but then no one looks at the cards. The cards may simply be allowed to remain in a pile, and the subject's job is to write down the order of the cards; or the cards may be taken off one by one without being looked at. Although one would think the latter procedure would be easier, both turn out to be equally successful in terms of ESP results. In some fashion, then, the mind has to be able to perceive the patterns of ink on pieces of cardboard in order to produce successful results. Clairvoyance generally works about as well in the laboratory as telepathy. The clairvoyance experiment is easier to carry out in terms of avoiding sensory cues, since one need only shuffle the cards and put them back into their box before the subject enters the room to completely shield the subject from all relevant physical information.

As with telepathy, there is no clear-cut relationship of clairvoyance to any physical variables, but it is strongly affected by psychological variables.

PRECOGNITION

Precognition refers to the extrasensory ability to predict *future* events, events which have not yet come into existence. Since the events do not yet exist, they cannot give off any physical energies which constitute information about them. Further, the event must not be predictable from knowledge of the current state of events: if I'm holding an object in my hand and let go of it, it is not unusual to predict that it will fall to the floor. Nor is it impressive to predict that there will be an earthquake in California. There are earthquakes here all the time, so you're bound to be right sooner or later. If, as in any spontaneous ESP case, one predicts months in advance the *precise* day and hour and intensity of the earthquake, that is another story, and may be precognition.

The laboratory procedure for testing and studying precognition with cards is very straightforward. The subject is told that at some specified time in the future a deck of cards will be shuffled thoroughly and then its order recorded. The subject's task is to write down *now* what the order of the deck of cards *will be* at the future time. In various experiments the future time has ranged anywhere from a few minutes after the subject finishes his calls to weeks or months after the subject finishes his calls.

Many precognition experiments have yielded results not due to chance variation, sufficiently so as to establish the reality of precognition beyond any doubt.

(I find this a striking instance of the case in which a scientist's commitment to form his belief system on the basis of data conflicts with personal preferences. I personally cannot understand how precognition can take place, and wish it didn't happen, but there is no doubt in my mind of its existence because of the strength of the evidence.)

Generally speaking, precognition experiments do not seem quite as successful as telepathy and clairvoyance experiments, so in some sense precognition is a harder phenomenon to produce. As with the other two ESP phenomena, telepathy and clairvoyance, physical variables do not seem to be meaningfully related to precognition: there is no clear-cut relation between the time distance or the spatial distance of the events to be precognized and the rate of success. Using both spontaneous case data and experimental data, it is clear that ESP (telepathy, clairvoyance, and precognition) can transmit information between any two points on the surface of the earth, and, judging from one experiment carried out by the astronaut Captain Edgar Mitchell (1971), telepathy or clairvoyance can work between a spacecraft in earth orbit and the surface of the earth.

These three phenomena, telepathy, clairvoyance, and precognition, are the three well-established types of extrasensory *perception*, direct mental perception of events outside of ourselves without the use of the known senses, in ways which make no sense in known physical energies. As human beings, we not only sense the world, we act on it, so analogous to our motor skills in affecting the world there is a fourth well-established paranormal phenomenon that is a kind of extrabodily motor action or direct effect of the mind on matter, psychokinesis.

PSYCHOKINESIS

Psychokinesis (PK) literally means the ability of the mind or psyche to move something. An older and still widely used term for this is *telekinesis,* indicating action at a distance, in this case direct action of the mind on objects at a distance without the intervention of the physical body.

Interest was very high in apparent psychokinetic phenomena around the turn of the century because of the rather spectacular events often reported at spiritualistic meetings. Trumpets apparently floated in the air, voices seemed to issue from them, forms of deceased persons were supposed to materialize into a semimaterial or completely material form, rappings and explosive sounds were heard coming out of solid objects, tables sometimes floated completely free from the floor, and, in a few cases, the medium was observed to levitate many feet into the air. As mentioned before, however, there were many quite scandalous cases of fraud, so most investigators were hesitant to build any case for psychokinesis on these types of events.

The main laboratory evidence for psychokinesis has come from experiments in rolling dice. In rolling dice with a machine and wishing a particular face to come up, one knows statistically that the desired target should come up one-sixth of the time, and can then evaluate any significant deviation from this. In a typical experiment, a machine rolls one or more dice over and over again for a predetermined number of trials while the subject, according to another predetermined schedule, wills certain target faces to come up. The subject is not allowed to touch the dice or the surface on which they fall in any way. There are several dozen experiments on this, yielding results significantly different from chance, which have established the reality of psychokinesis. As with ESP phenomena, physical variables, such as how far from the table a subject is, do not seem to affect results, while psychological variables do. If a subject *believes* that being closer to the table gives better results, then he gets better results, while if he believes being farther from the table gives better results, that is what happens.

LACK OF FIT BETWEEN THE PHYSICAL WORLD AND PARANORMAL PHENOMENA

Let us consider in more detail how these four psi phenomena fail to fit in with our otherwise brilliantly successful physical world view.

To get information about an event from one location in space and time to another location in space and time, some form of energy must be modulated in such a way as to contain the relevant information, and must pass from one location to the other. Thus when we talk we modulate sound waves which spread through the air as a carrying medium from one location to another. If we talk into a radio transmitter, these sound waves modulate an electromagnetic wave which propagates through space in a well-understood way to another location where the appropriate apparatus turns it back into sound waves.

All physical energies that we know of interact with the physical world in various ways: indeed, this is how we determine they exist. Paranormal phenomena do not interact with the world in any known way, but nevertheless the information is transmitted; this is the reason why they suggest how vastly incomplete our current physical world view is. They seem to "contradict" the rather nice view of the physical world we have built up. To look at this in detail, let us consider the effects of distance, shielding, detectability of energies, focusing of energies, and time.

Most physical energies that we know of show an attenuation of intensity with distance. If I sit beside you and talk you can hear me clearly, but as you get farther and farther away the sound becomes softer and softer and eventually the intensity of the sound reaching you from me is not sufficient to overcome the noise level of both the environment you find yourself in and/or the electrical noise level of your own nervous system, and communication is impossible. We could increase the distance of communication with known energies by increasing the energies, or finding a special medium where attenuation is less, or by using a highly focused beam of energy that does not show much attenuation with distance.

Paranormal phenomena show no clear-cut effect with distance at all. Astoundingly spectacular telepathy cases have been reported from one side of the earth to the other. There is no strong evidence to indicate that being two feet away from the person attempting to send a telepathic message has any advantage over being two thousand miles away. Thus there is no clear attenuation effect shown for telepathy, clairvoyance, precognition, or psychokinesis.

One might imagine some physical phenomena analogous to a laser beam, such as a tight beam of subatomic particles like neutrinos, showing little attenuation with distance, which acted as the carrier of energy for telepathy, but then one runs into a related problem even though one has solved the attenuation one. If you are trying to telepathically communicate with someone a thousand miles away, how in the world do you know which direction to aim your tight beam in? The probability of actually hitting the person you are aiming at over these kinds of distances where paranormal phenomena have been highly successful is almost infinitesimal. And what gives off this hypothesized tight beam in clairvoyance?

Physical energies that we know about can also be shielded in various ways. You can be put in a soundproof room and a person on the outside cannot hear you. If you are using radio waves, if you are put in a sufficiently thick metal enclosure they will not penetrate. No one has found any kind of shield that seems to affect paranormal phenomena, although research on this has been very small because it is expensive, and parapsychologists have never had much money to support their work. As an example of lack of effect of shielding and distance, Douglas Dean had highly successful ESP results with one sender skindiving off the coast of Florida and being shielded by more than one hundred feet of water and more than two thousand miles' distance to Zurich (Dean, 1969). Russian parapsychologists (Vasiliev, 1963) did experiments over a distance of several hundred miles with one of the participants in a solid iron room, completely shielding out most electromagnetic radiation. If anything, this kind of shielding seems to slightly improve telepathy, a result also reported by Puharich (1962) for copper-shielded rooms.

Another way in which we might try to find a basis in the currently known physical world for psi, in spite of the lack of effect of distance and shielding, is to assume that the human organism is capable of generating such a high level of energy for ESP processes that, within the earth-scale distances that we know of, attenuation is seldom a severe problem. After all, with a very powerful radio transmitter you can communicate with any spot on the earth's surface. The problem with this approach is that it requires such high levels of energy that it should be very readily detectable. If, for example, the energy for telepathic transmission fell anywhere in the radio wave spectrum, all the fluorescent tubes near someone sending out a very powerful telepathic message should glow! But the various attempts that have been made to measure physical energy emission from human beings using extrasensory abilities have had no clear-cut positive results at all, even when extremely sensitive instruments were used.

Finally, the apparent independence of extrasensory perception from the time dimension, as manifested in precognition, does not fit with our view of the physical universe. While some of my physicist colleagues assure me that certain equations in physics have mathematical solutions that are dual, allowing for normal time flow and time flow in a reverse direction, these second solutions to the equations are generally not thought of as representing anything real, and are certainly at variance with our ordinary picture of the physical universe.

THE PSYCHOLOGICAL NATURE OF BASIC PSI PHENOMENA

Scientifically, we know essentially nothing about the specific nature of psi phenomena. Progress in understanding their nature has been slow, for despite our best efforts, they are elusive and generally will not appear on demand in our laboratories in any quantity. Nevertheless, a general picture has now emerged from investigations that indicates that the four basic psi phenomena are affected by various psychological factors in ways similar to known sensory, motor, and cognitive processes. Psi phenomena so far make basic *psychological* sense in being rather like other things we are familiar with, even if they remain a mystery from the physicalistic world view.

Let us take a brief look at the psychological nature of psi phenomena.

Figure 1 sketches a simplified model of perception for us to orient our overview around. I have presented a more detailed model elsewhere (Tart, 1966a; 1973c). Let us look at it first as a model of perception in general, rather than ESP. In any perceptual process you start with a target or object to be perceived, something that is out there with respect to you. Information from that target, carried as modulation of physical energies present in the environment, proceeds from the distant target to you over some sort of channel, such as the air in the case of hearing, or simply the physical space between us in the case of vision. Some kind of transducer converts the physical energies arriving at your skin boundaries into neural impulses suitable for passing on to your brain. For ordinary perception, we call such transducers sense organs. The eye converts light, for example, into neural impulses. These neural impulses receive all sorts of further processing before they arrive at our consciousness. I have shown this as an arrow from the transducer to what I shall call input processing, the many nonconscious, automatic, habitual processes that take raw sensory data and translate it into units of meaning. Thus you look out your window and do not see an assortment of lights, lines, and colors from which you consciously hypothesize that this best fits the idea of an automobile: you simply "see" an automobile. You may then say, "I see an automobile outside"; information flow from your consciousness to your motor or muscle system results in an overt response.

The main function of input processing is to throw away most information and present only "meaningful" information to you, present a useful abstract of the world so that you do not have to deal with its infinite details. But not all information which doesn't reach consciousness is totally lost: some of it goes from the transducers or sense organs into what we may loosely call the unconscious mind, where further reactions to it and processes based on it may take place without any conscious awareness. In many psychological studies, for example, where emotionally charged input has been presented to a person under difficult perceptual conditions, such as embedding dirty words in a complex figure or presenting other emotionally loaded material in such a brief flash of light that conscious recognition is difficult, it has been shown that there is nevertheless an effect on a person's behavior, even though he is not consciously aware of it. *Subliminal perception* is the common term for this effect. The effect may be on the order of changing the contents of our conscious mind in ways which we do not see as related to the stimulus, the arrow from the unconscious to consciousness, or direct effects on the body with no conscious awareness involved at all, such as an increase in heart rate after a threatening stimulus even though a person is not consciously aware of having seen it. Ordinary perception, then, is very complex, and in addition to the obviously conscious parts of selectively perceiving the environment, there are many unconscious processes that may go on simultaneously and affect us.

When dealing with extrasensory perception, telepathy, clairvoyance, or precognition, similar psychological considerations hold. By definition we have a target to be perceived that is outside the subject, and information is transmitted from the target through a channel to the subject. We do not know the physical nature of this information, whether certain types of targets are more readily picked up by whatever energies transmit this information or not, or what the nature of the channel is: these are the "physics" of extrasensory perception that we've hardly begun to investigate. All we know so far is that known physical energies cannot account for what we observe.

We have no idea what the transducer or "extrasensory sense organ" is that takes some unknown form of energy and converts it into neural impulses (or simply mental information, if we do not wish to assume that brain processes are at the basis of consciousness) that we can perceive. We can say that whatever the nature of this sense organ, we very seldom realize that we are getting information

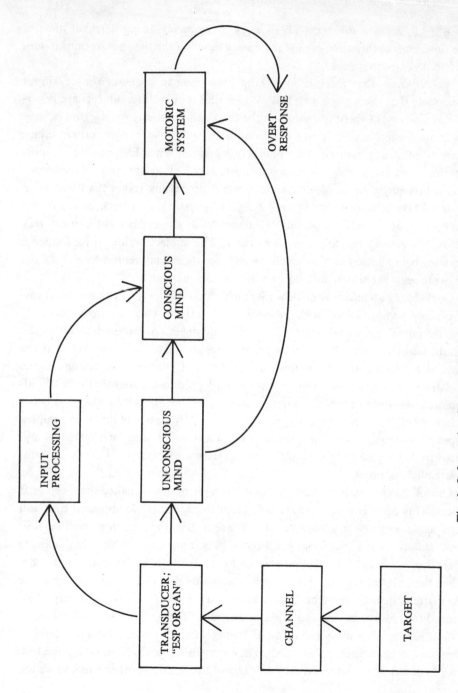

Fig. 1: Information flow and processes in extrasensory perception.

by ESP, so perhaps this sense organ works very rarely, being dormant most of the time, and/or this sense organ* may work much of the time but its output does not reach consciousness.

We do know that there is something analogous to ordinary sensory input processing that takes place with ESP. When ESP is operating, subjects are generally partially right about the nature of the target and partially wrong; that is, they are getting some aspects of information about the target but not others. Since there is no strong evidence that puts any limits on what ESP can do—almost anything and everything has been transmitted by ESP at one time or another—this is probably a result of some kind of input processing rather than limitation in our "extrasensory sense organ." Subjects guessing at a deck of cards, for example, may do well on getting the numbers of the cards right and do very poorly on getting the colors of them right. The subject trying to reproduce a drawing being looked at by someone in another room may reproduce part of the drawing very accurately and do very poorly on the rest of it.

Considering an information flow route which goes from the extrasensory transducer, via some kind of input processing, directly to consciousness, generally oversimplifies the actual operation of ESP, however. A more adequate model would be that extrasensory information flows in unknown quantities into the unconscious mind and there stimulates all sorts of processes, including simple, selective, input processing-type processes, and produces a slightly-to-greatly altered output to the conscious mind. Rather than extrasensory perception being relatively direct, psychologically speaking, it seems to be one of the most complex types of processes, with the information subject to all sorts of alterations and distortions because of the subject's belief systems, psychological needs, and unconscious dynamics.

One of the most striking examples of this is a phenomenon called the sheep-goat effect. This effect is hard to see in individual cases, but it has appeared over and over again when large groups of subjects are tested. Before being given an ESP test, usually a card test, subjects fill out a questionnaire on which they indicate their degree of belief in whether they can exercise ESP in the testing situation. Then the ESP test is given. For analysis, you divide the subjects into believers (the sheep) and disbelievers (the goats), and analyze their scores separately. This procedure, instituted by Gertrude Schmeidler (Schmeidler and McConnell, 1958), has consistently yielded the following sorts of results. Believers tend to score above chance: they show ESP. They were asked to do so in taking the test, they believed they could, and they did. Disbelievers, on the other hand, score too

---

*There may be many specialized receptors for different kinds of ESP, but we will treat them here as if they were one.

low: they score significantly *less* than chance expectation. Now most people do not realize that scoring too low on this kind of repeated guessing test is just as statistically significant as scoring too high. You cannot score too low unless you use ESP to tell what an occasional card is and then "deliberately" give a wrong answer.

Looking at the behavior of the goats in terms of our model, they have made a conscious commitment to try to use ESP, but they do not believe in it and so want to disprove it. Since they do not understand that scoring too low is just as improbable as scoring too high, they hold a naïve belief that scoring badly on the test disproves ESP. Thus, in addition to their simple guessing, they must use their transducer for ESP to occasionally pick out what a card is, but, without having this come into their conscious minds, their *un*conscious minds, operating in accordance with their belief system, send information to consciousness that results in a wrong guess. On seeing their poor scores when the results are checked, the goats feel that their own point of view was right; they have "proven" there is no ESP.

This phenomenon of getting scores that are too low, of "psi missing" as it is called, shows that ESP is like our ordinary perception: our psychological defenses raise our threshold for perceiving things we don't want to perceive, or distort our perceptions of them to fit in with our belief system.

Probably the strength of our belief system is important here too: in one study Schmeidler did psychological testing on subjects as to their degree of psychological adjustment, as well as classifying them into sheep and goats, and she found that the above-chance scores came from the psychologically well-adjusted sheep, the significantly below-chance scores came from the well-adjusted goats, and those people who were not very well adjusted tended to score around chance regardless of their belief.

So we can unknowingly use ESP to prove that there is no such thing as ESP, just as we can often unknowingly distort our ordinary perceptions to uphold our beliefs.

Sometimes ESP can manifest more strongly if one deliberately gets his conscious mind out of the way. Automatic writing, in which one practices sitting down with a pencil in his hand and waiting for it to write, while giving no conscious attention to it, is an example of this.* Some of the material produced this way is psychologically meaningful but just "gibberish" so far as verifiable ESP is concerned. But sometimes the material will contain genuine extrasensory information about distant events.

An experiment I carried out a decade ago (Tart, 1963) demonstrated the value

---

*A typewriter can also be used, with far more legible results.

of bypassing one's ordinary conscious mind under laboratory conditions. Subjects were individually tested in a study of "subliminal perception." The subject would sit in a darkened, soundproof chamber while various physiological measures were recorded from his body. He was told that at random intervals a "subliminal stimulus," whose nature was unspecified, would reach him: when he thought he had received one, he was to tap a telegraph key strapped to the arm of his chair. Unknown to the subjects, there was no subliminal stimulus at all. Rather, a sender in another soundproof chamber several rooms away received a severe electrical shock at random intervals. While receiving the shock the sender tried to make the subject react and tap his telegraph key by telepathy. The analysis of the data showed that subjects' taps of the telegraph key were completely unrelated to the times that the telepathic attempts had taken place, but their bodily responses were related. Whatever extrasensory sense organ they had was either directly influencing their bodily responses or doing so via the unconscious mind, and these could be detected in brain waves and heart rate measurements. So we can be influenced by extrasensory stimuli even when we are not aware of it.

Although consciously recognized ESP experiences seem to be relatively rare for most people, I suspect that we do make responses to extrasensory stimuli far more often than we realize, either not knowing why we wanted to do a particular thing or calling it just a "hunch" or some other familiar word that dismisses the significance of the occurrence.

Let us now consider the other half of psi phenomena, the motor output side or psychokinesis. Figure 2 sketches the general psychological process for affecting something outside of ourselves. We consciously have a wish to do something: using various learned patterns of how to operate our body (the patterns are largely outside of consciousness, but we can become aware of them) we use our transducer or power generator, our muscles, to produce the required physical energy which flows through a channel and affects the target. Thus if I want to open the door I (automatically) use my body in learned ways to walk over to it, put my hand on the handle, turn it, and pull on it; the power is generated by the muscles of my hand and arm; the channel in this case is the layer of skin and tissue between my muscles and the doorknob which transmits the force to it, and the target is the door handle.

If the task is at all complex I need feedback on what I'm doing; I need to see the results of my muscular action and make corrections. I may turn the handle and pull on the knob and then receive the feedback, via my eyes and touch sense, that the door is not opening. I then try pushing instead of pulling, the door does open, and the action is successful. I learn effective action by trying, getting feedback, correcting, a process that should work for learning psi processes (Tart, 1966b).

It is sometimes the case that, in terms of my conscious experience, I cannot

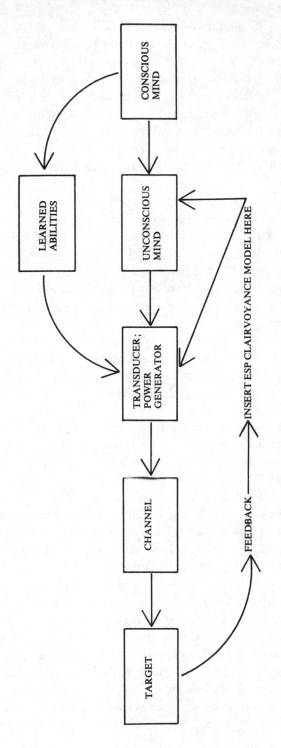

Fig. 2: Information flow and processes in psychokinesis (PK).

"directly" activate the transducer which produces some kind of effect. If I want to profoundly relax, for example, I do not know how to make my mind directly contact each and every tight muscle in my body and relax it. Rather I form mental images of warmth and relaxation which are, as it were, cast into my unconscious mind, and there, outside of my direct perception, something takes place which does affect the muscles and I relax. When I play badminton I have a goal of scoring points by hitting the birdie in certain ways. As I am a poor badminton player, I have very little direct feel for what the right things to do are; I can only drop the wish into my unconscious mind and, sometimes, it knows just how to hit the birdie.

PK, as it has been scientifically studied, is psychologically the latter kind of process. The subject doesn't know how to directly contract the "muscle" that will make some dice being shaken from a cup across the room fall in a certain kind of way. He wishes, he hopes, that they will fall the way he has been instructed they ought to on this trial, and sometimes some unconscious part of his mind activates whatever power generator or transducer produces the right kind of nonphysical energy to actually affect the dice. Psychological factors again affect this ability. Earlier I mentioned that a subject's actual physical distance, close to the table where the dice are thrown or far from it, does not seem to affect the results, but his belief in how that physical distance will affect things does affect results. Similarly if many dice are being thrown simultaneously versus one die being thrown at a time, a subject's belief about which kind of situation he can do best in will affect the results.

PK may be a far more complex phenomenon than ESP. Consider the problem of trying to influence a falling die. The die is spinning through the air and going to hit the tabletop somewhere, bounce several times, and finally come to rest. You are trying to make the two face come up this time. In terms of what we know about mechanical processes, you must do more than simply "push" on that die with PK, you must (1) "push" with exactly the right amount of force (2) on exactly the right part of the die (3) at exactly the right moment, taking into account (4) its mass, (5) its rotational velocity in all three dimensions, and (6) the characteristics of the tabletop where it is going to bounce, in order to get what you want. All this must take place in an extremely rapid period of time. Insofar as PK is analogous to ordinary physical action, then, some kind of clairvoyance must be operating to perceive all these energetic and mass properties of the die and tabletop, along with some very complex calculations on a nonconscious level, which influence the power generator to give just the right push at the right time at the right place. PK experiments remind us that many important mental processes can go on outside of consciousness.

In general, many psychological variables have been found to affect psi performance. Personality characteristics, mood, attitudes toward the experiment, effects of differing instructional sets and the like—all have effects. All of these effects are small ones: the degree of psi shown in experiments with groups of subjects is generally quite small, and the size of the correlations with psychological factors is small. A practical consequence of this smallness is that while findings may be replicated with large samples of subjects, it is not very useful to try to apply them to individual subjects, there are many individual exceptions to the group results.

PSI PHENOMENA AND ALTERED STATES OF CONSCIOUSNESS

Because many very powerful, spontaneous psi cases have occurred in conjunction with one or more of the participants being in a d-ASC, such as dreaming or mediumistic trance, there is now considerable interest in whether d-ASCs might provide a better way of both controlling and understanding psi phenomena. I have discussed this issue in detail elsewhere (Tart, 1973b), so we shall look at it only briefly here.

In considering the psychological nature of psi phenomena, we saw that information may be received by ESP by a person on a nonconscious level and, for a variety of psychological reasons, never make it into conscious awareness. Unless there are useful indirect effects on a person's behavior or experience, he might as well not have received the psi information at all. Because d-ASCs involve a temporary but radical restructuring of the mind, perhaps one or more of such restructurings might allow psi-obtained information to reach consciousness more frequently and/or activate whatever the psi reception process is more frequently.* A good deal of spontaneous case evidence indicates that this is so, but we are far from being able to produce it reliably at will. Hypnosis, for example, can give subjects very impressive experiences that they believe are psi phenomena, but they may not be valid. In general, hypnosis has been found to help psi perception to some degree, although far from always, and sometimes to have no effect at all (Honorton and Krippner, 1969; van de Castle, 1969).

A very promising d-ASC for enhancing psi perception is ordinary dreaming. Many exceptionally accurate, vivid, emotional, and highly detailed cases of ESP have been spontaneously reported in conjunction with dreams. The dreaming state, more specifically the stage 1 (rapid eye movement) sleep state associated with ordinary dreaming, has now been explored in some detail by Stanley Krippner, Montague Ullman, Charles Honorton, and their associates at the Maimonides Medical Center in New York City. Their many studies have recently been summarized in book form (Ullman, Krippner, and Vaughan, 1973). Their general experimental procedure is to have a subject sleeping in one room, moni-

---

*The same reasoning applies to PK, even though here we shall discuss only ESP.

tored for brain waves and rapid eye movements by a technician who wakes them near the end of each stage 1 (rapid eye movement) dream period. Meanwhile, an agent or sender in a distant room looks at a randomly selected target picture on a given night and tries to telepathically send it to the sleeping and dreaming subject. The results are evaluated objectively across subjects and across nights by having judges match dream protocols with target material when they do not know which pictorial targets were supposed to go with which nights. It is worth taking an example in detail from their results here, as it illustrates not only how dramatic and accurate the ESP process can be, but also how much (nonconscious) psychological factors can simultaneously alter and distort the information. The process here is of an unknown amount of information about the target picture being received by the subject, worked over outside of consciousness, and then woven into the psychological processes that would ordinarily create and control the dream.

The target painting that was transmitted all through the night was a reproduction of the Salvador Dali painting *The Sacrament of the Last Supper,* which portrays Christ sitting at the center of a table surrounded by his twelve disciples. A glass of wine and a loaf of bread are visible on the table, while a large body of water and a fishing boat can be seen in the distant background. From many awakenings from stage 1 (rapid eye movement) periods, the subject reported eight separate dreams, as well as associating to the dreams in the morning. I shall quote only extracts from the dream reports that are relevant to the target picture. Readers who are familiar with psychoanalytic theories of the unconscious can see the typical sorts of distortions that keep the target picture from being directly represented in dreaming consciousness, even though it is clearly influencing the dream.

S's first dream: "There was one scene of an ocean. . . . It had a strange beauty about it and a strange formation."

S's second dream: "I haven't any reason to say this, but somehow boats come to mind. Fishing boats. Small-size fishing boats. . . . There was a picture in the Sea Fare Restaurant that came to mind as I was describing it. It's a very large painting. Enormous. It shows, oh, I'd say about a dozen or so men pulling a fishing boat ashore right after having returned from a catch."

S's third dream: "I was looking at a catalog. . . . a Christmas catalog. Christmas season."

S's fourth dream: "I had some sort of a brief dream about an M.D. . . . I was talking to someone and . . . the discussion had to do with why . . . a doctor becomes a doctor because he's supposed to be an M.D., or something of that nature."

S's fifth dream: "It had to do with doctors again. . . . The picture . . . that I'm thinking of now is the doctor sitting beside a child that is ill. . . . It's one of those classical ones. . . . It's called *The Physician.*"

S's sixth dream: "I was in this office—a doctor's office again. . . . We were talking about

Preston. . . . He's a psychiatrist. A supervisor I had. Before he became a psychiatrist he was a pathologist."

S's seventh dream: "The only part that comes to mind is the part where I'm in a kitchen, and there is a restaurant that I was planning to go to."

S's eighth dream: "I was sampling these different articles that looked like spices. Herbs. Grocery store. Place to eat. Food of different types."

From S's associations: "The fisherman dream makes me think of the Mediterranean area, perhaps even some sort of Biblical time. Right now my associations are of the fish and the loaf, or even the feeding of the multitudes. . . . Once again I think of Christmas. . . . Having to do with the ocean—water, fishermen, something in this area."

, Many of the spiritual psychologies say that states of consciousness that can be reached in the course of their practices are highly favorable to psi abilities. We cannot scientifically say yes or no to this claim at present, but certainly it is possible in the light of what we do know.

We have now looked, all too briefly, at the four well-established psi phenomena, their lack of fit with the current picture of the physical universe, and their psychological nature. Now we shall consider some other psi phenomena whose existence is not overwhelmingly documented like the basic four, and about which we know much less, but which are clearly relevant to the claims of the spiritual psychologies.

PSYCHIC ENERGY AND HEALING

Many of the spiritual psychologies postulate various kinds of psychic energies, energies which are not physical but which exist on some nonphysical level and can influence living organisms and sometimes nonliving matter. PK, of course, must be one such form of energy, with its observable manifestation being a change in physical objects. An energy manifesting only in terms of its effect on life and consciousness has been called such names as *prana* in India (Garrison, 1964), *chi* in China, and *ki* in Japan (Frager, 1970). Some Western scholars have attempted to deal with it: Franz Mesmer (1774) called it *magnetic fluid,* and von Reichenbach (1968) called it *odic force,* but these conceptions have never been accepted in orthodox, Western science. Some people experience unusual sensations they consider psychic energy in their ordinary state of consciousness, and many more have experienced it in some d-ASC. When I surveyed experienced marijuana users, for example, 35 percent of them said they experienced it very often. Nine percent said they usually experienced it (Tart, 1971b).

The ability to produce, control, and direct this energy is often used to explain the basis of paranormal healing, the alleviation of physical ailments when there seems to be no adequate physiological or medical explanation for the healing. This is a difficult area to investigate, for so many physical ailments actually have a partial or completely psychosomatic basis, and the *belief* that a treatment is going to be effective may be sufficient to produce a cure, without involving any paranormal elements. Some excellent experiments by Bernard Grad, at McGill University, have now established a substantial case for the existence for some kind of psychic energy being involved in at least some cases of healing. Since Grad's experiments are the best in the field on psychic healing and energy, let us look at them in some detail.

Grad worked with a Hungarian healer, a Colonel Estabani, who had a long history of healing both animals and people by laying his hands on the afflicted areas for some time. The basic experimental question Grad addressed himself to was whether there was some sort of nonphysical energy emanating from Estabani's hands that could affect wound healings. In a number of studies (Grad, 1963; 1965; 1967; Grad, Cadoret, and Paul, 1961), experimental organisms were mildly wounded and then received a healing treatment in a way that eliminated known physical and psychological factors. In one early experiment, mice received small, surgically inflicted wounds on their skins, and the rate of healing of the wounds was objectively measured daily. The mice were divided into an experimental and a control group, and those in the experimental group were treated by Estabani. Each mouse in the experimental group was put into a paper bag by an experimenter, and Estabani held the bag and its contained mouse in his hands while doing his healing. Mice in the control group were put in paper bags for equivalent periods of time but not held by Estabani. The results showed that the wounds healed much more rapidly in the mice who received the healing treatment.

Because there might be some sort of physical handling factors or warmth factors involved in such an experiment, Grad then did a series of experiments eliminating even this possibility. The experimental organisms were seeds which had been "wounded" by being heated in an oven in a temperature that would kill some of them and adversely affect those that survived. These seeds were then planted in pots and watered with sterile, saline solution, mild salty water of the sort used for transfusions. The baking and the use of the mild saline solution for the seeds were to simulate conditions of illness, nonoptimal conditions for the organisms. The saline solution came in hermetically sealed jars. Some of the jars were held between Estabani's hands, and he did a healing treatment on the saline, presumably passing nonphysical energy through the walls of glass into the water. The seeds watered with this treated water were the experimental group. Seeds in the control group were watered with jars of sterile saline solution that had simply sat around in the room without receiving a treatment from Colonel Estabani. A technician who did not know which water had received the healing treatment took care of the actual watering of the plants; and another technician measured the number of seeds which actually sprouted and the heights to which the seeds grew in a certain period of time, as well as the final weight of the plants at the end of the experiment. The results showed repeatedly that for seeds watered with the treated solution, more seeds sprouted, the seedlings grew faster, and the final plants weighed significantly more at the end of the experiment.

The only thing that could happen in physical terms as a result of Estabani's healing treatment was that the water in the jar that he held would get slightly warmer. Since all bottles, control and experimental, were allowed to sit around and come back to room temperature before watering the plants, this variable was canceled out. No known form of physical energy emanating from the healer could get into and be stored in the water. Thus we can argue strongly that some nonphysical (in terms of our current understanding of the universe) kind of energy, a psychical energy, must be capable of attaching itself to water and then affecting growing organisms.

It is good to remind ourselves here, however, that because psi effects have been shown to exist in certain experiments, every unusual experience that people have should not be attributed to psi. We are quite good at misinterpreting things and fooling ourselves. But psi is a possibility in apparently inexplicable happenings. And probably a lot of "explicable" happenings are actually caused by psi, but we rationalize an ordinary explanation for them, since it fits our belief system better.

In spite of difficulties with our interpretations and misinterpretations, personal experience is generally more convincing than the best sort of experiments done by someone else, and readers who have had tingling, vibrating, flowing sensations they thought were energy moving around in their body or coming out of their hands are more likely to be convinced than those who simply rely on experimental method.

ANIMAL PSI

The orthodox view of man makes him rather special, the only creature on the planet with intelligence, in a class by himself. Might this also be true for psi abilities, that they are possessed only by man?

For years the main evidence on this issue was anecdotal accounts that seemed to indicate that animals might possess psi abilities. There are a number of well-documented "psi trailing" cases, for instance, in which a pet was left when a family moved a distance of dozens and sometimes hundreds of miles, and then some time later an animal showed up which could be recognized as the pet. Since there would be no physical clues for the animal to trail its owners, it must have relied on psi. These cases are difficult to evaluate, as often there is no way of being *absolutely* certain that the animal is actually the original pet and not one that greatly resembles it.

In the last decade a number of excellent laboratory studies have shown that many animals apparently have psi abilities.

Early experiments (Osis, 1952) suggested that cats could use ESP to find food. More recent studies have suggested psi abilities in experimental animals such as mice (Duval and Montredon, 1968). A recent review of this literature can be found in Morris (1970). Certain animal studies must now be discounted due to a discovery of fraud (see Rhine, 1974).

Assuming that results suggesting animals have ESP continue to be replicated and extended, the results are rather staggering to our ordinary view of the universe. Even simple organisms may be capable of responding to and affecting their environment in ways totally at variance with our physical view of the world. This kind of finding seems more in accordance with the view of the spiritual psychologies that life is a dynamic force in the universe, that mind is just as real as matter, rather than the orthodox, physicalistic view that life is strictly a physical reaction and consciousness merely a by-product of physical reactions.

A word should be said here about possible psi effects with plants. There has been much national publicity about "primary perception in plants," the apparent ability of plants to show a change in their electrical resistance when some other plants or living organisms are killed in their immediate vicinity, suggesting some kind of telepathic interaction at this very low level of life. Unfortunately, in spite of the amount of popular press coverage, only one experiment claiming this effect has ever appeared in a scientific journal (Backster, 1968), and there has not been a single replication published in a scientific journal in the many years since the original publication, although a number of parapsychologists have tried to repeat the experiment.* This phenomena cannot be considered as established, although the possibilities are intriguing.

PSI AND INANIMATE OBJECTS

If psi is not the exclusive property of man, even though it may be more developed in him, if it seems to extend down to at least some of the lower organisms, might its distribution and function in the universe be even broader, possibly extending to inanimate objects? The answer to this question is probably yes, in the sense that inanimate objects seem to be capable of storing or being associated with nonphysical psi information.

---

*Brier (1969) did show a *psychokinetic* effect on the electrical resistance of plant leaves, although there are conceptual difficulties in clearly discriminating telepathic and psychokinetic effects on living organisms.

The popular name for this phenomenon is psychometry,* and the concept generally takes the form that if an inanimate object is associated with particular persons or events or places for some time, some sort of nonphysical "traces" are created in the object which constitute a kind of stored memory about the owners of the object or the events or places with which it has been associated. A psychic or sensitive, a person possessing the requisite psychic ESP abilities, can then read out this information through some kind of clairvoyant ESP.

Many psychics have claimed to have this ability, and its use is mentioned on one spiritual path (see Chapter 11). The psychic, for example, may take a ring worn by a person he has never seen and give all sorts of descriptions that are purportedly about the owner's personality, life history, and so forth. Insofar as these statements are more than mere guesses, such psychometry or object reading makes no physical sense at all, as a person's personality and the events in his life do not affect the metal molecules comprising the ring in any physical way that we know of.

Although the phenomenon of psychometry has been known for a long time, it has been difficult to make an objective evaluation of whether there is any kind of psi operating. People doing psychometry may say many things about the owner of an object, and the owner may later agree with some of these and disagree with others. How many correct statements do you have to have compared with a certain number of incorrect statements before you decide more than chance is operating? How many of those correct statements are simply guesses, general sorts of statements which might apply to a lot of people and just happen to apply to the owner of this particular object? Too, if a person having a psychometric reading on an object of his wants to believe psi is operating, he will agree to almost anything and consider it a striking description of himself. If he doesn't want to believe in psi phenomena, he may take very specific statements that are correct and dismiss them as coincidence.

J. G. Pratt, a parapsychologist, and W. R. Birge, a statistician, worked out a method for objectively evaluating psychometric and similar readings (Pratt and Birge, 1948). The basic method is to have the psychic do readings on objects from a number of different owners, without the owners being present to give any sensory clues. The information statements from these readings are then transcribed and coded so that it is not clear in the final transcript which statements are supposed to go with which objects. Statements that obviously reflect sensory characteristics of the objects are not included. All of the people contributing psychometric objects then rate *every* statement for its truth or falsity: since they do not know which statements were intended for them (their object) and which

---

*Psychologists later took over this term to refer to psychological testing.

were intended for others, they cannot be systematically biased in their ratings in a way that will affect the outcome. The results are then analyzed statistically to see if correct statements are being made specifically on the people they were intended for, rather than just being generalities that are checked true by many people.

Several studies using this technique have now shown that there can be some degree of psi involved in psychometric readings. This supports the idea that some kind of psychic "traces" can be "deposited in" or somehow associated with material objects and then utilized by a person with the requisite abilities later on.

A brief word is appropriate here about the use of material objects to alter the functioning of psi abilities. Many psychics use some sort of object or another for this purpose, and occult traditions indicate that certain jewels or metals are favorable or unfavorable to the operation of various psychic powers. The idea has been covered in science fiction writing by the term "psionic machines," to indicate devices whose functioning makes no sense in physical terms but which amplify and direct psychic abilities.

There has been very little formal investigation of psionic machines and the like among parapsychologists, for two reasons. First is that almost inevitable reason of insufficient manpower and resources to devote to the investigation. Second, there is a general feeling that all these devices or psionic machines are simply psychological aids to a person and have no abilities in themselves. That is, in many cases it may be psychologically easier for a person to disown any unusual abilities himself and say he is merely using a machine that he knows how to use well. This not only avoids a certain amount of personal ego involvement in what he does, but brings the prestige of the whole machine culture to his side. A common example of this would be water dowsing, in which the dowser holds a forked twig, metal rods set in sleeves that act as bearings, or the like in his hands and walks around unknown terrain until the rods either swing together or apart (depending on the particular dowser's beliefs) to indicate water underground. The amount of swing of the rods or the degree of force the dowser senses may be used as an indication of the depth and quantity of the water. Most dowsers believe in very elaborate "physical" theories to explain their abilities, such as variations in the gravitational field, electrical or magnetic waves emanating from the water, or various postulated forms of energy emanating from the water which directly affect the rods. I put quotes around *physical* because these explanations would all look nonsensical to a physicist, clearly involving misunderstandings of basic physical principles and logically incorrect applications, as well as numerous contradictions.

Almost all parapsychologists would be of the opinion that the reason the rods move in a dowser's hands is because of unconscious muscular action. There is no evidence that any mysterious form of energy directly affects the rods. The unconscious muscular reactions that move the rods may be caused by a dowser's unconscious or semiconscious knowledge of geology which allows him to infer that water is likely at a particular spot and/or by clairvoyance of some sort operating and expressing itself through unconscious muscular action. Referring back to Figure 1 earlier in this chapter, this would be an example of the information flow route in psi perception being from the target through the channel to the transducer to the unconscious mind and directly to the musculature, without the direct participation of the dowser's conscious mind.

Many claims have been made for various kinds of psionic machines over the last hundred years. Most of these have received only preliminary investigation from parapsychologists, but the clear feeling seems to be that none of these machines works by itself. If a psychic uses them, they may get results, but probably only as a result of the user's psychic abilities. That is, the machines do nothing by themselves, they serve as readout devices for the psychic's own abilities.

Thus while we may say that the idea of a psionic machine or special psi properties of objects is possible, given what we know of clairvoyance, PK, and psychometry, there is no good scientific evidence for it at present and some good indications that in most of the cases we know about, the apparent psi properties of machines and other kinds of physical aids are merely psychological properties.

SURVIVAL AFTER DEATH

The historical phenomenon most responsible for the inception of a scientific look at the paranormal, psychical research as it was originally called, or parapsychology as we call it today, was the rise and tremendous growth of modern spiritualism in the latter half of the last century. Spiritualists believe that every individual has some sort of a soul which survives the physical death of the body and maintains the memories and personality of the living person. Specially talented psychics called mediums can communicate with the surviving entities. Usually a medium goes into some kind of d-ASC where his or her personality lapses into unconsciousness and he or she is then temporarily controlled by the surviving entity. The surviving entity may then talk with the sitters who attend the séance at which the mediumistic activities take place.

Many skeptical people went to mediumistic séances after the loss of a loved one and found that the medium's personality did indeed seem to be replaced by that of the lost loved one, or at least they got information relayed by the medium's control personality that seemed proof of the fact that the loved one had survived.

At worst, most mediumistic phenomena seem to be demonstrations of the psychology of belief. Many mediums and their alleged spirit controls (intermediate entities who may relay messages from the deceased) or the temporarily possessing entities seem only figments of the medium's unconscious mind, who speak in generalities and platitudes. But in some cases, many of them well documented, the alleged surviving person gives such highly specific details about his life, his history, and information about relatives that he seems identifiable beyond reasonable doubt as the formerly living person. It is this latter kind of mediumistic activity that provides the best sort of evidence for possible survival of an individual after death.

Psychical researchers spent a great deal of time decades ago in finding mediums who could produce this highly evidential kind of material. Basically they looked for mediums who had no ordinary knowledge of the deceased, and instances in which the apparent deceased communicators could give highly specific information about their past lives, such as specific names and addresses of friends, recollection of particular important events in their lives that they had shared with others, and so on. This included discovering a good many cases of outright fraud, including mediums who had employed private detectives to check up on the background of sitters and their deceased relatives in order to produce a good impression and thus acquire financial gain. But a number of excellent mediums were found who did produce evidence for the survival of the deceased personalities.

At the same time, the evidence for the existence of ESP was steadily mounting, and as it became clear that some individuals could occasionally exercise enormous amounts of ESP, such that no information could be said to be definitely *un*available to an individual using psychic abilities, a counter hypothesis to that of surviving entities developed. The counter hypothesis is that nothing survives physical death, but because of our intense desire to believe that this is not so, a good medium is someone who unconsciously uses his or her ESP abilities in the service of his or her belief system to unconsciously find out factual, verifiable information about the deceased persons. This information is woven into an excellent impersonation of the deceased person by a fragment of the medium's unconscious mind. Since the psychological evidence that human beings will engage in incredible distortions of perceptions and use unconscious processes to support belief systems is very solid, and since the evidence for the existence of extrasensory perception is now very solid, this is a powerful hypothesis.

Ingenious measures have been devised to try to collect evidence that will fit more with the survival hypothesis than the ESP plus unconscious impersonation hypothesis, but it is beyond the scope of this chapter to go into them. I would particularly recommend Gardner Murphy's and Laura Dale's *Challenge of Psychical Research* (1961) to the interested reader. There has been little research on the survival-after-death question in the last several decades because of the enormous difficulties in trying to distinguish between these two hypotheses, and also because spiritualism has not been an important cultural phenomenon for the last few decades. Interest in the survival question is building up again among parapsychologists, and we will probably see more sophisticated research approaches being applied within the next decade.

There is no doubt that sometimes mediums provide information about deceased personalities that is definitely paranormal: the doubt is whether to interpret this as indicating the personality has indeed survived or to explain it "away" on the ESP plus belief system hypothesis. But enough evidence has been collected that should allow one, on a scientific basis, to take the possibility of survival seriously, even if it can hardly be said to be unequivocally proven.

Perhaps the most amazing aspect of investigations of survival is the fact that the question of whether one might survive death or not is an incredibly important question to a human being, yet there is practically no social desire to really look at the question scientifically. Most people seem content either to believe in it on faith from some traditional religious background or to simply adopt the physicalistic world view that there is no survival beyond physical death. One would think that such an important human question would not be neglected for investigation by scientific method, the most powerful question-answering tool man has devised.

We should also briefly look at the possibility of reincarnation, an idea accepted in many of the spiritual psychologies, although quite alien to our Western, Judeo-Christian tradition. As a result of its social unpopularity and the lack of manpower, very little scientific investigation of reincarnation has been done. What little has been depends mainly on finding a spontaneous case in which someone claims to remember a previous incarnation, checking to see exactly what information about the previous personality he claims to remember, checking on the accuracy of that information if there are any living people or historical records available that are relevant, and then trying to establish whether the person could have known that information by ordinary means and worked it into a belief system of having been reincarnated.

When one attempts to fulfill all of these criteria, many cases of apparent reincarnation turn out to be very dubious: the historical details are too vague to allow checking on, or the historical records don't exist, or the apparent reincarnation is about some historical figure who is so well known that it is much easier to hypothesize that the person drew on memories acquired earlier in this life and then forgotten in order to support a fantasy about reincarnation.

Nevertheless, some excellent cases meeting many stringent criteria do exist. The interested reader should refer to a book by Ian Stevenson (1966), the world's foremost scientific investigator of reincarnation cases. Stevenson's work alone, as well as other investigators' works (with two more books of cases by Stevenson scheduled for publication in 1975), has produced enough excellent cases to say that the idea of reincarnation is well worth looking at scientifically, even though we would not want to say that it has been proven in any sense. As with the survival hypothesis of spiritualism, another kind of hypothesis of ESP being unconsciously used to support a belief system must also be entertained.

Note that reincarnation is such an emotionally loaded topic that it may be very difficult for Westerners like us to look at it objectively. Some readers will remember *The Search for Bridey Murphy* (Bernstein, 1956), a book that became very popular in the late 1950s. The author, a Colorado businessman, claimed that during experiments with hypnosis he regressed a housewife back to a previous life as Bridey Murphy in Ireland. She provided many details: some of them could not be checked up on, some could and were found to be true, some could and were found to be questionable. As cases of reincarnation go, the Bridey Murphy case was a fairly good one and was presented quite soberly by Bernstein.

I happened to pick up this book accidentally before it became a best-seller, and read it because it was concerned with hypnosis. A few months later I began hearing about the book in newspapers and magazines, and reading reviews of it, and I became convinced that there must have been two books with the title *The Search for Bridey Murphy,* since the reviewers didn't seem to be talking about the book I had read at all. Reviewers ranted and raved about how anyone could be so crazy as to present such a weird idea, made up all sorts of "facts" that had not come out of the book that they purported to be quoting from, and so on. It was a striking demonstration of how the idea of reincarnation was to be greeted within the cultural context of that time.

Note also that while there is enough scientific evidence to warrant seriously *investigating* the idea of reincarnation, especially because of its importance to our human lives, it, like all other spiritual beliefs, can be turned into a multitude of neurotic games. Too many people who embrace the idea of reincarnation are avoiding confrontation with the reality they have created and live in now by distracting themselves with fantasies about how important and wonderful they were in a past life.

OUT-OF-THE-BODY EXPERIENCES

A phenomenon with direct bearing on the possibility of some sort of postmortem survival, as well as one dealt with in some of the spiritual psychologies, is an *out-of-the-body experience* (OOBE). An older term for this is "astral projection," but this term is metaphysical rather than scientific. An OOBE occurs when one finds himself at a location that is clearly different from where his physical body is located.* He feels disconnected from his physical body and is unable to

---

*Given that the usual ideas of a space-time framework and being located within it hold.

sense it, although his state of consciousness seems completely clear and normal. (Ordinary dreaming is not an OOBE, for, in retrospect, one realizes that one's state of consciousness was not at all ordinary.)

As defined thus far, an OOBE is a psychological phenomenon and one of particular interest because of its effect on most people who experience it. The effect is generally a statement on the order of: "I no longer *believe* in survival of my personality after death—I know it to be a *fact* because I have experienced being conscious and functioning without being in my physical body." This does not follow in an absolutely logical fashion, for one might argue that no matter how impressive the experience, the person's physical body was alive and well, otherwise he would not have been able to give a report of the experience. And so one may dismiss the experience as some sort of interesting d-ASC (even though consciousness feels perfectly normal except for the sensation of being out of one's body) or a hallucination. Such reasoning seldom affects people who have actually had the experience, however, who *know* that they will survive physical death.

What makes the OOBE of *para*psychological interest is that it sometimes involves paranormal elements: the experiencer not only *feels* himself to be at some location distant from his physical body, he accurately describes what is going on at that location, the description is later verified, and we can be reasonably certain that there was no ordinary way in which he could have acquired this information. Hundreds of excellent cases of this sort have been collected by parapsychologists.

OOBEs are a once-in-a-lifetime experience for most people, often brought on by accident or illness that almost kills, sometimes occurring with emotional stress or for other reasons. The psychological OOBE can be produced in hypnosis fairly readily, but often descriptions of distant places the person feels he was at turn out to be purely imaginary. I have had the luck to be able to work with two people in my laboratory who had OOBEs very frequently. One of them, Robert Monroe, has since described his hundreds of OOBEs in a recent book (Monroe, 1971). The other, a young woman I called Miss Z, showed distinct brain wave patterns during her OOBEs in the laboratory, as well as providing very strong evidence as to their paranormal nature. These studies have been described elsewhere (Tart, 1967; 1968; 1974b). I feel they demonstrate more the feasibility of studying this phenomenon scientifically than providing any final conclusions on it. Research at the American Society for Psychical Research (K. Osis, personal communication, 1973) and the Psychical Research Foundation (W. G. Roll, personal communication, 1973) is extending these studies. As with reincarnation, we can hardly call the phenomenon well established, but there is enough evidence to warrant serious scientific study of it.

THE PSYCHICAL AND THE SPIRITUAL

Because of a historical association of unusual, "miraculous" happenings with various religious traditions, as well as for numerous other reasons, many people associate psychical or paranormal happenings and abilities with the spiritual. Whether it is done with full consciousness or not, this association often takes the form of believing that if a person displays any kind of paranormal abilities, he or she is therefore more evolved spiritually than ordinary human beings.

Many of the spiritual psychologies discussed in this book do indeed indicate that various paranormal abilities become available as certain states of consciousness are attained. Speaking as a parapsychologist, however, it also seems clear that people who would not be classified as particularly mature or spiritual may also possess paranormal abilities to various degrees, and it is very unlikely that the possession of such abilities may be used per se as a criterion of maturity or spirituality. I have met many psychics: some of them strike me as exceptionally mature people, and others are obviously as neurotic and into as much game playing as the rest of us.

The spiritual psychologies generally stress that the acquisition of paranormal abilities per se is not necessarily desirable, and may be a diversion from real spiritual growth. Further, it may be a particularly dangerous diversion, for one may become attached to such powers and use them in ways that are not conducive to one's spiritual growth or may actually hinder it. The old adage that power corrupts can be as true for spiritual paths as it is true for ordinary life. This does not seem to mean that power *must* corrupt, but that it is a very tricky thing to handle, and the acquisition of spiritual understanding and wisdom must be given priority.

If you think about it, the idea that having some special power automatically gives one more spirituality can be seen to be silly. For example, I now possess a power, as do you, which would have been considered absolutely miraculous or even impossible throughout the vast span of man's history. I can talk to any one of untold millions of people anywhere in the world with practically no exertion at all. I simply pick up the instrument whose functioning would have been considered totally magical even a few hundred years ago, the telephone. The fact that I can do this, however, says nothing about what the *quality* of my conversation with some person on the telephone will be. We may have an honest, open, growthful exchange, or I may lie or mislead or play all sorts of neurotic games. The fact that I am able to do this over distances of thousands of miles is no guarantee that my conversation will be any more mature than if I do it over a distance of a few feet.

The essence of this brief discussion on the psychic and spiritual, then, is that while there may be *relationship,* the two domains should not be *equated.* I think it is hard not to equate them on an emotional level, for we have a lot of drives to gain power, and if we can rationalize these drives as spiritual growth it will be more pleasing to our ego. Before we put a lot of effort into acquiring more power, however, we would do well to see what use we make of the power we already have.

This concludes our all too brief overview of the paranormal. It is a vast area, containing, as far as information goes, an incredible mixture of the scientific, the spiritual, the pathological, and the nonsensical, with a little touch of the just plain fraudulent. I have appended a list of a few of the better books at the end of this chapter for the interested reader who wants to pursue information about scientific parapsychology further. What we do know scientifically already, such as the undoubted existence of telepathy, clairvoyance, precognition, and psychokinesis, reminds us that our physicalistic view of the universe is limited, and opens us to a wider view that may be quite compatible with many of the ideas of the spiritual psychologies.

RECOMMENDED READING IN PARAPSYCHOLOGY

I am greatly indebted to McConnel's *ESP Curriculum Guide* (1971) in preparing this partial listing of good books on parapsychology, and I recommend the guide also.

Gudas, F., ed. *Extrasensory Perception.* New York: Scribner's, 1961.

Heywood, R. *Beyond the Reach of Sense: An Inquiry into Extrasensory Perception.* New York: Dutton, 1959.

———. *ESP: A Personal Memoir* New York: Dutton, 1964.

Mitchell, E. *Psychic Exploration.* New York: Putnams, 1974.

Murphy, G., and Dale, L. *Challenge of Psychical Research.* New York: Harper & Row, 1961.

Pratt, J., Rhine, J., Smith, B., Stuart, C., and Greenwood, J. *Extrasensory Perception after Sixty Years.* Somerville, Mass.: Bruce Humphries, 1940; reprinted 1966.

Rhine, J. *Extrasensory Perception.* Somerville, Mass.: Bruce Humphries, 1934; reprinted 1964.

Rhine, Louisa. *Hidden Channels of the Mind.* New York: Apollo, 1961, 1966.

———. *Mind over Matter: The Story of PK Research.* New York: Macmillan, 1970.

Schmeidler, G., ed. *Extrasensory Perception.* New York: Atherton, 1969.

Smythics, J., ed. *Science and ESP.* New York: Humanities Press, 1967.

Soal, S., and Bateman, F. *Modern Experiments in Telepathy.* London: Faber & Faber, 1954.

4 ZEN BUDDHISM

CLAIRE MYERS OWENS

CLAIRE MYERS OWENS (1896–1983) was born in Temple, Texas and received her B.S. from Texas Woman's University. She went on to do postgraduate work in psychology at Yale University. She did settlement house and social work in Chicago, New York City, and in an Alabama mining camp. Her wide range of experience included living in a commune in the Blue Ridge Mountains of Virginia, working in the book business in New York, and having a long, happy marriage.

In the early 1960s she had a spontaneous self-realization experience that greatly vivified her interest in the spiritual. In 1969 she began intensive training in Zen meditation (Zazen) at the Rochester, New York, Zen Center under Philip Kapleau, which led her to write and lecture on Zen. Her published books include *Awakening to the Good—Psychological or Religious* (1958), *Discovery of the Self* (1963) (reprinted as *Small Ecstasies* in 1983), and *Zen and the Lady* (1979). She also published several scholarly papers, such as "The Mystical Experience—Facts and Values," now reprinted in John White's *Highest State of Consciousness* (1972), "Self-Realization—Spontaneous and Induced," a talk given at the 1973 conference of the R.M. Bucke Memorial Society, which appeared in a book edited by Raymond Prince (1966), and "Implications of Consciousness—Changing Drugs" (1965), as well as a number of popular articles on psychology.

Is Zen a psychology, a philosophy, or a religion? Or a life style that actualizes man's noblest potentials? There is some controversy on this subject. It is suggested here that it may belong in all four categories. By any name it is a powerful movement now proliferating across the United States. It is especially favored by disillusioned but idealistic college youth—and other peaceful dissidents.

Zen Buddhism has been introduced into America by way of Japan. According to the Zen masters, its psychology of self-realization, however, is universal, applicable to anyone, anywhere.

Enlightenment is a religious experience but also a psychological one. A presentation in this paper of the parallels and distinctions between the spiritual psychology of Zen and the psychologies of the West—first growth, or transpersonal, psychology and then orthodox psychology—seems relevant if Zen is to be widely accepted by scientifically oriented Western man. At this time, an attempt to synthesize different disciplines may create a strange mixture of terminologies: lyrical and religious, psychological and scientific.

This modest attempt, it is hoped, may be a small part of a worldwide movement —the reconciliation of science and the religion-of-experience, the meeting of the scientific West and the spiritual East on a level deeper than the economic.

Today the ordinary unenlightened man is distraught because his values— rationalism, science, materialism, dualism, and individualism (despite their benefits)—have created a dangerous dichotomy between the conscious mind and the unconscious. This dichotomy appears to be the major cause of the present tragic crises in Western civilization in general and perhaps the revolt of youth in particular.

It is generally conceded that our civilization has presently reached a crucial turning point. Drastic measures seem indicated before it destroys the very world it has created.

ENLIGHTENMENT

The actualization of man's noblest potentialities by Zen or other systems of self-realization may offer a solution. The goal of Zen Buddhism is enlightenment (*satori* in Japanese) and ever-deepening enlightenment. This includes the wisdom derived from intuitive insights, the transformation of personality, and the new life style that ensues. The nature of Zen is difficult to describe and even more difficult to believe—unless one has experienced it.

Buddha's first statement immediately following his awakening is purported to have been: "Wonder of wonders! Intrinsically all living beings are Buddhas, endowed with wisdom and virtue, but because men's minds have become inverted through delusive thinking they fail to perceive this" (Kapleau, 1967, p. 28). In other words, a basic tenet of Buddhism is that a True-self or Original-nature (the deeper unconscious) is inherent in all men and that it is perfect. This Real-you is a treasure house of virtues—compassion, selflessness, love of one's fellow man, desire to serve, serenity, certitude, spirituality. The paramount function, therefore, of every man, Buddhism teaches, is to see into his own True-nature and thereby into the nature of all existence.

How is this to be accomplished?

Through the practice of *zazen* (Zen meditation), when the discriminating mind (the conscious mind) is quieted and the intuitive mind (the unconscious) is liberated and identifies with the universal Mind. During enlightenment the individual returns to his origin, ultimate reality, the Void, Emptiness—which yet contains everything.

The bliss and awe of enlightenment are indescribable. The whole experience of self-realization is ineffable because it is beyond the limits of reason and words— whether the method is one of induction, as in Zen, or spontaneous.

The enlightened man emerges from this overwhelming experience a new person. A transformation of his character, behavior, and hierarchy of values has occurred. A new life style arises without his volition, astounding no one so much as the person to whom it happens. His ego has mysteriously diminished. He experiences a selflessness of which he did not know himself capable, a certitude for which he longed, a love of the human race that astounds him, harmony with the universe that his rational mind had assured him was impossible, and a joy unlike any other (as I discovered in my own spontaneous self-realization).

The enlightened person feels as if realization of the self answers all questions, dispels all doubts, abolishing fear and anger, hate and jealousy. It ends alienation. It brings a new kind of harmonious identity with the self, others, nature, and the universe. The rational mind becomes clarified, functioning with intuition—which is in harmony with the universal law.

Many consider actualization of one's noblest potentials the supreme experience possible to mankind. Kapleau describes its results in the *Three Pillars of Zen:* "... self-centeredness [gives] way to flowing warmth, resiliency, and compassion, while self-indulgence and fear are transmuted into self-mastery and courage" (1967, p. 14). Self-realization sounds too good to be true. But history proves its validity in innumerable cases—Buddha being a supreme example.

Growth psychologists (or transpersonal psychologists) describe this process of realizing one's potentialities as quieting the conscious mind (seat of the ego) and awakening of the unconscious (seat of the Self). Then comes penetration to the deepest Integral level of the unconscious, to use Houston and Masters's (1967) terms for what Jung calls the collective unconscious, which is universal. It is in this deepest level that the religious experience transpires.

ZEN BUDDHISM

Zen asserts that it does not add anything to the individual. It merely shows him the way to uncover, recover, discover, the neglected part of his nature that too often lies dormant—his Essential-mind. Zen is a way to become what one already is. Zen training involves the daily practice of zazen, living in a Zen community *(sangha),* following a spiritual teacher *(roshi)* who is himself enlightened, and the teachings of the Buddha (the *Dharma*) recorded in the Buddhist scriptures *(sutras).*

Zen Buddhism is a strenuous body-mind discipline. It requires great effort, perseverance, and idealism. It also necessitates faith in the fact of the Buddha's enlightenment and in one's own ability to attain enlightenment. It is not esoteric but exoteric. It is simple, direct, and practical. It is concerned with the here and now. It solves the concrete problems of daily life in a way beyond the credence of the skeptic. This is especially emphasized by Philip Kapleau, founder and spiritual director of the Zen Center of Rochester, New York, with which I am most familiar. Current examples from this center leap to mind. Doubtless they are also typical of other centers.

A woman member is separating from her husband. She admits that ten years ago this traumatic experience might have left her a candidate for a mental institution, but thanks to her Zen practice it is a friendly separation. Sitting in zazen, she finds, causes a diminution of the ego and deeper concern for others.

A woman has just been informed by her doctor that she has a heart condition. Fortunately the bad news was received immediately following a profound Zen experience of purgation. Having the relaxation of zazen practice to aid her, she feels able to support what otherwise might have been a tragedy. She says her illness is actually a spur to deeper practice.

A young man was afraid he might lose his wife and baby in a difficult childbirth.

He informed me that it was daily sitting in zazen in his own home that supported him during this ordeal. Practice awakens the latent strength and courage inherent in all sentient beings, according to Buddha's teachings.

Recently I made a significant self-discovery. I was not participating in the week of intensive training (a *sesshin*) at the Zen Center. Consequently I was obliged to practice zazen at home. If I failed to sit an hour on rising every morning, my whole day was decidedly out of tune. If I practiced with intense concentration, however, I noticed afterward that my muscular coordination was smoother while I prepared breakfast. The creative stream flowed more freely when I began to write; my thinking was more lucid. Practice sweetened my disposition and improved my relations to others.

Prolonged zazen also releases energy. Hakuin, a great Japanese Zen master of the eighteenth century, wrote:

> Even though I am past seventy now my vitality is ten times as great as it was when I was thirty.... I find no difficulty in refraining from sleep for ... even seven days without suffering any decline in my mental powers. I am surrounded by ... five-hundred demanding students.... I lecture ... for thirty to fifty days in a row, it does not exhaust me. I am quite convinced that all this is owing to the power gained from practising this method of introspection [zazen]. [Hakuin, 1971, p. 32]

The word Zen is "an abbreviation of the Japanese word *zenna,* which is a transliteration of the Sanskrit *dhyana* (ch'an ... in Chinese), i.e., the process of concentration and absorption" (Kapleau, 1967, p. 350). Zen is a sect of Buddhism. Houston Smith states in his *Religions of Man* that "many students of religion believe [Zen] is the purest form of spirituality in the Far East today" (1958, p. 133). Goddard in *The Buddhist Bible* says that "Ch'an [Zen] Buddhism seems to have discerned the essentials of Shakyamuni's teachings and spirit better than any other sect, and to have developed their implications more faithfully" (1970, p. 672). To understand Zen it is necessary to understand something of Buddhism in general. But to know Buddhism, one must know Buddha.

SIDDHARTHA GAUTAMA, THE BUDDHA

The historical figure Siddhartha Gautama, later to be known as the Buddha, was born in Northern India about 563 years before Christ. "His historicity is indisputable" (Sangharakshita, 1970, p. 3). Siddhartha's father was a wealthy ruler of a large principality. He surrounded his son with every luxury, protecting him assiduously from knowledge of the miseries of the world.

The most meaningful incident of his youth occurred one day while he was sitting under a rose-apple tree. He was observing his father, who was engaged in ceremonial tilling with a jeweled plow. Suddenly Siddhartha was visited by a spontaneous experience which Govinda (1969) terms "mystical." It was so intense that recollection of it influenced him in the greatest crisis of his life, years afterwards. No details are proffered in the sutras. Evidence shows that it did not transform his life. Consequently it can be assessed as a temporary awakening of his intuitive mind and a brief experience of universal Consciousness.

As a young man Siddhartha was reputed to be handsome, possessing magnetic charm and a brilliant intellect. He appeared delicate almost to the point of effeminancy. He was also heir to a throne. At twenty-five, however, to the distress of his father, he became seriously concerned with the problems of human suffering caused by birth and death, old age and disease. Was there no solution to the problem of suffering? he asked. Suddhodana, his father, was unable to answer this question.

Consequently, when twenty-nine, Siddhartha renounced his wife, small son, wealth, and life of luxury and ventured forth into the world to search for ultimate Truth. He adopted the life of a spiritual mendicant—a custom not uncommon in India at that time.

Withdrawing to the forest, he first studied with a Hindu sage. He learned raja yoga, philosophy, and the theory of self-realization. Also he experienced a super-conscious stage, the Sphere of *"akimcanyayatana* or Sphere of No-thing-ness" (Sangharakshita, 1970, p. 13). This is the seventh state of consciousness, characterized by equanimity, one-pointedness, fatigueless energy, equanimity, and cessation of pain. Yet he felt this was not the highest mind-state attainable (Sangharakshita, 1970). Then he joined a group of five ascetics near Uruvela. Here for six years he meditated continuously and practiced severe austerities—fasting to excess, exposing himself to extremes of heat and cold, and undergoing other painful mortifications. He hoped by subduing the body to awaken his True-nature. One day, on the point of death from starvation, he recalled his childhood experience under the rose-apple tree. He asked himself: "Now, is this a way to enlightenment?" He determined that "the Way" was neither through the extremes of asceticism or sensuality nor through intellectual effort or no effort at all.

Siddhartha was now thirty-five—considered in India an especially spiritual time of life. On the memorable night of April 8, 508 B.C., he sat down under a peepul tree, determined not to rise again until he had attained enlightenment. This famous tree was later to be known as the bodhi or bo tree, meaning the tree of enlightenment.

He meditated all night long. Sangharakshita (1970) writes that Buddha traversed the first four levels of concentration *(dhyanas)*. Then he recollected his former births—he had visions of human beings vanishing from one state of existence and appearing in another according to their good and evil deeds. This led to his conviction of the truth of rebirth and the law of cause and effect *(karma)*, a concept long accepted in Indian religion. Now he was free from the bondage to the cycle of death and rebirth in the phenomenal world. When dawn came he was Buddha, the Enlightened One. In Sanskrit the word Buddha means not only one awakened to the true nature of existence but also ultimate Truth itself, or absolute Mind.

He sat in a state of bliss for forty-nine days assimilating the profound truths he had discovered. His compassion for humanity filled him with a strong urge to share his new knowledge with others, but he hesitated, fearing he would not be believed.

Soon, however, he delivered his first sermon. For forty-five years, until he was eighty, he walked across India preaching the Dharma, which is at once his doctrines and the universal Law. He was said to be radiant, compassionate, gentle, and charismatic. He converted his family and many others, "as numerous as the sands of the Ganges," and established a monastic order. He became not a saint or savior or god but one of the greatest spiritual teachers the world has ever known, it is generally conceded.

HISTORICAL DEVELOPMENT OF BUDDHISM

Buddhism did not spring full-grown from the brow of the Buddha. He asserted that there had been twenty-seven Buddhas in the past and there would be others in the future. Initially he was imbued with the prevailing religion of India: Brahmanism. Buddhism evolved out of Brahmanism and yoga as Protestantism developed from Catholicism. The youthful Buddha's new religion was a protest against the rigid caste system of Hinduism, against the spiritual emptiness of the prevailing Brahmanism and its overemphasis on ritual and ceremony. Buddha's goal was to create and disseminate a religion that would be a practical way of life —everyday life for laymen as well as monks. Zen particularly emphasizes this point. Lay Buddhists have always far outnumbered monastics. The goal of monks is not to withdraw from the world but to aid others in coming to enlightenment.

Today American young people also are protesting against traditional values, social inequality, and materialism. They are rebelling against the failure of Christianity and Judaism to provide the individual with a method of solving practical problems by his own efforts through religious training. Today, as in Buddha's time, this means specifically that man needs a valid method of awakening the deeper levels of the unconscious where man's moral, ethical, and spiritual values apparently lie buried and by means of which he can identify himself with "the beyond within."

After Buddha's death Buddhism divided into two main branches: the Southern

Therevada or Hinayana School, that spread through Ceylon, Vietnam, Cambodia, Thailand, and Burma; and the Northern School, Mahayana, that spread to Tibet, Mongolia, China, Korea, and Japan.

In the sixth century, Bodhidharma, the twenty-eighth Indian Patriarch of Buddhism, carried Buddhism to China and founded the Ch'an sect. There it flourished, incorporating elements of Taoism into its system. In the twelfth century the monks Eisai and Dogen brought Ch'an (now Zen) from China to their native Japan, where it has flourished for nearly a thousand years. In both China and Japan, Zen gave birth (as a by-product, as it were) to notable painting, sculpture, architecture, and poetry that have endured through the centuries.

The literature of Buddhism is voluminous. Buddha's teachings were memorized and transmitted orally by his disciples. After 300 to 500 years his words were written down by his later followers. They form the 10,000 Buddhist scriptures, or sutras, extant in various languages.

The earliest scriptures in Pali are considered the most authentic by the Therevada branch. The later sutras in Sanskrit are considered by the Mahayanists as more developed. The canonical Pali literature is called the Three Baskets (Tripitaka). The third "basket," the Ultimate Doctrines (Abhidhamma), contains an analysis of the early Buddhist teachings and metaphysics accepted by the Theravadist.

Zen refers to the sutras as it sees fit, also transmitting its principles through the teachings of its successive masters. Of the Mahayana sutras that Zen uses and comments on are: the Lotus of the Wonderful Law (Saddharma-Pundarika). This is the final discourse of the Buddha, in which he expounds the Mahayana teaching in great depth. Zen also esteems the Lankavatara Sutra. It concerns the doctrine and realization of nondualism and nondifferentiation. There is the Perfect Wisdom Sutra (Prajna Paramita), of which the Diamond Sutra is a part. Its theme is that all phenomena and ideas are of the relative world and therefore unreal. The essence of the Prajna Paramita is in the Heart of Perfect Wisdom Sutra (Prajna-Paramita-Hridaya), which is chanted in Zen monasteries and centers daily. The Crown Sutra (Surangama) contains the elucidation of the secret of the Buddha's supreme attainments. Awakening of the Faith is a sutra that gives a comprehensive summary of the essentials of Mahayana Buddhism.* The Kegon Sutra, though important in Zen, has not yet been translated into English.

Zen emphasis is not primarily on the sutras but always on practice and experience and the application of Zen principles to daily life. Ch'an and Zen, however, produced their own classics. Among them now in English is the *Eye of the True*

---

*The five Mahayana sutras above in English translation can be found in Goddard, ed., *Buddhist Bible*, 1970.

Law (Shobogenzo) by the Japanese master Dogen (1200–1253), edited by Masunaga (1971). Also notable are the writings of Japanese Zen Master Hakuin (1686–1769)—*Orategama, Hebiichigo,* and *Yabukoji* in English (Hakuin, 1971). These are Hakuin's letters to laymen and monks concerning Zen practice. His writing is extremely vigorous, colorful, and humorous. *Introduction to Zen Training,* by a contemporary Japanese master, Yasutani, has recently been translated into English for the first time by Philip Kapleau in *The Three Pillars of Zen* (1967).

In Chinese Zen there is the classic *Platform Scripture* by Hui-neng, translated into English by Win-tsi Chan (1963). It deals with pairs of opposites. Its principle theme is the attainment of the highest wisdom by liberating the mind from attachments.

PHILOSOPHY OF BUDDHISM

It cannot be emphasized too strongly, however, that Buddhism—from Buddha to the present American teachers of Zen—discourages the intellectual approach. Knowledge of the sutras, scholarship, dialectics, and understanding of the philosophy and psychology of Buddhism are not the measure of the Zen man. They are often an obstruction in the spiritual path of the aspirant. Emphasis is laid on the practice of zazen and implementation of it in a daily life of selflessness and oneness. After satori is attained, however, the self-realized man is in a proper mind-state to pursue abstract matters.

Despite these injunctions, in the West today prospective students exist who may long to enter Zen but find it impossible until their rational minds are first convinced of the validity of its philosophy and psychology. Buddhism often enters a disclaimer that it is not a philosophy at all. And certainly it is not "the search for truth through logical reasoning," as philosophy is defined in the West. Yet Buddhism is primarily the search for truth, the ultimate truth of all things. Much of its philosophy is based on assumptions ultimately incapable of proof but also on concepts derived from experiential knowledge and intuitive insights.

Is the philosophy of Buddhism the basis of its psychology or vice versa? Or are the two disciplines mutually reinforcing? Govinda states that "it is the close interweaving of philosophy and psychology which protects Buddhism from stagnation" (1969, p. 37). Suzuki, however, says that Zen is not to be conceptualized . . . it is to be experientially grasped. . . ." He admits nevertheless that "the conceptualization of Zen is inevitable; Zen must have its philosophy" (1956, p. 260).

Zen philosophy is, of course, Buddhist philosophy to a large extent. It may clarify the Eastern discipline if it is viewed very briefly against the background of the more familiar Western systems of philosophy and psychology. First philosophy, then psychology. In the West, philosophy usually includes five fields of study: metaphysics (epistemology, cosmology, and ontology), aesthetics, logic, politics, and ethics.

Buddhist philosophy includes metaphysics which involves not only logical but also intuitive and empirical study of the following: knowledge—its limits, validity, and source; the universe as an orderly system; and the nature of being.

Buddha, like modern philosophers, believed the first duty of a philosopher is to consider knowledge itself. And this concept of knowledge is one of the chief points of divergence between East and West.

The Western world for 2,500 years, ever since Plato, has postulated that reason (deriving from the conscious mind) is the sole source of truth. Plato asserted that intuition is the feminine principle of the universe and actually evil. Truth and wisdom, he maintained, can be attained by logical reasoning.

Buddha, however, during his enlightenment-event attained intuitive insights into the nature of things. He stated that there is a universal Mind, a discriminating mind, and an intuitive mind. He believed the discriminating mind (intellect or the conscious mind) is limited, that knowledge derived from it (and from the senses) continually changes, is impermanent; therefore reason is not a trustworthy guide to ultimate truth. Intuitive mind, on the other hand, is capable of partaking of the universality of the universal Mind, is also changeless and permanent, therefore cannot be in error and consequently is a valid guide to absolute reality. Intuition, then, not reason, is the source of ultimate truth and wisdom, Buddha concluded.

Despite his exalting of intuition, Buddha himself possessed a brilliant intellect, paradoxically enough. Burtt states that Buddha was "a thinker of unexcelled philosophic power. His was one of the giant intellects of human history, exhibiting a keenness of analytic understanding that has rarely been equaled. . . . Buddhism is the only one of the great religions of the world that is consciously and frankly based on a systematic . . . analysis of the problem of life and of the way to its solution" (1955, p. 22).

Buddha's dialectical skill is displayed in the Surangama sutra, for instance. His questioning of his favorite pupil, Ananda, is reminiscent of Socrates' dialectic in the Platonic dialogues. Despite his great intellectual powers Buddha contended that "the deepest secrets of the world and of man are inaccessible to abstract, philosophical thinking" (Govinda, 1969, p. 36). In the Abhidhamma, Buddha divided knowledge into three categories:

Opinions, which are not guided by reason . . . but by desires (tanhā) . . . which are based on sense-impressions. The second is based on reasoning . . . and leads . . . to scientific and philosophical knowledge. . . . The third degree, the highest state of knowledge, is *"bodhi"* or illumination which is attained with the help of *pannindriya* [reason], the guiding principle of the mind, and is based on meditation *(bhavana)*, the intuitive state of consciousness *(jhana)* which means "the identity of the mind knowing with the object known" *(appana bhavana)*. . . . Intuitive knowledge . . . is . . . the experience of cosmic consciousness in which the Infinite is not only conceptualized but realized. [Govinda, 1969, pp. 41–42]

In addition to the antithetical views of reason and intuition as valid means of knowledge, there is a controversial point between East and West on the nature of the universe, between oneness and dualism. The philosophy of Judeo-Christianity postulates the separation of creator and creature, also of body and mind, good and evil. It considers continual warfare between opposites a natural element of the human predicament. Classical Greece taught the West the separation of man's intellect and senses. Dualism is the Western concept.

Buddha, however, during his enlightenment saw the oneness of all existence, the oneness of man with the universe, with all people and all things, the inherent unity of body and mind. He experienced the reconciliation of opposites—time and eternity, life and death, reason and intuition. Hence his doctrine of oneness.

Enlightenment means "seeing things as they are." During that memorable night under the bo tree Buddha saw into the nature of the universe, into ultimate reality. "Seeing *(darsana)* here involves not only sense perception—direct and immediate—but also a noetic quality" (Sangharakshita, 1970, p. 51). He saw that the universe is an orderly system, not chaotic, that as constructed it is perfect, though only the self-realized man sees this.

He also saw into the nature of being and the different kinds of existence. On the practical level they were *nirvana, samsara,* and *sunyata.* Kapleau explains nirvana as "changelessness, of inner Peace and Freedom. *Nirvana* . . . stands against *samsara,* i.e., birth-and-death. *Nirvana* . . . is also . . . a return to the original purity of the Buddha-nature after the dissolution of the physical body . . . to the . . . unconditioned state (1967, pp. 339–340). Buddha said, "Nirvana is bliss."

On this subject of being Suzuki writes,

Zen . . . has developed from the enlightenment experience of Sakyamuni Buddha. This experience is best expressed by the doctrine of *sunyata,* which means "emptiness" or void. . . . It is not a negative term . . . it is a positive concept. . . . *Sunyata* envelops . . . the whole world, and yet is every object existing in the world. The doctrine of *sunyata* is neither an immanentism nor a transcendentalism . . . it is both. . . . A contradiction is felt only when we are out of *sunyata.* . . . it is to be experienced and not conceptualized. . . . To be aware of *sunyata,* according to Zen, we have to transcend this dichotomous world. [1958, p. 261]

So as to knowledge, Buddha said that reason is limited as a means to ultimate truth, that intuition provides valid knowledge difficult to refute because it conforms to universal law—its source.

Other fields of study in philosophy in the West include aesthetics and the ideal form of beauty. This is not a subject of theoretical inquiry in Buddhist religious philosophy. Beauty is rather the result of awakening the creativity in the True-self or Buddha-nature inherent in all men in varying degree. Logic (and ideal methods of thought) is not pursued as a subject per se. Logic is employed as a useful tool, but reason is not considered a reliable guide to the absolute. Politics is not a subject of Buddhist inquiry, but the ideal society is implied as a possible consequence of universal enlightenment of mankind.

Ethics, ideal conduct, however, was a field of intense study by Buddha. Ethics involves the taking of the ten precepts—not to kill, lie, steal, and so on. It includes an intellectual confirmation of experiential truths revealed during his enlightenment and also the results of logical reasoning. It embraces the nature of man and his function in the universe, his relationship to spiritual and animal entities, the relation of mind to matter, the role of the senses and the body.

MAN'S NATURE AND FUNCTION

Buddha saw into the nature of man during his enlightenment. He realized intuitively that his own True-self was intrinsically perfect, that all men are inherently perfect—that is, every man possesses the potentials of perfection waiting to be actualized.

Man's function in the universe, Buddha concluded, is to awaken his Original-mind that has been covered over by the dust of intellection and delusions of the relative world, to identify with universal Consciousness through zazen and self-realization, then to live a life of selflessness, wisdom, and compassion and eventually to attain nirvana.

Ideal conduct necessitates liberation from attachment to the ego, reason, and the senses, yet, paradoxically, gratitude for the possession of a body, "the material aspect of mind," as Kapleau commented after his own enlightenment.

Man's relationship to higher spiritual and lower animal entities, and to matter, is one of unity, resulting automatically from the experience of the oneness of all things. It precludes killing of any sentient being, including animals and even insect life. As a consequence of this principle Buddhists do not eat meat.

DEATH, REBIRTH, KARMA

Other tenets in Buddhist and Zen philosophy also relate to ethics and ideal conduct. They involve the concepts of survival, karma, rebirth, and death. These evolved partially from Buddha's intuitive insights and experiences during enlightenment. He reported that he saw his own numerous rebirths and those of others resulting from each individual's previous acts and thoughts. This convinced him of the truth of the prevailing beliefs in rebirth and karma, the law of cause and effect. Logical reasoning did the rest.

Buddhism teaches that there is a form of survival because it recognizes one of the essential laws of physics—the law of conservation of energy. Yasutani says, "No energy is ever lost. [It merely changes form.] To claim that this tremendous force behind our human activities permanently disappears at the moment of death is like saying that one wave on the ocean does not produce another" (Kapleau, ed., 1967, p. 43).

Blofeld explains further:

The bundle of characteristics which constitute a man's personality does persist from life to life. . . . Thus the Buddhist equivalent of the Christian concept of a soul is a continuum. . . . Everything observable (matter and energy) is subject to change but never to creation out of nothing nor to total extinction. . . . the same laws (may) apply to what is not observed. [1970, pp. 55–56]

Kapleau warns that "no meaningful discussion of rebirth is possible without an understanding of *karma.*" Every intentional deed and thought of our past lives affects our present life, and our present voluntary deeds and thought will determine the nature of our future lives. To be free of the bondage of this cycle of birth-and-death is one of the chief objects of Buddhist practice. Karma, however, is not fatalism. Buddha condemned this idea. There is a fixed karma (such as being born a man instead of a woman) and there is a variable karma (such as the state of one's health over which one may exert control). It is always possible by one's own efforts to alter one's destiny to a limited extent.

The belief in survival and rebirth logically led to the doctrine that death is a transient state and not to be feared as a tragic end. It is inevitable, natural, and transitory. "Life and death present the same cyclic continuity observed in all aspects of nature" (Kapleau, 1971, p. xvii).

In brief, Zen philosophy postulates that there is a survival of energy and a rebirth in accord with the person's karma; consequently, both death and life are transitory. This law of causation (karma) lends incentive to seek an ethical and spiritual life. Only *full* enlightenment can terminate the bondage of death and rebirth on earth.

SUFFERING AND THE HUMAN PREDICAMENT

In addition to a fallacious concept of death, Buddha inquired into other causes of the human predicament. Why are men unhappy? He systematized this answer in his philosophy of suffering, its cause and alleviation.

Buddha stated in his first sermon after his enlightenment that he was not assured of his own self-realization until the Four Noble Truths, the Noble Eightfold Path, and the Middle Way became quite clear to him. These principles were incorporated into the Therevada school of Buddhism but not specifically into the Mahayana. Suzuki says they are "not in the scheme of Zen." Huston Smith, however, maintains that these are the basic postulates from which all of Buddha's teaching unfold.

Briefly, Buddha postulated in the *Moojjhima-Nikaya* (Goddard, 1970, p. 22) that the Four Noble Truths are: (1) life is mainly suffering; (2) suffering is caused by desire for the wrong things; (3) the way to extinguish suffering is to extinguish desire; (4) the way to extinguish desire is to follow the Eightfold Noble Path. This comprises rightness in: understanding, aspiration, speech, behavior, livelihood, effort, attentiveness, and concentration.

Suffering in the unenlightened man, Buddha believed, is caused chiefly by (1) death; (2) sickness and old age; (3) sorrow, despair, and pain; (4) birth; (5) the failure to obtain desires. Buddha observed that ordinary man's strongest desires were *not* to be subject to death, sickness and old age, sorrow and pain, *not* to be subject to failure in obtaining desires or obtaining happiness, even after such wishes are fulfilled (*Digha-Nikaya,* Goddard, 1970, pp. 23–56). Today, because of our value system in the West, individuals usually desire pleasure from wealth, power, fame, and success, or undying love and passion, or eternal youth and beauty or sometimes the acquisition of knowledge.

It is only too obvious that wealth is easily spent, lost, or stolen; power corrupts or is easily lost; fame is fickle and fleeting—love and passion, youth and beauty, more so. Knowledge changes—even scientific knowledge. Opinions, ideas, and political ideologies are perpetually perishing. Such goals in the relative world constitute conditioned reality and are impermanent. Man's desire for transient things and compulsive clinging to them is one cause of his suffering.

On the other hand, the universal law (dharma) is unconditioned and imperishable. Oneness with it brings the eternal into the now. This means it brings permanent joy. But why is man unable to derive greater happiness from transient things? It is because he expects from them the supreme happiness that only the permanent unconditioned is able to bestow. Another cause of his suffering, Huston Smith explains, is a selfish craving for private fulfillment. Man's egocentricity compels a desire for personal identity. Enlightenment, however, endows the individual with a new kind of identity—of the one with the All and the "vast expanse of universal life."

SOLUTION TO THE PROBLEM OF SUFFERING

Death, birth, sickness and old age, sorrow, pain, and despair, and failure to obtain permanent happiness from impermanent things cause our suffering. They seem to be the law of life. They cannot be changed. Govinda elucidates the problem: "The analysis of the symptoms of suffering shows that in each of them our desire is in conflict with the laws of existence, and as we are not able to change these laws, *the only thing that remains is to change our desire*" (1969, p. 53).

This transformation of desire is accomplished by the practice of zazen and the attainment of enlightenment. For the enlightened man no longer desires wealth and fame and power. He is no longer *compulsively* attached to personal love and sensuous pleasures, prolongation of youth and beauty, or knowledge gained by rational methods. He no longer fears old age, sickness or death or poverty. His joy lies in his newly awakened Buddha-nature, his identity with universal Consciousness, his harmony with his fellow men, and his desire to serve them selflessly. He is at home in the universe.

In other words, the chief cause of man's suffering and delusion in the relative world, according to Buddha, is that somehow mankind has become estranged from his own Essential-self and from the laws of the universe (dharma). Consequently, if the desires of the ordinary man are a prime cause of his suffering, the way to extinguish suffering is to extinguish his desire for transient things by awakening his desire for the permanent and universal.

Zen finds that after the individual experiences self-realization, he follows the Noble Eightfold Path effortlessly and the Middle Way naturally even if he has never heard of them. The Middle Way is the mean between self-indulgence and asceticism, between making no effort and too great an effort, between free will and blind chance.

Certain skeptical intellectuals may derive deep satisfaction from theoretical knowledge of Zen Buddhism. To experience the benefits of Zen, however, not everyone finds it necessary to accept or understand its philosophy. Zen masters teach that all that is necessary is to practice prolonged zazen with ardor, feel faith in the Buddha's enlightenment and the possibility of one's own self-realization. The aspirant may thereby learn during the actualization of his noblest potentials that many of the philosophic assumptions of Buddhism are ultimately capable of experiential verification by the Seeker.

Buddha's disciples asked him repeatedly if man has an immortal soul, if there is a god, if man lives on after death. He refused to answer such questions. He asserted that such speculations were futile. It was more profitable to work on one's practice of meditation. He did, however, state in the Pali scripture, Udana: "There is an Unborn, Unoriginated, Uncreated, Unformed. . . . If there were not,

... escape from the world of the born, the unoriginated, the created, the formed, would not be possible" (Goddard, 1970, p. 32).

The philosophy of Buddhism is empirical in that its principles derive chiefly from experience, though observation and logic play their role. If the purpose of philosophy is to recognize unity in diversity, and if the purpose of religion is to attain self-realization and participation in the universal Consciousness in which all opposites are reconciled—matter and mind, self and others, subject and object, good and evil, reason and intuition—then Buddhist religious philosophy might be said to have achieved its purpose.

CONSCIOUSNESS

The philosophy of Zen Buddhism becomes especially interwoven with psychology when the study of consciousness is approached. What does Zen consider the basic nature of human consciousness to be? Zen experience has led to the conclusion that "human consciousness arises from pure consciousness and is indistinguishable from it—the Void-universe. The life of the individual is linked to the Formless Self. Man's life is like a wave of the ocean, apparently separate from it but having arisen from the sea will return to become the sea, then to emerge again as a new life in the next rebirth" (Kapleau, 1971, p. 327).

ZEN AND WESTERN PSYCHOLOGY

Perhaps the spiritual psychology of Zen may be clarified by an exposition of its parallels with Western psychology—first with transpersonal or growth psychology of the unconscious, then with the orthodox psychology of the conscious mind. In Zen even the conscious mind and behavior are influenced by the awakening of the various levels of the unconscious. In fact, consciousness arises from the unconscious, according to Jung.

The view of the unconscious held by Zen, Jung, and Houston and Masters will be presented separately. Then, employing Houston and Masters's discoveries as a scientific frame of reference, the other systems will be related to it—each illuminating and strengthening the other.

All three disciplines have established techniques and systems for inducing self-realization. All three offer data concerning the psychological processes and their results. Other transpersonal psychologists such as James, Bucke, and Maslow have contributed invaluable data on the results primarily, not on the process, of actualizing man's potentials. They investigated the spontaneous variety of self-realization, not that which is induced. If distinction between the two varieties is borne in mind it may prevent confusion. We are discussing here primarily the induced variety.

In all three systems—Zen, Jung, and Houston and Masters—the goal of self-realization, the psychological process, and the transformation of the personality seem similar. Methods and means, however, terminology and the subsequent intellectual interpretations, differ bewilderingly. Even the views concerning the location of consciousness are divergent. Unlike the West, Zen does not consider the brain the sole seat of consciousness. In Japanese "the word *kokoro* [mind] . . . also means 'heart,' 'spirit,' 'psyche,' or 'soul'. . . . Mind with a capital 'M' stands for absolute Reality. From the standpoint of Zen experience, Mind (or mind) is total awareness" (Kapleau, 1967, p. 338).

Buddhism and Hinduism also consider that yoga has demonstrated the existence of other centers of consciousness called psychic centers of energy or chakras. Govinda explains them as the focal points in which cosmic and psychic energies merge into bodily qualities, which in turn are transmuted again into psychic forces.

CLASSES AND LEVELS OF CONSCIOUSNESS

Buddhism distinguishes eight classes of consciousness. The first six are the senses of sight, hearing, smell, taste, touch, and thought (intellect). The seventh is manas (mind), which has two aspects, the lower concerned with the world of sense, the higher illumined by intuition. Manas acts as a conveyor of sensory experience to the eighth level of subconsciousness. The eighth class is universal consciousness *(alaya-vijnana)*. The first six classes involve the conscious mind and the relation of subject and object and are linked to birth and death. The seventh and eighth classes involve the conscious and unconscious, and when the eighth state is attained there is no more bodily birth and death.

Zazen and satori are psychological and spiritual processes occurring in the various levels of the unconscious. According to Yasutani, Zen divides the subconscious or unconscious into two main levels of experience—*makyo* and enlightenment. Makyo includes the images, visions, fantasies, and horrible monsters (in some cases) that may appear during zazen.

Based on empirical evidence, both the observed and the experiential, the suggestion is offered here that makyo appears to embrace the first three levels of the unconscious, and enlightenment occurs in the fourth and deepest level; the four levels of the unconscious in Zen might be termed: (1) imagery; (2) neurosis (if any); (3) historical and symbolical imagery; (4) self-realization that in rare instances rises to nirvana.

IMAGERY

When the first level of the unconscious is activated it often may project count-less, apparently meaningless images from memory. One recent example from personal experience comes to mind. It occurred during a three-day sesshin (inten-sive Zen training period). For twelve consecutive hours, from 5:00 A.M. until 5:00 P.M., thousands of beautiful images bombarded me. The blank wall in front of me was covered with moving colorful images like a continuous motion picture. They filled my entire field of vision, obliterating the meditation hall (zendo) and the other aspirants practicing zazen all around me.

Paraded before me were images of pink satin damask, figured green wallpaper, castles, gold statues of Buddha, a bust of Buddha with the face of my teacher, Mary holding the infant Jesus, a stage with actors, a green jungle with playful monkeys—all with a small bright spotlight playing across them. A very large disconcerting white enamel fern leaf glittering like silver was encrusted with amethysts. A detached arm and hand gestured wildly, turned black, every finger suddenly outlined with golden light. These images undulated ceaselessly—mad-deningly. I also beheld a small mythical golden dragon that completely mystified me at the moment, as it was not something once seen and remembered. Later I learned its meaning in Houston and Masters.

This surrender of the rational mind and opening of the door into the transra-tional is a deep, nerve-shaking experience. It shook my body uncontrollably and caused deep painful sobbing—hour after hour. Its effect was exhausting yet exhilarating.

NEUROSIS (IF ANY)

In this age of the "unloved generation" in America, a Zen center composed primarily of young people affords evidence of makyo that sometimes includes memories of childhood miseries and neuroses.

Yasutani warned beginners not to cling to any vision, fantasies, or prophecies or be alarmed by any terrible things that might appear from the unconscious. To dwell on these makyo may be a hindrance to progress. Practice should be con-tinued more devotedly because it has been shown that intensive zazen may alleviate some neurotic problems. For zazen may cause the aspirant to relive painfully his childhood problems and even to analyze them and to find a solution. Sometimes a difficult neurosis requires psychiatric treatment.

Training in Zen, long before enlightenment is attained, may unexpectedly come to the trainee's rescue in moments of crisis. For instance, a young woman of twenty-four returned home for Christmas. Her father, with whom she had always had a difficult relationship, drank a great deal on Christmas Eve. He forced his daughter against the wall, placed his hands around her throat, and harangued her angrily because she was living with a man to whom she was not yet married. In the past she would have felt fear and hate and retorted angrily. To her surprise she now felt great compassion for him, spoke calmly, and the possible tragedy was averted. She reports that her training in zazen enabled her to cope with a painful situation because it imbued her with compassion and courage. A Zen center provides many such reports of vastly improved relations between young people and their parents—whether neurotic or otherwise.

Some of the young members of the Zen Center of Rochester may unconsciously regard their spiritual teacher or the institution of the Zen Center itself as a surrogate father. Either transference may deflect their emotional dependence away from their father. Many marry while in Zen training and often transfer the images of their parents to husband or wife. These transferences are well recognized in Freudian and Jungian psychology.

Jung stated that all religions are a form of therapy. In some cases the Zen spiritual teacher in the West may himself recommend a competent psychiatrist, preferably one of the rare species who is religiously oriented.

In the Western world, the psychology of Freud apparently must be introduced into all religions, as the Christian churches realized to their dismay more than twenty years ago when the clergy formed a national organization with psychoanalysts.

Freud's special field was the neurosis in the personal unconscious or the second level of the unconscious. His successors have modified his views. In the book he wrote just before his death, however, he still attributed neurosis to repressed sexuality in childhood or infancy: "The symptoms of neuroses are exclusively . . . either a substitutive satisfaction of some sexual impulse or measures to prevent such satisfaction" (1949, p. 85).

When Freud's patients lay on a couch, they not only recollected but also relived painfully the repressed memories of their infancy and childhood in relation to their parents and/or siblings. He interpreted dreams as a clue to the meaning of the contents of their unconscious. All Americans are familiar with the symbolic meaning of a post representing the phallus, a cave representing the womb; and so forth. By free association, unconscious material was brought up into consciousness. Verbalization and understanding were supposed to cure the neurosis.

Freud's system was not designed to activate the inner spiritual development originating in deeper levels. He alerted Western society, however, to the presence and dangers of neuroses which appear to be more tragically prevalent today in the younger "unloved generation" than ever before in American history. His psychoanalysis throws an illuminating light on one form of makyo—that arising from the second or neurotic level during zazen.

Freud's followers have modified his theories of sexuality. One of them, Dr.

Flanders Dunbar, expresses today's prevailing feeling about the causes of neurosis:

It soon ceases to be surprising to the psychiatrist how frequently his patients turn out to have been children . . . rejected by their parents. . . . [She found that numerous psychomatic ills—allergies, hay fever, asthma, eczema—were traceable to lack of parental love. Or paradoxically enough occasionally "smother love" was the culprit.] The typical sufferers from skin disease have a deep-seated emotional conflict between desire for affection and fear of being hurt if they seek it. . . . They have been hurt in childhood at the same time that they developed their strong craving for affection [Dunbar, 1947, pp. 7, 191].

Sometimes the skin will literally "weep" instead of the eyes. Death, divorce, or quarreling of parents often produces neurotic children.

HISTORIC AND SYMBOLIC IMAGERY

At this level occasionally purposive images from history occur that seem symbolic and helpful to Zen students. DeLancey Kapleau during her enlightenment experience beheld a Roman centurion, who seemed to her a symbol of courage, with whom she apparently identified and who aided her immensely.

The four levels of the unconscious do not inevitably yield their contents in logical sequential order. Apparently, being over thirty-five, I omitted the second level and penetrated to the third at the end of the twelve-hour activation of the first level. At that time I beheld projected images of Egyptians and Jews of Biblical times in their striped costumes walking endlessly around a well and gazing at me expectantly with great intensity. But it was nearly five o'clock. The bell soon rang for supper, interrupting this scene at the well which I was unable to interpret.

In zazen it is usually when the third level is liberated that supernormal psychic powers may sometimes manifest themselves. Zen in general and Roshi Kapleau in particular discourage the cultivation of such powers until after one is fully enlightened and a proper judge of the appropriate way to use powers for the benefit of others. They are considered an obstacle in the path toward self-realization, partly because they may inflate the aspirant's self-esteem. Ego is the enemy.

Buddha warns of fifty of the commonest kinds of makyo. Yasutani says:

The disciple may develop the faculty of seeing through solid objects. . . . When the thought waves which wax and wane on the surface of the sixth class of consciousness are partly calmed, residual elements of past experiences "lodged" in the seventh and eighth classes of consciousness bob up sporadically . . . conveying the feeling of expanded reality.
. . . Such visions are certainly a sign that you are at a crucial point in your sitting, and

that if you exert yourself to the utmost, you can surely experience *kensho* [a mild form of enlightenment]. [Kapleau, ed., 1967, pp. 39–41]

In the Visuddhimagga (a summary of the Abhidhamma made by Buddhaghosa of the sections on meditation and consciousness) there are listed such psychic powers as clairvoyance, telepathy, walking on water, and so forth. Goleman (Chapter 5), referring to Buddhaghosa's discussion, states that "Western science at present cannot reconcile the possibility of [these states]." The Zen trainee, however, to whom they happen, cannot fail to find them awe-inspiring and incredible, and also a means of increasing his respect for the powers of zazen tenfold, even if no scientific explanation is yet available.

Recently an incredible experience was visited upon me. It may be significant that this psychic power occurred immediately following another very deep experience of resistance and expiation. Before this seven-day sesshin began and also during the first three days, the resistance of my rational mind was stultifying. As I sat in the zendo supposedly concentrating on my practice, I heard the interior dialogue of my rational mind: All my life I've fought for my freedom. Why am I now allowing someone else to tell me when to get up (at 4:30 A.M.), when to eat breakfast (after two hours of sitting), when to bathe, what to wear, what to do, what to think? That's why I left home as a girl—as a protest against parental rules, school, and church. That's why I have rebelled for years against the invisible pressure society exerts on women—concerning fashion, conventions, and morals. Why have I now, like a schoolgirl, deliberately submitted myself to a training school, an institution, with the strictest rules I ever encountered? *I am a fool!*

Despite such intellectual rebellion, however, I continued to sit, and finally was able to concentrate. As I stared at the blank surface of the low divider wall in front of me I suddenly beheld a row of people—my mother (dead), my brother, and a young woman, my friendly enemy. They were all gazing at me with sad accusing eyes. I knew I had hurt them in real life in various ways, though not always intentionally. Suddenly such powerful repentance and desire to expiate seized me that my very body shook uncontrollably. Sobs tore up from the depths of my being. It was like tearing up the roots of my ego, annihilating lifelong delusions of my own goodness. This emotional storm continued hour after hour. I was oblivious, blind, to everything and everybody in the zendo.

After five hours two monitors came and lifted me up. My body was so heavy and my legs so weak I was unable to walk. They carried me upstairs and placed me on the bed. After an hour's rest I returned to the zendo and commenced concentration with renewed assurance. As I gazed at the low wooden dividing wall in front of me it seemed to abruptly turn a beautiful luminous blue with lights flickering at the lower edge. Then it changed to thick silvery ice, next to gauze.

Then I saw right through the wall and beheld two men sitting on the other side. I was incredulous even while this phenomenon was occurring. When it happened again the next day I accepted it as makyo, a psychic power, encouraging, but not worth clinging to.

The experience itself was so convincing I needed no rational verification. Furthermore, no trainee during a tense solemn religious session like a sesshin would dream of disrupting her own practice or that of the fifty other aspirants in the zendo. She would be severely reprimanded, if not thrown out of the sangha.

I related the experience of my expiation to the girl who was my friendly enemy. At once all the latent hostility between us that had lasted for two years disappeared and a firm foundation for our friendship established itself. Zazen accomplished what I had been unable to accomplish alone.

SELF-REALIZATION LEVEL

In Zen the activation of the fourth level often induces the religious experience. The individual's deeper unconscious feels as if it merges with Pure Consciousness, or Formless Self.

A contemporary illustration can be found in the enlightenment experience of Philip Kapleau. It occurred in Japan after five years of pain and arduous effort in and out of monasteries. One day during a *dokusan* (private interview) with Yasutani-roshi, his spiritual teacher, Kapleau found that:

All at once the roshi, the room . . . disappeared in a dazzling stream of illumination and I felt myself bathed in a delicious unspeakable delight. . . . For a fleeting eternity I was alone—I alone was. . . . Then the roshi swam into view. Our eyes met and we burst out laughing. . . .

I exclaimed more to myself than to the roshi, "I have it! I know! There is nothing, absolutely nothing. I am everything and everything is nothing." (Kapleau, 1967, p. 228).

Later Zen Master Yasutani told Kapleau, "It is your duty to carry Zen to the West."

Many descriptions of the enlightenment-event can be found in Buddhist literature—Japanese, Chinese, and Sanskrit. The four levels of the unconscious traversed in zazen and satori, with variations of course, seem fairly well differentiated: the levels of meaningless imagery; neuroses, when present; purposive imagery of historic and symbolic events or persons; and self-realization.

JUNG'S PSYCHOLOGY AND ZEN

Does Jung's analytical psychology confirm or contradict the premise that there are four levels of the unconscious such as those found in Zen Buddhism?

Jung has said that the psychological methods of the East "have been developed to a degree which simply put all Western attempts along these lines into the shade" (1958, p. 554). He agreed with the Eastern assertion that the Universal Mind is without form, yet is the source of all forms, and that when the rational mind is quieted, "the Zen aspirant receives an answer—the only true answer from Nature herself. Then the meaning of *satori* is understood."

Jung divided the unconscious into two main levels—the Personal level (the seat of neuroses, if any) and the Collective Unconscious which, however, includes the purposive Historical and Symbolic Images (or level three as in Zen) and the religious experience of Self-realization (or level four).

IMAGERY

Imagery per se does not seem to play a role in Jung's process of inducing self-realization in his patients by analytical psychology. Images that arise, as in dreams, are used as indicators of activity at deeper levels.

THE PERSONAL LEVEL

Jung states: "The personal unconscious contains lost memories, painful ideas that are repressed (i.e., forgotten on purpose), subliminal perceptions by which are meant sense-perceptions that were not strong enough to reach consciousness, and finally, contents that are not ripe for consciousness" (1953, p. 65). "The conscious realization of unconscious compensations, transform[s] one's mental condition and thus [one] arrive[s] at a solution of painful neurotic conflicts" (1958, p. 491).

He says, "For young people a liberation from the past may be enough. . . . the life urge will do the rest" (1953, p. 59). Today this may not always be true. Members of the younger generation passionately seek spiritual experience, hoping in the process to alleviate their neuroses—if any. Jung says that the "neuroses of the young generally come from the abnormal dependence on the real or imaginary parents" (1953, p. 58). "If ever we succeed in liberating young people from the past. . . . they always transfer the imagos of their parents to more suitable substitute figures. . . . The feeling that clung to the mother now passes to the wife, and the father's authority passes to respected teachers and superiors or to institutions" (1953, pp. 59–60).

It was well known that Jung preferred to work with patients on the deeper spiritual levels, not the personal and neurotic level. He also interpreted patients' dreams at all stages of the journey into the self as valuable signposts.

THE HISTORIC OR SYMBOLIC LEVEL (part of the collective unconscious)

The penetration of this level often precedes the fourth level. Jung observed that all sorts of ancient mythical and Judeo-Christian occurrences and archetypes appear in the dreams, visions, waking fantasies, and projected symbolic images of modern man—even in normal persons, who constituted a third of his patients and who were seeking a meaning to life. Among his numerous case histories the most famous is that of Mrs. Christina Morgan (now deceased), who experienced vivid and numerous projections on the Symbolic and Historical level. She experienced in detail her own participation in the dramatic origin of the Mithraic religion and the Christian. Jung interprets her experiences of these inner events in *Spring* (1960–68) in great detail, illustrated by her paintings. The projection of such symbolic events and participation in them seems very helpful to the patients in solving their own problems.

THE COLLECTIVE UNCONSCIOUS OR LEVEL OF SELF-REALIZATION

In the psychotherapy of Jung, the primary aim is to arouse the deeper level of the Collective unconscious. He stated that:

the personal level ends at the earliest memories of infancy . . . but the collective layer comprises the pre-infantile period, that is, the residues of ancestral life. . . . When psychic energy regresses going beyond the period of early infancy, and breaks into the legacy of ancestral life then our interior spiritual world, whose existence we never suspected, opens out. [1953, p. 76]

Psychological experience has shown time and again that certain contents issue from a psyche that is more complete than consciousness. They often contain a superior analysis or insight or knowledge which consciousness has not been able to produce. We have a suitable word for such occurrences—intuition. . . . Everything must be done to help the unconscious to reach the conscious mind. . . . For this purpose I employ a method of active imagination, which consists in special training for switching off consciousness . . . thus giving the unconscious contents a chance to develop. [Jung, 1958, pp. 41, 537]

Jung found the problems of the adult, however, different from those of the young, unless the adult had remained infantile too long. "To the man in the second half of life [after thirty-five] the development . . . no longer proceeds via the solution of infantile ties . . . it proceeds via the problem of opposites" (1953, p. 60).

In the un-self-realized person there is continual conflict of opposites—body and mind, self and others, the individual and the universe, good and evil, reason and intuition, the phenomenal world and the spiritual world. In the fully individuated or self-realized person all opposites are reconciled and he is able to become the Whole person.

The eighteen volumes of Jung's collected works (1953–1958) contain many living examples. From nearly fifty years of practice with hundreds of people from all over the world he deduced his conclusions. Many of his patients became individuated, attained the religious experience, and witnessed the subjective light —a light even Jung has not explained scientifically. No one has. He observed that few of his patients were cured entirely of their neurosis until they had the great spiritual experience; in other words, until their lives ceased to be guided by the neurotic distortions operating in conjunction with their selfish, egotistic conscious minds. Instead they were thereafter guided daily by their awakened collective unconscious, their intuition functioning harmoniously with their conscious mind in tune with the cosmic order.

The three levels of the unconscious in Jung seem to be quite similar to levels two, three, and four in Zen.

Jung believed that the analyst is unable to guide a patient to heights (or depths) greater than he himself has attained. Without a self-realized analyst, no self-realized patient. Jung describes his own encounter with the unconscious and his self-realization in his autobiography *Memories, Dreams, Reflections* (1961).

ZEN AND HOUSTON AND MASTERS'S LEVELS

How do the scientific discoveries of Houston and Masters concerning the unconscious confirm or contradict the concept of four levels of the unconscious found in Zen and the three in Jung? Houston and Masters's experiments were conducted in a laboratory using scientific methods and are repeatable, public, and verifiable. That is the reason why their categorization is employed here as a frame of reference, and both Jung and Zen fitted into this frame.

As a surgeon resorts to a dangerous but effective scalpel to explore man's internal bodily organs, so this wife and husband team employed a dangerous but invaluable instrument, psychedelic drugs, to explore the various levels of the unconscious. Their experiments were performed before hallucinogenic drugs were considered as injurious as they are today. Their experiments are reported in *Varieties of Psychedelic Experiences* (1967).

They discovered four levels in the unconscious, which they term: (1) the Sensory; (2) the Recollective-analytic; (3) the Symbolic; (4) the Integral.

Houston and Masters carefully screened 206 subjects to obtain average, "normal" persons. They administered LSD to the majority and peyote to a few. Then they expertly guided each subject on his "trip." Of the four levels of the unconscious thus revealed, the first to manifest itself was usually the Sensory level.

THE SENSORY LEVEL

[The subject] may be confronted with a succession of vivid eidetic images brilliantly colored and intricately detailed. . . . [Many objects may be studded with jewels, often they undulate]. . . . The eidetic images [are those] . . . previously recorded by the brain or . . . a part of the phylogenetic (or "Racial") inheritance. . . . The images are most often of persons, animals, architecture, and landscapes. Strange creatures from legend, folklore, myth. . . . [On the sensory level] the images are almost always meaningless. . . . This type of functionless . . . image we have termed the *aesthetic* image, so distinguishing it from the highly meaningful . . . purposive images met with on the deeper drug-state levels. [1967, pp. 143, 156, 157]

Apparently trivial activity of the early images may be the means of one's descent to a deeper level.

RECOLLECTIVE ANALYTIC LEVEL

When this level was penetrated, Houston and Masters observed:

Images no longer are only aesthetic but become unconsciously purposive. . . . The usual boundaries between consciousness and the unconscious have been breached. . . . [The subject may] experience the emotional as well as the other contents of important forgotten or repressed events . . . as child or even infant. . . . [He] may discover that he misinterpreted the real event at the time of its occurrence. . . . He may find that what he has long remembered as an actual occurrence . . . never happened at all but was only a fantasy. . . . personal problems . . . past experience may be lived through with much accompanying emotion. . . . The subject see[s] what needs to be done as he has never seen it before. [His journey may be therapeutic . . . including the remission of some symptoms.]

An example on this level was S-1, a businessman of about fifty, who after the session confessed that at the time he had been on the brink of suicide. During the session he regressed to an infantile state, curling himself up into the foetal position, in which he remained without speaking for thirty minutes. . . . [Later he explained that during that period he felt] he had "died" and been "reborn" . . . leaving behind all the torments of the old life. [1967, pp. 184, 185, 144, 188]

THE SYMBOLIC LEVEL

Houston and Masters found that a third level of the unconscious was sometimes released by psychedelics, especially with careful guidance and suggestion. Of their 206 subjects, 40 penetrated to this deeper layer.

The symbolic images are predominantly historical, legendary, mythical, ritualistic and "archetypal." The subject may experience a profound . . . sense of continuity with evolutionary and historic process. He may act out myths and legends and pass through initiations and ritual observances often seemingly structured precisely in terms of his own most urgent needs. . . . Where the symbolic dramas unfold, the individual finds facets of his own existence revealed in the person of Prometheus or Parsifal, Lucifer or Oedipus, Faust or Don Juan . . . or in rites of passage. [1967, pp. 147, 214]

S-2, for example, was a twenty-four-year-old Jewish college graduate working in a law office. During the session he felt he was engaged in an initiation rite with other young men being flagellated by older men. The guide asked him if he minded the beating. He said it was necessary if he was to be reborn. "The mystery of initiation (whether culturally staged or psychedelically induced) can deliver the young man from shallow and adolescent understanding. . . . He must die to his shallow nature and rise to his deepened one" (1967, pp. 220–221).

Man's nature appears to need rituals and rites through which he experiences catharsis, symbolic death, and rebirth. Psychedelics offer one means of inducing them.

THE INTEGRAL LEVEL

In Houston and Masters's experiments, only 11 out of 206 subjects descended to the fourth level. "On this level ideation, images, body sensation (if any) and emotion are fused . . . culminating in a sense . . . of self-transformation, religious enlightenment and, possibly, mystical union. The subject here experiences what he regards as a confrontation with the Ground of Being, God . . . Essence or Fundamental Reality. . . . Validation is . . . in the . . . after effects . . . the behaviorai and other changes" (1967, p. 148).

With unjust brevity only one of their examples is offered here:

. . . S-3, in his late thirties, is a successful psychologist who has received much recognition in his field. [Under LSD he later said to his guide] "I had the sense . . . at birth . . . as if somebody wanted me to die. . . . I feel also that my father flung me snarling and gnashing my teeth like some kind of dragon or mad dog against the whole material world.". . .

He always felt himself to be "alien," not really a member of the human race. . . . He felt an irresistible attraction toward what others regarded as evil. . . . he was an atheist with scientific interests. [1967, pp. 268–287]

He manipulated others and wished to make others evil just as he was evil so that they could accept him. He was promiscuous, having hundreds of lovers. Anxiety, however, caused him to drink heavily. He was seized by rage whenever he found himself in a subordinate position. This rage, he realized, came to the surface as symptoms.

Under the influence of LSD and careful guidance he traversed the sensory, the recollective-analytic, and the symbolic levels, having many profound experiences as he approached the integral level. They were not always in orderly fashion. Sometimes he plunged to deep levels, then came up and descended again. Like Lucifer, he wanted to be God and had been punished by his pride. He fought against God in an effort to preserve his own identity. During the session he launched into a scathing attack upon Christ. Once he spoke from a deep quiet place: " 'Everything is . . . serpentine, often undulating.' He perceived everything as 'potentially beautiful' in its own right and as formless matter. . . . 'I was told that matter was evil. This teaching I have associated with Christianity.' " (1967, pp. 286–287)

At one point when he described his infancy he sat with his thumb in his mouth. He went to the bathroom and looking into the mirror felt his was no longer the face of the devil. . . . Now his face was surrounded with light and he felt for the first time hope for himself —hope that he might be delivered from all the punishments he felt he had to bear for what he had never done.

S now . . . physically felt himself to be standing in a brilliantly illumined hall where shone a preternatural light . . . , "an indescribable blending of white and gold." The Presence of God was tangible and overpowering . . . [there were] many complicated symbols encrusted with precious stones. . . . The initiation, S now understood, was for . . . investing him with "The Order of the Lion." [He had seen and identified with the Lion as an archetype and now identified with it as a creature of wisdom. He asked questions of God and came to realize that] "I can love God without being diminished as a man any more than a lion need be diminished by loving a human person." [1967, pp. 273–294]

He wept tears of gladness for the first time in his life. He felt wonderfully free. He had a sense of being reborn, energized, better coordinated, transformed, integrated, and happy. All his senses were more acute. He experienced a sense of unity and harmony in his relation with externals. His mind was stimulated. In the days that followed he noticed that his work capacity was greater and that his literary output increased. He felt no wish to be promiscuous. He fell in love and was to be married soon. One year after his psychedelic session he still felt and behaved as if transformed.

If we accept Houston and Masters's discoveries as a scientific frame of reference, how do we relate Zen and Jung to it?

THE SENSORY LEVEL

In Zen the contents of the first level, imagery, bear a startling resemblance to those of the sensory level in Houston and Masters—the same kind and sequence of images. Zen labels such images as "makyo" and dangerous to be clung to. Houston and Masters believe they may be remembered and meaningless. They do not appear in Jung. If they are remembered images why do unfamiliar jeweled objects appear and why do they often undulate? Why golden dragons?

Aldous Huxley found that such imagery is universal and has a prescribed order of appearance. He believed it has meaning. It is: "A manifestation . . . of the non-human otherness of the universe. . . . The raw material for this creation is provided by the visual experience of ordinary life. . . . [Such images constitute the mind's antipodes.] Every paradise abounds in gems. [Jewels have the power of transporting the beholder to the other world, to paradise]" (1955, pp. 13–19).

Be that as it may, these sensory images apparently indicate that a breach has been made in the highly resistant psychological barrier between the conscious mind and the unconscious. Yet the psychological union is very difficult to achieve by conscious effort.

THE RECOLLECTIVE-ANALYTIC LEVEL

The neurotic level in Zen and the personal level in Jung seem to show little divergence from the recollective-analytic in Houston and Masters—each involving problems with parents and/or siblings stemming from infancy and early childhood. A neurosis is a neurosis is a neurosis.

THE SYMBOLIC LEVEL

This third level is activated in Zen, although the evidence is slight. In Houston and Masters and Jung its existence is frequently manifested and its contents are dramatic and colorful.

THE INTEGRAL LEVEL

From the evidence, the level of self-realization in Zen and of individuation in Jung both appear to be similar to the integral level in Houston and Masters, though doubtless each discipline might dispute this. So the four levels of the unconscious penetrated in self-realization seem to be virtually the same in Zen and Jung (with exception of the first level) and Houston and Masters. Various means and methods are employed to arrive at, apparently, similar ends.

Incidentally, new light has been shed by science on the location of the unconscious. In the dialogue between Raymond Prince and Roland Fischer in the Bucke Society *Newsletter-Review,* Fischer states:

> The right hemisphere [of the brain] is concerned with nonverbal information processing, visuo-spatial gestalts . . . music, imagery . . . it is our analogical, intuitive mind. The left hemisphere is concerned with analytical, rational . . . survival-subserving, decision demanding tasks and information processing, represented in language, speech and arithmetic. The two hemispheres are separated and mediated by the *corpus callosum.* . . . Within this "one brain-two minds division," the left hemisphere is called "dominant.". . . "Dominant" . . . is restricted mostly to righthanded and about half of the lefthanded people. [V, 1 and 2, Spring, 1972, pp. 40–43]

Some day intuition may be regarded even in the West as equally important as reason. Buddha, Jung, and Houston and Masters foresaw the unconscious as a counterbalance to the conscious mind.

But what of the psychological process? Are the similarities not inevitable in the Zen, Jung, and Houston and Masters systems of actualizing man's noblest potentials? Each offers a technique for activating man's unconscious, which functions according to the fixed laws of the human psychology. This involves quieting the conscious mind and awakening the unconscious, unawareness of the physical world, death of the ego, seeing a subjective light, merging of individual consciousness with universal consciousness (briefly, not permanently, as a rule), ecstasy, oneness, intuitive insights, wisdom, identity with mankind, and afterward presumably a transformation of character, behavior, values, and life style.

It is the results of each system of self-realization that might develop into a controversial issue. In all three systems the consequences may be similar in kind but vastly different in degree, varying in sequence, quality, and duration. The truth may be presented explicitly or implicitly.

Do the results depend on the *ultimate* goal following self-realization? The goal of Jung's analytical psychology is the religious experience and individuation or wholeness of the patient—not specifically service to others. The aim of Houston and Masters was primarily research, though it involved many benefits to their subjects and in some cases induction of the religious experience. Service to mankind was not an objective.

The final goal of Zen is not enlightenment but a desire to dedicate one's life to service to all sentient beings on this earth. Zen records reveal such lives among monks and nuns in the monasteries and in laymen such as the famous householder Vimalakirti. Even laymen who are still in training at Zen centers today often find themselves, to their own surprise, living more selflessly for others then they ever dreamed possible. Also there exist numerous Bodhisattvas, those persons who have attained full enlightenment yet deny themselves the final bliss of nirvana in order to assist others in attaining enlightenment.

In other systems, self-realization may be full or shallow—that is, there may be continuous or intermittent identification with ultimate reality. In Zen the goal is full enlightenment, that is, experience of Being as distinct from Becoming. Also, nirvana is regarded as the highest state of consciousness, after which there is birthlessness and deathlessness. This state is not mentioned in Jung or Houston and Masters.

Does the role of the teacher, analyist, or guide influence the results? Jung and Houston and Masters guide and aid their patients or subjects almost continuously. Zen is a method of self-effort. The teacher is dedicated to the policy that the trainee must learn by personal experience. So doubtless Zen may feel that its strenuous methods and means of self-help may produce more continuously religious and selfless lives, more enduring compassion, more innate wisdom, more final bliss.*

To sum up, it seems evident that there is a parallelism in self-realization in the levels of the unconscious which are penetrated, the psychological process, and the kind of results, though not necessarily the degree, of Zen, Jung, and Houston and Masters. Dissimilarities occur in means and methods, terminology, quality and duration of achievement, and dedication to service. Nevertheless, if a Western scientific skeptic doubted the validity of Eastern Zen he might feel reassured by the correspondence of Zen psychology to that of Jung and Houston and Masters.

ZEN AND ORTHODOX WESTERN PSYCHOLOGY

Is Zen psychology concerned solely with the unconscious or also with the conscious mind and the harmonious union of the two opposites to create the whole man? What, in short, is the relation of Zen to the orthodox psychology of the conscious mind in the West?

Many textbooks define psychology as a science of human behavior (deriving from the mind), usually observed during scientific experiments in a laboratory. Today, however, psychology is becoming the spearhead of the disciplines engaged in research in all aspects of the human mind, conscious and unconscious, normal and pathological. It also is concerned with the integrated man.

---

*Those who want to compare the healthy normal psychology of the religious experience with unhealthy abnormal psychosis and infantile regression, as some psychologists do, might be referred to my essay "The Mystical Experience—Facts and Values" (Owens, 1972).

Buddha states that "getting rid of the discriminating mind removes the cause of errors." Stilling the discriminating conscious mind is certainly one objective of zazen. Is this a stumbling block, an irreconcilable difference between Zen and orthodox psychology? Much of the baffling language of Buddhism in general, and Zen in particular, however, refers to the brief enlightenment-*event,* not to the years of the enlightened-*state* that ensues. It is certainly true that in the fleeting moment of the enlightenment-event the discriminating mind is obliterated. There is a vast nothingness, a void, an emptiness—which paradoxically enough contains everything. During the enlightenment-*event* one is unable to see, think, talk, eat, walk, or function on the phenomenal plane. During the enlightenment-*state,* however, which follows the numinous event, one returns to consciousness of the body and its needs, of society and one's relations to it. Discriminating thought returns, but it is no longer dominant.

Zen embraces the whole mind; consequently a study of the psychology of the enlightened man's discriminating conscious mind cannot be separated from a study of his intuitive unconscious and the Universal mind with which it identifies. The rational mind, after enlightenment, functions in harmony with both. All three become integrated in the individual man.

Briefly treated here will be some of the chief agreements and disagreements between Zen and orthodox psychology concerning the following subjects which are the areas of psychological research: personality, its structure and functioning, emotion, motivation, memory, learning, mind-body relationship, psychopathology, perception, social relationships, cognitive processes, new faculties, and altered states of consciousness.

PERSONALITY

Personality to the academic psychologist is the complexities of characteristics that distinguish one individual from another. These characteristics, it is believed, are determined by inherited predispositions, innate abilities, culture, and learning in the family (Morgan and King, 1956).

The personality of the self-realized man also is determined by his inherited propensities but, it is hoped, more strongly by those propensities which are inherent in everyman's unconscious such as compassion, selflessness, and love. The desirable propensities have been awakened during zazen training and enlightenment. One's propensities that are undesirable have been modified during prolonged zazen and suppressed, if the enlightenment is shallow, or eliminated, if it is full enlightenment. Shallow and full enlightenment need to be differentiated to avoid seeming contradictions. Zen believes that every man possesses a predisposition to actualizing his spiritual potentialities partially or fully.

Buddha is purported by the Visuddhimagga to have said: "*Nirvana* destroys 'defiling' aspects of ego—hatred, greed, delusion, etc.—whereas *jnana* [a degree of absorption on a continuum] suppresses them. . . . Their seeds remain latent . . . [and] on emergence from the *jnanic* state these acts again become possible as appropriate situations arise" (Goleman, Chapter 5). This means that all enlightened persons should not be expected to be perfect at all times.

Innate abilities determine the personality of the enlightened Zen man also— in fact, such abilities are strengthened. Activation of the deeper unconscious and its Buddha-nature intensify creative abilities especially.

The personality of the enlightened man may or may not be determined by his culture and learning in the family. In the religiously oriented East, family and culture may be determining factors. In the modern West, however, where culture and family values are likely to be materialism and rationalism, individualism and competition, an enlightened person may reject such influences. He prefers the influence of spirituality and intuition, oneness and cooperation in the cultural climate created by Zen and the "family" in the sangha.

Even awakened personalities display certain unchangeable and distinguishing characteristics such as femininity or masculinity. Yet all enlightened persons possess many characteristics in common, such as compassion, selflessness, and desire to serve others. The experience of the identification of the individual's intuitive mind with the universal Mind creates the universal man. There is a universality in the deeper levels of man's unconscious, as Jung has stated. This has given rise to mankind's perennial dream of the universal brotherhood of man, a dream of all Buddhists—Zen and otherwise.

DYNAMICS AND EMOTIONS

The dynamic that enlivens the structure of personality (that is, the motivational influence of traits upon adjustment) in the fully awakened person is primarily *selflessness;* in the ordinary man it is *egoism,* or dominance, to use the orthodox psychological term. Our Western culture teaches that ego, aggressiveness, and competition are necessary to engender progress. Anyone who has witnessed a Zen group working together toward a common objective sees that cooperation and selflessness may also accomplish surprising results.

In the realm of emotions, diversities and analogies between the ordinary man and the Zen-realized man are most readily discernible. Emotions, of course, supply the motive power for much of our human behavior. Psychologists today believe that "emotional responses are learned. They generally accept a certain amount of negative emotions as inevitable, part of the human condition. But they have worked on modification of emotion in psychotherapy and behavior therapy" (Tart, personal communication, 1973).

Zen also attempts to diminish or eliminate undesirable emotions, whether inherited, learned, or conditioned. Selfishness, hate, anger, fear, and suffering— all have their roots in delusion, in desires of the ego, according to Buddhism. Incredible as it may seem—even to the aspirant himself—during prolonged zazen undesirable emotions gradually diminish and during the enlightenment-state disappear. Opposites are reconciled, selfishness becomes selflessness, hate becomes love—even of one's enemies, to one's own astonishment.

It is one of the paradoxes of Zen, which delights in paradox, that Zen masters may sometimes display genuine anger. The effect is to shock the pupil out of his delusive thinking or even into sudden enlightenment, if he is known to be on the verge. Such displays of other "undesirable" emotions seem not to occur.

Through persistent zazen, fear vanishes, because one feels secure, at home in the universe, able to cope with any difficulty. Suffering and pain may not disappear, but are transcended. Documentation of the alteration of these emotions may be found throughout the literature of Buddhism. Or in a Zen center, living mutations are noticeable, in the emotions of the practicing members. Apparently all these phenomena are attributable to the intrinsic nature of man's True-self and the intrinsic nature of dharma.

Psychologists and psychiatrists have learned that emotions cause physical changes especially in the autonomic nervous system and its two main divisions, the parasympathetic and the sympathetic. "Chronic emotional reactions may cause psychosomatic illnesses—high blood pressure, peptic ulcers, asthma, dermatitis, and obesity" (Morgan and King, 1956, p. 266). The effect of the mind on the body explains the reason zazen is regarded as a discipline for improving the health.

MOTIVATION, NEEDS, AND PLAY

Emotions may supply the motive power for motives, but what of the motives themselves? The Harvard Psychological Clinic has classified motives into seventeen categories, including their goals and effects. For example, "Achievement— to accomplish difficult tasks; to rival . . . others. Aggression—to overcome opposition forcefully . . . to belittle . . . others" (Morgan and King, 1956, p. 466).

Zen doubtless would agree that desire for achievement is a human motive— especially attainment of satori. In the self-realizing person, however, the goal is not to rival others but to attain greater empathy and harmony with them. One of the Zen precepts members take is "not to speak of the misdeeds of others."

Zen spiritual psychology recognizes some of the same motives as those in the Harvard table, such as Deference and Nurturance, though Zen might extend them to include one of the oft-repeated Four Vows—"All beings one body, we vow to liberate." The Harvard diagram lists "play—to devote one's free time to sports, games or parties." The ultimate meaning of play in Zen is explained by Reikieki Kita (a member of the Japanese parliament) and and Kiichi Nagaya (one of the leaders of Zen in Japan today) in their paper "How Altruism Is Cultivated in Zen." They say that "when utilitarianism ideas . . . have been transcended, every activity naturally accords with the law *(Dharma)* and there is . . . the *samadhi* (effortless concentration) in which all activity is play" (1954, p. 135). In other words, to the man in a certain stage of development even menial work is as effortless as play, and creative work doubly so.

Recently I experienced briefly this delicious form of play. A young Zen man came to help me with this very manuscript. No one else can read my execrable handwriting. He had offered to type the first draft. He read aloud to me the pages I had written by hand. He had majored in philosophy at the university and was well versed in Zen. He made suggestions. Some I gratefully accepted—others not. We discussed controversial points—no arguments—and verified them in the Zen books stacked high by my writing chair. We laughed often in the midst of great seriousness. We stopped at times and discussed Zen—surprised anew at its profundity and its unforeseen manifestations in our own daily lives.

The work progressed, and the hours flowed on and on like music. The whole afternoon was like a beautiful symphony composed of various instruments playing harmoniously together. We experienced a deep sense of oneness with the creative work, ideas, the religion of Zen, each other, and the dharma. The work developed into sheer joy. It became effortless, like child's play. It made us feel free, joyous, egoless, fulfilled, pure, innocent—like children walking in the morning of the world. Now we knew why Roshi Kapleau at the Zen Center continually urges us all to become one with all our daily activities. This is "living Zen," he says, and the sense of play which comes from it is the spirit of the universe.

To those to whom it happens, such phenomena seem nothing short of a miracle. It lends unbelievable magic to what might otherwise be arduous work. For hours afterward one feels buoyant, happy, in tune with the dharma, as if all questions were answered, all problems solved—for a few golden hours.

There are many theories concerning motives. One is that motives are caused by needs. Abraham Maslow evolved such a theory. He, as a psychologist, developed out of orthodox psychology and psychoanalysis into a prime mover and shaker in the growth (or transpersonal) psychology movement in the United States. In *Motivation and Personality* he presented a hierarchy of man's basic needs: "(1) physiological needs; (2) . . . security needs; (3) social or interpersonal needs; (4) . . . self-esteem needs . . . (5) . . . self-actualization needs" (as quoted in Peterman, 1972, p. 72). He postulated that higher needs cannot be effectively met until the lower ones are already being satisfied.

For many men this undoubtedly is true. In monastic training, however, or even in the intense training of a sesshin, the Zen person may find the reverse true for long periods. The need to actualize one's religious potentials may be so urgent that it may take precedence over all other needs—hunger, thirst, sex, sleep, and social life—for a long while.

MEMORY

The nature and function of memory is probably the same in the ordinary man and the enlightened man—up to a point. Orthodox psychology studies the memory process originating primarily in the conscious mind, and briefly the repressed neurotic memories in the unconscious. The spiritual psychology of Zen embraces all four levels of the unconscious. It recognizes the "remembering" and projection of what may or may not be eidetic images in the first level, and the reliving of repressed memories of early childhood (the neurotic level). It recognizes the emergence for the first time into consciousness of symbolic and historical events buried in the depths of the racial unconscious—events beyond the grasp of ordinary memory (the third level). It includes preinfantile and racial memories lying dormant in the deepest religious level of the unconscious, whose contents are universal (the fourth level). Might the experience of returning to one's source be termed a "memory" of one's origin? If so, this form of "memory" induces enlightenment and transformation of character.

Buddhism has also discovered that during the higher states of consciousness memory is capable of reaching much further back in time than in the usual conscious state. One's successive births and deaths in former lives through thousands of years may be recalled, as in the case of Buddha. There is no scientific proof of the validity of of such apparent memories, but abundant experiential data exist that seem to Buddhists to substantiate them. Govinda maintains that an advanced disciple may even remember, behold, and foresee world arisings and world dissolutions.

LEARNING

It is more baffling to compare orthodox psychology and Zen spiritual psychology in the field of learning than in any other area. Are zazen and enlightenment forms of learning? Or are they, as Buddhists often assert, merely the uncovering of the perfection of man's Original-nature which is already present but covered over by the dust of intellection? What is learning? The definition authored by the orthodox psychologists is "any relatively permanent change in behavior which occurs as a result of experience or practice." That seems applicable not only to the ordinary man but also to the enlightened man, yet why are the kinds of things "learned" so radically different?

Is it because they occur in different areas of the brain and mind? Do the learning processes researched by the orthodox psychologists occur only in the conscious mind or also in the unconscious? Are there learning areas or simply repositories in the seven psychic centers, the chakras? Until these questions are answered scientifically, it is difficult to approach the process of learning in Zen scientifically. In the meantime, however, an attempt to discover correspondences is possible and perhaps illuminating.

Academic psychologists find three processes of learning: classical conditioning, instrumental, and perceptual. Is "learning" to become a Buddha conditioned in the trainee by zazen, the presence of the spiritual teacher, and the exposure to Buddhist iconography?

In the process of instrumental learning, "The learner . . . is motivated toward some goal, and general exploratory activity ensues. In the course of such activity, a response happens to be emitted, which is instrumental in achieving the appropriate goal" (Morgan and King, 1956, p. 90). This response is *instrumental* in producing a reinforcing stimulus. In Zen the instrumental form of learning appears to function. With enlightenment as the goal, zazen practice may produce a response (a samadhi condition) which is a taste of self-realization. This response in turn may act as a reinforcing stimulus toward attaining the goal.

Perceptual learning, the third process, is also applicable to zazen. Concerning this category, however, the psychologists themselves disagree. One theoretical approach is the association theory, in which a cognitive map is used. Gestalt psychologists, however, "view perceptual learning as a reorganization of the perceptual field. . . . [It] is akin to insight which is relatively sudden. . . . Solution to a problem appears to come by a sudden insight . . . without trial-and-error fumbling" (Morgan and King, 1956, pp. 103–104). One of the most desirable results of enlightenment, or even advanced zazen, is a new ability to solve heretofore insoluble problems intuitively. And enlightenment itself is sudden, as are the intuitive insights that precede, or follow, or accompany it.

We usually see such sudden solutions in organisms that have had considerable opportunity—and capacity—for previous learning. [In Zen, years of arduous training usually precede sudden enlightenment.] Insight experiments are also sometimes cited as giving evidence for learning as perceptual reorganization in the face of an obstructed need. [Morgan and King, 1956, pp. 110–111]

The need for enlightenment, for instance, is a strong motive to learning the difficult method of zazen.

Psychologists have discovered four *methods* of learning. The Zen outlook might accord more thoroughly with them than with the three *processes.* The matter learned through Zen, however, differs drastically from that usually discussed by the psychologist. These four methods are:

1. Distribution of practice. Zen discovered pragmatically long ago that interspersing short periods of the practice of zazen sitting with short periods of rest, or with variety such as walking zazen *(kinhin)** or working zazen, increases the rate of learning.

2. Knowledge of results. Academic psychologists contend that ideally a person should know immediately after each trial exactly how well he has performed. During zazen often nothing seems to happen by which one can measure his progress. Yet, between sittings, benefits accrue in the aspirant's daily life which he may fail to relate to its cause—zazen. The spiritual teacher often points out this kind of feedback.

3. Reading versus recitation. In uttering the Four Vows and in chanting words that favorably affect the mind-state, it is found by Zen that active recitation is more effective than reading. Psychologists contend that some individuals learn more by reading than by listening. Buddhists in our Zen Center seem to prefer the lectures *(teisho)* delivered by the roshi to reading the sutras and commentaries themselves.

4. Whole versus part learning. In Zen there is no choice. The policy is that learning should be experiential, not theoretical. This entails the part method of learning to which some intellectual novices are opposed. They would prefer to learn the whole philosophy and psychology of Zen before submitting to the practice of zazen. Zazen and satori, however, should eventually reveal the whole empirically. Teisho and dokusans as well as the study of the sutras comprise secondary ways of learning. The meaningfulness of the material accelerates learning in both disciplines—Zen and orthodox psychology.

MIND-BODY RELATIONSHIP

Biological psychology studies the relation between the body and behavior and experience. The scientific experiments of psychologists have revealed the inextricable interrelation of the body and mind as in psychomatic illness, for instance.

Zazen is a discipline of the body and mind, each trained to aid the other on the path to Buddhahood. The experience of some Zen Buddhists has shown that psychosomatic illness and neuroses may be alleviated or cured by the practice of zazen. The body also may acquire unprecedented energy (Hakuin is an outstand-

---

*Kinhin is walking around the zendo between sittings in single file, mind concentrated on one's koan. Working zazen is concentrating on one's koan while working, hoping thereby to become one with one's work.

ing example); it may feel buoyant as if levitating through the joy of Oneness with everything. A relaxed, yet erect, posture is related to clarity of mind. Fatigue and sleeplessness during a sesshin, by weakening the hold of the conscious mind, may be conducive to an awakening of man's Essential-nature. The body-mind relationship is dramatically obvious in all altered states of consciousness.

PSYCHOPATHOLOGY

Orthodox psychology, psychoanalysis, and psychiatry have brilliantly analyzed the behavior disorders in the pathological states of neurosis and psychosis. Doubtless Zen would agree—up to a point—with the *analyses* of the origin and nature of neurotic symptoms: anxiety, defense mechanisms, withdrawal, depression, sexual deviation, antisocial criminality, addiction, and maladjustment. The effect of zazen on neurosis is different from the treatment of psychoanalysis. The simple reason is that orthodox psychotherapy "is . . . directed toward improved ego function and therefore places emphasis on the personal ego; meditation moves toward dissolution and transcendence of the ego" (Weide, 1973, p. 13).

Zen finds that some neuroses in some people may be alleviated or cured through zazen, whereas others cannot. To become a *fully* self-realized person the individual apparently must not only free himself of his neurosis but also activate the deeper levels of his unconscious until he experiences the death of the ego and unites with universal Consciousness. The combination of these processes appears to be in an experimental stage in America in Freudian psychiatry and in Zen training in the West, confronted as it is by the force of contemporary Western neuroses. Jung stated that few of his patients achieved *complete* individuation until they had a religious experience.

Weide, however, says, "People at any level of pathology may have important transpersonal experiences. . . . Neurosis may exist in a . . . person who . . . has 'mystical experiences.' . . . At the level of psychosis . . . transpersonal experience is often mixed with important delusions" (1973, p. 8). Weide does not state, however, that complete self-realization is possible in pathology. The intricacies of the unconscious, normal or pathological, offer a challenge both to psychology and to Zen.

The Zen teacher will screen applicants for membership in a Buddhist center to eliminate persons with psychological illness, such as psychosis, with which Zen is not prepared to deal. Yet it is only natural that those of the younger generation suffering from an emotional disturbance and having failed to find a cure in the indiscriminate ingestion of psychedelics, radical politics, violence, or perhaps psychoanalysis should seek aid in one of the religions-of-experience such as Zen. They not only seek relief from neurosis but also long for the spiritual experience.

Zen regards as makyo all mind states short of enlightenment; but there are different kinds of makyo. If the neurotic disturbance is severe, any competent Zen teacher, as stated previously, might advise psychotherapy. Otherwise he advocates more arduous zazen as well as serious reflection if the disturbance is a great obstacle to practice. More concentrated zazen activates the neurotic level of the subject. Consequently he may relive his childhood problems, discovering the solution to them during zazen or enlightenment.

The mundane world regards the ordinary unenlightened person as normal, and only the neurotic and psychotic (and sometimes the enlightened) as abnormal. Zen regards all unenlightened people as "abnormal." The normal person, it teaches, is the one who has realized his Original-nature, who has become what he was born to be—the natural creature whom our nurture has misled, but who instinctively longs to live in harmony with Tao, the Way of ultimate Reality.

SENSORY AND EXTRASENSORY PERCEPTION

"Perception refers to the world of immediate experience—the world as seen, heard, felt, smelled, tasted by a person" (Morgan and King, 1956, p. 367). This is the definition offered by orthodox psychologists.

Zazen may alter sensory perception. During zazen there is an effort to diminish sensory input as a distraction from concentrating on one's practice. Between sittings, however, the senses may become very acute. Aristotle said that the primary function of art is purification. And the Zen aspirant's sensory reaction to beauty, in art or nature, may be so purifying that it serves as a step forward on the spiritual path. Yet, paradoxically enough, the senses lose their importance the higher one ascends. In the eighth stage of consciousness there is "neither-perception-nor-nonperception."

In advanced stages of concentration, extrasensory perception may emerge without one's volition. Telepathy, clairvoyance, precognition, and other new faculties are fairly common. Zen discourages clinging to these faculties, which would block one's progress in the path. (Such faculties are, of course, sometimes possessed by nonspiritual persons.)

Behavior is determined largely by the way in which the world is perceived, the psychologists maintain. The ordinary man perceives the world through his senses and acts accordingly. The fully self-realized person becomes detached from his senses. He intuitively sees ultimate Reality as the only real "world" and acts to maintain his harmony with it and to remain detached from the unreal world of appearances. His behavior may appear odd by conventional standards.

SOCIAL RELATIONSHIPS

Traditional psychology researches the almost irresistible influence of social relationships with parents, peers, and educators on the behavior of the un-self-realized person. Zen teaches that individual behavior should be determined not by the values or pressures of any nonspiritual group but primarily by one's own fully functioning Essential-nature. Buddha teaches that man's inherent values are love and compassion, wisdom and selflessness. Even before these are established by self-realization, however, the Zen aspirant finds to his astonishment that there gradually occurs a diminution of the influence of inhabitants in the conventional world. In the East there is a tradition of enlightenment that is universally respected if not universally achieved. In Western culture there is no such tradition. Consequently critics and friends, failing to understand his ideals, may look at the Zen trainee askance. And worldly friends and relatives, however well loved, may distract him from his practice. The congeniality of the sangha is always available.

Many members of the younger generation apparently feel a basic need to live naturally, simply, and spiritually, to obey the laws of their inmost nature and of the cosmic principle rather than the artificial rules of man-made ego-based society.

MENTAL PROCESSES

Not only the intellect but the senses and intuition may also be avenues of "knowing," Zen believes. When the unconscious is awakened, it speaks to the conscious mind in images. Most people, however, do not experience the intensity of eidetic images, Morgan and King maintain (1956, p. 197). In the psychedelic drug state, Houston and Masters found, subjects were bombarded with eidetic images.

Especially during intensive training periods in sesshin, a person engaged in deep concentration may see many images—eidetic or otherwise. After going to bed he may be plagued by hypnagogic images and by hypnopompic images on first awakening. The cause of these apparently is unknown. They can be fascinating but extremely annoying if persistent. Many images may appear on the path to self-realization, but during the enlightenment-event itself there is only the Void, Emptiness, without images but followed by the profoundest cognition, for then one knows that one knows.

Set and setting are important factors in cognition both in orthodox psychology and in Zen because they may unconsciously influence thinking. The person's set may cause him to think or respond in a predetermined way. During Zen's intense training it is not the thinking of the aspirant that is governed by his set. It is his readiness to respond in a predetermined way, that is, to awaken his Essential-nature and hopefully to attain sudden enlightenment. The trainee is also affected by the setting of the sangha, especially the zendo in which he sits with other members, and also affected by the presence of his spiritual teacher—ever watchful, exhorting, and inspiring.

During zazen the aspirant strives to penetrate his koan (a nonrational question), which quiets thinking, and awaken his True-self, through which he may realize Truth in its essence. He concentrates assiduously on his practice to prevent distraction by discursive thoughts. After enlightenment, of course, the laws governing his thinking *process* are similar to those governing the ordinary man except that they are strongly influenced by his awakened unconscious. Zen psychology is not so concerned with the process of thought as with content.

Conceptualization is avoided by the Zen student as nearly as possible during his training hours, and even while performing many types of work. Concepts diminish during zazen and disappear entirely, though temporarily, during the enlightenment-event. After enlightenment this ability to generalize naturally reasserts itself, but is altered dramatically by the actualizing experience. For example, a brash young man may state that all girls are inferior to men. After Zen training, however, he may realize that all sentient beings are equal in their possession of a latent True-nature, though it may vary in potentials.

Creative thinking, the psychologists say, is "similar to insight . . . the ideas rise to consciousness after much unconscious rearrangement of symbols" (Morgan and King, 1956, p. 184). Undoubtedly Zen would concur in this. Zazen and self-realization stimulate creativity. Problem solving by methods other than reasoning is aided by intuitive insights that arise from the practice of zazen. Wise solutions become spontaneous after the self is realized. Everything in life seems to fall into its appointed place. This might be explained partially by the fact that the enlightened man has "entered the stream," the universal current.

Zen considers that a certain form of creative thinking, involving the truth of Noble Wisdom, is beyond the reasoning powers of the philosophers. In the Lankavatara Sutra, Buddha offered four categories of knowledge:

Appearance, relative, perfect and Transcendental Intelligence. Appearance-knowledge belongs to the ignorant. . . . It is subject to birth and death. Relative-knowledge belongs to the mind used by the philosophers. It is able to peer into the meaning . . . of things. Perfect-knowledge *(jnana)* belongs to the mind of the *Bodhisattvas* who recognize that all things are but manifestations of mind. . . . who are free from dualisms of being and non-being, no-birth and no-annihilation.

Transcendantal Intelligence is the inner state of self-realization. It is realized suddenly and intuitively as the "turning about" takes place in the deepest seat of consciousness. . . . [It] is not subject to birth nor destruction. [Goddard, 1970, pp. 301–309]

To sum up the cognitive process: during zazen, thinking, reasoning, conceptualizing, and logical problem solving are diminished, and during the moment of enlightenment they are impossible. Later they are resumed, influenced by the awakening of the deeper unconscious. So some *processes* of cognition in the ordinary man and the enlightened man are related but not identical. In Zen, imagery, set and setting, language, creative thinking, and symbolization are different, and the results produced are dissimilar. In Zen, the emphasis is primarily on knowledge gained through experience and intuition, not through reason. It is concerned more with the values than the facts that knowing produces.

New faculties, as already mentioned, may be acquired on the path even before the greatest potentials are realized. Psychic powers and extrasensory perception may be experienced without one's volition. It is only logical for scientists such as Daniel Goleman, when reading of such strange faculties, to pronounce them incredible. Not until one has experienced them oneself is it possible to believe that the mind possesses potentials of expansion of which we in the West have been skeptical. These extensions of mind, however, have been known for centuries in the East. Zen urges trainees not to cling to them—they may become obstacles on the path.

Today, investigators are conducting scientific physiological tests on Zen practitioners and yogis while they are in deep states of concentration. For example, Kasamatsu and Hirai (1966) find a reduced rate of metabolism. Wallace (1970) finds the amount of oxygen consumed was decreased by 20 percent. Datey et al. (1969) report that cardiac output was reduced by 25 percent, and muscle activity to nothing. Daniel Goleman reports these findings in *The Journal of Transpersonal Psychology:* (1971, p. 5). He states that these measurements indicate a degree of relaxation more profound than deep sleep. It is therefore invigorating to meditate or practice zazen.

ALTERED STATES OF CONSCIOUSNESS

The purpose of Zen is to alter the individual's states of consciousness. During zazen the aspirant "clearly feels a qualitative shift in his pattern of mental functioning." His center of gravity shifts from his ego to the self. A strikingly different structuring of mind occurs in zazen and satori. He is aware that the independent parts have changed their pattern of organization and become interrelated to each other and newly related to the whole. In approaching satori he becomes unaware of his physical surroundings, then traverses the four levels of the unconscious. In enlightenment he loses or virtually loses all consciousness. He identifies with universal Mind. Afterward, in his altered state, his conscious mind functions in harmony with his deeper unconscious, seeming to be guided by the irresistible force of transcendent Consciousness.

What is the Zen attitude toward drugs? The ingestion of psychedelics and alcohol is proscribed by the ten cardinal precepts of Buddhism accepted by its members. Their use is deplored as injurious to body and mind. It seems remarkable that young people voluntarily remain in a Zen center, where discipline is strict and practice strenuous and often painful. Roshi Kapleau comments that it may be that the younger generation by means of drugs caught a glimpse of the possibility of self-realization, but find the results of zazen more satisfying and less dangerous.

In conclusion we see that the structure and functioning of human consciousness in the ordinary man and the enlightened man are different in some ways and similar in others. It would be far simpler for the investigator if the two systems were entirely in conflict. We find, however, that like the opposites, yin and yang, the two psychologies invade each other's territory. Can the reconciliation of the opposites—religion and science—offer a solution?

Neither the rational man of the West nor the intuitive man of the East has been able *alone* to solve the problems of the world. The West has contributed reason, science, technology, and wealth, but suffered spiritually. The East has contributed intuitive wisdom, the religious life, and spiritual art, but suffered from poverty, disease, and illiteracy. Nations and cultures as well as individual man may be moving in the direction of wholeness. The West is in need especially of training in self-realization.

THE ZEN PATH

What is the Zen Path to self-realization? Zazen is the Path to enlightenment. There are two methods of understanding Zen Buddhism: "intellectually and more than intellectually," meaning experientially.

Can an unenlightened person of the West read the sutras and commentaries and accept Zen intellectually? It might be difficult without the interpretation of an enlightened teacher. To the ordinary man, Zen's claims may sound fantastic even when explained. It can, however, be apprehended intellectually through philosophy or psychology (which can be mutually reinforcing). In our scientifically oriented culture the science of psychology may offer the greater conviction. For Zen would appear to be a spiritual psychology based on the laws of the human psyche. The many parallels with Western psychology, Freud, Jung, Houston and Masters, seem to corroborate this. And doubtless Charles Tart's state-specific sciences of the future (see Chapter 1) will prove the validity of the religion-of-experience scientifically.

Intellectual understanding, however, does not transform the character and behavior. Experiential understanding is necessary for that. Consequently the policy of Zen is to teach the practice of Zen, leaving intellectual understanding until after enlightenment. Or it can be absorbed gradually from the roshi during his teisho. Zen maintains that no one is able to thoroughly understand this religious discipline unless he experiences it. The reason is that the experience of enlightenment occurs beyond the limits of intellection, words, and concepts. There are those, however, who seem to require both experience and intellect.

In the United States, the experiential method of understanding Zen begins, usually, with attendance at a workshop of one day or more at a Zen center or in a university. There are lectures, brief practice of zazen, question-and-answer periods, and interviews for membership. The prospective member must strive for moral purity and possess faith in the reality of Buddha's enlightenment and in the possibility of his own. Then if the student lives near a center or affiliate group he goes there to practice zazen, usually four or five times a week. The periods of sitting are customarily two hours, though on Sundays it sometimes continues all day—eight hours. Out-of-town members from all over the United States attend the sesshins of approximately sixteen hours daily of seven days' duration.

ZAZEN

What are the specific methods of sitting? In the zendo the student traditionally sits on a round, firm cushion, placed on a mat. His legs are folded, preferably crossed in the full lotus position. In the full lotus, illustrated in Figure 1, the right foot is placed on the left thigh, then the left foot on the right thigh. This provides a solid foundation for prolonged sitting. The pain in the knees and back may be excruciating at first, but pain can be a spur to practice.

There are other postures: the half lotus with the left foot placed on the right thigh; the Japanese style with the heels under the buttocks with a cushion between *(seiza)*, illustrated in Figure 2. It is admissible to sit in a chair if one places a cushion under the buttocks so that the angle of the torso to the legs is about 95 degrees. This angle is necessary in order to maintain a straight spine.

The trainee faces a blank wall in order to prevent distractions. His eyes are almost closed. He relaxes his muscles, yet his spine must be held erect at all times. He is urged to sit with dignity and grandeur, like a mountain. He sits silent and motionless. He never scratches his ear or blows his nose. "Profound silence in the deepest recesses of the mind . . . [aids in establishing] the optimum preconditions for looking into the heart-mind and discovering the true nature of existence" (Kapleau, 1967, p. 9).

When the aspirant first sits in zazen his mind may feel like a highly agitated pond of muddy water. Motionless sitting, however, affords an opportunity for the

Fig. 1: An American Zen student sitting in the classical full lotus posture. It is important to keep the head, neck, and spine in a straight vertical line. A cushion several inches in height is usually used to raise the buttocks.

Fig. 2: An American Zen student sitting in the *seiza* posture for meditation, a position much used in Japan. The cushion, firm and several inches in height, under the buttocks takes most of the weight off the lower legs and feet. A small bench rather than a cushion may be used, bridging the legs. As with the full lotus position, the head, neck, and spine must be in a straight, vertical line. (Drawings by Patricia Simons of the Rochester Zen Center.)

sediment or defilements to settle to the bottom so that eventually he feels strangely purified by his own immobility, relaxation, silence, and concentration.

During zazen, as instructed by the roshi, the student may count his breaths up to ten and then begin at one again. Breathing can become a vehicle of spirituality. Or he may question endlessly the koan assigned to him. The koan is an extraordinary device used by all sects of Zen. It is an intellectually meaningless question such as: "What is Mu?" or "What is the sound of one hand clapping?" The purpose of the koan is to so frustrate the discursive intellect that it will surrender its domination of the personality and allow the True-self, or the deeper unconscious, to function freely. In all Zen sects the monitors employ the *kyosaku*, a wooden stick, with which they strike the sitters on the shoulders at specified intervals. It is claimed that they stimulate the acupuncture meridians which carry psychic energy to the *hara*, the region immediately below the navel. While probing his koan the devotee concentrates on the hara. The hara is considered the wellspring of vital psychic energies and apparently is related to the solar plexus.

Usually the rounds of sitting are thirty-five minutes each; then the monitor rings a bell and mobile zazen, or kinhin, is practiced for five minutes. Everyone walks slowly about the zendo in single file, still silently concentrating on his koan, or other practice.

At the termination of a long sesshin the members usually feel so blissfully happy they laugh and cry, hug and kiss each other. Their muscles are weary, therefore the roshi advises rest for a few days, but at the same time they are surcharged with *joriki*—the dynamic power deriving from concentration when the mind is unified and one-pointed.

The object of zazen of course is to attain not merely one enlightenment but ever-deepening enlightenment experiences by stilling the discursive intellect and awakening the individual's Buddha-mind and compassionate heart. The purpose of the awakening is to open the door to the treasure house of virtues inherent in all man—compassion, love, desire to serve, selflessness, certitude, and creativity. At the Zen Center of which I am a member the young people are amazingly creative. They paint, sculpt, write, carve wood, compose music and poems, cook and sew, plan and produce ceremonies, do plastering, electric wiring and edit a house organ, the *Zen Bow*.

Long before enlightenment, zazen gradually alters the aspirants' states of consciousness, which in turn alters their characters, behavior, and system of values. It makes them less egotistic, more generous, more selfless. They share apartments, cars, money, problems, and work with each other. When I moved to Rochester seven young members appeared to unpack my many cartons of books and dishes. When I had flu ten of them rushed to my apartment to cook my meals—unasked and unexpected. A sangha (or Zen community) becomes truly like an affectionate family. A sangha offers not only warm companionships but also a goal to strive for, and expert directions along the way.

The members also attend Zen weddings, picnics, and many ceremonies to celebrate Thanksgiving, Buddha's birth and enlightenment, and so forth. The gold figures of Buddha placed throughout a Zen center are symbolizations of enlightenment, of the Dharma, and in the case of figures of Kannon, of compassion. They are, as well, objectifications of each individual's own Original-nature. To prostrate before them is not to bow to a heathen idol as the ignorant assert. It is to "lower the mast of the ego," to pay respect not to a god but to a great spiritual teacher, to a perfected human being and also to the personification of one's own potentials.

Buddha described his teachings as a raft to carry one across the river of life to the other shore—of enlightenment. Once arrived there, one is encouraged to discard the raft and even the Buddha, to stand alone, free, and self-reliant.

DANGERS

Are there any dangers along the Path? Yes. If one has reached a shallow enlightenment one may display pride in one's accomplishment. This is called the "Zen sickness." Also the deep, emotionally disturbing problems aroused by zazen may at times seem unbearable. Some trainees may faint, sob, shout, or occasionally become hysterical. Breaking the barrier erected by the strong egocentric rational mind and liberating the virtues imprisoned in the deepest levels of the unconscious, by one's own strenuous efforts is a painful, powerful, wonderful operation. If persisted in religiously, however, it is rewarding beyond the credence of the inexperienced.

SUMMARY

Zen abounds in negations, paradoxes, and contradictions—in curt, pithy expressions. This brief paper, however, is obliged to confine itself primarily to the positive psychology of zazen and self-realization, rather than to attempt an analysis of the entire Zen system which has lent itself to thousands of volumes.

The culmination of zazen is, hopefully, enlightenment. Then the True-self becomes identified with the universal Mind. One returns to one's origin, ultimate reality, the Void, Emptiness—which contains everything. One experiences a bliss beyond description, is visited by intuitive insights. One sees into the nature of all existence, feels a oneness with all things. Opposites are reconciled—reason and intuition, the individual and the universe, the self and others, life and death. One emerges from enlightenment with an incredibly different personality—selfless, loving, compassionate, strong, honest, creative, wise, able to solve daily problems. One experiences a sense of universal brotherhood. For in Zen one is unaware of differences of race, age, sex, or social status. One is aware of everyone's True-nature, even if dormant. One feels that perhaps the self-realized man may, by whatever system, become the man of tomorrow, who will, it is hoped, create the golden age of which mankind has so long dreamed.

CONTACTING ZEN

How can contact be made with the living tradition of Zen in modern America? There are centers and affiliate groups in several cities.

The Zen Center of Rochester, New York, was founded by Philip Kapleau, a former businessman. He spent thirteen years in the East training in various monasteries. He is an ordained Zen monk and the spiritual teacher of the Rochester Center. Membership is restricted to 500 members because of limited facilities: 250 are local residents; 250 in other states and Europe. They attend sesshin of four to seven days of intensive training. There is a full-time staff of forty-five. Roshi Kapleau frequently holds seminars at various universities. He is the editor of *The Three Pillars of Zen* (1967) and author of *The Wheel of Death* (1971).

The Rochester Center has twenty affiliate groups: the Toronto, Canada, Zen Center is composed of forty-five members and a resident adviser; the Zen Zendo in Sharron Springs, New York, is directed by Professor Richard Clarke, and there are groups practicing in Ann Arbor, Atlanta, Chicago, and elsewhere.

In California there is the San Francisco Zen Center, of which the roshi is Richard Baker. They also have a center in the Big Sur mountains, Tassajara. Forty are on the staff, and there are accommodations for both married and unmarried priests. Neither is a monastery. It also has zendo affiliates in Berkeley, Los Altos, Mill Valley, Santa Cruz, and Carmel. In Los Angeles there is the Zen Center, the zendo seating about thirty persons. And there is the Cimarron Zen Center with monastics—both men and women.

In New York City there is the First Zen Institute. It also owns a large country place. Mary Farkas has been the secretary of the Institute since 1938. Its membership numbers 150, mostly young people. Its practice is Rinzai. There is also the Zen Study Society with 170 members. Its teacher is Tai Shimano-Eido, an ordained monk. It is also a Rinzai sect. A Soto Zen Center is directed by Nakajimo. It has established affiliate groups in Philadelphia, Washington, and Florida.

In Maine near Bar Harbor, Walter Nowick created a Zen group after his return from Kyoto, Japan.

Most Zen centers are financed by membership fees, donations, fund-raising events, and contributions from nonmembers. They usually hold monthly sesshins and require sitting in zazen several hours a day as well at home. A variety of bells and drums are used to signal various activities. Certain general Japanese training methods are followed. American-born teachers adapt them to the American psychology and experience.

Currently Buddhism claims a quarter of the human race as members. Zen is still active in Japan with 20,000 temples and is spreading in America and Canada. Apparently it meets the urgent needs of many who wish to actualize their own finest potentials and create a peaceful world for all.

5   THE BUDDHA ON MEDITATION
AND STATES OF CONSCIOUSNESS

DANIEL GOLEMAN

DANIEL GOLEMAN is a psychologist who regularly reports on the behavioral sciences for the *New York Times*. Before joining the *Times* in January 1984, Dr. Goleman was a Senior Editor at *Psychology Today*, where he was on the editorial staff for nine years.

Dr. Goleman's most recent book is *Vital Lies, Simple Truths: The Psychology of Self-Deception* (1986). Dr. Goleman has received dozens of journalistic awards for his writing. He is a four-time winner of National Media Awards from the American Psychological Association, including a Lifetime Achievement Award in 1988. He was twice nominated for the Pulitzer Prize for articles in the *New York Times*. In recognition of his efforts to communicate the behavioral sciences to the public, he was elected a Fellow of the American Academy for the Advancement of Science.

Born in Stockton, California, Dr. Goleman attended Amherst College, where he was an Alfred P. Sloan Scholar, and graduated magna cum laude. His graduate education was at Harvard, where he received his M.A. in 1973 and Ph.D. in 1974 in clinical psychology and personality and development. While at Harvard, Dr. Goleman did research on meditation, relaxation, and stress.

As a Harvard Pre-Doctoral Travelling Fellow, and then as a Post-Doctoral Research Fellow of the Social Science Research Council, he spent two years in India and Sri Lanka studying Asian psychological systems and techniques of relaxation and self-regulation. His study of Buddhist psychology was done mainly under the guidance of Anagarika Munindra, then with the Mahabodhi Society of Bodh Gaya, India, and with Nyanaponika Mahathera, of the Forest Hermitage in Kandy, Sri Lanka. His book *The Meditative Mind* (rev. 1988) was based on that research, as is this chapter.

Manifestation is mind;
And so is Voidness too.
Enlightenment is mind;
And so is blindness too.
The emergence and extinction
Of things are also in one's mind.
May I understand that all and everything
Inhere only in the mind.

—Tilopa, *The Vow of Mahamudra*

The predicament of Westerners setting out to explore those states of consciousness discontinuous with the normal is like that of the early sixteenth-century European cartographers who pieced together maps from explorers' reports of the New World they had not themselves seen. Just as Pizarro's report of the New World would have emphasized Peru and South America and underplayed North America, while Hudson's would be biased toward Canada and North America to the detriment of South America, so with explorers in psychic space: each report of states of consciousness is a unique configuration specific to the experiences of the voyager who sets it down. That the reports overlap and agree makes us more sure that the terrain within has its own topography, independent of and reflected in the mapping of it. The differences in maps show us that there are many routes to these states, and that they can be reached in distinct ways and told of within disparate systems of language, metaphor, and symbol.

Perhaps the most thorough maps of the realms of consciousness today are among the teachings of the religious systems of the East. The Tibetan *bardo* or the *loca* of the Vedas and Buddhism are in their esoteric sense metaphors for those mental states traditionally dealt with by Western psychology, as well as for a range of states not yet widely acknowledged by psychology in the West. Buddhadasa Bhikku (1968), for example, gives the esoteric meaning in Theravadan scriptures for these terms: "hell" means anxiety; *preta loca,* the "realm of hungry

To Acharya Anagarika Munindra of the International Meditation Center, Bodh Gaya, India, for his instrumental instruction in the teachings of the Visuddhimagga; to Baba Ram Dass for conversations during the preparation of this paper; to Joseph Goldstein for his seminal comments on the mathematics of higher states of consciousness; and to Maharaj-ji for arranging the author's stay in India so as to make possible this work; the author is deeply and humbly grateful.

This chapter is taken from a much longer pair of articles by the author in the *Journal of Transpersonal Psychology,* 4 (1972), 1–44 and 151–210, with the permission of the author and the journal. Readers interested in research applications, particularly psychophysiological, should consult the original articles.—ED.

ghosts," refers to motivation based on craving or deficiency; *asura loca,* the "realm of frightened ghosts," is irrational fear; and "heaven" is sensual bliss of the highest order. All these states exist here and now. Beyond these more familiar states the Eastern systems go on to describe realms of mind that have only recently begun to be recognized and investigated by psychologists in the West. What has for ages constituted a fundamental transcendental religious experience, and so been described in the terminology of religious belief systems, is on the verge of being translated into the framework of modern psychology, itself a belief system, as "altered" or "higher" states of consciousness (ASC and HSC, respectively).

This paper is concerned with a subcategory of ASC: meditation-specific states of consciousness, or MSC. Meditation states are distinct from ASC in that they include only those states attained through meditation that transcend normal conditions of sensory awareness and cognition. ASC subsumes a wider range than does MSC: altered states include, for example, those induced by hypnosis and psychedelics (topics beyond the scope of this chapter) as well as MSC. In their *effects* on the three normal states of waking, dreaming, and sleeping, MSCs produce a higher state, in accord with Tart's (1971a) criterion for HSC: (1) all functions of "lower" states are available—that is, waking, dreaming, sleeping— and (2) some new functions derivative of meditative states are present in addition. What I have called elsewhere (1971) the "fifth state" has by definition the attributes of an HSC; the meditation-specific states to be discussed here are not HSC within Tart's formulation.

As systematic investigation of states of consciousness comes to fruition, seeming differences among traditional sources in descriptions and delimitations of meditation and higher states may prove to be due to the individual idiosyncrasies of those who have experienced and told of them, rather than to the innate nature of the states themselves. Since most of the teachings about MSC and HSC are within a religious framework, the particular belief system in terms of which the experiences of an HSC are interpreted also must be seen as accounting for some of the variance. Here, as elsewhere, the Schachter (1962) effect prevails: cognitive predispositions determine the interpretation and labeling of internal stimuli. Ramana Maharshi, for example, a being who has experienced higher states himself, says of St. Paul's great experience on the Damascus road that, when he returned to normal consciousness, he interpreted it in terms of Christ and the Christians because at the time he was preoccupied with the thought of them; St. Paul then identified his realization with this predominant thought (Chadwick, 1966). A more recent example is R. M. Bucke (1961), who spontaneously entered a high state while riding home after an evening of reading Whitman's Vedantic poetry, and subsequently saw his experience in terms of "cosmic consciousness." As Suzuki (1958) points out, in every religion it has been the core experience of an altered state which has preceded and been foundation for the subsequent structures of institution and theology. Too often it is the latter that have survived rather than the former; thus the modern crisis of the established churches might be seen in terms of the disappearance in our age of personally experienced transcendental states, the "living spirit" which is the common base of all religions. Still, for each being who enters these states without a guide, it is as though he were discovering them for all the world for the first time. A biographer of Sri Aurobindo, for example, notes:

One may imagine that Sri Aurobindo was the first to be baffled by his own experience and that it took him some years to understand exactly what had happened. We have described the . . . experience . . . as though the stages had been linked very carefully, each with its explanatory label, but the explanations came long afterwards, at that moment he had no guiding landmarks. [Satprem, 1970, p. 256]

This chapter is a detailed discussion of the Visuddhimagga account of Gautama Buddha's teachings on meditation and higher states of consciousness—perhaps the most detailed and extensive report extant of one being's explorations within the mind.

VISUDDHIMAGGA: THE BUDDHA'S MAP OF HIGHER STATES OF CONSCIOUSNESS

"In the Buddhist doctrine, mind is the starting point, the focal point, and also, as the liberated and purified mind of the Saint, the culminating point" (Nyanaponika, *Heart of Buddhist Meditation*).

Perhaps the broadest and most detailed treatment of higher states of consciousness is the encyclopedic Abhidhamma, attributed to the disciples' rendition of more than forty years of Gautama Buddha's discourses. The Abhidhamma was summarized in the fifth century by Buddhaghosa in his voluminous Visuddhimagga, the "path to purification."* Buddhaghosa explains that "purification" should be understood as nirvana. In the course of delineating this path virtually every other path to meditative states is touched on; the Buddha, it is said, traversed them all before attaining the nirvanic state. Indeed, the system of paths and their respective states given in the Visuddhimagga encompasses or intersects the major practical teachings of most all the Eastern schools newly transplanted to the West.

---

*In addition to the translation of Bhikku Nanamoli, I have also consulted contemporary commentaries on the Visuddhimagga by: Bhikku Soma (1949), Conze (1956), Dhammaratana (1954), Kashyap (1954), Lama Govinda (1969), Ledi Sayadaw (1965), Mahasi Sayadaw (1965, 1970), Narada Thera (1956), Nyanaponika Thera (1949, 1962, 1968), Nyanatiloka (1952a,b), and Mahathera (1962).

PURIFICATING SILA

The Buddha's system begins with *sila*—virtue or moral purity—the systematic cultivation of thought, word, and deed, converting energies spent unprofitably into profitable or wholesome directions. "Wholesome" is understood in its dharma language sense as that which leads one toward meditative states of consciousness, to nirvana. In the process that culminates in nirvana, sila is the essential foundation, the "cool-headedness" which serves as the basis for attaining MSC. Sila is one of three major divisions of training in the Buddha's schema, the other two being *samadhi* or concentration and *prajna* or insight. There is a psychological interaction effect between sila, samadhi, and prajna. Effortful sila facilitates initial concentration, which enables sustained insight. Established in either samadhi or prajna, sila, formerly an act of the will, becomes effortless and natural. Prajna can reinforce purity while aiding concentration; strong concentration can have both insight and purity as by-products. The dynamic of interaction is not linear; the development of any one of the three facilitates the other two. There is no necessary progression, but rather a simultaneity and spiral of interactions in the course of traversing any given meditation path. Though the presentation here is of necessity linear, it should be kept in mind that in actuality there is a complex interrelation in an individual's development of moral purity, concentration, and insight. These are three facets of a single process.

To attain effortless sila, ego must "die"—that is, desires originating from thoughts of self cease to be the primary determinants of behavior. According to the Visuddhimagga, if this "death" comes about through development of samadhi, ego will remain in the form of latent tendencies which will remain inoperative so long as mind is concentrated and will bloom again when concentration wanes. If ego death is due to maturing of prajna, ego will cease to exist as an operative force in behavior, though it may continue in thought as old habits of mind; with full insight mind remains disenchanted with ego desires which are now realized to be impermanent, unsatisfactory, and nonself. On full attainment of nirvana, sila is perfected, the potential for impure acts having been utterly relinquished. From the Eastern viewpoint, this endstate is *vairagya,* choiceless sila. Sila is not merely abstention from acting in proscribed ways, but also involves restraint from even thinking in those ways, for thought is seen as the root of action. Thus, for example, the Visuddhimagga urges the meditator, should lustful thoughts arise, immediately to counter those thoughts by contemplating the loathsomeness of the body. The object of the practice of moral purity is to free the meditator from thoughts of remorse, guilt, or shame.

What was initially effortful practice facilitates a change in consciousness to higher states where the attitudes embodied in sila are an effortless and natural by-product of the state itself. In these states the laws of thought and behavior are determined by the experiences of bliss, contentment, and detachment that prevail there. The old psychologies of the West, based on fundamental assumptions such as sexual dynamisms and the urge to power, cease to apply in these new realms of the mind, just as Newtonian physics was found to be inadequate for understanding physics within the atom.* Meditative and higher states are from the perspective of most Western psychology "transcendental" in that they are a realm beyond that particular body of thought, but MSCs and HSCs are not without laws and rules of their own.

Sila in the Visuddhimagga tradition begins with the observance of the codes of discipline for laity, novices, and fully ordained monks. The precepts for laity are but five: abstaining from killing, stealing, unlawful sexual intercourse, lying, and intoxicants. For novices the list expands to ten; for monks it mushrooms to 227 prohibitions and observances regulating monastic life. While the practice of sila varies in accord with one's mode of life, its intent is the same: it is the necessary preparation for meditation. On one level these are codes for proper social behavior; in this Buddhist tradition, that level is secondary in importance to the life of motivational purity that proper behavior foreshadows. Sila is to be understood not only in the ordinary external sense of propriety, but also as mental attitudes or as psychological preconditions out of which right speech, action, and thought arise. Behavior is to be controlled insofar as it affects consciousness. Sila is conscious and intentional restraint of action designed to produce a calmed and subdued mind. Purity of morality has only the purity of mind as its goal.

MINDFULNESS AND MEDITATION

Because a controlled mind is the goal of sila, its practices include restraint of the senses. The means for doing so is *satipatthana*, or mindfulness. Control is exercised over the sense organs through cultivation of the habit of simply noticing sensory perceptions, and not allowing them to stimulate the mind into thought chains of reaction to them. This attitude of paying sensory stimuli bare attention, when systematically developed into *vipassana*, seeing things as they are, becomes the avenue to the nirvanic state. In daily practice it facilitates detachment toward one's internal universe of perception and thought. One becomes an onlooker to his own stream of consciousness, preparing the way to those states that transcend normal consciousness.

In the initial stages, before becoming firmly grounded in mindfulness, one is

---

*One exception is the late Abraham Maslow's (1970) "Theory Z," which could, along with the work of R. Assagioli and C. G. Jung, become for the West the cornerstone for a psychological understanding of HSC.

vulnerable to distractions from external circumstances. Accordingly the Visuddhimagga gives instructions to the would-be meditator for what constitutes an optimum life setting. One must engage that "right livelihood" so that the source of financial support will not be cause for misgivings. In the case of monks, professions such as astrology, palm reading, and dream interpretation are expressly forbidden, while the life of a mendicant is recommended.

Possessions should be kept to a minimum. A monk is to possess only eight articles: three robes, a belt, a begging bowl, a razor, a sewing needle, and sandals. Food should be taken in moderation, enough to ensure physical comfort but less than would make for drowsiness. One's dwelling should be aloof from the world, a place of solitude; for householders who cannot live in isolation, a room should be set aside solely for meditation. Undue concern for the body should be avoided, but in case of sickness appropriate medicine should be obtained. The four requisites of possessions, food, dwelling, and medicine are to be acquired only insofar as they are necessary to well-being, and without greed, so that even one's material necessities will be pure and untainted.

Since the state of one's mind is seen to be affected by the state of mind of one's associates, it is recommended that the meditator surround himself with like-minded people. This is one of the advantages of a *sangha* (Sanskrit: *satsang*), narrowly defined as those who have attained the nirvanic state and, applied, in its widest sense, the community of people on the path. Meditation is facilitated by the company of mindful or concentrated persons, and is impeded by "hanging out" with those who are agitated, distracted, and immersed in worldly concerns. The latter are likely to engage in talk which does not lead to detachment, dispassion, or tranquillity. The sort of topics typical of such unprofitable talk are enumerated by the Buddha as:

> Talk about kings, thieves, ministers, armies, famine, and war; about eating, drinking, clothing, and lodging; about garlands, perfumes, relatives, vehicles, cities and countries; about women and wine, the gossip of the street and well; about ancestors and various trifles; tales about the origin of the world, talk about things being so or otherwise, and similar matters. [Mahasi Sayadaw, 1965, p. 232]

Having gained the advantages and encouragement to be found in a sangha and become firmly set in meditation, the determined meditator at a later stage may find to be obstacles what once were aids. The Visuddhimagga lists ten categories of potential attachments or hindrances to progress in meditation: (1) any fixed dwelling place if its upkeep is the cause of worry, (2) family, if their welfare causes concern, (3) accruing gifts or reputation which involves spending time with admirers, (4) a following of students or being occupied with teaching, (5) activities or projects, having "something to do," (6) traveling about, (7) people dear to one whose needs demand attention, (8) illness involving treatment (9) theoretical studies unaccompanied by practice, and (10) supernormal psychic powers, the practice of which becomes more interesting than meditation. The principle underlying this list is that release from worldly obligations frees one for single-minded pursuit of meditation. This is purification in the sense of freeing the mind from affairs that might disturb it.

ASCETICISM

There is a further set of thirteen practices of self-purification treated in the Visuddhimagga apart from sila. These ascetic practices are optional in the "middle way" of the Buddha. If someone set on a contemplative life should find any of them conducive to that aim, he may practice them but in their observance must be discreet, preferably doing them without anyone's noticing. These ascetic means to purification include wearing robes made only of rags; begging for food; eating only one bowl of food, and just once a day; living in the forest under a tree; dwelling in a cemetery or in the open; sitting up throughout the night. Though such practices are optional, the Buddha praises those who follow these modes of living "for the sake of frugality, contentedness, austerity, detachment," while criticizing those who pride themselves on practicing austerities and look down on others. In all facets of sila, spiritual pride mars purity. The goal of sila is a mind unconcerned with externals, calm and ripe for the inward turning of attention that is meditation.

SAMADHI: THE PATH OF CONCENTRATION

With the development of sila a psychological base is prepared for training in samadhi, concentration. The essence of concentration is nondistractedness; sila is the systematic pruning away of sources of distraction. Now the meditator's work is to attain unification of mind, one-pointedness. The stream of thought normally contains myriad concomitants. The goal of samadhi is to break and steady the thought continuum by fixing the mind on a single thought. That one thought is the subject of meditation. In samadhi the mind is not only directed toward the subject, but penetrates it, is absorbed in it, and becomes one with it. The concomitants of the thought stream are prevented from dissipation by being firmly fixed on that one point.

Anything that can be the object of attention can be the subject for samadhi meditation. Samadhi is simply sustained attention to a single point. But the character of the object attended to has definite consequences for the outcome of meditation. The compilation of sutras known as the Nikayas gives the fullest list of subjects of meditation recommended by the Buddha, elaborating 101. The Visuddhimagga enumerates forty meditation subjects:

ten *kasinas,* contemplation devices: earth, water, fire, air, dark-blue, yellow, blood-red, white, light, bounded space;

ten *asubhas,* loathsome and decaying corpses: e.g., a bloated corpse, a gnawed corpse, a worm-infested corpse, a skeleton;

ten reflections: on the attributes of the Buddha, his Teaching, the sangha, one's own sila, one's own liberality, one's own possession of godly qualities, or on the inevitability of death; contemplation on the 32 parts of the body, or on in-and-out breathing;

four sublime states: lovingkindness, compassion, joy in the joy of others, and equanimity;

four formless states: contemplation of infinite space, infinite consciousness, the realm of no-thing-ness, and the realm of neither-perception-nor-nonperception;

the loathsomeness of food; and

the four physical elements (earth, air, fire, water) as abstract forces.

Each of these subjects has characteristic consequences for the nature, depth, and by-products of concentration. All of them can serve as bases for developing concentration to the depth necessary for attaining the nirvanic state. The concentration produced by those of a complicated nature—such as the attributes of the Buddha—will be less unified than that produced by a simple object—for example, the earth kasina, a clay-colored wheel. Apart from the quality of concentration produced by a given meditation subject, each has distinct psychological by-products. The meditation on lovingkindness, for example, has among its fruits: the meditator sleeps and wakes in comfort, dreams no evil dreams, is dear to all beings, his mind is easily concentrated, his expression serene, and he dies unconfused. Perhaps the most important consequence of a subject is the depth of absorption—*jhana*—it will produce.

The Buddha recognized that persons of different temperaments would be more suited to some meditation subjects than to others. The typology of temperaments he set down as guidelines for advising which person should be given which subject has four main types: (1) one disposed to hatred, (2) the lustful, deluded or excitable, (3) one prone to faith, (4) the intelligent.* Subjects suitable for type (1)

---

*This typology parallels a psychoanalytic scheme of character types based on cognitive styles; in the same order (Shapiro, 1961): (1) the "paranoid," who sees others as separate and suspect, (2) the

Meditation Subject	Highest Jhana Level Attainable
Kasinas; Mindfulness of breath; Neither-perception-nor-nonperception	Eighth
No-thing-ness	Seventh
Infinite consciousness	Sixth
Infinite space	Fifth
Equanimity	Fourth
Lovingkindness; Selfless joy; Compassion	Third
Body parts; Corpses	First
Reflections; Elements; Loathsomeness of food	Access

are the four sublime states and the four color kasinas; for type (2) the ten asubhas, body parts, and respiration; for type (3) the first six reflections; for type (4) reflections on death, the loathsomeness of food, and the physical elements. The remaining subjects are suitable for all cognitive dispositions.

The ideal meditation teacher was the Buddha, who, it is said, had developed the power to know the mind and heart of others, and so could match perfectly each person with the appropriate subject for concentration. In lieu of the Buddha, the Visuddhimagga advises the would-be meditator to seek out a teacher according to his level of attainment in meditation, the most highly accomplished being the best teacher. His support and advice are critical in making one's way through unfamiliar mental terrain. The pupil "takes refuge" in his teacher, and must enter a contract of surrender to him. What is surrendered is the propensities of ego—"hindrances"—which might prevent the student from purposefully pursuing meditation to the point where those ego propensities are transcended. But the responsibility for salvation is laid squarely on the student's shoulders, not on the teacher's; the teacher is not a traditional Eastern guru, but a "good friend" on the path. The teacher will point the way; the student must walk for himself. The essence of the role of teacher in this tradition is given in the lines from the Zenrin:

> If you wish to know the road up the mountain,
> You must ask the man who goes back and forth on it.

"hysteric," who judges and acts on the first impulse, (3) the "obsessive-compulsive," who looks to others for direction, and (4) the "psychopath," who perceives accurately but restructures reality as he wishes.

JHANA: LEVELS OF ABSORPTION

Having found a suitable teacher and been instructed in an appropriate subject, and established to some degree in sila, the meditator begins in earnest. This first stage is marked by an internal psychological tension between concentration on the primary object of attention—the meditation subject—and distracting thoughts, which hinder concentration. These hindrances mainly take the form of: desires; ill will, despair, and anger; sloth and torpor; agitation and worry; and doubt and skepticism. With sustained effort there comes the first moment when these hindrances are wholly subdued, marked by a quickening of concentration. At this moment those concomitants of consciousness that will mature into full absorption come into dominance. This is the first noteworthy attainment of samadhi; because it is the state verging on full absorption, it is called "access" concentration.

This state of concentration is comparable to a child not yet able to stand steady but always trying to do so. The factors of mind characteristic of full absorption are not strong at the access level; their emergence is precarious, and the mind fluctuates between them and "inner speech," the usual ruminations and wandering thoughts. The meditator is still receptive to sensory input and remains aware of environmental noises and body states. The primary object is a dominant thought, but it does not yet fully occupy the mind. At this stage there may emerge (though not always) any of the following: strong feelings of zest or rapture, happiness and pleasure, equanimity, initial application to the primary object as though striking at it, or sustained application to the primary object as though repeatedly noting it. Sometimes there are luminous shapes or flashes of bright light, especially if the meditation subject is a kasina or respiration. Visionary experiences associated with MSC occur at this level, where mind is purified but still can be occupied with name and form. There may also be a sensation of bodily lightness, as though floating in the air. Access concentration is a precarious attainment, and if not solidified into full absorption at the same sitting, it must be guarded between sessions by avoiding distracting endeavors or encounters.

With continued application of mind to the primary object comes the first moment marking a total break with normal consciousness. This is full absorption, or jhana. The mind suddenly seems to sink into the object and remains fixed in it. Hindering thoughts totally cease. There is neither sensory perception nor the usual awareness of one's body; bodily pain cannot be felt. Apart from the initial and sustained attention to the primary object, there are only rapture, bliss, and one-pointedness. There is a subtle distinction between "rapture" and "bliss": rapture at the level of this first jhana is likened to the initial pleasure and excitement of getting a long-sought object; bliss is the enjoyment of that object. Rapture may be experienced as raising of the hairs on the body, as momentary joy flashing and disappearing like lightning, as showering through the body again and again in waves, as the sensation of levitation, or as the pervasive suffusion of thrilling happiness. Bliss is a more subdued state of continued ecstasy. One-pointedness is the property of mind that centers it in the jhanic state. The first experience of jhana lasts but a single moment of consciousness. With continued practice the jhanic state can be maintained for progressively longer intervals. Until the jhana is mastered, it is an unstable attainment which might be lost. Full mastery is stabilized when the meditator can attain this first jhana whenever, wherever, as soon as, and for as long as he wishes.

PATH OF CONCENTRATION

	Eighth	Neither-perception-nor nonperception. Equanimity and one-pointedness.
FORMLESS STATES	Seventh	Awareness of no-thing-ness. Equanimity and one-pointedness.
	Sixth	Objectless infinite consciousness. Equanimity and one-pointedness.
	Fifth	Consciousness of infinite space. Equanimity and one-pointedness.
	Fourth	Equanimity and one-pointedness. Bliss and all feelings of bodily pleasure cease. Concentration imperturbable. Breath ceases.
	Third	Feelings of bliss, one-pointedness, and equanimity. Rapture ceases.
	Second	Feelings of rapture, bliss, and one-pointedness. No thought of primary object.
MATERIAL STATES	First Jhana	Hindering thoughts, sensory perception, and awareness of painful body states all cease. Initial and unbroken, sustained attention to primary object. Feelings of rapture, bliss, and one-pointedness.
	Access	Hindering thoughts overcome; other thoughts remain— awareness of sensory inputs and body states. Primary object dominant thought. Feelings of rapture, happiness, equanimity; initial and sustained thoughts of primary object; flashes of light; or bodily lightness.

In the further course of meditation one-pointedness will become more and more intensified by the successive elimination of rapture, bliss, and attention; the energy invested in the eliminated factors becomes absorbed by one-pointedness at each higher jhanic level (see above). The process of becoming totally one-pointed proceeds, after mastery of the first jhana, with the systematic elimination of initial and sustained attention to the primary object, which, on reflection after emerging from the jhanic state, seems gross relative to the other mental factors. Just as the hindrances were overcome in attaining access, and all thoughts were stilled in attaining the first jhana, applied and sustained attention to the primary object are abandoned at the threshold of this second jhana. The procedure for this requires entering the first level of absorption on the basis of the primary object, and then, having previously so resolved, turning the mind toward the feelings of rapture, bliss, and one-pointedness, free of any idea of the primary object. This level of absorption is both more subtle and more stable than the first; mind is now totally free of any verbal formations or ideas of form embodied in the primary object. This jhana is to be mastered as before.

After mastery, on emerging from and reviewing the second jhana, the meditator sees the factor of rapture—a form of excitement—as gross compared to bliss and one-pointedness. The third level of jhana can be attained by again contemplating the primary object, and abandoning sequentially thoughts of the object, and then rapture. The third level of absorption is marked by a feeling of equanimity and impartiality toward even the highest rapture, which manifests with the fading away of rapture. This jhana is extremely subtle, and the mind would be pulled back to rapture without this newly emergent equanimity. An exceedingly sweet bliss fills the meditator, and on emerging from this state he is aware of bliss throughout his body. Because the bliss of this level is accompanied by equanimity, mind is kept one-pointed in these subtle dimensions, resisting the pull of rapture. Having mastered the third jhana as before, and on reviewing it, the meditator sees bliss as gross and disturbing compared to one-pointedness and equanimity.

Proceeding again through the jhanic sequence, with the abandonment of all forms of mental pleasure, the meditator attains the fourth level. With the total cessation of bliss, the factors of equanimity and one-pointedness achieve full strength and clarity. All mental states that might oppose these remaining two factors have been overcome. Feelings of bodily pleasure are fully abandoned; feelings of pain ceased at the first jhana. There is not a single sensation or thought. Mind rests with one-pointedness in equanimity at this extremely subtle level. Just as mind has become progressively more still at each level of absorption, breath has become more calm. At this fourth level breath, it is said, ceases altogether. Concentration here is imperturbable; the meditator will emerge after a time limit set before entering this state.

Each jhana rests on that below. In entering any jhana, mind traverses successively each lower level, eliminating its constituents one by one. With practice the traversal of jhanic levels becomes almost instantaneous, the mind residing at each level on the way for but a few moments of consciousness. As mental factors are eliminated, concentration is intensified.

THE "FORMLESS" JHANAS

The next step in development of concentration culminates in the four states called "formless." While the first four jhanas are attained by concentration on a material form or some concept derived therefrom, the formless states are attained by passing beyond all perception of form. While the first four jhanas are attained by removing mental factors, with the formless jhanas the complete removal of one stage constitutes the next attainment. All the formless jhanas share the factors of one-pointedness and equanimity, but at each level these factors are progressively refined.

The first formless absorption—the fifth jhana—is attained by first entering the fourth jhana through any of the kasinas. Mentally extending the limits of the kasina to the largest extent imaginable, the meditator turns his attention to the space touched by it. With this infinite space as the object of contemplation, and with the full maturity of equanimity and one-pointedness, mind now abides in a sphere where all perceptions of form have ceased. Mind is so firmly set in this level of sublime consciousness that no external sensory input can perturb or disrupt it. Still, the tendencies of the mechanisms associated with sensory perception exist in the fifth jhana, though they are not attended to: the absorption would be broken should attention turn to them.

The next level is attained (fifth jhana having been mastered) by achieving the consciousness of infinite space, and then turning attention to the element of infinite awareness. Thus the thought of infinite space is abandoned, while objectless infinite consciousness remains. This marks the sixth jhana. Having mastered the sixth, the meditator attains the seventh jhana by first entering the sixth and then turning contemplation to the nonexistence of infinite consciousness. The seventh jhana is thus absorption with no-thing-ness, or the void, as its object. That is, consciousness has as its object the awareness of absence of any object. Mastering this jhana, the meditator then reviews it and finds any perception at all a disadvantage, its absence being more sublime.

So motivated, the meditator can attain the eighth jhana by first entering the seventh, and then turning attention to the aspect of peacefulness, and away from perception of the void. The delicacy of this operation is suggested by the stipulation that there must be no hint of desire to attain this peacefulness, nor to avoid perception of no-thing-ness.

Attending to the peacefulness, he reaches the ultrasubtle state where there are only residual mental formations. There is no gross perception here at all: thus "no-perception"; there is ultrasubtle perception: thus "not-nonperception." This eighth jhana is called the sphere of "neither-perception-nor-nonperception." The same degree of subtlety of existence is here true of all concomitants of consciousness. No mental states are decisively present, yet residuals remain in a degree of near-absence. The Visuddhimagga says of mental states in the eighth jhana, "not having been, they come to be; having come to be they vanish." Lama Govinda (1969) describes it as the ultimate limit of perception. As with mind, so with body: metabolism becomes progressively more still through the formless jhanas until the eighth, where Kashyap's (1954) characterization of cognition applies, too, to physiological processes: it is a state "so extremely subtle that it cannot be said whether it is or is not."

The states of consciousness embodied in the jhanas are characteristic of what are called in the Visuddhimagga system the "Brahma realms," the "planes of illumination," and the "pure abodes." Just as the jhanas are out of the relative world of sense perception, thought, time, and space, are permeated with bliss and/or equanimity, embody infinite consciousness, and so on, so these other planes of existence are seen as existing solely in those jhanic dimensions. Beings may be born into an existence on one or another of these planes according to karmas of past lifetimes, especially the degree to which one has mastered jhanas in a human birth.* Thus, for example, developing the second jhana and practicing it to the highest degree is said to bring rebirth in the realm of "radiant Brahmas," from whose bodies rays of light are emitted like flashes of lightning.

SUPERNORMAL POWERS

The section on supernormal powers is the one part of the Visuddhimagga most dubious from the standpoint of the West, since it treats as real certain events that overleap the bounds of even the most advanced physical sciences. The Visuddhimagga enumerates among these supernormal accomplishments: knowing the minds of others, knowing any past or future event, materialization of objects, seeing and hearing at great distances, walking on water, flying through the air, and so on. More interesting, the Visuddhimagga describes in technical detail how these feats are performed, while Western science at present cannot reconcile their possibility.** Yet every school of meditation acknowledges them as by-products of advanced stages of mastery, if only to caution against their misuse. The Visuddhimagga sees them as fruits of concentration but a hindrance to full insight, and sets down stiff provisos as prerequisites for supernormal powers, warning that they are hard to maintain and the slightest thing breaks them. The required degree of mind-mastery for their use is formidable. One must first have full proficiency in fourteen methods of mind control, beginning with achievement of all eight jhanas, using as a base each of the eight kasinas up to the white one,

---

*These "kingdoms of heaven" are sometimes called in other cosmological teachings "astral planes," *deva locas, bardos,* and the like.

**Tart (1971a; 1972; also Chapter 1) describes as a "state-specific science" one in which practitioners are able to achieve a certain state of consciousness and agree with one another on their common attainment of that state, and then investigate further areas of interest—e.g., the interaction of that state with "reality." By these criteria, the Buddha and his meditating disciples are analogous to a principal investigator and coinvestigators in the science of MSC, the Visuddhimagga and other Buddhist teachings are their findings, and the supernormal powers described here are a representative body of technology generated by their research efforts.

and including such feats as skipping both alternate kasinas and alternate jhanas —that is, attaining first jhana on the earth kasina, then third jhana of the fire kasina, and so on—in both forward and reverse order. The Visuddhimagga estimates that of those who try, only one person in 100,000 or one million will achieve the prerequisite level of mastery. It further marks as a "blemish" wanting it to be known that one can practice these things (little wonder that Western parapsychological researchers have yet to encounter a subject capable of the supernormal feats of mind—such as telekinesis and supernormal hearing—described).

From the Buddhist point of view, the attainment of powers is a minor advantage, of no value in itself for progress toward liberation. Powers in one who has not yet attained the nirvanic state are seen as an impediment, for they may endanger progress by enhancing his sense of self-esteem, thus strengthening attachment to self. In Buddhist tradition powers are to be used only in circumstances in which their use will be of benefit to others. It is an offense against the community of monks for a Buddhist monk to display before laity any psychic powers that are beyond the capacity of ordinary men; a false claim to their possession would mean expulsion from the Order.

PRAJNA: THE PATH OF INSIGHT

From the standpoint of the Visuddhimagga, mastery of the jhanas, and the sublime bliss and supernormal powers that may accrue therefrom, is of secondary importance to the cultivation of *prajna,* discriminating wisdom. Jhana mastery is part of a fully rounded training, but the advantages are seen in terms of making the mind wieldy and pliable for speeding the training in prajna. Indeed, the deeper stages of samadhi are sometimes referred to in Pali, the language of the Visuddhimagga, as concentration games, the "play" of those well advanced in the practice. But the crux of this training is the path that begins with mindfulness (satipatthana), proceeds through insight (vipassana), and ends in nirvana.

The first phase, mindfulness, entails breaking through habits of stereotyped perception. The natural tendency is to "habituate" to the world surrounding one, to substitute abstract cognitive patterns or perceptual preconceptions for the raw sensory experience. The practice of mindfulness is purposeful dehabituation: to face the bare facts of experience, seeing each event as though occurring for the first time. The means for dehabituating is continual observation of the first phase of perception when the mind is in a *receptive,* rather than reactive, state. Attention is restricted to bare noticing of objects. Facts of perception are attended to as they arise at any of the five sense-doors or in the mind, which in the Visuddhimagga constitutes a sixth sense. While the meditator attends to sense impressions, reaction is kept to a bare registering of the facts of impression observed. If further mental comment, judgment, or reflection should arise in one's mind, these are themselves made objects of bare attention; they are neither repudiated nor pursued, but dismissed after their noting. The essence of mindfulness is, in the words of Nyanaponika Thera (1962), "the clear and single-minded awareness of what actually happens *to* us and *in* us, at the successive moments of perception."

It is in the thorough pursuit of mindfulness that the concentration developed previously finds its utility. In adopting and applying this new habit of bare perception, one-pointedness and the concomitant factors of concentration are essential. The optimal level of concentration in practicing mindfulness is, however, the lowest: access. Mindfulness is to be applied to the perceptual process of normal consciousness, and from the first jhana on, those processes cease. A level of concentration less than that of access, on the other hand, would be overshadowed by hindering thoughts and mental wandering, and so be dysfunctional for practicing mindfulness. It is only at the access level that there is a perfect balance: perception and thought retain their full strength, but concentration is powerful enough to keep the mind from being diverted from steadily noting the processes of perception and thought.

The preferred method for cultivating mindfulness is to precede it with training in the jhanas. Having some degree of mastery in samadhi, the meditator then applies his power of concentration to the task of mindfulness. There is, however, a method of "bare insight," in which these practices are undertaken without any previous attainment in absorption. With bare insight the prerequisite level of absorption is attained through the practice of mindfulness itself. During the first stages of bare insight, the meditator's mind will be intermittently interrupted by wandering, hindering thoughts which will arise between moments of noticing. Sometimes they will be perceived, sometimes not. Gradually the momentary concentration of mind in noticing will strengthen until virtually all stray thoughts are noted; such thoughts will then subside as soon as noticed, and the practice will resume immediately afterward. Finally the point will be reached where the mind will be unhindered by straying. Then the noticing of perceptual and cognitive processes wll proceed without break; this is functionally equivalent to access concentration.

In practice there are four varieties of mindfulness, identical in function but distinguishable by virtue of their point of focus. Contemplation can focus on the body, on feelings, on the mind, or on mind-objects. Any one of these serves as a fixed point for bare attention to the processes of experience. Mindfulness of the body entails attending to each moment of bodily activity, such as posture and movement of limbs, regardless of the nature of the activity engaged in. All functions of the body in daily experience are to be clearly comprehended by simply registering their occurrence; the aim of action is to be disregarded—the focus is on the bodily act itself. Mindfulness of feeling involves focusing on

internal sensations, disregarding whether pleasant or unpleasant. All propriocep-
tive stimuli are simply noted as they come to attention. Some will originate as
the initial reaction to sensory input, some as physiological concomitants of psychological states, some as by-products of physiological life processes; whatever
the source, the sensation itself is registered.

In mindfulness of the mind, it is mental states as they come to awareness that
are objects. Whatever mood, mode of thought, or psychological state presents
itself, it is simply to be registered as such. If, for instance, there is anger at a
disturbing noise, at that moment one simply notes: "anger." The fourth technique, mindfulness of mind-objects, is virtually the same as the one just described
save for the level at which the mind's workings are observed. Rather than noting
the quality of mental states as they arise, the meditator notes the objects of the
thoughts which occupy those states—for example, "disturbing noise." When a
thought arises it is noted in terms of a schema for classifying mental contents
which broadly categorizes all thought forms as either hindrances to, or factors
of, enlightenment.

THE STAGES OF INSIGHT

As any of these four techniques of mindfulness are persistently pursued, they
break through the normal illusions of continuity and reasonableness that sustain
cognitive and perceptual processes. The mind begins to witness the random and
discrete units of stuff from which a reality is continually being structured. There
emerges a series of realizations concerning the true nature of these processes, and
mindfulness matures into insight. The practice of insight begins when contemplation continues without lag; mind is fixed on its object so that contemplating mind
and its object always arise together in unbroken succession. This marks the
beginning of a chain of insights—mind knowing itself—culminating in the nirvanic state (see following table).

The first cognitive realization is that the phenomena contemplated are distinct
from mind contemplating them. The faculty whereby mind witnesses its own
workings is experienced as different from what is witnessed. As with all the stages
of insight, this realization is not at all on the level of verbalization at which it is
expressed here, but rather at the level of raw experience. The understanding
arises, but not necessarily an articulation of that understanding.

Once the twofold nature of mind and its objects is realized, there arises in the
meditator a clear understanding that these dual processes are devoid of self. They
are seen to arise as effects of their respective causes, not as the result of direction
by any individual agent. All come and go according to their own nature, regardless of "one's will." It becomes a certainty to the meditator that nowhere in the
mind's functioning can any abiding entity be detected. This is direct experience

of the Buddhist doctrine of *anatta,* literally "not-self," that all phenomena are devoid of an indwelling personality, including "one's self." All one's past and future life is understood as merely a conditioned cause-effect process. Doubts whether "I" might really exist have gone: "I am" is known to be a misconception. The truth of these words of the Buddha (Samyutta-Nikaya, 135) are realized:

> Just as when the parts are set together
> There arises the word "chariot,"
> So does the notion of a being
> When the aggregates are present.

PATH OF INSIGHT

Cessation	*Nirodh:* Total cessation of consciousness.
	Nirvana: Consciousness has as object total cessation of physical and mental phenomena.
Effortless Insight	Contemplation quick, effortless, indefatigable. Instantaneous knowledge of *anatta, anicca, dukkha.* Cessation of pain; equanimity pervades.
Realizations Leading to Desire to Escape	Realizations of dreadful, unsatisfactory, and wearisome nature of physical and mental phenomena. Physical pain. Arising of desire to escape these phenomena. Perception of vanishing of mind objects. Perception fast and flawless. Disappearance of lights, rapture, etc.
Pseudonirvana: Knowledge of Arising and Passing Away	Clear perception of arising and passing of each successive mind moment accompanied by:

brilliant light	strong mindfulness
rapturous feelings	equanimity toward objects of contempla-
tranquillity	tion
devotion	attachment to these newly arisen states
energy	quick and clear perception
happiness	

Stage of Reflections	These processes seen as neither pleasant nor reliable. Experience of *dukkha,* unsatisfactoriness.
	These processes are seen to arise and pass away at every moment of contemplation.
	Experience of *anicca;* impermanence.
	These dual processes seen as devoid of self.
	Experience of *anatta,* "not-self."
	Awareness and its object are perceived at every moment as distinct and separate processes.
Mindfulness	Mindfulness of body function, physical sensations, mental states, or mind objects.

	Access Concentration:	Bare Insight:
Applying Concentration	Previous practice of samadhi.	No previous practice. Samadhi developed to access level by mindfulness.

Further contemplation reveals that witnessing mind and the phenomena it takes as objects arise and pass away at a frequency beyond the meditator's ken. Flux and change are seen to characterize the whole field of consciousness. The realization strikes the meditator that his world of reality is continually renewed every mind-moment in a seemingly endless chain of experiences. The fact of impermanence (Pali: *anicca*) is known in the depths of his being. Seeing that these phenomena arise and pass away at every moment, the meditator comes to see them as neither pleasant nor reliable. Disenchantment sets in: what is constantly changing cannot be the source of lasting satisfaction. The psychological process, begun with the realizations of reality as devoid of self and ever-changing, culminates in a state of detachment from one's world of experience to the point where it can be seen as a source of suffering (Pali: *dukkha*).

Without any such further reflections, contemplation continues. A stage follows where the beginning and end of each successive object of contemplation is clearly perceived. With this clarity of perception there arise:

the vision of a *brilliant light* or other form of illumination, which may last for just one moment or longer;

rapturous feelings causing goose flesh, tremor in the limbs, the sensation of levitation, and so on (as described above in the factors of the first jhana);

a calm *tranquillity* of mind and body, making them light, plastic, and easily wielded;

devotional feelings and faith, which may take as their object the meditation teacher, the Buddha, his Teachings—including the method of insight itself—and the sangha, accompanied by joyous confidence in the virtues of meditation and the desire to advise friends and relatives to practice it;

vigorous and steady *energy* in contemplation, neither too lax nor too tense;

sublime feelings of *happiness* suffusing the whole body, a wholly unprecedented bliss which seems never-ending and motivates the meditator to tell others of this extraordinary experience;

quick and clear perception of the phenomena noticed: noticing is keen, strong and lucid, and the characteristics of impermanence, non-self, and unsatisfactoriness are understood quite clearly and at once;

strong mindfulness in practicing insight so that all successive moments of phenomena present themselves effortlessly to noticing mind;

equanimity toward all mental formations: neutral feelings prevail toward the objects of insight, which proceeds of itself without effort;

a subtle *attachment* to the lights and other factors listed here, and to pleasure in contemplation.

The meditator is elated at the emergence of these ten signs, and may speak out his experiences, thinking he has attained enlightenment and finished the task of meditation. Even if he does not think they mark his liberation, he may pause from the task of insight to bask in their enjoyment. For this reason this stage, called "Knowledge of Arising and Passing Away," is subtitled in the Visuddhimagga "The Ten Corruptions of Insight"; it is a pseudonirvana. The great danger here is in "mistaking what is not the Path for the Path," or, in lieu of that, faltering in the pursuit of insight because of attachment to these phenomena. When the meditator, either by himself or through advice from his teacher, realizes these experiences to be a landmark along the way rather than his final destination, he turns his focus of contemplation on them, including his own attachment to them.

Proceeding, the meditator finds that these experiences gradually diminish and the perceiving of objects becomes clearer. The discrimination of successive phenomena becomes increasingly finer; perception is flawless. The perception of objects becomes faster, and their ending or vanishing is more clearly perceived than their arising. Only their vanishing comes to be perceived at every moment of contemplation: contemplating mind and its object are experienced as vanishing in pairs at every moment. The meditator's world of reality seems to be in a constant state of dissolution. A series of realizations flows from this experience. The mind becomes gripped with fear and dread; all mental formations are seen to be dreadful in nature. Becoming—that is, the coming into being of thoughts—is regarded as a state of terror. The occurrence of mental phenomena—ordinarily reckoned a source of pleasure—is seen only as a state of being continuously oppressed, which mind is helpless to avoid.

Then arises realization of the faults and unsatisfactoriness of all phenomena. All mental formations are seen as utterly destitute of any core or satisfaction. In them is nothing but danger. The meditator comes to feel that in all the kinds of becoming there is not a single thing that he can place his hopes in or hold on to. All mental formations—whether the objects noticed or the consciousness engaged in noticing, or in any kind of existence brought to mind—appear insipid. In all the meditator perceives, he sees only suffering and misery.

Having known the misery in all phenomena, the meditator becomes entirely disgusted with them. Though he continues with the practice of insight, his mind is dominated by feelings of discontent and listlessness toward all mental formations. Even the thought of the happiest sort of life or the most desirable objects will seem unattractive and boring. He has become absolutely dispassionate and adverse toward the multitudinous field of mental formations, and to any kind of becoming, destiny, or state of consciousness.

Between the moments of noticing, the thought will arise that only in the ceasing of all mental formations is there relief. Now mind no longer fastens on to formations; the meditator becomes desirous of escape from suffering on account of these phenomena. Painful feelings may arise throughout his body, and he may be unwilling to remain long in one posture. The comfortless nature of mind-stuff becomes more evident than ever; motivation for deliverance from it emerges at the root of his being. With this strong motivation for surcease from mental formations, the meditator intensifies his efforts of noticing these formations for the very purpose of escaping them. Then the nature of these phenomena—their impermanence, the element of suffering, and their voidness of self—will become clearly evident. Also at this stage the meditator's body will usually undergo severe, sharp pains of growing intensity. His whole body and mind will seem a mass of suffering; restlessness may overwhelm his application to insight. But by applying the practice of noticing to these pains, they will come to cease. At this point noticing becomes strong and lucid. At every moment he knows quite clearly the three characteristics of these phenomena, and one of the three will come to dominate his understanding.

Now contemplation proceeds automatically, without special effort, as if borne onward of itself. The feelings of dread, despair, misery, and so on which formerly arose cease. Bodily pains are absent entirely. Both dread and delight in mental objects have been thoroughly abandoned. Exceedingly sublime clarity of mind and pervasive equanimity toward all mental formations emerge. The meditator need make no further deliberate effort; noticing continues in a steady flow for hours without interruption or tiredness. Contemplation proceeds by its own momentum, and insight becomes especially quick and active.

Insight is now on the verge of its culmination; noticing is keen, strong, and lucid. All mental formations are instantly known to be impermanent, painful, or without self simply because one sees their dissolution. All formations are seen either as limited and circumscribed or as devoid of desirability, or as alien. Detachment from them is at a peak. Noticing no longer enters into or settles down on any formations at all. Then consciousness arises that takes as its object the "signless, no-occurrence, no-formation": nirvana. Physical and mental phenomena cease entirely. This moment of realization of nirvana does not, in its first attainment, last even for a second. Immediately following, mind reflects on the experience of nirvana just past.

NIRVANA

The experience of nirvana is a cognitive shock of deepest psychological consequence. Its nature is of a realm beyond that of the consensual phenomenal reality from which our language is generated, and so nirvana, the unconditioned state, is describable only in terms of what it is not. It is the "Unborn, Unoriginated, Uncreated, Unformed." The word itself is derived from the negative prefix *nir* and the root *vana*, to burn, a metaphorical expression for the extinction of all forms of becoming: desire, attachment, and ego. Decisive behavior change follows from this change in consciousness. With the realization of nirvana, aspects of ego, or normal consciousness, are abandoned, never to arise again. The path of insight differs significantly from the path of samadhi on this point: nirvana destroys "defiling" aspects of ego—hatred, greed, delusion, and such—whereas jhana suppresses them. Nirvana makes sila effortless; in fact, sila becomes the only possible behavior. Jhana supplants defilements, but their seeds remain latent in personality as potentialities; on emergence from the jhanic state these acts again become possible as appropriate situations arise.

There are four levels of realization of nirvana, contingent upon the depth of insight attained in approaching it. Persons who have achieved nirvana are distinguished according to their level of attainment. The number of times one enters the nirvanic state determines his degree of mastery—that is, the ability to attain nirvana whenever, wherever, as soon as, and for as long as he wants—but is not related to the level of attainment. One can enter nirvana with a given level of insight countless times without any change of level. The deeper the development of insight prior to entering nirvana, the higher the level of attainment, and the more pervasive the consequent personality changes. The experience of nirvana itself is identical at each level of attainment; the difference between levels is reckoned in terms of the consequent permanent loss of ego on emergence from nirvana. Entering the nirvanic state is one's "awakening"; subsequent ego loss is one's "deliverance" from bondage to personality. D. T. Suzuki (1957, p. 55) says of the Buddha's prototypic experiences of enlightenment: "The enlightenment feeling affects the whole personality, his attitude toward life and the world. . . . Buddha's experience was not just a matter of feeling which moves on the periphery of consciousness, but something awakened in the deepest recesses of a human being."

The first level is that of *Sotapanna*, "Stream Enterer." One becomes a Stream Enterer at the first moment of the first experience of nirvana, and remains so until insight deepens to the degree necessary to mark the next level of attainment. The "stream" entered is that leading to the total loss of ego, the cessation of all becoming. This final liberation, it is said, is sure to occur "within seven more lifetimes." At this first level the following strata of personality traits and attitudes drop away: greed for sense desires and resentments strong enough to produce anxiety; greed for one's own gain, possessions, or praise strong enough to cause inability to share with others; failure to perceive the relative and illusive nature of what seems pleasurable or beautiful; the misapprehension of permanence in what is impermanent (anicca); and of self in what is devoid of self (anatta); adherence to mere rites and rituals, and the belief that this or that is "the Truth"; doubt or uncertainty in the utility of the path of vipassana; lying, stealing, sexual misconduct, physically harming others, or earning a livelihood at the expense of others.

When insight deepens so that the realizations of dukkha (suffering), anatta, or anicca more fully pervade one's being, there comes a quantum-level intensification of insight: nirvana is now attained at a level where both greed for sense desires and ill will become attenuated. One is now a *sakadgami,* "Once-Returner," who will be fully liberated in this lifetime or the next. Added to the elements of ego abandoned with Stream Entry are gross feelings of desire for sense objects, and strong resentment. The intensity of experiences of attraction and aversion undergoes a diminution: one can no longer be strongly impelled toward or put off by any phenomena; sex, for example, loses its appeal, thought it might still be engaged in for procreation. An impartial attitude toward any and all stimuli is typical.

At the next quantum-level intensification of insight, both greed for sense desires and ill will are abandoned without remainder. What was diminished on attaining to Once-Returner is now wholly extinguished. One's status becomes *anagami,* "Nonreturner," and one is bound to become totally liberated from the wheel of becoming in the present lifetime. In addition to previously abandoned ego elements, the last remaining residual propensities for greed or resentment drop away. All aversion to worldly states such as loss, disgrace, pain, or blame ceases. Malicious motivation, volition, or speech becomes impossible—one can no longer even have a thought of ill will toward anyone; the category of "enemy" vanishes from thinking, along with that of "dislike." Similarly, even the subtlest desire for sense objects disappears. Sexual activity, for example, is now extremely unlikely, because feelings of craving or lust are extinguished. Equanimity prevails toward all external objects; their valence to the Nonreturner is absolutely neutral.

The final and full maturity of insight results in overcoming all fetters of ego, and the dissolution of any subjective meaning in the consensual conceptual universe. One is now an *arahant,* a "Fully Realized Being" or saint. He is absolutely free from suffering and from the generation of any new karma. Having no feelings of "self," any acts will be purely functional, either for maintenance of the body or for the good of others. There remains not a single unabandoned internal state from one's past owing to which thoughts of greed, hatred, and such could come to mind. All past deeds are erased, as is all future becoming; only pure being remains. The last vestiges of ego relinquished in this final stage include: all feelings of approval for or desire to seek the worldly states of gain, fame, pleasure, or praise; any desire for even the bliss of the material or formless jhanas; mental stiffness or agitation, covetousness of anything whatsoever. The least inherent tendency toward an unvirtuous thought or deed is literally inconceivable.

From the level of arahant the validity of the noble truths of impermanence, suffering, and nonselfhood is evident at every moment. Wei Wu Wei says of the meaning of suffering from this level of consciousness:

When the Buddha found that he was Awake . . . it may be assumed that he observed that what hitherto he had regarded as happiness, as compared to suffering, was such no longer. His only standard henceforward was *ananda* or what we try to think of as bliss. Suffering he saw as the negative form of happiness, happiness as the positive form of suffering, respectively the negative and positive aspects of experience. But relative to the noumenal state which now alone he knew, both could be described . . . as *dukkha* (suffering). *Dukkha* was the counterpart of *sukha* which implied "ease and well-being," . . . to the Buddha nothing phenomenal could appear to be *sukha* although in phenomenality it might so *appear* in contrast to *dukkha.* [1968, p. 61]

Understanding the truth of nonself for an arahant is more straightforward. Suzuki (1958, p. 293) puts it simply: when one attains that level he finds "by immediate knowledge that when one's heart was cleansed of the defilements of the ordinary ego-centered impulses and desires, nothing was left there to claim itself as ego residuum." Impermanence is perceived at the primary stage of cognition. For an arahant, perception in vipassana is perfected: he is a witness of the most minute segments of the mind's working, the chain of mind-moments. According to this tradition, the Buddha witnessed 17×10^{21} mind-moments in "the wink of an eye," each one distinct and different from the one preceding and the one following it. Like him, the arahant sees that elementary constituents of the flow of consciousness are changing at every moment. Nothing in the universe of one's mind is constant, and one's external reality follows from one's internal universe. Nowhere, then, is there any stability or permanence.

NIRODH

There is a state apart from nirvana, little known in the West, called *nirodh,* cessation. In nirvana, awareness has as its object the cessation of consciousness: in nirodh, awareness ceases altogether. It is the absolute cessation of consciousness and its concomitants. Nirodh is accessible only to a Nonreturner or an arahant who has also mastered all eight jhanas. Neither a Stream Enterer nor a Once-Returner has relinquished enough strata of ego to muster the superconcentration required for nirodh—in the access process to this state of total nonoccurrence even the slightest residuum of sense desire will be an obstruction.

The path to nirodh entails the practice of vipassana using as a base each jhana in succession up to the eighth, neither-perception-nor-nonperception. With the cessation of this last state of ultrasubtle consciousness, one enters nirodh. Cessation is "differently real," all the data of our experience of reality, even the most sublime states, being absent. Although nirodh can last for up to seven days of the human time-rhythm, there is no time sequence in the state itself: the moment immediately preceding it and that immediately following it are experienced as of immediate succession. The limit of seven days given for the duration of nirodh may be due to its unique physiology: heartbeat and normal metabolism, it is said, cease along with consciousness, though metabolic processes continue at a residual level so that the meditator's body can be distinguished from a corpse. Prior to entering this state the meditator must set a predetermined length of time for staying in it. On emergence, he will go through the jhanas in reverse order to normal consciousness. At the eighth jhana, awareness resumes; at the third, normal bodily function; at the first, discursive thought and sense perception.

THE TWO PATHS: THEIR HIGHEST EXTREMES

At their highest extremes, the path of samadhi through the jhanas and the path of insight to nirvana tend to meet. But between these ultimate states of rarefied consciousness there remain extremely subtle but crucial differences. The seventh jhana is a state of awareness of consciousness that has no object: no-thing-ness. In the eighth jhana the consciousness of no-thing-ness cannot even be said to be operative, but yet remains as a latent function, and so cannot be said not to exist: this is the realm of neither-perception-nor-nonperception. At nirvana the final extinguishing of consciousness begins, with a state that is the awareness of no consciousness at all. This process of extinguishing culminates in nirodh, where there is no awareness whatsoever. The attainment of even the highest jhanas does not on emergence necessarily affect normal ego function, while the experience of nirvana irrevocably alters ego function.

These different paths mark two extremes on a continuum of exploration and control of mind. One who could marshal enough one-pointedness to attain, say, the formless jhanas might easily attain the nirvanic state should he choose to turn his powerful concentration ability to watching his own mind. And, conversely, one who had entered the nirvanic state might well possess a mind so indifferent to hindrances and distractions that should he choose to focus on a single object of awareness, he would readily enter and proceed through the jhanic levels. Thus those beings who have traversed these distinctly different paths to their highest extremes may no longer belong solely to one, but rather to both. With full mastery of either samadhi or insight, the other is readily attainable, the distinction between meditation avenues melts. As the Zenrin puts it:

From of old there were not two paths
"Those who have arrived" all walked the same road.

MAPS OF CONSCIOUSNESS IN PERSPECTIVE

This exposition, based on Buddha's map of MSC, may be an aid to those who seek to formulate theories or conceptualize and design research in this area. This was my intent.

Those who through personal practice are themselves exploring these states may or may not find these thoughts or this map helpful. The work of *sadhana* is often amorphous, its delimitation fluid, and the stages of progress as intricate as one's life experience. There is as much variety in paths to higher states of being as there are persons on the path; any one map does not necessarily apply to a given person's situation. There is a Sufi saying, "He who tastes knows." In the words of Meher Baba:

In the spiritual life it is not necessary to have a complete map of the Path in order to begin traveling. On the contrary, insistence upon having such complete knowledge may actually hinder rather than help the onward march. . . . He who speculates from the shore about the ocean shall know only its surface, but he who would know the depths of the ocean must be willing to plunge into it. [1967, p. 191]

6 YOGA PSYCHOLOGY

HARIDAS CHAUDHURI

HARIDAS CHAUDHURI (1913-1975) was founder, president, and professor of philosophy of the California Institute of Asian Studies in San Francisco (now called the California Institute of Integral Studies). He was also founding president of the Cultural Integration Fellowship, Inc. a nonprofit organization dedicated to the promotion of intercultural understanding between East and West.

He was born in Calcutta in May 1913 and had his first direct experiential understanding of higher states of consciousness at the age of fourteen, the beginning of his own spiritual search. This search formed the experiential basis of his scholarly career.

Dr. Chaudhuri received his Master's and Doctor on Philosophy degrees from the University of Calcutta (1927 and 1947, respectively) and went on to serve in the educational service of the government of West Bengal and as chairman of the department of philosophy at Krishnagar College before he came to the United States.

In addition to teaching and lecturing on integral philosophy, yoga psychology, and various spiritual disciplines, Dr. Chaudhuri contributed numerous articled on these subjects to both scholarly and popular periodicals and wrote many books, including *Being, Evolution and Immortality* (1974), *Prayers of Affirmation* (1956), *The Rhythm of Truth* (1958), *Sri Aurobindo: The Prophet of Life Divine* (1951), *Integral Yoga: The Concept of Harmonious and Creative Living* (1965), *Philosophy of Meditation* (1965), *Modern Man's Religion* (1966), and *Mastering the Problems of Living* (1968). He edited *Indian Culture: A Symposium* (1951), *The Integral Philosophy of Sri Aurobindo: A Symposium* (1960), and *Mahatma Ghandi: His Message for Mankind* (1969), and wrote several books in Bengali.

Posthumous books are: *The Evolution of Integral Consciousness* (1977), *Philosophy of Love* (1987), and *Essence of Spiritual Philosophy* (in press).

He participated in many international conferences, including the U.S. National Commission for UNESCO, San Francisco, 1957; Parliament of World Religions, University of Oregon, 1962; U.N. Convocation of Religion for World Peace, San Francisco, 1965; International Seminar on Human Unity, Government of India, New Delhi, 1972.

During his lifetime Dr. Chaudhuri was acclaimed as a profoundly effective educator, philosopher, and spiritual leader. His focus was on the integration of the human being, a synthesis of Eastern and Western thought, and the future of our world cultures.

HISTORICAL ORIGIN

Psychology occupies a preeminent position in the cultural history of India. It was realized as far back as the Upanishadic period, that is to say about 1500 B.C., that the psyche and the cosmic whole are inseparably interrelated. The universe is in ultimate analysis the psychocosmic continuum. Apart from the psyche the universe is an unknown X. Apart from the universe the psyche is an uprooted abstraction. This profound insight was crystallized in the supreme identity formula: the Self is one with Being* *(ayam atma brahman)* (Radhakrishnan, 1953, p. 695). This has the threefold implication of "I am Being," "The world is Being," and "Thou art That."

The Nature-oriented mystics of Vedic times around 3000 B.C. discovered Being as the ground of the universe. The Self-oriented mystics of the Upanishads around 1500 B.C. first discovered the Self *(atman)* as the ground of our psychic existence. But later on they arrived at a comprehensive synthesis affirming the identity or nonduality of the Self and Being.

The ontological** experience of the oneness of the Self and Being gave rise to

---

*I am using the word "Being" as a synonym for the Sanskrit Brahman. It has been described in the Upanishads as the nondual and nontemporal ground of the cosmic manifold. It is the ultimate experiential datum of transcendental consciousness or supreme mystic experience variously known as *turiya, nirvikalpa samadhi, nirvana, sambodhi,* etc. All the great yogis in India testify that on gaining the highest kind of mystic realization one makes an immediate experiential contact with the ultimate reality designated here as Being. Being in its inmost essence is eternal, nondual, and logically indeterminable. But in its function it is the creative ground of the universe or the cosmic manifold.

Be it noted here that all man-made words and statements are to be understood in a relative sense. For instance, when I say "Nontemporal nondual Being is logically indeterminable," what I mean is that it cannot be defined in terms of such determinate structures of existence as Personal God, Cosmic Mind, Universal Will, Matter, Life, etc. But nonetheless the words "nontemporal, nondual," ground of the universe, are still modes of determination. Only, such words represent the irreducible minimum of determination necessary to convey the central meaning of supreme mystical experience.

**By "ontological" I mean relating to the ultimate ground of all existence, i.e., logically indeterminable Being. Reference is to Ontology as the theory of Being or ultimate reality. A substitute word could be "spiritual," but it is extremely ambiguous and multivalued.

two important, interrelated cosmological theories. One is the theory of the universe as a psychocosmic continuum in which subject and object, psyche and cosmos, inseparably intermingle. The other is the theory of psychocosmic correspondence according to which various aspects of Being correspond to various phases of human experience.

When meditation leads on to deeper self-realization, the supreme truth dawns upon the mind that one's own authentic Self is the master key to the essential structure of the universe and to the mystery of the Being, the ontological root of the universe. So the ancient sages of India were convinced that search for the supreme truth or for the mystery of the universe must assume the form of search for one's own true self. "Realize the Self" was the proclaimed motto of life. The process of psychological self-inquiry, dauntless adventure in the domain of the psyche, was early established as the foundation for all philosophical disciplines including metaphysics (science of eternal principles) and ontology (science of Being).

Not only that, but the psyche as the organizing unity of all human experiences was believed to resemble in its essential structure that of the universe as a whole, just as according to modern physics the atom resembles in its essential structure the vast solar system. The Self is the inmost center of such diverse experiences as waking *(jagrat),* dream *(swapna),* sleep *(susupti),* and the superconscious experience *(samadhi).* In Western thought, all of these except waking experience are regarded as merely subjective. According to Indian thinkers the dichotomy of subjective and objective is a false creation of man's conceptual understanding. All experience represents an interpenetration of subject and object, a dynamic interaction between the psyche and the cosmic field. All psychic functions are reality-oriented. And all cosmic events are psychically reflected.

According to the Upanishadic seers, the four aforesaid phases of the human psyche correspond to four dimensions or aspects of Being (Radhakrishnan, 1953, pp. 695–699). Waking experience corresponds to Being in its gross sensory manifestation *(virat).* Dream or imaginative experience corresponds to Being in its subtle energy-vibratory manifestation or to Being in respect of its manifold potentials (*hiranyagarbha,* the golden-egg form of the real). Sleep corresponds to Being in its aspect of undifferentiated or equiliberated energy (causal energy, *karana, ishwara*). Samadhi, or superconscious experience, corresponds to Being in its aspect as pure transcendence or as the nontemporal ground of the cosmic manifold *(Brahman, Karanatita).* This psychocosmic correspondence constitutes the essential interdependence of psychology and philosophy.

No philosophy can reveal the essential nature of existence without adequate psychological discipline leading to superconscious awareness of Being. Likewise no psychology can reveal the true nature and function of the psyche without grasping the dimensions of Being corresponding to our various phases of experience.

An important methodological postulate that follows from the above is that in order to know the cosmic whole in its fullness, one must know the psyche in its fullness. Then again, in order to know the psyche in its fullness, one must know through analysis and evaluation all the altered states of consciousness. It is a welcome sign of the present day that Western psychologists have come to realize this important truth. Dr. Charles Tart has rendered in this respect a signal service to modern Western psychology by editing and publishing his monumental work *Altered States of Consciousness* (1969).

In the Taittiriya Upanishad,* it is shown how as a spiritual seeker grows and evolves to higher and higher levels of self-awareness his metaphysical world view begins to change in a corresponding manner. When a person is completely identified with the body he looks upon the world as an extension of his body. He is predominantly a materialist in outlook, and affirms matter as the creative source of all existence (Radhakrishnan, 1953, p. 554). When a person is identified with his life force, he looks upon the universe as the flux of vital energy. In other words, he is predominantly a vitalist in outlook and affirms life as the creative source of all existence. When he is identified with his mind, he is a subjective idealist in his outlook, and affirms mind as the creative source of all existence. When he identifies with his pure reason, he becomes an objective idealist in philosophy and affirms reason as the creative source of all existence. When he identifies with his pure transcendental awareness, which is a blissful experience, he becomes a mystic-seer or spiritual idealist in outlook, and affirms existence-consciousness-bliss as the creative source of all existence. When finally he identifies with pure indeterminable Being or Nothingness, he becomes a transcendental ontologist like Buddha (the founder of Buddhism) and Samkara (the most-well known exponent of Vedanta), and affirms Nothingness or indeterminable Being as the ultimate ground of all existence.

The psychological approach to philosophical knowledge and spiritual wisdom as adumbrated in the Upanishads set the pattern for all search for truth in the subsequent periods of the cultural history of India. In consequence, all kinds of

---

*The Upanishads, altogether 108 in number, represent the logical culmination and the most philosophical portion of the Vedas. Vedas and Upanishads are regarded as the most authoritative and sacred ancient scriptures of India. They are a veritable treasure house of spiritual wisdom inspired by most authentic mystic experiences of the ultimate. Taittiriya Upanishad is one of the ten major Upanishads in which the most fundamental and eternal spiritual truths are believed to be enshrined.

There are many commentaries and translations of the Upanishads. Professor S. Radhakrishnan's *The Principal Upanishads* (Harper & Brothers, 1953) is especially good for serious students and scholars.

psychophysical disciplines known as yoga systems evolved over the centuries. They represent an enormous variety of experiments with the spiritual truth resulting in different kinds of religious, mystical, or ontological experience. Such experiences have been interpreted in various ways, giving rise to the fundamental concepts of India's spiritual psychology.

From the fifth century B.C. to the eighteenth century A.D., as a result of intensive systematization of thought and codification of the fundamental principles of self-development, various well-defined yoga disciplines came into existence. Most important among them are:

> The yoga of breath control *(hatha)*
> The yoga of mind control *(raja)*
> The yoga of action *(karma)*
> The yoga of love *(bhakti)*
> The yoga of knowledge *(jnana)*
> The yoga of being-energy *(kundalini)*
> The yoga of integral consciousness *(purna)*

The ultimate goal of all the above self-disciplines is blissful union with the Self in its transcendental dimension of oneness with the timeless Being. They differ in starting point and mode of procedure, each emphasizing one of the various closely interrelated ingredients of personality such as the vital breath, mental functioning, social action, search for love, knowledge, power, or integral consciousness.

Be it finally noted that yoga psychology is the art as well as the science of the human psyche as a growth process. It is recognized that the full mystery of the psyche can hardly be disclosed to the eye of detached observance and analysis. It stands revealed only to one who is existentially involved in personal self-realization and ego-transcendence, in other words, in the practice of self-discipline. Dr. Indra Sen has rightly observed that in Indian psychology "the theoretical and the practical motives of life are combined" (Sen, 1960, p. 186). A person can truly know the Self only by becoming one with the Self.

CURRENT ACTIVITY

In modern times, especially since the beginning of India's spiritual renaissance movement in the nineteenth century, yoga psychology has taken on new dimensions. Whereas in ancient times there was an overemphasis on the transcendental dimension of the psyche, a growing awareness of the value and importance of the existential, social, and historical dimensions of life began to dawn. Attempts began to be made to integrate in various ways the transcendental or pure spiritual dimension with the latter.

In the Ramakrishna-Vivekananda order the ultimate goal of the evolving psyche was affirmed to include not only blissful union with the supreme Being, but also selfless social service and humanitarian work. Being *(brahman)* is not only the indeterminable ground of the Self but also the creative divine presence in all human beings. So service of the Divine present in the poor and the downtrodden *(daridra narayana seva)* emerged as an important part of the yoga discipline.

Those who derived inspiration from the writings of India's great poet-laureate Rabindranath Tagore, among them Mahatma Gandhi, Jawaharlal Nehru, and Vinoba Bhave, realized that the ultimate freedom of the spirit in man must be in the nature of creative freedom, not negative-transcendental freedom of the aescetic (Chaudhuri and Spiegelberg, 1960, pp. 18–21). To create new values in culture and civilization, to create a new society free of man's inhumanity to man, and to create a new international order free of recurrent global catastrophes are essential aspects of the spiritual goal of life. In Tagore's World University (Viswabharati) in Santiniketan, West Bengal, yoga assumes the dominant form of creative art expression and union with the historical world-spirit through comprehensive understanding of the richly variegated cultural values of East and West.

Mahatma Gandhi looked upon Tagore as his divine teacher *(Gorudev)*, appreciated the ideal of spiritual liberation as creative freedom, and applied it in the sphere of sociopolitical action. He demonstrated how a whole subcontinent of 400 million people can attain political independence with the spiritual weapons of truth and nonviolence. This is yoga in action, karma yoga, in its modern historically oriented form. Its ultimate goal is the kingdom of righteousness in society *(Ramrajya)* (Chaudhuri and Spiegelberg, 1960, p. 230).

In the integral psychology of Sri Aurobindo emphasis is laid upon the integral structure of the human psyche. The psyche is on the one hand a creative center of action of Being, and on the other a unique focus, an instrumentality of the process of planetary evolution. He envisions the goal of the evolving psyche as illumined participation in planetary evolution striving for the emergence of a new global society mediated by the manifestation of the higher supramental consciousness in man's collective living.

Besides the aforesaid historically oriented developments in yoga psychology, there are other directions in which experiments are being made today.

Swami Pratyagatmananda, Gopinath Kaviraj, Gopi Krishna, and others have given a new form and an evolutionary orientation to the psychosomatic self-energizing process of kundalini yoga. Thus a whole new field of fascinating research relating to the psychonuclear energy has been opened (Pratyagatmananda, 1961; 1971; Kaviraj, 1966; Krishna, 1971; 1972). The present writer, deeply interested in this approach, has been long engaged in systematic research, both theoretical and existential, in this area.

Sri Raman Maharshi (1880–1950) of Arunachal, Madras, has synthesized some of the essential principles of raja and jnana yoga. (Maharshi, 1962; 1967). He has laid stress on the techniques of critical self-inquiry and search for one's ultimate spiritual identity. He has also emphasized the need to establish Self-realization as an egoless natural condition in life ("Who," 1967, p. 11). This is a straight path to the traditional goal of Self-realization in a balanced form. But no attempt is made to come to grips with the problems of society, the dialectic of history, and the challenge of the modern West.

Swami Sivananda (1887–1963) of Rishikesh emphasizes modern man's need for some kind of syncretic or eclectic yoga (Sivananda, 1950). He uses the term Integral Yoga (purna yoga), which was first coined by Sri Aurobindo, in the eclectic sense. He shows how one can incorporate in his enormously complex life schedule of modern times elements of value extracted from all the different yoga systems I have listed. This is without doubt a very useful approach so long as one does not wish to be bothered with the crucial issues of history and evolution as related to the existential dimension of the human Self.

Swami Kuvalayananda of Lanovla, Poona, has initiated scientific investigation into the changing physiological processes accompanying the altering states of consciousness produced by yoga and meditation. Enhanced understanding of the manifold therapeutic value of yoga practice is a very fruitful result of his psycho-physiological approach (Kuvalayananda, 1966, ch. 13).

Maharishi Mahesh Yogi in his theory of transcendental meditation has laid major emphasis on the need for psychic relaxation with the aid of a nonconnotative mantra or sound formula. In order to gain a popular appeal, he also stresses the hedonic value of meditation as a means of enjoying life. "Life is absolute in bliss consciousness and relative in the variety of phenomenal joy" (Maharishi, 1963, p. 61). There is no appreciation of the tragic aspect of life, nor of the dialectical forces which make life a battleground for the creative manifestation of higher values.

Transcendental meditation has gained much popularity in Western countries. But in India there is a widespread mood of suspicion and criticism. Transcendental meditation is considered an oversimplification, and therefore incapable of leading people beyond the spiritual kindergarten. Its main value consists in psychophysical relaxation, which is undoubtedly the first important step in all yoga systems. But in T.M., there is little training in value consciousness. Nor is there any methodology for critical evaluation of the bewildering variety of mystical experiences and changing patterns of self-image.

At the California Institute of Asian Studies, San Francisco, some new research projects in yoga psychology are under way. Workshops in meditative explorations in the domain of the psyche are supplemented by sessions in critical analysis and constructive evaluation. In probing the depths of the psyche in all its aspects, an objective survey of all the various yoga disciplines, both traditional and modern, is encouraged. The focus is, however, on the psychology of integral yoga, its goal of total psychointegration, and today's imperative need for reformulation of the basic yoga insights in nonmetaphysical language (Chaudhuri, 1965a; 1966).

The psychology of integral yoga derives its unique characteristics from the practice of integral yoga in the original Aurobindonian sense of the term. A restructuring of the priorities of value consciousness is at the heart of this practice. Total psychointegration implies not only realization of the mystical or transcendental dimension of the Self. It also requires actualization of psychic potentials of the individual as a creative unit of the evolutionary process. A newly developing technique of integral self-realization is the delicate balancing of reason, sexual libido, and transpersonal Being-energy (logos, eros, and ontos; *brahma, visnu,* and *siva-sakti*).

PHILOSOPHICAL BASIS OF YOGA PSYCHOLOGY

At the very heart of the philosophy of yoga is the concept of the Self (purusa, atman). It is the inmost center, the unifying principle, of the total personality, including the physical, instinctual, intellectual, ethico-religious, and ontological dimensions. It is the integrative principle of the total psyche whose enormously complex structure includes such apparently divergent aspects as the self-conscious, the unconscious, and the superconscious. This true self is one with Being. So to know the true self is to experience, with all the ecstasy of intimate knowledge, oneness with Being, the eternal ground. Then again to experience oneness with Being is to experience oneness or kinship with all fellow beings and with all living things. A spontaneous outflow of the experience of oneness with others is the spirit of universal love and compassion which knows no bounds and brooks no prejudiced discrimination.

This experience of spontaneous joy and love inspired by the vision of the unity of all existence provides the philosophical basis for all yoga disciplines.

Philosophically significant yoga disciplines are broadly speaking, five: the yoga of mind control, the yoga of love, the yoga of knowledge, the yoga of energy, and the yoga of total integration. A brief outline of these philosophical bases, somewhat different in emphasis and orientation, is given below.

The yoga of mind control is based upon the dualistic philosophy of nature and spirit (prakriti and purusa). All the components of human personality, including body, senses, mind, reason, memory, and ego, are affirmed as diversified modes of expression of nature.

Nature is unconscious creative energy. The three basic constituents of nature are (1) inertia, passivity, resistance, opaqueness *(tamas);* (2) activity, motion, projection *(rajas);* and (3) transparency, expressiveness, harmony *(sattva).* At the human level the creativity of nature assumes the form of psychic energy *(chitta).* Nature, even though unconscious, has some kind of purposiveness of its own inspiring all its actions. Whatever nature does is done either for the enjoyment* or for the liberation of the spirit. Such psychic functions as sensation, perception, memory, imagination, reasoning, decision, resolution, action, and ego are various modes of operation of the psychic energy. Nature's energy has no consciousness of its own. It becomes more or less conscious as psychic energy reflects the light of self-shining spirit, just as the moon becomes luminous by reflecting the light of the self-shining sun. Or it is like a piece of iron which becomes red hot through contact with fire.

The human personality consisting of mind, intellect, memory, and ego is designed as a practically useful apparatus for participation in the world. But spiritually speaking these psychic functions impose restrictions upon the spirit, and obstruct its authentic self-awareness. The root cause of all human suffering is the individual's alienation from his own true self or spiritual essence, and false identification with the different functions and modes of expression of nature.

When through regular practice of yoga discipline—the celebrated eightfold path of Patanjali—all psychic functions and modifications cease, the true Self shines out in its intrinsic glory. Or the Seer is established in his own essential nature (Taimni, 1967, p. 10).

The Self is not a substance endowed with consciousness as an attribute. It is pure consciousness itself, eternally perfect, absolutely free, and intrinsically luminous.

The ultimate goal of yoga discipline is true transcendental self-realization and peaceful self-sufficiency. This entails transcendence of all psychic polarities such as love and hate, pleasure and pain, creation and destruction, and consequent indifference *(udasinata)* to the affairs of the world.

---

*This does not mean that life is all pleasure and happiness. Yoga philosophy recognizes the problem of evil and suffering, death and tragedy. In its view all evil and suffering stem from ignorance *(avidya)* about the true nature of self and reality. That is why yoga discipline is designed to liberate man from evil, tragedy, and suffering through the attainment of illumination.

The word enjoyment *(bhoga)* is used by yoga psychology in a pickwickian sense. It means participation in the dualities of pain and pleasure, joy and sorrow, agony and ecstasy, tragedy and comedy. In one sense, the whole business of living is suffering, because even the pleasures and ecstasies of life are evanescent and ephemeral. So Buddha characterized all life as suffering *(dukkha).* In another sense, all life is enjoyment; because underlying the dualities of pain and pleasure, there is the overall experience of the checkered joy of being. The joy of living is prepotent over sorrow. That is why in spite of all sorrow, all living creatures want to live and cling on to life desperately unless pathologically disturbed. Yoga psychology emphasizes the intrinsic and spontaneous joy of being, living, and becoming.

The yoga of love is based upon the monistic spiritual philosophy. The individual self is not absolutely independent and self-sufficient. It is a unique spiritual substance and an eternal portion of the supreme Godhead, the creator, supporter, ruler, and dissolver of the universe. Its essential attributes are consciousness, bliss, immortality, and freedom from ignorance and egotism. The ultimate goal of life is loving communion with the supreme Godhead. Since all living things are creatures of God, compassion toward and service of all living creatures is an implication of the full-blown love of God.

The yoga of knowledge is based upon nondualistic spiritual philosophy. The idea of Personal God as one infinite and creative spiritual substance is self-contradictory. The substance is a category of the human intellect which cannot be applied to ultimate reality. Second, God as a person is related to the world and to finite spirits and is therefore relative, not absolute. So God is not ultimately real, even though from the relative standpoint of man and the world, the ultimate appears as God. The absolute appears as God just as the boundless sky appears blue to the human eye.

Since the individual Self *(jivatman)* is conceived as a spiritual substance, it is an intellectual construct. Raja yoga is right when it says that the true self is pure formless consciousness. But the contradiction in raja yoga is that it both denies and affirms the substantive reality of the individual self. To say that the individual self is eternally self-subsistent, absolutely independent, existing all alone, sufficient unto itself, is to bring in surreptitiously the metaphysical notion of substance. Moreover, the concept of an eternally self-subsistent individual self is in discord with the supreme mystical experience of an individual's oneness with the all of existence and the ground of all beings. So according to the yoga of knowledge, the true Self is indeed pure formless consciousness in the true sense of the word. But there can be only one infinite boundless pure consciousness which knows no divisions or limitations within itself, just as there is only one infinite space within which finite spaces are merely unreal and artificially constructed divisions.

In fine, according to the yoga of knowledge the ultimate reality is one infinite boundless consciousness. The Self is nondifferent from the ultimate reality, Being, just as finite space is nondifferent from infinite space. The distinctions of subject and object, individual and universal, creative and creature, one and many, are only relatively valid but ultimately unreal phenomenal appearances. The ultimate goal of the yoga of knowledge is the immediate apprehension of this supreme nonduality.

The yoga of superconscious energy (kundalini) holds that unconscious nature does not exist by itself. It is the lower form of manifestation of the superconscious creative energy of Being. The same superconscious energy is present in the psychophysical system of man, his empirical personality, in a latent form. It lies dormant within him at the base of the spinal cord. So it is known as the coiled-energy (the kundalini). The awakening of the coiled energy through yoga practice indicates that the yogi is now ready to make the final transition from the realm of darkness to the realm of pure spiritual wisdom, from death to immortality. When it reaches the highest brain center (known as *sahasrara*) the yogi is fully liberated, and he experiences immortality* and supreme bliss; he is totally united with the timeless Being or the supreme spirit.

On close inspection it will be found that the aforesaid traditional yoga systems are caught between the world transcending on one hand and cosmic action or participation in the world on the other. Integral yoga, which in some form or other has been the major source of inspiration during the spiritual renaissance of India, is an attempt to bridge the gulf between transcendence and participation. The renaissance movement (Chaudhuri, 1951a), spearheaded by such outstanding leaders as Ramakrishna, Vivekananda, Rabindranath Tagore, Gandhi, Aurobindo, and others, is an attempt to harmonize the values of time and eternity, of nature and spirit, of the imperfect world and the supreme Good. It has received its most comprehensive philosophical articulation in the writings of Sri Aurobindo. (1950; 1953; 1957; 1964).

Let me say a word here about the philosophical basis of Integral Yoga as interpreted and developed by the present author.

The authentic individual Self is neither detached, eternally perfect, isolated, pure consciousness, nor an eternal portion of the divine personality, nor pure consciousness nondifferent from undifferentiated Being. It is the unified and integrated whole of body, instinct, emotion, intellect, and intuition. Self-integration is a process of the total harmonization of one's being. Out of total integration of personality is born the integral, experientially comprehensive awareness of Being. Being is reality in its integral fullness. The nontemporal, logically indefinable depth dimension of Being is inseparable from its cosmic creativity. Being as cosmic energy produces the evolutionary process leading to the emergence of higher and higher values and patterns of creation and levels of consciousness. The fully integrated individual, aware of the basic trend and potential of human evolution, actively participates in the affairs of the world even after the attainment of personal liberation. The integral yoga is the kind of integrated self-development which helps him bring to full flowering his own potential to realize Being as the unity of spirit and nature, of perfection and process, of value and action. On the

---

*I have deliberately said *experiences* immortality. First, immortality in the Vedantic sense is not infinite duration in time but *beyond time*. So immortality is the essence of spaceless, timeless Being. To experience timeless Being is to experience immortality. Such an experience is therefore truly the meeting point of time and eternity. Whether the individual self itself is an immortal entity or substance is at this point debatable matter. According to the Yoga of Knowledge, the *individual* self is *not* immortal. He realizes full immortality by transcending his individuality and recognizing it as a product of *maya*, an appearance. The Self alone is immortal.

basis of such self-perfection, he makes his own little contribution to the consummation of planetary evolution in the emergence of a new world order. His integrated action is oriented to the dawn of a new age characterized by freedom for all, social justice, international harmony, and creativity of ever new values.

THE YOGIC THEORY OF PERSONALITY

According to yoga psychology, personality is a multilevel or multidimensional structure. It has such different levels or dimensions as the physical *(annamaya)*, the vital or instinctual *(pranamaya)*, the mental *(manomaya)*, the rational or gnostic *(vijnanamaya)*, the ego function *(ahamkara)*, the memory function with its latent impressions and dispositions *(smriti* and *samskaras)*, the pure spiritual *(anandamaya)*, and the ontological *(brahman, sunyata)*.

The physical aspect of personality consists of the visible, tangible organism comprising vital organs and glands of the body as well as the highly developed nervous system crowned with the brain.

The vital aspect of personality consists of the various instinctual drives such as desire for food and drink, sexual appetite, destructive impulsive, and creative tendency.

The mental aspect of personality is the organ of perception both external and internal (for example, perception of the tree over there or that of the feeling of anger inside). It also includes ordinary and extraordinary perceptions (perception of an automobile accident in front of me or perception of a plane crash ten thousand miles away). The mind has five sense powers, seeing, hearing, smelling, tasting, and touching, which ordinarily function through corresponding bodily sense organs. These sense powers, as distinguished from corresponding sense organs, are essentially mental powers and are not to be equated with the corresponding bodily organs, even though they ordinarily operate through them. The external sense organs obstruct the free functioning of the internal sense power of the mind. They impose limitations upon the mind in order to focus attention on the practical needs of life. But since the senses are essentially mental powers, they are capable of functioning independently of bodily sense organs (eye, ear, and so on) under special circumstances, giving rise to such extraordinarily subtle sense perceptions as clairvoyance, clairaudience, precognition, and prophetic vision. Since these are subtle paranormal sense perceptions, the designation ESP or extrasensory perception is not quite accurate.

The rational mind *(buddhi)* includes such functions as identification; inference, judgment, discrimination, evaluation, and so on. It is the power of expanding the frontiers of knowledge by inferentially passing from the known to the unknown. The buddhi also includes such functions of the rational will as deliberation, decision, determination, resolution, perseverance, systematic research, affirmation of intrinsic values, and value-oriented self-discipline.

The subconscious mind *(citta)* consists of memory, imagination, and preservation of the impressions of past experiences which in turn produce subtle tendencies and dispositions *(samskaras)*.

All psychic functions have an affective tone. They are accompanied by ever-changing feelings of pleasure and pain, like and dislike, love and hate, or indifference and apathy. It does not take very long for these feelings to turn into one another.

Besides the above, there is a supersensory and supraintellectual level of personality (turiya) which consists of pure spiritual intuition. It is known as the transcendental or fourth-dimensional consciousness. As a mode of knowledge beyond normal and paranormal psychic functions, the fourth-dimensional consciousness is the pure, unclouded cognition of the nontemporal Being.

The traditional view is that the fourth-dimensional Being-cognition unerringly reveals the Self as it is, the nontemporal Being as it is, and the variegated universe as it is. The individual in the course of his personality growth through yoga and meditation eventually attains this level of Being-cognition when all the modifications of the psyche *(citta vritti)* are completely restrained or hushed into silence (Taimni, 1967, p. 6).

The development of personality from infancy is punctuated with changing patterns of self-image or self-identity. When the growing infant becomes aware of himself as an individual entity separate from the mother, he identifies himself with the body. This is his material self *(anamaya purusha)*. Next, he identifies himself with his vital nature—that is, with various impulses, passions, and desires. This is his vital self *(pranamaya purusha)*. Next he identifies himself with his mental nature as a sentient percipient being *(manomaya purusha)*. This is his aesthetic nature. Next, he identifies himself with his rational nature and perceives himself as a thinking, deliberating, choosing being *(vijnanamaya purusha)*. Finally, through a bold meditative breakthrough in consciousness he discovers the transcendental level of existence and finds his true self there *(anandamaya purusha)* (Radhakrishnan, 1953, pp. 503–509).

There is a controversy among different schools of yoga psychology regarding the precise nature of the ultimate self. According to bhakti yoga psychology the essential Self is a permanent spiritual substance eternally subsisting as a dependency or portion of the absolute Spirit of which the material world is the outward expression. According to raja yoga psychology the essential Self is not a spiritual substance or entity but is pure formless individual consciousness itself—eternally subsisting in its intrinsic glory and freedom. According to the jnana yoga psychology, the essential self is pure formless supraindividual consciousness (beyond substance-attribute category) which is nondifferent from the one infinite existence-consciousness-bliss that is the ultimate reality of the universe.

According to some jnana yogis even the transcendental level of blissful Being-cognition falls into the realm of cosmic ignorance (maya, relativity) inasmuch as it is rooted in a new sense of distinction from undifferentiated Being. The ultimate self is absolutely nondifferent from Being-itself and is therefore even beyond the blissful self. Ultimate self-realization would consist in being perfectly one with Being (Radhakrishnan, 1953, p. 547).

But according to the yoga of love, the blissful self is the individual self in its ultimate essence. The spirit of devotion and love is its essential structure. So it is in accord with the highest truth that the illuminated individual soul can enter into loving and rapturous communion with the supreme Godhead (Ishwara).

The blissful Self is what may be called the Self in its pure spiritual dimension. If the nontemporal Being, the ultimate ground of the universe, is equated with pure bliss, as Samkara often does, then the spiritual dimension is certainly identical with the nontemporal ontological dimension. In that case there is no reality, whether individual or cosmic, which is beyond pure bliss (mystical or transcendental idealism).

But according to the teaching of Buddha, the ultimate is even beyond bliss. It is emptiness, void (sunyata). Existence, conscious bliss—such categories do not truly belong to the ultimate. Consistent with his doctrine of indeterminable Being, Samkara also is sometimes inclined to this Buddhist position. He rightly argues that the ultimate, which is indeterminable Being, must be beyond the blissful Self. This is necessary in order to vindicate the doctrine of the absolute nonduality of Self and Being (absolute nondualism), to which he stands committed. But this strikes at the root of his other favorite doctrines, namely, the reality of the Self (atman), and the reality of the supreme Spirit (Saccidananda). So Samkara finds himself on the horns of a real dilemma—the horns of the bull of Lord Shiva, of whom he is believed to be an incarnation.

I think an honest solution of the problem would consist in unequivocally agreeing with the Buddha that the ultimate, the nontemporal ground of the universe, is Emptiness—that is, indeterminable Being—void of even consciousness and bliss. It follows that the ontological root of the individual Self also is Emptiness. But, be it noted, that does not reduce the blissful Self to an unreality. Samkara is perfectly right in affirming the reality of the transcendent blissful Self (atman).

But to hold, as Samkara and all other Vedantists do, that the blissful Self is an eternally self-existent entity or reality is to commit the metaphysical fallacy of substantializing a mode of experience or poise of consciousness. The metaphysical fallacy is a persistent refusal to acknowledge the finitude of human consciousness.

The basic experiential datum of samadhi is the experience of freedom, immortality, transcendence of subject-object dichotomy, inexpressible bliss, boundless expansion of consciousness. There is no questioning or denying this immediate datum of the highest kind of spiritual or mystic experience that has ever fallen to the lot of man.

But then the question arises: What is the metaphysical or philosophical or psychological significance of this experience? What conclusions can be reasonably drawn from this indubitable experiential situation?

Both during the duration of this samadhi experience and also while describing it later on in verbalized form, every mystic or sage does some unconscious interpreting of his own. A metaphysician or philosopher waxes even more eloquent with his own tacit assumptions and interpretations.

For instance, some draw the conclusions that the individual soul or self is immortal and that God, a determinate mode of spiritual or supernatural Being, is also undoubtedly immortal. This is what both Buddha and Samkara denied as intellectual constructions of the basic experience. The ultimate as revealed in that experience was declared by Samkara as indeterminable Being *(nirguna Brahman)*. Buddha thought that even the word "Being" was a determination and so referred to the ultimate as Void or Emptiness. But both Buddha and Samkara further agreed that samadhi or nirvana reveals one's individual empirical existence as evanescent and unreal.

I am inclined to agree with Buddha and Samkara on most of the major points of philosophic importance. However, I cannot accept their unfortunate use of the words "unreal" and "illusory" as adjectives of individuality or empirical personality. Individual, empirical existence is no doubt transitory and evanescent. Whatever is temporal is certainly mortal—destined to be dissolved in the unfathomable vastness of Being sooner or later. But it was the unconscious, uncriticized, but unwarrantable assumption that *"whatever is impermanent is unreal"* which produced the world-negating attitude of these two great spiritual masters.

INTUITION

Intuition is immediate apprehension of some aspect, form, feature, or dimension of the real. It is the basic function of that structural element of psychic energy which is known as sattva. It is central to all psychic functioning and is therefore operative on all levels of psychic existence.

On the sensory level intuition is direct apprehension of sense data (such as a patch of color, a rap of sound). On the intellectual level it is the insightful awareness of fundamental assumptions, postulates, and underlying principles of logical thinking (such as the law of contradiction, the law of uniformity of Nature).

In the mystical sense of the term, intuition can be conscious, unconscious, or superconscious. Conscious spiritual intuition reveals the meaning of life in terms of images and symbols during waking hours. It can also operate during altered states of consciousness, such as the burning-bush experience of Moses and the descent-of-dove experience of Jesus. Superconscious spiritual intuition is meditative experience in its most sublime form (for example, cosmic consciousness, transcendental Being-cognition). It provides insight into the spiritual oneness of all existence and into the mystery of Being as the nontemporal ground of the universe. Superconscious spiritual intuition is the kind of ontological experience in which the subject-object dichotomy is completely transcended. It transcends the realm of objects, images, and symbols on one hand, and also the subjective I-sense or the knower-identity on the other.

Unconscious spiritual intuition, which operates through various symbols and images, musical sounds and colorful visions, mandalas or geometrical patterns, lies at the source of the rich mythological literature of the world.

Ever since Dr. Carl Jung announced his theory of archetypal images in the collective unconscious, immensely valuable and very extensive psychological research has been going on in this field. Let us have a quick look at some of the symbols of mythological intuition in India.

When in dream or creative imagination there is a stirring of the deeper levels of the psyche, the consciously held ideals and aspirations and the repressed unconscious impulses become symbolically involved in a dance drama of spiritual growth. The masculine and feminine aspects of personality—*prakriti* and *purusa, siva* and *kali, krishna* and *radha*—dance together with ecstatic joy with a view to refashioning the personality into a growing image of wholeness. In this refashioning or rebirth process strange combinations of opposites appear. For instance, the lion (the will to conquer) becomes the obedient vehicle of the divine mother Durga, the spirit of progress in self and civilization (Thomas, 1961, p. 57). The serpent (the sexual libido) becomes a willing servant in the churning of the ocean of the unconscious leading to the discovery of the nectar of immortality (symbol of spiritual fulfillment) (Chaudhuri, 1965a, p. 44). Life is experienced as a battleground of gods and demons, where the luminous powers of value-consciousness constantly wage war upon the dark forces of ignorance offering resistance and opposition. In every critical phase of history, god-man (avatar) appears on the cosmic scene to destroy the forces of darkness and establish the kingdom of truth and righteousness *(dharma samsthapan)* (Radhakishnan, 1952, p. 155). The godman is of course the embodiment of the time-spirit or of the creative impetus of planetary evolution.

EMOTION

We have seen that emotion is the hedonic tone of all psychic functions. But the emotions of ordinary life undergo constant fluctuation and agitation. Emotional fluctuations are a potent cause of human suffering and disorientation.

When an individual in the course of his spiritual unfoldment transcends his psychic level and is reborn on the pure spiritual level, the level of no-mind, no-intellect, no-ego consciousness, he experiences the peace that passeth understanding, which is the same as transcendental bliss *(ananda)*. The transcendental emotion of bliss is of the very essence of one's true Self. It is intrinsic to one's pure existence. Therefore, it is spontaneous and uninterrupted. It is not dependent upon any object, or possession, or activity, or desire fulfillment. It is one with pure existence and pure consciousness.

Pure egoless consciousness is the consciousness of the fundamental unity of all existence, of the interrelated coexistence of all in the One. So the experience of transcendental bliss is also the experience of universal unmotivated love. On the attainment of transcendental consciousness (turiya), one spontaneously feels like embracing the whole world in the spirit of joy and love. Not because he expects anything or reaches out for something, but because that is the essence of his inmost being, like the singing of a bird, or the blossoming of a flower, or the shining of a star.

Pure egoless consciousness perceives the multitudinous things of the world as crystallized expressions of infinite creative joy in the heart of Being. Everything or every being proclaims that creative joy.

Transcendental bliss in yoga psychology is qualitatively and ontologically different from ordinary joys and pleasures. Ordinary pleasure is the effect of fulfilling a desire for some object, perhaps good food, an automobile, or a sex partner. Transcendent bliss is not dependent upon any object or thing. It is the essential structure of the authentic transcendent self or pure formless consciousness. The true self is described as pure existence, Consciousness-bliss *(sat-cit-ananda)*. So to know the self is to experience this kind of bliss. It is the spontaneous outflow of true self-realization.

The goal of yoga is to go beyond object-dependent pleasures and pains and to realize the Self or Being which is existence-consciousness-bliss. This realization does not preclude one's recognition of the presence in the world of the dualities of life and death, good and evil, pain and pleasure, as characteristics of empirical or phenomenal existence.

A blissful self-realized yogi is therefore in a position to accept a lot of suffering in life, to bear a heavy burden or cross in the world, without being terribly affected by it. He can participate in a spirit of nonattachment and without expectation of reward and recognition because he is already full inside. He has already received the highest reward of life, to wit, the unity of wisdom, spontaneous bliss, and unconditional love.

MEMORY

Memory is the reproduction of past experiences in their original form. All past experiences and activities leave their impressions and images in the mind. These are known as samskaras.

Interest and attention, controlled by the requirements of survival and growth, play a vital role in the functioning of memory. Those elements of past experiences which made a vivid impression on the mind-body and those from which we should profit in the interest of survival and progress in the world are easily remembered. This shows the pragmatic design of our brain structure and mental functioning. The most overwhelming tragic experiences of life, likely to interfere with the growth process, are prone to be repressed. This selection-rejection function of memory (smriti) is evidence of its origination from maya,* the principle responsible for the practically useful mode of living.

But a person determined to transcend the boundaries of the world of pragmatic validity (maya) experiences the expanding horizons of memory. It is said of Gautama Buddha that in the course of his meditative exploration of the psyche, not only experiences of infancy but also those of his past incarnations began to emerge. Long-past experiences both useful and useless, happy and unhappy, good and evil, began to emerge in procession before his retrospective survey. This is an important step forward in search of one's total being which is beyond good and evil. Such a quest for the total self must not be hampered by conventional value distinctions or considerations of practically useful adjustment to the environment.

It follows that we can enlarge our memory in two ways. First, by sharpening our interest and attention in regard to the things we wish to remember. Second, by intensifying our search for truth as it is, undaunted by the practical consequences thereof.

It is not necessary to remember everything of the past in order to attain enlightenment. When necessary, significant memories of the past can certainly be reviewed and evaluated at an exceedingly higher rate. In the case of Buddha, a rapid survey and integration of the past was necessary toward the fulfillment of his historic mission of helping all classes of people.

---

*There is a huge amount of misunderstanding in this country about the doctrine of maya. It does not mean illusion and such. It refers to the world of dualities—pain and pleasure, suffering and enjoyment, good and evil, God and devil—which are all relative. So maya means the world of impermanence and relativity. It has pragmatic validity but not ultimate reality. A person who realizes the ultimate stops craving for ever-changing things of the world of maya.

MOTIVATION

Different instinctual drives and desires of the mind, impulses and passions, are often equated with motives. This is true of those psychologists who believe in unqualified psychological determinism and, in consequence, deny freedom to man.

According to yoga psychology, consciousness is the essential structure of man. It is coextensive with his whole being. Only, it should be noted, there are different degrees and various levels of consciousness. Consciousness is present in the so-called unconscious mind in implicit and unreflective form. It is present in the superconscious dimension in expanded and self-luminous form, independent of bodily sense organs and conceptual tools. Then again, whereas mind is object-dependent consciousness, the pure self is objectless, self-luminous consciousness *(swayam jyoti)*.

Pure, objectless consciousness is compared to the sun, which shines by its own intrinsic light, whereas the object-dependent mental consciousness is compared to the moon, which shines by borrowed light.

Coextensive with human reality, consciousness also is the central unifying principle of all healthy human life. Without the sanction, acceptance, or choice of the active principle of consciousness (buddhi), nothing happens in human life, no performance, no participation. If a drive, desire, or impulse is socially unacceptable for some reason, a different personal reason has to be invented, a plausible pretext has to be found, before receiving the sanction from the ruling principle of consciousness, the indwelling ruler of the body-mind. That is how the device of rationalization comes into play. No human being can do anything, however irrational it may look, without a reason for it, even though this reason might be pure fabrication of the mind. A bank robber may feel rationally justified in his act by considering the bank as a symbol of capitalistic exploitation of downtrodden people. The murderer of an innocent man may feel justified on the ground that his victim was a symbol of the society which had done great injustice to him.

What I am driving at is that an impulse, a desire, an inner drive, becomes a motive only when it is reflectively or unreflectively chosen, accepted, or sanctioned by the dynamic principle of consciousness (buddhi).

Let us now turn to a discussion of the different kinds of motivation operative in human life according to yoga psychology.

Broadly speaking, there are three kinds of motivation: instinctual, cultural, and pure spiritual or onto-aesthetic.

Instinctual motivations again are of three kinds according to the three modalities of nature: rajas, tamas, and sattva. The power drive, the domineering urge, the aggressive impulse, and the will to overcome and conquer form the group of motivations which might be called self-assertive *(rajasic)*.

Inertia, the tendency to follow the line of least resistance, preoccupation with personal safety, security and creature comfort, and excessive fear of risk, danger, and death form the group of motivations which are called self-protective *(tamasic).*

The desire to know, striving for growth and perfection, search for truth, freedom, justice, and harmony, and altruistic and humanitarian impulses of sympathy and fellow feeling belong to the group of motivations which may be called transpersonal or self-transcending *(sattvic).*

Cultural motivations derive from the educational process of the society. The ethical notions of good and evil, and the religious ideas of divine and undivine, heaven and hell, salvation and bondage, instilled in the mind from early childhood, are the matrix of cultural motivations. When, for example, a person sacrifices his life for the sake of his community or country, when he suppresses his instinctual nature in order to lead the life of pure reason, when he practices penances and religious ceremonies in order to go to heaven (ritualism), or engages in holy crusades or national wars of liberation (ideological indoctrination), they are all motivations rooted in cultural background.

But cultural motivations as well as those of the instinctual nature still belong in the realm of maya (ignorance and egoism). A person is still bound by fixed ethico-religious notions of his own cultural system of the time, without any personal realization of his own true self, or the ultimate ground of his own being.

Transcending cultural as well as instinctual motivations, both of which are more or less ego-tainted, is the spontaneous egoless motivation of authentic Self-realization. When the light of true Self-realization is kindled in the soul, instinctual and culturally conditioned motivations are burned to ashes. All impulses stemming from ignorance and egoism are consumed in the flaming vision of supreme truth born of spiritual liberation *(moksa or mukti).*

Immediately after full liberation, a person finds himself for a while doing nothing but contemplating in detachment the ultimate meaning of life and existence. All inner urge or incentive to action is knocked out. Enlightenment is inevitably followed, at least for a brief length of time, by what is called mystic inaction.

Some self-realized yogis come back to the social life of action just to wear out their past karma through detached and disinterested performance of egoless action directed to cosmic welfare. They see no point in further emotional involvement in the being of the world, or in initiating any substantial change in the conditions of living or in the power structure of the world. The sole motivation for them is that of the fading momentum of the past life of ignorant action. It consists of the residual traces of past ignorance *(avidyalesa)* like the lingering smell of garlic even after it has been removed from the room, or the continuing movement of a wheel even after its engine has burst into flame. A fully liberated person may also be motivated by what has been called the *lila* motivation of divine play (Radhakrishnan, 1960, p. 362), onto-aesthetic motivation. The liberated person sees through the relativity and ultimate unreality of the world, but he also perceives the game character of the world. Even though perfectly self-sufficient, still he participates in worldly action until one day the body automatically drops from his liberated consciousness.*

According to the spiritual outlook of the leaders of modern India, especially as it takes mature shape in the purna yoga of Sri Aurobindo, after a brief period of quiet contemplation and inaction, suddenly a new kind of motivation is freshly born in the self-realized yogi. It is the Being-motivation of union with the superconscient creative energy of Being. His personal will, whether egoistic or altruistic, whether patriotic or philanthropic, whether serious or playful, whether powered by maya or prompted by *lila,* is replaced by the Being-energy. To put it in another way, his personality is transformed into a perfect center of action of Being's pure creative impetus. So he is now in a position to practice to perfection the principle of nonaction in action. He is in a position to say with all sincerity: "I act, yet it is not I but Being acts through me." This may be aptly called the Being-motivation of a fully liberated and perfectly self-realized person (Aurobindo, 1950, pp. 526–529).

Being-motivation does not impose limitations upon a person's scope of action. In other words, a self-realized person does not have to choose only an ethico-religious field of action. In accordance with his perceived sense of destiny, he may function as a statesman or an artist, as a businessman or a soldier, as a cook or a carpenter. The unmistakable mark of his authentic self-realization would be his egoless dedication to cosmic welfare.

---

*I am still continuing here the traditional view of Indian philosophy. Most yogis and philosophers of India (except ancient Charvakas and modern agnostics) believe in the survival after death of the spirit as pure consciousness lodged in a subtle body *(suksma deha).*

My own position is this. I consider survival a distinct possibility. But I am also aware of some crucial facts. First, the theory of survival has not yet been empirically established to the satisfaction of open-minded skeptics. Second, I am mainly concerned with establishing the paramount value, both pragmatic and cognitive, of authentic mystical or yogic experiences within the framework of firmly established empirical truths. This can be done without having to bring in the theories of reincarnation and supernatural existence. From the practical standpoint, concentration upon the potentials of life here and now is far more important anyway.

Third, the theories of reincarnation and subtle psychic existence in supernatural planes belong, in ultimate analysis, in the realm of *maya* or relative truth, as Buddha and Samkara would say. Fourth, the theories of survival, supernatural existence, reincarnation, etc., involve a metaphysical interpretation of otherwise very real and meaningful parapsychological experiences. By metaphysical interpretation I mean interpretation in terms of relatively self-subsistent substances or entities like soul, disembodied spirit, the personal God as the first cause, etc., or separate planes of existence such as the supernatural realms of heaven and hell existing independently of human consciousness.

THEORY OF LEARNING

The theory of learning is influenced by the fundamental concepts in Indian thought of individual self, the human society, and the ultimate reality.

Since the individual self is a free unique focus of the cosmic whole, he cannot be treated as a mere stimulus-response phenomenon, nor as a cog in the wheels of the sociopolitical apparatus of a country, nor as a mere cell in the national organism. It is possible for him to have a mode of fulfillment even outside of the society, even though that may not be the highest ideal from a spiritual point of view.

Since freedom is of the very essence of the individual self, the first principle of teaching is, as Sri Aurobindo says, that nothing important can be taught from outside. The best thing to do is to create a peaceful and beautiful atmosphere of free growth, rich in various learning facilities. What a growing child sees in his environment, what he takes from his teacher—all that is unconsciously regulated from within by the unique needs of the growing psyche, restricted only by his own past karma. When enlightened, he becomes what he essentially is, namely, a self-conscious center of Being—*lila sathi*—that is to say, a spontaneously joyful medium of manifestation of such supreme values as peace, love, justice, and creativity.

True learning is the art of living in harmony with the essential needs of the growing psyche, with the essential needs of the growing society, and with the growing light of true self-realization.

In early childhood, a process of sociocultural conditioning is necessary to produce some healthy habits of eating and sleeping, work and play, as well as proper social customs and manners. Later on it is also necessary for an individual's close acquaintance with the cultural heritage of his society *(samaj dharma),* including aesthetic forms, ethical norms, religious injunctions, and spiritual aspirations. Close contact and sustained personal dialogue with a good teacher *(guru)* is considered essential in this respect. The force of example and inspiring touch of an illumined preceptor play a vital role in the learning process, a role far more vital than massive accumulation of factual information about the world around us.

Since the human individual is a free spiritual entity, a cardinal principal of learning is increasing self-awareness. It implies awareness of one's unique talent and potential which must be constructively developed. It implies awareness of one's own becoming *(swadharma),* instead of blind conformity to some fixed external standard or model.

A traditional interpretation of swadharma is that it is the law of one's own social position or caste role, and the rights and responsibilities defined by the caste role. But in yoga discipline proper, which aims at spiritual self-realization beyond the limits of conventional morality and religious taboos, swadharma means the unique rhythm and pattern of one's own personal growth. It is in recognition of this ideal that in yoga psychology, instead of one standardized path, different spiritual disciplines are recognized as different pathways leading to the same goal. Every individual has a free choice to accept and follow any particular system of yoga discipline, helping him along on the path to independent self-existence and unique self-expression.

It also implies appreciation of the four intrinsic values of life, such as law and order *(dharma)*, wealth and material resources *(artha)*, lawful satisfaction of natural human desires for food, sex, and comfortable living *(kama)*, and striving for liberation from ignorance and egoism resulting in authentic self-realization *(moksa)*.

Acceptance of all these four intrinsic values of existence gives rise to a hierarchically structured scheme of balanced living. An essential part of learning is a clear insight into the scale of values. The four essential values provide satisfaction to the four essential aspects of human personality. Respect for the law (dharma) satisfies the socioethical side of human nature. Lawful satisfaction of healthy desires (kama) brings fulfillment to the vital or instinctual aspect of human nature. Lawful acquisition and intelligent use of material goods and wealth provide us with the resources for self-gratification and self-development as well as promotion of social welfare. Finally psychophysical and spiritual disciplines enable us to attain the ultimate goal of life, spiritual self-realization (moksa).

A mature spiritual guide (guru) sees to it that the disciple does not become emotionally fixated upon him. His main job is to help the disciple to discover the divine guru within the disciples' own unconscious psyche. As soon as the disciple learns to stand on his own feet, capable of treading the right path leading to the ultimate goal, the guru gracefully parts company, liberating the disciple from his last emotional bonds. This is what the Vedantic Guru Totapuri did to Ramakrishna, Ramakrishna did to Vivekananda, Vishnuvaskar Lele did to Aurobindo, and Aurobindo did to many of his disciples.

Unfortunately, however, so often in India, guru-realization unconsciously takes the place of Self-realization. An immature guru, and there are many of them, speaks no doubt of the value of self-realization but unconsciously takes many precautions to keep his disciples under his hypnotic spell. And most disciples love only to remain in the spellbound condition out of gratitude to the guru for something unique and unprecedented that they might have received. A powerful *(siddha)* guru can give something which nobody else indeed can give, not even a scholar or a philosopher or a psychiatrist. He can communicate or transmit the power of transcendental love which awakens the latent psychonuclear energy, or ignites the dormant spiritual spark in the disciple. This is an invisible, nonverbal communication endowed with something that may be felt as a high-voltage electrical charge. It brings about a new unprecendented spiritual awakening. But since the guru may yet be incapable of mature self-sacrificing love it may also impose new bondage on the disciple.

Little realized is the fact that the encouragement of emotional fixation is not only detrimental to the personality growth of the disciple but also degrading to the integrity and sense of responsibility of the guru. It hinders the independent thinking and decisionmaking of the disciple. It also beclouds the guru's inward truth-vision and imposes upon him the necessity to make constant concessions to the immature understanding of his growing number of disciples. The only justification may, however, exist in those cases in which the guru really thinks that some disciples are simply incapable of attaining independent self-realization, at least in this life. The best mode of self-fulfillment open to them is to attain guru-dependent self-realization and to make on that basis their best contribution to society or humanity under the guru's total guidance.

When authentic self-realization matures to the point of creative freedom or illumined creativity, the learning process bears final fruit. The Self-realized person now participates in the social process as a unique center of higher values. He is no more under any obligation or compulsion to act and serve in society. He is liberated from the conventional moral distinctions of good and evil, right and wrong. He sees through the relativity of all socioethical norms. In consequence, he perceives the game-character (lila-ness) of all life. But out of the fullness of his freedom and the spontaneity of his creative joy he participates in society and in world affairs with a view to playing his own distinctive role, however small, in the unfolding drama of human society, regardless of profit and loss, praise and blame, approbation or vilification. His own true Self becomes his ultimate guru.

Thus we see that the concepts of swadharma (unique law of one's own growth), *guruvada* (the vital role of the guru), *samaja dharma* (unique growth pattern of every society), civilization as the field of playful self-expression of Being *(lila bhumi),* and the perfect individual as a creative center of Being are postulated as guiding principles of true education.

MIND-BODY RELATIONSHIP

In yoga psychology the problem of mind-body relationship has never existed in the form in which it has plagued Western psychology.

The Cartesian dualism of mind and matter as heterogeneous substances gave rise in Western psychology to all kinds of fantastic notions regarding the interaction between them. Descartes himself thought that that the interaction took place through the pineal gland, ignoring the fact that the pineal gland itself is a part of the material body, not of the immaterial mind. Later on, some of his followers, especially Arnold Geulinex, invented a bizarre theory of occasionalism or that of "two clocks." According to occasionalism, there is no direct causal relationship between psychic functions and physiological processes. Mind and body are like two clocks keeping perfect time due to God's perfect preadjustment. Their interaction is an illusory appearance of divine preadjustment (Russell, 1945, p. 561).

In yoga psychology, mind and body are not heterogeneous but homogeneous. They are different evolutes or modes of manifestation of the same fundamental creative energy, to wit, Prakriti (Mishra, 1963). In the same way, the outside physical environment and the mind-body are evolutes of the same primal energy, too. Since there is homogeneous and existential continuity here, the fact of interaction between mind and matter causes no problem. The dualism of mind and body is a product of our discursive understanding. It is a division inserted by dichotomous thinking within the continuum of our multidimensional experience.

But in traditional yoga psychology there is a new kind of dichotomy: the dichotomy of body-mind on one hand and the self as pure matter-free, mind-free, consciousness on the other. The self is conceived as formless, objectless, imageless consciousness (purusa, atman), which is eternal, unchanging, imperishable, beyond life and death, good and evil, pleasure and pain, cause and effect. It is radically different from the mind-body apparatus which is a specifically organized structure of unconscious primal energy.

How does the purusa or atman, the principle of pure formless, objectless, imageless consciousness act upon the unconscious body-mind structure? What is the precise mode of relationship involved here? The usual assumption is that the mind-body reflects the light of pure consciousness just as the ocean reflects the light of the moon. But on closer scrutiny it should be evident that this analogy is misleading and incapable of solving the real problem. In the case of the moon and the ocean both are material objects existing in the same space-time continuum. They are different only in this respect, that one is active light energy and the other is relatively passive receptive energy. But this difference does not destroy the fundamental homogeneity and existential continuity of moon and ocean.

The case of nature and spirit, prakriti and purusa, is entirely different. Nature is ever changing, unconscious, and imperfect. Spirit is absolutely perfect, unchanging, and unchangeable, formless consciousness. The body-mind complex exists and functions in space-time, in the cause-effect relational scheme, but the pure spirit is absolutely beyond space-time and beyond all relations and distinctions. So no type of interaction—not even interaction in the form of spirit's cognition of nature, or nature's reflection of spirit—lends itself to rational comprehension.

The Indian tradition has, broadly speaking, three answers to the above problem. These answers are formulated by the yoga of love, the yoga of self-existence, and the yoga of nondual consciousness.

According to the yoga of love, the Self is *not* radically and absolutely different from Nature. Both Nature and Self are constituent elements of the creative energy of the same supreme Godhead (Ishwara). Nature appears unconscious because the spiritual energy of the Divine is operative in Nature in its most externalized and objectivized form. The individual Self in its essence is a differentiated portion of the same divine energy in its most luminous form. So between body and soul or Self there is both homogeneity of quality and substance as well as ontological continuity.

According to the yoga of nondual consciousness (jnana), the problem itself is simply fictitious. It is a mere fabrication of the human intellect. The metaphysical dualism of Nature and Spirit is a pure illusion. So the question of interaction between them does not really arise. The Self, which is nondifferent from Being, is infinite, formless, undifferentiated consciousness. Consciousness knows no bounds, divisions, differentiation, or fragmentation. The empirical self consisting of body and mind is indeed made of the energy-stuff of Nature. But Nature herself has no ultimate, independent reality. She is the energy of Nescience or Ignorance (maya, avidya). Since body, mind and the empirical self are made of the same energy of Nescience, they can certainly interact. But since from the standpoint of ultimate Being, neither Nature nor the body-mind personality nor the empirical person exists, their seeming interaction is only an illusory appearance.

In the view of the present writer, all the above theories involve untenable metaphysical assumptions. There is no experiential evidence to support the theory of an eternally self-existent and absolutely perfect, unchanging, and unchangeable Self, finite or infinite, individual, universal, or transcendental. The human individual does indeed have the characteristic of pure formless consciousness capable of cognizing body, mind, Nature, and their functions, processes, and phenomena. But the utmost that can be said about pure consciousness without overstepping the limits of experience is that pure consciousness is an emergent characteristic of the human psychophysical system. As the human organism endowed with the brain emerged in the course of evolution, pure formless consciousness also emerged as an essential characteristic of man. Thus the integral view of human personality is firmly established on the empirical foundation.

The distinction between mind and the Self is emphatically not a metaphysical or ontological difference. The human mind is in its essential structure an empirical, object-oriented modality of consciousness. It is an emergent characteristic possessed by the highly developed human organism endowed with the brain. What is mystically described as the spiritual or transcendental Self is a further refinement of mental consciousness. As the brain-energy of the evolving human organism attains to a higher degree of complexity of structure and function, it acquires the still higher emergent characteristic of pure self-luminous consciousness.

When man's self-luminous consciousness in its turn rises to the height of its potential, it leaps forth into the pure flame of unclouded Being-cognition. In other words, at the highest point of development, man's pure consciousness acquires the transcendental dimension of intuitive apprehension of Being as the nontemporal ground of both Nature and Spirit.

To know Being is to experience oneness with Being. So when an individual intimately knows Being, he also partakes of the life eternal of Being via his sense of identification. To transform this experience of identity or oneness into the doctrine of individual or personal immortality is an unwarrantable metaphysical or theological construction. Such a construction evidently bears the marks of wishful thinking.

The foregoing remarks express in a nutshell the integral theory of personality as developed by the present writer on the basis of his own pursuit of integral yoga. The central core of the theory is that man's total personality is an undivided and indivisible continuum of existence-consciousness-joy.

SOCIAL RELATIONSHIPS

According to yoga psychology, society is the organized structure of collective living for creative self-expression of the spirit in man, his authentic self. History is the unfolding of the drama of human relations, social, economic, political, cultural, national, and international. But history in its turn is an integral part of the drama of evolution of cosmic nature.

The cosmic process is the spontaneous and unceasing expression of the creative impulse *(ananda)* inherent in the heart of Being. The historical process comprising the changing phases of man's sociocultural and economic-political relations is spontaneous expression of the creative joy inherent in the human psyche. The creative joy of the human psyche, both individual and collective, is, of course, in ultimate analysis, the creative joy* of Being, the ground of human existence. The

---

*As applied to Nature, the word "joy" simply means the free spontaneity of her creative energy which finds expression in the blossoming of flowers, the shining of stars, etc. Since man has some freedom, his creative self-expression assumes many forms. Some people experience joy in killing and mass murder; some people experience joy in self-sacrifice for a noble cause; and some people experience joy in protecting the virtuous and punishing the lawbreakers. Moral evil consists in the distorted joy of selfish or egoistic action—whether of the individual or collective ego—in disregard of collective good or cosmic welfare. When spiritually blind ego-dominated people are bent on perpetrating evil —which is unquestionably a terrible social reality—it becomes the duty of more value-conscious or humanized men to deliver the counterblow with a view to paving the way of evolutionary programs. This is what Krishna advised Arjuna to do in the Bhagavad-Gita.

It follows that even though everybody is motivated by the joy of self-expression, not all such joys are good. That is where comes the need for yoga, meditation, spiritual discipline, psychophysical purification, etc., designed to lead to the bliss of Being-realization. The creative joy of Being-realiza-

human psyche is in ultimate analysis no different from the creativity of Being operative on the level of the human consciousness.

So the history of civilization is in ultimate analysis the story of man's creative self-expression. It is the story of "an eternal child," as Sri Aurobindo says, "playing an eternal game in the eternal garden" of life (1964, p. 8). The spontaneous creativity, the archetypal child, is constantly making, unmaking, and remaking ever new designs, perpetually building, unbuilding, and rebuilding ever new castles, with the countless sands of the seashore of life.

Let us now turn from poetic expression to psychological data. The closer man gets to his true Self (atman) which is one with Being, the ground of the universe, the more he experiences a feeling of self-sufficiency, a transcendent emotion of unconditional joy and love, the spontaneity of freedom and creativity.

A fully self-realized person perceives that his social existence and behavior pattern before enlightenment was largely a product of sociocultural conditioning. On the basis of his newly gained enlightenment he realizes that he is not only a member of the social organization but also beyond society, a unique, creative center of Being. He feels himself in society and yet not of society. On the basis of his blissful self-realization, he feels free to decide either to keep away from society or to participate in society. He may feel free also to decide that the conventional game of life being over for him, it is now time to leave the playground and be restored to the peaceful self-existence of his transcendental poise of Being.

In expressing the possibility of free choice, *sankhya* yoga gives the simile of a dancing girl. The flux of social existence is like the enchanting dance drama of the creative dynamism of Nature (prakriti). So long as a person is under the spell of ignorance (avidya) or nonapprehension of his true Self he is bewitched with the wonderful dance of Nature, gets actively involved, and goes through emotional fluctuations. But sooner or later the time comes when he gets fed up with Nature's dance-drama, withdraws and searches within, and becomes one with the true Self. He then perceives the artificiality of the social distinctions of class and creed, the relativity of socioethical laws of good and evil, and the mutability of all social roles and duties.

But according to Vedantic yoga, especially neo-Vedantic yoga, after the game of ignorance is over, a new game of creative freedom can begin. This is a higher choice open to the liberated person. He becomes aware of the meaning and secret purpose and dynamic potentials of human evolution on earth. So out of the spontaneity of his illumined freedom and creative joy he may decide to participate

---

tion fully takes into account the forces of good and evil, progress and regress, operative in society. On the basis of dispassionate evaluation it may seek expression through destruction of the forces of evil as a prerequisite to a new order of creation in tune with life's intrinsic values.

in social, economic, and political activities. Unconcerned with personal profit or loss, praise or blame, public applause or denunciation, he freely decides to participate in the social game of countless interpersonal relations, with a view to making his own little contribution to the growth of civilization or the blossoming of the evolutionary potential of human society.

In integral yoga this is called the *lila of divine action,* the creative joy of cooperation with the spirit of evolving earth-consciousness. It is the action of creative freedom toward the building of divine life on earth—that is, toward the establishment of a unified world order of peace, plenty, and progress.

In the yogic attitude to human relations and to society as a whole there are three changing phases of dialectical inner growth. These are the phases of attachment, renunciation, and renewed participation; obedience, rebellion, and joyful reconstruction.

A child first affirmatively feels himself as an integral part of his mother and father. As he begins to grow up, he rejects this relationship of utter dependence and asserts himself as an independent entity in order to feel his independent existence. In the course of his search for personal identity, he one day gains profound insight. The meaning of his unique existence as an individual dawns upon his mind. As this precious insight is fully assimilated, transforming his outlook and inner being into a strong center of independent existence, he now finds it a greater joy to reestablish affectionate relationships with parents without sacrifice of individuality.

The same is true with regard to our relationship to society itself. In the course of responsible social participation, it is natural to get involved more and more. Increasing possessiveness and commitment, mounting rights and privileges on the one hand, and duties and obligations on the other, build up to a dizzying height. Then the need for individuation asserts itself. One decides to renounce all possessions and social bonds in search of the inmost Self. Far away from the maddening crowd, one finds a place of solitude where the flame of self-inquiry may shine undisturbed, burning through the layers of false identification.

Finally, the moment of revelation comes. The voice of truth speaks in the stillness of the soul. From the sunlit summit of illumined consciousness one beholds the stream of social existence (samsara) with calm objectivity, from the perspective of the eternal. But the light of such wisdom not only dissolves all personal problems but also illuminates the path back to society. The retreat is followed by return. Renunciation is followed by joyful participation. Because the seeming gulf between nirvana and samsara, between enlightenment and bondage, vanishes like mist before the rising sun, one is inspired afresh to take part in the drama of life, in selfless dedication to human welfare.

The same is true of all interpersonal relations. Emotional maturity in all human relations is oftener than not the fruit of dialectical evolution. The initial attraction between two persons is inspired by mutual admiration of obvious good qualities satisfying deep-seated psychic needs. But as the previously hidden shadow side begins to show up, the honeymoon period fades away. The process of disenchantment sets in. Mutual withdrawal may quickly pass over into mutual recrimination. The first day's overflowing love suddenly turns to strange hatred, foreboding the last day, and threatening total severance of relations. But should favorable circumstances provide the opportunity for patiently endured further growth, the parties concerned come out of the fiery ordeal and rededicate themselves to a more meaningful relationship, broad-based upon realistic understanding of each other. Without going through the fire of realistic and balanced assessment, the interpersonal relations of affection, respect, and love do not get a chance of mature fruition.

VARIETIES OF MYSTIC EXPERIENCE

Yoga is practiced in India as the art of fearless adventure in the domain of consciousness. All kinds of experiments with the spiritual truth, conventional or unconventional, traditional or iconoclastic, have been made over the centuries in the yoga laboratories known as ashrams. A rich harvest of diversified mystic experiences has been the consequence thereof.

A brief outline of ten clearly distinguishable authentic* mystic experiences is presented below in an approximate order of increasing profundity.

1. Experience of the Self as transempirical subject.

Our ordinary self-identity is that of the physical-social self: Mr./Ms. X, child of so-and-so, holding a specific position in a specific community.

As a person withdraws into the silence of his meditation room and turns the searchlight of his attention inward, introspection reveals his identity as a stream of consciousness, a flux of cognitions, emotions, and conative urges. This is his empirical self *(manomaya purusa)*. At this stage his inner self is likely to be disturbed frequently. Every now and then he is unhinged from his self-poise and unconsciously hurled into the sphere of objectivity. Sometimes he finds himself lifted into a romantic land of sexual fantasy, and sometimes again he finds himself

---

*The following are a few inauthentic mystic experiences:

1. Regression to the oceanic feeling of the infant to whom the world appears as a vast undifferentiated "presentation continuum" or "a big looming buzzing confusion" (William James). It can be very delightful.

2. Regression to the primitive's "participation mystique," when the sense of individually has not yet emerged.

3. The false feeling of omnipotence or I-am-God-ness resulting from extreme introversion and ego inflation or artificially triggered premature kundalini-awakening.

thrown into a shadow land of threatening phantoms. Sometimes he is delighted with delusions of grandeur, and sometimes again he is horrified with the upsurge of unsuspected dark forces. The meditator is helplessly tossed to and fro on the stream of his consciousness.

But as from day to day, from month to month, a person continues the meditative inquiry into the inmost center of his being, one day a sudden leap, a spiritual saltus, takes place. The meditator discovers with profound joy a deeper level of consciousness. Quietly taking his stand on the newly discovered level, he is now in a position to watch and survey the unceasing stream of his psychic contents and functions. His self-identity now is that of a detached spectator unaffected by changing images and ideas, unperturbed by external disturbance or internal agitation. He is now the calm witness-consciousness *(saksi)*, indifferent to the spectacular dance of Nature (prakriti). The play of hide and seek between mind and spirit is now over for him. This is the experience of *savikalpa samadhi* in the discipline of raja yoga. It reveals the Self as the center of awareness of the cosmic whole *(vijnanamaya purusa)*.

2. Experience of the Self as pure transcendence beyond subject-object.

As the meditation process further continues and matures, one day, without any advance notice, another spiritual jump takes place. This is a jump to a still deeper level of consciousness beyond the subject-object dichotomy. This jump from the transempirical to the transcendental as well as the previous jump from the empirical to the transempirical is as spontaneous and mysterious as the sudden jumps of a moving electron from one orbit to another within the structure of an atom. As the meditator discovers this deeper level of pure transcendence, he perceives himself as the great Silence, as the unutterable Peace that passeth understanding. The dancing girl Prakrit suddenly vanishes from his field of vision. The dichotomy of subject and object, spectator and spectacle, witness and his field of observation, is entirely dissolved. The silent Self shines as the absolute *(kevala)*. This is the experience of *nirvikalpn samadhi* in the discipline of raja yoga. It reveals the Self as pure formless eternal consciousness *(nitya suddha purusa)*.

3. Experience of the creative ground of all existence.

When a person treads the path of devotion (bhakti yoga) following the principles of total self-surrender (letting go), constant remembrance (one-pointed concentration), repetition of the Name (taming the restless mind), and so on, he one day makes an immediate contact with the creative ground of his being. This is objectively and symbolically represented to him as God. He may hear the voice of God disclosing the unique creative potential of his life. Usually this happens when the forehead center of consciousness is opened. Or he may enter into rapturous communion with the indwelling divine presence within the unconscious psyche. Usually this happens when the soul-center behind the heart is opened.

4. Experience of the oneness of all existence.

The mystic experience of the all-pervasive oneness of all existence may be mediated either by the Self or by the image of God. In ultimate analysis, the image of God is no other than the projection of the Self. Subjectively, the yogi experiences the whole world within himself and experiences himself within all things and living beings of the world. Objectively, the same God that the yogi perceives within himself, he also beholds pervasively present everywhere in the world.

5. Experience of an eternal Thou.

A further intensification of consciousness following the direction of devotion produces the mystic experience of Being or the higher Self as an eternal Thou. At this stage Being is intimately perceived either as the Heavenly Father or as the Divine Mother. Being may also be perceived as an unfailing companion or an eternal child. Furthermore, Being may even be perceived as the Lord of one's soul, or as the supreme Lover with whom some kind of most exciting mystic marriage is possible. The bhakti yoga literature of India abounds in elaborate accounts of such mystic experiences of divine love (Bhattacharyya, 1953, 371–372).

6. Experience of the transpersonal Being-energy.

Most yogis of India would agree that the creative energy of Being is present in man as the psychonuclear energy. It has been variously described as the coiled energy or serpent power (kundalini), or as the mystic fire *(divya agni)*. It is the transpersonal Being-energy in the sense that, when awakened, it is capable of carrying the individual beyond the furthest boundaries of his personal consciousness into the realm of all-sustaining, all-generating, and all-fulfilling transcendence. When evoked into full operation by yogic methods of breath control and undivided concentration, the swiftly moving Being-energy is experienced as the dance of Kali beating down all opposition with lightening speed and consuming with her fiery tongue all impurities of the psychophysical system. As the irresistible Being-energy, drunk as it were with the ecstasy of inner expansion, begins to move in all directions clearing up the enormously complex network of nerve channels in the human organism, she is sometimes experienced as the divine mother Durga battling with the forces of darkness with her ten invincible arms. Blessed with her grace—the same as the grace of Kali or the mystic fire Agni—the yogi is empowered to capture the kingdom of heaven by storm and enjoy the expanding vision of boundless Being.

7. Experience of Being as infinite existence-consciousness-bliss.

This is the most exalted mystic experience in jnana yoga. Being is experienced as the superpersonal spiritual mystery, or as God beyond God. This God beyond God is not any determinate mode of existence but the indeterminable nontemporal ground of all determinate forms of existence. This ultimate ground is perceived not as an infinite spiritual substance endowed with immortal existence, infinite consciousness, and boundless joy and love. That would make the ultimate finite, limited, and determinate, a manifest absurdity. In point of truth, the ultimate is infinite consciousness as such, which is inseparable from boundless bliss as such, which is inseparable from imperishable existence as such *(Sat-Cit-Ananda).* So the nontemporal ground is perceived as the all-encompassing medium of all existence, just as the infinite span is perceived as the boundless medium of the material world.

8. Experience of Being as the absolute void.

Gautama Buddha bore testimony to the most austere and logically perfect experience of Being. He experienced the ultimate ground as the absolute void or emptiness *(sunyata)* in the sense that it is void of all determinations without exception. Strictly speaking, it is a violation of the indeterminable character of Being to describe it even as existence-consciousness-bliss, which are obvious determinations of our experience.

At the core of both the Vedantic and the Buddhist forms of mystic experience, there is a perception of the unreality or falsity of the world of imperfection, change, and multiplicity. So both the schools postulate the principle of cosmic ignorance (avidya, maya) to account for the appearance of the ever-changing cosmic manifold.

9. Experience of Being as one with cosmic energy.

Tantric mystics who follow the discipline of kundalini yoga reject the notion of Being as empty or void of energy. Their mystic experiences are charged through and through with the power dance of the coiled energy. Naturally therefore they experience the ultimate ground of the universe as Being-Energy (siva-sakti). In consequence, the world of change and multiplicity also is perceived as the real manifestation of the creative energy of Being.

10. Experience of Being-Energy as creative evolution.

This means that Being-Energy is perceived not only as the creative ground of the real universe but also as the impetus of the evolutionary processes giving rise to higher and higher forms and functions, and to ever-new values and patterns of perfection. Evolution is a constant interaction between nature and spirit, always giving birth to fresh novelties and ever new creative syntheses. Experience of the process of evolution as a meaningful expression of Being-Energy has been described by Sri Aurobindo as supramental or integral consciousness (purna jnana). It is the inspiring source of integral self-discipline.

The light of integral consciousness is not only revelatory of the fullness of Being, it is also effectively transformative. A person first achieves this light of total truth on a transcendent level of consciousness. But then it is possible for him to bring this integral light down to the lower levels of his existence: to his physical and social consciousness; to the emotional and vital levels of his being; and even to the most obscure recesses of his unconscious mind. By doing so the entire personality of man can be transformed into a fit instrument for the increasing manifestation of higher values such as truth, love, and beauty in human life and society.

VARIOUS ENERGY CENTERS (CHAKRAS)

A very interesting feature of yoga psychology is the doctrine of energy centers *(chakras)*. It has been most elaborately developed in the psychology of tantra or kundalini yoga.

The doctrine of energy centers implies that our central nervous system is a hierarchically organized structure, that energy and consciousness are inseparable.

There are seven major energy centers in the human organism. Many Western writers are inclined to equate the chakras with different nerve plexuses, ganglia, and glands. But this is contrary to the view of the tantric masters (Woodroffe, 1964, p. 164), who maintain that whereas the nerve plexuses, ganglia, and glands control the ordinary physiological and psychological processes of a person, the chakras or energy centers, which exist only in the living organism and never in the dead body, are located inside the innermost channel *(brahmanadi)* of the spinal cord as consciousness potentials. These consciousness potentials can be actualized only with the aid of the awakened coiled energy (the transpersonal Being-energy). So long as the Being-energy lies dormant at the base of the spinal cord, the chakras exist only as inoperative spiritual potentials of man.

The chakras as consciousness potentials relate to, although they are not equivalent to, various nerve complexes, ganglia, and glands. Purification of these nerve complexes by yogic methods is a *sine qua non* of the opening of the chakras, or actualization of the spiritual potentials. We already referred to the root center *(muladhara)* at the base of the spinal cord. The release of the coiled energy means the opening of the root center. It signifies the shifting of consciousness from the ego-centric to the cosmo-centric or Being-centric focus, and a discovery of the transmental dimension of existence. At this stage the flux of mental thoughts, desires, feelings, and tendencies appears, at least to some extent, like a flight of birds or clouds, passing before the steady light of inward consciousness without affecting or disturbing the latter.

Psychologically, the root center is the center of organic consciousness. It is a matter of opinion whether the root center corresponds to the sacral plexus in the region of the anus or to the sacro-coccygeal plexus midway between genitals and anus. Cosmologically, the root center corresponds to the material world. On the opening of this center, the yogi experiences matter as the womb of the spirit.

The second chakra, known as the *swadhisthana,* is the transmental consciousness center of our vital or instinctual nature. One becomes aware of one's vital nature as the microscopic representation within oneself, of the macroscopic subtle vital level of existence-consciousness, or of the biosphere, to use an expression of Teilhard de Chardin (1959, p. 78). It is possible at this stage to tap the vital currents of energy flowing in one's environment.

The instinctual center corresponds to the prostatic or epigastric plexus, which again is vitally related to the endocrine gland known as the gonads. When the energy consciousness is lifted to this center through the activity of the kundalini, one may experience a tremendous upsurge of sexual energy. If a person has not previously come to terms with the sexual libido, he may get at least temporarily "blocked" in his spiritual progress. Much of his meditation may be reduced to a phantasmagoria of hallucinatory sexual gratification. One may be inwardly prompted to set aside the spiritual pursuit, at least temporarily, in order to finish the unfinished business of settling accounts with the sexual drive. Or, with the help of a protective environment, such as an ashram or a monastery, one may violently suppress the sexual urges and forge ahead on the path at the cost of mutilation of a vital aspect of personality.

On the opening of the second chakra, one experiences Being as vital energy, the élan vital *(prana),* the universal life force, as Henri Bergson puts it.

The third chakra, known as the *manipura,* is the center of higher ambition and the will to power. It is the naval or umbilical center, corresponding, according to some, to the solar plexus, and according to others, to the lumbar plexus. The solar and lumbar plexuses, again, are vitally related to the adrenal gland (Tiller, 1971).

The third center is cosmically related to the psychosphere—that layer of the global atmosphere which is surcharged with the vibrations of psychic experiences. This is another danger zone for the spiritual seeker. At this level there is the danger of being enchanted with the various possibilities of power grandeur. One gains the ability to tap the streams of psychic energy flowing through the human environment. The successful dictators of history, such as Napoleon, Caesar, Hitler, Mussolini, and Stalin, had access to the power region. When a person concentrates his whole being on the glory of power, his power chakra is activated. They also felt that they were omnipotent instruments in the hands of Destiny.

At this stage, Being is experienced as the cosmic will to power, as Nietzsche experienced it.

The fourth center, known as the *anahata,* is the center of the soul or psychic being. Psychologically speaking, the soul is the seat of unselfish love and the sense of higher values. On the opening of this center, one experiences for the first time in life the pure flame of spiritual love, unconditional, unmotivated love directed to man or God. One also experiences the spontaneous and intrinsic joy of Being. Furthermore, one hears at this stage the music of the cosmic harmony, the music of the spheres, or the music of the cosmic sound vibration which was at the beginning of creation. That is why it is called the center of anahata, which means the original sound not produced by any friction. Religious poetry in India describes this enchanting sound as the celestial music flowing from the flute of Krishna, the higher Self or the Divine playmate of man.

Physiologically, the soul center corresponds to the cardiac plexus, which is vitally related to the thymus gland. Cosmically, it is related to the realm of beatitude *(janaloka),* an essential part of what Teilhard de Chardin calls the Noosphere. At this stage a person, filled with the spirit of pure love and spontaneous joy, can bestow healing and wholeness upon all those whose various ailments are traceable to the lack of love in life. One experiences Being as the personal Godhead who is the unity of wisdom, love, joy, and beauty. One enters into loving and blissful communion with one's Supreme Beloved in an eternal I-Thou relationship. Or one may experience in one's heart the birth of a new celestial light, perhaps the light of Krishna-consciousness or Christ-consciousness or Buddha-consciousness.

The personal God is the symbol of the unity of all supreme values. Or personal God may be experienced as the phenomenal manifestation of Being under a certain degree of intensity of love and devotion, just as the colorless, shapeless water of the ocean appears under a certain degree of temperature as the white iceberg with a definite shape and size.

The fifth important chakra, known as *vishuddha,* is the center of pure and distinctive awareness of things as they are in their uniqueness or suchness. It is an effective center of communication and powerful self-projection. One realizes one's own Self as a unique individual, as an intrinsically valuable spiritual being, as an active center of creative energy. The vishuddha center corresponds to the phalangeal or laryngeal plexus, at the base of the throat, which is vitally related to the thyroid gland.

Being is experienced here as the creative word, as Vak, or Bharati, the goddess of speech (Woodroffe, 1964, p. 122).

A person in whom this consciousness potential has been actualized can transmit the power of existence with the help of a suitable word or mantra, and can serve as a source of great creative inspiration to others.

The sixth important center is known as the wisdom center, or as the divine command center *(ajna)*. It is also known as the center of the third eye of philosophic knowledge.

Physiologically it corresponds to the cavernous plexus, located at the midregion between the two eyebrows. The cavernous plexus again is vitally related to the pineal gland. It has command over all efferent or motor nerves. Some connect it with the pituitary gland, and some connect it with the cerebellum.

Psychocosmically, the command center corresponds to the cosmic level of self-fulfilling ideas, another important dimension of the Noosphere. In yoga philosophy it is specifically known as the *maharloka,* the realm of cosmic consciousness or synoptic vision of the world as a whole.

There are various reasons why this center is called the command center. It is not the center of ineffectual intellectual knowledge divorced from the power of self-fulfillment. It is the center of spiritual enlightenment, which carries its own authority and power of self-fulfillment. Second, on the opening of this center, a person gains self-mastery, perfect control over various urges, impulses, and tendencies of his personality. Third, he receives the unconditional imperative of his higher self, the pure spiritual self. This imperative is not externally communicated to him by any divine authority existentially separate from him. It is the command of the divine presence dwelling within himself. It is the imperative of his own destiny, the freely chosen mission of his life.

Being is experienced here as destiny or the purpose of life, freely chosen on the basis of awareness of one's true Self as related to the cosmic whole. So, self-realization takes place on this level as awareness of one's true Self as a creative center of the cosmic whole.

The highest center, known as the crown center, is metaphorically called the thousand-petaled lotus *(sahasrara)*. The opening of this center means the full blossoming of man's spiritual potential at the thrilling touch of the sunlight of pure timeless Being. It is the center of genuine transcendental consciousness or transcendent cognition of the nontemporal depth dimension of Being.

The opening of the crown center produces what may be called the transcendental experience of Being as the nontemporal ground of the universe *(nirvikalpa samadhi, nirvisesa nirvana)*. Physiologically, the crown center corresponds to the top of the skull or upper brain, which is closely related to the pituitary gland. It corresponds to the highest level of spiritual consciousness, that of existence-knowledge-bliss. It may aptly perhaps be called the pure ontosphere *(satyaloka)*.

It is the loftiest level of consciousness that man has ever attained.

Being is experienced here first as supracosmic existence—consciousness-bliss, as ineffable superconscience, or absolute void (Buddha) or indeterminable Being (Sankara). The present writer is inclined to describe this center as that of indefinable cosmic creative energy, or Being-Energy *(Brahma-Sakti)*.

On the attainment of this level of consciousness a person gains enormous power for healing people and making them whole by transmitting the power of illumined and integrated consciousness. The built-in healing power of the psyche reaches the highest point of development on the activation of this center. It is the revitalizing, rejuvenating, and inspiring power of the perfect unity of wisdom, love, and peace. On this level a person realizes oneness with the nontemporal Being. Such an enlightened person can awaken the transpersonal Being-energy of other people with a loving embrace or touch on the head or a compassionate glance or a softly spoken word, piercing the heart like a shaft of light. It is the alchemy of luminous Being-energy, capable of transforming clay into gold, ordinary men into heroes and saints, as demonstrated in the lives of such great masters as Jesus, Gautama, Lao-tzu, Ramakrishna, Aurobindo, and others.

Being is experienced here as the logically indefinable unifying ground of Nature and Spirit, of universe and self. All that can be said about this experience is: Being is Being. Being must not be equated with any such determinate mode of existence as matter, life, mind, and spirit.

PSYCHEDELIC EXPERIENCES

It is common knowledge today that there are varieties of psychedelic experience produced by such mind-changing drugs as mescaline, marijuana, LSD-25, and so on.

According to the yogic methodological postulate of comprehensive experientialism as outlined before, our psychological knowledge will ever remain incomplete without careful analysis and unbiased evaluation of the various types of psychedelic experience. Since all human experience has in it an element of truth-revelation (sattva), an open-minded examination of psychedelic experiences is sure to be richly rewarded in terms of psychological understanding, therapeutic efficiency, and even ontological insight into the structure of Being.

It is well known that the precise nature of psychedelic experience depends upon both set and setting. It depends upon the physiological and psychic conditions of the subject at the time of ingesting the drug. But then it also depends upon the setting or environmental arrangement. A harmonious, softly musical, tastefully decorated environment occupied by friendly and trustworthy persons is likely to lend a spiritual dimension to the drug experience. On the contrary, a discordant, disorderly, and boisterous environment occupied by suspicious-looking people is likely to produce a frightful and grueling effect.

For our purpose let us classify psychedelic experiences as bad trips and good trips.

Bad psychedelic trips such as excessive depression, exposure to dreadful phantoms, suicidal tendencies, feelings of utter helplessness, and such reveal to the subject the deep, dark abysses of his unconscious psyche. These dark abysses again are not absolutely subjective but are causally related to his objective physiological conditions on one hand and his distorted views of life and reality on the other.

Good psychedelic trips, which usually take place under favorable conditions in a proper setting, can provide a person with profound insight into his own hidden potentials, into the relativity of conventional ethico-religious conceptions, into the pervasive oneness of all existence, and into the immeasurable vastness of Being, far transcending the limits of the previously known world with its established value system. The world of daily existence, structured in accord with an unconsciously operative system of set values, is known in yoga psychology as the world of maya, that is, the world of limited pragmatic validity.

Let us now make some comments on the standard yogic attitude to the use of drugs. Some yogis do use what may be called psychedelic drugs and derive benefit therefrom. But they are also aware of the dangers involved. So their general advice is: "Never use a drug just for fun or curiosity. That would be like drinking poison or playing with fire." But moderate use at the right time and in the right place during worship or meditation, after getting into the right spiritual frame of mind and after strictly following the instructions of a competent guru, can without doubt accelerate the pace of spiritual progress.

Many yogic teachers, however, especially those who serve society in responsible leadership positions, have warned against the use of psychedelic drugs and prohibited them in their own ashrams. For instance, the foremost yoga teachers—Ramakrishna, Vivekananda, Raman Maharshi, Mahatma Gandhi, Aurobindo, Sivananda, Ramdas, Mother Mira, and Mother Anandamayi—desist from recommending drugs to any disciple. Going back to earlier times we find that Gautama Buddha, Mahavir, Shankara, Ramanuja, Chaitanya, Nanak, Kabir—the foremost yoga teachers of the past—never recommended drugs. Ramakrishna used to describe drug use as the back-door method to God.

Various reasons account for this negative attitude to drugs. First, drugs, oftener than not, interfere with the natural integrative and maturing process of the evolving psyche. It is not enough to have an exciting and mind-expanding experience, however exalted or powerful it may be. It must be fully assimilated and properly interpreted, coordinated with other areas of life and other experiences, and transformed into a harmonious ingredient of the psyche's Being-cognition.

Otherwise, it would remain like oil in water, an unassimilated alien factor, or like a spark of fire in a heap of straw, consuming the previously organized psychosocial life structure. It might inflate the ego, stimulate the feeling of omnipotence, pervert the world image, beyond all reasonable proportions. Second, there are alternatives, the many time-tested techniques of yoga discipline, such as spiritually oriented emotional experiences and devotional exercises. These include the use of a potent sound formula, repetition of God's name, devotional song, and musical expression of adoration. Then there is physiological discipline consisting of the relaxing and harmonizing bodily postures and breathing exercises. Then again there are concentration, discrimination, evaluation, and meditation, which are far better and safer alternatives to drugs in one's search for soul-satisfying peak experiences.

Third, no drug, neither mescaline nor marijuana, nor LSD-25, can produce the highest form of transempirical Being-cognition experience, known as nirvikalpa samadhi or nirvana. Nirvana presupposes a sufficient degree of integration of intellect, emotion, and intuition, which is contingent upon a long period of adequate training and psychic growth from within. Even the highest psychedelic experiences take place within the realm of maya. Neither the ego nor the empirical self is completely transcended, nor is the boundary of the objective manifold of images, symbols, sounds, and colors crossed in order to step forth into the pure emptiness of Being.

ON DEATH

From the traditional yogic standpoint, exposure to the phenomenon of death and discussion of the meaning of death are considered necessary and valuable in order to gain a mature attitude to life and the right perspective on the world.

In Katha Upanishad we find that a young seeker after truth (Naciketa) has to go to the god of death in order to learn the law of life and the secret of immortality. Encounter with the phenomenon of death enables a person to place himself in the heart of nonbeing and thus behold the totality of existence from the right perspective. It cuts the umbilical tie to the life of instinctual union with the flux of time.

There is a practice among many yogis, especially Tantrics, to resort to the cremation ground to engage in meditation there. The most heroic of them do this at midnight on special occasions when the whole world is asleep and impenetrable darkness reigns supreme.

The supreme God Shiva dances on the cremation ground with the music of creation in one hand and the flame of death in another. His dance is the dance of cosmic rhythm. Those who understand that rhythm attain immortality. Their own heart is reduced to a cremation ground on account of the burning of all vanity and selfishness, greed and aggressiveness. That is when they hear in their own heart the dancing footsteps of the lord of eternity who liberates man through the baptism of death.

There are, broadly speaking, four aspects of immortality as the traditional goal of yoga discipline (Chaudhuri, 1954, chs. 13, 14).

First, immortality means continuation of life after death and the soul's evolutionary passage through subtle planes of existence.

Second, immortality means a long series of reincarnations as successive material embodiments of the soul's evolutionary career until complete liberation is attained.

Third, immortality is conscious union with the eternal here and now in this world as a result of full enlightenment.

Fourth, after death the fully enlightened individual can freely choose (a) to get absorbed in the vastness of the Absolute, or (b) to continue to act for the good of humanity and/or in the service of God on some higher level of consciousness, or (c) voluntarily to return to earth and assume another body to do God's will in the world in a spirit of total unselfishness.

THE YOGIC PATH

The methodology of yoga psychology has two interrelated aspects: theoretical and practical. The theoretical aspect is concerned with the method for determining the truth about the essential structure of the human psyche. We have already seen that on the theoretical side the yogic method consists of comprehensive experientialism. The approach of careful observation, analysis, and evaluation of all the fundamental phases of human experience is considered vital to complete psychological understanding.

On the practical side, the yogic method consists of various disciplines which are immensely helpful to gradual self-unfoldment and eventual self-realization. This may be called the yogic path.

The yogic path is a multidisciplinary approach to ultimate self-realization. Broadly speaking, there are three kinds of discipline involved in the pursuit of the ultimate goal. These are: ethico-religious, physico-vital, and psycho-spiritual.

The ethico-religious discipline. Since man is a sociocultural animal, he always finds himself born in a definite cultural milieu. He grows up unconsciously imbibing from his environment certain moral and religious ideas and values.

Ethico-religious discipline makes positive use of the norms and ideas of sociocultural conditioning in the search for self-realization.

Satisfactory spiritual growth is not possible without a harmonious and peaceful environment. Social position, physical strength, and mental brilliance are of no avail for lasting happiness, if there is constant discord and friction with those who belong to our social orbit. Ethico-religious ideas, even when they are imperfectly and inadequately formulated, have at least a limited value insofar as they emphasize man's organic relationship to society. According to Patanjali, there are ten fundamental ethico-religious principles which may be described as the imperatives of the authentic Self. These ten principles are as follows:

1. Do not injure or kill, physically or mentally, any living being (*ahimsa*, nonviolence).

2. Affirm truth in thought, speech, and deed (*satya*, truthfulness).

3. Don't steal; abstain from theft (*asteya*, nonstealing).

4. Discipline and organize your various impulses and desires (*brahmacharya*, self-discipline).

5. Do not be greedy and do not accept any unnecessary gifts or bribes from people of questionable motive (*aparigraha*, nongreed).

6. Observe purity, both external and internal, physical and mental (*shaucha*, purity).

7. Cultivate the spirit of contentment. Don't multiply your desires for material goods (*santosha*, contentment).

8. Train yourself in enduring changes of environment and reverses of fortune (*tapas*, self-training).

9. Regular study, with devotion and an open mind, of books of spiritual wisdom (*swadhyaya*, study of scriptures).

10. Constantly remember God and surrender to the Divine Will (*Ishwarapranidhana*, love of God).

The first five principles are known as restraint *(yama)*. The next five are known as regulation *(niyama)*. They are all designed to establish harmonious relationship with the environment and a spirit of dedication to life's intrinsic values.

All the above guiding principles can be interpreted in various ways. In modern India, the interpretation of some of them radically differs from the traditional view. For instance, the first principle of nonviolence is the principle of self-perfection within a harmonious environment, but in modern times it is interpreted more positively as the practice of love, compassion, appreciation of opposite viewpoints, and unselfish social service. Mahatma Gandhi even transforms it into a uniquely powerful technique for humanistic improvement of socio-economico-political, interracial, and international relations. He shows how nonviolence can be used as a potent spiritual weapon to conquer the social evils of injustice and inequality, the political evils of imperialism and colonialism, and the interpersonal evils of hatred and violence.

In yoga psychology the notion of God used in the tenth imperative is not a theological dogma but a pragmatically useful concept which can serve the purpose of heightening one's value-consciousness and channeling instinctual energy in the direction of the spiritual goal of enlightenment. Patanjali's yoga is based upon the sankhya system of philosophy, which is avowedly atheistic and does not accept God as the ultimate reality. An elucidation of the manifold implications of the above principles as interpreted in modern times can easily occupy a whole volume.

In the light of the fundamental trend of ethico-religious discipline in India today, two more principles can be added to the above ten.

11. Do not develop a rigidly doctrinaire attitude in the practice of the above laws, which are only abstract guidelines, not unconditionally valid criteria for final decision.

12. In cases of conflict of principles or laws, the overriding consideration should be the spirit of active concern for the collective good of society and humanity.

Physico-vital discipline (Asana, pranayama). The yogis of India early recognized the close interdependence of body and mind, and the function of the body-mind as the necessary foundation for optimum spiritual growth. It has been stated in the Upanishads that "the strong alone can realize the Self" (Munkaka Upanishad, III, 2, 4; see Radhakrishnan, 1953, p. 690).

There are two main reasons for this.

First, an abundant supply of vital energy is necessary to draw from in order to develop sufficient brain power by stimulating the normally unused cells of the brain. There are yogic techniques capable of transforming vital *(prana)* and sexual *(retas)* energies into a very refined kind of luminous energy *(ojas)* (Narayananda, 1951), which is, in a sense, superconscient *(chit shakti)*, transcending the dichotomies of discursive understanding. Second, authentic mystic realization is an overwhelmingly powerful experience. It puts tremendous pressure on the brain and the central nervous system. An untrained person with a weak nervous system is hardly able to stand the impact and quietly assimilate it. He is likely to shake and tremble, shout and scream, excitedly dance and roll on the floor, instead of being able to direct meaningfully the newly generated energy of mystical experience or Being-cognition. He would be inclined to dissipate it in unconstructive forms, and perhaps become confused, disturbed, or psychotic.

So Patanjali recommends the regular practice of certain bodily postures *(asanas)* which are relaxing, revitalizing, and harmonizing. The headstand, shoulder stand, spine twisting, plow and bow and other postures are immensely beneficial in this respect. They are eminently suitable for people committed to intellectual and spiritual pursuits. They are aimed not so much at muscle building as for the strengthening of the nervous system, stimulation of the endocrine glands, the elimination of impurities from the body, as well as recuperative relaxation. Second, an essential supplement of bodily postures is the training in breath control *(pranayama)*. There are breathing exercises for psychophysical relaxation, for rejuvenation, for release of dormant energies, and also for mental serenity through the equalization of the two breath currents, left and right *(ida* and *pingala)*. These breath currents are known as the feminine and masculine currents (moon and sun, water and fire). The first is soothing like water and the second one is electrifying like fire. The equalization of the two is the happy marriage of negative and positive vital energies, generating a new kind of energy, extremely subtle, and upward-moving toward the seat of consciousness in the brain.

It may be added that there are three other aspects of the physical-vital discipline, which are:

1. A regimen of well-balanced, easily digestible nutritious diet.

2. Close contact with the vitalizing forces of Nature such as fresh air, sunshine, and pure water.

3. Pursuit of the middle path, avoiding the extremes of epicureanism and asceticism, restless pleasure seeking, and puritanical suppression of instincts and emotions.

As the Bhagavad-Gita puts it, "A yogi should not eat too much nor eat too little. He should not talk too much nor talk too little. He should not sleep too much nor keep awake too much" (Radhakrishnan, 1952, p. 199). A fuller discussion of this concept of balanced living is to be found in the author's *Mastering the Problems of Living* (1968, ch. 11).

Psycho-spiritual discipline. Psycho-spiritual discipline consists in the constructive channeling of the psychic energy in the quest of the Self. The goal is to know the Self in itself, the Self as related to the mind-body structure, and also the Self as related to Being.

Patanjali's Raja Yoga emphasizes four factors under this heading:

1. Withdrawal of attention from the outside world *(pratyahara)*.

2. Concentration of energy in a definite direction *(dharana)*.

3. Contemplation or uninterrupted flow of thought-energy in the chosen field of attention *(dhyana)*.

4. Unitive or Identity Consciousness *(samadhi)*.

The technique of withdrawal consists in the ability to withdraw one's interest and attention from the outside world and focus mental energy upon the mystery of one's own being. It is the cultivitation of one's capacity to be alone with the alone—with one's true Self—which is unique and independent.

The world in which we live is, in ultimate analysis, a projection into the sphere of objectivity of what we are within. So a person cannot know the meaning of the world without knowing his own self. Moreover, a person lacking inner peace and joy, serenity and compassion, cannot be of much help to others in spite of all his good intentions and efforts. A self-integrated person alone can spontaneously function as a source of peace and joy, hope and faith, wholeness and healing, to all who come in his contact.

So the first step in meditation is withdrawal of attention, temporarily bidding farewell to the outside world, and entering into the quiet privacy of one's meditation room. Then you take an easy and comfortable seat in erect posture, close your eyes, and enter into the silence of your being.

The second step in meditation is training in one-pointed concentration (dharana). You focus attention upon something pleasant, beautiful, and attractive to you, say a lovely flower or a vast ocean. Or concentrate on something spiritually meaningful to you, like a prophet or messiah or God or a specific center of consciousness within you, or on the natural flow of your breath as the symbol of the universal life-force operative within you.

One-pointed concentration is the technique of mobilizing the usually diffused mental energy in a definite direction. It is like transforming an ordinary lamp into a powerful searchlight. It gives you the power of penetrative vision and effective self-actualization.

The use of a suitable mantra or a spiritual formula such as "I am an integral part of cosmic consciousness" *(Om Sivoham),* or "I am a unique creative center of Being" *(Aham Brahmo smi),* is worthy of recommendation. It helps focus attention upon one's true spiritual identity or essential oneness with the universe.

At the beginning one is likely to encounter many difficulties in keeping the mind fixed in one direction for long. When the mind is found to be jumping around too much like the monkey, relax, give it free play for a while, become a detached onlooker, and quietly keep a watch. Eventually, with regular practice, the mind will increasingly come under control.

When concentration becomes deep, it develops into contemplation (dhyana),* which consists in uninterrupted flow of thought-energy around the object of

---

Dhyana has been defined in various ways. According to Patanjali, it is the more mature form of concentration in which there is a spontaneous and uninterrupted flow of consciousness, directed no longer by the conscious ego, but from a deeper level of the psyche.

In a second definition, whereas concentration is the focusing of mental energy on any object holy

concentration. It reveals much truth about the nature of the object.

The next higher phase of the psycho-spiritual discipline is the experience of oneness or identity, unitive experience. This is authentic mystical experience of the superconscious order (samadhi).

DANGERS ON THE PATH OF YOGA

There are many traps and temptations, many hazards and dangers, besetting the yogic path. That is why the ancient sages of India warned: "The spiritual path is sharp like the razor's edge."

A few temptations and dangers are briefly outlined here:

1. *The danger of extreme introversion.* As a person embraces the path of yoga and meditation, he begins to discover the hidden springs of joy and ecstasy within himself. This tempts him to withdraw more from society. The more he withdraws, the more he feels alienated from society. And the more he feels alienated, the more the chances of his return journey are destroyed.

2. *The danger of spiritual hedonism or gluttony.* Gurus often lay an exaggerated emphasis upon transcendental bliss as the ultimate goal of life. This is an exaltation of the infantile pleasure principle. As a result, many yogis happily withdraw into the shining shell of their transcendent blissful Self. The Samkhya doctrine of the alienness and nonspirituality of the world and the Vedantic doctrine of the world's unreality provide them with ample justification for this withdrawal. Furthermore, the transcendent Self has been described as essentially aloof, alone, eternally perfect, self-sufficient, and therefore indifferent (Ballantyne, 1963, p. 270). So the self-realized yogi often fails to understand the meaning of responsible participation in the being of the world with a view to effectuating essential changes in the conditions of living. He finds it much easier and convenient to renounce and reject.

One needs competent guidance and maturity of experience to discover that the bliss which is the essence of being holds within itself the dynamic factor of the joy of creative self-expression and environmental transformation for the glory of Being.

3. *The danger of regression.* Such yogic techniques as mantra repetition and thought suppression are often used without a prior clear-cut understanding of the ultimate goal of dynamic self-integration on a higher level of consciousness. To

---

or profane, sacred or secular, meditation is intensified and spontaneous concentration on spiritual truth or value (Chaudhuri, 1965b, of pp. 26–28).

According to a third definition, meditation may assume a form entirely different from concentration. Instead of exercising the mind, it lets the mind go. One assumes the position of a detached onlooker, more and more withdraws from all mental processes with a view to waking up on a deeper no-mind, no-ego, level of consciousness (Chaudhuri, 1965a).

the unprepared novice this immediately provides a delightful escape from the dizziness of freedom—from the challenge and hardship of adult life. The young meditator easily feels tempted to regress to the lost paradise of childhood.

4. *The danger of emotional fixation upon the guru.* There is no doubt that a perfect guru can play an immensely valuable role in the spiritual growth of people. A perfect guru is one who, by virtue of the awakening of his dormant Being-energy, has attained not only cosmic consciousness but also superconscient Being-cognition. Such a guru can awaken the latent Being-energy of another person with one compassionate glance, or a loving embrace, or a single electrifying touch on the head. This is indeed an overwhelming rebirth experience. But herein also lurks the possibility of a great danger.

The disciple who has received the blessings of a great guru feels overwhelmed under the shadow of his towering personality. He knows that he has received something of unique and paramount value which he cannot possibly get anywhere else—neither in scriptures nor in schools, neither in seminars nor in group encounters. So he may respond with an attitude of adoration, deification, or idolization. As a result, in spite of many delightful mystical experiences, his independent personality growth may get arrested.

In this regard my strong personal conviction is that there is a great need today for a constructive and fruitful dialogue between yoga and psychotherapy, between the guru and the psychotherapist.

The Western psychotherapist and the Indian guru can indeed learn a good deal from each other. The guru can learn from the psychotherapist the value and essential conditions of independent personality growth. The psychotherapist can learn from the guru the value and essential conditions of transcendent Self-realization and the dynamics of the transpersonal Being-energy.

5. *The danger of self-mutilation.* The traditional guru has a compulsive negative attitude to the elements of the so-called lower nature—sex, intellect, and ego. There is little understanding of the vital role that they are designed by nature to play in independent personality growth and in constructive development of one's unique potentials. The negative policy of suppression is bound to produce mutilation of one's total being, resulting in lopsided, neurosis-tainted spiritual development. Pathological conditions are bound to result therefrom.

What is imperatively necessary for balanced spiritual growth is not suppression, but intelligently organized fulfillment of normal healthy desires and intellectual urges. It is only out of the legitimate satisfaction of the so-called lower nature that the glory of the higher spiritual dimension can evolve. One has to obtain a passport from mother nature herself in order to enter the kingdom of heaven, as the Tantric school of psychology would say.

ON CONTACTING THE LIVING TRADITION

It is important to understand that there are three types of guide or guru who may help in contacting the living yoga tradition. First, one may contact a sincere *swami* (one who has renounced social life in search of spiritual truth) or *acharya* (accredited teacher or professor), or *bhakta* (one who lives in society and follows the devotional approach to God). In India the acharyas, religious teachers, philosophers, or professors of philosophy, are also practitioners of yoga and meditation. They try to combine intellectual development with spiritual realization.

People belonging to all the aforesaid categories may be called yogis insofar as they practice yoga successfully. They are called *rishis* (Rajarshi, Maharshi, and Maharishi are exalted variations of rishi) insofar as they are believed to have attained direct vision of truth.

In India no philosopher is recognized as a true philosopher unless his systematic world view is based upon personal self-realization or yogic experience.

A Westerner planning to visit India to contact the living yoga tradition will be well advised to visit some good ashrams, and meet some living yogis renowned for personal enlightenment.

SUMMARY

The methodology of yogic psychology includes comprehensive experientialism and the yogic path. Comprehensive experientialism means that all possible types of human experience, including waking, dream, sleep, psychedelic, mystical, and Being-cognition modes, must be carefully investigated and analyzed in order to obtain adequate knowledge of the human psyche. The yogic path consists of various self-disciplines, ethico-religious, physico-vital, and psycho-spiritual, which must be followed in order to attain the ultimate goal of Self-realization.

The distinction between the psyche (citta) and the Self (purusa, atman) is of vital importance in yoga psychology.

The psyche consists of the mind with its sense powers, instincts, memory, intellect, and ego. The Self is pure egoless, formless consciousness, eternally perfect and free. A sufficient measure of integration of the various components of the psyche combined with an awareness of their essential distinction from the true Self is essential for Self-realization.

Broadly speaking, there are seven important systems of yoga discipline: breath control (hatha), mind control (raja), egoless action (karma), egoless love (bhakti), pure Being-cognition (jnana), transpersonal Being-energy (kundalini), and integral-evolutionary self-integration (purna). They all emphasize the goal of Self-realization, but differ in respect of its true meaning as well as the methodological procedure. There are, however, many essential principles common to all the yogic paths.

In medieval times, major emphasis was upon the concept of Self as eternally perfect, unchanging, and unchangeable consciousness. In modern times, a reorientation of outlook shifted the emphasis to the integral view of the Self as a creative center of the evolutionary process as well as a unique focus of the supreme Being.

SELECTED BIBLIOGRAPHY ON YOGA

Aurobindo, Sri. *The Synthesis of Yoga.* Pondicherry: Sri Aurobindo Ashram, 1953.
Bernard, Theos. *Hatha Yoga.* New York: Samuel Weiser, 1971.
Brena, Steven. *Yoga and Medicine.* New York: The Julian Press, 1972.
Chaudhuri, Haridas. *Integral Yoga: The Concept of Harmonious and Creative Living.* London: George Allen & Unwin, Ltd., 1965.
_____. *Sri Aurobindo: Prophet of Life Divine.* San Francisco: Cultural Integration Fellowship, 1973.
Krishna, Gopi. *The Secret of Yoga.* New York: Harper & Row, 1972.
Mishra, Rammurti S. *The Textbook of Yoga Psychology.* New York: The Julian Press, 1963.
Radhakrishnan, S., trans. *The Bhagavadgita.* George Allen & Unwin, Ltd., 1958.
Woodroffe, Sir John. *The Serpent Power.* Madras: Ganesh & Co. 1963.

7   GURDJIEFF

KATHLEEN RIORDAN

KATHLEEN RIORDAN has been connected with the Gurdjieff Work all her life. Born into a family of the students of Gurdjieff and Orage, she became familiar with *Beelzebub's Tales to His Grandson*. (Gurdjieff, 1950) read from the manuscript as a children's story, and grew up in a world in which those who are now the leaders of the Gurdjieff groups were everyday influences. Gurdjieff himself, so shockingly real and full of love for young people, made an indelible impression. These early influences, perhaps, produced a growing commitment to study the mechanics of human behavior which led to a decade of work in the kind of behavioristic research usually associated with the name of B. F. Skinner, culminating in a doctorate in psychology from Columbia University in 1967. It also produced an orientation toward what Aldous Huxley called the "perennial philosophy," leading to persistent study in Gurdjieff's ideas, system of movements, and practice of meditation in action in various Gurdjieff groups, with brief excursions into the more exoteric forms of Christianity.

A continued interest in human beings drew Dr. Riordan into the newly developing field of educational technology, where the effort was made to apply Skinnerian laboratory principles to the complexities of human learning. During the 1960s she developed materials and systems for schoolchildren and physicians, salesmen and computer operators, graduate students and Job Corpsmen, and wrote a number of scholarly articles on methodology, motivation, programed instruction, educational media, and computer-assisted instruction.

In the early 1970s Dr. Riordan became interested in the psychotherapeutic aspect of human behavior, first through the medium of Skinnerian behavior therapy and then through training in Gestalt therapy, which led to an enlarged involvement in the humanistic as well as the transpersonal aspects of psychology. She also edited *Introductory Psychology* (1971), wrote *Recent Developments in Psychology* (1972), and continued the study and practice of Gurdjieff's teachings. Her more recent books include *Gurdjieff, Seeker of the Truth* (1979)(with Ira Friedlander), *The Essential Psychotherapies* (1981)(with Daniel Goleman), *The Gurdjieff Work* (1989), and *Generativity* (1990).

At present, Dr. Riordan, who also uses her full name, Kathleen Riordan Speeth, is a psychologist in private practice in California and New York.

In most of the major cities in the Western world you can, if you make a serious attempt to do so, find a group of people who are, as they say, "in the work"— that is, who attempt, together and as individuals, to function more consciously and harmoniously by studying the ideas and practicing the techniques given by George Ivanovitch Gurdjieff. Gurdjieff groups generally avoid publicity. They do not proselytize. They are relatively invisible in the world, being as hard to find as a particular piece of hay in a haystack because their members lead ordinary lives while devoting themselves to their inner work. This work is designed to engage many aspects of human functioning: it involves a wide range of activities including intellectual study, self-observation, daily meditation, sacred dances or "movements," cooperative efforts, and, more often than not, manual labor performed under special conditions.

The extraordinary being and "rascal sage" to whom all this activity is due devoted his life to the study of Eastern esoteric teaching and the translation of the knowledge of theory and practice he acquired into forms assimilable by people living in the Occidental world. He was careful to create a fog around himself during his lifetime, just as don Juan, another man of knowledge, was to recommend to all who tread the path (Castaneda, 1973). Thus we know relatively little about Gurdjieff, and although some information can be pieced together from more or less reliable sources, the specific influences on and sources of his teaching will probably remain as mysterious as he intended them to be.

He was born in the 1870s in Alexandropol, in the Caucasus region of what is now Russia, of a Greek father and an Armenian mother. Some insist that December 28, 1877, his passport date of birth, is accurate, and yet his own reports of his age and the events of his life seem to point to an earlier birthdate, perhaps about 1872. When he was still a boy his family moved to Kars, where he had the good fortune to become the student of Dean Borsh of the Russian Military Cathedral, who, with Gurdjieff's own father, became an important influence on his development. According to Gurdjieff these two men were chiefly responsible for his " 'irrepressible striving' to understand clearly the precise significance, in general, of the life process on earth of all outward forms of breathing creatures and, in particular, of the aim of human life in the light of this interpretation" (Gurdjieff, 1933, p. 13). He lived in a place that was particularly rich ground for unearthing answers to such perennial questions, or at least for finding clues. Kars and the surrounding region lying between the Black and Caspian seas had been invaded and occupied by many different peoples and was, at the time of Gurdjieff's formative years, a place of great cultural ferment owing to the interpenetration of Christian, Armenian, Assyrian, Islamic, and even Zoroastrian sources. He had access to "the so-called 'holy-of-holies' of nearly all hermetic organizations such as religious, philosophical, occult, political and mystic societies, congregations, parties, unions, etc. which were inaccessible to the ordinary man" (Gurdjieff, 1933, p. 17).

Gurdjieff gathered much in this context, particularly from Christian monastic sources. Very much later in his life, when he had begun to teach, he was asked about the relation of the system of self-development he was offering to students to Christianity.

"I do not know what you know about *Christianity,*" answered G., emphasizing the word. "It would be necessary to talk a great deal and to talk for a long time in order to make clear what you understand by this term. But for the benefit of those who know already, I will say that, if you like, *this is esoteric Christianity.*" [Ouspensky, 1949, p. 102]

There was considerable knowledge about Christian ritual and practice to be had in Kars, and Gurdjieff learned much about the ancient symbolism of the liturgy and the techniques of rhythmic breathing and mental prayer that were still part of the orthodox monk's religious duty. Yet, despite the fertility of his native land and the religious tradition into which he was born, he was not at all satisfied with the progress of his understanding of the basic question he had posed himself. He went in search of knowledge.

Accompanied by a band of friends who called themselves "Seekers after Truth," Gurdjieff set off, in his teens or early twenties, toward the east in wanderings through Central Asia and to such far-flung regions as Ethiopia and the Solomon Islands. During these travels he was undoubtedly in contact with esoteric circles in several Islamic orders, most notably the Sarmouni and the Naqshbandi, and it is to these Sufi sources that much of his teaching can be traced, even without the account, written after Gurdjieff's death and repudiated by his students, of his dervish teachers (Lefort, 1966). Anyone familiar with the Nasrudin corpus of Sufi teaching stories (Shah, 1966; 1968c; 1973) will recognize the same character in Gurdjieff's "Mullah Nassr Eddin." Another Sufi influence appears, according to J. B. Bennett, who was a disciple of Gurdjieff, in the character of the Bohkarian dervish Boggo-Eddin, who is none other than the great Sufi teacher and the founder of the Naqshbandi order, Bahaudin Naqshband. The central symbol of the Gurdjieff work, the enneagram, is certainly of Sufi origin, and it is fairly well established that many of the sacred dances done as meditations in movement by students of Gurdjieff were also inspired by Sufi contacts, most particularly the Sarmouni.

Sufi teachings certainly contributed much to Gurdjieff's thought in ways that can be noted more or less exactly. Another esoteric influence was also important, though less easily specified. This was the Vajrayana Buddhism of Tibet. Louis Pauwels writes in his book *Gurdjieff* (1972, p. 31):

Gurdjieff was the principal Russian secret agent in Tibet for ten years.[*] (Kipling knew this.) He was given important financial posts by the Tibetan authorities and control over the equipment of the army. He was able to play a political role, as they knew him to possess spiritual powers and in this country that is all-important, especially among the high-ranking priesthood. He was tutor to the Dalai Lama, and escaped with him when the English invaded Tibet.

Bennett (1974) suggests that Gurdjieff's travels in search of esoteric knowledge, in which he seems to have crossed a great many national borders with peculiar ease, were facilitated by his secret connection with the tsarist government, though his alleged connection with the Dalai Lama is corroborated neither by Bennett nor by other Gurdjieff sources. Very little is known about the period in Tibet and Central Asia, which may have lasted from the early 1890s until perhaps 1910 or 1912, except that Gurdjieff was on the track of archaeological and religious keys to unlock the secrets of his "fundamental question." He carried on his researches into lamaism and prelamaistic practice, into tekkias and monasteries where ancient knowledge was preserved, and even, it seems likely, into Siberian shamanism, often referred to as the original matrix from which religions developed. Apparently, during these wanderings, Gurdjieff pieced together a world view that he found satisfactory and became aware of his mission: to bring this understanding of the "terror of the situation" and the possible way out to the Western world.

The next time Gurdjieff's whereabouts are certain is the year 1915, when he first appeared as a teacher in the Russian towns of St. Petersburg and Moscow. There he found, or was found by, Peter Ouspensky, the man who was to become Plato to his Socrates, as Colin Wilson put it in his book *The Outsider* (1967). Ouspensky had himself just returned from travels in search of genuine esoteric knowledge, and was amazed to find that what he had been looking for was in his

---

[*]This statement of Pauwels, from vague sources, is strongly disputed by some people who knew Gurdjieff.

native land, and, in fact, in his hometown. He describes their first meeting in his book *In Search of the Miraculous* as follows:

I remember this meeting very well. We arrived at a small cafe in a noisy though not central street. I saw a man of an oriental type, no longer young, with a black moustache and piercing eyes, who astonished me first of all because he seemed to be disguised and completely out of keeping with the place and atmosphere. I was still full of impressions of the East. And this man with the face of an Indian raja or an Arab sheik whom I at once seemed to see in a white burnoose or a gilded turban, seated here in this little cafe, where small dealers and commission agents met together, in a black overcoat with a velvet collar and a black bowler hat, produced the strange, unexpected and almost alarming impression of a man poorly disguised the sight of whom embarrasses you because you see he is not what he pretends to be and yet you have to speak and behave as if you did not see it. He spoke Russian incorrectly with a strong Caucasian accent; and this accent, with which we are accustomed to associate anything apart from philosophical ideas, strengthened still further the strangeness and unexpectedness of the impression. [Ouspensky, 1949, p. 7]

Ouspensky was impressed. Gurdjieff, alien as he still was to the Westernized Russian mind, was presenting ideas in a way that rang true, that threw new light on basic questions about man in relation to the universe, levels of consciousness, the human condition, mortality and immortality, and the possibility of self-realization—and he was encouraging and even insisting upon personal verification. So Ouspensky joined a group of Gurdjieff followers who were meeting secretly in Moscow and worked with them until the group disbanded under the threat of revolution.

As Olga de Hartmann, one of his earliest Russian students, describes this period: "Russia in 1917 was torn by war and revolution. Mr. Gurdjieff was an unknown person, a mystery. Nobody knew about his teaching, nobody knew his origin or why he had appeared in Moscow and St. Petersburg. But whoever came in contact with him wished to follow him, and so did Thomas de Hartmann and I" (de Hartmann, 1964). So the de Hartmanns, Peter Ouspensky and his wife, and a number of other students fled Russia, in a tortuous journey over the mountains on foot, to Essentuki in the Caucasus, and then, when life became impossible there, to Tiflis. Here Gurdjieff was joined by other students, including Alexander and Jeanne de Salzmann from Paris, and together they began a new group that continued to work under his guidance. Within a matter of months, however, the effects of the revolution were felt in Tiflis, and Gurdjieff took his followers to Constantinople, then to Berlin, and finally, after five years of hardship and refugee existence, to Paris. Here Gurdjieff decided to settle and within a year gathered the money necessary to acquire the Château of Avon, near Fontainbleau, where he founded the Institute for the Harmonious Development of Man.

The decade from 1923 to 1933 was spent in intense work with students at the

Institute, during which time Gurdjieff tested and revised a system of study, self-observation, physical work, and exercise aimed toward the reconciliation and union of the three basic human functions of thinking, feeling, and physical activity. Many pupils came to stay at the Institute, including such notables as Katherine Mansfield (who died there), A. R. Orage, Maurice Nicoll, and the de Salzmanns. Gurdjieff, however, made no distinctions on the basis of eminence, and whoever came to study with him could be sure to be required to make consistent and intense efforts and also to be exposed to Gurdjieff's particular style of work on ego reduction, which involved planned interpersonal friction and the public acknowledgment, if not actual ridicule, of personal patterns of malfunction. Every moment at the "Prieure," as the château was called, was regarded as an opportunity for developing self-awareness and attuning personal attitudes— from work in the gardens, to housebuilding, to cooking and cleaning as well as in the more formal instruction. Mealtimes were particularly likely to produce talk and teaching by Gurdjieff, who would often end a dinner with toasts to specific members of the group as various kinds of idiots—round idiots, square idiots, compassionate idiots, and nineteen other varieties. These celebrations of individual personality weaknesses were part of the attempt, carried on by Gurdjieff on many fronts simultaneously, to invalidate and detoxify patterns of conditioning so that the student's more essential nature could begin to appear.

This period of intense work included exhibitions and lectures in Europe and America. It was punctuated by a serious accident which occurred while Gurdjieff was driving alone in a powerful car, and from which physicians were amazed to see him recover. He began, while still recuperating, to give some of his attention to writing and eventually completed his three major works, which consist of ten books divided into three series. Of these the first series *All and Everything,* and the second series, *Meetings with Remarkable Men,* are available. The third work, *Life Is Real only Then, When "I Am,"* has so far been transmitted only orally and in fragmentary form to those actively engaged in the Gurdjieff work.

These books deserve and, in fact, need some introduction. According to Gurdjieff (1950), they are written to solve the following fundamental problems facing mankind:

FIRST SERIES: To destroy, mercilessly, without any compromises whatsoever, in the mentation and feelings of the reader, the beliefs and views, by centuries rooted in him, about everything existing in the world.

SECOND SERIES: To acquaint the reader with the material required for a new creation and to prove the soundness and good quality of it.

THIRD SERIES: To assist the arising, in the mentation and the feelings of the reader, of a veritable, nonfantastic representation not of that illusory world which he now perceives, but of the world existing in reality.

The first series concerns the "three-brained beings"—mankind—on planet earth as described by Beelzebub to his grandson Hassein as they travel in the spaceship Karnak. Beelzebub recounts what he saw and learned about humanity during his six visits to this unhappy planet, how the inhabitants function and how they could function, what has been done by cosmic forces to provide aid, and how the situation has continued to deteriorate. The magnum opus of Gurdjieff's life, this work is an encyclopedic commentary on the most urgent questions facing every individual. It is difficult to read in part because, in his wish to avoid words that had incorrect connotations and past associations (or perhaps in order to require an additional committed effort on the part of the reader) Gurdjieff has chosen to introduce new vocabulary, including such words as Heptaparaparshinokh (roughly translated as "sevenfoldness"), Hanbledzoin ("that substance that arises in the common presence of a man from all intentionally made being-efforts") and even Tescooano (telescope). The serious reading of this book is virtually guaranteed by the use of this new and unfamiliar vocabulary. Students of the work will be aided by a concordance prepared recently by a Gurdjieff group (Plewes, 1971).

The second series is very easily penetrable and is as enjoyable as a good adventure story. It seems to tell the story of Gurdjieff's early years, his first tutors, and the extraordinary individuals he met on his journeys in search of esoteric knowledge, but actually includes a good deal of teaching material and allegory.

The third series is much more direct than its antecedents. It gives an account of Gurdjieff's personal development and describes specific practices which develop attention and awareness of self; thus, like the oral tradition in any spiritual technology, it is reserved for those who have left idle curiosity behind.

After completing these works, Gurdjieff wrote and distributed another, smaller book, *The Herald of the Coming Good* (1933), in which he introduced the ideas on which his work rests, described the Institute for the Harmonious Development of Man, and announced the forthcoming publication of the first and second series.

The years between 1933 and 1949, when he died in Paris, marked a new phase of Gurdjieff's activity in which he closed the Prieure and traveled widely, starting new groups in several American cities. At the time of his death he may have had several hundred pupils, mainly in New York and Paris. Ouspensky had broken sharply with him and had died before him, leaving a group of students committed to Ouspensky's version of the work in London. Gurdjieff's writings were practically unknown, and his influence on European thought and culture, apart from the deep impressions made on his pupils, was virtually nil.

Yet now the students of his teachings number in the thousands. His birthday is ritually celebrated on the first day of the year according to the Russian calendar, January 13, with festivities, music, and sacred dances, and the anniversary of his death, October 29, is honored with Russian Orthodox memorial services. The ideas Gurdjieff offered to the Western world continue to ring true. The growth of his influence must be due, at least in some measure, to the current resurgence of interest in self-realization that has led those suffering from what Jung called "holy neurosis" to seek out spiritual guidance wherever it is authentically present. In part, however, it must be due to the fact that Gurdjieff was successful, at least in a considerable degree, in the effort he made to translate Eastern methods and ideas related to the unfolding of man into terms that were specifically evocative for Westerners. Whether he was "the first emissary to the West" from a great Middle Eastern teaching school, as he has been called by some, or whether he was working under his own auspices, he undertook the heroic task of the cultural translation of esoteric ideas, and his efforts deserve the consideration—and perhaps even the gratitude—of postindustrial seekers after truth who, tired of what the material world, the world of business and even the world of academia can offer, turn inward to find reality.

THE PHILOSOPHICAL BASIS OF GURDJIEFF'S IDEAS

According to Gurdjieff, man lives in a very poor place in the universe, from the point of view of possible evolution. Self-realization is almost maximally difficult owing to the extreme density of mechanical laws that operate on our planet so that, although man is designed, so to speak, with the potential for increasing the level of his being, the chance that any particular individual will succeed is very slim. Because of the factors operating against him, man must expect that inner growth will not be easy: on the contrary, it will require great understanding and skillful effort, and this effort can begin only when man realizes the truth about the human condition. Plato likened man to someone fascinated by the shadows dancing on the rear wall of a cave, who is so engrossed that he is heedless of the world behind him. Gurdjieff compares man's state to that of a prisoner:

You do not realize your own situation. You are in prison. All you can wish for, if you are a sensible man, is to escape. But how escape? It is necessary to tunnel under a wall. One man can do nothing. But let us suppose there are ten or twenty men—if they work in turn and if one covers another they can complete the tunnel and escape.

Furthermore, no one can escape from prison without the help of those *who have escaped before.* Only they can say in what way escape is possible or can send tools, files, or whatever may be necessary. But *one* prisoner alone cannot find these people or get in touch with them. An organization is necessary. Nothing can be achieved without an organization. [Ouspensky, 1949, p. 30]

Liberation, then, depends first upon the realization of the truth about our condition. Once this understanding has hit home, it is not enough to be very intelligent or very highly motivated to do something about it: precise instructions, maps, and knowledge are needed by those who have already liberated themselves, and these "tools" must be used cooperatively.

One of the obstacles facing those who seek to liberate themselves is that humanity exists on this planet for a definite purpose, and that purpose would not be served if more than a certain percentage of people attained extraordinary levels of being—in fact, the flow of substances from the highest levels to the lowest would be severely disrupted if mankind's general level of consciousness were to change. The biosphere serves as an energy transducer at a critical place in a constantly evolving universe, serving to bridge the gap between sun and solar system and our own moon.

In order to understand this fact about man's situation we must look at his place in the cosmos. We will designate the prime mover, or origin, the Absolute. Out of the Absolute proceeds a very great number, perhaps an infinite number, of *rays of creation.* Looking down one of these (the one that interests us most, namely our own), we see that out of the Absolute emanate all possible systems or worlds, and from all worlds come all suns, our sun, the planets in our solar system, our planet, the earth, and finally the moon. These steps in the ray of creation differ in the number of laws under which they operate. At the level of the Absolute there is only one law, the unity of the will of creation; in the next world there are three orders of laws; in the next, six; in the next, twelve. On our earth there are forty-eight orders of laws under which we must live. The only place on the ray of creation in which it would be more difficult to strive for liberation would be the moon, which is governed by ninety-six orders of laws.

The will of the Absolute is manifest only on the level of all worlds, which it creates directly. The plan or pattern created at that level proceeds mechanically, level after level, until it reaches the very end of the ray of creation which is, in our case, the moon. Because we live under forty-eight laws we are very far from the will of the Absolute. If we could free ourselves from half of those laws we would be one step closer, and if we could reduce the number of laws we live under to only twelve we would be still closer. Moving toward the Absolute by liberating oneself, stage by stage, from the mechanical laws constraining us is the path of self-realization.

Everything in the universe is weighable and measurable, although the matter from which everything is made exists in differing degrees of materiality. The seven steps in the ray of creation may be thought of as the seven levels or orders of materiality, each differing in the rate of vibration: the Absolute vibrates most rapidly and is least dense, and the levels below it become more dense and slower in rate of vibration until the moon, the slowest and densest place on the ray, is reached. Of these orders of matter the finer permeate the denser and coarser ones, so that everything around us and familiar to us is in fact permeated with all the levels of matter that exist, including the Absolute.

There is no need to study or investigate the sun in order to discover the matter of the solar world: this matter exists in ourselves and is the result of the division of our atoms. In the same way we have in us the matter of all other worlds. Man is, in the full sense of the term, a "miniature universe"; in him are all the matters of which the universe consists; the same forces, the same laws that govern the life of the universe, operate in him; therefore in studying man we can study the whole world, just as in studying the world we can study man. [Ouspensky, 1949, p. 88]

Of these universal laws the most basic, perhaps, since it applies to every event, everywhere, is called by Gurdjieff the Law of Three. This law states that every manifestation is the resultant of three forces, which may be called active, passive, and neutralizing or Holy Affirming, Holy Denying, and Holy Neutralizing or, more simply, first force, second force, and third force. These forces are present everywhere, even in the very first step of the ray of creation, where they are unified, as reflected in many of the world's religions as Brahma, Vishnu, and Shiva, Father, Son, and Holy Spirit, and other trinities.

The Ray of Creation

Absolute	①	
World 3 under 3 laws	③	All Possible Systems of Worlds
World 6 under 6 laws	⑥	The Milky Way
World 12 under 12 laws	⑫	The Sun
World 24 under 24 laws	㉔	The Planets as One Mass
World 48 under 48 laws	㊽	The Earth
World 96 under 96 laws	�996	The Moon

Creation depends on the conjunction of these three forces: nothing can take place unless all three are present. Without neutralizing force, active and passive forces stand in useless opposition and nothing new can emerge, but when this third force is present, active and passive forces can join and produce results. Man in his present state of consciousness is blind to third force: it requires a higher level of awareness than man's ordinary state to see more than duality in things. But there are a few examples that may be readily pointed out in the sciences, such as the action of catalysts in chemistry, for purposes of illustration.

When the three forces do meet and an act of creation takes place, a chain of manifestations may develop in which third force in one event becomes active force in the next event—for the three forces change sign with respect to one another as they go about spinning or braiding the thread of occurrences. Now the second fundamental law, the Law of Seven, begins to operate.

The Law of Seven governs successions of events. It states that whenever any manifestation evolves, it does so nonlinearly. There is an orderly discontinuity in every progression of things, in every series. This lawful discontinuity is preserved in our musical scale which, as singing up and down any octave will show, is composed of unequal steps. Do, re, and mi are equally distant from one another, but between mi and fa there is a half-step instead of a full step. Proceeding up the scale, we have sol, la, and si (ti in some usages) separated by full intervals, but si and do having a half-step between them again.

The Law of Seven explains why when something begins it does not just continue and continue, ad infinitum: why a rainstorm abates or a grudge finally loses its venom. And the Law of Seven is behind the fact that there are no straight lines in nature. It is also reflected in the ray of creation.

If we redraw the ray of creation so that it is a descending octave going from the level of the Absolute to the level of the moon, the discontinuities appear between the Absolute and the level of all worlds, and between all planets and the earth. The first of these gaps or discontinuities is bridged by the force of creation engendered by the Absolute itself. The second requires our biosphere: the sensitive living film of organic life on earth acts as a transmitter of energy between the planetary level of the ray of creation and our own planet and its satellite moon, the lower part of the ray.

The Law of Seven may also be called the law of shock, for if an additional force or energy enters a process between mi and fa it will proceed on course until the

The Ray of Creation as an Octave

Level of the Absolute	①	Do
		SHOCK
Level of All Possible Systems of Worlds	③	Si
Level of Our Milky Way	⑥	La
Level of Our Sun	⑫	Sol
Level of Planets	㉔	Fa
		SHOCK
Level of Our Earth	㊽	Mi
Level of Our Moon	⑳⑥	Re

si-do interval, and if another shock or influx of energy is given at that point, the process continues to its conclusion at do. In the ray of creation this additional energy is generated by mankind and other living things. In this sense we exist to serve nature and it is not in the interests of nature that man develop further. In another perspective, man is created in an incomplete form and has the potential of evolving to the level of the sun—world 12—and even further. In this sense there are forces at work that are striving to complete an ascending octave in man, forces that work toward his realization.

The union of the Law of Three and the Law of Seven is represented in a diagram that is central to Gurdjieff's teaching—the enneagram. The enneagram is a circle divided into nine equal parts. Numbering the points by moving around the circumference clockwise, we can then form a triangle by connecting the points at 9, 3, and 6. This triangle represents the trinity, or the Law of Three. If we think of the whole of creation as manifestation seeking to be reabsorbed into the Absolute, or unity, then we can see the three perpetuated: 3 tries to return to 1 —this is, in mathematical terms, 1 divided by 3, which is a recurring series, .333333. . . . The other points around the circle are connected in such a way that they reflect the striving of all seven points on the ray of creation to return to unity: one divided by seven is a recurring series of six digits, .142857, which contains no multiples of three. Thus both laws are represented on one symmetrical diagram in a way that reflects their independence as well as their interrelationship.

The enneagram can be used in the study of all processes, since it must be present in all sequences of events. The days of the week can be laid out around the circle, for example, with Monday at one and Sunday at point nine, the point of rest where the Law of Three and the Law of Seven are (in this case) joined. There is a progression, the sequence of chronological time, around the circle and there is also an inner flow from Monday to Wednesday and back to Tuesday, from Tuesday to Saturday and thence to Thursday, and from Thursday to Friday. (Notice that the points on the triangle, 3 and 6, have been left out.) There is some nonobvious relationship indicated between these days. Something that I do, or am about to do if you want to think linearly, on Wednesday may affect what I experience on Tuesday. Extending this idea we can consider the possibility that there are connections between events that are outside of chronological progression of cause and effect that might, for instance, modify today's pattern of events on account of a *future* calamity or victory. Reflection on such possibilities in one's personal experience can be very fruitful.

Points 3, 6, and 9 on the enneagram represent shock points. Animals can experience only the first shock, the one that occurs between mi and fa in the octave. This shock is delivered automatically to all sentient beings with every breath. The shock is air. The other two shocks are represented by points 6 and

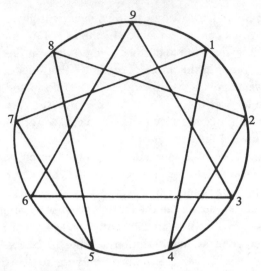

9, and they are not given automatically. They are called First Conscious Shock and Second Conscious Shock.

In ordinary man the transformation of food is accomplished with the shock of air coming between mi and fa, as shown on the enneagram of metabolism in man. The influx of air both furthers the assimilation of food and begins a new octave which, because it does not receive the shock necessary for it to pass from mi to fa, dies at mi. If this shock were given it would initiate a new octave of the assimilation of impressions which would require the Second Conscious shock to pass into its fa. A person must give these shocks to himself by, in the case of the First Conscious Shock, receiving impressions consciously, remembering himself, and, in the case of the Second Conscious Shock, transmuting the negative emotional energy produced by external circumstances into positive emotions. The First Conscious Shock involves body awareness, while the second, higher shock involves awareness of the emotions. If man fully metabolized the food, air, and impressions he receives he would live to the fullest, but, as he ordinarily lives, only the assimilation of food is carried out properly. The assimilation of breath is halted, and its octave stopped, for lack of a shock at its mi-fa interval, and the octave of the assimilation of impressions, which are also a kind of nourishment that is vital to life, is aborted at its very inception. The octaves can be brought to completion if shocks are delivered at the right points in these processes. It is about the production and absorption of these shocks that all esoteric teaching is ultimately concerned.

THE PSYCHOLOGY OF MAN

It will be convenient, in studying Gurdjieff's teachings about man's psychology, to look at the issues from two points of view: man's condition as he is now, and man's condition as it would be if he were to realize his possibilities, his destiny, to the fullest.

MAN AS HE IS NOW

The human condition, as made manifest in almost every one of us, is, according to Gurdjieff, substantially different from our ordinary notions of it. This difference between how man thinks he is and how he is in actuality is most strikingly evident with respect to notions about personal identity, responsible action, and free will, though it applies with equal validity to hosts of other, lesser, human functions as well. Take, for example, the idea we all have deeply ingrained in us that each of us is one consistent person. It is generally accepted by students of personality and by practically everyone else also that except in cases of hysterical dissociation, which are very rare, when a person says "I" he refers to himself in his entirety. And each person who says "I" assumes that he speaks for himself as an entity that persists hour after hour, day after day. That is how we represent ourselves to others and what we generally accept as a self-evident truth. After all,

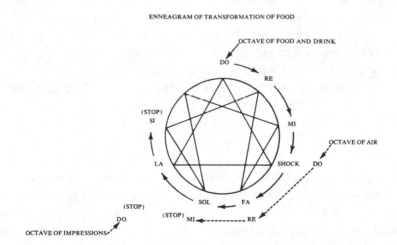

ENNEAGRAM OF TRANSFORMATION OF FOOD

each individual has one familiar body that is a consistent factor in daily experience. "The illusion of unity or oneness is created in man first," says Ouspensky,

by the sensation of one physical body, *by his name,* which in normal cases always remains the same, and third, by a number of mechanical habits which are implanted in him by education or acquired by imitation. Having always the same physical sensations, hearing always the same name and noticing in himself the same habits and inclinations he had before, he believes himself to be always the same. [Ouspensky, 1954, p. 13].

In reality, however, man's psychological structure and function are better explained by looking at behavior in terms of many "I's" rather than one. These "I's" are very numerous—an adult may have thousands. At one moment one "I" is present and at another, a different "I" who may or may not be in sympathy with the previous "I." This "I" may not even know that the other "I" exists, for between these "I's" there are often impenetrable defenses, called *buffers.* Some "I's" are clustered: there are subpersonalities made up of "I's" for professional functions and others comprised of "I's" for the supermarket, and still others for parental and conjugal situations. These subpersonalities consist of "I's" which, because they are related by association, are generally familiar with one another, yet they are isolated by barriers of unawareness, the buffers, from other clusters of "I's" with which they are not related by associations. One "I" may promise and another may have no knowledge of the promise, owing to buffers, and therefore no intention of honoring it. One group of "I's" may rush enthusiastically into a marriage that makes others resentful and withdrawn. Certain "I's" may value and work toward an aim that others subvert, and man may suffer "the nature of an insurrection." Seen from Gurdjieff's perspective, then, psychotherapeutic techniques that bring the various fragments of ego into awareness, from the basic rule of psychoanalysis to the explicit inner dialogues of Gestalt, would have the important function of gradually reducing the effects of buffers and acquainting the "I's" with one another.

MAN IS A MACHINE

Not only is human psychological functioning characterized by inconsistency, but this inconsistency is entirely determined by mechanical laws. The "I" that is in control of a person's behavior at any given moment is determined not by his personal choice but by his reaction to the surrounding environment which evokes one or another "I." Man as he is cannot choose which "I" to be, much as he would like to: his situation chooses for him. His behavior is elicited, not emitted, and what happens to him occurs entirely because of external influences and the "accidental" associations of his conditioning history. He has no capacity to do, no "free will"—in fact, he has no function of will at all. Attractions and aversions, tendencies to approach or avoid whatever stimuli impinge upon a man, act as the invisible strings that animate the marionette that he is. In Gurdjieff's words,

Man is a machine. All his deeds, actions, words, thoughts, feelings, convictions, opinions, and habits are the result of external influences. Out of himself a man cannot produce a single thought, a single action. Everything he says, does, thinks, feels—all this happens. . . . Man is born, lives, dies, builds houses, writes books, not as he wants to, but as it happens. Everything happens. Man does not love, hate, desire—all this happens. [Ouspensky, 1949, p. 21]

Man is a machine, then, a very complex and intricate machine that, unlike other machines, has the potentiality of knowing it is a machine. Man can study himself, and this study may give the clues necessary to attain another, higher level of being in which true will is possible. But this study, like the study of any other complex system, may take a long time and require much persistence and attention.

THE THREE BRAINS OF MAN

In Gurdjieff's *All and Everything,* Beelzebub tells his grandson all about the "inexplicable behavior of those three-brained beings on that strange planet Earth." These three brains correspond, like stories in a building (and in particular, a food factory), to three distinct levels of function. The upper story is the intellectual center, the middle story contains the emotional center, and the lower story is the locus of control for three functions which sometimes work independently but often do not. These are the moving center, the instinctive center, and the sexual center. In addition to these five centers, which are operative in every normal person, there are two more centers which, although they are perfectly formed and always functioning, have no connection to the others unless one is intentionally and skillfully made. These are the higher intellectual center in the top story and the higher emotional center in the middle story.

In ordinary man the five lower centers function inefficiently and out of harmony with one another and the higher centers are not used. The lower centers use different forms of energy, yet they borrow and steal energy from one another even though it cannot be properly used. They waste virtually all the energy they have at their disposal in leaks that are so chronic and so debilitating that unless measures are taken to stop them there is no way to raise the level of functioning of centers at all. And they habitually perform functions that are not their own, interfering with one another and degrading the work output. All the centers habitually rob sex center of its energy, which is of a higher vibrational level than that used by the other centers and therefore not necessary for their proper

THE CENTERS OF MAN

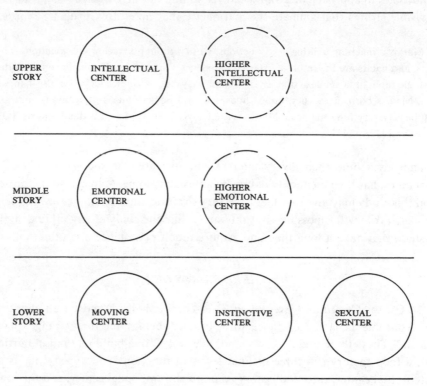

UPPER STORY	INTELLECTUAL CENTER	HIGHER INTELLECTUAL CENTER
MIDDLE STORY	EMOTIONAL CENTER	HIGHER EMOTIONAL CENTER
LOWER STORY	MOVING CENTER	INSTINCTIVE CENTER	SEXUAL CENTER

functioning. This finer energy leaks away in expressions of fanaticism, vehemence, and misplaced enthusiasm while sex center, like a powerful car filled with low-octane fuel, works with inferior energy and virtually never functions to its fullest capacity.

Other centers, too, do not work at nearly their full potential. If the emotional center were operating to the fullest it would become connected with the higher emotional center and if the intellectual center were operating correctly it, too, would become connected with the higher center corresponding to it. These connections require a match in vibrational levels between lower and higher centers. Permanent connections with the higher centers can, therefore, be forged only when the work of the lower centers has been regulated and quickened. Temporary connections do occur spontaneously in ecstatic moments, but these must be brief until the lower centers are prepared for the energy flow involved. Man as he is could no more tolerate such connections than, say, an appliance designed for 110 volts could stand connection with a 220-volt power supply.

Not only do the lower centers function below their capacity, waste energy, rob and steal from each other, and function unharmoniously with respect to one another in a host of ways, but even within centers there is a misapplication of effort. Each center is divided into intellectual, emotional, and moving parts, and each of these parts typically (though not always) has a positive and negative aspect, and is further subdivided into intellectual, emotional, and moving aspects. As an example of the wrong work of intellectual center, Nicoll gives the following:

The mechanical part includes in itself all the work of registration of *memories, associations and impressions,* and this is all the work it should do normally—that is, when the other centers and parts of centers are doing *their* proper work. It should only do the work of registration or recording, like a secretary taking down what is said and arranging it, etc. And, as was said, it should never reply to questions addressed to the *whole center* and should never decide anything important: but unfortunately it is always deciding and always replying in its narrow limited way, with ready-made phrases, and it continues to say the same things and work in the same mechanical way under all conditions. [Nicoll, 1952, p. 72]

This part of intellectual center has been given a special name: formatory center or formatory apparatus. When it usurps the work of the entire intellectual center what results is "formatory thinking," characterized by stock phrases and slogans, and the black-white, wrong-right, either-or comparisons that lack the depth and subtlety of intellectual thought.

The study of wrong work of centers is one of the keys to understanding the mechanics of human psychology. Some approximate descriptions of correct functions are summarized in the table (modified from Nicoll, 1952) to give a wider, though still incomplete, perspective.

Man's three stories have separate memory banks, each of which records impressions appropriate to it. Gurdjieff describes the mechanism of memory as follows:

In a newly-born child these three diverse parts of the general human psyche may be compared to a system of blank gramophone rolls upon which begin to be recorded, from the day of its appearance into the world, the external significance of objects and the subjective understanding of their inner significance, or the sense of the results of all actions taking place in the outer world, as well as the inner world already forming in him: all this is recorded in accordance with the correspondence between the nature of these actions and the nature of the distinct systems which form themselves in man.

All kinds of these recorded results of environing actions remain unchanged on each of these "depository rolls" for life, in the same sequence and in the same correlation with the impressions previously recorded, in which they are perceived. [Gurdjieff, 1933, p. 30]

Theoretically, according to Gurdjieff, impressions can impinge upon an individual in different ways: they can come from mechanical associations or completely

*The Functions of Centers**

	MOVING PART	EMOTIONAL PART	INTELLECTUAL PART
MOVING CENTER	Automatic reflexes Imitation on small scale Limited adabtability to learning new movements	Pleasure in movement Normal love of games Higher imitation: some forms of acting	Inventing things and machines Making adaptations
INSTINCTIVE CENTER	Pleasant sensations Unpleasant sensations	Blind animal love "Instinctive" love Animal jealousy Animal rage: desire to kill	Many so-called intuitions
SEXUAL CENTER	Sexual sensations (can only be pleasant or neutral)	Sexual attraction and gratification or frustration feelings	Assumptions about sex Perceptions of sex
EMOTIONAL CENTER	Mechanical expression of emotions All emotions relating to one's likes and dislikes: personal emotions Small desires: little daily "wills"	Religious emotions Aesthetic emotions Moral emotions: may lead to conscience	Artistic creation Chief seat of magnetic center
INTELLECTUAL CENTER	Repetition of words and phrases: mechanical talking Inquisitiveness; curiosity Shrewdness; craftiness	Desire to know and understand, search for knowledge; higher kinds of imagination	Intellectual construction Creative thought Discovery

*After Nicoll, 1952.

unconscious sensation of the world; they can come from voluntarily received impressions, active thinking, and conscious feeling; or they can come from a higher state of direct and conscious perception which is only a remote possibility for ordinary man, depending on how many shocks are received. As consciousness changes in level, the quality of impressions received changes as well. Most of life is spent in a dulled state of consciousness that is our ordinary waking state, and which we will discuss in more detail below. At this point it is sufficient to say that, in this state, impressions are related only by the mechanical laws of association, and it is thus that they are recorded by the centers. Consciousness varies in level, however: people bob up and down from level to level, sometimes more, sometimes less submerged in identification with actions and events in their experience. There are, occasionally, moments of higher states of consciousness. At these times, memory is quite different. It is far more vivid and immediate.

THREE TYPES OF MAN

The relative importance in an individual's patterns of functioning of each of the three stories of his "food factory" determines his place in a scheme of classification used by Gurdjieff to characterize man. One person may depend more on his head than on his heart, for example, while another may allow emotion to sway him where logic fails. Everyone is born with one "brain" predisposed to predominate over the other two. According to Gurdjieff's scheme, Man Number One has his center of gravity in moving and instinctive functions, Man Number Two gives more weight to feelings, and Man Number Three bases his actions on his knowledge or theoretical perspective. These individuals are more or less on the same level of being, since they all lack inner unity and will. They differ, however, in their reliance on one function or another.

Men Numbers One, Two, and Three differ from one another in their habits, tastes, and styles of life. They correspond roughly to Sheldon's varieties of temperament. Man Number One is visceratonic; Man Number Two, somatotonic; and Man Number Three, cerebretonic. In literary terms, we can see them as three familiar Shakespearean characters: Falstaff is Man Number One; Prince Hal, Man Number Two; and Hamlet, Man Number Three. Much has been said about these three types in the literature written about Gurdjieff's teaching. Some notions of characteristics of each are given here in the form of a table.

The Three Types of Man

MAN NUMBER ONE	MAN NUMBER TWO	MAN NUMBER THREE
Moving/Instinctive Man	Emotional Man	Thinking Man
Rote memorization and imitative learning	Knowledge of likes and dislikes	Logical thinking and literal interpretations
Primitive, sensual art	Sentimental art	Intellectual, invented art
Religion of rites and ceremonies	Religion of faith and love, and of persecution of heresy	Religion of proofs and arguments
Fakirs	Monks	Yogis
Karma yoga	Bhakti yoga	Jnana yoga

MAN IS ASLEEP

In his ordinary state of awareness man, whether he be One, Two, or Three, does not pay attention to himself the way he likes to think he does. Awareness of moving, emotional, and intellectual functions is consciousness, and his consciousness is very hazy and inconsistent, very much below capacity. Any person, chosen at random in a business office, social club, or university lecture hall and imperceptibly followed throughout a normal day's routine by a trained observer, would be seen to be very seldom aware of who he is and where he is, and even more rarely to register on what he knows and does not know.

Gurdjieff distinguishes between four states of consciousness that are possible for man: sleep, ordinary waking state, self-consciousness, and objective consciousness. Although all these states are possible for man, they differ widely in duration and in probability of occurrence. Typically man divides his life between sleep and ordinary waking state, which may be thought of as a form of sleep. In sleep he may spend a third or even more of his time on earth. In ordinary waking state, if asked whether he is conscious of himself, he will assuredly say that he is—and in fact for that moment he may be—but the next moment he will lapse into the fragmentary, inconsistent, and clouded attention that characterizes this state.

Ordinary waking state is more difficult to appraise, at first, in oneself than in others. Anyone who has a difficult time accepting the notion that man as he is has but few moments of true self-consciousness can make a study of the loose jaws and vacant stares of people in public places and in situations where they do not think that they are being observed—the streets of any city or the buses or department stores. Extrapolating from the realization that others walk, talk, eat, work, marry, divorce, and in general spend their lives in a state of almost complete inattention to the application of this knowledge to one's own life and the acceptance of this truth about oneself may be painful and daring, but it requires only a minimally small deductive leap.

Above the states of sleep and ordinary waking consciousness there are the possibilities of self-consciousness and even of what is called objective or cosmic consciousness. Self-consciousness occurs spontaneously for brief moments that often leave particularly vivid memories behind them. These are the high moments that occur in situations of great danger, intense emotion, or extraordinary stress. Then attention is clear, impartial, and relatively complete, and is divided between self and environment so that action unfolds spontaneously, appropriately, and sometimes even heroically. This is the state that could be, but is not, normal waking consciousness for mankind.

Objective consciousness also occurs in spontaneous flashes. Such moments are life's "peak experiences"—or they are totally forgotten as lower centers fall into unconsciousness to protect the body's delicate machinery from unbearably high energy. During states of objective consciousness higher centers are connected to the ordinary ones. Man is fully attuned to, and aware of, cosmic laws. He understands. He knows. Along with the *knowing* comes an ecstatic or blissful quality of joyful acceptance.

States of objective consciousness have been reported by people of all religious traditions and also by those who experiment with mind-altering drugs. According to Gurdjieff, drugs are useful to give a taste of what these states might be like, but objective consciousness can be approached legitimately only through the careful development of sustained self-consciousness. Only then can the state become part of what a man can call his own experience.

As we are now, we can know little more of objective consciousness than what we can assimilate from reports collected in such works as William James's *The Varieties of Religious Experience* (1961) and Richard Bucke's *Cosmic Consciousness* (1901). Such experiences are as relatively inaccessible to modern man as was Tibet to his medieval counterpart. He is like a householder who owns a beautiful mansion of four levels, each more sumptuous than the one below it, but he has forgotten how to get upstairs and lives in ignorance and privation in the kitchen and the basement.

THE PSYCHOPATHOLOGY OF ORDINARY WAKING STATE

What keeps man out of the upper floors of his mansion? Obstacles to higher levels of consciousness are abundant in daily life. Perhaps the most important is *identification* which is, according to DeRopp, the essence of ordinary waking state. "In this state man has no separate awareness. He is lost in whatever he happens to be doing, feeling, thinking. Because he is lost, immersed, not present to himself, this condition is known . . . as a state of 'waking sleep' " (DeRopp, 1968, p. 62). Identification is the opposite of self-consciousness. In a state of identification man does not remember himself. He is lost to himself. His attention is directed outward, and no awareness is left over for inner states. And ordinary life is almost totally spent in states of identification.

Identifying with other people's expectations is called *considering.* We can distinguish two kinds of considering, internal and external. Internal considering is based on the feeling of deficiency that man in his less developed states feels most of the time—in this case the deficiency is felt when people fail to give us sufficient attention or appreciation. It is keeping internal accounts of what we have given and what is, therefore, owed us, and feeling bad, stepped upon, and hurt when others don't pay up. It cannot occur without identification.

External considering, on the other hand, is the practice of empathy and tact. It is true considerateness. It is dependent, therefore, on a certain reliability and consistency of attention and effort on the part of the one who aspires to practice it. Interestingly, attempts at external considering often turn into internal considering when the person making the effort to consider another in the external sense finds no gratitude or caring given him in return. External considering must be its own reward and can expect nothing in return.

Inability to love is directly related to the inability to be truly considerate, the inability to pay attention, the plurality of "I's" that is man's plight. Although we all need love, we are unable to provide it as we are. "Begin by loving plants and animals, then perhaps you will learn to love people," says Gurdjieff (Nott, 1961, p. 23). In the Gurdjieff literature there are very few references to love, since it is beyond the capacity of ordinary man. Man the machine can react only to stimuli according to the laws of mechanical association, and according to which "I" is in charge at the moment. In response to a question about the place of love in his teaching, Gurdjieff once said,

With ordinary love goes hate. I love this, I hate that. Today I love you, next week, or next hour, or next minute, I hate you. He who can really love can *be;* he who can be, can *do,* he who can do, *is.* To know about real love one must forget all about love and must look for direction. We love because something in ourselves combines with another's emanations; this starts pleasant associations, perhaps because of chemico-physical emanations from instinctive center, emotional center or intellectual center; or it may be from influences of external form; or from feelings—I love you because you love me, or because you don't love me; suggestions of others; sense of superiority; from pity; and for many other reasons, subjective and egoistic. We allow ourselves to be influenced. Everything attracts or repels. There is the love of sex, which is ordinarily known as "love" between men and women—when this disappears a man and a woman no longer "love" each other. There is the love of feeling, which evokes the opposite and makes people suffer. Later, we will talk about conscious love. [Nott, 1961, p. 23]

The search for sources of love and objects of love must be disappointing and fruitless, based as it is on the mechanical orientation of sleeping man, and the degree to which it is given energy and to which it fascinates the attention is a major obstacle in the development of self-consciousness.

Lying is another inevitable aspect of ordinary waking state and is so pervasive that Ouspensky (1954) said that the psychology of man could be renamed the psychology of lying. Lying, in Gurdjieff's sense, is speaking about that which we do not know. Lying is obviously present in the chatter of cocktail parties and the lectures of those who know only partially or theoretically and yet profess to have real understanding. Since all knowledge is interconnected, the presentation of one aspect of truth usually involves lying.

Gurdjieff differentiates between knowledge and understanding, and this distinction is relevant to the idea of man's lying. Knowledge—the acquisition of facts, data, information—is useful in man's development only to the degree that it is absorbed or assimilated by his being, that is, to the degree to which it is understood. If something is known but not understood there will be lying about it, for one cannot convey a truth one does not understand.

The thinking of ordinary man occurs when something "occurs to him." It is *mechanical chatter,* colored by lying, which is not under his control. Formatory apparatus, the moving part of intellectual center, is incapable of comprehending orders of truth higher than the dualistic: thus ordinary man is third-force blind. He sees things in terms of opposites—cause and effect, good and evil, truth and falsity, seeing duality but not trinity. Since, as we have seen, the laws of nature are trialectic rather than dialectic, lying and all other mechanical thought must be considered serious impediments to self-development.

This brings us to the idea of *imagination,* the body of unrealistic notions about himself that ordinary man holds as unquestionable truth. When the word "imagination" is used in the Gurdjieff sense the creative imagination of Leonardo, Rembrandt, Bach or Beethoven or Brahms is not meant. What is meant is something far more commonplace—the delusional system that each of us learns to believe to be the facts of life. This is a form of lying. For example, man is not typically conscious of himself and yet he believes he is. He is not able to control his actions and yet he thinks he can. Imagination goes on overtly and covertly all the time. It saps motivation for self-development, for if I do not admit that I am in a state of inattention, what will cause me to wish to change? The urge or impetus to work toward self-consciousness can arise only when the illusion of having capacities we do not actually possess falls away.

Another, related characteristic of ordinary waking state that is a useless energy leak and an obstacle to the development of higher states of consciousness is *unnecessary talking.* We spend our lives talking, either outwardly or inwardly. Idle talk is mechanical, involves imagination and lying, and encourages identification. It is related to other *unnecessary physical movements* and bodily tensions, twitches, fidgeting, finger drumming, foot tapping, grimacing, and so on, which serve to drain the daily ration of energy that might, if man but knew how, be used for increasing the level of available attention.

Let us consider, finally, the emotional manifestations of ordinary waking state. The feelings of ordinary man are made up almost entirely of *negative emotions,* although they are often successfully hidden by a polite mask. These negative emotions are triggered by identification and internal considering. Much of what motivates human activity is negative emotion, as anyone who picks up a newspaper can see. Man has an enormous repertoire of negativities: there are the basic passions of anger, envy, pride, vanity, hate, sloth, fear; the negative moods such as self-pity, depression, resentment, despair, boredom, irritability; the forms of sentimentality, including much of what is called humanitarianism and love; the forms of negative intellectual bias such as cynicism, argumentativeness, pessimism, suspicion. The list could go on and on. And what seems to be positive in the emotional states experienced by people in ordinary waking state can go sour and turn into negativity with just a little pressure on one of what Gurdjieff called our "corns"—sensitive psychological issues and images which are generally founded on pride or vanity.

THE SYSTEMATIC DISTORTION OF EXPERIENCE OF ORDINARY WAKING STATE

According to Gurdjieff, ordinary man experiences the world in such a way that he is generally content with his situation, attains a certain amount of pleasure and enjoyment, and finds life tolerable without progress toward self-realization. This feeling of contentment keeps man from striving for higher levels of consciousness and thus ensures that he will continue to serve nature's immediate purpose of transmitting energy from the upper realms of the ray of creation to its growing tip, the moon. It arises from the effects of "a special organ with a property such that, first, they should perceive reality topsy-turvy and, secondly, that every repeated impression from outside should crystallize in them data which would engender factors for evoking in them pleasure and enjoyment . . ." (Gurdjieff, 1950, p. 88). This "organ" he calls *Kundabuffer.* Kundabuffer has been removed, but its effect lingers on, its residue producing a kind of "opiate of the people" that makes man forget about the terrors of his mortality and his lack of will and control and helps him rationalize and lie to himself about his state, and to so misperceive the world that he shudders when a mouse runs across the room and feels no fear—in fact, cannot even imagine—the prospect of his own death.

The effects of Kundabuffer are such a serious impediment to self-realization that Beelzebub remarks, in the concluding statements of *All and Everything:*

The sole means now for saving the beings of the planet Earth would be to implant again into their essences a new organ, an organ like Kundabuffer, but this time of such properties that every one of these unfortunates during the process of existence should constantly sense and be cognizant of the inevitability of his death as well as of the death of everyone upon whom his eyes or attention rests. [Gurdjieff, 1950, p. 1183]

THE DEVELOPMENT OF PERSONALITY

Every human being is, according to Gurdjieff, born with an essential nature. This "essence" is not a tabula rasa, a blank or amorphous mass, although it has blank areas in which the influences of life experience make their imprints. It is a real individual identity with its own tendencies and predispositions, and it will grow, if not stifled, into self-conscious adulthood. Yet virtually every one of us, like the king's son, Prince Dhat, in the ancient Sufi allegory, falls into the stupor that is ordinary waking state and forgets his origin and destiny (Shah, 1967).

A little child acts in ways that reflect the truth about his being. He is not manipulative; he acts in good faith, as it were. But as socialization begins, personality begins to form. The child learns to modify his behavior to fit in with culturally approved patterns of conduct. This learning occurs partly through intentional training and partly through a natural tendency to imitate. As a natural consequence of the lengthy period of human social dependence (and the lack of instinctive constraints that are present in lower animals) we thus acquire sets of habits, roles, tastes, preferences, concepts, preconceptions and prejudices, desires and felt needs, all of which reflect family and cultural milieu and not necessarily innate tendencies and predispositions. These make up personality.

In the best of all possible worlds the acquired habits of personality would be available to man's essential nature and would help him to function adequately in the social context in which he lived, and for a realized being this is undoubtedly the case. Ordinary man, unfortunately, lacks the ability to make use of personality to carry out his essential wishes. What is essential in him can manifest only in the simplest instinctive behavior and in his primitive emotions. The rest of his behavior is controlled, as we have seen, by an accidental progression of "I's" that comprise his personality. And personality may or may not resemble essence.

People who lead simple lives close to nature may develop in such a way that personality is a minor part or passive element in their psychological makeup, but they are the rare exceptions in a world in which each adult relies almost totally on personality in whatever he does for a living, in public behavior, in intimate relationships, in virtually all aspects of daily existence. In most people personality is active and essence passive: personality determines their values and beliefs, profession, religious convictions, and philosophy of living. Personality, not essence, is responsible for the vast quantities of books and articles that fill the libraries of the world, for very few indeed speak to essence; personality creates most visual art; it speaks in the highest sentiments of statesmen. Personality even projects a God and prays to that projection.

Essence is what is man's own. Personality is what is not his own, what may be changed by changing conditions or artificially removed with hypnosis, drugs, or special exercises. Gurdjieff demonstrated this to his early pupils dramatically by temporarily stripping two individuals of their personalities for purposes of comparison (Ouspensky, 1949, pp. 251ff.). Those who have had some acquaintance with psychedelic drugs may have experienced essence in themselves or observed it in others, for some psychotropic substances have the effect of anesthetizing personality briefly, so that essence can appear without distortion.

All this is not to say that man's essence is always noble and beautiful while his personality is an alien crust of useless cultural barnacles. According to Gurdjieff, "as a rule a man's essence is either primitive, savage and childish, or else simply stupid" (Ouspensky, 1949, p. 163). The essences of many are actually dead, though they continue to live seemingly normal lives. The development of essence to maturity, when it will embody everything that is true and real in a person's being, depends on work on oneself, and work on oneself depends on a balance between a relatively healthy essence and a personality that is not crushingly heavy —as it is in the case of the "rich man" who cannot get into heaven. Both are necessary for self-development, for without the acquisition of personality there will be no wish to attain higher states of consciousness, no dissatisfaction with everyday existence; and without essence there will be no basis of development.

Essence and Personality Compared

ESSENCE	PERSONALITY
Innate	Acquired
What is a person's own	What is "not one's own"
The truth in man	The false in man
Develops into man's individuality	Provides the information necessary to work on self
Controlled by fate	Controlled by accident

MAN'S POSSIBILITIES

Although the picture of man's ordinary state as presented by Gurdjieff might be thought of as quite grim, it is not at all without hope, for man does have the possibility of change. The qualities he attributes to himself in his imagination and lying can actually be attained: there can be a real and unchanging "I," there can be action that is not reaction—the virtues are not entirely beyond our reach.

Every human being is born with the same right to develop, yet there are noticeable degrees in potential for inner growth. Man Number One is somewhat less permeable to the kinds of influences that attract people to inner work than is Man Number Two, and Man Number Two, in turn, is not as likely to heed these messages as is Man Number Three.

Looking at the possibilities of man's inner growth from the point of view of attitude, it is important that ordinary man be a "good householder" rather than a "tramp" or a "lunatic" if he is to begin to realize his full potential. A good householder is a person who is capable, well oriented in life, able to do his duty —and who no longer believes fully in life's goals or aims. A tramp is someone who believes in very little at all, who cannot or does not wish to live up to any responsibility. Tramps are more open-minded than lunatics who think they can do, think they know, believe in unrealities. Each of us has a tramp and a lunatic within, so to speak, which provide resistance to personal development through their antagonistic attitudes.

In order to be attracted to ideas related to self-development, a person must have developed a *magnetic center*. Each person grows up surrounded by influences coming from within life and other influences coming from sources outside of ordinary life. These latter influences begin to collect within an individual, and eventually, if there are enough of them, they develop sufficient mass to affect orientation, to cause a feeling of the need for self-development or at least a vague feeling of discontent. The values and goals of everyday life are then coupled with a search, looking for a certain kind of reading, and a growing inclination to be with people who are also concerned with such ideas. Ouspensky quotes Gurdjieff's description of the effect of magnetic center on personal orientation:

> If the magnetic center receives sufficient nourishment and if there is no strong resistance on the part of the other sides of a man's personality which are the result of influences created in life, the magnetic center begins to influence a man's orientation, obliging him to turn round and even to move in a certain direction. When the magnetic center attains sufficient force and development, a man already understands the idea of a way and he begins to look for the way. The search for the way may take many years and may lead to nothing. This depends upon conditions, upon circumstances, upon the power of the magnetic center, upon the power and the direction of inner tendencies which are not concerned with this search and which may divert a man at the very moment when the possibility of finding the way appears. [Ouspensky, 1949, p. 200]

If he is lucky, a man may come upon another person who has true knowledge about how to develop. Then he comes under the sway of a third kind of influences: those that can only be transmitted personally from master to pupil. He begins a course of instruction that may lead him to inner harmony and unity and to higher and higher levels of being.

HIGHER ORDERS OF MAN

In addition to the three types of men we have already classified according to the predominance of thinking, feeling, or moving-instinctive functioning, there are other and higher possibilities for man. Man Number One, Two, or Three is born, but the higher categories of men, that is, Men Number Four, Five, Six, and Seven, are always the results of efforts at self-development that have come to fruition.

Man Number Four has a permanent center of gravity which consists of his ideas about self-study and his firm aim to develop, by which he judges all other aspects of his life. He is man in the beginning of real evolution. His centers are beginning to become balanced and harmonious in operation. He is collecting real information about himself. His foot is on the path. He is in the process of getting to know himself and to know where he is going.

Man Number Five has reached inner unity. He has undergone the process of the crystallization of a permanent "I." He cannot become Man Number One, Two, or Three again except by a very painful process of decrystallization that is necessary only in the rare event that the process of crystallization has taken place on the wrong foundation. Unless crystallization takes place correctly an individual may become Man Number Five without having been Man Number Four, and in that case there is no possibility of further development into Man Number Six or Seven. "Hasnamuss" individuals belong to this category of man: they are people crystallized from the wrong substances or in the wrong way. If a permanent "I" develops before personality is sufficiently weakened, an individual may have the ability to do that characterizes Man Number Five, but this force will inevitably be misdirected and will become the cause of suffering to others.

The next two levels of man's attainment represent the highest an individual can possibly achieve. Man Number Six has all the attributes of Man Number Seven except that some of them are not permanent. Man Number Seven possesses all the qualities a human being can have: will, consciousness, a permanent and unchanging "I," individuality, and immortality.

EVOLUTION, DEATH, AND IMMORTALITY

Immortality is possible for man only to the degree to which he has developed embodiments of himself beyond his ordinary physical body. Many esoteric traditions describe the evolution of man in terms of the development of four bodies, each finer or more subtle than the last, which stand in a definite relation with one another.

The first body of man is the familiar physical body that each human being possesses. This body is called the *carnal body* in Christian terminology. It is all that a person has without work on himself, and when physical death occurs it returns to dust.

Under certain conditions a second body, called the *astral body* or body kesdjan, sometimes grows within the physical body. This body is not at all necessary for a person to have, and in fact it is possible to appear to be very highly developed intellectually and emotionally and even spiritually without one. Body kesdjan is something of a luxury. The physical body has all the functions of the astral body or analogues of them and, indeed, of all the higher bodies as well. It can work with the same energies and process approximately the same substances. The difference is that while the physical body can use these energies and substances, they pass through it and are not, so to speak, owned. Thus the functions of the physical body govern all processing of substances, and they, in turn, are under the control of environmental stimuli. Will does not exist. Reaction is all that is possible for man at this level of development, although his reactions may seem at first glance to be as subtle and finely attuned as the actions of a more highly evolved man.

The third body, called the spiritual or *mental body,* is related to the intellectual function or mind of man. The fourth body is called the causal or *divine body* and is related to the function of will. Only Man Number Seven, man who has developed all four bodies, can be called, in Gurdjieff's phrase, "man without quotation marks."

Gurdjieff compares a contemporary man with his thoughts, feelings, and physiology to a hackney carriage, horse, and coachman. The carriage is analogous to the physical body, the horse is the emotions, the coachman is the consciousness, and there is also a passenger in the box—that which we call "I." The carriage, though it may be the latest style, must function at the mercy of the coachman, who has never understood it and who, therefore, does not clean the parts with kerosene or oil them appropriately, and although the carriage was originally designed to oil itself naturally as the shocks and bumps of byroads spread lubricant around the moving parts, today's smooth highways render that kind of greasing unlikely. The horse, says Gurdjieff,

has never received any special education, but has been molded exclusively under the influence of constant thrashings and vile abuse. It has always been kept tied up; and for food, instead of oats and hay, there is given to it merely straw which is utterly worthless for its real needs. Never having seen in any of the manifestations towards it even the least love or friendliness, the horse is now ready to surrender itself completely to anybody who gives it the slightest caress. [1950, p. 1195]

The coachman sits sleepily on the box, ready to go anywhere (as long as it doesn't cause him too much trouble) for anyone who offers him a fare, and anywhere at all for a fare plus a tip.

Looking at this analogy from the point of view of what man might become, the carriage corresponds to the first or physical body, the horse to the astral body, the coachman to the mental body, and the passenger to the master, who, unlike any passer-by who might rent the carriage, actually owns, maintains, and directs the carriage. Ordinary man is an automaton whose actions, desires, and thoughts are the products of environmental stimuli, and who is plagued by contradictory "wills" created by desires which are, in turn, created by external influences. The direction of control goes from outer world to man. The development of all four bodies reverses the direction of control: the permanent "I" or master is obeyed by the mind and emotions, and the body obeys thoughts and feelings in its turn.

Seen in terms of the ray of creation, the first body is created with the materials of this earth and is therefore destined to return to the earth. The second body is made of a finer level of material; that of level 24, and can last after the death of the physical body but is not, strictly speaking, immortal. It will be survived by the third body in an individual in whom this body is developed. The fourth body is immortal within the limits of this solar system, since it is composed of materials that do not belong to the solar system, but to the level beyond it. Thus one person may be immortal and another not at all so. It all depends on the level of inner development.

The possibility of relative levels of immortality which are based upon the degree to which psychological work has evolved evokes the idea of reincarnation or recurrence, which states, in many versions (depending on the theological or cosmological context), that something in each human being must return again and again to life after life until it works through its psychological tendencies and biases. On this topic Gurdjieff was often abrupt and unwilling to teach, since it has the flavor of intellectual fitting games rather than practical import. Ouspensky once plied him for a statement on this subject.

"This idea of repetition," said G., "is not the full and absolute truth but it is the nearest possible approximation of the truth. In this case truth cannot be expressed in words. But what you say is very near to it. And if you understand why I do not speak of this, you will be still nearer to it. What is the use of a man knowing about recurrence if he is not conscious of it and if he himself does not change? One can say even that if a man does not change, repetition does not exist for him. If you tell him about repetition if will only increase his sleep. Why should he make any efforts today when there is so much time and so many possibilities ahead—the whole of eternity? This is exactly why the system does not say anything about repetition and takes only this one life which we know. The system has neither meaning nor sense without striving for self-change. And work on self-change must begin today, immediately. All laws can be seen in one life. Knowledge about the repetition of lives will add nothing for a man if he does not see how everything repeats itself in one life, that is, in this life, and if he does not strive to change himself in order to escape this repetition. But if he changes something essential in himself, that is, if he attains something, this cannot be lost." [Ouspensky, 1949, p. 250]

THE FOUR BODIES AND THE RAY OF CREATION

ABSOLUTE		
ALL WORLDS	3 LAWS	FOURTH BODY DIVINE OR CAUSAL BODY I, CONSCIOUSNESS, WILL
ALL SUNS	6 LAWS	THIRD BODY MENTAL OR SPIRITUAL BODY MIND
OUR SUN	12 LAWS	SECOND BODY ASTRAL BODY OR BODY KESDJAN FEELINGS, DESIRES
ALL PLANETS	24 LAWS	FIRST BODY PHYSICAL OR CARNAL BODY
EARTH	48 LAWS	
MOON	96 LAWS	

This kind of inner change is the goal of every real religious teaching and practice, for it may give man the capacity to live virtuously, harmoniously, and forever. Man in his highest form assimilates the food, air, and impressions he receives as his daily bread to the fullest extent possible, for he is wise in the ways of delivering to himself the two conscious shocks necessary to bring his inner metabolism to completion. This is the aim of the system of study and practice that was transmitted by Gurdjieff to his pupils, and which is now known as the "Gurdjieff work."

THE GURDJIEFF WORK

If a man could understand all the horror of the lives of ordinary people who are turning round in a circle of insignificant interests and insignificant aims, if he could understand what they are losing, he would understand that there can only be one thing that is serious for him—to escape from the general law, to be free. What can be serious for a man in prison who is condemned to death? Only one thing: How to save himself, how to escape: nothing else is serious. [Ouspensky, 1949, p. 364]

The method of self-development taught by Gurdjieff is an attempt to liberate individual people from the heavy burden of laws under which our place in the universe compels humanity to live. It is the technology of subverting the effects of the organ Kundabuffer, of plugging up energy leaks and tuning the body's machinery for the transformation of various foods, of making personality passive with respect to essence, of increasing knowledge and being, of developing the four bodies of man, of delivering the first and second conscious shocks.

In order to develop from any of the three types of ordinary man into higher orders of being it is necessary to crystallize and temper essence into a permanent and unified "I." This is done to a large extent by instigating a struggle between essence and personality. Both essence and personality are necessary for this work: essence must have personality or it will have no wish to develop. Personality provides the material to study, the obstacles to overcome, the temptations to resist, the delusions to invalidate, and in the process of struggling with and testing itself against personality essence gains in strength and maturity. This battle is what Islam originally meant by a holy war, and in this war the more evenly matched the opposing sides, the greater the friction and the more rapidly crystallization, which depends upon the heat thus generated, will occur.

The work, or war, can most profitably take place in the conditions that make up man's daily routine for the environment, relationships, habits, and responsibilities in which a person finds himself are yet another reflection of the patterns of habitual functioning he has acquired in the formation of his personality. They can be watched, analyzed in terms of energy wastage and wrong work of centers, and to some degree modified. Self-study is aided and made more effective when it is carried out in everyday conditions.

Because there is no requirement to leave home, family, and profession, the Gurdjieff work is perhaps more accessible and easier to begin than any of the paths of self-development that require withdrawal from the world. Once fully engaged, however, the process is no less arduous.

THE FOURTH WAY

The Gurdjieff work makes use of each of man's three stories or brains—the intellectual, emotional, and moving-instinctive functions—in an attempt to balance and harmonize their activity. It does not focus more on one than another, though for individuals it is often necessary to concentrate on one of the centers for a while in order to make up for atrophy that may have occurred through disuse in life—as, for example, when a coldly rational person must painfully learn to express himself emotionally, or an impulsive one to stop and think.

In working on all three functions simultaneously and in allowing and even requiring life in the world, the Gurdjieff work differs from the three traditional religious paths. These paths or ways correspond to the three types of ordinary man: Man Number One, Man Number Two, and Man Number Three. They are also related to the relative importance or stress they give to the three functions. These traditional ways are:

1. The way of the fakir.
2. The way of the monk.
3. The way of the yogi.

The fakir develops mastery of the lowest story, the physical body, by enduring tortuous physical postures or exercises. Some fakirs assume a painful position such as standing on one leg or balancing on fingers and toes, and they maintain it for years. In so doing they strengthen will. The way of the fakir requires very little knowledge. Disciples simply stay in the general vicinity and learn by imitation. If a fakir does actually achieve an unbendable will he must still develop the other two basic functions and sometimes, in the rare event that he is found and taken on by a skilled master, this may be possible.

The way of the monk is the way of devotion, religious sacrifice, and faith. The emotional center is central in work in this way, which appeals to Man Number Two. Emotions are transcended and self-mastery attained when all petty desires are subjugated to the love of God. But even if this state of being is attained, the monk can only be a "silly saint" if he does not go on to develop his physical and intellectual functions correspondingly.

The way of the yogi is the path of knowledge, corresponding to the intellectual center and to Man Number Three. Again, though the yogi achieves his aim, he will still be without mastery of the emotional and physical aspects of his being, and these will require new efforts and new study if unity is to be achieved.

The fakir, monk, and yogi must renounce the world, give up their families, and devote their full energies to personal development, for at the very beginning of each of these ways an individual must die to his past if he is to accomplish anything of value.

The fourth way demands that the individual aspirant be "in the world but not of it," as the Sufi saying goes. In following this approach to self-realization the seeker renounces renunciation. It makes use of a person's own life situation and is thus a possible path for all types of people. Work goes on in all three stories of the "food factory" at once, and therefore, when the end result is attained, it is already attained in all three of the basic functions. The Gurdjieff work is in the tradition of fourth-way schools.

The names of the four ways need not be misleading to students of world religion if it is remembered that whether a particular sect or tradition belongs to one or another of the ways depends not on whether its adherents call themselves monks or yogis but on the relative predominance of centers. A Zen monk meditating on a koan is, though called a monk, following the way of the yogi as defined here; those practicing bhakti yoga, the yoga of devotion, are on the way of the monk.

Fourth-way schools are sometimes found hidden within Eastern and Middle Eastern religious groups. They are, however, very rare in the East and even rarer in the West.

THE BEGINNING

Those who wish to engage in work on themselves according to the methods of Gurdjieff can expect obstacles to be thrown up in front of them at the beginning. First there is the problem of finding a group, which is not as easy as finding a monastery or the ashram of a yogi. People who are practicing Gurdjieff's techniques are relatively invisible as they go about their daily round of activities. And they have very little missionary inclination; groups that proselytize are very likely to be imitators.

Gurdjieff emphasized that knowledge cannot belong to all or even to the majority of people, not because anything must be kept secret or retained by an elect few, but because the acquisition of real knowledge requires great effort on the part of both teacher and student, master and disciple, and this effort is not often considered valuable by those who consider themselves seekers. Like everything else in the cosmos, knowledge is material in nature, and like any other form of matter it must exist in a limited quantity at any given place and time. Gurdjieff once compared knowledge to gold:

If we take a certain quantity of gold and decide to gild a certain number of objects with it, we must know or calculate, exactly what number of objects can be gilded with this quantity of gold. If we try to gild a greater number, they will be covered with gold unevenly, in patches, and will be much worse than if they had no gold at all; in fact, we shall lose our gold.

The distribution of knowledge is based on exactly the same principle. If knowledge is given to all, nobody will get any. If it is preserved among a few, each will receive not only enough to keep, but to increase what he receives.

At first glance this theory seems very unjust, since the position of those who are, so to speak, denied knowledge in order that others may receive a greater share appears to be very sad and undeservedly harder than it ought to be. Actually, however, this is not so at all; and in the distribution of knowledge there is not the slightest injustice. [Ouspensky, 1949, p. 37]

Nothing is concealed, no knowledge is witheld, yet Gurdjieff stresses: "He who wants knowledge must himself make the initial efforts to find the source of knowledge and approach it, taking advantage of the help and indications that are given to all, but which people, as a rule, do not want to see or recognize. Knowledge cannot come to people without effort on their own part" (Ouspensky, 1949, p. 39).

And then there is the question of payment, which is very closely related. Some people think that anything related to the spiritual or to self-development should be given away free, but this, to Gurdjieff, is a radical misunderstanding. Esoteric knowledge, like anything else in the universe, must be paid for—by the effort it takes to find it and assimilate it and even by actual payment in money as well. Like Freud, Gurdjieff recognized that people do not value a thing if they do not pay for it. Ouspensky put it this way:

Payment is a principle. Payment is necessary not to the school but to the people themselves, for without paying they will not get anything. The idea of payment is very important and it must be understood that payment is absolutely necessary. One can pay in one way or another way and everyone has to find that out for himself. But nobody can *get* anything that he does not pay for. Things cannot be given, they can only be bought. It is magical, not simple. If one has knowledge, one cannot give it to another person, for only if he pays for it can the other person have it. This is a cosmic law. [Ouspensky, 1954, p. 280]

The notion of good householder is relevant here. Competence and strength in the world are predictive of strength in the work. The most likely candidates for this sort of inner work have a trade or profession that they know well and that is valued by the world. Knowing something well gives a person experience in doing a task thoroughly—beginning, middle, and end. It also provides financial solidity that frees the attention for inner work.

STAGES ON THE WAY

The Gurdjieff work is very much a group activity. Several people gathered together around a teacher can form a center of gravity for their mutual benefit that one person working independently, however dedicated, cannot have. The group is used to create conditions favorable to work on oneself, to generate energy, to produce psychological heat through interpersonal frictions, to provide mutual support and for many other purposes as well. This becoming part of such a group and relating to a teacher is the very first stage of the Gurdjieff work. Reading books and articles and attempting to carry out practices on one's own can serve as an important preface, but without the group situation and the guidance of another who is somewhat more advanced in the work, even the best intentions will gradually but inevitably be diverted from their original orientation by the discontinuities inherent in all processes, as we have seen in the study of the Law of Seven.

After one takes the initial step of finding a group with which to work, the exact order of stages and phases of work will depend on each individual pattern of unfolding. What is the most basic preparation for one will be useless or even

deleterious for another. It is for this reason, among others, that the actual practices of esoteric teaching are always transmitted orally. Yet, however individual
the actual course of work on oneself must and will inevitably be, some general
directions of work can be discerned and described.

Three "lines of work" exist in Gurdjieff's teaching: work for and on oneself;
work with and for others; and work in relationship to the ideas of the work, in
and for the work itself. These lines correspond roughly to the three basic functions
of moving-instinctive, emotional, and intellectual centers. They may begin simultaneously or not, but in any case the first line is stressed at first, later more
attention is given to the second line of work, and only the more advanced students
focus most of their energies on the third line of work.

THE FIRST LINE OF WORK

The first line of work is an extended attempt to follow the ancient injunction,
"Know thyself." Knowledge about oneself and the order of things is sought
through many channels, and at the same time awareness is enlarged and strengthened to increase the level of being. Work in this line typically begins with the
collection of information about personal functioning without any attempt to
change. It is possible, even in the dulled state of inattention that is the ordinary
human condition, to catch glimpses of one's characteristic activities such as gaits,
postures, tones of voice, and facial expressions. The data amassed through repeated, though brief, moments of self-observation may be used to understand the
concept of many "I's" as it applies to one's own life, to study the relative activity
of centers, to watch the ways in which energy leaks away in the course of every
day, to detect the presence of buffers, and to attribute specific reactions to the
parts of centers to which they are due.

As the work of getting to know oneself proceeds from the observation of bodily
habits to the observation of emotional reactions and patterns of thought, moments
of "self-remembering"—flashes of the third level of consciousness—may occur
and may become more lucid and more frequent. Nicoll describes the process:
"*Self-Remembering* is the most important thing of all and has many degrees and
stages. Everyone can, to a limited degree, begin to practice and understand
Self-Remembering. Full Self-Remembering is one thing, but many degrees exist
in the approach to it" (Nicoll, 1952, p. 457).

Self-remembering is not merely the observation of self, though that is difficult
enough; it has a quality of attention that is unmistakable though difficult to
convey, just as the taste of salt would be almost impossible to describe to someone who had never tasted it but once known is easily recognized thereafter.
This particular sensation is that of delivering to oneself the First Conscious

Shock. Tracol (1968) asserts that "whether or not it be active in me, the possibility is given to me to become aware, at certain moments, of my own presence: I, here, now. This, when I experience it, is accompanied by a strangely familiar taste, a particular sensation that might be called 'genuinely' subjective. It is, quite simply, I. I recognize myself. I remember myself. I." During moments of self-remembering, attention is divided between the surrounding environment and one's inner self. Perceptions are clear and undistorted, both interiorly and exteriorly. According to Ouspensky (1949, p. 121), moments of self-remembering do occur spontaneously in life, and most of what we can remember vividly is recorded during these flashes. The deliberate attempt to produce such moments, to sustain them and to deepen them, is the backbone of the first line of work.

Along with efforts at self-observation and self-remembering there can be a parallel attempt to extend and deepen self-understanding through active interventions carried out on a small scale. It is possible to change certain aspects of overt behavior and to use such changes as reminders for flagging attention. Minor variations in the way habitual actions are carried out—as, for example, when a cigarette is held with the unaccustomed hand or the normal pace of walking is speeded up or slowed down—may foster significant improvement in the general level of awareness. Great caution must be used in making changes in habits, since, as Gurdjieff repeatedly pointed out, the organism is a delicately balanced mechanism and any modification in one habit always brings about a corresponding adjustment in some other manifestation. This adjustment is often unpredicted and sometimes quite unwelcome.

Efforts to remember oneself during the day are sustained through a connection with a state produced in quiet meditation before the activity of daily life begins each morning. At first this period of sitting will involve only a sequence of physical relaxations and the enhancement of a general awareness of the body fostered by focused attention to physical sensations. As the student progresses, many techniques, all predicated on the assumption that a firm foundation in sensing the body has been established, are introduced. Sometimes the technique of bare attention is used in this period of quiet sitting; at others a repeated question such as "Who am I?" is used as the object of contemplation.

Progress through the various stages of inner development in meditation follows the general course that is usual in such practice. At first the mind is found to be exceedingly active and its chatter defies all attempts to move toward interior silence and simple attention to the physical body. Eventually and gradually a familiarity with inner process permits some of the identification with its vagaries to lighten, and there are moments of clear consciousness. As meditation deepens, the moments of self-remembering during active life can be linked to the meditation state, and they, too, become stronger and more reliable.

As the effects of self-remembering accumulate and produce an improvement in level of being, knowledge of various manifestations is also increasing. Patterns begin to emerge that permit true self-understanding and produce the kind of heat and light that characterize the struggle between essence and personality. Nicoll describes one of the many stages in this process:

The side of what we actually are, and the side of what we pretend and imagine we are, are two contradictory sides. These two contradictory sides, however, exist in everyone without exception. The action of the Work, once it is beginning to be wished for, makes us become gradually aware of this contradiction—over many years. Then we begin to have traces of real suffering—interspersed with all sorts of attempts at self-justifying and excuses and reactions—until we become, by inner taste, sick of self-justifying, excuses and so on. This marks a stage in the Work, a definite point in self-development. [Nicoll, 1952, p. 456]

Self-understanding develops, and with it arises a clearer and clearer conception of personal aim. Commitment to the "voluntary labor and intentional suffering" involved in the Gurdjieff work must increase as friction between essence and personality increases or else a person will become unwilling to endure the attendant pain. A personal aim may be stated in one way or another: it is an individual matter. For one it is: "I wish to be master of myself," while for another it is: "I wish to be able to do good." However it is stated, it represents the level of a person's understanding at any given moment in time about his orientation in working on himself. It is against this aim that all other motives, actions, and directions must now be measured, and upon which a new sense of morality is founded, for what aids my inner work is good and what does not must fall away.

First line of work blends into second line of work with the practice of external considering. But first a word about what is known as chief feature. As we have seen, the adult personality is characterized by many "I's," by plurality and inconsistency. Nevertheless each person has a central attribute, a pillar on which the rest of personality rests or around which it could be said to revolve. This "chief feature" is almost always invisible to a person himself, but the people around him can usually give accurate enough information about it. Nicknames are often telling clues to chief feature.

Although hints and other aids in working on oneself are given the student, it is typically his task alone to determine what chief feature is by piecing together the data collected through self-observation. Once chief feature is known, it can provide a key to the invalidation of personality so that essence is relatively stronger in its struggle against it. In describing Gurdjieff's presentation of their chief features to people in his group, Ouspensky relates this incident:

"There cannot be proper outward considering while a man is seated in his chief feature," said G. "For instance So-and-So" (he named one of our party). "His feature is that he is *never at home.* How can he consider anything or anybody? . . .

To another in our party he said on the question of feature that his feature was that *he did not exist at all.*

"You understand, *I do not see you,"* said G. "It does not mean that you are always like that. But when you are like you are now, you do not exist at all."

He said to another that his chief feature was a tendency always to argue with everybody about everything.

"But then I never argue," the man very heatedly at once replied.

Nobody could help laughing. [Ouspensky, 1949, p. 268]

As self-study brings to light the facts about a person's actual functioning and as personality is, to some extent, seen through, it loses some of its stranglehold on essence and loses some of its force. It is no longer quite so believable: identification is not always inevitably present. Work that required a certain degree of self-control begins to be possible, and this includes work in relationship with other people, the second line of work.

THE MOVEMENTS

Rhythmic gymnastic movements and dances, adapted by Gurdjieff from many Middle Eastern and Eastern sources, are used as aids in the first line of work. They may be thought of as a form of meditation in action, though they also have the properties of an art form and a language. In practicing these movements an effort is made to divide attention and remember oneself, for often the head, arms, hands, and feet must follow different rhythms, and without a great effort of attention, performing them is quite impossible. Right working of centers and consistent awareness are necessary to perform the movements correctly. One error, one moment of inattention, may involve the loss of an elaborate count and render the student unable to deny his lack of awareness.

The Gurdjieff movements are a unique contribution to the resources of those who are able, to some extent at least, to meditate while sitting still and quiet and who are ready to try to extend their state of recollected attention to a more active state of being. They are done to music, which engages the emotional center in the effort joined by the intellectual center, which much keep track of what is to be done next, and the moving-instinctive level of function which must go against all personal and idiosyncratic biases and do the movements exactly as indicated.

The movements are said to be a form of objective art—an art form that comes from conscious sources and produces, without any variation, the effects upon participants and audiences that it is intended to have. Like some Balinese and

Indonesian dances, the movements often represent a kind of bodily semaphore or symbolic method of communication. Each position has its own meaning and presumably can be deciphered by those initiated into the code. Although the movements come from many sources, perhaps the chief of these is a hidden monastery in the Hindu Kush to which Gurdjieff was taken, and in which he saw priestess-dancers taught sacred temple dances using a most peculiar piece of equipment:

> The external appearance of these peculiar apparatuses gave the impression, at first glance, that they were of very ancient workmanship. They were made of ebony inlaid with ivory and mother-of-pearl. When they were not in use and stood grouped together, they reminded one of "Vasanelian" trees, with branches all alike. On close examination, we saw that each apparatus consisted of a smooth column, higher than a man, which was fixed on a tripod. From this column, in seven places, there projected specially designed branches, which in turn were divided into seven parts of different dimensions, each successive part decreasing in length and width in proportion to its distance from the main column. . . . [Gurdjieff, 1963, p. 160]

A more recent account of what must be the same monastery is given by Desmond Martin:

> An articulated tree, of gold and other metals, which seemed to me unbelievably beautiful and resembled a Babylonian work of art which I had seen in the Bagdad Museum, was by far the most impressive. It served to indicate the postures assumed by dervishes in their yoga-like exercises, which, performed to special music, they studied for self-development. [Martin, 1966, p. 22]

The monastery was that of the Sarmouni Brotherhood, a Sufi order whose ideas of the materiality of knowledge and of universal laws may also be the source of the fundamental principles of Gurdjieff's cosmology.

SECOND LINE OF WORK

"The hardest thing for man," said Gurdjieff," is to endure the manifestations of others" (Nott, 1961). The second line of work provides special conditions and support in the effort to become aware of one's ways of relating to other people, and opportunities to practice new ways of being with others.

Just as habitual reactions of the physical body can become the subjects of a detailed study, patterns of emotional reaction can undergo observation and analysis. They have been the prime targets of psychoanalytic investigation since its inception. The Gurdjieff work differs radically from other methods of self-study in this domain, however, in its insistence that negative emotions are entirely unnecessary and we may suppress their outward expression (although observing them internally) without the danger of provoking an unwanted compensatory adjustment in some other habit pattern. Thus, for those who have undertaken the effort of self-remembering, the nonexpression of negative emotions (which even a relatively superficial survey will show to be the vast majority of all emotional experiences ordinarily encountered in daily life) will soon be required. Nicoll describes the process in its first stages:

> I will remind you of the first step—namely, we are not asked to like, but to stop dislike and all its ramifications. This makes a very practical starting point. Later, when you feel the presence of a negative emotion in you as a foreign substance, as acutely as a stomach-ache, then you will seek, for your own reasons to work on yourself and transform your inner state for your own inner health. [Nicoll, 1952, p. 695]

The suppression of negative emotions is an immensely difficult task, and one which intensifies the struggle between essence and personality in a way that is often very painful. As essence matures, standardized patterns of feeling that personality has acquired through accepting the labels that parents and teachers have transmitted become weaker and eventually begin to drop away. True feelings begin to appear, changing the quality of emotion that is available to be directed outward toward others and inward toward one's own being. According to Nicoll the signs of the raising of emotional life to a higher plane include "a change in the feeling of 'I' " and the "ability to control lower emotion" (Nicoll, 1952, p. 696).

Gurdjieff was expert in provoking interpersonal friction in order to highlight the emotional habits of his pupils. Fritz Peters describes how Gurdjieff actually paid one man, "who without conscious effort, produced friction in all the people around him," to live in the Prieuré (Peters, 1964, p. 72). The Gurdjieff work continues this form of help in self-development by requiring collaboration in many kinds of physical labor and arts and crafts projects that groups undertake. During these periods of work together special tasks are given. Sometimes the tasks are attention sharpeners or dividers, as, for example, counting forward and backward in an unfamiliar language while working. Others, and most particularly external considering, which may be thought of as a fundamental exercise in the practice of love, are given to provide further material in the study of the working of emotional center and also to lay the groundwork for the practice of a truly moral life. Discussion of the inevitable problems that arise between people whose personalities clash from the point of view of inner considering, identification, lying, and useless negativity furthers understanding of what emotional function is and is not.

The suppression of negative emotions requires a long and often painful period of inner effort. It serves as a preface for the phase of the work that involves the transmutation of negative emotions into positive energy. With this effort, an individual begins to be able to give himself the Second Conscious Shock and thus to complete the full assimilation of food, air, and impressions that characterizes the evolved human being.

THE THIRD LINE OF WORK

The first line of work might be thought of as being self-centered, as an individual concentrates on his own process in order to gain in awareness and increase his level of being. The second line of work involves relationship, interaction with other people, but still the attention is focused on individual patterns of reaction to others and to the social context. In both the first and the second lines of work the indications of a teacher are followed. In the third line of work, which is work done for the benefit of the ideas of the work itself, initiative is allowed and even encouraged and personal growth or gain is not the main thrust of effort.

In the third line of work the needs and requirements of the organization, the group of people who have come together to work on themselves, are considered. Selfless service is the heart of the third line of work, and since any selfless action is beyond the capacity of man in his ordinary level of consciousness, this line of work cannot involve any sustained effort until personality is, at least to some degree, disarmed.

THE ROLE OF PHYSICAL LABOR IN THE WORK

Contemporary man has lost the opportunity, if he is urban and educated, to engage in the kind of manual labor for which his body evolved, and yet physical exertion helps the centers to work in the ways they were intended to work and to stop stealing energy from one another and interfering with each other's functioning. People who work on themselves according to Gurdjieff's system, therefore, create opportunities to do farm work, construction work, and other heavy tasks in order to balance and harmonize centers. There are some things that are possible for the body only when it is given additional burdens of great energy expenditure, little sleep, and complicated efforts to make that require great attention. Under such stress, centers have no leeway to work wrongly. Furthermore, efforts made to and beyond the point of exhaustion may allow access to a special reservoir of energy which Gurdjieff calls the "large accumulator," as contrasted with the small, peripheral energy accumulators that are routinely available to us:

Small accumulators suffice for the ordinary, everyday work of life. But for work on oneself, for inner growth, and for the efforts required of a man who enters the way, the energy from these small accumulators is not enough.

We must learn how to draw energy straight from the large accumulator. [Ouspensky, 1949, p. 235]

The large accumulator provides the "second wind" that comes when, completely spent from the tremendous effort of climbing a mountain or fighting off fatigue in tending the sick throughout the night, one suddenly feels an influx of energy and the strength to go on as if after a refreshing sleep. Although man naturally switches from one small accumulator to another in the course of a day or night, switching to the large accumulator, which can happen only in great exhaustion, gives him the possibility of making superefforts, impossible for him in his ordinary state, which may, like the powerful first stage of a rocket, allow him to liberate himself from laws which now bind him to the level of the earth.

EXPERIENTIAL EXERCISES

Work on oneself according to Gurdjieff's teachings is individual and empirical, and results are directly proportional to understanding. Nothing must be accepted unless it has been compellingly proved by personal experiment, and, in fact, blind faith is not in accordance with the principles underlying the work. "No faith is required on the fourth way; on the contrary, faith of any kind is opposed to the fourth way," Gurdjieff insisted. "On the fourth way a man must satisfy himself of the truth of what he is told. And until he is satisfied he must do nothing" [Ouspensky, 1949, p. 49].

Consider the basic premise that man's ordinary waking state is very limited and inconsistent. Ouspensky demonstrated this fact in a lecture given in 1934:

Take a watch and look at the second hand, *trying to be aware of yourself,* and concentrating on the thought, "I am Peter Ouspensky," "I am now here." Try not to think about anything else, simply follow the movements of the second hand and be aware of yourself, your name, your existence, and the place where you are. Keep all other thoughts away.

You will, if you are persistent, be able to do this *for two minutes. This is the limit of your consciousness.* And if you try to repeat the experiment soon after, you will find it more difficult than the first time. [Ouspensky, 1954, p. 19]

A. R. Orage, who headed the Gurdjieff work in New York for many years, gave these additional instructions:

Now take another step. Keeping the focus as before, count mentally the numbers one to ten backwards, slowly, during the course of one revolution of the hand. This requires a double attention, as it were. You are observing the movement and counting deliberately at the same time. At first it may be easy, but do it again and again until it becomes difficult; and *then do it!* This is a very important piece of advice. [Orage, 1954, p. 12]

The exercise can be made more and more complex until the limits of one's attention are clearly evident. Then these limits may be, with persistent effort, expanded.

Because we have such inconsistent awareness, and because what we do have is so often distorted by identification, it may be difficult to conceive of the degree to which we act mechanically and are unable to "do." It is necessary to take some distance from personal involvement in one's own life experience in order to see it as an impartial witness. Orage described a procedure of reviewing the events in a day that, when practiced regularly, ought to yield a great deal of information that would enrich the understanding of the notion: "Man is a machine." Here is a condensed version of his technique:

Before going to sleep, begin to count slowly to yourself a series of simple numbers, backwards and forwards, such as 2,4,6,8,10—10,8,6,4,2. Continue this repetition rhythmically. Having got this rhythm moving, almost but never quite automatically, deliberately try to picture yourself as you appeared on getting up that morning.

You woke, you got out of bed, you proceeded to dress, to breakfast, to read the paper, to catch a bus and so on. Try to follow this sequence of yourself pictorially observed, from moment to moment, exactly as if you were unwinding a film. At first you will find the exercise difficult . . . the necessity to count continuously will trouble you at this stage. Nevertheless, continue; for the fact is that counting occupies the thinking brain and thus naturally allows the pictorial memory to work more easily. . . . Thinking not only impedes the pictorial representation but it subtly but surely falsifies the pictures. [Orage, 1954, p. 94]

Other difficulties that may be encountered, according to Orage, are the interruptions due to failures in memory that everybody experiences and the likelihood that when thinking and worrying, which generally keep us interested in the inner chatter we know as ordinary waking consciousness, cease or are drastically attenuated, sleep may put an end to this exercise before the day's review is complete.

If the nightly review of each day's activities is practiced consistently it may happen that moments of self-observation begin to occur spontaneously during the day. The locus of awareness may move up in time so that it occasionally appears in the here and now rather than in memory or the anticipation of future events. It is at this point that the collection of data about thinking, feeling, and sensing functions might begin. Moments of self-observation, or "snapshots," may be taken of gestures, tones of voice, facial expressions, and ways of habitual interaction with others to form a collection in which the patterns of functioning that make each of us a recognizable individual can, when the gallery of pictures is extensive and exhaustive enough, be discerned. As the details of mechanical functioning emerge from the study of these "snapshots," wasteful and inefficient kinds of reaction will be identifiable and what to do about them (if anything) will become clear. And during each step of this process a thorough understanding, based on experience that is so personal that it cannot be forgotten or denied, is a fundamental necessity. Some of this self-study can be accomplished on one's own, but, as the Sufis say, "He who has no guide has Shaitan (the devil) as his guide." Observations made without the context of a teaching situation must inevitably be subject to the falsifications that Orage warned about; thinking mind is full of biases and tricks of distortion that make these biases look to oneself as if they were the pure truth. Exercises on one's own are fine for a preface, but not for the body of the work.

HOW TO CONTACT THE LIVING TRADITION

In late October 1949, in the American Hospital in Paris, the dying Gurdjieff spent long hours in a private interview with Jeanne de Salzmann, who, with her late husband, had been his student from the very early days in Tiflis and Constantinople. Since that time Mme. Salzmann has served as the head of a network of Gurdjieff groups throughout the world. There is undoubtedly one near any interested reader. The way to contact the one nearest you is to write to the publisher of Gurdjieff's works.

Groups that are connected with and headed by the Gurdjieff Foundation in Paris are typically led by those who knew Gurdjieff personally and who can, therefore, be expected to render his ideas with some authenticity. In addition to this network, which can be thought of as the Gurdjieff orthodoxy and which has been criticized by some as rigid and even as lacking in the ineffable ingredient that is present around a living master, there are several groups run by students of Gurdjieff and Ouspensky under their own auspices. Of these the best-known are Willem Nyland in upstate New York and California; pupils of the late John Bennett, in England; and Robert DeRopp, in California.

In addition to groups deriving from Gurdjieff's teaching, the kind of work that has come to be associated with Gurdjieff has recently become available through other channels that are not Gurdjieff groups but trace their sources to the background of Gurdjieff's teaching: Pir Al-Washi's group in Crestline, California; Oscar Ichazo's Arica Institutes in New York and other major cities; and SAT, a school founded in Berkeley, California, by Claudio Naranjo with the purpose of establishing a living synthesis between various Eastern traditions and the contributions of contemporary psychology which has generated a form of work that is very much in the same spirit as Gurdjieff's.

Gurdjieff movements are available to students at all the Gurdjieff Foundations related to Mme. de Salzmann's Paris group, at Nyland's, Bennett's, and De-Ropp's groups, and at SAT. The legacy of music left by Gurdjieff and arranged by Thomas de Hartmann has been, to some extent, recorded. Sheet music of "Seekers of the Truth," "Journey to Inaccessible Places," and "Rituals of a Sufi Order" and long-playing records of these works, plus "Chants for an Essene Order," may be obtained by those who join Gurdjieff groups.

FURTHER READING

A basic overview of Gurdjieff's ideas is given in:
Bennett, J. G. *Gurdjieff: Making a New World.* New York: Harper & Row, 1974.
Ouspensky, P. D. *In Search of The Miraculous.* New York: Harcourt, Brace and Co., 1949.

Other accounts may be found in Kenneth Walker's books:
Walker, K. *Venture with Ideas.* London: Jonathan Cape, 1951.
Walker, K. *A Study of Gurdjieff's Teaching.* London: Jonathan Cape, 1957.

Gurdjieff's own works are:
All and Everything. New York: Harcourt Brace and Co., 1950.
Meetings with Remarkable Men. New York: E. P. Dutton and Co., 1963.
Herald of the Coming Good. Paris, 1933. Reprinted New York: Weiser, 1970.
Views from the Real World: Early Talks of Gurdjieff as Recollected by His Pupils. New York: E. P. Dutton, 1973.

Accounts of personal experience with Gurdjieff are many. Particularly vivid descriptions of his personality and teaching are given in:
De Hartmann, T. *Our Life with Mr. Gurdjieff.* New York: Cooper Square Publishers, Inc., 1964.
Peters, F. *Boyhood with Gurdjieff.* New York: E. P. Dutton and Co., 1964.
Bennett, J. *Witness.* New York: Dharma Books, 1962.
Nott, S. C. *Teachings of Gurdjieff: The Journal of a Pupil.* London: Routledge and Kegan Paul, 1961.

Descriptions of Gurdjieff's teaching by his pupils, including actual teaching material, may be found in:
Ouspensky, P. D. *The Psychology of Man's Possible Evolution.* New York: Alfred Knopf, 1954.
Ouspensky, P. D. *The Fourth Way.* New York: Alfred Knopf, 1957.
Nicoll, M. *Psychological Commentaries on the Teaching of Gurdjieff and Ouspensky.* London: Vincent Stuart, 1952.

8 CONTEMPORARY SUFISM

ROBERT E. ORNSTEIN

ROBERT ORNSTEIN received his Ph.D. in psychology from Stanford University in 1968 and was awarded the American Institutes for Research Creative Talent Award for his work. He is the author of twenty books that relate body, mind, health, and the human spirit, including *The Psychology of Consciousness*, *The Amazing Brain*, *Multimind*, and *Ready for the Tiger*.

To be a Sufi is to become what you can become and not to try to pursue what is, at the wrong stage, illusion.

It is to become aware of what is possible to you and not to think that you are aware of that of which you are heedless.

Sufism is the science of stilling what has to be stilled and alerting what can be alerted; not thinking that you can still or alert where you cannot, or that you need to do so when you do not need it.

—*Sayed Imam Ali Shah*

[Shah, 1968. Frontpiece]

THE HIGH KNOWLEDGE

Anis was asked:

"What is Sufism?"

He said:

"Sufism is that which succeeds in bringing to man the High Knowledge."

"But if I apply the traditional methods handed down by the Masters, is that not Sufism?"

"It is not Sufism if it does not perform its function for you. A cloak is no longer a cloak if it does not keep a man warm."

"So Sufism does change?"

"People change and needs change. So what was Sufism once is Sufism no more.

"Sufism," continued Anis, "is the external face of internal knowledge, known as High Knowledge. The inner factor does not change. The whole work, therefore, is the High Knowledge, plus capacity, which produces method. What you are pleased to call Sufism is merely the record of past method." [Shah, 1971, p. 153]

If one can speak so loosely and generally, the "aim" of Sufism is to open another mode of knowledge to the practitioner, one which is spoken of as "High Knowledge," "Deep Understanding," or sometimes "Wisdom." These words have a technical meaning within Sufism, and refer to the experiential, not merely intellectual, understanding of many of the ultimate questions of philosophy and psychology.

The methods of Sufism are the means by which this is brought about. The "knowledge" has at times been the province of philosophical, religious, esoteric, and occult systems. Many of the rituals and practices with which we are most familiar today are the remnants of those systems, altered and lessened over time. Therefore, the first order of business is to distinguish past practices from current

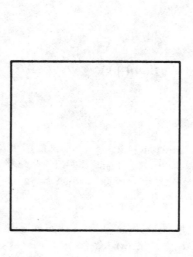

methodology. The "body of knowledge" which is Sufism has taken many forms, depending upon the culture and people who contact it. It has existed within Hindu, Zoroastrian, Jewish, Christian, and nonreligious frameworks. It is, of course, best known in the West as a development of Classical Islam, yet one can see that it is not dependent on Islamic study for a predominantly Western audience.

Within Islam, Sufism has been considered its "flower" or its highest development. With a current revival of interest in Sufism, sparked mainly by the writings of Idries Shah, many have extended their interest to the classical, theological versions which are the product of the Middle East. But some of this interest is archaeological and anthropological as well as spiritual: these two separate factors must be distinguished at the outset. The stream of knowledge is continuous, say the Sufis, from the beginning of recorded history through Zoroaster, Moses, Jesus, Mohammed, and many others. It exists today as well, in a new form, and a fresh adaptation.

THE TALE OF THE SANDS

A stream, from its source in far-off mountains, passing through every kind and description of countryside, at last reached the sands of the desert. Just as it had crossed every other barrier, the stream tried to cross this one, but it found that as fast as it ran into the sand, its waters disappeared.

It was convinced, however, that its destiny was to cross this desert, and yet there was no way. Now a hidden voice, coming from the desert itself, whispered: "The wind crosses the desert, and so can the stream."

The stream objected that it was dashing itself against the sand, and only getting absorbed: that the wind could fly and this was why it could cross a desert.

"By hurtling in your own accustomed way you cannot get across. You will either disappear or become a marsh. You must allow the wind to carry you over, to your destination."

But how could this happen? "By allowing yourself to be absorbed in the wind."

This idea was not acceptable to the stream. After all, it had never been absorbed before. It did not want to lose its individuality. And, once having lost it, how was one to know that it could ever be regained?

"The wind," said the sand, "performs this function. It takes up water, carries it over the desert, and then lets it fall again. Falling as rain, the water again becomes a river."

"How can I know that this is true?"

"It is so, and if you do not believe it, you cannot become more than a quagmire, and even that could take many, many years; and it certainly is not the same as a stream."

"But can I not remain the same stream that I am today?"

"You cannot in either case remain so," the whisper said. "Your essential part is carried away and forms a stream again. You are called what you are even today because you do not know which part of you is the essential one."

When he heard this, certain echoes began to arise in the thoughts of the stream. Dimly, he remembered a state in which he—or some part of him, was it?—had been held in the arms of a wind. He also remembered—or did he?—that this was the real thing, not necessarily the obvious thing to do.

And the stream raised his vapour into the welcoming arms of the wind, which gently and easily bore it upwards and along, letting it fall softly as soon as they reached the roof of a mountain, many, many miles away. And because he had had his doubts, the stream was able to remember and record more strongly in his mind the details of the experience. He reflected, "Yes, now I have learned my true identity."

The stream was learning. But the sands whispered: "We know, because we see it happen day after day: and because we, the sands, extend from the riverside all the way to the mountain."

And that is why it is said that the way in which the Stream of Life is to continue on its journey is written in the Sands. [Shah, 1967, pp. 23–24]

THE HANDICAP

A Persian carpet-weaver challenged a Turkish weaving master to a contest.

Each was to make the best carpet that he could, so that a panel of judges might finally decide who was the greatest weaver in the world.

But the Turk was a philosopher whose teaching for many years had been summed up in this phrase:

"Never refuse, but never contend."

So he accepted the challenged, saying only:

"I must make one proviso, because of the known disparity between your work and mine."

"Yes, indeed," said the Persian, "I am prepared to agree to a handicap."

"Very well," said the Turkish master, "the condition shall be that I give you a start of twelve thousand years." [Shah, 1970, p. 123]

IN CHINA

It is related of a Sufi visiting China that he was approached by a group of traditionalist priests who said:

"In our country there have been sages who have interpreted the sayings of great men for many thousands of years. How then could someone come to us from outside and say or act in a manner not foreseen in our philosophy?"

He answered:

"When it is desired to bring a piece of land to fertility, the trees may have to be felled. Such an enterprise is conceived and carried out by men of wisdom. Then, perhaps when they have died, it is needful to break the soil and add to it materials which will help to support a new growth. This is carried out by people worthy of respect and admiration. When the time comes for the introduction of a perhaps formerly unknown vegetable, those who bring it are as important as those who went before in the succession; even though to an outward observer they may be outside the succession of ploughing and harrowing.

"Before the stage of tasting of the vegetable there will assuredly be many who will say, 'This is no action foreseen in our agriculture.' " [Shah, 1970, p. 71]

Another, equally important, reason for the lack of a fixed system in Sufism is that the questions which may lead one to this study, such as "What is the meaning of Life?" and "What is the Nature of Man?" cannot be *answered* systematically. These questions lie in the domain of personal, experiential knowledge within the lives of many men and women. To pose the question in purely academic terms is therefore inappropriate and often is the stimulus for incomprehensible doctrine. That many bizarre and absurd notions have been advanced in this area in print does not mean, as the positivists would have it, that the questions should never be asked. It is a matter of the appropriateness of the response and the mode of the asking.

THE SUFI QUEST

Man, we say we know, originates from far away; so far, indeed, that in speaking of his origin, such phrases as "beyond the stars" are frequently employed. Man is estranged from his origins. Some of his feelings (but not all of them) are slight indicators of this. This is why we speak of "separation from the beloved"; but these are technical terms, and those who employ them to increase their emotional life are—increasing their emotional life.

Man has the opportunity of returning to his origin. He has forgotten this. He is, in fact, "asleep" to the reality.

Sufism is designed as the means to help awaken man to the realization, not just the opinion, of the above statements. Those who waken are able to return, to start "the journey" while also living this present life in all its fullness. Traditions about monasticism and isolation are reflections of short-term processes of training or development, monstrously misunderstood and grotesquely elaborated to provide refuges for those who want to stay asleep.

However improbable all this seems, it happens to be true. It is, of course, no less probable than many other things believed by man. Some such beliefs are certainly erroneous: we all know individuals with beliefs which we are convinced *are* erroneous. On the other hand, since Sufism depends upon effectiveness, not belief, Sufis are not concerned with inculcating and maintaining belief. "I believe this is true" is no substitute for "This is how it is done." The two things are in reality, if not in appearance, poles apart.

If man finds himself again, he will be able to increase his existence infinitely. If he does not, he may dwindle to vanishing-point. Those who see a threat or promise in such a statement are unsuitable for this work. There is no threat or promise in facts: only in the interpretation man makes of them.

People have been sent, from time to time, to try to serve man and save him from the "blindness" or "sleep" (which today would be better described as "amnesia") which is always described in our technical literature as a local disease. These people are always in

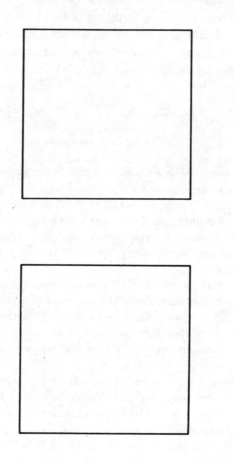

touch with the Origin, and they bring the "medicine" which is half the cure. The other half, as in orthodox terrestrial medicine, is the activity of that which is acted upon, to attain its own regeneration with the minimum of aid. These cosmic doctors—a literal translation of a most ancient term—often live in the world almost unnoticed, like the camel in the desert. They have been of all races, and they have belonged to all faiths.

Essentially, religion has two roles, which in all surviving systems have become confused through the absence of specialist knowledge in the publicists and most visible and active theoreticians. The first is to organize man in a safe, just, and peaceful manner, to establish and help maintain communities. The second is the inward aspect, which leads people from the outward stabilization to the performance which awakens them and helps to make them permanent.

Numerous residual systems for human progress continue to float around in the world, but virtually all are devoid of value in this inner aspect, though they may not be without historical interest. Certainly they can show us at a glance that they are only employed for personal and community sentimental satisfactions—whatever their own imaginings about the matter may be. They can most charitably be described as vehicles abandoned by their builders and now occupied by half-comprehending amateurs who seek only a relief from thought about their predicament.

"The Teaching," however, operated by those whom we call "The Wise," continues and may take any form. It is preserved intact and constantly nurtured by certain Sufis. Well-meaning but imitative groupings based on Sufism, and of no value to this inner side of "the Work" exist side by side with real ones.

Recognizing a "True Master" is possible only when the postulant, man or woman, is what we call "sincere." This technical term refers to his condition, not his opinions. Sincere means that he is objective enough to recognize the specialist and the nature of the task. To reach this stage, the Seeker has to learn to set aside, at least for a time, superficial assessment about the teachers, the Teaching, and himself. By superficial we mean something quite precise: automatic assumptions based upon rules employed in testing a different type of phenomenon.

A person may be attracted to Sufism because of the wrong motives—such as curiosity, desire for power, fear, insecurity—but in spite of this he has a chance to develop understanding of the work. If, however, he merely deepens his attachment and increases his acquisitiveness, he is not a Sufi, and is most unlikely to become one. He is taking and consuming smaller stimuli than he needs, though perhaps unable to prevent himself from craving such stimuli.

Sufism has two main technical objectives: (1) to show the man himself as he really is; and (2) to help him develop his real, inner self, his permanent part.

Though man "originates from far away, is asleep and may return after he has attained the means" he can do so only if he works from a sound environmental base in the world in which we find him: our slogan is "Be *in* the World, but not *of* the World."

The Sufis, it is admitted on all sides by externalist students, have produced some of the world's greatest literature, particularly in tales, illustrative recitals and poetry. Unlike professional literary workers, however, they see this as a means to work, not an end of their work:

"When the Higher Man does something worthy of admiration, it is an evidence of his Mastership, not the object of it." [Shah, 1971, p. 196]

> Show a man too many camels' bones, or show them to him
> too often, and he will not be able to recognize a camel when
> he comes across a live one.
>
> *[Shah, 1970, p. 18]*

There is no fixed system in Sufism, no dogma which one must follow. If Sufism is "too sublime to have a history" this is the reason. As it has existed in different guises at different times, it has become impervious to literalism. If it were possible to attain the aim of Sufism—to "open one's eyes" —in a systematic manner, then this would have been done long ago, as has been done in many other areas of study such as mathematics. This is not possible because people differ at different times—what is appropriate for one person in one civilization may not be useful for another. Conditions of life change, understandings progress and regress, and the "ground" on which Sufism is based changes. Since Sufism is a "growing, organic, process," it becomes different in different eras. Ideas and practices which may have been of use in a rural economy two hundred years ago are no longer of such import. The system is always temporary.

Most Sufi writers maintain, then, that the "system" (or methodology) of Sufism and the "knowledge" of Sufism should be distinguished. Too often adherents of one system (which may originally have been of great use) tend to identify it with "the only Way" and the only Knowledge. This is the first stage in the degeneration of a school. Then the system becomes permanent and fixed, a process similar to the bureaucracy of a government taking over a program or an idea. The original aim and the knowledge are subverted to that of perpetuating the system. Great care is then necessary, as a preparatory communication in Sufism, to divorce the system from the thing gained. The interested student can then consider many diverse systematic approaches, and can learn to understand their workings and relevance to him, yet remain inoculated to the exclusivistic claims.

CONTRARY TO EXPECTATION

"A wise man, the wonder of his age, taught his disciples from a seemingly inexhaustible store of wisdom.

He attributed all his knowledge to a thick tome which was kept in a place of honour in his room.

The sage would allow nobody to open the volume.

When he died, those who had surrounded him, regarding themselves as his heirs, ran to open the book, anxious to possess what it contained.

They were surprised, confused, and disappointed when they found that there was writing on only one page.

They became even more bewildered and then annoyed when they tried to penetrate the meaning of the phrase which met their eyes.

It was: "When you realise the difference between the container and the content, you will have knowledge." [Shah, 1969a]

OIL, WATER, COTTON

A certain man who was fond of studying all kinds of systems of thought wrote to a dervish Master asking whether he could talk to him in order to make comparisons.

The dervish sent him a bottle with oil and water in it, and a piece of cotton wick. Enclosed in the package was this letter:

Dear friend, if you place the wick in the oil, you will get light when fire is applied to it. If you pour out the oil and put the wick in the water, you will get no light. If you shake up the oil and water and then place the wick in them, you will get a spluttering and a going out. There is no need to carry out this experiment through words and visits when it can be done with such simple materials as these. [Shah, 1971, p. 59]

If the principles of Sufism are not systematizable, neither, unfortunately, is "progress" in this area. The two concepts, however, are related. There are many people who are excessively interested in whether they are "progressing" or "improving" in any endeavor. This does set the stage, even in formal metaphysical writing, for the conception of Levels of Development. These are generally studied well by the person looking for the fast answer, or looking to become "enlightened" and to have others know and judge him or her as such. There is, however, little place or consideration in Sufism for the anxiety-ridden obsessional, no matter how attractive Sufism may be to such a person. The difficulty is that obsessional thought tends to capture anything of value in *any* system. Spiritual progress can then become the substitute for progress in one's job or family life.

This type of thought (and it is quite common) is at once the product of miseducation and personal derangement, merely applied to the process of mysticism. For it must be clearly stated that many individuals who seek relief from their personal incompetence or from their "inability to relate" (in any culturally approved manner) to others are not likely to find a haven for themselves in Sufi studies. Sufism is not mushed-under psychotherapy or a substitute for on-the-job training. Neither is it an *extension* of psychotherapy or any other problem-solving institution. The difficulty here is that many people who believe that they need help in their personal life mistakenly assume that they will obtain it in "higher studies." But probably worse is the confusion of these areas in the practitioners of therapy *themselves*, who come to offer a mash of warmed-over religion, an attempt at "good feeling" and degenerate mysticism, to their clients.

This is not to state that personal problems should just "go away," be ignored, are irrelevant, or that they should not be met and answered. They should be, but

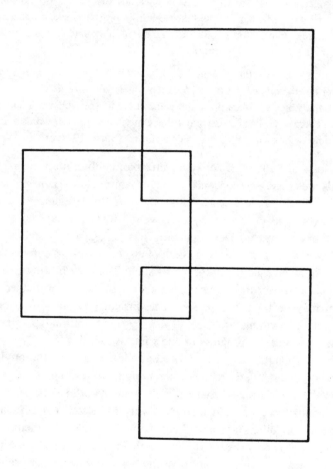

before one's involvement in Sufi studies begins, else this study will become an extension of the person's difficulty, and may be captured by it. Once these problems are met and properly treated, the irrational desire for progress and a comforting system may be lessened.

The miseducation component remains. This is our lack of appreciation that people at different times differ and that "steps on the path" or "entry into another world" will not fall along the same lines for everyone. Even the discussion of "another world" is a device, to put in metaphor another kind of thought, consciousness and being, which has been romanticized and made external. All people are not the same, and what is opportunity at one occasion for one person may not be for another. The common error includes "looking to the heavens" for some sign or some comforting system when opportunities may abound in the life of the person, although these may not be "systematic" enough for him to notice.

THE MAN WITH THE INEXPLICABLE LIFE

There was once a man named Mojud. He lived in a town where he had obtained a post as a small official, and it seemed likely that he would end his days as Inspector of Weights and Measures.

One day when he was walking through the gardens of an ancient building near his home Khidr, the mysterious Guide of the Sufis, appeared to him, dressed in shimmering green. Khidr said: "Man of bright prospects! Leave your work and meet me at the riverside in three days' time." Then he disappeared.

Mojud went to his superior in trepidation and said that he had to leave. Everyone in the town soon heard of this and they said: "Poor Mojud! He has gone mad." But, as there were many candidates for his job, they soon forgot him.

On the appointed day, Mojud met Khidr, who said to him: "Tear your clothes and throw yourself into the stream. Perhaps someone will save you."

Mojud did so, even though he wondered if he were mad.

Since he could swim, he did not drown, but drifted a long way before a fisherman hauled him into his boat, saying, "Foolish man! The current is strong. What are you trying to do?"

Mojud said: "I do not really know."

"You are mad," said the fisherman, "but I will take you into my reed-hut by the river yonder, and we shall see what can be done for you."

When he discovered that Mojud was well-spoken, he learned from him how to read and write. In exchange Mojud was given food and helped the fisherman with his work. After a few months, Khidr again appeared, this time at the foot of Mojud's bed, and said: "Get up now and leave this fisherman. You will be provided for."

Mojud immediately quit the hut, dressed as a fisherman, and wandered about until he came to a highway. As dawn was breaking he saw a farmer on a donkey on his way to market. "Do you seek work?" asked the farmer. "Because I need a man to help me to bring back some purchases."

Mojud followed him. He worked for the farmer for nearly two years, by which time he had learned a great deal about agriculture but little else.

One afternoon when he was baling wool, Khidr appeared to him and said: "Leave that work, walk to the city of Mosul, and use your savings to become a skin merchant."

Mojud obeyed.

In Mosul he became known as a skin merchant, never seeing Khidr while he plied his trade for three years. He had saved quite a large sum of money, and was thinking of buying a house, when Khidr appeared and said: "Give me your money, walk out of this town as far as distant Samarkand, and work for a grocer there." Mojud did so.

Presently he began to show undoubted signs of illumination. He healed the sick, served his fellow men in the shop during his spare time, and his knowledge of the mysteries became deeper and deeper.

Clerics, philosophers, and others visited him and asked: "Under whom did you study?"

"It is difficult to say," said Mojud.

His disciples asked: "How did you start your career?"

He said: "As a small official."

"And you gave it up to devote yourself to self-mortification?"

"No, I just gave it up."

They did not understand him.

People approached him to write the story of his life.

"What have you been in your life?" he asked.

"I jumped into a river, became a fisherman, then walked out of his reed-hut in the middle of one night. After that, I became a farmhand. While I was baling wool, I changed and went to Mosul, where I became a skin merchant. I saved some money there, but gave it away. Then I walked to Samarkand where I worked for a grocer. And this is where I am now."

"But this inexplicable behaviour throws no light upon your strange gifts and wonderful examples," said the biographers.

"That is so," said Mojud.

So the biographers constructed for Mojud a wonderful and exciting history; because all saints must have their story, and the story must be in accordance with the appetite of the listener, not with the realities of the life.

And nobody is allowed to speak of Khidr directly. That is why this story is not true. It is a representation of a life. This is the real life of one of the greatest Sufis. [Shah, 1967, pp. 155–57]

THE INITIATION OF MALIK DINAR

After many years' study of philosophical subjects, Malik Dinar felt that the time had come to travel in search of knowledge. "I will go," he said to himself, "seeking the Hidden Teacher, who is also said to be within my uttermost self."

Walking out of his house with only a few dates for provision, he came presently upon a dervish plodding along the dusty road. He fell into step alongside him, in silence for a time.

Finally the dervish spoke. "Who are you and where are you going?"

"I am Dinar, and I have started to journey in search of the Hidden Teacher."

"I am El-Malik El-Fatih, and I will walk with you," said the dervish.

"Can you help me to find the Teacher?" asked Dinar.

"Can I help you, can you help me?" asked Fatih, in the irritating manner of dervishes everywhere; "the hidden Teacher, so they say, is in a man's self. How he finds him depends upon what use he makes of experience. This is something only partly conveyed by a companion."

Presently they came to a tree, which was creaking and swaying. The dervish stopped. "The tree is saying," he said after a moment: " 'Something is hurting me, stop awhile and take it out of my side so that I may find repose.' "

"I am in too much of a hurry," replied Dinar. "And how can a tree talk, anyway?" They went on their way.

After a few miles the dervish said, "When we were near the tree I thought that I smelt honey. Perhaps it was a wild-bees' hive which had been built in its bole."

"If that is true," said Dinar, "let us hurry back, so that we may collect the honey, which we could eat, and sell some for the journey."

"As you wish," said the dervish.

When they arrived back at the tree, however, they saw some other travellers collecting an enormous quantity of honey. "What luck we have had!" these men said. "This is enough honey to feed a city. We poor pilgrims can now become merchants; our future is assured."

Dinar and Fatih went on their way.

Presently they came to a mountain on whose slopes they heard a humming. The dervish put his ear to the ground. Then he said: "Below us there are millions of ants, building a colony. This humming is a concerted plea for help. In ant-language it says: "Help us, help us. We are excavating, but have come across strange rocks which bar our progress. Help dig them away." Should we stop and help, or do you want to hasten ahead?"

"Ants and rocks are not our business, brother," said Dinar, "because, I, for one, am seeking my Teacher."

"Very well, brother," said the dervish. "Yet they do say that all things are connected, and this may have a certain connection with us."

Dinar took no notice of the older man's mumblings, and so they went their way.

The pair stopped for the night, and Dinar found that he had lost his knife. "I must have dropped it near the ant-hill," he said. Next morning they retraced their way.

When they arrived back at the ant-hill, they could find no sign of Dinar's knife. Instead they saw a group of people, covered in mud, resting beside a pile of gold coins. "These," said the people, "are a hidden hoard which we have just dug up. We were on the road when a frail old dervish called to us: 'Dig at this spot and you will find that which is rocks to some but gold to others.'"

Dinar cursed his luck. "If we had only stopped," he said, "you and I would both have been rich last night, O Dervish." The other party said: "This dervish with you, stranger, looks strangely like the one whom we saw last night."

"All dervishes look very much alike," said Fatih. And they went their respective ways.

Dinar and Fatih continued their travels, and some days later they came to a beautiful riverbank. The Dervish stopped and as they sat waiting for the ferry a fish rose several times to the surface and mouthed at them.

"This fish," said the Dervish, "is sending us a message. It says: 'I have swallowed a stone. Catch me and give me a certain herb to eat. Then I will be able to bring it up, and will thus find relief. Travellers, have mercy!'"

At that moment the ferryboat appeared and Dinar, impatient to get ahead, pushed the dervish into it. The boatman was grateful for the copper which they were able to give him, and Fatih and Dinar slept well that night on the opposite bank, where a teahouse for travellers had been placed by a charitable soul.

In the morning they were sipping their tea when the ferryman appeared. Last night had been his most fortunate one, he said; the pilgrims had brought him luck. He kissed the hands of the venerable dervish, to take his blessing. "You deserve it all, my son," said Fatih.

The ferryman was now rich: and this was how it had happened. He was about to go home at his usual time, but he had seen the pair on the opposite bank, and resolved to make one more trip, although they looked poor, for the "baraka," the blessing of helping the traveller. When he was about to put away his boat he saw the fish, which had thrown itself on the bank. It was apparently trying to swallow a piece of plant. The fisherman put the plant into its mouth. The fish threw up a stone and flopped back into the water. The stone was a huge and flawless diamond of incalculable value and brilliance.

"You are a devil!" shouted the infuriated Dinar to the dervish Fatih. "You knew about all three treasures by means of some hidden perception, yet you did not tell me at the time. Is *that* true companionship? Formerly, my ill-luck was strong enough: but without you I would not even have known of the possibilities hidden in trees, anthills and fish—of all things!"

No sooner had he said these words than he felt as though a mighty wind were sweeping through his very soul. And then he knew that the very reverse of what he had said was the truth.

The dervish, whose name means the Victorious King, touched Dinar lightly on the shoulder, and smiled. "Now, brother, you will find that you can learn by experience. I am he who is at the command of the Hidden Teacher."

When Dinar dared to look up, he saw his Teacher walking down the road with a small band of travellers, who were arguing about the perils of the journey ahead of them.

Today the name of Malik Dinar is numbered among the foremost of the dervishes, companion and exemplar, the Man who Arrived. [Shah, 1967, pp. 148–51]

WISDOM FOR SALE

A man named Saifulmuluk spent half of his life seeking truth. He read all the books on ancient wisdom which he could find. He travelled to every known and unknown country to hear what spiritual teachers had to say. He spent the days in working and the nights in contemplation of the Great Mysteries.

One day he heard of yet another teacher, the great poet Ansari, who lived in the city of Herat. Bending his steps thither he arrived at the door of the sage. On it he saw written, contrary to his expectation, a strange announcement: "Knowledge is Sold Here."

"This must be a mistake, or else a deliberate attempt to dissuade the idle curiosity-seeker," he said to himself, "for I have never before heard it said that knowledge can be bought or sold." So he went into the house.

Sitting in the inner courtyard was Ansari himself, bent with age and writing a poem. "Have you come to buy knowledge?" he asked. Saifulmuluk nodded. Ansari told him to produce as much money as he had. Saifulmuluk took out all his money, amounting to a hundred pieces of silver.

"For this much," said Ansari, "you can have three pieces of advice."

"Do you really mean that?" asked Saifulmuluk. "Why do you need money, if you are a humble and dedicated man?"

"We live in the world, surrounded by its material facts," said the sage, "and with the knowledge that I have I gain great new responsibilities. Because I know certain things that others do not, I have to spend money, among other things, to be of service where a kind word or the exercise of 'baraka' is not indicated."

He took the silver and said, "Listen well.

"The first piece of advice is: 'A small cloud signals danger.'"

"But is this knowledge?" asked Saifulmuluk. "It does not seem to tell me much about the nature of ultimate truth, or about man's place in the world."

"If you are going to interrupt me," said the sage, "you can take your money back and go away. What is the use of knowledge about man's place in the world if that man is dead?"

Saifulmuluk was silenced, and he waited for the next piece of advice.

"The second piece of advice is: 'If you can find a bird, a cat, and a dog in one place, get hold of them and look after them until the end.'"

"This is curious advice," thought Saifulmuluk, "but perhaps it has an inner metaphysical meaning which will become manifest to me if I meditate upon it long enough."

So he held his peace until the sage brought forth the last piece of advice:

"When you have experienced certain things which seem irrelevant, keeping faith with the foregoing advice, then and only then will a door open for you. Enter that door."

Saifulmuluk wanted to stay to study under this baffling sage, but Ansari sent him away, rather roughly.

He continued his wanderings, and went to Kashmir to study under a teacher there. When he was travelling through central Asia again, he reached the marketplace of Bokhara during an auction sale. A man was leading away a cat, a bird, and a dog which he had just bought. "If I had not tarried so long in Kashmir," thought Saifulmuluk, "I would have been able to buy these animals, because they certainly are a part of my destiny."

Then he started to worry, because although he had seen the bird, the cat, and the dog, he had not yet seen the small cloud. Everything seemed to be going wrong. The only thing that saved him was looking through one of his notebooks in which he had recorded, though not remembered, the advice of an ancient sage: "Things happen in succession. Man imagines this succession to be of a certain kind. But it sometimes is another kind of succession."

Then he realized that, although the three animals had been bought at an auction, Ansari had not actually told him to buy them at an auction. He had not remembered the words of the advice, which had been, "If you can find a bird, a cat, and a dog in one place, get hold of them, and look after them until the end."

So he started to trace the buyer of the animals, to see whether they were still "in one place."

After many inquiries, he found that the man was called Ashikikhuda, and that he had only bought the animals to save them the pain of being cooped up in the auctioneer's rooms, where they had been for several weeks, awaiting a buyer. They were still "in one place" and Ashikikhuda was glad to sell them to Saifulmuluk.

He settled in Bokhara, because it was not practicable to continue journeying with the animals. Every day he went out to work in a wool-spinning factory, returning in the evening with food for the animals which he had bought from his day's earnings. Time passed, three years.

One day when he had become a master-spinner, and was living as a respected member of the community with his animals, he walked to the outskirts of the town, and saw what seemed to be a tiny cloud, hovering almost on the horizon. It was such a strange-looking cloud that his memory was jogged, and the First Piece of Advice came into his consciousness, very sharply:

"A small cloud signals danger."

Saifulmuluk returned immediately to his house, collected his animals, and started to flee westwards. He arrived in Isfahan almost penniless. Some days later he learned that the cloud which he had seen was the dust of a conquering horde, which had captured Bokhara and slain all its inhabitants.

And the words of Ansari came into his mind: "What is the use of knowledge about man's place in the world if that man is dead?"

The people of Isfahan were not enamoured of animals, wool-spinners, nor strangers, and Saifulmuluk was before long reduced to extreme poverty. He threw himself down on the ground and cried: "O Succession of Saints! O Holy Ones! Ye who have been Changed! Come you to my aid, for I am reduced to a state in which my own efforts no longer yield sustenance, and my animals are suffering hunger and thirst."

As he lay there, between sleeping and waking, his stomach gnawed by hunger, and having resigned himself to the guidance of his fate, he saw a vision of something as clearly as if it were there. It was a picture of a golden ring, set with a changing lighted stone, which flashed fire, glowed like the phosphorescent sea, and in its depths gave off green lights.

A voice, or so it seemed to be, said: "This is the golden crown of the ages, the Samir of Truth, the very Ring of King Solomon, the son of David, upon whose name be peace, whose secrets are to be preserved."

Looking around him, he saw that the ring was rolling into a crevice in the ground. It seemed as though he was beside a stream, under a tree, near a curiously-shaped boulder.

In the morning, rested and more able to bear his hunger, Saifulmuluk started to wander around the periphery of Isfahan. Then as he had half-expected for some reason, he saw the stream, the tree, and the rock. Under the rock there was a crevice. In the crevice into which he interposed a stick, was the ring which he had already seen in the curious way related above.

Washing the ring in the water, Saifulmuluk exclaimed: "If this is truly the Ring of the Great Solomon, upon whom be the Salute, grant me, Spirit of the Ring, a worthy end to my difficulties."

Suddenly it was as if the earth shook, and as if a voice like a whirlwind was echoing in his ears: "Across the centuries, good Saifulmuluk, we bid you peace. You are the inheritor of the power of Solomon, the son of David, upon whom be peace, Master of the Jinns and Men, I am the Slave of the Ring. Command me, Master Saifulmuluk, Master!"

"Bring the animals here, and food for them," said Saifulmuluk at once, not forgetting to add: "In the Great Name and in the Name of Solomon, our Master, Commander of the Jinns and Men, upon him be the Salute!"

Almost before he had finished saying this, there were the animals and each had set before him the necessary food, that which he liked best.

Then he rubbed the ring, and the Spirit of the Ring again answered him, like a rushing in the ears.

"Command me, and whatever you desire shall be done, save only that which is not to be done, Master of the Ring."

"Tell me, in the Name of Solomon (peace upon him!) is this the end? For I must look after the welfare of these companions of mine until the end, according to the command of my own master, The Khoja Ansar of Herat."

"No," replied the Spirit, "it is not the end."

Saifulmuluk stayed at this spot, where he had the Jinn build him a small house and a place for the animals; and he passed his days with them. Every day the Jinn brought them all sufficient for their needs, and passersby marvelled at the sanctity of Saif-Baba, "Father Saif," as he was called, "who lived on nothing, surrounded by tame and wild animals."

When he was not studying the notes of his travels and contemplating his experiences, Saif-Baba observed the three animals and learned their ways. Each responded to him in its own way. He encouraged their good qualities and discouraged their bad ones, and he often spoke to them about the great Khoja Ansar and the Three Pieces of Advice.

From time to time holy men passed his habitation, and often they invited him to dispute with them, or to learn their own particular Ways. But he refused, saying, "I have my task to perform, given me by my teacher." Then one day he was surprised to find that the cat was speaking to him in a language which he understood. "Master," said the cat, "you have your task, and you must carry it out. But are you not surprised that the time which you call 'the end' has not come?"

"I am not really surprised," said Saif-Baba, "because for all I know it might last for a hundred years."

"That is where you are wrong," said the bird, which was now talking too, "for you have not learned what you could have learned from the various travellers who have passed this way. You do not realize that although they appear different (as we animals all appear different to you) they were all sent by the source of your teaching, by Khoja Ansar himself, to see whether you had acquired enough insight to follow them."

"If this is true," said Saif-Baba, "which I do not for a moment believe, can you explain to me why it is that a mere cat and a tiny sparrow can tell me things which I, with the miraculous benefits which I have received, cannot see?"

"That is simple," they both said together. "It is that you have become so accustomed to looking at things in only one way that your shortcomings are visible even to the most ordinary mind."

This worried Saif-Baba. "So I could have found the Door of the Third Piece of Advice long ago, if I had been properly attuned to it?" he asked.

"Yes," said the dog, joining the discussion. "The door has opened a dozen times in the past years, but you did not see it. We did, but because we were animals, we could not tell you."

"Then how can you tell me now?"

"You can understand our speech because you youself have lately become more human. But you have only one more chance, for age is overcoming you."

Saif-Baba at first thought: "This is a hallucination." Then he thought: "They have no right to talk to me like this, I am their master and the source of their sustenance." Then another part of him thought: "If they are wrong, it does not matter. But if they are right, this is terrible for me. I cannot take a chance."

So he awaited his opportunity. Months passed. One day a wandering dervish came along and pitched a tent on Saif-Baba's doorstep. He made friends with the animals, and Saif decided to take him into his confidence. "Away with you!" snapped the dervish, "I am not interested in your tales of the Master Ansari, your clouds and your seeking and your responsibility to animals, even your magic Ring. Leave me in peace. I know what you *should* be talking about, but I do not know what you *are* talking about."

Saif-Baba in desperation called the Spirit of the Ring. But the Jinn merely said: "I am not to tell you those things which are not to be told. But I do know that you are suffering from the disease called 'Permanent Hidden Prejudice' which rules your thoughts and makes it difficult for you to progress in the *way*."

Then Saif-Baba went to the dervish who was sitting on his doorstep and said: "What should I do, for I feel a responsibility for my animals, and a confusion about myself, and there is no more guidance in my Three Pieces of Advice."

"You have talked sincerely," said the dervish, "and this is a beginning. Hand your animals over to me, and I will tell you the answer."

"But I do not know you, and you ask too much," said Saif-Baba. "How can you ask such a thing? I respect you, but there is still a doubt in my mind."

"Well spoken," said the dervish. "You have revealed not your concern for your animals, but your own lack of perception about me. If you judge me by emotion or logic, you cannot benefit from me. You are still covetous in some way, maintaining proprietorship over 'your' animals. Go away, as sure as my name is Darwaza."

Now, "Darwaza" means "door," and Saif-Baba thought very hard about this. Could this be the "door" which was foretold by his sheikh, Ansari? "You may be the 'Door' I am seeking, but I am not sure," he said to the dervish Darwaza. "Be off with you, you and your speculations," shouted the dervish. "Don't you see that the first two pieces of advice were for your mind and that the last piece can be understood only when you perceive it yourself?"

After nearly two more years of confusion and anxiety, Saif-Baba suddenly realized the truth. He called his animals and dismissed them, saying, "You are on your own now. This is the end." As he said so, he realized that the animals now had human forms, and that they were transformed. Standing beside him was Darwaza, but his form was now that of the great Khoja Ansar himself. Without saying a word, Ansari opened a door in the tree beside the stream, and as he walked over the threshold Saif-Baba saw written up in letters of gold in a wondrous cavern the answers to the questions about life and death, about mortality and humanity, about knowledge and ignorance, which had plagued him all his life.

"Attachment to externals," said the voice of Ansari, "has been what held you back all these years. In some ways because of this, you are too late. Take here the only part of wisdom still open to you." [Shah, 1967, pp. 169–76]

BAHAUDIN NAQSHBAND: DISCIPLESHIP AND DEVELOPMENT

Extracts from the Testimony of Bahaudin the Designer (Naqshband):

We are adjured constantly to study and make ourselves familiar with the lives, doings, and sayings of the Wise because a link of understanding exists between these factors and the potentiality in ourselves.

But if, as have the literalists, we soak ourselves in these elements from motives of greed or marvelling at wonders, we will transform ourselves indeed; but the transformation will be animal into lesser animal, instead of animal into man.

The test which is placed in man's way is to separate the real Seekers from the imitation ones by this very method. If man has not addressed himself to this study through his simplest and most sincere self, he will be in peril. It is therefore better, did man but know it, to avoid all metaphysical entanglements rather than to allow himself to be acted upon by the supreme force which will amplify, magnify, his faults if he lacks the knowledge of how to cure the fault, or of how to approach the teaching so that his faults are not involved in the procedure.

It is for this reason that we say that there are many different spheres, levels, of experience of the truth.

The Wise have always concentrated upon making sure that their disciples understand that the first stage towards knowledge is to familiarize themselves with the outward, factual, appearance of that knowledge, so that, preventing it from rushing into the wrong area of their minds, it might await development when the possibilities exist.

This is the analogy of a man taking a pomegranate and keeping it until his stomach is in a condition to digest it correctly. If a man eats a pomegranate when there is something wrong with his stomach, it will make the ailment worse.

One manifestation of man's ailment is to want to eat the pomegranate at once. Should he do this, he will be in serious difficulties.

Now you have the explanation as to why the Wise continually supply materials to be stored in the heart, as grain is stored, with a view to the making of bread. Because this is

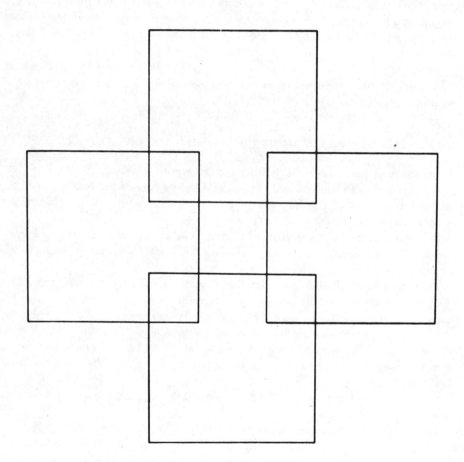

experience and not grain, man in his crudity does not customarily feel able to understand this great truth and secret. The man to whom we speak is, therefore, a specially attuned sort of man—"The Generous Miser"—that is, the man who can hoard when hoarding is indicated, and who will make available that which there is as and when it is able to exercise its optimum effect.

I was mystified for many months by my esteemed mentor's giving me things to speak, to think and do which did not seem to satisfy my craving for the spiritual life. He told me many times that the craving which I felt was not for spirituality at all, and that the materials which he was giving me were the nutritions which I needed. It was only when I was able to still my maniac desires that I was able to listen to him at all. At other times I said to myself, "I have heard all this before, and it is highly doubtful," or else, "This is no spiritual man," or, further, "I want to experience, not to listen or to read."

The wonderful thing was this, that my teacher continually reminded me that this was my state of mind, and although I was outwardly trusting him and serving him in everything, I was not able to trust him to the necessary extent, nor in the vital direction. Looking back, I realized later that I was willing at that time to yield far more far-reaching parts of my sovereignty than were needed; but I was not prepared to yield the minor ones which alone were the pathways to my understanding.

I refer to this because it is by rehearsal of the experience of others that people at a similar stage in the Path may be able to recognize their own state and profit by it.

I remember that I was always magnetized, transfixed by the dramatic, and became attentive whenever anything of great stimulation was said or done, but that the significant factors in my association with my teacher were the ones which I missed, sometimes almost entirely. Because of this, in spite of being continually employed in the work, I wasted as much as eight years of my life.

Then it must be remembered that there are the two kinds of everything. This is something which we normally do not imagine as existing, but it is fundamental. There is the keeping of company with a wise man and learning from him, in the right way, which is productive of human progress. Then there is the counterfeit, which is destructive. What makes us completely confused in this matter is that the feeling which accompanies the false discipleship or the ordinary keeping company, as well as its external manifestations in courtesy and seeming humility, is so able to make us imagine that we are religious or dedicated people that it is possible to say that this is due to what has been called the entry of a demonic, counterfeiting power, which persuades most of the very distinguished and compelling spiritually reputed people and also their followers, even down the generations, that they are dealing in spirituality. It even enables them to communicate this belief to those who are not of their number, so that their reputation gains credibility through the very people who misguidedly say, "I do not follow his path, but I do not deny that he is a spiritual and a good man. . . ."

The only corrective to this is the making use of the special-occasion timing by the Master who alone is able to say as to when and where and in what manner the exercises and other activities, even those which do not appear to have the smallest connection with spirituality, may be carried on. There is a confusion here because this is sometimes taken to mean that one must never read books or carry out processes without the direct supervision of the

Master. But this common and shallow mistake is seen to be absurd when we realize that the Master may specify courses or reading or action for a number of people or for an individual, and that he may find it necessary from time to time for these to take what seems a conventional, indeed, a seemingly scholastic course. But what is vital here is not how things appear to the student, but that the Master has prescribed them and that he will intervene as and when there is a need for a change. All manifestations of opposition to this curriculum or any other disharmony with the Master are manifestations of the rawness of the pupil, and may not be taken into consideration by the Master or any of his intermediaries (deputies), since the student can either follow the course dutifully or he cannot. If he cannot, he ceases at that moment to be a student, and hence has no right even of comment. Only true students have the right of comment, and those who draw attention to themselves by questioning the course itself are not in the condition of being students at all.

Failure to observe this is common among scholastic emotionalists who have adopted Sufi procedures, because they do not realize that the curriculum is already erected on the basis of all the possible contingencies which include any and all feelings of the pupils. What is aimed at here is the operation of the teaching through the capacity. If he is disturbing the progress of the session or the work of the deputy, he is the opposite of a student, and this should be observed as a lesson by the company.

I am well aware that the principles are far from the accepted ones in the shallow world which is balanced on the basis of what people think of one another, including the problem which false teachers continually feel, which is the question of what other people think of them. But the central factor is whether the Teaching is operating, not whether people feel through their ordinary sense that they are being fulfilled.

In the latter case, you may be sure that nothing of real worth is happening at all.

This is the end of the first section of the Testimony of Bahaudin Naqshband, the Designer. [Shah, 1971, pp. 183–86; the second section may be found in the same work, pp. 187–90]

If the foregoing may seem to deal largely with what Sufism is *not*, I hope that the reader will appreciate the need to clear away many common misconceptions as the first order of business. There are, of course, contemporary aspects of Sufism which are publicly available. Its prime exponent, Idries Shah, has now published more than one thousand teaching tales in English as well as in other contemporary Western languages. These stories and tales are not designed to inculcate moralisms or to be learned as rote facts, but to provide the means of communication of this consistent teaching. The earliest Sufi tale to bear the authentic stamp of a constructed artifact designed to point to a form of reality normally imperceptible to man is in the Koran, the tale of Khidr and Moses, reproduced by Shah in *Tales of the Dervishes*.

Although these tales, brilliantly presented and translated, have earned many general plaudits, used on television, film, and radio, their origins are of more serious intent. Although they were originally intended by the dervish storytellers from the Middle East as "teaching stories," these tales have little in common with the parable or didactic story of most Western cultures. The main difference is that instead of convincing the reader that a certain type of thought or action is Good or Moral, these teaching stories illustrate patterns of behavior or events to provide a lesson which could not be put in any other way.

These stories guide the reader along unfamiliar paths; some contain a pattern of activity so that the reader can become familiarized with the unusual, and some are intended as "shock"—a fresh stimulus to the mind to upset the normal paths of thought and consciousness.

In the stories, many of which are in the form of recitals of the sayings and doings of wise men and fools, we often find the sage playing the part of the ordinary man, demonstrating some course of action or a train of thought which he is attempting to criticize. Other stories are open-ended; they provide no automatic solution, but rely on members of the audience to find their own often individual interpretations.

Until 1964 this function of the "story of inner meaning" was all but completely unknown to most Western thinkers. Jalaluddin Rumi (in *Fihi ma Fihi* and *Masnavi-i-Maanavi*) employed some types of these tales quite extensively, yet, oddly, until Idries Shah's *The Sufis* explained the special application of tales among the Sufis, many scholars regarded Rumi as something of a storyteller in the folklore and parable tradition, and some seemed even embarrassed by the Master's apparent fondness for mere jokes, anecdotes, and folk tales.

The literary and entertainment quality of these stories is their "Moses' basket" aspect—their key to continued use and survival and their lack of dependence on specific cultural mores. But their aim is to "connect with a part of the individual which cannot be reached by any other convention, [and to] establish in him or in her a means of communication with a non-verbalized truth beyond the customary limitations of our familiar dimensions." (Shah, 1968a, p. 96)

LITERATURE

Yakoub of Somnan, explaining the function of the literature which he used, said:

"Literature is the means by which things have been taken out of the community, such as knowledge, can be returned.

"The similitude is as of a seed, which may be returned to the earth long after the plant from which it grew is dead, with perhaps no trace of it remaining.

"The learned may be millers of the grain-seed, but those whom we call the Wise are the cultivators of the crop.

"Take heed of this parable, for it contains the explanation of much irreconcilability of attitudes in the two classes of students." [Shah, 1971, p. 166]

THE QUESTION

A rich braggart once took a Sufi on a tour of his house.

He showed him room after room filled with valuable works of art, priceless carpets, and heirlooms of every kind.

At the end he asked:

"What impressed you most of all?"

The Sufi answered:

"The fact that the earth is strong enough to support the weight of such a massive building." [Shah, 1971, p. 162]

UNANSWERABLE

When Jalaludin Rumi started to recite his couplets of wisdom, it is reported, people had not had enough time to form any opinion of him.

Some were interested, some were not. Others, following an inevitable human pattern, resented him. They said, "We hope that you do not think that you are a second Aesop or something." [Shah, 1971, p. 151]

HOW AND WHAT TO UNDERSTAND

This interchange between the Sufi mystic Simab and a nobleman named Mulakab is preserved in oral transmission as a dialogue often staged by wandering dervishes:

Mulakab: "Tell me something of your philosophy, so that I may understand."

Simab: "You cannot understand unless you have experienced."

Mulakab: "I do not have to understand a cake, to know whether it is bad."

Simab: "If you are looking at a good fish and you think that it is a bad cake, you need to understand less, and to understand it better, more than you need anything else."

Mulakab: "Then why do you not abandon books and lectures, if experience is the necessity?"

Simab: "Because 'the outward is the conductor to the inward.' Books will teach you something of the outward aspects of the inward, and so will lectures. Without them, you would make no progress."

Mulakab: "But why should we not be able to do without books?"

Simab: "For the same reason that you cannot think without words. You have been reared on books, your mind is so altered by books and lectures, by hearing and speaking, that the inward can only speak to you through the outward, whatever you pretend you can perceive."

Mulakab: "Does this apply to everyone?"

Simab: "It applies to whom it applies. It applies above all to those who think it does not apply to them!" [Shah, 1971, p. 109]

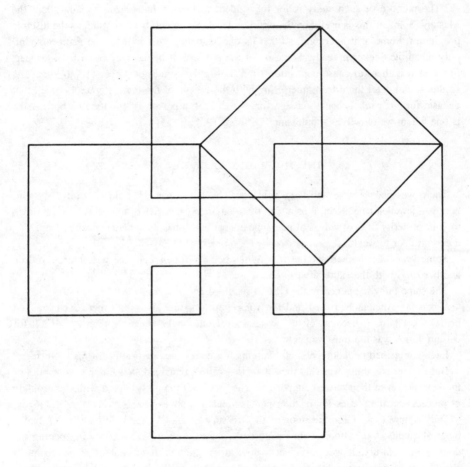

THE LIVES AND DOINGS OF THE MASTERS

A dervish of the first rank was asked:

"Why is it that people spend so much time and effort studying the lives and doings of the Masters of the past, when their lives may have been misreported, and their doings may have been for effects to be seen at that time, and their words may be full of hidden meaning?"

He said:

"The purpose of such study is for the student to know what is said by and about the Masters. Some of this is useful on the ordinary level. Some will become plain as the disciple progresses. Some of it is cryptic, so that its understanding will come at the right moment, only when the Seeker is ready. Some is for the purpose of being interpreted by a teacher. Some of it is there to cause opposition from those who could not proceed along the Way, so that it will deter them from interfering with the People of the Path. Remember well that distaste for our work is usually a sign for us that such a person is shunning us because he is one whom we ourselves should shun." [Shah, 1971, p. 55]

THE THREE JEWELLED RINGS

There was once a wise and very rich man who had a son. He said to him: "My son, here is a jewelled ring. Keep it as a sign that you are a successor of mine, and pass it down to your posterity. It is of value, of fine appearance, and it has the added capacity of opening a certain door to wealth."

Some years later he had another son. When he was old enough, the wise man gave him another ring, with the same advice.

The same thing happened in the case of his third and last son.

When the Ancient had died and the sons grew up, one after the other, each claimed primacy for himself because of his possession of one of the rings. Nobody could tell for certain which was the most valuable.

Each son gained his adherents, all claiming a greater value or beauty for *his* own ring.

But the curious thing was that the "door to wealth" remained shut for the possessors of the keys and even their closest supporters. They were all too preoccupied with the problem of precedence, the possession of the ring, its value and appearance.

Only a few looked for the door to the treasury of the Ancient. But the rings had a magical quality, too. Although they were keys, they were not used directly in opening the door to the treasury. It was sufficient to look upon them without contention or too much attachment to one or the other of their qualities. When this had been done, the people who had looked were able to tell where the treasury was, and could open it merely by reproducing the outline of the ring. The treasuries had another quality, too: they were inexhaustible.

Meanwhile the partisans of the three rings repeated the tale of their ancestor about the merits of the rings, each in a slightly different way.

The first community thought that they had already found the treasure.

The second thought that it was allegorical.

The third transferred the possibility of the opening of the door to a distant and remotely imagined future time. [Shah, 1967, pp. 153–54]

> The Sage said:
> "Fate continues. But on no account abandon your own intentions.
> "For if your plans accord with the supreme will, you will attain a plenitude of fulfillment for your heart."
>
> *Anwar-i-Suhaili*
> (Shah, 1970, p. 61)

Many people have expressed some difficulty in understanding the idea of submission and that of alignment. The concept of submission often conjures a grotesque image of a person giving up his attainments to "humbly" serve another. Or the selling of one's possessions and belongings and the total renunciation of the products of contemporary life. These, again, are remnants of previous systems, which have so degenerated that the essence of the concept is forgotten. These concepts are maintained by people who are interested mainly in keeping themselves away from any real contact with Sufi study or those who confuse Sufism with some kind of therapy. The idea of submission, in contemporary terms, is related to the understanding that our conventional sources of education have not yielded answers to the basic questions of life, and therefore we must turn to those who specialize in such matters. There is no mortification of the person who submits in this manner. There is, however, the need for a clear distinction between what *should* be surrendered and what need not. Recall Naqshband relating his experience that he was ready "to yield far more far-reaching" parts of himself than were necessary, and was not prepared to yield the *minor* ones which were the barriers to his understanding.

There is then no need to give up meat, or reading, or normal social endeavors. There is no celibacy in Sufism, no mortification. To shift the example, consider a parallel—what sort of surgeon would demand it? He would not ask that one dress in rags in order to obtain his specialized service, even though he may be the only one specially trained to aid in a life-threatening situation. One does not owe one's life to him after an operation, yet he may have saved a life. Such behavior obviously is inappropriate submission. Also inappropriate is the relinquishing of skills and competence in other areas, such as business or science, since they are separate from the event in question. It is an unfortunate accident of our times that the area of metaphysics is now littered with submissive and "humble" occultists, neurotics, and others who feel that their intellectual, emotional, and family development must be discarded. They confuse "piety" and "humble" behavior with "humility." No doctor would put up with his kind of nonsense. Neither will the Sufi.

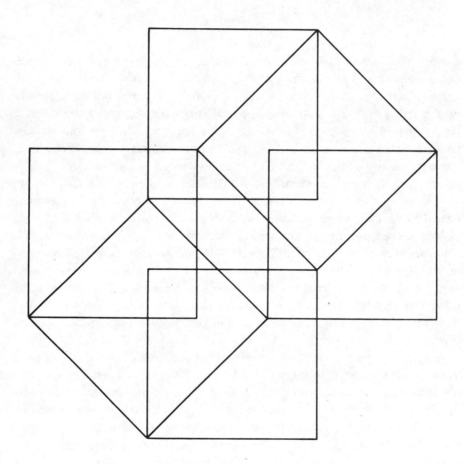

The "submission" that the doctor *does* need, however, is the agreement to follow his regime of treatment and to employ the materials provided in the manner prescribed. At some moment in many ordinary endeavors we place ourselves in the hands of others, when we learn to swim, when we have a suit made, when we learn a foreign language, or when we obtain treatment for a health problem. Sufi studies are no different.

There is no requirement to divest oneself of autonomy and identity. A proper approach is to learn to put what is to be put into "abeyance," to "wake up" in order that one's proper role may be assumed. This "alignment" is not then a submission of identity, a smoothing out of "rough edges" or personality change to conform to an agreed-upon ideal. Here is a tale in which the Sufi does not try to divest the student of his identity, no matter how negative his strongest characteristic might appear.

THE MAN WHO WAS EASILY ANGERED

A man who was very easily angered realized after many years that all his life he had been in difficulties because of this tendency.

One day he heard of a dervish deep of knowledge, whom he went to see, asking for advice.

The dervish said: "Go to such-and-such a crossroads. There you will find a withered tree. Stand under it and offer water to every traveller who passes that place."

The man did as he was told. Many days passed, and he became well known as one who was following a certain discipline of guidance and self-control under the instructions of a man of real knowledge.

One day a man in a hurry turned his head away when he was offered the water and went on walking along the road. The man who was easily angered called out to him several times: "Come, return my salutation! Have some of this water, which I provide for all travellers!"

But there was no reply.

Overcome by this behaviour, the first man forgot his discipline completely. He reached for his gun, which was hooked in the withered tree, took aim at the heedless traveller and fired. The man fell dead.

At the very moment that the bullet entered his body, the withered tree, as if by a miracle, burst joyfully into blossom.

The man who had been killed was a murderer, on his way to commit the worst crime of a long career.

There are, you see, two kinds of advisers. The first kind is the one who tells what should be done according to certain fixed principles, repeated mechanically. The other kind is the Man of Knowledge. Those who meet the Man of Knowledge will ask him for moralistic advice, and will treat him as a moralist. But what he serves is Truth, not pious hopes. [Shah, 1967, pp. 79–80]

In our conventional way of thinking, there is nothing worse than anger and murder. The story is designed to "shock" by using his trait, as it illustrates the difference between conventional ideas of submission and "improvement" and the Sufi conception of alignment.

The Sufi does not attempt to "cure" the man of his difficulty. Rather, he attempts to align his dominant characteristic with a more comprehensive perception of the current activity, and places him in a spot in which his "difficulty" can be of use.*

Within Sufism, there is no adulation of the Final Mystic Experience or the retired life of the ascetic on a mountaintop. Somehow this experience has been considered the End Point, or the Pinnacle, of many religious and philosophical systems. This is an error. However true this may be in degenerate systems, it is not the case within contemporary Sufism. If one were to "wake up" and still remain in bed, then what is the use of awakening? How would the awakener differ from those also in bed, but asleep? For the Sufi, the "return to the world" is the return to and alignment with active life as it is lived, which distinguishes the full development of man.

APPETITE

Firoz was asked:

"The books and the very presence of a man of wisdom increase the appetite for learning in the public, and also in those who wish to understand the real meaning of man. Is it not harmful to excite the anticipation of those who may not be able to profit from the Teaching, and who are incapable of recognizing its beauty, meaning, and significance?"

He said: "Water will attract the greedy man, but that is no argument against water. There are greedy men who are excited at the sight of apricots. If they try to steal them, they may be punished. If their greed causes them to gobble them so that their stomachs cannot sustain the load, they become sick. The owner of the orchard does not become sick."

The questioner continued:

"But in the interests of the thirsty man, could the water not be given to him in small amounts, so that he does himself no harm?"

Firoz said:

"Sometimes there is a kindly person present when he sees a crazed thirsty one, and he prevents him from killing himself through drinking too much. At other times, as you well know, the thirsty man comes across a well, and there is nobody there to prevent him destroying himself. Even if there were a well-meaning bystander to say 'Be careful!' the man crazed with thirst would thrust him aside and believe him to be his enemy."

The questioner asked:

---

*It may also be of some use here to consider the Sufi teacher, the man, the withered tree, and other elements in the story as aspects of one single personality.

"Is there no way in which a person may be safeguarded against these perils?"

Firoz told him:

"If you can find anything in this life which is without any danger of abuse and lacks risk for the stupid, tell me, and I shall myself spend all my time concentrating upon that thing. In the meantime learn, before it may be too late, that the guide exists because the path is rough. If you, so to speak, want to be able to breathe in without breathing out, or to waken up without facing the day—you are no Seeker, but a mere trumpery dilettante, and a hypocrite at that, for to call oneself something which one is not is contrary to the dignity of the people of dedication and straightforwardness." [Shah, 1971, pp. 57–58]

The living Sufi tradition can be best contacted by the study of the works of Idries Shah which are referenced in the Bibiliography. These works make available material which has not been seen in the West for thousands of years, suitably translated for our time and needs, adapted from the continuing "endowment" of Sufi tradition.

There is no profession which has any claim at being closer to Sufism than any other. This study is at the center of conventional thought in many areas, and carries nutrition for many groupings of people, of different countries, classes, and specializations. Here follow four stories on the relation of Sufi studies to ordinary activities.

MEATBALLS

Awad Afifi was asked:

"Which kinds of worldly happening can conduce towards the understanding of the Sufi Way?"

He said:

"I shall give you an illustration when it is possible."

Some time later, Awad and some of his group were on a visit to a garden outside their city.

A number of rough mountaineer nomads were encamped by the wayside. Awad stopped and bought a small piece of roast meat from one nomad, who had set up a Kebab stall there.

As he raised the meat to his lips, the stall-keeper uttered a cry and fell to the ground in a strange state. Then he stood up, took Awad's hand and kissed it.

Awad said:

"Let us be on our way." Accompanied by the roast-meat man, all proceeded along the highroad.

This nomad's name was Koftapaz (meatball-cook), and he was soon revealed as one whose *baraka*, spiritual power, gave meaning and effect to the spiritual exercises of the whole School.

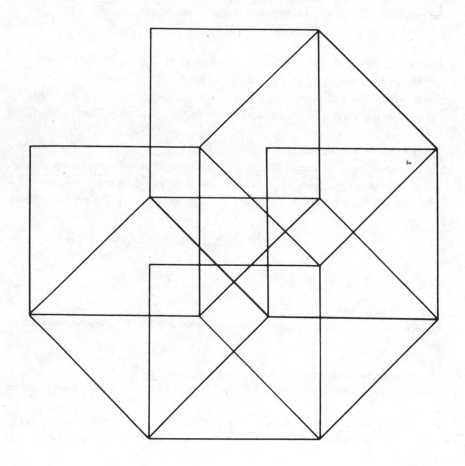

Awad called his followers together and said:

"I have been asked which kind of worldly happening can conduce towards the understanding of the Sufi Way.

"Let those who were present at the meeting with Koftapaz tell those who were not there, and then let Koftapaz himself give the explanation, for he is now my appointed Deputy."

When all had been informed about the encounter on the way to the garden, Sheikh Koftapaz stood up and said:

"O people upon whom the shadow of the beneficent bird Simurgh has rested! Know that all my life I have been a maker of meatballs.

"Therefore it was easy for me to know the Master by the way in which he raised a morsel to his lips—for I had seen the inwardness of every other kind of mortal by his outwardness; and if you are totally accomplished in your own work, you may recognize your Imam (leader) by his relationship with your work." [Shah, 1972, pp. 191–92]

SERVICE

"How," said a seeker to a well-known Sufi, "can one do even the minimum service towards helping the teaching?"

"You have already done it," he said, "for to ask how to serve is already a contribution towards service." [Shah, 1972, p. 161]

DUTY

A certain Sufi was asked:

"People come for companionship, discourses, and teaching. Yet you plunge them into activity. Why is this?"

He said:

"Though they—and you—may believe that they come for enlightenment, they mainly desire engagement in something. I give them engagement as a means of learning.

"Those who become totally engaged are they who sought only engagement, and who could not profit by self-observation of themselves so uselessly engaged. It is, therefore, not the deep respecters of activity who become illuminated."

The questioner said:

"Who, then, is it who does become illuminated?"

The Sufi replied:

"The illuminated are those who perform duties adequately, realizing that there is something beyond."

"But how is that 'something beyond' to be reached?"

"It is always reached by those who perform adequately. They need no further instruction. If you were doing your duty adequately, and were neither neglectful nor fanatically attached to it, you would not have had to ask the question." [Shah, 1972, p. 151]

SERVICE

Baba Musa-Imran lived the life of a rich merchant, although his sayings were accepted as those of a saint. People who had studied with him were to be found as teachers in places as far apart as China, it was said, and Morocco.

A certain man of Iran, assuming the garb of a dervish wanderer, found the Baba's home after much searching. He was received kindly and assigned the work of keeping the garden's irrigation channels clear. He stayed there for three years, without receiving any instruction in the mysteries. At the end of this time, he asked a fellow-gardener: "Can you tell me if I may expect to be admitted to the Path, and how much longer I might have to wait? Is there anything which I should do, in order to qualify for the *Iltifat*, the kindly attention of the Master?"

The other man, whose name was Hamid, said:

"I can only say that Baba Musa has assigned us tasks. Performing a task is a period of Service, known as the Stage of Khidmat. A disciple may not move out of the stage assigned to him. To do so is to reject the teaching. To seek something else or something more may be an indication that one has not, in reality, even been properly in the Stage of Service."

Less than a year later, the Iranian gardener asked permission to leave, to seek his destiny.

Another thirty years passed and this same man one day found himself in the presence of his former companion, Hamid, who was now Murshid of Turkestan. When Hamid asked if there were any questions, the Iranian stood up and said:

"I am your former fellow-pupil from the Court of Baba Musa-Imran. I quitted the studies in the phase of *Khidmat,* Service, because its relevance to the Teaching was incomprehensible to me. You, too, at that time, were performing menial tasks and attending no lectures.

"Can you tell me the particular point at which you began to make progress in the Path?"

Hamid smiled and said:

"I persevered until I was truly able to exercise service. This only happened when I ceased to imagine that menial work was in itself enough to denote service. It was then that its relevance to the Path became comprehensible to me. Those people who left our Baba did so because they wanted to understand without being worthy of understanding. When a man wants to understand a situation when he only imagines that he is in it, he is sure to be at a loss. He is incapable of understanding, so desiring is not enough. He is like a man who has placed his fingers in his ears and shouts 'Talk to me!' "

The Iranian asked:

"And after you had perfected your Service, did the Baba confide the Teachings to you?"

Hamid said:

"As soon as I was able to serve, I was able to understand. What I understood resided in the surroundings prepared for us by the Baba. The place, the others there, the actions, could be read as if he had painted a picture of the mysterious realities in their own language." [Shah, 1972, pp. 94–95]

And yet can so many of the most grand metaphysical problems be subject to such an elegantly simple formulation? One cannot answer these kinds of questions directly. As an illustrative example, one can note that the simplest of elements, if aligned correctly, can produce an entity of great interest and complexity, one to which many would attribute very grand and complex origins. To take an example, the final figure in this chapter is comprised "simply" of eight squares, set at 45-degree angles to one another, yet . . .

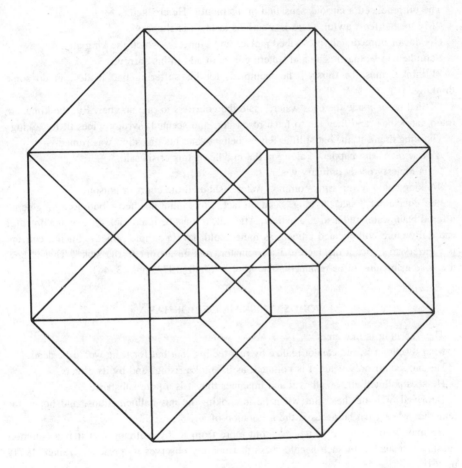

THIRSTY

There once was a king who was thirsty. He did not quite know what the difficulty was, but he said:

"My throat is dry."

Lackeys at once ran swiftly to find something suitable to alleviate the condition. They came back with lubricating oil. When the king drank it, his throat did not feel dry any more, but he knew that something was not right.

The oil produced a curious sensation in his mouth. He croaked:

"My tongue feels awful, there is a curious taste, it is slippery . . ."

His doctor immediately prescribed pickles and vinegar—which the king ate.

Soon he had stomach-ache and watering eyes to add to his sorrows.

"I think I must be thirsty," he mumbled, for his suffering had made him do some thinking.

"Thirst never made the eyes water," said the courtiers to one another. But the kings are often capricious, and they ran to fetch rosewater, and scented, syrupy wines fit for a king.

The king drank it all, but still he felt no better—and his digestion was ruined.

A wise man who happened along in the middle of this crisis said:

"His Majesty needs ordinary water."

"A king could never drink common water," shouted the court in unison.

"Of course not," said the king, "and, in fact, I feel quite insulted—both as a king being offered plain water and also as a patient. After all, it must be impossible that such a dreadful and daily more complicated ailment as mine could have a simple remedy. Such a concept is contrary to logic, a disgrace to its originator, and an affront to the sick." That is how the wise man came to be renamed "The Idiot." [Shah, 1972, pp. 43–44]

WORDS OF ISRAIL OF BOKHARA

The Teaching is like air.

Man dwells in it, but cannot realize by real feeling that but for it he would be dead.

He can see air only when it is polluted, as in smoke rising, and by its effects.

He sees polluted air, breathes it and imagines that it is a pure substance.

Deprived of it he dies. But when he is choking he has hallucinations, and hopes for remedies when what he needs is the restoration of air.

He may become aware of it, and profit more from it, by realizing that it is a common substance treated with such heedlessness that nobody observes its presence. [Shah, 1971, p. 26]

9 PSYCHOLOGY AND THE CHRISTIAN MYSTICAL TRADITION

WILLIAM McNAMARA

WILLIAM MCNAMARA, O.C.D., was born in Providence, Rhode Island, on Valentine's Day 1926. He became a Disclaced Carmelite monk in 1944 and was ordained a Roman Catholic priest in 1951. Since then he has been a lecturer and retreat leader in every state of the country except Alaska.

After an audience with the visionary Pope John XXIII in 1960, Father William founded the Spiritual Life Institute of America, a small monastic community of men and women, Roman Catholic in origin and universal in outreach.

The community is rooted in Christ, characterized by earthy mysticism and a Christian Humanism that lays the foundations for contemplation in a vibrant natural life enhanced by the primitive Carmelite spirit of the prophet Elijah, St. Teresa of Avila, and St. John of the Cross.

Beginning in Sedona, Arizona, the first center, Nada Hermitage, moved to Crestone, Colorado in 1983. Nova Nada, a more primitive wilderness hermitage, is located in North Kemptville, Nova Scotia, Canada. Both centers are open for retreats year round and welcome men and women, married couples and singles, Christians, practitioners of other spiritual traditions, and those without any religious affiliation.

"It is ironic, and yet a typical trait of history, that the most contemporary form of religious life in the modern world should also by the most primitive," says Father William. "Our eremitical life is very similar to that of the original Carmelite hermits in the early centuries of the Church who lived on Mt. Carmel under a common rule characterized by its simplicity and minimal structure to enable the hermits to offer God a pure heart."

Father William now spends less time traveling and lives more of the year in his hermitage at Nova Nada. He stays in silence and solitude and takes his meals with the rest of the eremitical community only once a week. Nova Nada had no electricity, no phone, or running water in winter, and mail service only weekly. (The Colorado hermitage has all these.)

Father McNamara, who received his Bachelor of Arts in theology and philosophy from Catholic University and his Master of Arts in education and psychology from Boston College, founded *Spiritual Life Magazine* in 1955 and served as its editor until 1962. He now publishes *Desert Call*, a quarterly on contemporary spirituality, and *Desert Express*, his tape-of-the-month club.

He is the author of *The Human Adventure* (1974), *Mystical Passion* (1977), and *Christian Mysticism* (1981), republished as a trilogy by Amity House in 1987. Other works include *The Art of Being Human* (1967), now out of print, and Earthy Mysticism (1983). All publications are available from the Spiritual Life Institute.

The life of man is meant to be a personal response to a personal God. It is not as important or as close to the truth to speak of God as a Person as to speak of him as personal, or superpersonal. He is not strictly speaking the Absolute but rather the *absolutely loving superpersonal Being* in whom all being subsides. The Christian way of emphasizing the superpersonal nature of God is through the altruistic love-life of the Trinity in which each person is eternally constituted by being totally related to the other.

To respond to God means to be alive to God. In fact, St. Irenaeus, one of the Fathers of the Church, boldly insisted that *"the glory of God is man fully alive!"* In the Christian Mystical Tradition it is the whole man whom God calls and the whole man who responds. The Christian mystic or religious man remains human even in his most transcendent moments. He remains in continuity with the world of physical, biological, and psychological phenomena, a feeling, thinking, imagining, remembering, perceiving, socializing body-person, with a distinct life history, a unique and unrepeatable personality, his own mind sets and major project of existence, his own interests, inclinations, desires, and needs. To deny this fundamental fact is to build on utter unreality.

The transcendent moments inspired by divine initiative in the Christian Mystical Tradition are experienced by flesh-and-blood human beings and are therefore part of human behavior, that area properly relegated to psychology. Man's final goal is transcendent, but it is a goal of *man,* a fulfillment of his nature. "Grace" does not destroy nature—it perfects it, according to St. Thomas Aquinas, whose *Summa Theologiae* (Aquinas, 1964), perhaps the greatest theological accomplishment in the whole of Christian history, might also be understood as a Summa Psychologiae. Psychology can make an enormous contribution to the Christian Mystical Tradition by helping us to understand and foster the psychologically integrated man, who can thus be far more receptive to the workings of the divine in him than the unintegrated, disintegrated, or maladjusted man. This neither denies the reality of God's intervention nor overestimates the value of a psychology of Christian Mysticism. It merely keeps things in proper perspective.

For ages we have ceased to be at home with our bodies. Because of the Incarnational basis for all Christian Mysticism, the Christian mystic is *required* to be at home with his body, affirming the goodness and beauty of it and recognizing the body as the only possible agency through which he can *be* effectively in the world. In view of this, the original purposes of such growth centers as Esalen, namely to enable man to live in harmony with his body and to be sensitively in touch with others, are highly commendable. The trouble with many programs thus far has been such a fascination with this new and delightful experience of the body and all the possible tactile concomitants of a full-bodied existence that programs have bogged down on that level, therefore missing the opportunity to move into the deeper spiritual dimensions of human growth.

Psychotherapy and other humanistic growth techniques which help people find out what they genuinely feel are not only compatible with the Christian Mystical Tradition but can be extremely helpful. The divinizing process which leads to transforming union, the ultimate stage of the Mystic Way, depends upon a healthy and harmonious individuation. That is why at certain early stages of spiritual development, far from a denial of the senses, Christian Mysticism requires a thoroughgoing exercise and development of the senses. Long before the approach of the Dark Night or the dominance of the Cloud of Unknowing, the Christian is required to develop the senses and come into touch through the senses with a highly perceived world.

Developing a psychology of Christian Mysticism is a vastly important endeavor. But the project is extremely young and characteristically, at this stage of development, noticeably confused. Many of the conclusions of the investigators conflict with one another, and most of the helpful insights are, at best, tentative and provisional. Understandably so, since psychology is just one, limited, and isolated science, it cannot be expected to plumb the depths of the whole multileveled mystery of man.

For instance the idea of nonconceptual workings of the mind is abhorrent to most psychologists, and so their disposition is to reduce the state of mystical union to a mental blank, a mere unconsciousness. While admitting that this may be true of certain kinds of quasi-mystical absorption, often deliberately induced by methods akin to hypnotism, it is an entirely untrue and inadequate description of the ecstatic union of the great mystics, their ecstasies being highly wrought states of religious consciousness and of spiritual activity. If we were to accept the former superficial and *merely* psychological explanations, we would have to reject the wholy body of testimony of the mystics.

"Ask the mystic if you will," says the late Dr. Joseph Maréchal, professor of experimental psychology in Louvain and author of one of the pioneer works in the field of the psychology of mysticism.

Ask the mystic which of the following hypotheses corresponds most completely to the *ensemble* of his internal experiences: The hypothesis of a supernatural action directing the whole of his intimate life and mingling itself with his own natural activity, or the hypothesis which would reduce this intimate life of his to be nothing but a mechanical combination of mental phenomena modified psychologically by the representation of a religious ideal. The reply is not doubtful; it may be read in the writings of the saints and of truly religious men; and the conviction which it expresses goes far beyond the exigencies of dogma on the subject of grace.

We should make a great mistake in forming our personal point of view, to despise the suggestions of theology and the divinations of traditional piety: without bringing us full light, they have the appreciative advantage of keeping us in close contact, and so to speak, in sympathy with the original documents which we will have to utilise: when all is said, thanks to the modest and always reformable "prejudice" with which they inspire us, we run less risk of misunderstanding important shades of thought or feeling of the mysteries themselves, while a premature psychological theory would certainly involve such sacrifices. [Maréchal, 1964, p. 50]

The proper scientific attitude is to accept the testimony, even though it transcends the data of psychology. The phenomenal dimension of all the experiences of the mystic lie within the range of psychological science except the very highest, that of full union, as described by St. Teresa's Fifth Mansion in her *Interior Castle* and in similar narrations of other mystics. It is, therefore, impossible to understand the mystical experience unless considerations derived from ontology and theology are introduced to supplement those of experimental psychology.

For example, the prodigious talent and work of C. G. Jung in the field of psychology is unassailable, but his attempts to engage the interest and sympathy of religious people by his references to God are bound to confuse more than enlighten. According to Augustine Leonard (1956), a man deeply and extensively versed in philosophy and contemporary psychology, the Divine Quaternity postulated by Jung is a result of confused deductions, and consequently:

Those who christen the psychology of Jung as a *mystic psychology* are certainly not entirely wrong. In comparison and because his method is more strict, Freud is less dangerous (from the religious point of view). That which Jung calls religion, that which he honestly believes to be religion, is not religion at all; *even from the empirical point of view.* It appears to be only a very incidental manifestation.

There is a consensus on this according to Dr. Gregory Zilboorg, a psychologist and one of America's foremost historians and philosophers of medicine. He says that while psychology can throw a great deal of *psychological* light on religious experience, and religious faith may enrich one's psychological functioning, psychology as a scientific discipline can shed no light whatsoever on the relations between man and God. And so Leonard (1956) says:

> The religious act is an intentional act and is related to an object which is situated beyond the reach of our (practical) experience. Consequently, an empirical study of the relationship between man and God can never reach the second number of this relationship. What we are apt to observe is only the reaction of a person, without our knowing the nature of the stimulus that originated the reaction.

With that limitation in mind we are now ready to suggest a psychology of Christian Mysticism. We need to know first of all the nature of Christian Mysticism. It is the Christian form—on the deepest and most personal level—of religious experience. In fact, it is the God-man experience of Christ prolonged by the Church and participated in by the community of believers, the Mystical Body of Christ. Since mysticism is an experience, we had better grapple with the latter concept first.

OVERALL DESCRIPTION IN TERMS OF EXPERIENCE

EXPERIENCE

The key word running through this whole chapter is *experience*. Only the experienced man knows what it is because he knows what it feels like: the sand, the mud, the stone, the water, the grass, the fire, the wind, the peach, the body of the dog, the cat, the man, or the woman, working hands and dancing feet, the agony and ecstasy of death and rebirth, the many different kinds of human love and hate, the touch of God.

We smother ourselves in monumental mounds of ideas, problems, projects and programs, a million meanings and purposes, and a veritable Vesuvius of words —with no experience; and so we suffer and die without ever having lived. You can skim along the surface of life with information enough to be buried in and meaning enough to make a derivative existence seem plausible. But without firsthand experience you don't really know and you don't really live. Observation, conceptualization, conversation, or pedantic dithering cannot take the place of the direct awareness of experience. Subsequent reflection and interpretation can and often do enlarge and enrich the experience; and the experience can be partially shared by careful articulation. But the heart of the experience is being in a predominantly conscious love relationship with the other.

Read the opening paragraph of St. John's Epistle:

Something which has existed from the beginning, that we have heard and that we have seen with our own eyes; that we have watched and touched with our own hands: the Word who is life—this is our subject. That life was made visible: we saw it, and we are giving our testimony, telling you of the eternal life which was with the Father and has been made visible to us. What we have seen and heard we are telling you so that you too may be in union with us, as we are in union with the Father and with his Son Jesus Christ. [1 John 1:1–4]

That's experience. It is the stuff of life and the cornerstone of Christianity. Experience is so elemental to life that it cannot be fully described or defined. But something must still be said.

Experience is extremely personal, unique, and unrepeatable. It cannot even be fully captured by subsequent reflection. One can focus only on certain aspects of it, though permanent effects remain in the psyche. A lifetime of conceptualization will not match the range of data supplied to the psyche in one single rich experience. The conscious part of the psyche cannot absorb the multiple stimulations and resonances that occur in a striking experience.

Experience is not simply a result of conscious activity. In fact, experience is a wider concept than that of consciousness. Experience issues from both conscious and unconscious areas of the psyche. It comprises an awareness of both the extent and the limitations of consciousness. Experience is founded primarily on consciousness. If there is no consciousness there is no experience. But the conscious aspect of an experience is only part of it. An experience involves awareness of some stimulus and a simultaneous recognition of the limits or boundaries of consciousness. Although it may not be possible to recall or conceptualize or articulate this dimension of the experience, what lies on the other side of the boundary of consciousness can at times be apprehended as a significant part of an experience. Experiments have shown that what lies beyond the boundary of consciousness in the dark area affects the experience itself. And we know from experience that there is a persistent drive, often repressed or sublimated, to extend the boundaries and transcend the limits of ordinary consciousness.

If God is to be touched anywhere within the range of human experience, the area of *peak experience* would seem to be the most likely. In such an experience one is touched at his core and afterwards his life is profoundly and permanently altered. This kind of experience is not necessarily sudden and startling; it can also be slow and gradual: an example of the latter would be a baptismal experience, identification with Christ, lived out and deepened over a lifetime. In that case there would be no need for any other peak experience.

Abraham Maslow (1962) has made the characteristics of the peak experience well known. The peak human experience area involves a reconciliation of opposites (sinful and just, darkness and light, finite and infinite, and so on), the identity of subject and object; it makes a deep impression with permanent consequences and transcendent possibilities; it is mysterious and ambiguous, alogical, predominantly passive, unique, ambivalent, and involves heightened activity of all the senses guided by the enlightened mind. These same qualities are described by the mystics as characteristics of the "mystical experience."

RELIGIOUS EXPERIENCE

God is not just another object of human understanding. The subjective encounter with God is constitutive of the very being of man from the start. "Our hearts are restless, Lord, until they rest in Thee," believed St. Augustine. At the core or apex of his being, man is man by his relatedness to God. The unimpaired totality and lucidity of his essence are not his own: he possesses them in God. The religious act is thus man's consent to the transcendence of his own being. He is subject to God's sovereign claim. But far from enslaving him, this subjection or ontological humility, really a seductive and salubrious union, liberates him. By this ruling magnetism, this irresistible gravity, man not only stands naked and defenseless before God, but he becomes his best and most noble self in the most profound and comprehensive portrayal of his own being—which is the finite spirit's conscious relationship to the infinite mystery.

The positive nature of this "subjectism" is emphasized by existential psychologist Adrian van Kaam of Duquesne University's interdisciplinary Institute of Man, who uses the term "self actualizing surrender," which "arises from the authentic gift of oneself . . . [and] implies growth in maturity by constant participation in the Transcendent" (van Kaam, 1965).

Man's total and radical orientation toward God in the religious act is a function of the whole person. It is not the function of any isolated faculty or disposition: it is not the intellect as in Spinoza; nor the will as in Kant; nor religious feeling as in Schleiermacher; nor the urge to happiness and the fear of death as in Feuerbach; nor repressed sexuality as in (the younger) Freud.

Man is naturally religious. He has a transcendental hunger for what lies beyond his grasp. Man is mostly mind, and is by nature at least incipiently mindful of God consciously or unconsciously. His faith in God is therefore not subrational but superrational (more rational) and intelligent. The religious act, then, far from being opposed to metaphysics, is indeed the supreme manifestation of the metaphysical essence of man. That is why Alan Watts freely equates metaphysics with the life of the spirit. This rational structure indicates how the religious act does not ignore the question of truth as the pragmatism of William James would have us believe.

Perceptions are sensations endowed with meaning. Intuition is a direct mental apprehension. Some intuitions, such as the intuition of mathematical truths, are distinct but abstract. Others, such as the intuitions of the soul and God, are obscure but concrete. Such fundamental modes of cognition are ultimates. They cannot be adequately explained. Nor do they prove anything. As E. I. Watkin says, these truths of intuition are "monstrated" not demonstrated. The mind apprehends directly, that is intuitively, not when it strains to know but when in contemplative repose it actively receives the secret of being, the inner suchness of things. It is by intuition that man becomes, in Heidegger's striking phrase, "obedient to the voice of Being" (Watkin, 1920).

What is meant to be conveyed by the term "religious experience" is an experience of a distinctive and immediate religious quality, direct apprehension of a religious object, truth, or value. It is an ultimate kind of spiritual intuition. It is strongly subjective, though not exclusively or primarily so. Although God is not a separated being, he is wholly other and utterly distinct and absolutely transcendent, external to the experient and to the universe. The experience of the absolute transcendence and otherness of God is bound, therefore, to be obscure and its conceptual formulation inadequate. This is not to say that God as the object of religious experience is solely apprehended as transcendent. His intimate presence in the psyche and his infinite attraction as the fullness of value and the fulfillment of desire are also apprehended, at times more powerfully. The experience is essentially an intuition, not an emotion, though no doubt colored more or less strongly by emotion. The experience is more, not less, mindful and also more concrete than other operations of the mind.

Religious experience breaks through the narrow boundaries of individualism. His own experience is not enough for the man in touch with God. He leans heavily on the cumulative traditions of mankind and more specifically on the living tradition in which he is rooted and to which he contributes in some small way. He rediscovers for himself the insights of the Church, penetrates their dogmatic formulations, and in a secondary sense relives them and incorporates them by a fresh vital assimilation into his own religious existence.

Religious experience is normally accompanied by and requires a conceptual interpretation. It also demands for its full flowering and fruitfulness some exterior and sensible expression in the form of public worship, sacraments, and ceremonies. This is necessarily so because it is the experience of an embodied spirit. Religion without religious experience is a corpse. Experience is its soul. But the soul cannot operate without its body, namely, theology and external cults.

Religious experience is not only concerned with God in himself, but extends to his creative action and presence in creatures—mineral, vegetable, animal, and human—especially the Communion of Saints (the union and interrelatedness of all the people of God brought into at-one-ment with God by the redemptive love-act of Christ), which can be experienced by the soul, obscurely for the most part, but with a conviction more powerful than could be produced by mere reflection on a doctrine accepted only externally. So religion in its essence is wholly and solely the experiential element. To think or act otherwise, subordinating the experiential element of religion to its conceptual and institutional embodiments, is doctrinal and ecclesiastical materialism.

A good example of religious experience in the raw and its conceptual embodiment is Pascal's famous conversion experience, as recorded in the "Memorial" he sewed into his coat and wore for the rest of his life:

FIRE

God of Abraham, God of Isaac, God of Jacob.
Not of philosophers or men of learning.
Certainty, joy, certainty, feeling, sight, joy.
God of Jesus Christ.
My God and your God.
Thy God shall be my God. Truth.
Oblivion of the world and all outside God.
Joy, Joy, tears of Joy.

Blaise Pascal, who lived in seventeenth-century France, a mathematician, physicist, psychologist, and engineer, was one of the great intellectuals of the world. His "Memorial" (1966) is a historical document in the strict sense of the word—a turning point and decision which stands in history, which makes history: the inner Christian history of this man. It brings to its culmination everything experienced up to this point and fixes a new beginning.

"Fire"—that bare word, alone and unqualified, epitomizes the whole experience. Pascal was on fire, and his life blazed with a brand-new kind of light, from a source other than physical nature or psychic consciousness. It was an experience of the spirit, the Holy Spirit: Pentecostal Fire, the Fire that on the original Biblical Pentecost transformed sluggish, fearful, fishermen apostles into wild, contagious, courageous lovers of God.

Then came the staccato of words that highlight qualities typical of a direct religious experience: certitude, joy, and a new level of existence. But why does he stammer? Because he is dumfounded by the aweful and the unbelievably new reality of God. It is not the God he tried to fit into his head, the philosopher's God. His direct intuition of the absolutely, superpersonal being of God stands out in vivid contrast to the abstract ideas which are all that philosophers can attain without distinctively religious experience.

Pascal's response to this firsthand experience was radical amazement. One would have to grasp the enormity of the Christian insight of a philosopher and mathematician: that God is not the God "of philosophers and men of learning," but "the God of Abraham, God of Isaac, God of Jacob." What is being experienced by this towering man is the facticity, historicity, concreteness, and infinite freedom of God who cannot be had by man, but freely intervenes in the human domain when and however he chooses to.

"God of Jesus Christ." No other God, no projection. He whom Jesus embodied, he whom Jesus meant when he said, "my Father." There is no Christian conception of God or Christian truth apart from the concrete historical Christ. "To have seen me is to have seen the Father" (John 14:9). Apart from him there is no "essence of Christianity." The essence of Christianity is Christ. What must be faced once and for all is this: that the definitive category of Christianity is the particular, unique reality of the concrete personality of Jesus of Nazareth—who happens to be God.

MYSTICAL EXPERIENCE

No word is our language—not even "humanism" or "socialism"—has been employed more loosely than "mysticism." Cuthbert Butler, in a masterly book entitled *Western Mysticism* (1960), is quite specific on this point:

It has come to be applied to many things of many kinds: to theosophy and Christian science; to spiritualism and clairvoyance; to demonology and witchcraft; to occultism and magic; to weird psychical experiences, if only they have some religious color; to revelations and visions; to other-worldliness, or even more dreaminess and impracticability in the affairs of life; to poetry and painting and music of which the motif is unobvious and vague. It has been identified with the attitude of the religious mind that cares not for dogma or doctrine, for Church or sacraments; it has been identified also with a certain outlook on the world—a seeing God in Nature, and recognizing that the material creation, in various ways, symbolises spiritual realities: a beautiful and true conception . . . but which is not mysticism according to its historical meaning. And, on the other side, the meaning of the term has been watered down: it has been said that the love of God is mysticism; or that mysticism is only the Christian life on a high level; or that it is Roman Catholic piety in extreme form. [pp. 65–66]

Mysticism is the science of mystical experience. Mystical experience, the realization of union with God, is simply the highest or deepest form of religious experience. The claim consistently and unequivocally made by the whole line of great mystics found perhaps its simplest and most arresting expression in these words of St. Augustine in his *Confessions:* "My mind in the flash of a trembling glance came to Absolute Being—That Which Is."

Whereas the ordinary man is ruled and governed by the exigencies of his superficial ego, at the deep root of the mystic's being, at his center, there is a conscious direct contact with Transcendental Reality. This center or ground of being is the fount and unifying source of all the lower psychological functions, not another self, but the essential ego—the fundamental transcendent self—where man is most himself and most open to God. Here man's passion for God, which is a response to God's own divine pathos (God's tender "feeling" for man), comes to rest in the contemplation of the really Real and vital union with God who is Pure Love. The mystic knows God no longer by hearsay or information but by experience. He sees and is ravished and becomes him who ravishes him. He becomes God—not like God autonomously—but God, by participation in his Godhood. "The soul appears to be God more than a soul," wrote St. John of the Cross. "Indeed, it is God by participation. Yet truly, its being (even though transformed) is naturally as distinct from God's as it was before, just as the window, although illumined by the ray, has an existence distinct from the ray" (Bars, 1963).

In mystical experience, God is known as much as he can be known in this life; he is known in himself; but he is known through union of love. It is the supernatural love of charity which alone can connaturalize the soul to the Deity: this love becomes the objective means of knowledge. As Henry Bars points out:

A particularly important point of practical doctrine is thus established: supernatural mystical experience is bound to no condition of nature, to no particular temperament, or particular education nor to any technique whatsoever. It is bound only to the Gospel way of life pushed to its ultimate consequences, and in particular to "detachment from perfection in perfection itself," and finally to the unforeseeable choice of created liberty in its encounter with uncreated love. [van Kaam, 1965, p. 55]

The psychophysical phenomena—rapture, trance, ecstasy, cessation of the ordinary activity of the mind or the senses—that sometimes occur concomitantly at certain phases of the mystic life and during certain states of prayer are by no means essential to the mystical experience. In fact, if not treated with graceful, light-hearted detachment, they can and often do become impediments to the mystical union. This will be discussed in greater detail when we speak of the dangers along the path of the Christian Mystical Tradition.

Two questions must be raised here. The first question is: Can drugs cause a mystical experience? Definitely not. Mystical experience is a free gift of God. Drugs might heighten the possibility in the case of an individual already morally disposed by changing his temperament from dominantly opaque to dominantly transparent. This transparency due to drugs or even intoxication can expose the divine content of the soul otherwise imperceptible to the subject. The use of narcotics, however, generally leads to pseudomysticism. To say this much and no more is an enormously inadequate answer to the question, but the space of this chapter does not allow further comment.

The second question is: If only the mystic is in direct contact with the living God, then what does the conscious life of the rest of mankind feed on in its quest for the fullness of truth and love? It feeds on the surrogate of God that revelation and theology have provided for us, an abstract and metaphysical God who is the fruit of theological reflection. This surrogate of God does not represent the idolatrous whim of any individual or limited group but is an archetype that is the product of the collective unconscious of mankind. Although a substitute for the God-to-be-experienced, man needs something akin to God or that represents God verbally and conceptually to lead him to the possible experience of God as he is in himself.

SUMMARY OF EXPERIENCE

It is time to summarize the whole gamut of experience from beginning to end. The *human experience* of contemplation (seeing the Real) and vital union (enjoying the Good) becomes *religious experience* when God is recognized as the ultimate subject of the contemplative union. Religious experience becomes *mystical experience* when the direct object of perception is no longer the self, the other, or the event, but the "mysterium" which suffuses them and underlies the phenomenon. The mystical experience becomes *Christian* when Christ is seen to be the Way into the mystery, in fact the mystery itself, since he is not only the Way but the Truth and the Life as well. There is a *psychological factor* that identifies the mystic and distinguishes him from the grace-full spiritual man who is not a mystic, and that is that the mystic has become conscious of and passive to God active at the core of his being. All saints are mystical, though not to the same degree. The fact that some are easily recognizable mystics is due to their peculiar type of temperament.

The essence of the spiritual life is charity. When his love of God is perfect man is perfect. The santification of man consists in the union of his will with the will of God. The experience of this union is the natural psychological effect wherever the union reaches a particular degree of intense intimacy. The felicity and frequency with which one experiences divine union depends upon the psychophysical temperament of the subject. According to E. I. Watkin's helpful division, some persons are comparatively transparent, others opaque. The latter, for instance, sees the same comedy as the former but never laughs; hears the same music but never moves a muscle; suffers the same embarrassment but never turns red. The inner experiences of the transparent personality, however, always register on his countenance or in his external behavior. What happens in his spiritual depths, at the center of his soul, rises easily to the conscious surface. What occurs in the deep recesses of the opaque personality will seldom, if ever, rise to the surface. Transparent personalities are more subject to experiences such as telepathy and clairvoyance and to psychic phenomena such as ghostly sounds, movements, and apparitions; and they are much more likely to translate an inner experience into a painting, a song, or a poem.

That is why a transparent and an opaque person may both be in union with God but only the transparent one becomes conscious of it. Both are drawn by God into the deepest dimensions of the human adventure, the mystical depths of the spiritual life, but only the transparent personality has a mystical *experience.* The opaque personality, though raised by God into the mystical existence of God-manhood, does not experience it. Despite this, he may be just as holy as his transparent counterpart. If he is holy, then he enjoys, without experience, a supernatural union with God; whereas the person of transparent temper may enjoy nothing more than an experience of God's natural presence in the soul. As I have indicated in far more detail elsewhere (McNamara, 1974a), strictly or *theologically* speaking, both saintly persons—the transparent and the opaque—are mystics; but *phenomonally* speaking, only the transparent person is because he experiences God's active presence within him and is, obviously, recognizably a mystic.

PHILOSOPHICAL BASES OF THE CHRISTIAN MYSTICAL TRADITION

The Christian Mystical Tradition, like any other, is based on certain assumptions about man and the universe. According to Christian Mysticism, who is man? What is the structure and function of his human consciousness? What is the nature of the universe in which man must live and move and have his being? How does man contact the world of matter and beyond it? How does he communicate with it, in fact, become one with it in a union of love if he, indeed, has any such desire?

Much of the philosophical basis of Christian Mysticism can be deduced from our discussion of experience. But let us investigate more specifically.

BRIEF AND PARTIAL OUTLINE OF HUMAN CONSCIOUSNESS

According to the Christian Mystical Tradition:

1. Man is created in the *image and likeness of God.* Genesis, the first book of the Bible, tells us that God made man "in his image and likeness." The New Testament calls Christ "the likeness of God," or more precisely, "the image of the invisible God," while it insists that we are called to bear the image of Christ as the heavenly Man at the end of time, and to be now transformed in his image by reflecting it as in a mirror.

According to the Christian tradition, every man bears in his soul the image of God both because he is made an intelligent being "in the Word" and because the Word, the Son of God himself, became man and the supreme exemplar of all mankind so that every man is an image of Christ.

If man would seek the image of God within himself (for in man alone is the Trinity mirrored by an expressed likeness), he will find there in the depths of his soul his nearest approach to God. In this sense "know thyself" lies at the foundation of Christian contemplation, which is not a selfish preoccupation because it regards the image of God in the center of the soul. Such contemplation is perfected when all forms of egotism are burned away by the fire of purification. At this point when all voluntary attachments to evil and inordinate attachments to creatures have vanished, the soul is ready to be fully transformed into the living image of God. This likeness of God in man is noticeable in a certain conformation to the Word made flesh, to such an extent that sometimes extraordinary phenomena occur, for instance the stigmata, in which the image of Christ takes on a corporeal likeness and the body shares with the soul its likeness to Christ. St. Francis of Assisi is an outstanding example of such a striking conformation, including the stigmata.

2. Man is a *body-person*. But the true Christian concept and the central Christian tradition of man as a body-person has not been faithfully upheld. There have been both heresies and epochs in the history of Christianity that have held the body cheap and tried to foster the spiritual life by neglecting or even denigrating the body. Even today we suffer to some degree from the influences of Jansenism and Puritanism which did not prize the body. Yet the value of the body was overwhelmingly affirmed when God himself chose to take on a body and become man through the person of Jesus Christ. Ever since the Incarnation no man is permitted to scorn or disregard anything human or natural. Man does not *have* a body but is an embodied spirit (or an enspirited body). He exhibits certain needs and desires through his body (the need for food, drink, sex, rest, and so forth), but his being is not limited either to these drives or to his body itself.

3. Man is *emotional,* possessing the ability to feel. His emotions are sources of information which must be listened to; his emotions, in addition to gracing his personality with warmth, liveliness, spontaneity, and passion, also provide him with strong *motivating powers,* for if he does not feel a strong emotional attraction, for example, toward God, his will cannot be moved to love nor his intellect to know. Man's being, though colored by his emotions, is not limited to them or governed solely by them. Christ provides us with a stunning example of this:

He wept over Jerusalem and over the death of Lazarus. He could be moved by holy anger, as when he ejected the vendors from the Temple. His encounters with his friends and disciples were pervaded by an exquisite tenderness [his encounters with the Samaritan woman in John 4:1–30 and with Mary and her jar of ointment in Mark 14:3–9 are worthy of special note]. In the Garden of Olives he was terrified by the thought of the suffering that was awaiting Him. And still this sensitive, deeply emotional Man maintained in the core of his being an infinite poise, an unshakable serenity, an orientation of perception and purpose that never gave way under the torrents of His feelings. [Underhill, 1955, p. 55]

4. Man is both *social and solitary*. He is fundamentally in relation to others, but this does not mean he need always live in groups. Man must, in fact, act out his simultaneous ultimate aloneness before God. These aspects of beingfulness will be treated more detailedly in our discussion of the Path.

5. Man is a *lover*. With extra motivating power inspired by his emotions—"The heart has reasons the mind knows nothing about," said Pascal—he makes an act of love with his whole being: will, intellect, body, emotions, and so on.

6. Man is a *knower*. Through his *intellect* he is capable of discursive thinking and reasoning. Through his body's *senses* he knows through touch and taste and scent. But man's knowledge is not limited to sense impressions or any process of intellection. Man knows intuitively. *Intuition* differs radically from reasoning or any sensory awareness: (a) it cannot be produced and comes when least expected; (b) the inner suchness rather than the appearance of a person, a thing, or an event is penetrated immediately and directly without any interposed intermediary (of intellect or sense); thus (c) there is an "intimate compenetration" of subject and object; that is, subject-object duality is effaced. How similar to Maslow's description of the "peak experience" this is!

We will have more to say about the structure and function of human consciousness in our discussion of the Path.

If man's deepest and truest self is not limited to his body, his emotions, his intellect, or even so noble a power as his intuition, "where" is this deep center "located"? If man's essential unity is no mere composite of all these elements of human consciousness, what is his true self? It must be allied to that Christ-depth "that never gave way" despite vacillating surface conditions. It must be intuitive, too, penetrating beyond sense and discursive thought to the essential unity of things, the manifold in the One. Christ, the supreme psychologist, was both poetic and precise in his description of man's deepest self which alone is capable of mystical experience.

CHRIST THE PSYCHOLOGIST AND THE DEEP CENTER

"I am come that you may have life and have it more abundantly." Christ came to induce and empower man to live fully. The kingdom he preached was the realm of fullness of life. He himself was the perfectly live man. He summoned every man to the same kind of freedom, the same perfection of love: "You must become perfect as your heavenly Father is perfect." He points out in unmistakable terms the salient features of the *individuation process*, describing in detail both the dangers encountered and the means by which man and societies may become whole. The early Christian diagnosis of man makes Freud's comparable attempt seem like a very weak cup of tea indeed. The discoveries of analytical psychology do little else than repeat, in modern phraseology, and with detailed empirical evidence, the principle injunctions of the Christian way.

Above all, Jesus preached the deep center, man's truest self, that something indestructible in the depths that never gives way, the kingdom of heaven within a man. It is the smallest of all seeds which will become the greatest of all herbs, a tree. It is the leaven that works upon and transforms the lump. It is the treasure hidden in a field, the pearl of great price, for which a man gives all. It is the bridegroom who comes when least expected, for whom unremitting watch must be kept. It is the narrow way which few discover, the straight gate by which a man finds his way to God.

St. John of the Cross says in his commentary on the "Spiritual Canticle": "We must remember that the Word, the Son of God, together with the Father and the Holy Spirit, is hidden in essence and in presence, in the inmost being of the soul. The soul therefore that will find Him must go out from all things in will and affection and enter into the profoundest self-recollection." Hence St. Augustine said: "I found Thee not without, O Lord; I sought Thee without in vain, for Thou are within."

The center of the soul is not God, but it is so intimately grounded in God it can and sometimes is mistaken for God himself, as it was by mystic Meister Eckhart. The center is the *created* ground of being grounded in God's *Uncreated* Being and thus opened up into Eternity. This most profound and most sacred depth of the soul is the dwelling place of God. It is in this divine center that we are made in his likeness. Nothing can fill or satisfy this center except God himself. At this center God is more real than man is.

All the mystics discovered the deep center. That centeredness is one thing they have in common: Augustine, Eckhart, Teresa, Julian of Norwich, George Fox, John Wesley, John Woolman. The mystics have called this deep center by many names: the soul, the eye of the soul, the ground of the soul, the ground of being, the heart, and in more modern psychological terms, the organ of man's spiritual consciousness or the transcendental self. William Law, early eighteenth-century English mystic, described it thus: "There is a root or depth in thee from whence all thy faculties come forth as lines from a centre, or as branches from the body of a tree. This depth is called the centre, the fund, or bottom of the soul." We have used any number of these expressions interchangeably. The existence of this deep center is the "pivot of the Christian position," according to Evelyn Underhill:

It is the justification of mysticism, asceticism, the whole machinery of the self-renouncing life. That there is an extreme point at which man's nature touches the Absolute: that his ground, or substance, his true being, is penetrated by the Divine Life which constitutes the underlying reality of things; this is the basis on which the whole mystic claim of possible union with God must rest. [Underhill, 1955]

This deep center is not God, remember, as Underhill stresses, but rather that *point where God touches us.* The deep center expresses itself through emotion, intellect, and will, as we saw in the example of Christ, but it differs from and transcends each. "Heart, Reason, and Will are there in full action," says Underhill, drawing their center "from the deeps of true Being . . . not from the shadow-show of sense" (Underhill, 1955).

The deep center must not be confused with man's superficial self or *empirical ego,* which can respond only to the world of sense impressions and intellectual processes. Man's surface life or surface consciousness is but a scrap compared to the depths of which he is capable. The deep center lies dormant in the ordinary man precisely because he limits his life to his superficial self with its limited sets of perception through cognition and sense. The ordinary humdrum routine of his daily existence leaves his deep center unnoticed, and its resources untapped. This, despite Christ's own admonition tó "seek first the kingdom of God" and everything else will be thrown in free! The whole meaning of Christian asceticism— which is no repudiation of the self or the world but a positive dynamic discipline, meant to achieve fullness of being—is to diminish the pull of the phenomenal world to permit the emergence of this deep center, to still the superficial self in order that it may liberate another more deep-seated power, to bring the deep self out of hiding so that the kingdom of God within us can be made the dominant element around which the Christian personality is arranged. Man's superficial ego must capitulate to the claims of the authentic self. Surrender and not annihilation is the key to the Christian asceticism which necessarily precedes mystical experience.

Two questions arise here. Is the mystic in possession, then, of some new "organ" of perception or cognition that is not ordinarily possessed by ordinary people? The powers latent in every man's deep center have atrophied through lack of exercise and need to be rehoned. Mystical experience, the "peakest" of all human experience, opens up whole new horizons, layers of being, and styles of living. Mystical experience does not produce *new* faculties, then; rather, it enlivens, enlightens, and reactivates already present faculties, however atrophied or latent.

Does the mystic experience altered states of consciousness? Indeed he does. Total conversion or rearrangement of his feeling, thought, and will—his character —about God, who has become the new center of his life, a complete reevaluation of his own being-in-the-world, and rebirth or reform in the Gospel sense are instances of such altered states. Owing to his extraordinarily acute sensitivity, extraordinary states of consciousness such as clairvoyance and extrasensory perception also occur. Perhaps it would be better to speak of "heightened forms of loving awareness" rather than "altered states of consciousness." With a growing concerted effort to cultivate the whole mind, such heightened forms of loving awareness hitherto undreamed of will become eminently possible for a growing number of Christians who seek to be in closer touch with deeper dimensions of reality.

Lastly, man's deep center cannot be *equated* with what is popularly as well as psychologically termed "the subconscious." There is a definite *subliminal aspect* to the deep center, however.

There is every reason to believe that the subliminal (or superconscious?) sphere of the psyche is the seat of mystical experience. These depths of the soul are the special domain of the Divine Presence and Action, since they are the most remote and the most free from the conditions of sense, and so are the least limited by the limitations due to the senses and their material data. Thus the subliminal is the special organ through which the Absolute Being of God, wholly other than and outside of man, nevertheless touches man at the core of his being. It is an experience of a Transubjective Reality. So William James, despite the great stress he lays on the subliminal, distinctly says that "the reference of a phenomenon to a subliminal self need not exclude the notion of the direct presence of the Deity. The notion of a subconscious self ought not . . . to be held to exclude all notion of a higher penetration. If there be higher powers able to impress us, they may get access to us only through the subliminal doors" (James, 1961).

It seems clear that the central depths of the soul with the roots of man's spiritual functions are normally subliminal. Subliminal also, as E. I. Watkin (1920) points out, "is the ordinary supernatural union of the central ego and its radical functions with God through sanctifying grace. The ordinary soul in a state of grace has no direct consciousness of the special union with God thus constituted." The subliminal grace-union becomes conscious through the union-intuition of mystical experience. The essential and indispensable element of mystical union is not the consciousness of God as object of union but the union itself. That is precisely why all saints are mystical saints because they all enjoy the same gift: union with God. The realization of the union, however, is experienced in varying degrees which accounts for degrees of mysticism. This is true for the same reason that different liquids boil at different temperatures.

The mystic's intuition of the Truth and enjoyment of the Good is a gift received through the highest and most refined powers of his soul. The Divine Object cannot be represented by a logically coherent concept or conceptual system, but only, and then vaguely, through paradoxes such as John of the Cross's poetic "silent music" or "sounding solitude," stanza 15 of his poem "Spiritual Canticle."

SUMMARY

The Christian's goal is a transcendent one: union in love with the God of Abraham, Isaac, and Jacob. In this alone lies the ultimate fulfillment of his human personality. Living in a universe polarized by opposites, man cannot attain this "Goddened" Oneness through his sense perception or his intellectual prowess. He becomes one with God and all of creation simultaneously through a direct and firsthand peak human experience: an intuitive act welling up out of his deepest center where God touches him. Called by many names, this ground of being is man's most real self, the "still point" where he is most open to God. The deep self sustains and inspires the whole thinking-feeling man but cannot be identified with God, the empirical ego, or the "subconscious." The Christian attempts to liberate his deep center, to raise it to surface consciousness through his ascetical practice, thereby readying himself for intimate communion with the Deity. And so Christ prayed: "Father, may they be one in us as you are in me and I am in you . . . may they be one as we are one. With me in them and you in me" (John 17:21–23).

ORIGIN AND HISTORY: JESUS CHRIST

CHRIST: THE GOSPELS AND ST. PAUL

In her book *The Mystic Way,* Evelyn Underhill (1913) studies the mysticism of the New Testament. Writing to demonstrate that the Christian mystic has definite qualities which differentiate him from mystics who have evolved along other lines, Oriental, Neoplatonic, and Islamic, she claims that this differentiation is acknowledged by such independent investigators as Professor J. H. Leuba (1929) in his classic study, *The Psychology of Religious Mysticism,* and H. Delacroix (1900) in his *Essai sur le mysticisme,* and she sums up: "All the experiences characteristic of genuine Christian mysticism can be found in the New Testament; and I believe that its emergence as a definite type of spiritual life coincides with the emergence of Christianity itself in the Person of its Founder."

Christian Mysticism sprang from the heart of Christ. That was the gateway through which it emerged into history. In the Gospel we have a record of the words and teachings of Jesus. His characteristic teaching is found in the Synoptics: the Sermon on the Mount, the parables, the instructions to his disciples— all of which consistently stress the inwardness and mysticalness of religion. The record is a matter-of-fact account of ineffable experiences, for example the Baptism of Jesus, the Temptation or Desert Experience, the Transfiguration, and Gethsemane.

The whole monumental achievement of Christian apostolic action in the world

began with a mystical experience (John 1:35–39). A few earthy, untutored fishermen were hanging around the edge of the lake one day when the fascinating figure
of Jesus passed by. They followed him from a distance out of curiosity. He sensed
their presence, turned to them, and spoke: "Whom do you seek?" One of these
chaps, anxious to fill up an embarrassing silence, answered by asking him a
question: "Master, where do you live?" Christ said: "Come and see." They
followed him and they saw and they came to know him firsthand, and became,
of course, his faithful apostles—captivated forever by the divine force "that went
out from him."

The Fourth Gospel has been known always as the "spiritual" Gospel: it contains all the great words of mysticism. Paul, of course, is a master spirit. Though
he tries to write soberly of the profound psychical changes which came to him,
and of the heavenly manifestations he enjoyed, he cannot restrain his pen, and
he communicates something of his own rapture as he attempts to relate what
never can be told: his writings too—especially in relation to the soul, the sacraments, and the Church—are a treasure house of mystical doctrine.

DIONYSIUS AND THE SIXTEENTH CENTURY

Christian Mysticism, as we know it today in terms of a formulated doctrine
or a theology, began with a writer known as Dionysius the Areopagite, probably
of the fifth century. Until then (and afterwards, for instance in St. Augustine, St.
Gregory, and St. Bernard), contemplation is the word used to designate mystical
experience, and I adopt that same use in this chapter.

Christian Mysticism reached its peak at the time of St. Teresa of Avila and St.
John of the Cross in sixteenth-century Spain, when mystical experience turned
back on itself and came to know itself reflexively. This dramatic growth in
mystical awareness served as a mighty stimulant, and consequently there was a
veritable mystical tidal wave throughout Europe. It lasted about a century.

Teresa and John are both Doctors of the Church and psychologists *par excel-
lence* of the spiritual life. St. Teresa was the first to study the various phases of
Christian mystical union; she not only described them but classified them as well,
not in strict categorical divisions but in general, loose, overlapping, rhythmic
movements of spiritual growth. (See *Complete Works of St. Teresa,* translated by
E. Allison Peers, 1946.) At the same time, St. John was an innovator, but in a
narrower field. He analyzed the spiritual life more psychologically, not only
describing in detail the ways in which superficial, empirical ego can distort the
process of spiritual development but recommending concrete methods of preclud-
ing such distortion. "The progress achieved by these two great masters will
explain why later writers always come back to quoting them. . . . Since St. Teresa's
time, descriptive mysticism seems to have made but little progress. Scarcely any

new facts have been discovered," according to R. P. Augustin Poulain, whose *Graces of Interior Prayer* (1911) is probably still the definitive work on Christian Mysticism from an experimental viewpoint. Poulain worked forty years on his study, interrogating at great length numbers of Christian persons whose religious experiences were false as well as genuine. As a "check" on his findings, Poulain relied not merely on the "mystics" of his day, but even more so on the testimonies of the Church's traditional mystics: St. Bernard, Dionysius, as well as Teresa and John of the Cross and others. I personally know of no one who, following Christ, has paved and marked the *Way* into the center more effectively and surely than John of the Cross. We will refer to him later in greater detail. (See *Collected Works of St. John of the Cross,* translated by Kieran Kavanaugh and Otilio Rodriguez, 1973.)

The space of this chapter does not permit a broader outline of the history of Christian Mysticism. For a historical sketch from the beginning of the Christian era to the nineteenth century, consult the appendix to Evelyn Underhill's classic work entitled *Mysticism: A Study in the Nature and Development of Man's Spiritual Consciousness* (1955).

DISTINCT FEATURES OF CHRISTIAN MYSTICISM: PARTICIPATION, NOT TECHNIQUE; EARTHINESS; PRIMACY OF LOVE; ASCESIS: ORDINARY STUFF OF LIFE; CENTRALITY OF THE CROSS

Christian Mysticism is not the result of techniques, devices, and practices but is initiated and brought to fulfillment by contact with and participation in an organism, the Mystical Body of the Church. All genuine mystical experience occurs at the heart of the Church; the Church is to be understood as the community in which the raising of manhood to God-manhood, which we see in Christ, continues. That is why the Church is called the "body of Christ." The Church is the prolongation of Christ in the world of today. All Christian Mysticism is a mystique of Christ, through which man enters into relation with God. In the mystique of Christ, man participates in and reenacts Jesus' death and resurrection through the mediation of the sacraments: baptism and the Eucharist, celebrated in and by the Church. Christian Mysticism is inexplicable and inconceivable apart from its ontological but partly perceptible link with Christ, revelation, dogma, the Church, and the sacraments.

This mystical experience—the mystery of faith erupting at the creative center of the Church—is not the fruit of a direct and systematic effort, but a free gift from God. The desired goal is the perfection of charity and not, as in the case with other mystics, a mysterious means of acquiring transcendental knowledge. But the contemplative's intuition, born of love, is the result of a lively faith, a faith experienced in a particular psychological mode. It is precisely this highly developed faith issuing in love that makes the knowledge of God mystical and experiential.

There are other peculiar features of this mysticism that spring from the Gospels. For one thing, the mystic isn't the slightest bit spooky: for instance, he doesn't look like a zombie, talk in unctuous and banal platitudes, sit in solemn trances, or distinguish himself by weird forms of religiosity. Christian Mysticism is remarkably and refreshingly earthy, human, passionate, and worldly, meaning that it takes the world seriously. It is also wild. The mystic, in fact, is the disciplined wild man, in love with God and God's world. Discipline frees him to love. Love casts out fear and makes a man wild, which does not mean crazy but simply unfettered. He is moved now not by merely human motivations but by a divine mode of action, a divine madness. And as Zorba the Greek said, "every man needs a little madness; otherwise he will never cut the rope and be free," that is, free to love. Without love, self-mastery is a bore, yoga a drag, Zen a joke, and Christian asceticism a waste of time.

Although the Christian mystic may use yoga and Zen as means for achieving the proper dispositions for the loving awareness of God, he is much more adept at being disciplined by the ordinary duties and exigencies of daily life and is thereby readied for God in a much more natural, supple, and unselfconscious way. His prayer is not a discipline but a delight; he goes to prayer not to achieve higher states of consciousness but to savor the real presence of God and to attend to him with love. The Christian mystic, says John of the Cross, "enjoys a certain contact of the soul with the Divinity; and it is God himself who is then felt and tasted," not the self in a state of higher or altered consciousness.

The Christian mystic becomes more and more earthy, human, passionate, and worldly, more of a lover. You cannot love what you do not know; and the mystic knows. Above all, he knows the meaning of death and how to do his own death —not violently but gracefully—so that he can rise with Christ and live fully.

The Christian faces with a positive and joyful attitude the death of both his body and his ego. In every act of ego-reduction he prepares for the final act of death which will usher him into eternal life. In death man becomes capable of his first completely personal act; hence at death man is most disposed to respond to the divine summons, to achieve his vocation, his destiny with the total affirmation of his whole being. At that undivided and undistracted moment man encounters Christ completely and with all his being says "yes" to the sovereign claim of God, that is, to all the exigencies of love. The opportunity occurs not after death when our eternal destiny is already fixed, nor before death in the debilitating state of dying, but *in death*.

In that moment when the soul leaves the body, it awakes suddenly to its pure spirituality and reaches the complete unity of its being. Then man is free to decide —for Christ or against him. Death, then, is birth. All things and roles are shed, and man, liberated in death, stands in his naked essence, his authentic self, before God. No more escapes, no more subterfuges, no more postponements. Pure Reality. Ladislaus Boros describes this:

Here—in death—God has completely overtaken man. By taking death on himself, he has closed up all ways of escape. Man has to go through death. And in death he will meet Christ irrecusably. Here the terrible adventure into which man has thrown himself—the adventure of keeping at a distance from God—comes to its end. Christ is now standing there, before man in death: clearly seen, luminously perceived, he calls man to himself with the gesture of redeeming love. Christ will forever stand there, his love calling and seeking to give itself. If man in death decides against Christ, it makes no difference to Christ's love. But this love will burn him eternally, because he eternally experiences it as utterly close and nevertheless rejects it (and this is hell). But if he decides for Christ, then the same love of Christ becomes for him eternal light and final perfection in infinite happiness, the eternal acceptance of the closeness of our Lord (heaven). Thus the decision in the moment of death is the judgment itself. [Boros, 1966]

But we must not put off eternal life until then. The real Christian embraces death now by mortal blows to the false self, the grasping, craving ego.

Man is sick and neurotic precisely because, although he desperately wants to live, he cannot face life without facing death—and he is unwilling to face it. Instead of suffering life to the point of death he sublimates. He works to palliate his guilt, and it seems like life. It is a sophisticated sublimation that keeps death, and therefore new life, at a distance. He talks about life and analyzes it but doesn't live because he won't face and endure or embrace the kinds of death it takes to come magnificently alive. Frustration results. He works because he is afraid to play—that is, he is afraid to engage in activities that are so pure and intrinsically valuable that they need no extrinsic utilitarian justification. A few Americans play —football, for instance—and the rest of the country analyzes the game with painfully serious and ponderous scrutiny. We are dumb, deadly spectators.

And yet, the German mystic Jakob Böhme says that play is the fullness of life, and God is the God of play, not of work, a God of experience before reflection. Man, made in the image and likeness of God, graced to imitate God, should reflect on experience; but should never let reflection replace experience. Man keeps "cuddling up" to persons, institutions, and vices so he won't have to play. He escapes from death in all his cozy little huddles: in cliques, in crowds, in seminars, in pseudolife sessions, in nice churches, in petrifying prayer groups, in unleisurely schools, in massive religious campaigns and demonstrations and conventions. In all of this, how much has he sublimated the reality of death?

Man even resorts to the gospel message of peace and love to avoid the parlous adventure of life, the shame of the cross, and the challenge of death—the ineluctable fact of death in every genuine I-Thou relationship, in every soulful act of love. The peace and love of the Gospels wait for the courageous, wild man on the other side of death. In other words, once a man is liberated from the debilitating and conflicting demands of the ego, he is free to live.

The only way to life is through the darkness and death lurking in the subliminal depths. Repress it, and another man bites the dust. Better to face death now; let it come when it will but face it now, and live on the spot where you are. "In truth, in very truth I tell you, a grain of wheat remains a solitary grain unless it falls into the ground and dies, but if it dies, it bears a rich harvest" (John 12:24).

THE PATH

OVERALL VIEW

Almost twenty centuries of Christian mystical experience have resulted in a detailed description of the Mystic Way. The Christian's journey along the Path to Divine Union is well marked and divided into clearly defined stages. These phases, as we have commented earlier, are strict categorical divisions only in the abstract, for the sake of better analysis. In the real life of any "mystic" they are far more general, loose, overlapping rhythmic movements of spiritual growth, and the lines separating the stages from one another are nearly imperceptible.

The initial steps along the Mystic Way are more exterior and include an awakening of the self, a practical asceticism, practice of virtue, and a progressive turning to God. The later stages are characteristically more interior.

The Mystic Way is traditionally divided into three phases: purification, illumination, and union. In the first phase the Christian is purged of all self-centeredness; his experience of God is limited to "sporadic flashes." In the illuminative phase the Christian gains a real foothold and enjoys a certain fellowship with God. He is God-centered, but he still experiences God as a seperate entity. In the third phase, the self is utterly transformed into God. The Christian enjoys that full union with the Godhead which is often described as spiritual matrimony or mystical marriage.

Any treatise on the Christian Mystical Tradition will provide additional information about the purgative, illuminative, and unitive phases. For our purpose here we choose to describe the Mystic Way drawing on the remarkable work of E. I. Watkin, whose classic studies of Christian Mysticism are known and appreciated far less than they deserve.

In his *Philosophy of Mysticism,* Watkin (1920) describes twelve major characteristics of the Mystic Way—characteristics which pertain to all (neophyte and proficient alike) who have undertaken the Mystic Way; Watkin uses the words of Christ to elucidate each aspect (pp. 140–141). The parenthetical insertions relate Watkin's characteristics to our previous discussion; the commentary following each of the twelve aspects is my own. I draw heavily here, too, on the mystical poetry of John of the Cross (Kavanaugh and Rodriguez, 1973), for John's poetic descriptions of his personal mystical experience, holding a prominent place in the field of world as well as Spanish literature, perhaps give us greater insight into the Christian Mystical Tradition than any other sources quoted, short of the works of Christ himself.

TWELVE CHARACTERISTICS OF THE MYSTIC WAY

1. Emancipation from limits (of sense perception and intellectual processes).

I ascend to my Father and to your Father, to my God and to your God. I will come again and will receive you to myself that where I am you also may be.

The psyche through its reason and rationally directed will has a natural capacity and even a need for the infinite and unlimited, and consequently an enduring aspiration for God. Dehumanized man is confined within the limits of creatures as the objects of his desire and the conditions of his understanding. Man has lost his wildness, his zest for the All, his great passion for the Holy; and a thousand puny passions have tamed and profaned him. These limits must be, and by the divinizing power of a Goddened man are, transcended. The ordinary life of grace (unconscious union with God) is a gradual sundering of limits. The mystical life (union-intuition) is an emancipation of an enormously higher degree.

2. Conversion from creatures to God.

Every one that hath left house or brethren or sisters or father or mother or lands for my name's sake shall receive a hundredfold and life everlasting. Blessed are the poor in spirit: for theirs is the kingdom of heaven.

Gradually the confining barriers, concepts, and limited aims of the will and inadequate images which separate our life from the infinite Godhead immanent in all creatures are removed and destroyed. God gets all of man's attention, and the world—now diaphanous and crammed with God—is not slighted; nor is it any longer abused by this God-centered man. The mystic sees and presses on. Thus John of the Cross, wounded with love of the Beauty of the Beloved which it traces in created things, and anxious to behold that beauty which is the source of this visible beauty, sings in stanza 6 of his "Spiritual Canticle":

Ah, who has the power to heal me?
Now wholly surrender Yourself!
Do not send me
Any more messengers,
They cannot tell me what I must hear. [p. 713]

3. Introversion (in touch with the deep center where God touches).

When thou shalt pray, having shut the door, pray to thy Father in secret. The kingdom of God is within you.

Since God is progressively manifesting himself in a more intense and intimate way in the central depths of the soul, the individual becomes increasingly held and captivated from within. This is called recollection or the prayer of *loving attention,* which is not an egotistic preoccupation with the self nor a narcissistic fascination with the psyche, but a dwelling with God there present and operative. John of the Cross expresses it in his "Sum of Perfection":

Forgetfulness of creation
Remembrance of the Creator
Attention to what is within
And to be loving the Beloved. [p. 737]

The result of this introversion is that the soul, particularly when most exposed to the divine action—namely, in prayer—finds its peripheral activities, such as the formation of images and distinct concepts, impeded if not wholly inhibited.

4. Detachment from self (superficial self or empirical ego).

If any man will come after me, let him deny himself. For he that will save his life shall lose it, and he that will lose his life for my sake will find it.

Once touched by God, a man ceases to fuss about his little self. He seeks God with all his might and finds self-oblivious delight in doing God's will, which he discerns quite readily because the inflated ego is no longer an abstraction to his seeing things as they really are. Detachment from the superficial may be painful, as John of the Cross describes in stanza 2 of his poetic "Living Flame of Love," but the end result is the ecstatic enjoyment of the touch of God in the deep center, man's truest self:

O sweet cautery
O delightful wound!
O gentle hand! O delicate touch
That tastes of eternal life . . .
In killing You changed death to life. [pp. 717–718]

5. Conversion from matter to spirit (from a world of sense to an intuitive world).

That which is born of the flesh is flesh: and that which is born of the Spirit is spirit. The hour cometh, and now is, when the true adorers shall adore the Father in spirit. God is a spirit, and they that adore him, must adore him in spirit.

The liberating Christian adventure toward the Unlimited Center gradually frees man from the limitations of matter. Not that matter is abandoned. The entire Incarnational and Sacramental system, with its corollary, the resurrection of the body, emphasizes the fallacy of this belief. The life of the liberated spirit does not scorn or scrap matter; it transforms it.

6. *Increase of delicacy or subtlety* (greater sensitivity).

Be ye wise as serpents and simple as doves. Blessed are the eyes that see the things that you see. Think not that I am come to destroy but to fulfill. For I tell you that unless your justice exceed that of the scribes, you shall not enter into the kingdom of heaven.

The humanization of man by the increasing dominance of the Spirit endows the developing person with a marvelous kind of subtlety or delicacy. Such a person, as distinct from a thoughtless and tactless man capable of only small, vapid pleasures and narrow perceptions, is easily and deeply delighted because of his keenly perceptive appreciation of the transparency of things. The vulgar man craves and grabs what he can for his immediate satisfaction. The contemplative admires, discriminatingly chooses, and enjoys. The contemplative gets more pleasure out of one glass of beer than the vulgarian gets out of a tankful. But all the contemplative's small pleasures issue from and redound to his one ruling pleasure—the pleasure of God's company. And so the man of prayer (that's what a contemplative is) sees all the connections that hold the broken world together; and he does so by his apprehension of the spiritual unity underlying the superficial manifold. Without this kind of vision men perish.

So St. John of the Cross prays in the *Living Flame* (stanzas 2, 17):

O delicate touch, thou Word the Son of God, that through the delicacy of the divine Being dost subtly penetrate the substance of my soul and touching it delicately throughout dost absorb it wholly in Thyself in divine ways of delights and sweetness never heard of in Canaan nor seen in Teman. . . . O my God and my life, they only shall see Thee and shall feel Thy subtle touch who have made themselves alien to the world, and have made themselves subtle, for the subtle fits the subtle, and so shall they be able to feel and enjoy Thee. Such as those dost Thou touch with a subtlety proportionate to their condition seeing that the substance of their soul hath now been purged, purified and rendered subtle.

7. *Liberation.*

You shall know the truth and the truth shall make you free. The Spirit breatheth where he will. So is everyone born of the Spirit.

Freedom does not mean doing whatever one wants to do. It means, rather, really wanting to do what one must do to become whole and centered. Watkin (1920) puts it this way:

In its more superficial aspect, liberty is freedom to follow reason unhindered by external violence. In a deeper sense, it is this same freedom to follow reason unhindered by the force of our own lower passions and desires. Bondage to the latter is far worse slavery than slavery to the former, since it confines the inner life of the soul, not merely its external manifestations. Everything, therefore, that enables us to follow reason (including superrational intuition) sets us free, everything that hinders from following reason enslaves.

Watkin is not talking about *isolated* reason. That is another form of tyranny.

Ultimately what prevents liberty of soul is ego enslavement. Therefore, when self-will is destroyed, and God's will is perfectly chosen, the will is entirely free to attain its true good and end, which it has perversely sought from the outset. In the possession of this boundless Good it enjoys perfect freedom. "As mystical will-union through love thus emancipates the will from limited ends, the mystical intuition emancipates the spiritual consciousness in understanding from limited apprehensions" (Watkin, 1920). So St. John of the Cross sings again:

Now I occupy my soul
And all my energy in His service
I no longer tend the herd,
Nor have I any other work
Now that my every act is love. [p. 714]

8. *Unification* (human wholeness).

Martha, Martha, thou art careful and art troubled about many things. But one thing is necessary.

An outstandingly weak feature of man today and always, undoubtedly, is his uncollected dispersion. His life, his focus, his major project of existence, is fragmented. He needs to be pulled together. He needs a single compelling force, a personal gravity, one irresistible attraction, to give him a single-hearted mind and a pure heart. "But it is only in the order of grace and its sovereign manifestation, mystical experience, that this need of unification can attain full satisfaction. For in mystical experience the soul attains a supernatural union with the Absolute Unity of an infinite manifold, from whom all multiplicity proceeds and in whom it is all made one" (Watkin, 1920).

9. Purification.

Blessed are the clean of heart, for they shall see God. Now, you are clean by the reason of the word that I have spoken to you.

Spiritual purity is the energy or life of the psyche unimpeded in its passionate pilgrimage toward the Absolute by the limits that would necessarily accrue to it by attachment to sensible objects. Such attachments would repress this Godward life and energy of the spirit by confining our psychical activities and life within the limits of the sensible and the created. They would disperse that fullness of life by dissipating its energy among a multiplicity of objects.

10. The attainment of peace.

Peace I leave with you, My peace I give unto you. Take my yoke upon you and learn of me, and you shall find rest to your souls.

The peace of the mystic is not born of indifference but of hard-earned harmony with oneself and the universe. It is nothing like vapid quietude or inward torpor. It is a magnetic, mobilizing peace characterized by the wise passiveness of St. John of the Cross: "I abandoned and forgot myself . . . leaving my cares forgotten among the lilies" (p. 712). It is the highest form of action-contemplation: taking a long loving look at the Real, with no fussing or fretting and no utilitarian plans. The peaceful man doesn't just do something; he stands there. He doesn't even take a pole with him when he goes fishing because he has no need to justify doing nothing. Being compels him to do nothing. When God speaks, the soul must do nothing but listen; when he appears, the soul must simply behold; when he gives, the soul must do nothing but receive. Responding to God's initiative in this way distinguishes this positive and gracious quiet from the error of Quietism, the limp passivity of the sluggard often confused with the alert stillness of the spiritual athlete. English mystic Walter Hilton describes the paradoxical activity of such peace: "This restful travail is far from fleshly idleness and from blind security. It is full of ghostly work, but it is called rest . . . an holy idleness and a rest most busy." (Sitwell, 1953).

11. Will identification with the will of God (empirical ego surrender).

I came not to do my own will but the will of him that sent me. Thy will be done on earth as it is in heaven. Not as I will but as Thou wilt.

The mystic is in harmony with all things except sin because all is a product of God's will. He loves everything and everyone and enriches all by his love because he shares the universal and creative charity of God himself. He not only loves what he finds to be lovable but, by God, makes lovable whatever or whomever he decides to love.

As we mentioned earlier in this section, the surrender of the ego is painful, but John of the Cross, staunchest urger of such ego surrender, sings again and again of the love-ecstasy. "I abandoned and forgot myself," he says in the "Dark Night's" eighth stanza, but was graced with the privilege of "laying my face on my Beloved."

12. Progressive attainment of reality.

Not by bread alone man lives. Labor not for the meat that perisheth, but for that which endureth unto life everlasting. I am the bread of life. Give us this day our daily bread.

The Christian mystic neither overestimates nor underestimates creatures. They are real and good and not to be sniffed at. Their intrinsic value and goodness are to be recognized and loved. They are meant and deserved to be prized and reverenced. But compared to God's absolute self-subsisting Being, they are nothing. After "an ecstasy experienced in high contemplation," John wrote: "He who truly arrives there cuts free from himself; all that he knew before now seems worthless" (p. 719). Creatures have their being in God and from him and depend utterly upon his ongoing, processive, and creative act of love. And though they are real they are not all equally real. There is a hierarchy of beingfulness. The closer a creature approaches God, the more being it possesses, because it is less narrowly limited. This is what differentiates matter from spirit. Matter has more limits, therefore less being, less reality.

The mystic way, at least in its Christian form, is a positive penetration of reality even to its ultimate depths, and reception of greater fullness of being, as limits, which are scraps of reality, or isolated fragments of being, are gradually transcended in the ascent to the infinite.

TECHNIQUES AND EXPERIENTIAL EXERCISES

We have attempted to define and describe the Christian mystical experience. We have also given an overall view of the Mystic Way and described something of what "happens" to the mystic en route: emancipation from limits, detachment from self, liberation, and so on. It is time now to become as practical as the mystics themselves, for they are the greatest of all "experimentalists" or "experientialists."

The Christian Mystical Tradition is no mere theory or theology, but an active psychology, a body of practical knowledge with application to our own daily life. The mystics tell us not how they speculated but how they lived; they present themselves to us not as thinkers but as doers; they proclaim a "God known of the heart" rather than a "God guessed at by the brain." The Mystic Way shows the precise psychological processes to which everyone desiring union with the Living God of Abraham, Isaac, and Jacob, the God of our Lord Jesus Christ, must submit.

The Mystic Way is not easy. The serenity achieved by the mystics belies the arduous task and extraordinary effort involved in "arriving there." Many of their favorite symbols are those of battle, search, and suffering. "Let us arm ourselves," says St. Paul, and "let our armor be the Lord Jesus Christ." "Is it strange that the conquest of such a treasure should cost us rather dear?" asks St. Teresa in her *Way of Perfection.* "Why, since You wounded this heart, don't You heal it?" moans John of the Cross. His counsel to be inclined always "not to the easiest, but to the most difficult; not to the most gratifying, but to the less pleasant; not to what means rest for you, but to hard work" (*Ascent of Mt. Carmel* 1, 13, 6) is guaranteed to separate the lukewarm seeker from the enflamed and deadly serious one who is willing "to be nothing" in order "to arrive at being all."

Christianity's mystics assume that the aspirant about to embark on the Mystic Way has reached a certain stage in the development of the Gospel way of life: (1) his spiritual consciousness is awake and alive; he has turned to God wholeheartedly and converted from creatures; (2) he has restructured his personality, arranging his life style, interests, group affiliations, and such around his major project of existence: union with God; (3) he has developed a serious spiritual program of "experiential exercises" which he has adhered to over a long period of time with utmost regularity and generosity of spirit.

If mystical experience is bound to the Gospel way of life "pushed to its ultimate consequences," as we pointed out earlier, which experiential exercises of the mystic's spiritual program apply here in a more refined and deeply developed fashion?

1. Development of full humanness.

Although mystical experience is a free gift of God, and not the fruit of a direct and systematic effort, we can prepare for it indirectly by developing a good decent human being, a pure transparent human instrument. Spinoza emphasized this when he said: "Make the body [the psychophysical organism] capable of doing many things: this will help you to perfect the mind and so come to the intellectual love of God."

By a progressive enlightenment of the mind and enlargement of the heart— greater knowing and loving—the Christian becomes a more fully developed human being and is therefore capable of greater mystical depth. The Mystic Way, then, involves the cultivation of both mind and body.

When a group of sisters discovered St. Teresa of Avila in the kitchen avidly devouring a partridge, the mystic responded to their horror with: "When it's time for prayer—prayer; when it's time for partridge—partridge!" *That* is the sort of healthy humanism that has been too little emphasized in the Christian Mystical Tradition.

2. Prayer.

Prayerful exercise helps the Christian move into his deep center where he can be touched by the Mystery. When the Christian learns to pray he seldom meditates. Meditation is what we do to ready ourselves for prayer. As St. Teresa said: "Prayer is a heart to heart conversation with God, our Father, who we know loves us." By meditation we dispose ourselves for this conversational encounter with the loving Father. We reflect, for instance, on a passage of the Bible, or on an image of Christ or on an event in his life, and are led by this meditation into prayer, that is: *the loving awareness of God.* When this prayer becomes so simplified that we no longer find images, words, and concepts helpful, but a loving though obscure awareness remains, then we have reached one form of contemplation. In contemplative prayer God becomes more active, man becomes more passive. Man thinks less and loves more; he does less but is more. His prayer becomes progressively the prayer of Christ.

As we advance along the Mystic Way we move from meditation to prayer to contemplation: away from words and images and concepts into silent, rapt, loving attention to God. The ultimate criterion of growth in prayerfulness is the simplicity of our prayer. The mystic's prayer is not characterized by petition and thanksgiving for favors received but by adoration: self-oblivious delight in God. "He prays best who doesn't even know he's praying," said St. Anthony the hermit.

Prayer for the mystic is not a discipline but a delight, not a technique but a savoring of the real presence, an attending to him with love. We pray not to acquire transcendental knowledge but because God is there and infinitely attractive, compelling us to dwell with him and delight in him.

Because we are so denatured and dehumanized, however, we must take the proper steps to set the stage for this prayerful relishing of God's presence. The necessary recollection is not easily come by and demands regularity, stubbornness, and time each day set aside specifically. There are many books available on the practice of prayer: *Beginning to Pray* by A. Bloom (1970), *Conversation with Christ* by P. T. Rohrbach (1956), *Let's Start Praying Again* by B. Basset (1972), for example.

A regular program of spiritual reading is also requisite. Spiritual reading cannot be identified with prayer, but it can inspire us, give us food for thought, and lead us into prayer. A careful and discriminating selection of spiritual books is crucial. We haven't time to waste on "junk"; in fact, we haven't even time to waste on the good books but only the very best, such as *Seeds of Contemplation* (Merton, 1949), *The Jesus Myth* (Greely, 1971), *Resistance and Contemplation* (Douglas, 1972), *Principles of Christian Theology* (Macquarrie, 1966), *The Screwtape Letters* (Lewis, 1960), *The Great Divorce* (Lewis, 1946), and *The Chronicles of Narnia* (Lewis, 1971). The New Testament is best of all.

3. Asceticism.

The asceticism of the Mystic Way is far deeper than the simple custody of the senses which occurs at the premystical level of the spiritual life. St. John of the Cross calls this mystical process of detachment the Dark Night of the Soul. "The soul must of necessity—if he would attain to divine union with God—pass through the dark night of mortification of the desires and self-denial in all things." St. John sums up the negative dimension of his doctrine in the following paradoxes. They are of paramount importance:

To reach satisfaction in all
desire its possession in nothing.
To come to possess all
desire the possession of nothing.
To arrive at being all
desire to be nothing.
To come to the knowledge of all
desire the knowledge of nothing.
To come to the pleasure you have not
you must go by a way in which you enjoy not.
To come to the knowledge you have not
you must go by a way in which you know not.
To come to the possession you have not
you must go by a way in which you possess not.
To come to be what you are not
you must go by a way in which you are not.

When you turn toward something
you cease to cast yourself upon the all.
For to go from all to the all
you must deny yourself of all in all.
And when you come to the possession of the all
you must possess it without wanting anything.
Because if you desire to have something in all
your treasure in God is not purely your all.
In this nakedness the spirit finds
its quietude and rest.
For in coveting nothing,
nothing raises it up
and nothing weighs it down,
because it is in the center of its humility.
When it covets something
in this very desire it is wearied. [*Ascent of Mt. Carmel,* 1, 13, 11]

What John condemns is not the enjoyment of created goods, but the adherence of the *will* to those goods, not the use of created images and concepts, but the *resting* of the soul in them. Detachment leads the contemplative into the inner suchness of things. He ultimately enjoys them more not less (the partridge event is a good example of this!); is more in tune with the *real* world, not less. St. Francis of Assisi is an impressive example of such charming kinship with the world of "Brother Sun and Sister Moon."

In the opening chapter of the first book of the *Ascent of Mt. Carmel* St. John analyzes with amazing psychological skill the debilitating effects of desire for creatures *as ends in themselves*. He shows how such desires fatigue, torment, darken, pollute, and enfeeble the soul. "Does it make any difference whether a bird is tied by a thin thread or by a cord? For even if tied by thread, the bird will be prevented from taking off just as surely as if it were tied by cord—that is, it will be impeded from flight as long as it does not break the thread. . . . This is the lot of a man who is attached to something; no matter how much virtue he has he will not reach the freedom of the divine union" *(Ascent of Mt. Carmel, 1, 11, 4).*

Christian Mysticism does not demand the elimination of *desire,* however, as much Eastern Mysticism does, but, rather, the elimination of *conflicting* desires. All our little desires must fit into our major project of existence: our one big desire for God. Van Kaam (1965) describes the process more psychologically:

Very slowly those modes which do not fit into one's project of existence lose their appeal . . . these incompatible modes no longer participate in one's daily self-actualization as fully and continuously as the new compatible modes of life. . . . They are not forcefully ejected from one's existence; neither is their presence denied. They are simply taken for what they are; beautiful, valuable, attractive possibilities of existence which are no longer in harmony with one's new, freely chosen design of being.

As one deepens his spiritual life and comes closer to the center and enjoys God more, the negation of even *spiritual goods* will be required of him. For example, the mystic must remain detached even from the psychophysical phenomena which may accompany his interior mystical experience.

St. John indicates that the Passive Night of Sense is the negative entrance into the Mystic Way. Then follows the Passive Night of the Spirit which introduces the faithful lover of God, the steadfast man of prayer, into the final stages of prayer and the spiritual life: spiritual betrothal and mystical marriage.

John gives three signs for recognizing this night and the entry into the mystical life: (1) we find no pleasure in the things of God, nor any in created things; (2) we remain faithful and persevere despite our lack of enthusiasm in serving God; (3) we are unable to meditate. If this pervasive aridity is not due to lukewarmness or ill health, then it may indeed be indicative of the first stages of mysticism.

On a practical level, we must be ready at this point along the Mystic Way to be stripped of every spiritual as well as sensible consolation by the divine action.

4. Growth in personal perfection of charity.

A practical concern for moral perfection has always been the clear line of demarcation between true Christian Mysticism and its aberrations and counterfeits. Growth in virtue along the Mystic Way takes on *heroic* proportions, particularly in the growth of charity. The mystic is not one who engages in unusual prayer or ascetic practices but a person whose life is ruled by the primacy of charity. Our prayer or ascetic practice is valuable only insofar as it causes, fosters, or preserves charity: love of God first, and then of our neighbor, for the ultimate test of our love of God is its overflowing love of neighbor. A frenzy of activity in the name of brotherly love, however, is often a subtle and respectable escape from the devastating demand of God to "be still and see that I am God." Our own lives must therefore reflect the continuum of a contemplatively active life "for the others" and an actively contemplative life "from the Other."

5. Silence and solitude.

St. Teresa's own life is an example of this delicate balance. In addition to her charitable sharing of the fruit of her mystical experience through an active life as reformer of the Carmelite Order, she also spent a great deal of time in silence and solitude, though not as much as she wished.

Silence is not a negation but a positive absorption. As God becomes more real and active in our lives, he absorbs more and more of our attention all by himself. Since he alone is the Word, we are bound to become more and more silent as we hear him. If "I am no longer seen or found on the common," wrote John of the Cross, I have been guided

To where He waited for me
—Him I knew so well—
In a place where no one else appeared. [*The Dark Night,* stanza 4]

There is a great difference between solitude and isolation. Solitude is not an escapist's withdrawal from the hurly-burly of the world but a way of entering into the deepest possible communion with a consciousness of the solidarity of the human race, the Mystical Body of Christ, and the Communion of Saints.

If we cannot build some measure of silence and solitude into our daily life, a periodic retreat is a must sometime during the year.

6. Spiritual guidance.

The assistance which a guru, a spiritual teacher, or a father can render the mystic is of incomparable measure. Spiritual direction is a must for everyone— even, or rather, especially those in the highest stages of mystical union. St. Teresa not only highly recommended this but consulted a spiritual director throughout her entire life. In fact, her great mystical treatises were written at the request of her spiritual directors. It is important to remain under the direction of the same spiritual leader and not switch when "the going gets rough" and the director will not indulge our every whim and caprice. I must admit, however, that qualified, let alone willing, spiritual directors are rare these days, in the Dark Night of the Church described in our conclusion. But they do exist, if one can ferret them out of their hermitages or find them even in the marketplace.

7. Christ-consciousness.

"Once you get to know Christ, you cannot be cured of him," said François Mauriac. The mystic has been infected by Christ. Christ holds the central place in his life; his entire life revolves around him; all his decisions and plans are made in terms of him. The question "What think ye of Christ?" which Jesus asked Peter at Caesarea Philippi (Matt. 16:13–17), is the central Christian question. The only way to answer is through mystical knowledge: direct and firsthand experience of the Living Christ, which Peter had. And so Christ responded with: "It was not flesh and blood that revealed this to you [that is, your sense impressions and intellectual powers], but my Father in heaven." We must ask ourselves—and answer—the same question.

The mystic is not merely conscious of Christ; he shares intimately in Christ's own consciousness. "We have the mind of Christ," said St. Paul. And again, "I live now, not I, but Christ lives in me."

"All our trouble comes from not keeping our eyes on Christ," said St. Teresa. This is the essence of the Mystic Way: eyes on Christ in the neighbor, in prayer, reading of the New Testament, and the life of Christ in its various contemporary forms, identifying with Christ, imitating Christ, becoming Christ.

8. Summary: Divine action.

We have stressed the fact that mystical experience is a free gift of God and not the result of our own efforts. Not that we fall into the error of quietism and exert no effort at all, however! "We must pray as if all depends on Divine Action," said St. Ignatius, "but labor as if all depended on our own effort." We must develop our full humanity along with a regular program of prayer and ascetic practice (which in higher stages of mystical experience is more an acquiescence to the Divine Action in our life); we must seek and adhere to the counsel of a spiritual guide, allow ourselves copious supplies of silence and solitude, and grow in charity and Christ-consciousness. We must take Christ so seriously that we take all else—including ourselves—light-heartedly. The Mystic Way is also character-ized by good cheer and a sense of humor. "God deliver us from sour-faced saints," prayed the partridge-eating, castanet-playing, and dancing Teresa of Avila!

And all the while the Divine Action will penetrate and erupt out of our deep center when and how it will. This lies beyond the realm of psychology, as we stated in our introduction, but no discussion of the Mystic Way is adequate without at least mentioning the fact that it enters in. "If it does not help much empirically, it helps logically," admits social scientist Pitrim Sorokin: "It fills the hole of the unaccountable force."

DANGERS OF THE PATH

The dangers of the Mystic Way are legion and can be treated only summarily here. Among them are the following:

1. *Delusion.* The deluded man, most often without spiritual director, believes his experience is mystical when it is not. In her *Interior Castle,* St. Teresa tells us how to treat this deluded "mystic": "At times, indeed, very often this may be nothing but a fancy, especially with persons of a lively imagination or who are afflicted with melancholy to any marked extent. I think no attention should be paid to such people when they say they see, hear, or learn anything supernatu-rally" (Peers, 1946, Mansion VI, ch. 3, pars. 2–3).

2. *Hyperintrospection and Self-Consciousness.* The self-conscious man prowls around in the sanctuary of his soul, looking for kicks and trips and trouble instead of taking self-oblivious delight in God. This amounts to "psychidolotry," an attempt at titillation of the psyche rather than enjoyment of the spirit.

3. *Quietism.* The quietist becomes purely and totally passive in contrast to the intelligent action of the *wisely* passive mystic, who responds to the Superactive Vitality within him.

4. *Privation and Pride.* This individualist is so caught up in his own mystical experience that he forgets the larger world of men and events outside of himself. He becomes proud, overestimating his own achievements, forgetting that his mysticism is truly a divine gift.

5. *"Fakirism."* This fake mystic forgets the love which inspires a constructive asceticism and is concerned with a destruction rather than the regulation of his body-person. He falsely believes that he must annihilate a nature which is evil rather than master one which is rebellious. The castration and bodily mutilation of some of the early desert ascetics provide us with examples. No less excusable is the "psychological fakirism" which blunts and dulls the spirit. The fakir performs "strongman" acts of asceticism and knows nothing about an intelligent,

organic, ongoing, gradual, and gracious program of mortification. Just barely surviving the rigors of desert asceticism himself, St. Benedict grounded the monastic movement within Christian Mysticism with the principle that "all things be done in moderation."

6. *Contempt for the World.* The fakir is also guilty of disdain for the world, which he falsely views as a contemptible obstacle. The true mystic, on the other hand, who possesses all in the All, loves the whole of creation. He "perceives the true beauty of things, which appear to him transfigured . . . [and] becomes once more, in a certain fashion, what man [once] was . . . the 'priest of the sensible creation.' " He exults with John of the Cross:

Mine are the hills and the mountains are mine,
Mine are the just and the sinners are mine,
The nations are mine, the people are mine,
The angels are mine, the Mother of God is mine,
And God himself is mine and all for me
Because Christ is mine and all for me.
["Sayings of Light and Love," Prologue to 26, in Kavanaugh & Rodriguez, 1973]

7. *Attraction to Psychophysical Phenomena.* The somatic marvels which accompany mystical experience do not express the essence of mysticism; they are only accidental and secondary and must neither be sought after nor clung to, should they occur.

Both Baron von Hugel in his excellent work *The Mystical Element of Religion* (1908) and E. I. Watkin in *Philosophy of Mysticism,* so often quoted here, make very careful and important studies of this psychophysical aspect of mysticism. The whole question can be handled only briefly here.

In general these phenomena are neither purely subjective nor purely objective. In regard to objective validity and divine causality there are three levels:

a. *Pure subjectivity.* Here there is no divine causality; the phenomena are due to the abnormal psychophysical temperament of the mystics. A few cases could be cited: for instance, the hysterical phenomena of St. Catherine of Genoa's final illness: the yellowing of her skin, her arbitrary and shifting moods, her hyperesthesia. Baron von Hugel's book is a complete study of St. Catherine and her friends.

b. Phenomena due to a *natural effect of a supernatural cause.* Perhaps most visions and locutions (audible messages) belong to this category. John of the Cross admits this explanation himself in the *Living Flame of Love:*

If at any time God permits any external effect of a spiritual wound of love to appear in the bodily senses, the wound is manifested externally after the fashion of the interior wounding. This happened, for example, when the Seraph smote St. Francis. When his soul was wounded by love with the five wounds, after that very fashion was their effect communicated to the body, for the wounds were imprinted also in the body, which itself was wounded, even as they had been imprinted on the soul when wounded by love. It is indeed God's usual way not to bestow any favour on the body that he has not primarily and principally wrought in the soul.

Many cures fit into this category also; as does the concomitant phenomenon—the psychophysical effect—of ecstasy (to be distinguished from the mystical degree of union called ecstasy), which St. John says is nothing but the natural effect of physical weakness and the natural incapacity of the soul's lower functions to endure the special operation of God in the inmost center. "For in the perfect, these raptures and bodily torments cease, and they enjoy freedom of spirit without a detriment to or transport of their senses" (*Dark Night of The Soul*, 2, 1, 2). When a man has purified or harmonized his lower functioning sufficiently, he may still enjoy mystical experience but without the usual psychophysical manifestations.

c. On this level *even the psychophysical form* is not wholly subjective but has been externally *caused by God* or another spiritual being, for example the external vision of Bernadette at Lourdes, although given through the mode of images taken from Bernadette's subconscious.

With regard to all these phenomena, qua external sensible phenomena, they are worthless. Any value they may possess pertains entirely to an underlying spiritual communication made by God or another spiritual being through such phenomenal means. Since it is possible for a person to delude himself or to be acted upon by the devil or even to cling inordinately to a gift of God himself, St. John does not hesitate to urge all who desire union with the Unlimited Godhead to reject both external and internal visions, even when produced supernaturally. On the same principle, one cannot grasp the Unlimited Godhead, by loving faith, if and insofar as he clings to and rests in any essentially limited image, even the gift of tongues, a popular phenomenon today.

8. *Fixation and Fanaticism.* The fanatic forgets the end and multiplies the means. He fixates at one stage of growth and does not move on to greater heights and deeper dimensions. The true mystic, on the other hand, does not rest in legalism, formalism, or ritualism; he does not stop at liberation of the deep center or the awakening of his spiritual consciousness; he does not make silence and solitude, full humanity, prayer or asceticism final ends. As the author of the *Cloud of Unknowing* says in his "Epistle of Discretion": "For silence is not God, nor speaking is not God; fasting is not God nor eating is not God; solitude is not God nor company is not God . . ." (Knowles, 1961).

9. *Presumption.* The presumptuous "mystic" does not fixate on a particular

step like the fanatic does but instead skips them. He is falsely preoccupied with the end without having become sufficiently and suitably disposed through the purgative process.

10. *Psychopathology.* Finally, the mystic, because he remains in continuity with his physical-biological-psychological life, is as susceptible as the rest of us to both ordinary neuroses and full-blown psychoses which cannot be adequately investigated here. Let the example of St. Catherine of Genoa suffice. Most people assume that when one is "spiritually" inclined one somehow automatically transcends all the neurotic traps of life, and this is a dangerous assumption.

The question of the "normality" of the mystics arises. Is the mystic "normal"? Yes, in the sense that he lives and moves and breathes in the same world as we do without grotesque or bizarre behavior. No, in the sense that his vitality and sensitivity, his powers of knowing and loving, his humanness and his "divineness," are abnormally fuller, richer, and deeper than that of the mass of men.

CURRENT ACTIVITY: THE FAILURE OF CHRISTIANITY

We *should* be able to contact the living tradition of Christian Mysticism wherever there are Christians. This is not the case, however, because of the failure of Christianity.

If men who profess the faith are not drawn and captivated by the infinitely attractive Christ, then Christianity has failed.

If men in the Church are not driven by a transcendental hunger and thirst for God, then Christianity has failed.

If even morally upright men do not enjoy God, then Christianity has failed.

If even cold-bloodedly dutiful men have lost their taste and capacity for God, then Christianity has failed.

If God is not real enough to absorb in contemplation even the ecclesiastical leaders of the Church, then Christianity has failed.

If schools, parishes, convents, seminaries, and monasteries throughout our land are not at least half full of mystics—that is, people who know God by experience —then Christianity has failed.

If Christians are not, as a rule, more human, more integrated personalities because of their Christian spirit, then Christianity has failed.

The implication in each one of these instances, is, of course, that Christianity has indeed failed. It has not failed *finally,* in the sense that it is all over, and the battle is lost: but it is failing its mission here and now.

The mission of Christianity is to enable man to see God and to be with God. Christ is the supreme and most complete revelation of religious truth, of love, of the Godhead. He who sees Christ, sees God; who enjoys Him enjoys God; who does His will does the will of His Father.

It is the mission of Christianity to keep the image of Christ alive and bright enough for men to see, to contemplate; and to keep the presence of Christ concrete, strong, and compelling enough for man to desire and achieve vital union.

It is here, precisely, where Christianity has failed. It has, over the centuries, become so completely absorbed in jobs to be done—admittedly vastly important jobs—that it has neglected its mission.

It's so easy to blame the old myths, symbols, and structures, "the institution." But where does the trouble really lie? In our routine, barren experience of Christian truth. If we would really immerse ourselves in the Christian existence and discover ultimate reality—God—with the whole mind, heart, and soul, then this Truth would become our inner truth and be transmuted into terms and symbols which would reach our contemporary fellow men. What is required of Christians is that they develop a completely modern and contemporary consciousness in which their experience as men of our century is integrated in their experience of the fullness and richness of the perennially valid Christian Mystical Tradition.

The Church must grow into the stature of Christ. A growing Church—becoming Christ—will have its dark nights, pain, emptiness. It must be freed of everything except Christ. It must be stripped down and boned up for the Christ-dance, the Christ-fright, the whole Christ-life breaking through all the necessary ritual and conceptual embodiments. Such a Church will not be as tidy or formidable or even as respectable, but it will more readily draw and captivate people into mystical union with Christ. It will not be a big Church providing safety for millions; but will be a live Church creating live men to match its maker: Christ-men.

10   PATTERNS OF WESTERN MAGIC: A PSYCHOLOGICAL APPRECIATION

WILLIAM G. GRAY

WM. G. GRAY as he signs himself, dislikes personal blurbs, believing that literary work should stand or fall by its own intrinsic merits. This balding, heavily built, latter-life man does make some admissions about what he calls the "nonprivate" areas of his lifework.

Born March 25, 2:10 P.M. Harrow, Middlesex, England (Sun Aries, Leo rising, Moon Scorpio), he seems to have spent life since along two main levels: first in attempting to make a modest living as a regular soldier until invalided in World War II after Dunkirk, and mainly as a chiropodist since then; second, but of primary importance to himself, in gaining the needed knowledge and experience for writing his highly original books.

His advantages in this respect came chiefly through descent from a most literary family. A great-uncle of his mother, Professor Lemuel Chester, LL.D., of Columbia University, was one of the very few Americans to be commemorated in Westminster Abbey for services to English literature. Gray's mother, who later became a practicing astrologer, was a youthful associate of the poet Ezra Pound. His father was connected at one time in a business capacity with Katherine Tingley, the Theosophist leader. On his father's side also, the line leads back to Archbishop Walter de Gray, a founder of the famous York Minster.

Gray's life has been mostly a struggle against economic and other difficulties while remaining in dedicated contact with the Inner beliefs and traditions which compromise his whole modus vivendi. He is firmly Western in outlook, and would describe himself as protagonist of the Western Inner Tradition.

In 1970, Gray was British delegate to a semiprivate "Spiritual Symposium" held at Dallas, Texas, under the auspices of the Sangreal Foundation. Gray later conducted a short seminar on Theurgy at the Southern Methodist University, and was awarded an honorary Doctorate of Humanities.

Gray is married to a practicing astrologer. He likes a quiet life, interesting people, countryside rambling, cats, classical or folk music, and handicrafts; dislikes politics or politicians, TV, modern "music," and is saddened by the "Sex-Violence-Drug Culture" of contemporary living. He is far from a puritan (another dislike), but does value what he calls an "honest and upright standard of Life."

His published works on the Western magical tradition are *The Ladder of Lights* (1981), *Magical Ritual Methods* (1980a), *The Tree of Evil* (1984), *Inner Traditions of Magic* (1978), *Seasonal Occult Rituals* (1970), *Office of the Holy Tree of Life* (1970), *Magical Images of the Tree* (1972), *Simple Guide to the Tree of Life* (1973), *Rollright Ritual* (1975a), *The Talking Tree* (1975b), *The Rite of Light* (1975c), *Self-Made by Magic* (1975d), *Outlook on Our Western Inner Way* (1980b), *Western Inner Workings* (1983a), *The Sangreal Sacrament* (1983b), *Concepts of Qabalah* (1984), *Sangreal Ceremonies* (1986), *Sangreal Tarot* (1988a), *Temple Magic* (1988b), *Between Good and Evil* (1989), and *Invoking the Primal Goddess* (1990).

First, it is extremely important to recognize the fundamental difference between those Eastern and Western systems of spiritual development which might be classified as Magical. This is essentially one of Individuation aims and techniques. Briefly, the main Eastern aim is absorption of the Individuality into whatever Ultimate Nil lies behind all Life and Existence. The Western aim is actual achievement of Eternal Identity as a responsible integer living in the Unifying Principle of entire Existence. Thus, Occidentals would identify their beings with the "Energy of Existence" expressed as Eternal Entity, whereas Orientals evidently prefer identifying with the Inertia principle providing passivity for such a Primal Power to operate Itself from. Perhaps one might broadly say that the East favors a "feminine-passive" Life-angle, while the West prefers a "masculine-active" approach to problems of the psyche.

It should also be realized that neither Eastern nor Western systems actually oppose each other, both being complementary extensions of a central spiritual consciousness that will ultimately lead individuated members of Mankind toward the "Light of Truth" explaining the Eternal Enigma we all seek to solve. East and West simply approach the same solutions of spiritual living from alternative angles or "Paths." Nevertheless, it is a fact of Inner Life that those who belong fundamentally to any specific spiritual Path should develop themselves along its particular lines rather than attempt inherently alien Life attitudes. Since there is a definite "Way of the West," it is surely the responsibility of advancing Westerners to find and follow their own Inner Tradition. This means evolving within their natural Ethos.

THE IMPORTANCE OF ETHOS

Inner Traditions consist of inherited patterns of progress toward an instinctive Ultimate. Such patterns amount to our "spiritual genes" or "family Life-faith."

Just as we are born with specific ancestral traits and characteristics which condition our living consciousness, so do we have definite spiritual inherencies stemming from our people's past links with Life. The "Soul of a People," or Ethos, is shared proportionately by every member of that ethnic association. We establish either favorable or unfavorable working associations with these vital "trace elements" of our metaphysical makeup. This means it is best for all to acknowledge their inbuilt ethnical "psychosomes" and live along lines these indicate as aims for future Inner expansions of Identity. Conflicts of consciousness between surface interests and our deepest-seated basic beliefs implanted at Identity levels cause serious psychological damage. So it is just as wise to recognize our ethnic elements as to know our physical blood groupings.

Denying our deepest derivations results in a type of spiritual schizophrenia. Carl Jung had a great deal to say about this in his preface to Wilhelm's *Secret of the Golden Flower* (Wilhelm, 1962). The sum of his remarks comes to a conclusion that each ethnic grouping should support and follow its own Inner Tradition while reaching through this toward a sort of central Collective Consciousness. He put it quite bluntly that we of the West must make our own Inner way, rather than be beguiled by intricacies of Orientalism which have become alien to our present lines of advancement. Jung says finally: "It is sad indeed when the European departs from his own nature and imitates the East or 'affects' it in any way. The possibilities open to him would be so much greater if he would remain true to himself."

The broad spiritual spectrum of the Western Inner Tradition fines down to a number of parallel Paths, linked together on deep levels, yet offering opportunities for every different category of developing consciousness. Since the particular Path we shall consider here is so often called "Magic," we had best define this blanket term to fit present purposes.

DEFINITION OF "MAGIC"

There is much misunderstanding about defining the term "Magic." It means something different for most of its practitioners, and many people still think of it in childish terms like some sort of superior stage conjuring. The roots of this misused word stem from *maj,* meaning great, royal, and similar superlative states of being. Magic is properly "magistery," or *mastery* in the sense of mastering one's own self-state before contemplating control of anything else. Therefore the word "Magic" should stand for the means of attaining the greatest spiritual state of Selfhood reachable by initiated Individuants. As an art, it is consequently both sacred and secret, however much it has been misrepresented through the centuries. Reestablishment of its pristine meaning should be a major concern of Initiates in our modern era.

PSYCHOLOGICAL BACKGROUND OF WESTERN MAGIC

The historical origins and developments of Western Magic have a highly interesting social and psychological background. Because of its essentially individualistic nature, it largely became a secret or semisecret counterculture in which practitioners sought spiritual independence from imposed patterns projected by Temple, Church, State, and other organized establishments of human society in general.

There is a fascinating possibility that motivations behind Magic go back to our most primitive times when sharp distinctions appeared between the two main classes of Mankind dividing into Hunters and Herders. Man first *hunted* for food and essentials. In this practice, Hunters developed intensely individual skills, making great personal progress in all arts of sharpening senses and coordinating consciousness. Hunters became the chief providers for, and saviors of, their close family and tribal associates. A Hunter was virtually the "King center" of his own Magic Circle.

Later on, as the practice of herding arose, the old Hunter-King became increasingly deposed. Working collectively rather than individually, Herders became able to supply the foods and raw materials their contemporary civilization needed. They were probably the first supermarketeers in history. So the role of the Hunter slowly downgraded to that of soldier. His place became that of protector for the Herding Establishment's property against predators. The Hunter naturally resented this usurpation of his place and significance in human society. His individualism had been swamped by collectivism, and he felt frustrated and rejected. In fact he carries this sense of injury subconsciously to this very day.

Intelligent and Initiated human Hunters learned how to translate all their self-skills into Inner fields of action where the Quest became that of their own spiritual attainments, and the Quarry was Individuation into Eternal Entity. By and large, Hunters tended to become Western Magicians, while Herders remained Eastern ones. Looking at the general outlines of our world today, we should see this pattern fairly plainly.

There is a very interesting sidelight on this point in the present popularity of our "St. Christopher" image. Early representations of this Figure are those of the Hunter, with animal-skin cloak and club-staff like Heracles, whose name could stem from roots meaning "Earth-Keys." Christopher, (Christ-bearer) gained his name by carrying the "new" religion, but he himself is the old Hunter-God-Sacred-King Figure of the oldest faith known to Man on this earth. He typifies the fundamental Life-faith of humans for all time, and as such is instinctively revered today. Whenever humans feel their real spiritual roots threatened, they reach for these with every protective device they can find. The roots of our deepest beliefs lie with Magic in its real sense, and not all the intellectual influence in this world will alter our adherence to that ancient Inner anchor.

The modern resurgence of "Christopher" as a symbolic patron of those seeking their ways along Paths seems to be a cry for help from a humanity feeling the very foundations of its Life-faith shaking intolerably. This is a direct appeal not to the Christ-Image now associated with that Church-State establishment which has betrayed so many beliefs, but to the Old Avatar of the Hunter-King who might carry us through the dangers of our crazy civilization with some degree of spiritual safety. Today, Man needs Magic more than ever.

MODERN VALUE OF WESTERN MAGIC

The function of Magic in our times lies largely with fulfillment of an almost desperate need for advancing individuals to maintain a sense of spiritual Identity in the swelling seas of Collectivism threatening to swallow all our souls. If entities are ever to evolve efficiently, they need to become exactly what they ought to be in and *as* the Selves they fundamentally are: not anything they are told to be by others, compelled to seem by circumstances, or otherwise altered to suit anyone else's ideas of Selfhood, except their own *as conceived by the Consciousness of Cosmos working through them.*

Such a spiritual need may be felt as urgently as drowning people need air or starving folks crave food. It is actually our deepest Life-drive, transcending all others associated with purely physical functioning. In Mass-mankind, it is usually dormant like the senses of a fetal child, but once awakened (which was called the "second birth"), this drive becomes more and more dominant and directive of every individualizing instinct and activity.

Some Magical systems claim to awaken this spiritual Self-sense by processes often involving stress techniques and ritual psychodramatics. Be that as it may, the field of genuine Magic in the West does afford unique scope for souls struggling to Individuate in a modern world.

THE REAL INNER TRADITION IS INDEPENDENT OF EARTHLY ORGANIZATIONS

It will probably be most difficult for many to appreciate that the real Inner Way of Western Magic is something quite apart from all Earth-based organizations claiming connections with it. One hears of many different "schools" and systems such as Rosicrucian, Druidic, Hermetic, Templar, Martinist, and all the rest purporting Western ways of Initiation. At best, these are only *agencies* for the Tradition and are neither better nor worse than those operating them. The Tradition itself exists independently of them all, and can be contacted by whosoever has the needed links or "Keys" within himself.

The real home ground of the Western Inner Way is not in this world of material manifestation at all. It is in another level of spiritual consciousness which has to be reached from ordinary "Earthstates" by specific symbolisms or "consciousness converters" available to initiated intelligences at each end of the linkage. Different systems use different types of symbology and agreed arrangements of action to suit definite categories of human awareness seeking solutions to our Eternal Enigma: "What am I and It to each other?" Such variants, however, belong to the same Tradition, so they relate with each other at appropriate angles.

Once we can see our Tradition as something apart from its purely human makers, we must admit that other orders of Life than those are concerned in its construction also. Whatever we choose to call such orders is largely a matter of common convenience. They, however, deal with the spiritual structure of the Tradition on its own Inner ground, so to speak, whereas we in this world are concerned with it in the midst of material Time-Space-Event affairs demanding focal attention on much lower Life-levels. We are therefore likely to get somewhat distorted views of Inner actualities which would appear quite clear when seen from higher spiritual angles.

Providing we remember that whatever organizations we meet with in this world claiming contact with the Western Way can interpret it only along their particular lines, these may serve useful purposes. Yet it is the realization that the Tradition exists in its own right apart from incarnate individuals or combines which makes real spiritual sense of everything.

ELUSIVENESS OF WESTERN INNER WAY

Partly for these last-mentioned reasons, a remarkable characteristic of our Western Magical Tradition is its amazing elusiveness. In the East one finds gurus and expounders of spiritual systems everywhere, and evidence of Inner Traditions all over the place. In the West, things are quite the opposite. The harder one seeks an Inner Magical Tradition the more rapidly it recedes into near-inaccessibility. It is like following someone always disappearing around a corner ahead. What may not be so obvious is that such a withdrawal causes suitably sincere seekers to follow much further Inwardly than they might have done otherwise.

Actually the Western Way is far more mysterious, mystical, and truly Magical than its Eastern equivalent. It has to be sought out with considerable devotion, and its contacts are discovered only after some difficulty. Only those who locate the links leading through all the obstacles deployed before the "Doors of the Western Mysteries" are likely to penetrate those Inner portals. In other words, there is a sort of spiritual aptitude test for selecting worthwhile entrants.

This is why the overall picture of the Tradition is so puzzling until its structure is understood. Externally it presents a scattered and seemingly stupid medley of myth and muddle. Traces of fragmented old faiths, almost forgotten folk customs, and a welter of apparently isolated incidentals make everything look rather a silly and superstitious mess. This is just how it is meant to appear from a world's-eye view. It really offers a complicated yet spiritually soluble IQ problem, which only those who naturally belong inside the Tradition are likely to suspect, let alone solve. For IQ, read Inner Quest.

LINES OF WESTERN INITIATION

In earlier times, initiation into the Western Secret Tradition tended to be hereditary, more or less restricted to definite family frameworks which later widened into associative clans and classes of limited social structure. The "Passing of the Blood" from kingly levels to peasant ones was once enjoined as the sacred duty of a monarch or noble for the sake of his people's spiritual future. By implanting the "sacred seed" in selected virgins, it was believed that blood lines would go on incarnating which could eventually prove the people's ultimate salvation. That is to say, the psychogenetic patterns of human perfection and Individuation would become set up and consolidated by processes of biological breeding.

Later on, this custom was honored as a psychological rather than a physical actuality, although *droit de seigneur* continued for many centuries into its modern attenuated versions. The spiritual side of the Tradition was disseminated by secret or confidential communications handed through families from one generation to another. This always had to be from father to daughter and mother to son, or older generations of one sex to younger people of the other—a sex-polarized transmission of Tradition. Where this proved practical it worked out very well, but human nature being what it is, errors of teaching and other inaccuracies became far from few over the centuries.

With the rise of Church-State control of society, the older Western Tradition associations either had to go underground or else assume Christian disguise. This resulted in a wide division within the Tradition's framework. On one hand, the wealth-accumulating aristocracy commanded the best facilities and commodities, and on the other a poor peasantry possessed but the most elementary wherewithals, but held an inherited and instinctive faith in Nature and the Spirit it stood for. Between these two extreme Pillars of the Western Tradition developed the mysterious "Middle Way" which has become, as it were, a backbone of belief supporting so many seekers right into our present times, even though we may not yet be a completely classless society. We have to remember now how very sharply distinctions and divisions of human society were marked in olden days. It was almost inevitable that magical methodology had its corresponding divisions then.

Among the privileged circles of the Western Way, elaborate and expensive procedures were possible. There were writers, poets, artists, designers, and experts of all kinds to employ in this "spiritual secret service." Musicians arranged sonics, apothecaries compounded drugs and aromatics, while artificers made beautiful symbols and ceremonial accessories. Everything became expensively exclusive and eclectic. In some ways a good deal of progress was made, but in others a lot of touch was lost with Nature, the common Mother of Mankind.

Down at the other end of the Tradition, an illiterate and impoverished peasantry kept up what they could remember of "old times" with a kind of instinct that if they persisted long enough, things would come right for them in the end. As best they could, they contrived symbols and simples of their own from the commonest materials freely available from the countryside. Every flower and leaf had its Inner meaning for them, and they read the book of Nature for themselves in its oldest language that needs no speech for communication.

Against all Church-State ordinances, these simple folk still kept touch with their "Old Ones," now nameless verbally but always identifiable Inwardly. Here and there they met on hilltops or old-time sacred sites, unless the warmth of barns tempted them closer to civilization. It was almost inevitable that their customs coarsened and crudened until accusations of demonism and worse were hurled at them by members of Church-State society. Even so, such rustic rowdyism was true only among some circles of surviving pagan practice. Others went quietly along their own Inner lines, skillfully avoiding open conflict with authority, yet remaining loyal to the Tradition they honestly believed would always be best for them.

Those humble and faithful followers of the "Secret Faith" would have been horrified to hear themselves described as any kind of "witch." In those days, witches were just what the word meant: "workers of wickedness." It is only recent mistranslations and reiterations of error that have given the word "witch" its present ambivalent sense. An Anglo-Saxon dictionary will clear this point entirely. Adherents of the Old Religion had no special name for their religion among themselves, and they believed in nothing like the Christian devil at all. If anything, their beliefs were not unlike those of the American Indians. They certainly never bothered much about what Church people said of God, since they could seek this Spirit for themselves in all Nature around them. Such was their simple code of conscious Individuation.

THE TWO STREAMS OF WESTERN MAGIC

So along such main lines, Western Magic went two ways. It is tempting to call these the Magics of the Poet and Peasant. One was sophisticated, intellectual, artistic, and polished, the other home grown and instinctual. One might say Urban and Rural Magic, perhaps, or that of the Lodge and Land.

It is important to recognize this division of Western Magic into distinct streams, because that explains so much of the whole Tradition. Neither stream was the "one true, etc.," inheritor of the Tradition, and both distorted it in different directions.

There is one point for investigators to bear in mind. The Urbanites were usually literate, whereas Rustics were seldom so. What has been written of Rustic or "folk magic" was not put down by the people who practiced it, but often by "non-Magical" Urbans who wrote what the Rustics told them. This was often deliberately twisted or exaggerated, or else just muddled and misremembered. What country folk told "foreigners" with nice smiles, bright coins, and busy pencils was often very different from what they said to children and grandchildren in ways familiar to the family.

Therefore, whoever looks nowadays for traces of the Western Tradition in literary lines of approach needs great gifts of deduction, appreciation of inferences, not to mention quite real contacts with Inner sources of spiritual awareness, in order to make much of what is available in written shape. Most of what was written got cast into very involved allegories and complicated codes of consciousness. In those days of Church-State dominance, genuine Traditionalists no more dared express their deepest spiritual realizations in writing than a modern Moscovite would dare scrawl "Marx is a Bum" on the walls of the Kremlin. Points like that have to be borne in mind by moderns looking for Magic in old Western literature.

Possibly the best way to treat written relics of Magic from the past is to transcend their literality altogether and use them like "launching pads" for making excursions into Inner Space in search of the Tradition they link with so tortuously. There is more chance of reaching real truth that way than by trying to reconstruct it from mutilated mosaics of meaning scattered sparingly over such a wide field.

EXAMPLES OF THE TWO-STREAM TRADITION

Here are four examples, two good and two bad, from the Urban and Rustic streams of the Western Tradition. We will take the Urban Poetic stream first. The good example is the Grail Mythos. Under a light disguise of Christian symbology, the best aspects of the old Sacred-King sacrificial beliefs were perpetuated. All the elements of initiated circles, disciplined ideals, pure purposes, "in-group" phraseology, and the rest of those old Questings revolving around the Magical meaning of the Mass-Rite are to be found by anyone knowing what to look for.

The "Last Supper Cup," for example, was an euphemism well known to initiated members of the Mystery. The "Grail" was not so much of a "what" as a "who." Whoso "gained the Grail" was the one chosen to die Sacred-King fashion for the sake of salvation among the remainder: a noble death by a noble individual on behalf of his beloved people—a life-giving death, they all believed. Later, this extended to a "life-until-death" offering of a lifetime dedicated to spiritual service in the common cause of God and Man together. As such, this ideal is with us yet.

The bad example of the same stream was Satanism, or anti-God and anti-Man ideas and activities devoted to sheerly malicious destruction of ordered living so as to gratify the worst propensities of human people. It was sometimes called Black Magic. Here again, the system centered on the Mass-Rite perverted to its most horrible potentials. It is easy nowadays to suppose that the Evil Entity concept connected here might be some old Fertility Figure gone wrong, or perhaps vilified by Christian commentators. That could be most misleading. The intention behind Satanism under any name was and still is sheer Evil, and old Fertility Figures were never intended to be evil in any way. Therefore the personification of Evil conceived by Satanists was a product of their own relations with Evil as a Principle, and resemblances to previous God-Images of earlier generations was probably due to subconscious desires for denigrating those ancient deities, in addition to insulting the Christ-concept associated with the Church-State enemy.

At the opposite end of the Tradition, one good example of its "Peasant" part emerged as a "Fairy-faith." This was a hand-down from old animistic sources. Nature-spirits were believed to be involved everywhere with events influencing human affairs. In other words, learning how to make good spiritual relationships with the ordinary things and events of Life would lead more deeply Inward toward Individuation on higher levels right out of this world. The Fairies were the "Little People" or lesser beings of "Spiritland" who pointed out paths to the "Great Ones" behind them who were never to be mentioned except by inference or allusion. There was much more to the Fairy-faith than ever appeared in print, and there are still fascinating blanks to be filled in by whoever interprets the clues correctly.

The bad example of the Peasant end can be classed as witchcraft in the real sense of the word, "the skill of working wickedness." It was deliberate encouragement of Evil through applied spiritual and natural agencies. This included the use of herbal poisons and abortifacients, calling down curses, and what we would now call "psychological warfare" on other humans, such as preying on their fears and weaknesses. In fact the word "witch" stems back to "weak," and there is an implication that witchcraft involves working on people's weaknesses. Rustic witchcraft means an instinctive, inherited, or instructed ability for using the finer forces of Nature against one's fellow creatures for reasons of malice or personal profit. This type of spitefully directed subtle energy always works best within the relatively closed circles of association such as were commonly found among country communities. The wider the area the less effective it becomes as a rule, unless correspondingly larger groups of ill-wishers are involved.

So called "Witches' Sabbats" of medieval times were seldom more than orgiastic assemblies of an oppressed peasantry with undertones of pagan memories. That happens among humans without any witchcraft at all, being simply the worst elements of any community behaving badly, as they always do through all the centuries we have been trying to civilize ourselves.

THE MIDDLE MAGICAL WAY OF THE WEST

Very quietly and steadily, a main stream of "Middle Magic" grew up among the "Men of the West" who were far-sighted enough to consolidate workable ways of consciousness calculated to lift spiritual levels of living toward highest possible human aims. A central theme developed among the various branches of the Tradition in terms comprehensible to initiates from each separate system.

Perhaps the most significant item of this centralizing trend was the formation of what became generally known as Cabalistic philosophy and practice. This is often assumed to be purely of Hebrew origin because that language was largely used in its literary formulas. It actually derives from many spiritual sources, all Westernizing in nature. Its uniqueness lay in compressing the metaphysics of Western Magic into mathematically acceptable spiritual symbology serving as a central Codex from which advances of Inner awareness could be developed during successive generations. It was spiritually what the famous Einstein formula meant physically in later times, though of course it attracted far less publicity.

The word "Cabala" literally means "mouth to ear," or signifies the Secret Tradition which could only be whispered by Initiates directly into the ears of worthy recipients. It also implies transmission of the Tradition through "Inner ears" attuned to purely spiritual sources of instruction—that is to say, a kind of "Master method" or summation of Western Magic into a Key-symbology giving access to the truth behind the Tradition by making direct links with what could only be called Divine Consciousness. While so-called vulgar or mere gold-grasping Alchemists sought chemical formulas for discovering the principles of health (Universal Elixir) and wealth (Philosophers' Stone), initiated inheritors of the Sacred Science sought means of transmuting the earthiest parts of plain human nature into the finest states of being achievable. This was symbolically described sometimes as "making demons subject to God by means of angelic agencies." Unluckily a great deal of misunderstanding arose through wrong interpretation of such metaphors.

MAGIC MISUNDERSTOOD

It was the printing press which brought private Magic into public possession for the sake of profit regardless of authenticity or anything whatever except making money. There can scarcely be a bigger metaphysical muck-heap than most medieval books about Magic. Their badness lies mainly in their motivations, based on the meanest and nastiest aspects of human nature. Cast into contemporary commercial cant, their sales blurbs might have read something like: "Defy Demons and Find Fortunes! Eliminate Your Enemies and Fool Your Friends!" or maybe: "Millions by Magic. Wealth through Wickedness," or perhaps: "Fun with Fiends. Satanic Supersex, Masturbate by Magic!!" or just: "Glorious Grovels and Demonic Delights." One could go on inventing idiotic titles like those for a long time, but that was more or less the literary level of those books. Unhappily, they still sell, and many moderns get their inaccurate ideas of Magic from such stupidity.

Into print for profit went all the ridiculous rubbish and torrid trash that authors and booksellers could compile from available sources, especially including their inventive imaginations. Peppered among this, of course, were quite genuine items of folk faith and odd fragments of interesting information. Possibly the greatest sales promotor of this stuff was its illegality in the eyes of the Church-State enemy hated by more and more of mankind. This seemed like a chance of hitting back at resented authority, and books on Magic sold for big prices as status symbols of defiant daring. Their reputed wickedness made owners feel wonderful. Few feelings stimulate compulsive conventionalists so much as a luxurious sense of sin.

Sad to say, much of that same story applies today. The so-called occult explosion has probably pushed more mental junk into a buyers' market than most of the dangerous drugs causing chemical damage to physical brains. Moreover, if drugs destroy addicts in a few short years, whereas books produce mental effects lasting for centuries, one is tempted to wonder which evil is worse in the long run. Now that almost no publisher will handle material that does not promise computor-calculated sales well above a high profit mark, works of genuine scholarship are bound to be few in relation to the hackwork easily marketable among so much of Mankind.

This is a problem which has to be faced by all who seriously seek evidence of the Western Magical Tradition. Books are becoming very chancy means of making any true contacts with it through literary links. Besides, even if every book on the subject of Magic were read right through, these would only supply *information,* which is not the same as *initiation* into the actual Tradition at all. Everything depends on what will trigger the right reflexes in any entity to initiate a search for its own True Identity. The combines of consciousness needed for this most Magical of operations might arise from many suggestions over a wide reading area. On the other hand, some single symbol could initiate a chain reaction of consciousness leading in exactly the right direction. Sometimes it may take years of muddling around with Magical literary material before even a dull Inner Dawn begins to break. Magical Dawns are much more often leaden than Golden.

BASIC BELIEFS

Because of its essentially individualized character, there are no dogmatic beliefs imposed by any obvious authority in Western Magic. Nevertheless, owing to similar spiritual findings reached by independent Initiates, a convenient body of belief and practice has indeed grown up through the Tradition as a whole. It could, perhaps, be covered in very general terms something like this.

First, a belief in whatever amounts to the Ultimate of Unbeing, Zoic Zero, or Infinity of Inexistence, which has "No Name but NIL" behind all Being. This supreme act of Magic is regarded as emergence of Eternal Entitized Energy from a preprimal state of Perfect Peace Profound.* Something out of Nothing always symbolizes Magic to some degree, even with stage symbolism of a rabbit (a lovable living creature and fertility emblem) out of a hat (Emptiness—Ultimate Unconsciousness). Note the *white* creature from the *black* circular "creation-crater"— Birth of Being and so on.

After the Supreme Spirit of Life is accepted as the One Self in Which or Whom all other selves live, each individual self is considered as an idea conceived by Cosmic Consciousness. This could be simplified in childish terms by saying that we should be as God intended us to be originally. So why are we obviously not? Here, the "Fall" is postulated. The basics of this belief are briefly that Man was not meant to be a biologically bred entity on this Earth at all. This Earth was set up for animal ecology only, and Man, in spiritual shape, was supposed to lead those lesser beings up the Ladder of Life as they evolved into higher states of entity. Once the first "Adamic" specimens of Man had made the fatal mistake of "falling" into materialization and begun breeding as the prototypes of

---

*It is obviously impossible within the limitations of a wide coverage like this to develop very comprehensive and logical definitions. All that can be done is put forward leading ideas which it is hoped will encourage people to start seeking their own definitions along these lines from sources already within themselves.

humanity on Earth, the damage was done. More and more members of Mankind were dragged into incarnation through the gates of sexual intercourse, and humans became an almost alien species of being, having a spiritual entity attached to an animal body. Only a long series of evolving incarnations may breed out animal traits and breed in those more suited for essentially spiritual entities.

Thus, the "Great Work" or Life-aim of Magic is seen to be that of making the right relationships with Divinity and Humanity which will "redeem" our spiritual situation and result in attainment of original Intended Identity so that Cosmos can complete its Plan of Perfection through itself. This implies a belief in the principles of reincarnation, equation of energy,* cooperation of and with other orders of intelligent Life in Inner dimensions of Existence, and individual responsibility for self-salvation in the entire scheme of Corporate Cosmos. That not only means "Know thyself," but also *"Be* thy self."

Many attempts have been made to formulate a "Golden Rule" of Magical living. One such is phrased:

> These words our Ancient Rule fulfill,
> An thou harm none, DO WHAT THOU WILL.

The true meaning of this is the signification of the word "Thou," which is taken to be the Divine Will working in the individual, far above levels of personal wants or desires. However the formula may be expressed, it means the same thing— Individuate. The methodology by which this becomes possible is the only Magic recognized as such by Initiates of the Western Mysteries. Now let us see how the psychology of all this might work out under various suggested headings so that we can get a reasonable picture of the whole subject.

THE FUNCTION OF MAN IN THE UNIVERSE

From a Magical viewpoint, Man is a Microcosmos living in a Macrocosmos, and is himself a Macrocosmos relative to the lesser lives comprising his corpus: a sort of "atom in the Body of God, and God of an atomic body." One lovely old Magical legend says that when Archetypal Man fell to Earth, he broke up into millions of pieces which all became tiny men and women running around after each other. One day, they will discover the secret of coming together as One again, and then all will be happy forever in Heaven.

Magically, Man is seen as a sort of spiritual anomaly. Our proper place was

---

*Equation of energy could also be called "metaphysical metabolism," or balancing and harmonizing all one's Inner forces so that a healthy and workable "whole" results.

supposed to be a kind of Life-link between physical animals and nonincarnating orders of Life much higher up the spiritual spectrum. Since we "fell down on the job," our immediate function is perfection of our species until we evolve enough to Individuate away from Earth altogether. Sooner or later we have to learn living independently of incarnate bodies, and realization of this necessity is part of Magical practice.

Meanwhile, we have to act as agencies on these Life-levels for that Power which intends Perfection everywhere—in a sense, to become "Deputy-Divinities." Our finest function is becoming focal points for that single spiritual Universal Intention.

THE NATURE OF HUMAN CONSCIOUSNESS

Strictly speaking, there is only One Consciousness, that of Creative Cosmos Itself, the Life-Spirit as the Energy of Infinite Awareness. The reflective reaction of this Energy through every category of Creation can be considered as the consciousness of whatever class of created entity it may be. This again subclassifies until individual awareness is indicated in each and every entity.

Thus, human consciousness, per se, covers a fairly broad frequency band. If we accept the Consciousness of Cosmos to extend over the entire spiritual spectrum of what can only be called Divine Omniscience, we must also admit that humans are capable of consciousness through a segment of that spectrum however small in relative terms.

Our consciousness is therefore a limited waveband of the Inner spectrum which links with many Life-categories. We are rather like radios with transmission and reception covering a limited set of frequencies. Few humans bother to explore anything like their available range, let alone attempt to increase or improve it.

Because of our imperfect and unsatisfactory states of being, we are highly unstable and potentially dangerous creatures as "connectors of consciousness" in Cosmos. Conversely, on account of our unique positions in the Life-scheme, we may yet prove invaluable innovations for furthering its fulfillment.

Central control and correctly aligned arrangements of consciousness are considered a very major job of practical Magic. This is one "first on the list" exercise on all authentic training programs, and consciousness is treated as the natural "raw material," out of which a Magical artificer has to make everything he needs —especially his own entity.

Consciousness is undoubtedly the most important energy that humans have to handle. Since so much may go wrong with it or be deliberately misused for malicious reasons, we might say that our entire future as entities depends on our "Cosmic commodity of Consciousness." Genuine Magi respect their art as a means of controlling and directing this most elemental Energy of Existence for the sake of our spiritual safety and prospects of perfection.

PERSONALITY (OR PSEUDOSELF)

Personality is regarded as a fractional and frequently faulty presentation of energies from different Life-levels concentrated into incarnate organisms. It is virtually a buildup of bits obtained from many sources fitted into a fundamental framework integral to the presenting entity. Ideally the personality should disintegrate like a defunct physical body after its useful purpose has been served, and a finer fresh one be built up for future incarnations if these are unavoidable. This is why Western Initiates are so strongly discouraged from trying to remember past lives, or attempting to "bring back the dead" as they were known in personal guise.

Persistence of past personalities is normally a serious spiritual disadvantage to be dealt with very carefully. Personality is an *effect* of Identity, and not the Individuality at all. That is the reason why real Magic and so-called Spiritualism are incompatible. The Magical view is that recall of past personalities after physical death may interfere with the Individuals who should be in process of liberating themselves from these outworn encumbrances. Besides this, a disintegrating personality is a poor proposition to deal with. Much of the unreliable rubbish obtained via so many dubious "spirit-guides" comes from these low levels. Communication with discarnate entities is not denied as a possibility, but it is strongly discouraged as a practice confined to personality levels alone. The experience of centuries is that communication with disintegrating personalities is a waste of time and energy.

Persistence of personality from one incarnation to another eventually builds up a kind of artificial ego or Pseudoself which can cause very serious spiritual trouble if it tries to "set up in business for itself," regardless of best Individuating interests. This is something on the principle of a theatrical role specially created by an actor persisting after the play has ended and making difficulties for its designer. Just as such temporary constructions of consciousness have to be equated out of existence for the sake of mental health, so do our incarnationary personalities have to be dealt with likewise if spiritual health is to be safeguarded. Practical Magic offers many formulas for coping with this problem.

For reference purposes, it is generally taken that we derive our personalized presentations by combination of consciousness from Brain (our animal component), Mind (its metaphysical counterpart), Soul (feelings and emotions), and Spirit (our remotest Inner reality and True Identity). It should not be forgotten also that we have connections with the vegetable and animal kingdoms in us, and may present the best or worst of those Life-levels through our own living. In fact we are "compendiums of consciousness" coming from natural spheres as well as spiritual ones. Constructing worthwhile personalities amenable to Cosmos-control is a valuable project in the Western Magical program for the perfection of people.

EMOTION

Emotion (literally, "outmovement") classes as "Soul" or ability of empathy with Existence in general and specific spiritual qualities in particular. This pushes people between the Life-pillars of Pain and Pleasure up toward the "beatific balance" of Perfect Peace Profound which equates these exactly.

Emotion is the correct complement of Intellect, and those two faculties should always be kept in harness with each other if a straight course is intended along the Path of Life. This is very highly important. Employment of either Intellect or Emotion unilaterally always leads to spiritual trouble, and correct balance of both is regarded as a most vital Magical operation. Treated as a team, the qualities are invaluable and indispensable, but allowed to run wild they can be disastrous.

Unguarded emotions in Magical practice are a very real hazard, and a large proportion of early training is usually devoted to emotion employment and equation, balancing emotions so they can be kept hold of. Theoretically, emotions are used to contact many Inner sources of direct energy supply, and Intellect is applied to direct and dispose the power provided. Magic utilized irresponsibly is a potent producer of emotions, particularly in young people. Unless correct channeling is also available, far more harm than good is likely. Emotion, however, remains a principal provider of those "raw" energies needed especially during early stages of Magical practice. Hence the construction of an adequate "emotion apparatus" is a valuable procedure of primal Magical training.

MOTIVATION

All motivation goes back to a primarary "need to BE," and this diversifies through all Life-levels until there are so many varied needs and drives that they conflict with one another if improperly related in common areas. Our bodies alone have motivations coming from mineral, vegetable, and animal levels which all have to be mutually equated until we can begin living with them to any degree of success at all. Above animal levels, our metaphysical motivations come from every Self-state of spiritual being insisting on survival.

Magically, the only sensible thing to do is make all these motivations subservi-ent to our "One NEED" of Individuation into spiritual Selfhood. Otherwise the constant conflicts going on within our "invisible empires" will exhaust us by attrition if nothing else. Unless a clear line of consciousness connects our manifold motivations and "centers them in," so to speak, relative to a pivotal purpose-point, Life is liable to get very difficult for us. Therefore the establishment and maintenance of such a center line is very much part of Western Magic.

MEMORY

Strictly speaking, "memory" is intentional conscious contact with "stored" life experiences or information either in one's own brain cells or any other available supply. Theoretically we inherit all "memories" of every ancestor with our genes. Theoretically also one should be able to project these forward along Inner levels. The issue at stake is how from our "here-now" we might influence the course of such deep consciousness to our ultimate spiritual advantage. Through our genes, we should be able to remember all our ancestry and contact the Inner epitomization of their Life-experiences. By spiritual equivalents, we may "link in" with pre- and post-incarnationary processes not as pictorial representations, but as pure awareness translatable in symbolic or other terms.

One of the chief reasons why old-time Initiates attached so much importance to genealogical tables with all the "begats" was because when ritually recited these had an effect of extending an Identity-sense past personality levels into more spiritual spheres. So did poetic identifications with imagery such as: "I was a hart in the forest and the tree in which its horns were caught. I was a cloud in the lonely sky, and the shadow it cast on the cornfield beneath." Magical memory has to work in much wider fields than mere brain memories.

Equally important to memory is the faculty of clearing consciousness so as to remove from any Selfstore whatever might have harmful effects on future progress.

Manipulations of memory in order to improve Individuation are part of Magical practice. A great aim also in Magic is to transcend purely personal memories altogether and gain access to Cosmic memory banks. Mild examples of this may be found with what was once called "psychometry," or an ability for reading metaphysical "memory impressions" associated with inanimate objects, especially stones. The use of ESP can allow one person to read the memories of another. Once memories limited to a single physical brain are exceeded by Magical means, a very wide field of discovery awaits awakeners in Inner dimensions of living.

LEARNING

Learning is regarded as an ability of life-appreciation at all levels. To be useful in any degree it has to be backed by memory and spearheaded by interest. It is far more than feeding information into computer banks of consciousness and recalling this to order. True learning involves a faculty of some identification with what is learned. This means absorption of subject into Self, analogically to Self-absorption into an Ultimate Awareness. It is a vital part of the perfection process.

Magic postulates that humans increase learning by Inner contacts with superior sources of intelligence on higher Life-levels, not necessarily by specific conscious instruction, but mainly through opening out areas of awareness in line with human intentions of advancement. In other words, the knowledge already exists in different dimensions of living, and we simply catch up with it in ours —if we can.

Learning is the Inner equivalent of eating and drinking. Our bodies must feed or die, and our Selves must learn or cease living. Magic treats learning as "Inner alimentation," necessitating correct choice and diet. It is considered very important that learning should call for equal and more care than physical feeding. Just as food metabolizes in our bodies and builds them into whatever they are, so does what we learn metabolize in our minds and souls, making us Inwardly into the Self-states we assume. The related functions are very parallel indeed, and Magic makes much of this both symbolically and practically.

Magic especially recognizes the extreme importance of continuing with learning all through Life. Refusal to learn amounts to spiritual starvation, and mental malnutrition can be a severe complaint indeed. Most of all, Magic specializes in learning not so much from externals of any kind, but by looking inside one's own Self. Many Magical formulas are designed for that very purpose. They all amount to much the same message, which could perhaps be translated as something like: "You don't have to depend on somebody telling you or seeing it in a book. Go inside yourself and dig out what you need from there. That will also lead you to whatever externals are related which you may need."

MIND-BODY RELATIONSHIP

Here, the Magical view is that Body with its brain constitutes an animal in its own right, deserving the care and attention as a creature for which its attached Individuant is responsible to a common Creative Consciousness. The ideal should be to establish a relationship of friendly confidence between each end of the partnership. Mutual recognition of each other's faculties, functions, and potentialities is essential for a good working agreement between Mind and Body. Magic aims to inculcate such an awareness and develop it with advantages for both ends of entity.

In Magic, it is very necessary to realize that bodies are temporary focal accommodators of Mind in these material dimensions of Life. As a creature, the body has an instinctive awareness of its own. At physical death this either breaks up altogether and reverts to origins, or it may be absorbed into and integrate with surviving spiritual principles which it served faithfully during incarnation. This is how immortality works: the awareness of an entity withdrawing its focal projections from one Life-level into the wider field behind it. That in turn is focal in relation to levels behind it again, and so on until Ultimation.

Man has to learn how to live apart from embodiment, yet in close friendship with physical associations. That is one great value of fellowship with other animal dependents. This should teach us how to appreciate our bodies and what they mean for us. It ought also to remind us that the body can be a dangerous animal if ill-treated or not properly dealt with. Once good relationships can be established between the body and mind of an Individuant, Life becomes better for both, and many Magical methods are concerned with creating such a happy condition.

DEATH

With regard to this event of universal concern, the broad teachings of the Path of Magic are possibly the simplest of all. Fundamentally we are entities of pure energy temporarily inhabiting animal-type bodies in the biological range of existence which have very limited lives. Those bodies die, decompose, and are elementally recycled through natural channels. Assuming our entities have not evolved to a point of living entirely apart from physical projection, then we generally reincarnate to continue the course of our spiritual development. In ancient times, Celts believed this so strongly that instances were noted of some who actually lent money to friends for repayment in some future incarnation as cash or favors—possibly a graceful way of covering what was intended as a pure gift, but in any case indicative of faith extending beyond bodily bounds.

Ultimate immortality, however, is not considered automatic, but depends entirely on individual intentions and actions spread over a wide spiritual spectrum. In every being exists the "Original Intention" of the Supreme Life Spirit indicating the cosmic condition of such a being if it ever became "Perfect." That is to say that there is a Divine Intention of Ultimate Perfection behind all "Being" as a "Whole," and each individual item of that Whole has its own degree thereof integral to itself, what used to be called "the Will of God within oneself." That, and that alone, leads us through Life toward true Immortality by a process of Individuation.

As mortal humans in our present imperfect life state we have two mainstream options. We may follow the "Perfection-pattern" imprinted in our spiritual genetics and individuate toward our own Ultimate state of spiritual Entity in "PERFECT PEACE PROFOUND." Conversely, we may try breaking away from this pattern and setting up apparently on our own in a state of "pseudoself," which steadily separates from "Universal Life" until its eventual extinction as entity and reabsorption into the Life-cycle as raw energy. Put in crude old-fashioned metaphor, we either "Live with God or die with the Devil." Both processes take a very long time indeed in human terms, but they go on continually in the Cosmos. We are normally instinctively rather than consciously aware of this, but as we evolve we become more and more conscious of it, and increasingly able to influence its course volitionally. In fact a major aim of initiation on this Path is to train and develop this faculty advantageously.

During earthlife we build up a sort of artificial, personal pseudoself which should die a natural death subsequently to our bodies. Theoretically, our imperfect self states should become "absorbed back" into successively higher levels of Life until Ultimate Entity is reached. Failure to perfect this in practice leads to reincarnation or reprojection into higher than human biological conditions of consciousness. We simply become as and what we make of our own beings. To that extent, both "Heavens" and "Hells" as states of awareness have indeed reality for all sharing experiences of consciousness to any degree of those conditions. Both are purely self states, and no one gets us into or out of either except ourselves, however long it may take us to realize this and live accordingly.

Therefore the word "death" on this particular Path is purely a relative one signifying cessation of function along any specific line of living and redeployment of energy otherwise. Everything depends for us on our sense of identification. The more we "identify" purely with our physical bodies, then the more spiritually traumatic their deaths will be to us, unless a merciful unconsciousness supervenes, and "Inner reawakening" becomes a very gradual process. The more we learn to identify with our spiritual structure, the less losing our bodies will bother us. It should be noted that neither "Heavens" nor "Hells" are regarded as any kind of ultimate condition for advancing Individuals, but purely as "temporary accommodations," so to speak, for souls in such states of relation with the Spirit of Life.

"Death" in any sense of ultimate finality can be considered only as an eventual total loss of individual identity, which is normally determined by the entity concerned of its own accord. The pros and cons of this are quite beyond discussion within limits imposed here. The main issue is that the death of a physical body should be regarded as one incident in a very long chain of conscious life, whereas the death of an individual soul is to be deplored as a loss to Life as a Whole which cannot be replaced by any means so readily. A truly dead individual is a contradiction in terms, for the genuinely dead are altogether nonexistent. An individual apart from a physical body is *alive,* whatever state of being that entity may exist in. It is very important to realize this distinction between Life and death in relation to ourselves as principles of being and nonbeing.

It can scarcely be overstressed that this concept of Life-continuity through all levels of Cosmic Creation is virtually central to this Tradition. Unless our lives are realized to reach very far beyond the limits and death of one biological body, nothing else of the Tradition has the slightest meaning whatsoever. Furthermore, no amount of external teaching, offered opinions, or even spectacular demonstrations can really bring about such a realization for anyone. That is something we all have to reach for ourselves within ourselves entirely, by means of the relations we make with Life itself. All that this or any other Tradition can do to help is to provide integrals for people to build their own beliefs and experiences with. The Tradition does indeed appear to fulfill exactly that function for its mortal followers who have made themselves vital to its spiritual structure.

PSYCHOPATHOLOGY

Magically, psychopathology can be seen only as faulty relationships among the Body-Mind-Soul-Spirit combination comprising a human entity. Causes and remedies are quite beyond this basic introduction. States of Inner unbalance cannot be fairly described as "abnormal" in the sense that mass-average humans must necessarily be the norm. The only "Norm" (so far as this exists) recognized by Magical Initiates is the most direct degree of relationship between the center lines of Body-Mind-Soul-Spirit stages of both individual and collective Mankind.

Since this varies so greatly, it could be possible for a mass of "abnormals" to consider a few "normals" among them as quite crazy. Magic has no interest in enforcing a rubber-stamp artificial "abnormal-normality" upon anyone. Its chief concern is with establishing conditions of balanced relationships among integers of individuals and their collective Cosmic circles.

PERCEPTION

As an animal body and brain perceives by its sensory organs, so does our spiritual sensorium make relationships with environing and internal energies by equivalent Inner sensors. Again, as with physical sense organs which we must train to function well in our external world, these Inner "estimators" take a good deal of training and practice for accurate working and coordination. Many exercises are devoted to that purpose.

This is one reason why Magic makes use of symbology so very widely. It is about the most reliable "converter of consciousness" into terms relevant at all Life-levels. Moreover, it enables perception to be directed and controlled. Literally, perception means "by taking in," and signifies an admission of anything to at least "outer courts" of consciousness for examination. That would be the Magical definition of perception: a sort of preentry consideration of anything prior to acceptance or rejection of its significance.

In old Magical workings, this was symbolized by an external circle traced around the inner area into which "spirits" could be called for examination as to suitability for whatever purpose motivated the whole operation—a sort of preliminary interview as it were. If wanted, these "spirits" could be directed accordingly, and if not, dismissed forthwith. Making up an actual Inner "perception perimeter" around Individuants is part of Magical psychological practice.

SOCIAL RELATIONSHIPS

Magical Initiates are seldom noted as great seekers of human society for its own sake. Nor are they antisocial by nature. The general pattern is that of Individuation out of Mass-Mankind, and pioneering Paths for others to follow in their own ways if they will.

As a rule, Magical practice often begins with Lodges, Temples, Groups, and so forth, but eventually Initiates must progress on their own Inner Paths as these open up within themselves. Therefore very few really close contacts on ordinary levels are normally made. Initiates are not advised to intrude themselves into incompatible company, or court any kind of publicity whatever in connection with their Inner activities. In fact any television, radio, or press appearance by people claiming some special spiritual status or authority should be very highly suspect at once by those knowing what appertains to authenticity in these affairs. True Initiates do not advertise themselves as such in any way whatever, or even imply by hints or other means that they are at all different from other humans. It is strictly forbidden to do anything like this under commonly accepted ethical codes of conduct.

There is no actual injunction against Initiates making any social relationships they please with other people, *providing* these do not interfere with processes of Individuation. Most Initiates follow personal patterns of involvement with others up to a point, then withdraw quietly from social contacts periodically and switch over to spiritual ones for a while, something on the lines of a "retreat." Some organize this rather rigidly by daily, weekly, monthly, quarterly, and annual schedules, while others just "take a breather" at need. All would acknowledge that it is only their Inner periods of spiritual contacts which enable them to live and work in this world with sanity and stability.

Sooner or later, Initiates of every spiritual system are forced to face the fact that they cannot possibly fulfill all their needs from or with other humans only.

Human associations will take them so far and no further. To pass that point, they have to seek companionship from other Life-levels, and nothing else will answer their spiritual purposes and problems.

COGNITIVE PROCESSES

A major Magical method here is Inner imagery with creative consciousness controlled by intention—that is to say, treating consciousness as the basic material of an art, and making what is willed with it. Symbols have been described as the tools or implements of this "trade."

That is why Masonry, for instance, relates with symbolic tools of the building trade. The significance is to work with consciousness comparable to that of any skilled craftsman dealing with whatever materials and processes are appropriate for specific purposes. There is also an implication that if as much training, application, discipline, and other essentials were put into Magical practice as there must be for normal employments, Magic would become a much more practical proposition.

NEW FACULTIES

Properly speaking, humans do not so much gain any new faculties as develop inherent Inner potentials. We have only one real faculty, that of being. All whats, whys, and hows are extensions of this. As individuals progress along their Paths, cognition centers tend to rise, as it were, from physical to spiritual status. So our sense of values alters accordingly. As insight increases, knowledge is acquired by "whole understandings" rather than through serialized efforts.

ALTERED STATES OF CONSCIOUSNESS

There are only two ways of altering states of consciousness: from Within by intention and ability, or from without by intrusions and impositions. A main aim of Magic is to so cultivate the first method that it controls or equates effects of the second. This allows the "Central Consciousness" coming from True-Self level of Spirit to function more fully in such an altered area. That in turn should result in fractional changes of human awareness toward more perfect states of Life.

Therefore, in the higher echelons of the Western Magical Tradition, employment of chemical hallucinogens, hypnosis, and the like is strictly prohibited for altering states of consciousness. It is considered essential that the individual always be in command of the consciousness involved with any spiritual situation. That is why all exercises, customs, practices, and so forth are deliberately geared toward training Individuants to alter consciousness for themselves. Artificial aids are regarded as secondary and subservient to the will-work concerned with such changes.

THE PATH ITSELF

The authentic Western Way of Magic usually follows a general pattern. Applicants or candidates with interests awakened deeply enough to reach real Inner sources of guidance are normally dealt with something like this: From some established circle of consciousness operative in the Tradition, individuals are supplied with basic symbologies of spiritual significance, informed of disciplines and procedures for combining these into relevant structures, put into contact with Inner agencies of intelligence, then allowed to grow their own ways within that force-framework.

All this is not necessarily carried out in any physical Lodge, Temple, or anything of that nature. That is actually somewhat rare. A noticeable difference between Eastern and Western Traditions is an apparent absence of "Teachers," gurus, or whatever in the latter. This is especially so nowadays, when all initial information is lying around awaiting *discriminating* attention from interested Individuants. Formerly the various "primal points" could be imparted only orally in carefully closed circles of incarnate Initiates, or else learned instinctively from Inner sources. That often took a whole incarnation to absorb. Now, the symbology and instructions can be put into plain print or other very ordinary ways —except, of course, for private and confidential matters applying only within circles entitled to regard these as purely "family affairs." It must be fully realized that the onus is squarely placed on the spiritual shoulders of would-be Western Traditionalists to pick up its threads for themselves from the available keys placed before them, and follow these inside themselves until they encounter the experiences they seek on Inner Life-levels.

STARTING POINT

There is no starting point except one's own emergence into Existence as an entity. On ordinary levels of Life here on Earth, however, there does come a point of reaching realization right into incarnate awareness that one truly belongs to the Western Magical Tradition. This might be regarded as the starting point of each incarnation, where anyone picks up links which lead back to a sense of *belonging*—as, for example, one feels states of age, sex, nationality, or other distinctive status. Usually this happens via some symbolic impact which makes contact between ordinary consciousness and deep-down recognition of spiritual realities. A word, a place, an object perhaps, almost any symbol is likely to act as a key. Once this occurs, there will come a positive Inner certainty that an affinity exists with the Western Magical Tradition. There will be an unmistakable sense of "This is ME." The rest will follow quite naturally.

This may or may not be encouraged or enhanced by efficient ritual psychodramatics, assuming that competent practitioners of this art can be found. Nevertheless such is not entirely necessary for initiating anyone associating with the Western Way. It is an odd fact that so many inexperienced people who are at the stage of being "attracted to the Occult" have an almost pathetic belief or expectation that if only some marvelous Master or "Teacher-Figure" would consent to put them through an impressive form of ceremony, they would forthwith become altered and amazing persons, full of wisdom and other remarkable qualities. So much nonsense is supposed of initiation ceremonies by those knowing nothing of them that they have only themselves to blame for anything going wrong. Perhaps it may be as well to deal with this issue here.

Any real initiation ceremony is exactly what the phrase means, a ceremonious beginning of something, in this case, the commencement of specific spiritual courses of conduct. Such affairs can have a marked psychological effect upon subjects, *providing* adequate preparation has already created a condition of readiness for effects to take place. Not otherwise. All that any ceremony does is to act as a symbol linking very deep spiritual Self-states with ordinary conscious levels, so that the candidate may realize his own Inner potentials and is therefore likely to live accordingly. Unless such a prestate is already operative, no ritual initiation will be of the slightest use whatever. In any case, it is perfectly possible to arrive at an Inner awakening quite naturally of one's own accord. One mildly witty description of the difference between this and a ceremonial initiation is that the latter is like a friend waking one up with a cup of tea, and the former is like waking up by oneself and putting a kettle on. Either way, one still wakes up.

So whoever bewails his misfortune in never meeting great Masters and mighty Secret Orders willing to initiate him into the Mysteries of Magic merely reveals total ignorance of actualities. In point of fact, putting unprepared and inadequate people through inaccurate and badly presented initiation ceremonies has probably done more harm in occult circles than many less serious follies. A whole thesis could well be written on that one point alone.

INTELLECTUAL APPRECIATION OF PATH

This is mainly a matter of reading available material, making contacts with the oral Tradition where possible, and forming opinions out of collected items of consciousness. A very great deal of time, money, and effort can be spent on this pastime quite pointlessly apart from intellectual entertainment. Many people spend lifetimes at it and little else. They "shop around" from one system to another exploring something of each and gaining personal proficiency in none. It is always best to adopt some single system in particular and work with that until one is able to transcend it into auto-operative Inner areas.

The major system emerging as most suitable for present Western spiritual development in the Magical Tradition seems definitely that which is based on the Tree of Life and Circle-Cross symbology. From these fundamantals, any branch of the Western Inner Way may be entered and its Magic operated. The Tree of Life has mainly intellectual appeal, and the Circle-Cross has emotional attractions. A combination of both is thus ideal for a framework of Western Magical workings.

EMOTIONAL APPRECIATION OF PATH

The Western Magical Way is superlative in ritual and psychodramatic operations involving the deepest emotional levels of Life. Ritual is probably the most perfect tool which the Tradition has forged to suit all spiritual needs. Whether the simplest or most sumptuous type of rite, the West has brought ritualism to a high point of perfection.

Ritual is an activity and participatory practice in which all concerned can combine for a common cause. It might be described as a concert of consciousness through symbolic instrumentation. As an organ of occult energy operative between human and associated entities, ritual is Man's oldest and maybe most trustworthy Magical ally. Ideally, each ritualist should be capable of constructing individual rites from basic principles. Great spiritual satisfaction is possible, however, by working existent rites of reliable form, where these are obtainable.*

Successful management of ritual procedures is a highly skilled art demanding considerable practice and patient training. To suppose anyone could merely say some words, make vague gestures, and Magic happens would be utterly absurd, to put it very mildly. Unless external symbology can be used to raise and release actual associated Inner energies, no ritual will prove any more effective than amateur theatrical exercises.

---

*Given the large amount of readily available material on Magic, the aspirant must develop a great deal of discrimination. Ideally, ritual formulas evolve out of people themselves by their own efforts, and it is the basic principles of this which are important. Rites which work for some will not work for others. Some of the basics are given in my published works (Gray, 1968; 1969; 1970a; 1970b; 1971; 1972; 1973a; 1973b; 1974), but there is a vast amount of research and condensation to do in this area. As a rule, reputable occult groupings tend to adopt generalized basic rites and encourage initiates to develop their own workings out of these which, as one might expect, again tend to produce parallel patterns. The operative requirement here is realizing what to select and what to reject.

DANGERS OF THE PATH

There are many dangers on all Paths of Life, and the Western Magical Way is no exception. The worst danger is definitely *imbalance* in every imaginable direction. For this reason, most of the early advised exercises are concerned with poise, stability, and rapid recovery of Inner equilibrium. Then, exaggerations of character deficiencies are to be expected. It is a fact that frequently after initiation ceremonies there are sudden "flare-ups" of outrageous behavior in the subject, analogous to inoculation reactions. Also symptoms of paranoia may develop. All these possibilities arise from spiritual structural weaknesses existing already in the people concerned. What Magic does is apply Inner stresses which will naturally show up flaws lying dormant in the individuals themselves. In fairness it must also be said that Magic may also be used to remedy those very failings.

Overenthusiasm and overconfidence are very common dangers. Again and again, adherence to a "Middle Path" has to be emphasized and practiced until this becomes second nature. A chief hazard especially of the Magical Path is breakdown of mental and physical health if safeguards are ignored. Diseases are nonetheless real because of psychosomatic origins. Most of these troubles arise through misuse of Magic applied to mind or body, and are traceable to wrong intentions, disregard of calculable risks, carelessness, or just lack of common sense. Genuine accidents can occur as with everything else, but the majority of ills through Magic are invited ones. For example, those who poison themselves with chemical drug compounds and exhaust their physical energies while contorting their consciousness into painfully unnatural knots can scarcely complain when the account for all this has to be paid. Their mistreatment of Magic deserves small sympathy. Magic makes its own retribution on misusers.

It is also true with Magic that there are dangers arising from misinterpretation of intelligence gained from Inner sources, or acceptance of influences from antihuman entities. These latter were once called "temptations of the devil." By whatever name they are termed, they amount to pressures and persuasions contrary to our best spiritual interests. These affect humans in general, of course, but more especially those who have awakened Inner susceptibilities by Magic or similar means, yet have neglected to take even commonsense precautions against ill usage. This leaves them extremely vulnerable in sensitive Inner areas without adequate protection.

The upshot of this results very often in troubles coming from sheer gullibility, deceived Inner senses, and plain credulity due to inaccurate Self-estimates. Human beings enjoy flattery and Pseudo-Self aggrandisement. They like supposing they have been singled out for special spiritual messages, and are delighted to discover an awakened ability to make contact with other than human types of consciousness. This makes them liable to any kind of confidence trick or subtle manipulation they may meet with from immediate Inner quarters which are not necessarily in favor of human progress. In other words, they become common or garden-variety suckers—unless and until they learn better by sad experience. It is almost amazing how those who are too clever to be cheated by fellow mortals fall for the same hoary take-ins when these are slid over the edges of Inner dimensions in their directions.

Most of the "awful warnings" about dangers of Magic are uttered by non-Magical observers unable to distinguish between carts and horses. It is not so much that Magic is of great spiritual danger, but that spiritually dangerous people are so liable to suppose that Magic might be a wonderful weapon for their worst intentions. So many stupid, wicked, irresponsible, and other inadequate people are attracted to Magic for the wrong reasons that it is scarcely surprising that their mismanagement of it is apt to make a very bad impression upon un-Magically minded people. Nevertheless it should definitely be seen that such misfits are fundamentally bad to begin with, and Magic is simply their means of making themselves worse. They could have done as much by other means such as religion, politics, or anything else. Another thing we must remember is that the worst examples of Magic gone wrong get all the publicity, while spiritual successes normally remain secret in this world. There are no dangers in Magic that do not already exist in its practitioners.

The most sensible safeguard against misuse of Magic is adoption of and abidance by some clear spiritual standard of values against which all may be measured while decisions on energy applications are being made. Setting up and making real relationships with such a standard is a "first and foremost" in authentic circles of Western Magic. Probably the best-recognized and most practical of these standards is that of the Tree of Life.

TECHNIQUES OF PATH

Most of these are described in every book of mental and spiritual exercises. The essential elements are: understanding of requirements, dedicated discipline, and regularity of practice. Rituals combining physical, mental, and spiritual activities are normally in general usage. There should be no "dead letters" in Western ritualism, but only living experiences within a controlled framework of consciousness. Every system within the Tradition has whole collections of such practices and performances which they usually reveal to followers as they seem ready to benefit by them. The vast majority of such "secrets" are accessible in any public library nowadays. What makes them special is knowing just what will be right for any individual at particular points of his progress. It is the planning and layout of apparently quite simple factors which differentiates between an initiated expert and a dilettante. One knows how to do this, and the other does not.

Techniques of early training among responsible circles in the Western Way seem disappointingly simple or inadequate. They are specially designed along two main lines: to act as "character revealers," and to awaken the applicant's Inner attention, which is then directed into responsive spiritual areas already "staffed" by nonincarnates capable of dealing with exactly such types of contact—not by any spectacular or obvious objective means, but by arranging a return force-flow calculated to stimulate whatever point in the applicant seems likely to make a right Self-response. Whether or not this works depends on the inquirer's ability to answer the Inner impetus correctly.

Let us take an actual example of this. Students or candidates are told to do several quite simple things every day which differ only slightly, though significantly, from their ordinary living routines. The idea is to link spiritual progress with human activities, while initiating a gradual direction of attention away from merely mundane matters toward Inner areas of Magical importance. In addition to these acts, applicants are given a basic philosophy to follow, and a standard (often the Tree of Life) to set up for themselves.

The simple activities are frequently these: first, five minutes' meditation in the morning as soon after waking as possible. At commencement, these meditations are free choice, later going on to graduated subjects and symbols. Very brief tabulated notes are made afterward on crucial points, such as clarity of concentration, drift of attention, unusual impressions received, and so forth. At noon, a very brief but intense "Inner Call" is sent out. This is simply a momentary focus of all available Inner energy directed toward Divinity for aid and assistance through the Powers of the Path. Some verbal formula such as: "Lighten Thou my Way" may accompany this. It is meant only to be a "flash contact" for one precise instant. In the evening not more than ten lines on the "subject of the day" have to be written into what is called a "Magical Diary." This has to be confined strictly to subject, and be compressed into the smallest symbolic consciousness possible, though not in shorthand. To get this compression, a good method is taking a whole page of written material, condensing that to a paragraph, the paragraph to a sentence, and then to a word, finally finishing in a wordless awareness of meaning. By reversing this process, ideas may be obtained out of Nil which will gradually expand and unfold until maximum perception is reached.

Last thing at night just before going to sleep comes the "rapid reverse review." This consists of running *backwards* mentally and quickly through remembered events of the day, if possible going to sleep while doing so. The purpose of this is to push serialized consciousness out of its mundane groove, and also there is an aim of "event equation" which has an effect of balancing out long-term likelihoods, otherwise known as "converting karma." Dealing with events of the day this way tends to balance one instead of letting long-term, unfinished business accumulate.

All this sounds very simple and undemanding. To persist with it day after day as routine procedure for a year and more may not sound very profitable. Yet it works for Westerners who have to earn livings in this world while trying to earn rights of living away from it. There are other methods, of course, but all depend on the same principles of fidelity, devotion, and genuine spiritual humility which has nothing to do with masochism at all. It is simply a quiet confidence that the Emptiness in one's own entity will become filled with whatever is most fitting for the sake of true Selfhood in Perfect Peace Profound. In the words of an old initiation ritual:

> Q.   In what do you place your trust?
> A.   I trust in Truth alone.
> Q.   What is Truth?
> A.   [keeps silent]

TECHNIQUE TEMPTATIONS

In most Traditions, but particularly in the West, people are tempted to play around with practices regardless of abilities for working them properly. Mostly they only make a mess, or get themselves grubby like children who interfere with materials of adult art. Physically grownup humans seldom see their Inner conditions of spiritual childhood, and they behave with infantile abilities as they did during early days on Earth. It takes more than one human lifetime to reach spiritual maturity, and in this world we are a very much mixed-up assortment of Inner age groups.

Because desire to dress up and act like adults is a normal part of childhood, ritual Magic has an automatic appeal for those unable to handle it on higher levels. Playing with Magic is very different from working with it. Luckily, most muddlers with Magic seldom come to much harm unless they insist on releasing real evil from inside themselves or willingly act as agents for ill-intentioned entities capable of using their Magical efforts for malicious purposes. The real danger of things going wrong occurs in groups of virile energetic youngsters who get together and, as they believe, "make Magic." Their sex energies are an entirely natural supply of "wild" force which can be tapped fairly easily from Inside while they are throwing Magic around so freely.

This is actually where a good deal of harm comes through misused Magic. By itself, there would be relatively few results beyond an ebullience of energy something like a geyser or other natural phenomena exploding happily. The evil lies entirely in the deliberate exploitation of the energy by "baddies" who are able to divert and apply it for their own vicious purposes otherwise. There is nothing especially new about this, but it could be particularly nasty in modern times because of our recent relationships with Energy to such extremely dangerous degrees. This topic indeed deserves very careful study by competent investigators.

Much muddle in Western Magic comes from people trying to work its "big bits" before gaining proficiency with small ones. Overestimation of personal importance is a fairly common temptation leading in that direction. When would-be Magi learn to look for real powers in the least evident factors of Life, they might find something they snatched at and lost so often in sizes too big for them to handle. Maybe too many of them lose altogether, or never gain at all, one most precious power of very mighty Magical import: a genuine sense of humor and fun!

HOW TO CONTACT THE LIVING TRADITION

There is only one real way to contact the living Tradition of Western Magic: Live it oneself and become part of it. This may not sound a very encouraging answer, but it is the truth. Let us face the issue squarely.

If anyone seriously expects to meet up with incredible "Secret Brotherhoods of Magic" or the like outside the pages of occult fiction, he may as well forget the fantasy unless it amuses him to maintain it. Small secret and semisecret Lodges and Societies do indeed exist by the dozen, and fade out again. Some may, or may not, operate contact points within the Tradition, but none has exclusive entry rights or the power to prevent a single entitled entrant from "belonging" to what amounts to a spiritual birthright. Whether to spend time, money, and effort on membership with esoteric "culture clubs" must remain the decision of individual seekers. The thing to remember is that these may indeed be part of the Western Tradition, but it is much bigger than all of them by itself.

It is possible to encounter bits of the living Tradition almost everywhere: in books, conversations, pictures, buildings, designs, music—all over the place. One can make a fascinating Treasure Hunt or Grail Quest, following the Tradition around from point to point and trying to connect up a complete picture. This might take a whole lifetime, yet only provide interest. It would not make inquirers part of the Tradition themselves.

To discover the Tradition along living lines, one factor is essential: selective working with its fundamental frequencies *only.* This means strict spiritual discipline in working exclusively with Western symbology and terminology as well as employing its methods and customs. For instance, that calls for closing down all immediate channels leading directly to Oriental or other Traditions. These would still be contacted through common Inner meeting points, but because they are not appropriate to the Western Inner Way, they have to be cleared from the Paths of whoever would follow the Western Inner Way faithfully. A Tradition is a Tradition, and must be kept true to itself, or it dies out in the end.

As an example, it would be impossible to work true Western Magic while still employing Tibetan prayer wheels, African masks, Chinese drums, Egyptian jewelry, Asian costume, and a muddled medley of symbology regardless of derivation or Inner association. Then again, rituals fudged up from Tantric terms, invocations of Egyptian deities, bits of medieval misprints, and assorted junk from similar sources are not, and never will be, part of the true Western Way. To take items properly belonging elsewhere and force them into uneasy association with each other is simply incongruous and silly. Yet so many make that very mistake.

Any reputable or reliable group of initiated individuals trying to represent the Western Tradition in its best light has to insist that applicants sacrifice all such "un-Western" associations before admission—not from any kind of prejudice or aversion, but simply for the sake of keeping clear contacts along specific spiritual lines of development. A really strict set of Initiates who knew what they were doing would have to refuse admission to anyone in a state of "mixed Magic." It would be just as foolish to include such incompatibles among their company as it would be to mix unsuitable chemicals together.

So if anyone is seriously seeking contact with the living Western Tradition of Magic, let this be approached for itself, by itself, and as itself alone. Otherwise it will just elude all pursuit in a very maddening fashion, leaving an impression that it does not exist at all. There is only about one really sound piece of advice to offer anyone genuinely looking for the Inner Way of the West. It is this: Go down inside yourself as deeply as you can, and try to reach *your own* Western spiritual roots. No one else's. Yours alone. Never mind what other people do in different parts of the world, or even next door. You are not they, but only yourself. So dig down into your very depths and find whatever you can of a fundamental Life-faith. If this looks shaky or uncertain, then remember you weren't much to look at a few moments after conception, so do not worry if your beliefs seem crude or tenuous. If you believe you have found nothing, then hold on to that Nothing as hard as you can. Something will have to emerge from it in the end, because Everything comes out of Nothing.

Realize you came into this world through a long chain of Westernizing people. Their bodies may be dead and gone long since, but their spiritual legacy is still very much alive in you genetically. You can accept this and live happily with it, or you can try to deny it and live in a perpetual quarrel with your own Inmost nature. That last course makes trouble for anyone.

Believe in yourself and your inherent ability to reach a spiritual Tradition already existing in you, however much this may be obscured by accretions and importations from everywhere else. It is your own rightful heritage, so if you want it enough, then bend down to your roots and pick it up.

Do not be afraid to ask inside yourself for spiritual help from others whose consciousness connects with yours deep down. Call clearly, call confidently, and you will be heard. Just don't demand an instant reply in English or hard cash. That would cut off communication forthwith. If you use verbal symbology yourself, keep this very sincere and simple, such as: "Let me live as I belong." Keep sending this out repetitively like a radio call sign. Then keep quiet and very still. Try to follow the silence Inside until it speaks in its own way. Keep anything that comes to you secret. Remember the Four Maxims of Western Magic: Know, Dare, Will, Keep Silent. Those are all meant to be observed as One.

THE "BE-IT-YOURSELF" TRADITION

In bygone times, little or none of any Tradition came from books or written records. Only parts of it were transmitted orally. So where did the rest come from? Directly from within Initiates themselves by contact with higher levels of Inner consciousness. Furthermore, this is where all truly spiritual teaching *should* come from. We rely far too much nowadays on writings, records, mass media, and mechanistic means of bulk-storing information and computerized systems of collating it. This is having an effect of making us rely too little on our own powers of Inner perception, which means a loss of spiritual linkage with Life.

It was for that reason that Initiates of former days insisted on solitary Self-searches in quest of Inner Identity and a sound Life-faith. The sojourn of Jesus in the desert and the meditation of Siddhartha Buddha beneath his bo tree are examples. One way or another, all Initiates expected to undergo such an experience not only as a psychophysical actuality, but as a principle applied to living consistently. In the West particularly, the Druid system forbade learning from books past a certain point, and insisted on oral and meditational communication with other people and Nature. Most spiritual systems had formal bans of some kind on writing details of their Tradition down. No great Teachers wrote messages for posterity. Certainly Jesus left no written inspirations, and judging from his followers' behavior over the centuries, it may have been a mistake to have written what survives of his reputed speaking.

None of this arose from prejudice against literature or unnecessary "secrecy-mongering." It was entirely to emphasize and ensure the importance of sustaining spiritual Traditions through individual relationships with the Infinite, rather than by ready-made recitations from previous people's findings. Eventually the utility of recording routine run-of-the-mill information was accepted, but the real "live" spiritual side of any system continues to be communicated through purely Inner channels of consciousness. Learning what others have said or done is very valuable *providing* this stimulates or encourages souls to make their own ways from there along the Path of Inner Life. *That* is the only way the Western Tradition may be truly entered. Concentrating on the Key-Symbols will always be the best plan of asking admission. In the Western Magical Mysteries, those are the Rod, Sword, Cup, Shield, and Cord. "Five are the Symbols at your Door," as the old and most Magical song says. Those Symbols relate with both the Circle-Cross and the Tree of Life, so should be seen in that kind of Light.

SYMBOL WORKING

The fundamentals of Western magical ritualism are concerned with practical symbology specifically applied in and to the spiritual areas of activity. This basically means that the operating magician must learn how to make himself and his consciousness alter intentionally in character according to the symbol being used. That is entirely a matter of practice in what is essentially the acquired art of magic.

Thus the only real value of magical symbols is for "calling up" or "raising" *in the magician himself,* and consequently in his whole field of influence, whatever particular qualities or abilities those symbols demonstrate by themselves. Such a value is actually beyond all ordinary calculations and should on no account whatever be underestimated or treated casually. Symbols are virtually the literal Keys to an Inner Kingdom which Man makes for himself by means of Magic.

For example, to use a consecrated Cup and actually become in and as oneself a living vessel of Love embracing Entity at every level of Life from Divine to human and all lesser beings. To take up a Sword and focus every available quality of keenness, flexibility, and pointed purpose. To raise a Rod, and firmly uphold whatever spiritual standards are accepted as an authority in all life activities. To shelter with the Shield of a living faith in oneself and one's True Identity, from all adversities and oppositions we encounter on Earth. Those are Magical practicalities of the highest possible order.

Then there is the symbology of working in a Magic Circle. One way or another we all have to live and work in circles of some kind, but a Magic Circle is one constructed of careful and systematically arranged patterns of consciousness relating the magician and his environs of Inner energies with a maximum of meaning according to intention. In olden times this was often done by writing various names of God functions or antievil signs in a circle around the operator. Those, of course, were worth neither more nor less than the faith of an operator in their efficacy. The chalk marks did nothing of themselves unless they inspired someone to create their meanings around himself as an actual construction of consciousness and intentional arrangement of his own nature. That was the real Magic Circle.

A MODERN MAGICAL CIRCLE

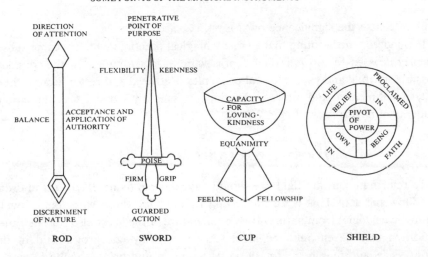

SOME POINTS OF THE MAGICAL INSTRUMENTS

ROD   SWORD   CUP   SHIELD

A modern initiate of Magic would make a "power perimeter" around himself consisting of specific spiritual qualities categorized consciously in relation to himself and all other living entities. This could be diagrammed or symbolically traced in what might nowadays be considered a "circuit layout." There are many possible designs for such a "Cosmic Compass," but a good reliable one is constructible from the Circle-Cross formula of: "In the Name of the Wisdom, the Love, the Justice, and the Infinite Mercy of the One Eternal Spirit, AMEN." These are the four Principles or qualities directly relating Humanity and Divinity. So the Circle is made with one Principle (or some sign thereof) at each quarter, the One Eternal Spirit (or acceptable signification thereof) around the outer edge, and the AMEN at center.

To make such a Circle effective, the magician in the middle must raise in himself and project intentionally the four basic qualities of its quarters, which have to harmonize as a single surrounding constant of consciousness. This not only amounts to a polarized power perimeter which relates the individual rightly with Life at all angles, but also becomes the "spirit" in which that individual actually lives. We might otherwise say that by making such a Magical Circle, the operator had achieved the right sort of spirit to live with. Few Magical operations can come much higher than that.

As a point of interest here, the central AMEN from which the operator works is capable of many interpretations. It is firstly the Name of Deity itself: AUM-En, "I Am the Mother (Creator) of all." The letters may be rearranged to give:

> NAME: The Name of whoso works the rite.
> MEAN: Median or balance of Life.
> MANE: "Soul."

Plus of course the significance of "May this be so."

It is indeed worth noting that so many magical practices which became subsequently debased to superstitial depths were in fact founded on the soundest possible spiritual and psychological principles. Retrieval and restoration of these in terms of modern and future realizations is assuredly a major task for serious students of our Western Inner Way.

LOOKING FOR LIGHT IN THE WEST

To remain in constant light, we should have to keep flying *Westward* in order to follow the sun. This is an interesting thought for those who like drawing symbolic analogies from nature. It is in the nature of the West also that its Inner Tradition may be encountered at closest quarters. Magic grows wild in the countryside, and may be met with on its home ground by those who learn the silent language of Life itself speaking through "stems and stones." This is meant quite literally.

Those sincerely seeking the spiritual Way of the West would be well advised to communicate directly with it through the natural features of its earthly environs. There are also many "sacred spots" where such communion seems clearer than at other places. These are not difficult to find by anyone with an inch of imagination. One condition is essential: a right relationship. There is no use at all, for instance, in visiting places with noisy parties of restless companions. It is always best to be alone, or with only another very trusted person. Silence and secrecy are keys that open many hidden Western Inner doorways. This may be difficult to observe in overcrowded areas, but with ingenuity it is still possible to contrive opportunities. It is tempting to wonder, however, if Jesus would have learned much in the desert had a major airway been overhead, or if Buddha could have coped with his consciousness if that bo tree had been beside a superhighway.

In these days of aerial and terrestrial motormania, it can be very difficult if not virtually impossible to isolate oneself in any Western countryside for a month in search of spiritual enlightenment. Nevertheless, it is possible with practice to make every moment rewarding that is spent in close contact with the "soul of the soil," or the Western Inner Tradition interlinking with the natural physical foci of its earthly embodiment. Learning the art of extracting this Inner content of consciousness from nonhuman sources is a fascinating facet of Western Magic by itself. It is possible only by real empathy, or one might as well say genuine *love* for the spirit hiding behind such ordinary and humble externals.

The action is simple enough. Make contact with the externals of whatever Western "pickup point" is chosen. This could be anything from a sacred site to a natural feature or a symbol. Realize that there is a special sort of "spirit" associated with whatever it is. Seek Inner relationship with that spirit in a friendly, welcoming, and loving manner. Let such feelings arise and be directed toward its Inner objective just as if a real person were present. Try to feel a return flow from Inside. An important point here is that *no deliberate attempt should be made to translate any such receptions into visual or verbal terms at that instant.* Simply experience the Inner contact and nothing else. Interpretations make themselves later on through subconscious symbology. During the "moment of mediation," words and pictures have to be transcended. When there is a sense of completion in this transaction, contact is best closed quietly and carefully before switching to more usual channels.

If this has been done with any degree of success, there will be a definite feeling of something "extra" entering the sphere of personal extensions. It is difficult to describe, but unmistakable when undergone. There is something of a spiritually satisfying sensation, as if something good had been ingested—which indeed it has along Inner lines of assimilation. Again it is important not to try analyzing, dissecting, criticizing, or otherwise interfering with the natural processes of "digestion" which should now be in progress. That should be left to take its normal course through the subconsciousness until effects show up by themselves on focal levels. Those vary greatly with different individuals. Some have definite dreams of significant character. Others might obtain realizations "out of the blue," and others again feel impelled to take some line of action which will lead to clarified consciousness on this or that issue. One way or another, the original act of empathy will enter the deep psyche of participators, eventually surfacing through the subconsciousness as some favorable evidence of progress. So works Western Magic.

AND SO

Perhaps this has all been very disappointing and disheartening for any who expected detailed descriptions of Magical rites and methods guaranteed to induce Godlike intelligence in plain human people. In one sense, these do exist as processes extending over very long periods of wide Life-experience. What most people suppose to be Magical rites that only take moments to work are actually symbolizations of spiritual dramas played out on much more significant stages of Life than Lodge or Temple floors. These do have their uses, for those capable of construing them correctly, yet Life itself will always be the Great Initiator of all systems, Eastern, Western, or otherwise.

The aim throughout this study has been to indicate that the Magic of the West is no less than whatever special spiritual disciplines and symbology may be needed to make each individual Initiate of the Western Way achieve Self-status as a true "Companion of Cosmos," responsible to Divinity on behalf of Humanity. This is not a matter of dogma, precept, rigid regulations, or so-called scientific techniques. It is essentially an affair of constant adaptions, right relationships, and empathic experience of Existence. This was once put: "Love God and fellow creatures as your True Self." That is the mightiest Magic of all, so why accept inferior imitations?

Real Western Magic is not in the least a curriculum of reading many mysterious tomes, concocting strange compounds, chanting weird words, wearing impressive robes, reveling in secret rites, and taking such incredible trouble for the sake of getting gods and demons alike eating out of one's hand, so to speak. Those are symbols of no value unless converted into currencies of consciousness exchangeable on much higher levels of living. They are means, not ends, and not even exclusive means. Western Magic is far wider and deeper than that. It is the root behavior of our reality in relation to Life.

Undoubtedly it is very clever to delve into past forms of belief and make speculations about primitive practices and previous Magical methods—quite fascinating in fact. It is undeniable, however, that we should be much more concerned with making the Magic of our own times good enough for leading us faithfully toward Enlightenment in the future. Magic is always modern for those capable of translating it into contemporary idiom while yet understanding its strange "secret speech" which is ageless and wordless. The Magic of today should matter most to us. Like the Living Tree symbolizing its spiritual structure, Western Magic should constantly be growing this year's branches for bearing next season's fruit.

TOWARD FURTHER AND FINER MAGIC

Just as, a few centuries back, a modernizing center stream of Magic produced a philosophy and practice which aimed the human psyche of the West in our present directions, so now should we "center up" the Magical methods and metaphysics which will carry us along the Line of Life ahead. This is actually being done in many ways that moderns might not term "Magic" at all, yet these have already become incorporated into the Western Tradition stemming from old systems of Initiation. Magic, far from being dead today, exists around us to such a great extent that we fail to see what we are standing in the middle of—the greatest Magic Circle of all, a worldwide circuit of common consciousness. What Man the Magician invokes therein will determine the fate of everyone on Earth. That is the way to look at Magic now. Once we recognize what it really is and what can be done with it, our Ancient Art will be identified with our most Advanced Arcana.

Surely few people would deny that civilization advances from the West? In that case it is our Magic which leads the world ahead to its ultimate destiny. If the least idea of how important this implication is awakens some awareness of spiritual "Westernism" in anyone seeking an Inner Way which is *already seeking that individual,* then the mission of this little "work within a Work" will come just that much closer to completion. For the rest, may everyone find his or her own Ways of Faith toward the same Self shared by all of us alike in

PERFECT PEACE PROFOUND.

SUGGESTED READING LIST

The Apocryphal New Testament. Trans., M. James. Oxford: The Clarendon Press, 1953.
The Apocrypha of the Old Testament. Ed., B. Metzger. New York: Oxford University Press, 1965.
The Holy Bible. King James Version. Reprinted, New York: AMS Press, 1967.
The New English Bible. New York: Oxford University Press, 1961, 1970 (1961 edition includes O.T., N.T., and Apocrypha).
Apuleius, L. "Madaurensis." *The Golden Ass.* Trans., R. Graves. New York: Pocket Books, 1954.
Butler, W. *The Magician, His Training and His Work.* London: Aquarian Press, 1959.
Constant, A. *The History of Magic,* by E. Levi [pseud.]. Trans., A. Waite. London: Rider & Co., 1957; New York: Samuel Weiser, 1969 (paperback).
———. *Transcendental Magic,* by E. Levi [pseud.]. Trans., A. Waite. London: Rider & Co., 1958; New York: Samuel Weiser, 1970.
Fortune, D. [pseud. of V. Firth]. *The Esoteric Orders and Their Work.* London, Rider & Co., 1928; St. Paul, Minn.: Llewellyn Publications, 1971.
———. *The Mystical Qabalah.* London: Williams & Norgate, 1935; New York: Samuel Weiser, n.d.
———. *The Training and Work of an Initiate.* London: Aquarian Press, 1955.
———. *The Cosmic Doctrine.* London: Aquarian Press, 1957; Hackensack, N.J.: Wehman Brothers, 1966.
———. *Sane Occultism.* London: Aquarian Press, 1967.

————. *Practical Occultism in Daily Life.* London: Aquarian Press, 1969; New York: Samuel Weiser, n.d.

Frazer, J. *The Golden Bough.* London: MacMillan & Co., 1911–15, 1922, 1935; New York: Limited Editions Club, 1970.

Graves, R. *The White Goddess.* London: Faber & Faber, 1952.

————. *The Greek Myths.* New York: George Braziller, 1957; London: Cassell, 1965.

————. *Mammon and the Black Goddess.* London: Cassell, 1965.

————. and Patai, R. *Hebrew Myths: The Book of Genesis.* Garden City, N.Y.: Doubleday & Co., 1964.

Gray, W. *The Ladder of Lights or Qabalah Renovata.* Toddington, England: Helois Book Service, 1968.

————. *Magical Ritual Methods.* Toddington, England: Helios Book Service, 1969.

————. *Inner Traditions of Magic.* London: Aquarian Pub. Co., 1971; New York: Samuel Weiser, n.d.

McNeill, W. *The Rise of the West.* Chicago: University of Chicago Press, 1963.

Malory, T. *Le Morte d'Arthur.* London: Medici Society, 1930; New York: Crofts, 1940.

Regardie, I. *Roll Away the Stone.* St. Paul, Minn.: Llewellyn Publications, 1968.

————. *The Tree of Life.* New York: Samuel Weiser, 1969.

————. *A Garden of Pomegranates.* St. Paul, Minn.: Llewellyn Publications, 1970.

————. *The Golden Dawn.* River Falls, Wisc.: Hazel Hills Corp. 1970 (distributed by Llewellyn Publications, St. Paul, Minn.).

Spence, L. *The Magic Arts in Celtic Britain.* London, New York: Rider & Co., 1945.

————. *British Fairy Origins.* London: C. A. Watts & Co., 1946.

————. *The Minor Traditions of British Mythology.* London, New York: Rider & Co., 1948.

————. *The History and Origins of Druidism.* London, New York: Rider & Co., 1949.

————. *An Encyclopedia of Occultism.* New Hyde Park, N.Y.: University Books, 1960.

Waite, A. *The Occult Sciences.* New York: Dutton & Co., 1923.

————. *History of the Rosicrucians.* Blauvelt, N.Y.: Rudolf Steiner Publications, n.d.

————. *The Book of Ceremonial Magic.* New Hyde Park, N.Y.: University Books, 1965.

————. *Alchemists through the Ages.* Blauvelt, N.Y.: Rudolf Steiner Publications, 1970.

Wentz, W. *The Fairy Faith in Celtic Countries.* New Hyde Park, N.Y.: University Books, 1966.

RECENT BOOKS ON
TRANSPERSONAL PSYCHOLOGY

Charles T. Tart

There have been many new books on transpersonal psychology since this book was originally published. Indeed, I am happy to say that the field is growing somewhat faster than I can keep up with it! This list of suggested books is to supplement the original bibliography and references. I cannot call it complete, but it should be very helpful to the interested reader.

The keys to the most up-to-date developments in humanistic and transpersonal psychology are the following two journals:

> *Journal of Humanistic Psychology*, Sage Publications, 2111 West Hillcrest Dr., Newbury Park, California 91320.
>
> *Journal of Transpersonal Psychology*, c/o Association for Transpersonal Psychology, Box 3049, Stanford, CA 94305.

Membership in the following two organizations, open to anyone with a sincere interest as well as to professionals, is also an excellent way to become acquainted with current developments. Subscriptions to the above journals can be gotten through membership.

> Association for Humanistic Psychology, 1772 Valejo St., San Francisco, CA 94123
>
> Association for Transpersonal Psychology, Box 3049, Stanford, CA 94305

Books on humanistic psychology are listed after these on transpersonal psychology.

BOOKS ON TRANSPERSONAL PSYCHOLOGY

Alexander, C., and Langer, E., eds. *Higher Stages of Human Development: Perspective on Adult Growth*. New York: Oxford University Press, 1989.

Anderson, W. *The Upstart Spring: Esalen and the American Awakening*. Reading, Mass.: Addison-Wesley, 1983.

Anthony, R., Ecker, B., and Wilbur, K., *Spiritual Choices: Recognizing Paths to Inner Transformation*. New York: Paragon House, 1986.

Atwater, P. *Coming Back to Life: The After-Effects of the Near-Death Experience*. New York: Ballantine, 1988.

Bleakley, A. *Fruits of the Moon Tree: The Medicine Wheel and Transpersonal Psychology*. London: Gateway Books, 1984.

Bolen, J., *Goddesses in Everywoman: A New Psychology of Women*. San Francisco: Harper & Row, 1984.

Boorstein, S., ed. *Transpersonal Psychotherapy*. Palo Alto, Calif.: Science & Behavior Books, 1980.

Brunton, P. *The Hidden Teaching Beyond Yoga*. York Beach, Maine: Samuel Weiser, 1977.

———. *The Spiritual Crisis of Man*. York Beach, Maine: Samuel Weiser, 1984.

———. *A Hermit in the Himalayas*. York Beach, Maine: Samuel Weiser, 1984.

———. *The Notebooks of Paul Brunton*. Vol. 4, Part I: *Meditation*. Burdett, N.Y.: Larson Publications, 1987.

Bugental, J., *The Search for Existential Identity*. San Francisco: Jossey-Bass Publishers, 1976.

———. *Psychotherapy and Process: The Fundamentals of an Existential-Humanistic Approach*. New York: Addison-Wesley, 1978.

Bulka, R., ed. *Mystics and Medics: A Comparison of Mystic and Psychotherapeutic Encounters*. New York: Human Sciences Press, 1979.

Capra, F., *The Tao of Physics: An Exploration of the Parallels between Modern Physics and Eastern Mysticism*. Berkeley: Shambhala, 1975.

Carrington, P. *Freedom in Meditation*. Garden City, N.Y.: Anchor, 1977.

Chogyam, N. *Journey into Vastness: A Handbook of Tibetan Meditation Techniques*. Worcester, Great Britain: Element, 1988.

Courtois, F. *An Experience of Enlightenment*. Wheaton, Ill.: Theosophical Publishing House, 1987.

Coward, H. *Jung and Eastern Thought*. Albany: State University of New York Press, 1985.

Cox, H. *Turning East: The Promise and Peril of the New Orientalism*. New York: Simon & Schuster, 1977.

Davidson, R., Schwartz, G., and Shapiro, D. *Consciousness and Self-Regulation: Advances in Research and Theory*. Vol. 3. New York: Plenum, 1983.

Dean, S., ed. *Psychiatry and Mysticism*. Chicago: Nelson-Hall, 1975.

Deikman, A. *Personal Freedom: On Finding Your Way to the Real World*. New York: Grossman Publishers, 1976.

———. *The Observing Self: Mysticism and Psychotherapy*. Boston: Beacon Press, 1982.

———. *The Wrong Way Home: Uncovering the Patterns of Cult Behavior in American Society*. Boston: Beacon Press, 1990.

Dhirivamsa. *The Way of Non-Attachment: The Practice of Insight Meditation*. Wellingborough, Northhamptonshire, England: Turnstone Press, 1984.

Dossey, L. *Recovering the Soul: A Scientific and Personal Search*. New York: Bantam, 1989.

Elgin, D. *Voluntary Simplicity*. New York: William Morrow, 1981.

Eliade, M. *The Encyclopedia of Religion*. New York: Macmillan, 1987.

Fadiman, J., *The Proper Study of Man: Perspectives on the Social Sciences*. New York: Macmillan, 1971.

Fadiman, J. and Frager, R. *Personality and Personal Growth*. New York: Harper & Row, 1976.

Feinstein, D., and Krippner, S. *Personal Mythology; The Psychology of Your Evolving Self: Using Ritual, Dreams, and Imagination to Discover Your Inner Story*. Los Angeles: J. P. Tarcher, 1988.

Ferguson, M. *The Aquarian Conspiracy: Personal and Social Transformation in Our Time*. New York: J. P. Tarcher, 1988.

Goldstein, J. *The Experience of Insight: A Simple and Direct Guide to Buddhist Meditation*. Boston: Shambhala, 1987.

Goldstein, J., and Kornfield, J. *Seeking the Heart of Wisdom: The Path of Insight Meditation*. Boston: Shambhala, 1987.

Goleman, D. *The Varieties of Meditative Experience*. New York: Dutton, 1977.

_____. *The Meditative Mind: The Varieties of Meditative Experience*. Rev. ed. Los Angeles: J. P. Tarcher, 1988.

Goleman, D., and Davidson, R., eds. *Consciousness, Brain, States of Awareness, and Mysticism*. New York: Harper & Row, 1979.

Grey, M. *Return from Death: An Exploration of the Near-Death Experience*. Boston: Arkana, 1985.

Grof, S. *Realms of the Human Unconscious: Observations from LSD Research*. New York: Viking Press, 1975.

_____. *LSD Psychotherapy*. Pomona, Calif.: Hunter House, 1980.

_____. *Beyond the Brain: Birth, Death, and Transcendence in Psychotherapy*. Albany: State University of New York Press, 1985.

_____. *The Adventure of Self-Discovery*. Albany: State University of New York Press, 1988.

Grof, S., and Grof, C., eds. *Beyond Death: The Gates of Consciousness*. New York: Thames & Hudson, 1980.

Grof, S., and Grof, C. *Spiritual Emergency: When Personal Transformation Becomes a Crisis*. Los Angeles: J. P. Tarcher, 1989.

Grof, S., and Halifax, J. *The Human Encounter with Death*. New York: E. P. Dutton, 1977.

Grof, S., and Valier, M., eds. *Ancient Wisdom and Modern Science*. Albany: State University of New York Press, 1984.

————. *Human Survival and Consciousness Evolution*. Albany: State University of New York Press. 1988.

Gyatso, T. [The Dalai Lama]. *Kindness, Clarity, and Insight*. Ithaca, N.Y.: Snow Lion Publications, 1984.

Hanh, Thich Nhat. *Being Peace*. Berkeley: Parallax Press, 1987.

Harding, D. E. *On Having No Head: Zen and the Re-Discovery of the Obvious*. London: Arkana paperbacks, 1986.

Harman, W. *An Incomplete Guide to the Future*. San Francisco: San Francisco Book Company. Trade distribution by Simon & Schuster, 1976.

————. *Global Mind Change: The Promise of the Last Years of the Twentieth Century*. Indianapolis, Ind.: Knowledge Systems, 1988.

Harman, W., and Rheingold, H. *Higher Creativity: Liberating the Unconscious for Breakthrough Insights*. Los Angeles: J. P. Tarcher, 1984.

Hastings, A. *With the Tongues of Men and Angels: A Study of Channeling*. San Francisco: Holt, Rinehart & Winston, 1991.

Hayward, J. *Perceiving Ordinary Magic: Science and Intuitive Wisdom*. Boulder: Shambhala, 1984.

Hendlin, S. *The Discriminating Mind: A Guide to Deepening Insight and Clarifying Outlook*. London: Unwin, 1989.

Hendricks, G., and Fadiman, J. *Transpersonal Education: A Curriculum for Feeling and Being*. Englewood Cliffs, N.J.: Prentice-Hall, 1976.

Hendricks, G., and Weinhold, B. *Transpersonal Approaches to Counseling and Psychotherapy*. Denver: Love Publishing, 1982.

Hoffman, E. *The Right to Be Human: A Biography of Abraham Maslow*. Los Angeles: J. P. Tarcher, 1988.

Holm, N., ed. *Religious Ecstasy*. Stockholm, Sweden: Amlqvst & Wiskell International, 1982.

Houston, J. *The Search for the Beloved: Journeys in Sacred Psychology*. Los Angeles: J. P. Tarcher, 1987.

Johnson, W. *Riding the Ox Home: A History of Meditation from Shamanism to Science*. London: Rider & Company, 1982

Kastenbaum, R., ed. *Between Life and Death*. New York: Springer, 1979.

Katz, R. *Boiling Energy: Community Healing among the Kalahari Kung*. Cambridge, Mass.: Harvard University Press, 1982.

Klimo, N. *Channeling: Investigations on Receiving Information from Paranormal Sources*. Los Angeles; J. P. Tarcher, 1987.

Kornfield, J. *Living Buddhist Masters*. Santa Cruz, Calif.: Unity Press, 1977.

Kornfield, J., and Breiter, P. *A Still Forest Pool: The Insight Meditation of Achaan Chah*. Wheaton, Ill.: The Theosophical Publishing House, 1985.

Krippner, S. *Human Possibilities: Mind Exploration in the USSR and Eastern Europe*. Garden City, N.Y.: Anchor/Doubleday, 1980.

Krippner, S., and Villoldo, A. *The Realms of Healing*. Millbrae, Calif.: Celestial Arts, 1976.

Krishna, G. *The Awakening of Kundalini*. New York: E. P. Dutton & Co., 1975.

Langer, E. *Mindfulness*. New York: Addison-Wesley, 1989.

Leff, H. L. *Playful Perception: Choosing How to Experience Your World*. Burlington, Vt.: Waterfront Books, 1984.

Leonard, G. B. *Education and Ecstasy*. New York: Delacorte, 1968.

————. *The Transformation: A Guide to the Inevitable Changes in Humankind*. Los Angeles: J. P. Tarcher, 1972.

————. *The Silent Pulse: A Search for the Perfect Rhythm that Exists in Each of Us*. New York: E. P. Dutton & Co., 1978.

Leshan, L. *Alternate Realities: The Search for the Full Human Being*. New York: M. Evans & Co., 1976.

Levin, D. *The Listening Self: Personal Growth, Social Change and the Closure of Metaphysics*. New York: Routledge, 1989.

Levine, S. *An Investigation of Conscious Living and Conscious Dying*. New York: Anchor Press/Doubleday, 1982.

Markley, O., and Harman W., eds. *Changing Images of Man*. New York: Pergamon Press, 1982.

May, G. *Will and Spirit: A Contemplative Psychology*. San Francisco: Harper & Row, 1982.

Metzner, R. *Maps of Consciousness: I Ching, Tantra, Tarot, Alchemy, Astrology, Actualism*. New York: Macmillan, 1971.

————. *Know Your Type: Maps of Identity*. Garden City, N.Y.: Anchor Press, 1979.

————. *Opening to Inner Light: The Transformation of Human Nature and Consciousness*. Los Angeles: J. P. Tarcher, 1986.

Mishlove, J. *The Roots of Consciousness: Psychic Liberation Through History, Science and Experience*. New York: Random House, 1975.

Mitchell, S. *The Enlightened Heart*. San Francisco: Harper & Row, 1989.

Moody, R. *Life After Life: The Investigation of a Phenomenon—Survival of Bodily Death*. Atlanta: Mockingbird Books, 1975.

————. *Reflections on Life After Life*. Atlanta: Mockingbird Books, 1977.

Murphy, G., and Murphy, L. B. *Asian Psychology*. New York: Basic Books, 1968.

Murphy, M., and Donovan, S. *The Physical and Psychological Effects of Meditation: A Review of Contemporary Meditation Research with a Comprehensive Bibliography 1931–1988*. Big Sur, Calif.: Esalen Institute, 1988.

Nalimov, V. *Realms of the Unconscious: The Enchanted Frontier*. Philadelphia: ISI Press, 1982.

Naranjo, C. *The One Quest*. New York: Viking Press, 1972.

_____. *The Healing Journey: New Approaches to Consciousness*. New York: Pantheon Books, 1974.

_____. *How to Be: Meditation in Spirit and Practice*. Los Angeles: J. P. Tarcher, 1990.

Needleman, J. *The Sword of Gnosis: Metaphysics, Cosmology, Tradition, Symbolism*. Baltimore: Penguin Books, 1974.

_____. *Lost Christianity*. Garden City, N.Y.: Doubleday, 1980.

_____. *Consciousness and Tradition*. New York: Crossroad, 1982.

_____. *The Heart of Philosophy*. New York: Bantam Books, 1982.

Needleman, J., ed. *Speaking of My Life: The Art of Living in the Cultural Revolution*. San Francisco: Harper & Row, 1979.

Needleman, J., and Baker, G., eds. *Understanding the New Religions*. New York: Seabury Press, 1978.

Needleman, J., and Lewis, J., eds. *Sacred Tradition and Present Need*. New York: Viking Press, 1975.

Neher, A. *The Psychology of Transcendence*. Engelwood Cliffs, N.J.: Prentice-Hall, 1980.

Norbu, N. *Dzog Chen and Zen*. Nevada City, Calif.: Blue Dolphin Publishing, 1986.

_____. *The Cycle of Day and Night: An Essential Tibetan Text on the Practice of Dzogchen*. Barrytown, N.Y.: Station Hill Press, 1987.

O'Flaherty, W. *Dream, Illusion and Other Realities*. Chicago: University of Chicago Press, 1984.

Osis, K., and Haraldsson, E. *At the Hour of Death*. New York: Avon Books, 1977.

Owens, C. M. *Zen and the Lady: Memoirs—Personal and Transpersonal—in a World in Transition*. New York: Baraka Books, 1979.

Palmer, H. *The Enneagram: Understanding Yourself and the Others in Your Life*. San Francisco: Harper & Row, 1988.

Panshin, A., and Panshin, C. *The World Beyond the Hill: Science Fiction and the Quest for Transcendence*. Los Angeles: J. P. Tarcher, 1989.

Pearce, J. C. *The Crack in the Cosmic Egg*. New York: Julian Press, 1971.

_____. *Exploring the Crack in the Cosmic Egg*. New York: Julian Press, 1974.

_____. *Magical Child: Rediscovering Nature's Plan for Our Children*. New York: E. P. Dutton & Co., 1977.

Peterson, S. *A Catalog of the Ways People Grow*. New York: Ballantine Books, 1971.

Peto, F. *Cosmic Psychology*. Houston: Yates Printing Company, 1976.

Prince, Raymond, ed. *Trance and Possession States*. Proceedings of the second annual conference, R. M. Bucke Memorial Society, 4–6 March 1966. Montreal: R. M. Bucke Memorial Society, 1968.

Progoff, I. *The Practice of Process Meditation*. New York: Dialogue House Library, 1980.

Rama, W., Ballentine, R., and Ajaya, S. *Yoga and Psychotherapy*. Glenview, Ill.: Himalayan Institute, 1976.

Ring, K. *Life at Death: A Scientific Investigation of the Near-Death Experience*. New York: Coward, McCann & Geoghegan, 1980.

_____. *Heading Toward Omega: In Search of the Meaning of the Near-Death Experience*. New York: William Morrow, 1984.

Robbins, T., and Dick A. *In Gods We Trust: New Patterns of Religious Pluralism in America*. New Brunswick, N.J.: Transaction Books, 1981.

Roberts, B. *The Experience of No-Self: A Contemplative Journey*. Boston: Shambhala Publications, 1982.

Roberts, T. *Four Psychologies Applied to Education: Freudian, Behavioral, Humanistic and Transpersonal*. New York: Wiley, 1975.

Rushbrook, L. *Sufi Studies: East and West*. New York: E. P. Dutton & Co., 1974.

Sabom, M. *Recollections of Death*. New York: Harper & Row, 1982.

Sayama, M. *Samadhi: Self-Development in Zen, Swordsmanship, and Psychotherapy*. Albany: State University of New York Press, 1986.

Sheikh, A., and Sheikh, K., eds. *Eastern and Western Approaches to Healing: Ancient Wisdom and Modern Knowledge*. New York: John Wiley & Sons, 1989.

Sinetar, M. *Ordinary People as Monks and Mystics: Lifestyles for Self-Discovery*. New York: Paulist Press, 1986.

_____. *Do What You Love, the Money Will Follow: Discovering Your Right Livelihood*. New York: Dell Pub., 1987.

Singer, S. *Androgyny: Toward a New Theory of Sexuality*. New York: Anchor Press/Doubleday, 1976.

Shafii, M. *Freedom from the Self: Sufism, Meditation and Psychotherapy*. New York: Human Sciences Press, 1985.

Shapiro, D. H. *Precision Nirvana*. Englewood Cliffs, N.J.: Prentice-Hall, 1978.

_____. *Meditation: Self-Regulation Strategy and Altered State of Consciousness*. New York: Aldine, 1980.

Shapiro, D. H., and Walsh, R., eds. *Meditation: Classic and Contemporary Perspectives*. New York: Aldine, 1984.

Smith, H. *Forgotten Truth: The Primordial Tradition*. New York: Harper & Row, 1976.

_____. *Beyond the Post-Modern Mind*. New York: Crossroad, 1982.

Snelling, J., Watts, M., and Sibley, D. *The Early Writings of Alan Watts*. Berkeley: Celestial Arts, 1987.

Sole-Leris, A. *Tranquility and Insight: An Introduction to the Oldest Form of Buddhist Meditation*. Boston: Shambhala, 1986.

Spretnak, C. *The Politics of Women's Spirituality*. Garden City, N.Y.: Anchor Press/Doubleday, 1982.

Stewart, R. *East Meets West: The Transpersonal Approach*. Wheaton, Ill.: Theosophical Publishing House, 1981.

Suzuki, S. *Zen Mind, Beginner's Mind: Informal Talks on Zen Meditation and Practice*. New York: John Weatherhill, 1970.

Tart, C. *Waking Up: Overcoming the Obstacles to Human Potential*. Boston: New Science Library, 1986.

_____. *Open Mind, Discriminating Mind: Reflections on Human Possibilities*. San Francisco: Harper & Row, 1989.

Thera, N. *The Heart of Buddhist Meditation: A Handbook of Mental Training Based on the Buddha's Way of Mindfulness*. York Beach, Maine: Samuel Weisner, 1962.

_____. *The Power of Mindfulness*. San Francisco: Unity Press, 1972.

Tibetan Nyingma Meditation Center. *Calm and Clear*. Berkeley: Dharma Publishing, 1973.

Trungpa, C. *Meditation in Action*. Berkeley: Shambhala Publications, 1970.

_____. *Cutting Through Spiritual Materialism*. Berkeley: Shambhala Publications, 1973.

_____. *The Myth of Freedom and the Way of Meditation*. Berkeley: Shambhala Publications, 1976.

Tulku, T., ed. *Reflections of Mind: Western Psychology Meets Tibetan Buddhism*. Emeryville, Calif.: Dharma Publishing, 1975.

Tulku, T. *Gesture of Balance: A Guide to Awareness, Self-healing and Meditation*. Emeryville, Calif.: Dharma Publishing, 1977.

_____. *Openness Mind*. Berkeley: Dharma Publishing, 1978.

Valle, S., and Halling, S., eds. *Existential-Phenomenological Perspectives in Psychology: Exploring the Breadth of Human Experience: with a Special Section on Transpersonal Psychology*. New York: Plenum Press, 1989.

Valle, R., and von Eckartsberg, R., eds. *The Metaphors of Consciousness*. New York: Plenum Press, 1981.

Vaughan, F. *Awakening Intuition*. Garden City, N.Y.: Anchor Press/Doubleday, 1979.

_____. *The Inward Arc: Healing and Wholeness in Psychotherapy and Spirituality*. Boston: New Science Library, 1985.

Vaughan, F., and Walsh, R., eds. *A Gift of Healings: Selections from "A Course in Miracles."* Los Angeles: J. P. Tarcher, 1988.

Walsh, R. *Staying Alive: The Psychology of Human Survival*. Boulder, Colo.: New Science Library, 1984.

_____. *The Spirit of Shamanism.* Los Angeles: J. P. Tarcher, 1990.

Walsh, R., and Shapiro, D. H., eds. *Beyond Health and Normality: Explorations of Exceptional Psychological Well-Being.* New York: Van Nostrand Reinhold Company, 1985.

Walsh, R., and Vaughan, F., eds. *Beyond Ego: Transpersonal Dimensions in Psychology.* Los Angeles: J. P. Tarcher, 1980.

Washburn, M. *The Ego and the Dynamic Ground: A Transpersonal Theory of Human Development.* Albany: State University of New York Press, 1988.

Weil, A. *The Natural Mind: A New Way of Looking at Drugs and the Higher Consciousness.* Boston: Houghton Mifflin, 1972.

_____. *The Marriage of the Sun and Moon: A Quest for Unity in Consciousness.* Boston: Houghton Mifflin, 1980.

Weinhold, B., and Elliot, L. *Transpersonal Communication: How to Establish Contact with Yourself and Others.* Englewood Cliffs, N.J.: Prentice-Hall, 1979.

Welwood, J., ed. *The Meeting of the Ways: Explorations in East/West Psychology.* New York: Schocken, 1979.

Welwood, J. *Awakening the Heart: East/West Approaches to Psychotherapy and the Healing Relationship.* Boulder, Colo.: Shambhala, 1983.

_____. *Challenge of the Heart: Love, Sex, and Intimacy in Changing Times.* Boston: Shambhala, 1985.

West, M. A., ed. *The Psychology of Meditation.* Oxford: Clarendon Press, 1987.

White, J., ed. *The Highest State of Consciousness.* Garden City, N.Y.: Anchor Books, 1972.

_____. *What is Meditation?* Garden City, N.Y.: Anchor Press, 1974

_____. *Kundalini, Evolution and Enlightenment.* Garden City, N.Y.: Anchor Press, 1979.

_____. *Frontiers of Consciousness: The Meeting Ground between Inner and Outer Reality.* New York: Julian Press, 1974.

_____. *A Practical Guide to Death and Dying.* Wheaton Ill.: Theosophical Publishing House, 1980.

White, J., and Krippner, S. *Future Science: Life Energies and the Physics of Paranormal Phenomena.* Garden City, N.Y.: Anchor Books, 1977.

Wilbur, K. *The Spectrum of Consciousness.* Wheaton, Ill.: Theosophical Publishing House, 1977.

_____. *No Boundary: Eastern and Western Approaches to Personal Growth.* Los Angeles: Center Publications, 1979.

_____. *The Atman Project: A Transpersonal View of Human Development.* Wheaton, Ill.: Theosophical Publishing House, 1980.

_____. *Up from Eden: A Transpersonal View of Evolution.* Garden City, N.Y.: Anchor Press/Doubleday, 1981.

————. *The Holographic Paradigm and Other Paradoxes: Exploring the Leading Edge of Science.* Boulder: Shambhala, 1982.

————. *A Sociable God: A Brief Introduction to a Transcendental Sociology.* New York: New Press, 1983.

————. *Eye to Eye: The Quest for the New Paradigm.* Garden City, N.Y.: Anchor Books, 1983.

————. *Quantum Questions: Mystical Writings of the World's Great Physicists.* Boston: New Science Library, 1984.

Wilbur, K., Engler, J., and Brown, D., eds. *Transformations of Consciousness: Conventional and Contemplative Perspectives on Development.* Boston: New Science Library, 1986.

Woods, R., ed. *Understanding Mysticism.* Garden City, N.Y.: Image/Doubleday, 1980.

Zukav, G. *The Dancing Wu Li Masters: An Overview of the New Physics.* New York: William Morrow, 1979.

————. *The Seat of the Soul.* New York: Simon & Schuster, 1989.

REFERENCES AND BIBLIOGRAPHY

Aquinas, T. *Summa Theologiae*. New York: McGraw-Hill, 1964.

Aurobindo, Sri. *Essays on the Gita*. New York: Sri Aurobindo Library, 1950.

_____. *The Life Divine*. New York: E. P. Dutton, 1953.

_____. *On Yoga I: The Synthesis of Yoga*. Pondicherry, India: Sri Aurobindo Ashram, 1957.

_____. *Thoughts and Glimpses*. Pondicherry, India: Sri Aurobindo Ashram, 1964.

Baba Ram Dass. *Be Here Now*. New York: Crown, 1971.

Backster, C. "Evidence of Primary Perception in Plant Life, *Inter. J. Parapsychol.*, 10 (1968), 329–348.

Ballantyne, J., trans. *Samkhya Aphorisms of Kapila*. Varanasi: Chowkhamba Sanskrit Series, 1963.

Barber, T. "Suggested ('Hypnotic') Behavior: The Trance Paradigm versus an Alternative Paradigm," in E. Fromm and R. Shor, eds., *Hypnosis: Research Developments and Perspectives*. Chicago: Aldine/Atherton, 1972. Pp. 115–184.

Bars, H. "Maritain's Contributions to an Understanding of Mystical Experience," in J. Evans, ed., *Jacques Maritain: The Man and His Achievement*. New York: Sheed & Ward, 1963.

Basset, B. *Let's Start Praying Again*. New York: Herder & Herder, 1972.

Bennett, J. *Witness*. New York: Dharma Books, 1962.

_____. *Gurdjieff: A Very Great Enigma*. New York: Samuel Weiser, 1973.

_____. *Gurdjieff: Making a New World*. New York: Harper & Row, 1974.

Bernstein, M. *The Search for Bridey Murphy*. New York: Doubleday, 1956.

Bhattacharyya, H., ed. *The Cultural Heritage of India*. Vol. III. Calcutta: The Ramakrishna Mission Institute of Culture, 1953.

Bhikku Soma. *The Way of Mindfulness*. Colombo, Ceylon: Vajirama, 1949.

Blackburn, T. "Sensuous-Intellectual Complementarity in Science, *Science*, 172 (1971), 1003–1007.

Blofeld, J. *Tantric Mysticism in Tibet*. New York: Dutton, 1970.

Bloom, A. *Beginning to Pray.* New York: Paulist Press, 1970.

Boros, L. *Pain and Providence.* Baltimore: Helicon Press, 1966.

Brier, R. "PK on a Bio-electrical System," *J. Parapsychol.,* 33 (1969), 187–205.

Broad, C. *Lectures on Psychical Research.* New York: Humanities Press, 1962.

Bucke, R. *Cosmic Consciousness.* New York, Dutton, 1901; reprinted New Hyde Park, N.Y.: University Books, 1961.

Buddhadasa, B. *Two Kinds of Language.* Trans., A. Bhikku. Bangkok, Thailand: Sublime Life Mission, 1968.

Burtt, E., *The Teachings of the Compassionate Buddha.* New York: Mentor, 1955.

Butler, C. *Western Mysticism.* London: Arrow, 1960.

Castaneda, C. *Journey to Ixtlan.* New York: Simon & Schuster, 1973.

Chadwick, A. *A Sadhu's Reminiscences of Ramana Maharshi.* Tiruvannamali, India: Sri Ramanasram, 1966.

Chaudhuri, H. *Sri Aurobindo: Prophet of Life Divine.* Calcutta: Sri Aurobindo Pathamander, 1951 (a); reprinted, San Francisco: Cultural Integration Fellowship, 1973.

―――――, ed. *Indian Culture.* Calcutta: Bharat-Sanskriti Parisat, 1951 (b).

―――――. *Philosophy of Integralism.* Calcutta: Sri Aurobindo Pathamander, 1954; reprinted, Pondicherry, India: Sri Aurobindo Ashram Press, 1967.

―――――. *Prayers of Affirmation.* San Francisco: Cultural Integration Fellowship, 1956.

―――――. *The Rhythm of Truth.* San Francisco: Cultural Integration Fellowship, 1958.

―――――. *Integral Yoga: The Concept of Harmonious and Creative Living.* London: George Allen & Unwin, 1965 (a); reprinted, 1970.

―――――. *Philosophy of Meditation.* New York: Philosophical Library, 1965 (b).

―――――. *Modern Man's Religion.* Santa Barbara: J. F. Rowny, 1966.

―――――. *Mastering the Problems of Living.* New York: Citadel Press, 1968.

―――――, ed. *Mahatma Gandhi: His Message for Mankind.* San Francisco: Cultural Integration Fellowship, 1969.

―――――― and Spiegelberg, F., eds. *The Integral Philosophy of Sri Aurobindo.* London: George Allen & Unwin, 1960.

Conze, E. *Buddhist Meditation.* London: Allen & Unwin, 1956.

Dasgupta, S. *Yoga as Philosophy and Religion.* London: Kegan Paul, 1924.

Datey, K., Deshmukh, S., Dalvi, C., & Vinekar, S., "Shavasan": a yogic exercise in the management of hypertension. *Angiology,* 20 (1969), 325–333.

Dean, D. "Long Distance Plethysmograph Telepathy with Agent under Water," *J. Parapsychol.,* 33 (1969), 349–350.

de Hartmann, T. *Our Life with Mr. Gurdjieff.* New York: Cooper Square Publishers, 1964.

Delacroix, H. *Essai sur le mysticisme: Speculatif en Allemagne.* Paris: F. Alcan, 1900.

DeRopp, R. *The Master Game.* New York: Delacorte Press, 1968.

Dhammaratana. *Guide through Visuddhimagga.* Varanasi, India: Mahabodhi Society, 1964.

Dogen. *Eye of the True Law* [Shobogenzo]. Ed., Masunaga. Honolulu: East-West Center Press, University of Hawaii, 1971.

Douglas, J. *Resistance and Contemplation.* New York: Doubleday, 1972.

Dunbar, F. *Mind and Body: Psychosomatic Medicine.* New York: Random House, 1947.

Duval, P., and Montredon, E. "ESP Experiments with Mice," *J. Parapsychol.,* 32 (1968), 153–166.

Ebon, M. *Maharishi, the Guru.* New York: The American Library, 1968.

Fischer, R. Letter in *Newsletter-Review* of (Montreal) Bucke Society, 1–2 (Spring, 1972), 40–43.

Frager, R. "On Vital Energy: Some Eastern and Western Conceptions." Paper, World Conference on Scientific Yoga, New Delhi, Dec. 1970.

Freud, S. *An Outline of Psychoanalysis.* New York: Norton, 1949.

Garrison, O. *Tantra: The Yoga of Sex.* New York: Julian Press, 1964.

Goddard, D., ed. *A Buddhist Bible.* Boston: Beacon Press, 1970.

Goleman, D. "Meditation as Meta-therapy: Hypotheses toward a Proposed Fifth State of Consciousness, *J. Transpersonal Psychol.,* 3:1 (1971), 1–25.

Govinda, L. A., *Foundations of Tibetan Mysticism.* New York: E. P. Dutton, 1960.

———. *Psychological Attitude of Early Buddhist Philosophy.* New York: Weiser, 1969.

Grad, B. "A Telekinetic Effect on Plant Growth, *Inter. J. Parapsychol.,* 5 (1963), 117–134.

———. "Some Biological Effects of the 'Laying on of Hands': A Review of Experiments with Animals and Plants," *J. Amer. Soc. Psych. Res.,* 59 (1965), 95–129.

———. "The 'Laying on of Hands': Implications for Psychotherapy, Gentling, and the Placebo Effect," *J. Amer. Soc. Psych. Res.,* 61 (1967), 286–305.

———, Cadoret, R., and Paul, G. "The Influence of an Unorthodox Method of Treatment on Wound Healing in Mice," *Inter. J. Parapsychol.,* 3 (1961), 5–25.

Gray, W. *The Ladder of Lights.* Toddington: Helios, 1968.

———. *Magical Ritual Methods.* Toddington: Helios, 1969.

———. *Seasonal Occult Rituals.* London: Aquarian, 1970 (a).

———. *Office of the Holy Tree of Life.* Dallas, Texas: Sangreal Foundation, 1970 (b).

———. *Inner Traditions of Magic.* London: Aquarian, 1971.

———. *Magical Images of the Tree.* Dallas, Texas: Sangreal Foundation, 1972.

———. *Simple Guide to the Tree of Life.* Labrys Press, 1973 (a). Distributed by The Technology Group, Box 3125, Pasadena, Ca. 91103.

_____. *Simple Guide to the Paths on the Tree.* Labrys Press, 1973 (b). Distributed by The Technology Group, Box 3125, Pasadena, Ca. 91103

_____. *The Tree of Evil.* Toddington: Helios, 1974.

_____. *Rollright Ritual.* Toddington: Helios, 1975 (a).

_____. *The Talking Tree.* New York: Weiser, 1975 (b).

_____. *The Rite of Light.* New York: Weiser, 1975 (c).

_____. *Self Made by Magic.* New York: Weiser, 1975 (d).

Greely, A. *The Jesus Myth.* New York: Doubleday, 1971.

Gudas, F., ed. *Extrasensory Perception.* New York: Scribner's, 1961.

Gurdjieff, G. *The Herald of the Coming Good.* Paris, 1933 (no publisher given); reprinted, New York: Weiser, 1970.

_____. *All and Everything: Beelzebub's Tales to His Grandson.* New York: Harcourt, Brace & Co., 1950.

_____. *Meetings with Remarkable Men.* New York: E. P. Dutton & Co., 1963.

Hakuin. *Selected Writings (Oratagama, Hebiichigo, and Yabukoji).* Trans., P. Yampolsky. New York: Columbia Univ. Press, 1971.

Heywood, R. *Beyond the Reach of Sense: An Inquiry into Extrasensory Perception.* New York: Dutton, 1959.

Honorton, C., and Krippner, S. "Hypnosis and ESP: A Review of the Experimental Literature," *J. Amer. Soc. Psych. Res.,* 63 (1969), 214–252.

Houston, J., and Masters, R.: see Masters, R., and Houston, J.

Hui-neng. *Platform Scripture.* Trans., Wing-tsit Chan. New York: St. John's Univ. Press, 1963.

Huxley, A. *Heaven and Hell.* New York: Harper & Bro., 1955.

James, W. *The Varieties of Religious Experience.* New York: Collier Books, 1961.

Jung, C. *Two Essays on Analytical Psychology.* New York: Pantheon, 1953.

_____. *Collected Works.* Bollingen ed. New York: Pantheon, 1953–58.

_____. *Psychology and Religion.* New York: Pantheon, 1958.

_____. "Interpretation of Visions," *Spring, Magazine of Jungian Thought.* New York: Analytical Club of New York, 1960–68.

_____. *Memories, Dreams, Reflections.* New York: Pantheon Books, 1961.

Kapleau, P., ed. *The Three Pillars of Zen.* Boston: Beacon Press, 1967.

_____. *Wheel of Death.* New York: Harper & Row, 1971.

Kasamatsu, A., & Hirai, T. An electroencephalographic study on the Zen meditation (Zazen). *Folio Psychiat. & Neurolog. Japonica,* 20 (1966), 315–336.

Kashyap, J. *The Abhidhamma Philosophy.* Vol. 1. Nalanda, India: Buddha Vihara, 1954.

Kavanaugh, K., and Rodriguez, O., eds. *Collected Works of St. John of the Cross.* Washington, D.C.: Institute of Carmelite Studies, 1973.

Kaviraj, G. *Aspects of Indian Thought.* Burdwan, India: University of Burdwan, 1966.

Kita, R., and Nagaya, K. "How Altruism Is Cultivated in Zen," in P. Sorokin, ed., *Forms and Techniques of Altruism and Spiritual Growth.* Boston: Beacon Press, 1954.

Knowles, D. *The English Mystical Tradition.* London: Burnes & Oates, 1961.

Krishna, G. *The Kundalini: The Evolutionary Energy in Man.* Berkeley: Shambala, 1971.

———. *The Secret of Yoga.* New York: Harper & Row, 1972.

Kuhn, T. *The Structure of Scientific Revolutions.* Chicago: Univ. of Chicago Press, 1962.

Kuvalayananda. *Pranayama.* Bombay: Popular Prakashan, 1966.

Ledi Sayadaw. *The Manuals of Buddhism.* Rangoon, Burma: Union Buddha Sasana Council, 1965.

Lefort, R. *Teachers of Gurdjieff.* London: Vincent Stuart, 1966.

Leonard, A. "Studies on the Phenomena of Mystical Experience," in *Mystery and Mysticism: A Symposium.* London: Blackfriars Publications, 1956.

LeShan, L. "Physicists and Mystics: Similarities in World View," *J. Transpersonal Psychol.,* 1:2 (1969), 1–20.

Leuba, J. *The Psychology of Religious Mysticism.* London: Routledge & Paul, 1972.

Lewis, C. *The Great Divorce.* New York: Macmillan, 1946.

———. *The Screwtape Letters.* New York: Macmillan, 1960.

———. *The Chronicles of Narnia.* New York: Colliers, 1971.

Lilly, J. *Man and Dolphin.* New York: Doubleday, 1961.

———. *The Mind of the Dolphin.* Garden City, N.Y.: Doubleday, 1967.

———. *Programming and Metaprogramming in the Human Biocomputer.* New York: Julian Press, 1968.

———. *The Center of the Cyclone.* New York: Julian Press, 1972.

McConnell, R. *ESP Curriculum Guide for Secondary Schools and Colleges.* New York: Simon & Schuster, 1971.

McDermott, R. *Cross Currents,* Winter 1972. West Nyack, New York: Cross Currents Corporation, 1972.

McNamara, W. *The Art of Being Human.* New York: Doubleday, 1962.

———. *The Human Adventure.* New York: Doubleday, 1974 (a).

———. *Mount of Passion.* New York: Doubleday, 1974 (b).

Macquarrie, J. *Principles of Christian Theology.* New York: Scribner, 1966.

Maharishi, M. *The Science of Being and Art of Living.* Fort Lauderdale, Fla.: Allied Publishers, 1963.

Maharshi, R. *Self-realization.* Madras: Tiruvanamalai, 1962.

———. *Maha Yoga.* Madras: Tiruvanamalai, 1967.

Mahasi Sayadaw. *The Process of Insight.* Trans., Nyanaponika Thera. Kandy, Ceylon: The Forest Hermitage, 1965.

————. *Buddhist Meditation and Its Forty Subjects.* Buddha-gaya, India: International Meditation Center, 1970.

Mahathera, P. *Buddhist Meditation in Theory and Practice.* Colombo, Ceylon: Gunasena, 1962.

Maréchal, J. *Studies in the Psychology of the Mystics.* Trans., A. Thorold. Albany, New York: Magi Books, 1964.

Martin, D. "Account of the Sarmouni Brotherhood," in R. Davidson, ed., *Documents on Contemporary Dervish Communities.* London: Society for Organizing Unified Research as Cultural Education, 1966.

Maslow, A. *Toward a Psychology of Being.* Princeton: Van Nostrand, 1962.

————. *The Psychology of Science: A Reconnaisance.* New York: Harper & Row, 1966.

————. "Theory Z," *J. Transpersonal Psychol.,* 2:1 (1970), 31–47.

Masters, R., and Houston, J. *The Varieties of Psychedelic Experience.* New York: Dell, Delta, 1967.

Meher Baba. *Discourses,* I, II, III. San Francisco: Sufism Reoriented, 1967.

Merton, T. *Seeds of Contemplation.* Norfolk, Conn.: New Directions, 1949.

Mesmer, A. *Memoire sur la décourverte du magnetisme animal.* Geneva: 1774. Available in *Mesmerism by Doctor Mesmer: Dissertation on the Discovery of Animal Magnetism, 1779.* Trans., V. Myers. London: Macdonald, 1948.

Mishra, R. *The Textbook of Yoga Psychology.* New York: Julian Press, 1963.

Mitchell, E. "An ESP Test from Apollo 14," *J. Parapsychol.,* 35 (1971), 89–107.

————, ed. *Psychic Exploration.* New York: Putnam, 1974.

Monroe, R. *Journeys out of the Body.* New York: Doubleday, 1971.

Morgan, C., and King, R. *Introduction to Psychology.* New York: McGraw-Hill, 1956.

Morris, R. "Psi and Animal Behavior: A Survey," *J. American Soc. Psychical Res.,* 64 (1970), 242–260.

Murphy, G., and Dale, L. *Challenge of Psychical Research.* New York: Harper & Row, 1961.

Narada Thera. *A Manual of Abhidhamma.* Vols. I, II. Colombo, Ceylon: Vajirarama, 1956.

Naranjo, C., and Ornstein, R. *On the Psychology of Meditation.* New York: Viking, 1971.

Narayananda, S. *The Primal Power in Man.* Rishikesh: N. K. Prasad, 1950.

————. *The Mysteries of Man, Mind, and Mind Functions.* Rishikesh: N. K. Prasad, 1951.

Needleman, J. *The New Religions.* New York: Doubleday, 1970.

Nicoll, M. *Psychological Commentaries on the Teachings of Gurdjieff and Ouspensky.* 5 vols. London: Vincent Stuart, 1952–56.

Northrop, F. *The Meeting of East and West.* New York: Macmillan, 1946.

Nott, S. *Teachings of Gurdjieff: The Journal of a Pupil.* London: Routledge & Kegan Paul, 1961.

Nyanaponika Thera. *Abhidhamma Studies.* Colombo, Ceylon: Frewin, 1949.

_____. *The Heart of Buddhist Meditation.* London: Rider, 1962.

_____. *The Power of Mindfulness.* Kandy, Ceylon: Buddhist Publication Society, 1968.

Nyanatiloka. *The Word of the Buddha.* Colombo, Ceylon: Buddha Publishing Committee, 1952 (a).

_____. *Path to Deliverance.* Colombo, Ceylon: Buddha Sahitya Sabha, 1952 (b).

Orage, A. *The Active Mind.* New York: Heritage House, 1954.

Orne, M. "On the Social Psychology of the Psychological Experiment with Particular Reference to Demand Characteristics and Their Implications," *Amer. Psychologist,* 17 (1962), 776–783.

Ornstein, R. *On the Experience of Time.* New York: Penguin Books, 1969.

_____. *Psychology of Consciousness.* San Francisco: W. H. Freeman, 1972.

_____, ed. *The Nature of Human Consciousness.* San Francisco: W. H. Freeman, 1973.

Osis, K. "A test of Occurrence of a Psi Effect between Man and the Cat," *J. Parapsychol.,* 16 (1952), 233–256.

Ouspensky, P. *In Search of the Miraculous.* New York: Harcourt, Brace & Co., 1949.

_____. *The Psychology of Man's Possible Evolution.* New York: Alfred A. Knopf, 1954.

_____. *The Fourth Way.* New York: Alfred A. Knopf, 1957.

Owens, C. *Awakening to the Good—Psychological or Religious.* North Quincy, Mass.: Christopher Publishing House, 1958.

_____. *Discovery of the Self.* North Quincy, Mass.: Christopher Publishing House, 1963.

_____. "Religious Implications of Consciousness—Changing Drugs," *J. for Scientific Study of Religion,* 4:2 (1965), 246.

_____. "Mystical Experience—Facts and Values," in J. White, ed., *Highest State of Consciousness.* New York: Doubleday, 1972.

_____. "Self-Realization—Induced and Spontaneous," in R. Prince, ed., *Transformations of Consciousness.* New York: Wiley, in press.

Pascal, B. "Memorial," quoted in Guardini, Romano, *Pascal for Our Time.* Trans., B. Thompson. New York: Herder & Herder, 1966.

Pauwels, L. *Gurdjieff.* New York: Samuel Weiser, 1972.

Peers, E., trans. and ed. *Complete Works of St. Teresa.* London: Sheed & Ward, 1946.

Peterman, D. "Toward Interpersonal Fulfillment in an Eupsychian Culture," *J. Humanistic Psychol.,* 1 (1972), 72–85.

Peters, F. *Boyhood with Gurdjieff.* New York: E. P. Dutton, 1964.

Plewes, E. *Guide and Index to G. I. Gurdjieff's All and Everything.* Toronto: The Society for Traditional Studies, 1971.

Poulain, R. *Graces of Interior Prayer.* St. Louis, B. Herder, 1911.

Pratt, J. *Parapsychology: An Insider's View.* New York: Dutton, 1966.

————, and Birge, W. "Appraising Verbal Test Material in Parapsychology," *J. Parapsychol.,* 12 (1948), 236–256.

————, Rhine, J., Smith, B., Stuart, C., and Greenwood, J. *Extrasensory Perception after Sixty Years.* Somerville, Mass.: Bruce Humphries, 1934; 2d ed., 1966.

Pratyagatmananda, S. "Philosophy of the Tantras." in H. Bhattacharyya, *The Cultural Heritage of India.* Vol. III. Calcutta: The Ramakrishna Mission Institute of Culture, 1953.

————. *The Fundamentals of Vedanta Philosophy.* Madras: Ganesh & Co., 1961.

————. *Japasutram: The Science of Creative Sound.* Madras: Ganesh & Co., 1971.

Puharich, A. *Beyond Telepathy.* New York: Doubleday, 1962.

Radhakrishnan, S., trans. *The Bhagavadgita.* New York: Harper & Row, 1952.

————, trans. *Principal Upanishads.* New York: Harper & Row, 1953.

————, trans. *The Brahma Sutra.* New York: Harper & Row, 1960.

Rao, R. *Experimental Parapsychology.* Springfield, Ill.: Charles C. Thomas, 1966.

Rhine, J. *Extrasensory Perception.* Somerville, Mass.: Bruce Humphries, 1934; 2d ed., 1964.

Rhine, J., A new case of experimenter unreliability. *J. Parapsychol.,* 38 (1974), 215–225.

Riordan, K. ed. *Introductory Psychology.* San Rafael, Cal.: Individual Learning Systems, 1971. (Published under author's married name, Speeth.)

————. *Recent Developments in Psychology.* New York: Appleton-Century-Crofts, 1972. (Published under author's married name, Speeth.)

Rohrbach, P. *Conversation with Christ.* Notre Dame, Ind.: Fides Publishers, 1956.

Rosenthal, R. *Experimenter Effects in Behavioral Research.* New York: Appleton-Century-Crofts, 1966.

Russell, B. *A History of Western Philosophy.* New York: Simon & Schuster, 1945.

Sangharakshita. *The Three Jewels: An Introduction to Modern Buddhism.* New York: Anchor, 1970.

Satprem. Trans., Tehmi. *Sri Aurobindo: The Adventure of Consciousness.* Pondicherry, India: Sri Aurobindo Society, 1970.

Schachter, S., and Singer, J. "Cognitive, Social, and Physiological Determinants of Emotional State," *Psychol. Rev.,* 69 (1962), 379.

Schmeidler, G., ed. *Extrasensory Perception.* New York: Atherton, 1969.

_____, and McConnell, R. *ESP and Personality Patterns.* New Haven: Yale University Press, 1958.

Sen, I. "The Indian Approach to Psychology," in H. Chaudhuri and F. Spiegelberg, eds., *The Integral Philosophy of Sri Aurobindo.* London: George Allen & Unwin, 1960.

Shah, I. *The Sufis.* Garden City, N.Y.: Doubleday & Co., 1964.

_____. *The Exploits of the Incomparable Mulla Nasrudin.* London: Jonathan Cape, 1966; New York: Dutton, 1972.

_____. *Tales of the Dervishes.* London: Jonathan Cape, 1967; New York: Dutton, 1970.

_____. *Caravan of Dreams.* London: The Octagon Press, 1968 (a); Baltimore: Penguin Books, 1972.

_____. *Reflections.* London: Octagon Press, 1968 (b); Baltimore: Penguin Books, 1972.

_____. *The Pleasantries of the Incredible Mulla Nasrudin.* London: Jonathan Cape, 1968 (c); New York: Dutton, 1972.

_____. *The Way of the Sufi.* London: Jonathan Cape, 1968 (d); New York: Dutton, 1970.

_____. *The Book of the Book.* London: The Octagon Press, 1969 (a).

_____. *Wisdom of the Idiots.* London: Octagon Press, 1969 (b); New York: Dutton, 1971.

_____. *The Dermis Probe.* London: Jonathan Cape, 1970; New York: Dutton, 1971.

_____. *Thinkers of the East.* London: Jonathan Cape, 1971; Baltimore: Penguin Books, 1972.

_____. *The Magic Monastery.* London: Jonathan Cape, 1972; New York: Dutton, 1972.

_____. *The Subtleties of the Inimitable Mulla Nasrudin.* London: Jonathan Cape, 1973; New York: Dutton, 1973.

Shapiro, D. *Neurotic Styles.* New York: Basic Books, 1961.

Sitwell, G. (Ed). *The Scale of Perfection.* London: Burnes & Oates, 1953.

Sivananda, S. *Raja Yoga.* Rishikesh: Yoga Vedanta Forest University, 1950.

Smith, H. *The Religions of Man.* New York: Mentor, 1958.

Smythies, J., ed. *Science and ESP.* New York: Humanities Press, 1967.

Soal, S., and Bateman, F. *Modern Experiments in Telepathy.* London: Faber & Faber, 1954.

Stevenson, I. "Twenty Cases Suggestive of Reincarnation," *Proc. Amer. Soc. Psych. Res.,* 26 (1966), 1–362. Reprinted Charlottesville, Va.: Univ. of Virginia Press, 1974.

Suzuki, D. *Zen Buddhism.* New York: Doubleday, 1956.

————. *Mysticism: Christian and Buddhist.* New York: Macmillan, 1957.

————. *Essays in Zen Buddhism.* 2d series. London: Rider, 1958.

Taimni, L. *The Science of Yoga.* Wheaton: Theosophical Publishing House, Quest Books, 1967.

Tart, C. "Physiological Correlates of Psi Cognition," *Inter. J. Parapsychol.,* 5 (1963), 375–386.

————. "Models for the Explanation of Extrasensory Perception," *Inter. J. Neuropsychiat.,* 2 (1966), 488–504 (a).

————. "Card Guessing Tests: Learning Paradigm or Extinction Paradigm?" *J. Amer. Soc. Psych. Res.,* 60 (1966), 46–55 (b).

————. "A Second Psychophysiological Study of Out-of-the-Body Experiences in a Gifted Subject," *Inter. J. Parapsychol.,* 9 (1967), 251–258.

————. "A Psychophysiological Study of Out-of-the-Body Experiences in a Selected Subject," *J. Amer. Soc. Psych. Res.,* 62 (1968), 3–27.

————, ed. *Altered States of Consciousness.* New York: John Wiley, 1969; New York: Doubleday, 1972.

————. "A Theoretical Model for States of Consciousness." Paper, Menninger Foundation Conference on the Voluntary Control of Internal States, Council Grove, Kansas, 1970.

————. "Scientific Foundations for the Study of Altered States of Consciousness," *J. Transpersonal Psychol.,* 3:2 (1971), 93–124 (a).

————. *On Being Stoned: A Psychological Study of Marijuana Intoxication.* Palo Alto, Cal.: Science & Behavior Books, 1971 (b).

————. "States of Consciousness and State-Specific Sciences," *Science,* 176 (1972), 1203–1210.

————. "Parapsychology," *Science,* 182 (1973), 222 (a).

————. "On the Nature of Altered States of Consciousness, with Special Reference to Parapsychological Phenomena." Parapsychological Assn., Charlottesville, Va., Sept. 1973 (b). In Roll, W., Morris R., and Morris, D., eds., *Research in Parapsychology, 1973.* Metuchen, N.J.: Scarecrow Press, 1974.

————. "Preliminary Notes on the Nature of Psi Processes," in R. Ornstein, ed., *The Nature of Human Consciousness.* San Francisco: Freeman, 1973 (c).

————. "Discrete States of Consciousness." Paper, American Association for Advancement of Science, San Francisco, 1974 (a).

————. "Out-of-the-Body Experiences," in E. Mitchell, ed., *Psychic Exploration,* pp. 349–374. New York: Putnam, 1974 (b).

————. *States of Consciousness.* New York: Dutton, 1975.

————, and Kvetensky, E. "Marijuana Intoxication: Feasibility of Experiential Scaling of Depth," *J. Altered States of Consciousness,* 1 (1973), 15–21.

Teilhard de Chardin, P. *The Phenomenon of Man.* New York: Harper & Row, 1959.

Thomas, G. *Epics, Myths, and Legends of India.* 12th ed. Bombay: D. B. Taraparevala, 1961.

Tiller, W. *Radionics, Radiosthesia and Physics, Varieties of Healing Experience.* Los Altos, Cal.: Academy of Parapsychology & Medicine, 1971.

Tracol, H. *George Ivanovitch Gurdjieff: Man's Awakening and the Practice of Remembering Oneself.* Bray: Guild Press, 1968.

Ullman, M., Krippner, S., and Vaughan, A. *Dream Telepathy.* New York: Macmillan, 1973.

Underhill, E. *The Mystic Way.* New York: E. P. Dutton, 1913.

_____. *Mysticism: A Study in the Nature and Development of Man's Spiritual Consciousness.* New York: Noonday Press, 1955.

van de Castle, R. "The Facilitation of ESP through Hypnosis," *Amer. J. Clin. Hypnosis,* 12 (1969), 37–56.

van Kaam, A. *Religion and Personality.* Englewood Cliffs, N.J.: Prentice-Hall, 1965.

Vasiliev, L. *Experiments in Mental Suggestion.* Church Crookham, Hampshire, England: Institute for the Study of Mental Images, 1963.

Vivekananda, S. *Raja Yoga.* 2d ed. New York: Ramakrishna-Vivekananda Center, 1956.

von Hugel, Baron. *The Mystical Element of Religion.* 2 vols. London: J. M. Dent & Co., 1908.

von Reichenbach, K. *The Odic Force: Letters on Od and Magnetism.* New Hyde Park, N.Y.: University Books, 1968.

Walker, K. *Venture with Ideas.* London: Jonathan Cape, 1951.

_____. *A Study of Gurdjieff's Teaching.* London: Jonathan Cape, 1957.

Wallace, R. Physiological effects of Transcendental Meditation. *Science,* 167 (1970), 1751–1754.

Watkin, E. *Philosophy of Mysticism.* London: Grant Richards, Ltd., 1920.

Weide, T. "Varieties of Transpersonal Therapy," *J. Transpersonal Psychol.,* 5:1 (1973), 7–14.

Wei Wu Wei. *Posthumous Pieces.* Hong Kong: Hong Kong Univ. Press, 1963.

"Who," *Maha Yoga.* South India: Sri Ramana-Ashram, 1967.

Wilhelm, R. *The Secret of the Golden Flower.* New York: Harcourt, Brace, & World, 1962.

Wilson, C. *The Outsider.* New York: Houghton Mifflin, 1967.

Woodroffe, J. *The Serpent Power.* Madras: Ganesh, 1964.

_____. *Sakti and Sakta.* Madras: Ganesh, 1965.

Yasutani. See Kapleau, *Three Pillars of Zen.*

INDEXES

INDEX OF NAMES

INDEX OF SUBJECTS